THE ECONOMIES OF ASIA 1950–1998

THE ECONOMIES OF ASIA 1950–1998

Critical perspectives on the world economy

Edited and with a new introduction by Robert Ash and Anne Booth

VOLUME I

China

London and New York

First published 2000
by Routledge
11 New Fetter Lane, London EC4P 4EE

Simultaneously published in the USA and Canada
by Routledge
29 West 35th Street, New York, NY 10001

Routledge is an imprint of the Taylor & Francis Group

Typeset in Times by RefineCatch Limited, Bungay, Suffolk
Printed and bound in Great Britain by Clays Ltd, St Ives plc

British Library Cataloguing in Publication Data
A catalogue record for this book is available from the British Library

Library of Congress Cataloguing in Publication Data
A catalogue record for this book has been requested

ISBN 0–415–14051–X (set)
ISBN 0–415–17947–5 (volume 1)

CONTENTS

VOLUME I CHINA

PART VI: POPULATION AND LABOUR

PART VII: WELFARE AND STANDARD OF LIVING

VOLUME II SOUTH EAST ASIA

PART I: THE CHALLENGE OF MACROECONOMIC RESTRUCTURING

PART II: THE ROLE OF GOVERNMENT ENTERPRISES AND MONOPOLIES, AND PRIVATIZATION

PART III: DEVELOPMENT OF THE FINANCIAL SECTOR

PART IV: FOREIGN INVESTMENT, TECHNOLOGY TRANSFER AND EXPORT PROCESSING ZONES

PART V: CHANGING LABOUR CONDITIONS

PART VI: THE CHANGING NATURE OF SOUTHEAST ASIAN CAPITALISM

PART VII: TRENDS IN POVERTY

PART VIII: ASEAN ECONOMIC INTEGRATION

CONTENTS

VOLUME III THE FOUR TIGERS: KOREA, TAIWAN, HONG KONG AND SINGAPORE

INTRODUCTION

Robert Ash

A conventional view of China's post-1949 history would regard the period of Mao Zedong's ascendancy (1949–76) as years of revolutionary change and upheaval. China's trajectory during this period was of course critically shaped by Mao's radical ideas. The political and economic revolutionary experiments which he and his colleagues in the Chinese Communist Party (CCP) had undertaken through the vicissitudes of the Party's previous 30-year history were also important shaping factors.

During Mao's lifetime, the powerful control mechanisms inherent in the system of government and Party control made independent debate, let alone criticism, of official economic strategy virtually impossible. Only after his death – and especially following the Third Plenum of the 11th CCP Central Committee (December 1978 – did a relatively objective critique of that strategy begin to appear. The emerging orthodoxy sought simultaneously to acknowledge both the strengths and weaknesses of China's economic performance during the previous three decades. Its most striking departure was, however, its open admission of the serious economic damage caused by the excessively "Leftist" policies espoused by Mao. Thus, on the one hand, there was praise for the buoyant performance of China's economy during the First Five-Year Plan (FFYP) (1953–57) and under the impact of the pragmatic adjustment measures introduced in the early 1960s. But there was also criticism of the economic dislocation and collapse attendant on those quintessentially Maoist adventures – the Great Leap Forward (1958–59) and the Cultural Revolution (1966–76). The implicit message was that China's economic interests had been better served through reliance on methods borrowed from other countries' experiences, whether socialist (the 1950s) or capitalist (early 1960s), than through the adoption of a more expressly indigenous developmental approach.

To emphasize the revolutionary thrust of Mao Zedong's approach to economic development is not to deny that, when necessary, Mao himself was capable of acting in a supremely practical manner.[1] Equally, it is simplistic

Source: The growth economies of Asia, volume 1, People's Republic of China.

and misleading to suppose that the reformist thrust of China's post-1978 strategy can be captured through recourse to simple epithets highlighting the supposed "pragmatism" of Deng Xiaoping.[2] The reality is that in their roles as economists as well as politicians, Mao and Deng shared many important similarities, at least one of which – a penchant for economic "great leaps forward"[3] – smacked of the very "Leftism" which the post-Mao economic critique had condemned.

Given China's circumstances after 1949, fulfilling the goal of rapid industrialization arguably made the adoption of a Soviet-style command system of economic planning inevitable. By 1956, the essential attributes of such a system were already in place in China. To argue that China's development during the last two decades of the Mao period demonstrates a similarly inevitability is, however, much more questionable. Nor does the suggestion that the post-Mao economic transition under Deng Xiaoping represented a "natural economic evolution"[4] do justice to the very radical nature of many aspects of the Dengist reforms. When set against their immediate historical background, some of the defining features of such reforms suggest less an evolutionary response to the Maoist economic legacy than a new economic revolution unfolding in China.

Whether viewed against the background of its own recent historical experience or that of other developing countries (including Japan and the "tiger" economies of East and South-east Asia at comparable periods of development), China's economic record since 1978 is an outstanding one. This is an assessment that is not materially affected by an upward bias concealed in some official growth statistics. It has been estimated that by 2020, the Chinese economy will be bigger than that of the United States and that its share of world markets will have risen from 4 percent to around 10 percent. Meanwhile, with US$ 145 billion, China already possesses the second-largest foreign exchange reserves in the world.[5]

But the overwhelmingly positive assessment of China's recent development experience suggested by the statistical record is by no means unqualified. The very nature of the Maoist economic legacy ensured that the challenges of modernization facing China in the post-Mao world would be formidable. Under the impact of economic reform, some of these challenges have been successfully met. Growth has been rapid across many sectors and industries; significant productivity gains have been realized in some areas of the economy; and associated structural modernization has shifted the economy towards higher value-added activities. Most significant of all has been the achievement of a high degree of marketization, with all that this implies in terms of price liberalization, competition and incentives, and the increasing use of economic levers at the heart of macroeconomic control and regulatory mechanisms.

But other challenges have yet to be overcome. Structural imbalances and resource bottlenecks – some of them inherited from the past, others arising out of the reforms themselves – are still in evidence. Not least, China's food and energy security must be assured. Despite some progress having been made towards rationalizing their structure and operational mechanisms, the state-owned enterprises (SOEs) currently pose the greatest reform challenge. Resolving the difficulties facing the SOEs rightly assumes a high priority within the government's strategic plans, not least because of its implications for financial reforms, employment and the closely linked goal of establishing a fully-fledged social security system. Meanwhile, the strong regional orientation of economic development has been the source of serious and worsening inter-provincial tensions. Environmental pressures have also intensified.

Such challenges cannot be addressed behind closed doors. Not only do they impact on the international community, but their resolution will depend to some extent on cooperation with and China's further integration into the regional and global communities. Not least, access to modern technology and foreign capital is likely to be a crucial determinant of China's sustained economic growth and modernization.

The failure to address such issues would pose a serious threat to China's future economic trajectory. But it is not only economic goals that are at risk. The maintenance of a virtuous circle of high growth, wealth creation and employment generation is also needed in order to contain social and political strains.

It is a remarkable feature of China's development in the last half century that during most of the period, the country has been largely shielded from the impact of external economic forces. It is true that during the FFYP period, the Chinese government's decision to "lean to one side" and take advantage of the assistance offered by the former Soviet Union was instrumental in promoting rapid economic growth and structural transformation. But from the late 1950s until the early 1970s, preoccupations associated with the Great Leap Forward and Cultural Revolution were reflected in the imperative of self-reliance and pushed China towards a more insular stance. As it turned out, the subsequent adoption of a genuinely open-door strategy in a buoyant and expansionary international economic environment (especially in Asia, where China's outward-orientated role was most apparent) worked overwhelmingly to China's advantage. From this latter perspective, the most recent challenge posed by the financial crisis in parts of East and South-east Asia is unprecedented in China's post-1949 history and serves to highlight the dangers, as well as the benefits of the Chinese government's pursuit of regional and global economic integration.

The nature and sources of China's growth record in the 1980s and 1990s are considered in many of the papers included in this volume. The accompanying analysis also offers valuable insights into the origins and likely outcome of many of the attendant problems to which reference has just been made. It is beyond the scope of this brief introduction to try to extend such analysis. Instead, the following remarks seek to lend a contemporary focus to the story and to highlight some of the major economic issues which confront China at the end of the 1990s and will shape its development trajectory into the next century.

REVIEWING THE RECORD OF GROWTH AND STRUCTURAL CHANGE

The remarkable changes that have taken place in the 1980s and 1990s are most obviously reflected in the unprecedented growth that has characterized this period of rapid economic expansion and modernization. Between 1978 and 1997, China's GDP grew, on average, by 9.8 percent p. a., compared with a corresponding figure of 6.1 percent during 1953–78.[6] To ignore the temporal fluctuations in growth in each period would, however, be disingenuous. Under Mao, for example, there was a sharp deceleration of growth after 1957 – a trend that was observable at an aggregate level as well as in all major sectors.[7] After 1978, as Table 1 shows, there was also a distinct slowing of growth during the mid-reform years.

The figures in Table 1 provide clear evidence of the very positive impact of economic reforms upon China's growth. The per capita GDP estimates are also eloquent testimony to the weakening erosion of the benefits of such growth as a result of population pressure, the rate of natural increase of total population having consistently declined in every year since 1987 to the extraordinarily low level of 10.06‰ (1997).[8]

The estimates of sectoral growth shown in Table 1 suggest that until the second half of the 1980s, agriculture remained an important engine of economic growth in China.[9] By the end of the decade, that situation had changed and in the 1990s, the resurgence in growth has been driven by a marked acceleration in the rates of growth of both secondary and tertiary sectors. In

Table 1 Growth in China's GDP, 1978–97 (In comparable prices: average % p.a.)

	GDP	*Per capita GDP*	*Primary*	*Secondary*	*Tertiary*
1978–97	9.8	8.4	5.0	11.9	10.6
6FYB 1981–85	10.7	9.2	8.2	10.0	15.2
7FYP 1986–90	7.9	6.2	4.2	9.0	9.4
8FYP 1991–95	12.0	10.7	4.2	17.4	10.0

Source: State Statistical Bureau, *Zhonggou tongji zhaiyao (A Statistical Abstract of China) (ZGTJZY)*, (Beijing: Zhongguo tongji chubanshe, 1998), p. 14.

this respect, it is noteworthy that during the most recent completed Five-Year Plan period (1991–95), the renewed surge in economic growth was carried almost wholly by secondary sector expansion, with industry and construction growing by 17.7 and 14.9 percent p.a. By contrast, agricultural growth remained unchanged, while average tertiary sector growth rose by less than a single percentage point.[10]

What the estimates in Table 1 conceal is the consistent decline in annual GDP growth that has occurred in the most recent past. Since 1992, statistics made available by the State Statistical Bureau show the rate of increase of GDP to have fallen from 14.2 percent (1992) to 7.8 percent (1998). It is no coincidence that during the same period, the Chinese government embarked on a programme designed to reduce growing inflationary pressures throughout the economy.[11] The rate of consumer and retail price rise peaked in 1994, when both indexes increased by more than 20 percent; in 1997, the corresponding figures were 0.8 and 2.6 percent. But no less significant than the reduction in inflation was the manner by which it was achieved, lending credence to government claims of having secured a 'soft landing'.

Parallel claims that the Chinese economy had entered a new stage of "development through stability" have, however, yet to be substantiated. Apparent economic buoyancy conceals serious underlying problems. Some of these reflect the persistence of problems from the past, although the regional financial crisis is a significant new element, the effect of which has already been to threaten China's growth momentum. These are issues to which we return below.

POPULATION, EMPLOYMENT AND MIGRATION

In the last 40 years, China's population has doubled.[12] The inevitable consequence has been to place its agriculture, energy supplies, forests, environment, cities and social system under increasing stress. The sharply downward trend of population growth since the mid-1970s to an annual rate of natural increase that is now little more than 1 percent has led some to argue that China no longer faces a serious problem of population growth.[13] But despite unprecedented success in implementing Draconian birth control policies, the population base is so huge that even low vital rates still result in the net addition of more than 12 million people each year (12.37 million in 1997). Projections of demographic changes in the medium term vary: some predict that total population will reach 1.5 or even 1.6 billion by 2025; more optimistically, another authoritative source suggests that it will stabilize at between 1.35 and 1.4 billion during 2012 and 2047 before starting to decline.[14]

In the foreseeable future, the key demographic variable in China will be the population age structure. The likelihood that this will remain largely unchanged until well into the next century has led some to argue that China has entered a demographic "golden age," characterized by a low dependency ratio in terms of both children and the aged. Until around 2030, the majority of Chinese will be of potentially productive working age, implying a demographic structure which, if properly mobilized, will be capable of enhancing productivity, maximizing savings and investment, and minimizing non-productive consumption needs (for example, for education and health). The delay in population ageing also promises to benefit China by a providing a breathing space in which to anticipate future longer-term demographic changes and generate the requisite resources to provide for the needs of the elderly.

The obverse of China's stable, low dependency ratio will, however, be an unusually high cohort of those of working age. This phenomenon serves merely to underline the enormity of the employment problem and the burden of job creation that now faces the Chinese government.

In the 1990s, more than half of China's population has been of working age.[15] Until the mid-1960s, some 6 million jobs were, on average, needed annually in order to accommodate new entrants into the labour force. Between 1965 and 1978, this figure rose to almost 9 million. Such was the delayed effect of burgeoning population growth in the mid-1960s that by the 1980s, more than 12 million job placements were required each year.[16]

Such figures are stark enough, but they are far from indicating the true burden of employment. For example, they take no account of rural underemployment. The collective framework, which evolved after the mid-1950s, afforded an effective means of maximizing employment opportunities in the rural sector, if at the cost of low levels of productivity, and thereby of concealing the true extent of underemployment. Part of the impact of early post-1978 rural reform was to raise labour productivity, reduce labour requirements in farming and eventually eliminate the institutional framework in which semi-productive agricultural labourers could be accommodated. The exact number of surplus agricultural labourers in China is subject to widely varying estimates, but cannot be less than 100 million and may be considerably in excess of this figure. One recent official projection concedes that even after making allowance for an expected 70 million new jobs during the current [Ninth] Five-Year Plan (1996–2000), the surplus rural workforce could reach 200 million by the turn of the century.

The existence of surplus labour on such a massive scale is part of the background against which, in recent years, large-scale rural-urban migration has become widespread in China.[17] By its very nature, the scale of migration is not easily measured, but that it runs into many tens of millions is not in doubt. There is a sense in which this huge movement of people has acted as a kind of safety-valve, dampening some of the social tensions associated with rural demographic and economic pressures.[18] Intra-rural economic diversification and rural-urban migration have also made available a motivated and, by the standards of poor countries, quite skilled pool of labour to sectors and regions of high growth in the national economy. The same process has facilitated capital accumulation and technical progress within the rural sector itself, as migrants send or bring back income and expertise gained from working outside farming and/or outside their native province.

Official sources also concede a significant rise in *urban unemployment* in recent years. Estimates of an unemployment rate of 3.1 percent in cities (1997) grossly understate reality through their exclusion of unemployed migrants and failure to make allowance for large numbers of workers who remain on the payroll of state enterprises but are in receipt of only a fraction of their stipulated wage (under-employment is not simply a rural phenomenon). To have acknowledged that urban unemployment might rise to 3.5 percent in 1998 is one indication, albeit probably a conservative one, of the scale of the challenge facing the government.[19]

How to provide productive jobs for new entrants into the labour force, as well as the backlog of unemployed and under-employed is a profound economic and social issue. Central to the Chinese approach towards job creation in recent years has been the development of rural industries, offering productive and well-paid employment to surplus rural workers, without requiring them to leave the countryside. In the 1990s alone, for example, the number of people employed by township and village enterprises (TVEs) has risen from 96 to around 130 million (about 30 per cent of the entire rural workforce). Tens of millions of other workers have found jobs in rural construction and tertiary occupations.

This massive achievement is no doubt unprecedented in terms of its scope and impact. Yet ironically, it has only partly accommodated the enormous reservoir of surplus farm labourers. There is evidence too that improved labour productivity and the use of increasingly capital-intensive techniques has dampened rural industry's demand for labour. This is one of the reasons why in recent years there has been increasing emphasis on the need for accelerated development of the tertiary sector, where the scope for the substitution of labour for capital is still considerable.

THE STATE-OWNED ENTERPRISES

The slow pace of reform of the state enterprises (SOEs) has been a major obstacle to continued growth. In the absence of a comprehensive social security system, fears of social unrest go some way towards explaining why the Chinese leadership for so many years felt unable to confront the problem head-on. Political concerns are also important, enterprise reform being a highly sensitive issue that impinges on the effectiveness with which the Party can continue to exercise its control.

The restructuring of the SOEs is essential for the restoration of public finances.[20] In recent years, the lagging growth of state enterprises has been mirrored in the sharp decline in their contribution to total industrial output (from 78 percent in 1978 to 27 percent in 1997).[21] But they remain pre-eminent in key sectors of the economy and in certain individual regions, they continue to dominate the industrial economy.[22] In addition, SOEs embody almost 60 percent of Chinese industrial assets and their workforce accounts for about 55 percent of the entire urban labour force.

The size distribution of enterprises is an important dimension of the physical profile of China's SOEs. Estimates showing half of all units to be loss-making conceal the fact that the SOE sector is dominated by small-scale enterprises, which account for less than 15 percent of industrial value-added (1996).[23] Moreover, although the output share of SOEs, taken as a whole, has fallen at the expense of that of the non-state sector, it is telling that the GVIO contribution of large and medium-scale units has actually risen since the mid-1980s.[24] The inference is quite clearly that the role of small enterprises has declined quite markedly during the same period, their share in industrial production having fallen by almost 10 percentage points.

The frequent inability of small units to realize economies of scale has inhibited their performance and is one of the factors that has encouraged advocacy of bankruptcies and mergers in recent years.[25] Hence too the government's strategy of 'grasping the large and letting go of the small.' This approach reflects not only the determination to retain control of key industrial units, but also the fact – sometimes imperfectly recognized – that output growth and technical modernization in large enterprises have actually been quite impressive. Indeed, outside fuel extraction industries, there are probably relatively few loss-makers in the large-scale state sector, which has benefited from significant economies of scale and scope, and only limited competition from the non-state sector.[26]

The ultimate institutional goal of enterprise reform is to facilitate the re-grouping of the old state enterprises into large multi-plant firms, with increasingly autonomous managers of large SOEs taking the lead in promoting strategic take-overs.[27] As the central government continues to retreat from direct involvement in enterprise activities, the managers of emergent large corporations are promised unprecedented independence and scope of decision-making power with which to advance their firm's cause. The evolution of associated property rights is a complex process and the second half of the 1990s has witnessed more diversified ownership of large SOEs. The state holding company remains a major actor, although its share of the firm's equity value has tended to contract, as other institutions (including multinational firms) have acquired ownership rights. This pattern has received official ratification through the government's formal approval of the establishment of joint stock companies, with clearly-defined and legally-binding identification of the ownership rights of the different owners.

But for the time being, the problem of indebtedness within the state-owned sector remains serious. For example, it is estimated that some US$ 120 billion have been sunk in so-called 'triangular debts', embracing government, enterprises and banks. Indebtedness on such a scale is a major impediment to reform of the banking sector. At the present time, three out of the four state-run commercial banks are technically insolvent and the level of bad loans is equivalent to over 20 percent of China's GDP.

THE AGRICULTURAL AND RURAL SECTORS

Although China's economic growth is no longer closely tied to the performance of agriculture, the potential role of the farm sector – and more broadly, of the rural economy – remains an important one. To ignore that role would be to ignore what is still a fundamental determinant of China's future economic trajectory.[28] China remains overwhelmingly a rural society, with some 70 percent of total population living and working in the countryside. In the Chinese context, the processes of urbanization, industrialization and even globalization are partly rural phenomena. In an effort to mitigate some of the pressures of urban-rural migration that have so scarred other developing countries, the Chinese government has successfully promoted the establishment of towns and cities in the countryside. It has also encouraged rural industrialization. In particular, the rapid expansion of township and village enterprises (TVEs) since the mid-1980s has made a notable contribution not only to domestic industrial and economic growth, but also to China's export performance.

It is important not to underestimate the importance of such developments. But it would also be foolish to ignore the serious challenges that still face the rural sector in China. Poverty is not only a rural phenomenon, but its worst manifestations are to be found in the countryside.[29] From this perspective, the rural population is bound to be a focus of efforts to improve welfare and living standards. Rural environmental problems associated with land loss, land degradation, water shortages and pollution are also very serious. There is evidence too that the growth and efficiency performance of rural industrial enterprises may be declining.

It is also of course in the countryside that the battle to provide sufficient grain to meet its food requirements will be won or lost. Many would find it surprising that at the end of the 1990s, the Chinese government should continue to be so exercised by the question of China's food security. China has, after all, for many years enjoyed a comfortable cushion above its subsistence needs and living standards have meanwhile improved markedly for the majority of the Chinese population, including those living in the countryside. Since 1978, grain imports have never exceeded more than 4.5 percent of total domestic output and China's agricultural trade balance has generally been in surplus. With its huge reserves of foreign exchange, China is also comfortably placed to finance major imports of foreign grain, should such purchases become necessary.

More than anything else, the continued imperative of grain self-sufficiency is an expression of an official perception of a problem in political-economy, rather than in mere economics.[30] Inside and outside China, the debate surrounding China's food security has also been fired by fears about the possible international dimensions of declining domestic food production. The most apocalyptic expression of such fears is the scenario outlined by Lester Brown, who has predicted that a combination of rising demand and contracting supply within China will, by 2030, necessitate imports on such a scale as to squeeze poorer, grain-deficit countries in Africa and South Asia out of international markets. Hence, the spectre of "China starving the world."[31]

It is beyond the scope of this introduction to extend what remains a continuing debate.[32] But it does deserve to be said that since 1995, China has enjoyed an unparalleled sequence of fine grain harvests. Between 1990 and 1994, there were sharp annual fluctuations in grain production, leaving no impression of sustained growth. By contrast, average growth since 1994 has been almost 2.5 percent[33] (more than two times faster than the rate of natural increase of total population). The recent (1995–98) run of fine harvests does admittedly conceal a declining growth trend, but the fact that despite the most serious flooding for many years, grain output in 1998 recorded its third highest level is also significant. In 1997, rice production for the first time in China's history exceeded 200 million tonnes, while that of wheat rose by a remarkable 11.5 percent.

Three further observations may be made here. The first is that, even allowing for the negative impact of economic and environmental forces,[34] the potential for continuing and significant increases in grain yields – above all, through the application of modern farm science and technologies – remains considerable.[35] The appropriate use of price incentives will of course be central to the effectiveness of policies designed to realize this potential.

Nevertheless (the second observation), it is noteworthy that China's record in terms of policy implementation in such areas is not wholly convincing. The government has often enough articulated sensible policy measures, but it has not always been successful in putting such measures into place. It has yet to be demonstrated, for example, that the kind of policies set out in the State Council's 'White Paper' on grain (October 1996) can be effectively and comprehensively implemented.[36]

There does, however, appear to be one respect in which a recent agricultural initiative – the 'grain bag' policy – has met with considerable success.[37] This strategy has been mainly directed towards some coastal and southern provinces, where neglect of agriculture (especially crop farming) had earlier generated increasing grain deficits. By placing the responsibility for maintaining regional grain balance and stability on individual provincial governors, it appears to have gone some way toward reversing the previous, serious decline in grain production in these regions.[38]

Third, even if the recent series of fine harvests proves to have taken grain output growth on to a new trajectory, demand pressures are still likely to generate a widening gap between availability and needs. Accordingly, there is a strong likelihood that in the medium term China will make increasing demands on international grain markets.

INFRASTRUCTURAL BOTTLENECKS – ENERGY SECURITY

For much of the Mao period, infrastructure was relatively starved of funds and associated bottlenecks were a major impediment to growth in the economy. Despite significant recent improvements, such bottlenecks have not been entirely removed and current levels of domestic infrastructural investment may well still be insufficient to sustain annual economic growth at 8–9 percent.[39] Even allowing for massive projected increases in such investment (including the involvement of overseas capital), the scale of the challenge remains a huge one.

In order to support rapid growth, China has already found it necessary to direct large amounts of investment to its energy sector. China is already the second-largest consumer of energy and the third-largest energy producer worldwide. It ranks sixth in the world as an oil producer, and it is the biggest coal producer. Between 1980 and 1995, it rose from being the sixth largest electricity producer in the world to become the second largest.[40]

But per capita energy consumption in China is very low by world standards and the energy sector continues to carry a heavy burden. Sustaining high growth during the next several decades will be critically dependent on the ability to secure access to affordable and clean energy supplies.[41] For the time being, the reality is that despite rapid growth, energy production is falling more and more behind its needs. A significant watershed was reached in the early 1990s, when China was forced to revert to the status of a net oil importer (oil accounting for about one fifth of its primary energy supplies).[42] Despite the existence of rich indigenous sources, there is widespread agreement that dependence on energy imports will rise still further, not least given the constraints on further efficiency improvements in energy use. It is against this background that China has become actively engaged in 'oil diplomacy' with Russia and other countries in Central Asia and the Middle East.

The global implications of China's involvement in world energy markets are not to be underestimated, even if world oil reserves are sufficiently large to accommodate its increasing demand. But shortfalls in domestic energy production might still have a short-run disruptive impact on international energy markets.[43]

Energy imports are costly and China is already making big efforts to enhance domestic supplies of energy. This is not easy, since rich domestic energy sources are often sited far from consumption destinations. Massive investment will undoubtedly be required to improve the energy infrastructure (including constructing gas and oil pipelines, modernizing port handling facilities and extending transport channels). The continuing dominance of coal as a source of primary energy makes the development of clean-coal technologies an obvious priority. Overall, the scale and complexity of all these tasks would seem to demand the involvement of foreign investors not only to provide the necessary funds, but also to furnish the requisite technology and expertise.

ENVIRONMENTAL CONCERNS

China's rapid economic growth has entailed a very high environmental cost. Population pressure has long placed a heavy burden on the country's natural resources. As a result, per capita availability of arable land, fresh water and forest stocks are all well below the world average. From an environmental perspective, the Dengist dictum that 'high growth is best' seems to have found expression in a belief that 'high growth is best, whatever the cost.' There is no shortage of evidence that misuse and inefficient use of limited resources have exacerbated problems associated with mere demographic pressures.

Out of many environmental issues confronting China at the present time, two which merit consideration here relate to land and water resources.[44]

There is no doubt that under the pressure of population size and growth, economic modernization and rising prosperity, some of China's best farmland has been lost. Increased numbers of cities and towns in what used to be rural areas have taken land out of farm production. So have residential, industrial and infrastructural construction activities – the building of roads, dams, reservoirs, factories, houses, etc. (whether undertaken by the state, collective or private sector). To attribute the contraction of China's arable land base to the effects of urbanization is, however, too simplistic and one of the most striking findings that emerges from an analysis of land loss is the even more important contribution of other factors. Of these, the two most important are likely to have been structural change within agriculture – transfers of land out of crop farming and into animal husbandry, aquaculture or forestry – and environmental change, such as the destruction of topsoil as a result of flooding or soil erosion.

This is a significant finding. The loss of farmland to urbanization and industrialization is likely to be irrevocable in the sense that once it is built over, such land is permanently lost to agriculture. The same does not necessarily apply to crop land that has been transferred to other kinds of farming. It is true that reclamation can compensate for land that has disappeared as a result of construction activity.[45] But there is an important qualitative dimension to the process of arable area contraction in China. Fertile, peri-urban land taken out of production in coastal areas has been replaced by inferior and marginal land – much of it in inhospitable and barren north-western provinces of the country – newly brought into production.[46]

Official legislation seeks to ensure that land losses resulting from industrial and infrastructural construction are offset by reclamation of the same amount of land of equivalent quality. It is significant that recent revisions to the Land Management Law seeks to restrain farmers from converting crop land to other agricultural uses, in addition to forbidding them from building kilns, tombs or houses on cultivated land, or letting land lie idle or go to waste.

The second environmental issue concerns water and poses what in many ways is a more serious problem than that of arable land loss. With an average per capita availability that is a mere 25% of the world average, China is inherently water-deficient. Some 20 million hectares of arable land are affected by drought each year, although the flood-affected area (some 8 million hectares) is also large. Irrigation accounts for about half of total water usage, but poor diversion facilities and inefficient water use result in the wastage of as much as 70 percent of irrigation resources. In northwest China, where half of the arable area is located, the arable land base is becoming more and more desertified, and sandstorms more frequent, as a result of improper water use. Scientists have warned that the Yellow River could dry up by 2020. Excessive use of groundwater is also causing ground subsidence and seawater intrusion in some coastal areas.By the mid-1990s, water shortages were costing China some 200 billion *yuan* annually, or about 5 percent of GNP – in lost output.[47] Excessive extraction of groundwater was the source of widespread land subsidence; salt water intrusion and a rapid fall in the level of water tables affected huge areas of China. In recent years, the lower reaches of the Yellow River has run dry for increasingly long periods as a result of excessive extraction of water from upstream stretches.

Water resources are distributed unevenly. Southern China contains some 82 percent of all water resources, but has only 36 percent of the national arable area. By contrast, the northern half of the country – the area which will carry the heaviest burden of China's future crop output growth – contains 64 percent of all arable land, but has access to a mere 18 percent of water resources. Hence, the emphasis on a colossal engineering project designed to divert and transfer southern water to northern regions.

Water pollution is also a serious problem. A fifth of Chinese rivers are polluted – 5 percent of them seriously and much of China's fresh water may not be directly usable by early in the next century because of pollution from waste water discharge. Meanwhile, water pollution seems to have been responsible for unusually high rates of cancer in some parts of the country.[48]

The pressures of economic development, and associated tensions between traditional means of water control and technical progress in water use have been important elements contributing to this situation. The failure to implement effective pricing mechanisms has been an added factor. In northern China, the threat posed to agriculture by water shortages is particularly acute, this being the region which carries a heavy burden in terms of generating the higher yields needed to generate sustained farm growth. Competition for limited water supplies for farm and non-farm use is growing more intense not only in the countryside, but also in the cities, where domestic and industrial consumers vie with each other for the scarce resource.

MACROECONOMIC CONDITIONS AT THE END OF THE 1990s[49]

In the face of serious structural problems and with few interruptions, the Chinese economy has maintained a remarkable record of sustained growth since the early 1980s. In 1997, the Chinese leadership's proud boast was that it had successfully engineered a 'soft landing' without sacrificing the momentum of economic growth. More recently, however, domestic economic problems have been exacerbated by the impact of the financial crisis in East and South-east Asia. The result has been to inhibit growth, threatening fulfilment of macro targets contained in the Ninth Five-Year Plan (1996–2000).

In the early months of his Premiership, Zhu Rongji spoke of the regional financial crisis as a "formidable challenge" to China's development programme.[50] Throughout 1998 and into 1999, he and other Chinese leaders remained consistent in their defence of the feasibility of immediate growth targets.[51] In the face of intense speculation overseas, they have also won plaudits for their refusal to contemplate devaluation. In fact, with the import content of finished Chinese exports in excess of 50 percent, the benefits of currency devaluation might be limited and could, if it led to a further round of competitive devaluations by other countries, be counter-productive. In any case, at the end of 1998, China's foreign exchange reserves (US$ 145 billion) were sufficient to cover its existing foreign debt four times over and to fund a whole year's worth of capital imports. Nor would devaluation serve to address the critical problem of slowing *domestic* demand.

Compared with those of many of its neighbours, the Chinese economy has remained buoyant. In some respects, China would also appear to be less susceptible to influences of the kind that precipitated financial crises in countries, such as Thailand, Indonesia and South Korea. At the end 1998, China's foreign exchange reserves stood at 141 billion dollars – the second highest in the world – and 80 percent of its foreign debt reflected long-term loans, many of them funded by international financial institutions, such as the World Bank.

Concern among Chinese leaders has therefore reflected less the comparative performance of the economy than the impact of external difficulties associated with the Asian financial crisis, which have exacerbated more deeply-rooted domestic problems in the Chinese economy. The impact of these forces has been to constrain economic growth and further threaten the remarkable development momentum of recent years.

Preliminary figures issued by China's State Statistical Bureau point to

GDP growth of 7.8 percent in 1998 and suggest that for the first time in the 1990s, the economy failed to fulfil the annual plan (8 percent). The small shortfall implied by these figures is likely to have understated by a significant margin the true gap between economic reality and aspiration. Many would argue that official growth estimates contain an upward bias, not least by including output that has merely been added to already-large inventories.

Slowing growth has serious implications for an economy in which urban unemployment is already rapidly rising. After a long period in which potential social and political unrest associated with lay-offs from SOEs inhibited urban industrial reform in China, after the Fifth Party Congress (September 1997) the government showed a greater willingness to embrace difficult reforms in the interests of enhancing enterprise efficiency and eliminating massive indebtedness within the SOE sector. In the first nine months of 1998, some 11.5 million lay-offs are estimated to have taken place in China and it has been suggested that by 2000, the number of urban jobless could reach 15–18 million, affecting up to 58 million people.

Even allowing for workers who subsequently find new jobs – a significant proportion of all lay-offs – the social costs of recent rises in urban unemployment have been high. The real income of laid-off workers who remained unemployed has fallen sharply, causing many of them to fall below the poverty line. Further consequences have included widening income disparities and burgeoning crime in many large Chinese cities, especially in the north-east.

In the face of such problems, the Chinese government during 1998 was compelled to retreat from its SOE reform programme in favour of increased investment in state-owned manufacturing industries (including loss-making units). As a short-term expedient, this response may have stemmed rising unemployment and encouraged growth. But as past experience shows, such measures are no substitute for the reforms that are essential to reviving the state enterprise sector. Moreover, since investment injections to SOEs derive from state-owned banks rather than government revenue, the government's action also has grave implications for reform of the financial sector and the creation of an accountable, commercial banking system.

The injection of extra investment funds into the SOE sector contradicts the policy goal of transforming China's banks into truly commercial entities. It has also exacerbated the problem of non-performing loans and caused a further deterioration in the quality of banks' loan portfolios. The intimate connection between China's SOE and financial reforms no doubt ensures that the Chinese government will eventually have to return to the reformist thrust of earlier policies. The success of such reforms are, however, likely to have been further delayed by the short-sighted expediency of the most recent stimulatory initiatives.

One of the clearest lessons of the regional financial crisis has been that China's macroeconomic policies can no longer be formulated without regard for international economic fluctuations. The impact of the regional financial crisis has been most obviously reflected in China's foreign trade performance. In 1998, the volume of such trade fell by 0.4 percent. The burden of this decline was carried entirely by imports, which declined by 1.5 percent (exports meanwhile rising by 0.5 percent).[52] The most telling sign of recent difficulties is the 9.9 percent decline in exports to Asian countries – a deterioration whose impact would have been much more severe, had it not been for offsetting rises in exports to Europe and North America (by 15.7 percent).

Meanwhile, the recent downward trend in inflows of foreign investment has continued. Official Chinese sources show that the peak level of foreign direct investment (FDI) (US$ 111.14 billion) was attained in 1993. In 1998, FDI rose by just 0.7 percent, although foreign loans fell by 8.5 percent. Meanwhile, the collapse (October 1998) of Guangdong International Trust and Investment Corporation (GITIC) – the 'investment arm' of the Guangdong provincial government – and Beijing's clearly-stated refusal to guarantee its unregistered debts served as a timely warning to foreign investors. Other provincial ITICs are thought to be under similar pressure. The recent downgrading of China's foreign currency debt status has merely added to the loss of confidence that seems to be growing amongst overseas investors.

CONCLUSION

Steady and sustained economic growth in the longer term will depend on China's ability to guarantee food and energy supplies, to contain environmental degradation, and to address major reforms – in particular, the transformation of state-owned enterprises, the implementation of financial reform and the establishment of a comprehensive social security system. Meanwhile, the financial crisis in Asia has taken its own toll on the prospects for China's future economic development. In particular, the impact of the crisis on access to urgently required capital could be serious, bearing in mind that some 80 percent of foreign capital inflows originate in East and South-east Asia. Foreign investors elsewhere in the world may also review their assessment of the region's prospects.

The challenges are formidable and although the experience of the last two decades may encourage an optimistic assessment of China's ability to address the underlying problems, it would be foolish to underestimate the scale of the task. Even if the recent pattern of growth is not reversed, a significant slowing of the growth momentum is already taking place. If this were to continue, the economic, social and political consequences could be severe.

NOTES

1 Many writers have highlighted Mao's delight in contradictions and drawn attention to inconsistencies in his behaviour. One outcome of these tensions was that "Mao's concrete actions . . . often cut against the grain of his core principles" (Kenneth Lieberthal, *Governing China: From revolution through Reform* (New York and London: W.W. Norton & Company, 1995), p. 61).

2 More often than not, Deng's vaunted pragmatism is evidenced in his famous statement (July 1962) that "it doesn't matter whether a cat is black or white, as long as it catches mice." For consideration of Deng's economic attributes, see Barry Naughton, "Deng Xiaoping: the Economist" in David Shambaugh (ed.), *Deng Xiaoping: Portrait of a Chinese Statesman* (Oxford: Clarendon Press, 1995), pp. 83–106.

3 Naughton refers to Deng's "tendency to push for unsustainably rapid economic growth rates" ("Deng Xiaoping: the Economist, p. 97).

4 The phrase is Y. Y. Kueh's (see his *Was Mao Really Necessary? An Economic Perspective* (Lingnan College, Hong Kong, Professorial Inaugural Lecture Series 1, 1996, p. 2).

5 Inclusion of Hong Kong's foreign exchange deposits would raise the figure to around US$ 230 billion – almost exactly the same as those of Japan.

6 See State Statistical Bureau (SSB), *Zhongguo tongji nianjian* (*China Statistical Yearbook*) (*ZGTJNJ*), 1998, (Beijing: Zhongguo tongji chubanshe), 1998, p. 38. The same source gives a comparable figure of 6.1% p. a. for 1953–78.

7 See Peter Nolan and Robert F. Ash, "China's economy on the ever of reform" in Andrew G. Walder (ed.), *China's Transitional Economy* (Oxford: Oxford University Press, 1996), p. 20, Table 1.

8 *ZGTJNJ*, 1998, p. 106.

9 The role of tertiary sector activities, especially wholesale and retail sales growth (up by 20.9% p. a. during the first half of the 1980s) was also an important contributory factor.

10 Relevant data can be found in *ZGTJNJ*, 1998, pp. 55–58.

11 In 1998, the impact of the regional financial crisis was for the first time significantly retarded growth.

12 Cf. total populations of 646.53 million (1957) and 1,236.26 million (1997). See *ZGTJNJ*, 1997, p. 69; 1998, p. 105. Peak population growth was reached in China during the 1960s.

13 E.g., see Judith Banister, "Population growth in China and its economic implications," Robert F. Ash (ed.), *China and Asia: Economic Security and Geostrategic Issues* (Curzon Press, forthcoming).

14 See Judith Banister, "Population, public health and environment in China," *The China Quarterly*, No. 156 (December, 1998), pp. 956–1015.

15 The corresponding figure was 37% in 1957.

16 Estimated from figures in *ZGTJNJ* (various issues).

17 Another major contributory factor is simply rural, especially agricultural poverty. The gap between rural and urban incomes has widened since the mid-1980s to the extent that it is now wider than it was at the beginning of the reform period. Crop farming is likely to be the principal expression of poverty among farmers.

18 But it has done so at the partial cost of transferring such pressures to cities, where the social consequences of migration have become very evident in recent years.

19 The figure of 3.5% is mentioned in *Liaowang*, 5 January 1998, quoted in British Broadcasting Corporation (BBC) Monitoring, *Summary of World Broadcasts: Part 3 (Asia-Pacific)* (*SWB*), FE/3136, 28 January 1998.

20 See especially Nicholas R. Lardy, *China's Unfinished Economic Revolution* (Washington, D.C.: Brookings Institutions Press, 1998).

21 *ZGTJZY*, 1998, p. 100. During the same period, the output shares of collectively-owned, private and foreign-funded enterprises industry have all increased sharply.

22 In the North-east, for example, SOEs account for about 60% of industrial gross value output.

23 *ZGTJNJ*, 1998, p. 448. By contrast, large-scale units, accounting for less than 6% of all SOEs, contribute 70% of industrial value-added.

24 The share of large and medium SOEs in GVIO rose from 47% (1985) to 52% (1990) to 55% (1996) (*ZGTJZY*, 1992, p. 70; and *ZGTJNJ*, 1997, p. 424).

25 It is instructive that not a single merger of a large-scale SOE with another has occurred in China and no doubt the more common future pattern will be mergers between smaller and larger units.

26 Cf. Peter Nolan: "in 1992, only seven of China's 100 largest enterprises were reportedly making losses. Among the top 500 enterprises, only 42 were making losses" (*Indigenous Large Firms in China's Economic Reform: The Case of Shougang Iron and Steel Corporation* (University of London, School of Oriental and African Studies, Contemporary China Institute: Research Notes and Studies, No. 12, 1998, p. 7.

27 For a good discussion of the emergence of large firms under the impact of economic reform in China, see Nolan, *op. cit.*, esp. pp. 6–10.

28 For more detailed consideration of the importance of the rural sector in China at the end of the 1990s, see Robert F. Ash, "Challenges and opportunities facing the rural sector in China," *China Review 1998* (Hong Kong: The Chinese University Press, 1998).

29 Official Chinese sources indicate that there are 50 million people still living in absolute poverty, although use of the World Bank's poverty criterion suggests that over 20% of China's population should be considered as poor. See World Bank, *China 2020: Development Challenges in the New Century* (Washington, The World Bank, 1997), p. 50.

30 On purely economic grounds, there is a strong case in favour of China seeking to produce more higher value-added crops and importing more grain. Indeed, such a strategy could best serve the needs of China's own sustainable development, as well as contributing to more stable world food prices and enhancing agricultural production in Europe and North America.

31 Lester R. Brown, *Who Will Feed China? Wake-Up Call for a Small Planet* (New York and London: W.W. Norton and Co., 1995). Brown's provocative thesis has attracted a considerable literature, most of which is very critical of his analysis. For a representative selection, see Frederick W. Crook, "Could China starve the world? Comments on Lester Brown's article," (Washington, D.C.: US Department of Agriculture, Economic Research Service, 1994), pp. 17–19; Scott Rozelle, Huang Jikun and Mark W. Rosegrant, "Why China will not starve the world," *Choices*, 1996, No. 1; Vaclav Smil, "Who will feed China?" *The China Quarterly*, No. 143 (Sept. 1995), pp. 801–13; Nikos Alexandratos, "China's projected cereals consumption and the capacity of the rest of the world to increase exports", *Food Policy* (June 1997).

32 E.g., see Lester Brown's recent interview in *China Perspectives*, No. 13 (Sept/Oct 1997), pp. 11–19; also a subsequent comment by Ash in *China Perspectives*, No. 16 (March/April 1998), pp. 25–28.

33 Cf. the following estimates (reproduced from *ZGTJZY*, 1998, p. 92) of total grain output:

1990–4 (av)	445.2 m. tonnes
1995	466.6
1996	504.5
1997	494.2

34 E.g., the effects of urban and industrial encroachment on arable land, worsening water shortages in northern China and rural environmental degradation.

35 The fact that official estimates seriously understate the reality of China's arable area and grain sown area merely underlines this point.

36 The text of the "White Paper" can be found in *Beijing Review*, 11–17 November 1996.

37 For more detailed consideration of this policy, see Song Hongyuan, "The 'grain bag' Governor Responsibility System (GRS) and its impact on grain production, grain marketing and macro-control," and Frederick W. Crook, "How will China's 'rice bag' policy affect grain production, distribution, prices, and international trade?" both in Organisation for Economic Cooperation and Development (OECD), *Agricultural Policies in China* (Paris: OECD, 1997), pp. 52–70. Also Ash, "The grain issue in China: domestic and international perspectives," *China Review 1997*, esp. pp. 141–44.

38 One of the most prominent features of China's grain output growth since the early 1980s has been the change in the regional centre of gravity of grain production away from southern China towards the northern half of the country (especially the North-east).

39 Transport bottlenecks alone may depress GDP growth by a percentage point. In recent years, infrastructural investment in China has been about 6.5% of GDP. See East Asia Analytical Unit, *China Embraces the Market: Achievements, Constraints and Opportunities* (Australian Department of Foreign Affairs and Trade, 1997), p. 225.

40 In so doing, China more than doubled its share of global electricity output. See Peter Nolan and Wang Xiaoqiang, "The battle for the Chinese power equipment market: Harbin Power Equipment Company – sub-contractor to the multinationals or integrated, globally competitive firm?" (1998) (mimeo), p. 12.

41 The industrial sector (especially iron and steel, and chemicals) accounts for about 60% of total energy consumption in China, compared with 29% in the USA and 49% in South Korea (estimates for 1993). Transportation absorbs a further 10% of consumption. See Unit I-2 (Policy Planning), Directorate General I (External Relations), "The European Commission, Economic security: the EU's stake in a sustainable development in China," in Werner Draguhn and Robert F. Ash (ed.), *China's Economic Security* (London: Curzon Press), forthcoming.

42 China is unusual in the extent of its dependence on coal, which still accounts for more than three quarters of primary energy (two thirds of final commercial energy consumed).

43 This could have serious consequences for EU member states, some of which are very vulnerable to price rises because of their dependence on oil imports.

44 For detailed consideration of these two environmental issues, see the papers by Robert F. Ash and Richard Louis Edmonds, James Nickum, Frederick W. Crook, and Liu Changming in *The China Quarterly*, No. 156 (December 1998).

45 Official SSB data suggest that in 1990, 1995 and 1996, reclamation more than offset the gross loss of farmland and thereby generated a net increase in China's arable area. See Ministry of Agriculture, *Zhongguo nongye fazhan baogao* (*China Agricultural Development Report*), 1997 (Beijing: Nongye chubanshe, 1997), p. 110. In 1997, however, a further 140,000 hectares of arable land were lost (net).

46 A similar argument is relevant to the interpretation of the under-estimation of China's arable area in that much of the under-reported land is likely to be marginal uplands in remote areas of the country.
47 Lee Travers, "Sustainable development without safeguards: the example of the Chinese water economy", Ash (ed.), *China and Asia: Economic Security and Geostrategic Issues* (Curzon Press, forthcoming).
48 *Ibid.*
49 This section was written at the beginning of March, 1999 and reflects quantitative indicators available at that time.
50 Zhu was appointed Premier in March 1998.
51 In 1998, planned growth was set at 8% for GDP, and 11% for industry.
52 The outcome was that China's trade surplus increased to US$ 43.6 billion: see Xinhua, 26 February 1999, quoted in *SWB* FEW/0578 WG/2 (3 March 1999). Note that in May 1998, China experienced *negative* export growth for the first time in almost two years and in September exports fell by 6.7% year on year.

Part I

THE CHALLENGE OF MACROECONOMIC RESTRUCTURING

1

HOW TO REFORM A PLANNED ECONOMY

Lessons from China

John McMillan and Barry Naughton[1]

I. INTRODUCTION

The countries of Eastern Europe and the former Soviet Union have been flooded with advice from the West on how to liberalize their planned economies. This advice is, unfortunately, offered in an empirical vacuum: no one knows how these economies will react to the proposed liberalization measures. There exists, however, a neglected source of information. China offers a long time-series of data—over a decade's worth—on the effects of reforms on a planned economy. China's reforms were gradual, but their cumulative effect has been large; and they have been remarkably successful. China's experiments provide some practical lessons on what kinds of reforms can work elsewhere.

The dominant school of thought among economists favours the 'big-bang' policy of reforming quickly and according to a comprehensive plan. Partial reforms, in this view, are useless: they will be negated by the remnants of the planning system. The proponents of big-bang reform have been influential, with Poland, Czechoslovakia, and Russia announcing plans for a rapid transition to capitalism.

China's reforms, by contrast, were not conceived as a grand plan; rather they have consisted of small, step-by-step changes. No ultimate goal was announced, nor any timetable for the transition. Some of the changes were initiated spontaneously at ground level and only later ratified by government regulation. The reforms have proceeded by trial and error, with frequent mid-course corrections and reversals of policy; the reformers were probing into the unknown. China has muddled through.[2] We shall therefore characterize China's approach (in keeping with the natural-science phraseology of 'big bang') as *evolutionary reform*.

Evolutionary reform is not intrinsically superior to big-bang reform: it is obviously desirable to create an efficient, market-based economy as quickly as

Source: *Oxford Review of Economic Policy*, Vol. 8(1), (1993), pp. 130–43.

possible. But, as is becoming increasingly clear, any reform process will be protracted. All the institutions of the planned economy were developed as component parts of that system; they are mutually consistent, but incompatible with a true market economy. The price, fiscal, monetary, ownership, and legal systems must all be changed. A big-bang transition can indeed cause the interconnected socialist system to collapse. But there is more to moving to a market economy than just removing government controls. New institutions must be created. Some government direction of the process of building the institutions of the market economy is needed. But, as we shall argue, this is a highly complex and unpredictable process, and so it is only in a limited way susceptible to planning and control.

China's example shows that there are specific characteristics of the centrally planned system that can he used to initiate a step-by-step reform process. Once a crack is opened in the monolith that is the centrally planned economy, cumulative forces take over and prise the crack open ever more widely.The crack, in the case of China, was the elimination of the state monopoly over industry, which began a process of change that became irreversible. This process is compatible with vigorous economic growth, so a reform-oriented government gains time and resources to build the new institutions required to run the market economy.

What are the lessons from China? While the exact sequence of events in China cannot and should not he replicated elsewhere, the key features of China's reforms can be adopted in other countries. China's reform success can be seen with hindsight to have resulted from, first, massive entry of non-state firms; second, a dramatic increase in competition, both among state firms and between state firms and non-state firms; and, third, improvements in the performance of state-owned firms resulting from state-imposed market-like incentives. The process in turn drove a realignment of prices, which caused an erosion in governmental resources and a shift of economic power towards households. China shows the potency of the fundamental market forces of entry and competition. China's example does not, however, justify *laissez-faire*: the state must monitor firms during the transition.

II. CHINA'S REFORMS HAVE BEEN SUCCESSFUL

China is a counter-example to the claim, often made by the proponents of big bang, that gradual reform must fail. Conventional wisdom notwithstanding, China's economic reforms have indeed been successful. This economic success is in glaring contrast to the deplorable lack of progress in political freedoms; China has had *perestroika* without *glasnost.*

Real *per capita* GNP grew 7.2 per cent annually from 1978 to 1990. Growth was particularly rapid between 1982 and 1988, averaging 9.7 per cent *per capita* over six years, among the best in the world, before slowing sharply in 1988–90 with the political crisis around Tiananmen. Vigorous growth did, however, resume in 1991. The increasing efficiency of China's industry is indicated by its success in selling in competitive world markets: exports grew in real terms at over 10 per cent per year between 1978 and 1990; the ratio of exports to GNP had risen to 17 percent by 1990 (compare this to Japan's 9 per cent). While growth of national income should not be the only criterion for evaluating the success of economic policies, it is the first and most important indicator of success. An economic system—especially in a poor country—must be judged by its performance in providing increased levels of goods to its citizens, and this can be roughly measured by the growth of GNP *per capita.*[3] By the simple criterion of making ordinary people better off (or, more accurately, less badly off), China has been spectacularly successful.

In many obvious cases, specific aspects of the Chinese reforms were misconceived or self-defeating. Thus, we are far from arguing that Chinese reforms were anything close to optimal. But it is precisely China's success in the face of initial poverty and repeated policy mistakes that makes its reform process interesting. It appears that the Chinese approach to reform has been quite robust, capable of producing good results in spite of large deviations from best practice. This is particularly significant as it becomes increasingly clear that all reform processes will be protracted and marked by significant policy errors and backtracking.

In some respects, Eastern Europe and the former Soviet Union face a more difficult transition than China. Macroeconomic imbalances have been more severe in Eastern Europe than in China, creating an urgent need for anti-inflationary policies. The need for macroeconomic stabilization complicates the reform transition, requiring some big-bang policies, at least in the macroeconomic sphere. China made great gains, as will be seen, through agricultural reforms; there is less scope for such gains in the more industrialized countries of Eastern Europe. In other respects, however, China has had the bigger impediments to transition. Education levels are much lower in China than in Eastern Europe. To the extent that institution-building is a crucial component of the reform process, China, like any developing country, faces greater challenges than the relatively wealthy countries of Eastern Europe. The rapid political change in Eastern Europe means that those countries have largely discarded political constraints to the reform process, while China continues to labour under the dead hand of a repressive and ideologically rigid group of Communist Party elders. How, if at all, the choice of reform policy—big bang vs. evolutionary—is constrained by the form of government—authoritarian vs. democratic—is a topic on which there are many strong opinions but few hard facts. Country-to-country differences such as these limit the transferability of any lessons from China. But China offers one of the few sources, as yet, of empirical information on the long-term effects of reforms on a planned economy. For a reformer, some data must be better than none.

III. PRIVATIZATION IS NOT CRUCIAL; COMPETITION IS

Many Western economists maintain that reform necessitates the rapid transfer of state-owned firms to private ownership; there are lengthy debates about the best way to achieve this (for example, Blanchard *et. al.*, 1991; Lipton and Sachs, 1990; Sinn, 1991). China's experience suggests that privatization is a red herring. Rapid privatization need not be the centrepiece of a reform policy. Scarce resources of economic and administrative expertise might better be directed into thinking about other problems. We see three reasons to delay privatization.

(i) Entrepreneurs set up new firms

Investment in new firms by profit-seeking entrepreneurs is the most potent force to be harnessed by reformers. China's most dynamic sector, particularly since 1984, has been non-state-owned industrial firms. These firms, mostly located in rural areas, have a range of formal organizational structures; but they are primarily profit-seeking firms (Byrd and Lin, 1990). The non-state sector has grown since 1978 at an annual rate of 17.6 per cent, such that in 1990 it accounted for a striking 45 per cent of total industrial output. While the output of state-owned firms has also grown in absolute terms (7.6 percent annually from 1978 to 1990), it has shrunk dramatically relative to the non-state Sector: state-owned firms accounted for only 55 per cent of industrial output in 1990, down from 78 per cent in 1978. China is growing out of the plan (Naughton, 1992*a*). Over time, the issue of how and when to privatize China's state-owned firms is becoming less important, as the state-owned firms weigh less and less heavily in the overall economy.

The scope for new entry in socialist economies is particularly great because of two fundamental characteristics of those economies. First, the size distribution of industrial enterprises is highly skewed towards large firms. In economies such as the Soviet Union or Czechoslovakia, there were virtually no small industrial firms. While China was known for the large number of 'small' firms in its pre-reform system, even these were relatively large, typically having over fifty employees. Rapid growth has occurred in 'micro-enterprises', those with less than fifty employees. The size distribution of industrial firms in market economies, developed and developing, is quite consistent: small firms typically account for around 25–30 per cent of industrial employment.[4] There are numerous niches in both modern and developing economies that are best filled by small firms. Since those niches are empty in socialist economies, the potential rewards to entrepreneurs who arrive first are quite large, ensuring rapid entry and at the same time, holding the promise of efficiency gains for the economy as a whole.

Second, the price system of socialist economies is skewed in a fashion that raises profitability in manufacturing. Socialist governments maintain high prices for manufactured goods (except for a small number of items judged to be necessities). The purpose is to concentrate taxable revenues in the large-scale, state-dominated manufacturing sector (we return to this point below). This means that once barriers to entry are lowered, new entrants will be able to reap high profits in the initial phase. This effect is magnified by the presence of shortages of certain essential goods and services. Rural enterprises in China in 1978, before reforms, were earning an average rate of profit on capital of 32 per cent. This very high profitability was not the result of superb efficiency on the part of these firms, but rather of the fact that they were able to share in a part of the monopoly profits created by state pricing policy. As entry has proceeded and the rural industrial sector has grown explosively, profitability has declined steadily, falling to below 10 per cent of capital.

Lenin understood that the state's monopoly on production was essential for the survival of the planning system: he wrote 'small production *engenders* capitalism and the bourgeoisie continuously, daily, hourly, spontaneously, and on a mass scale'. Lenin foresaw what China illustrates, the corrosive effect of the entry of non-state firms. 'The decisive thing is the organization of the strictest and country-wide accounting and control of production and distribution of goods.'[5]

The entry of new firms in China illustrates the vitality of market forces. Despite impressive impediments—little law of contract, weak property rights, underdeveloped capital markets—when the restrictions on the activities of non-state firms were loosened, a huge amount of entrepreneurial investment occurred, such that by 1990 non-state firms were producing almost a half of industrial output. Because of the pre-existing distortions both in the size structure of industry and in industrial prices, the economic forces that propel entry are particularly strong. Entry looks to be a fringe phenomenon in the early stages of reform; but in fact it attacks the heart of the planning system.

(ii) State-owned firms' performance can be improved

While shrinking relative to the rest of the economy, China's state-owned industry has itself achieved respectable productivity gains. This has been the result of liberalization measures that fall far short of privatization. China's state-owned firms are notoriously inefficient; press reports commonly describe them as 'dinosaurs' and 'terminally ill'. But recent empirical studies show they are significantly less inefficient than they used to be.

China's state-owned firms have been commercialized: they have been given some market or market-like incentives. State-owned enterprises are now allowed to keep some fraction of their profits, where before all profits had to be remitted to the state; enterprises now sell and buy in free markets, rather than selling and procuring everything at state-controlled prices; managers' pay is based on firm performance; and production decisions have been shifted from the state to the firm.

This commercialization has resulted in improved productivity. Under the system of enterprise contracting, state firms are required to deliver a certain fixed amount of profit to the government, and are allowed to retain a substantial fraction of any profits they generate beyond this fixed amount; many firms now keep as much as 100 per cent of residual profits.

The data show that, when firms' autonomy increased (in either of two senses: the firm's profit-retention rate was increased, or the responsibility for deciding output levels was shifted down from the state to the firm), managers responded by strengthening the discipline imposed on workers: they increased the proportion of the workers' income paid in the form of bonuses; and they increased the fraction of workers whom, since they were on fixed-term contracts, it was in principle possible to dismiss. The new incentives were effective: productivity increased significantly following the strengthening of worker incentives. Also, the extra autonomy was followed by an increase in productive investment by the state-owned firms (Groves *et al.*, 1992*a*).

Managers of state-owned firms are now paid according to their firms' performance: the data show a strong link between a firm's sales and its top manager's pay, and a weaker link between profits and pay. As well as these direct monetary incentives, managers can be demoted for sub-par performance by their firms, and promoted for unusually good performance. The data show that the careers of the managers of China's state-owned firms are in fact affected by how well or badly their firms do, so the prospect of promotion or demotion does work as an incentive (Groves *et al.*, 1992*b*).

Instead of auctioning off firms, the Chinese government has begun auctioning off top management jobs. Potential managers (including, often, the incumbent manager) vie for the right to be manager by submitting bids—promises of how the firm will perform in the future. This process has revealed information about the potential capabilities of both the firms and the potential managers. As a result, it has put better people in top managerial positions than the old system, under which managers were simply appointed by government bureaucrats (Byrd, 1991; Groves *et al.*, 1992*b*).

Firms in capitalist economies face discipline from their product markets (Schumpeter, 1950, ch. 7). In order to survive, a firm must produce at a high enough quality and low enough price to persuade customers to buy from it rather than its competitors. As a result of both the entry of non-state firms and the fact that state firms have begun to sell on free markets, China's state-owned firms now face active product-market competition. This market-based discipline has given the state-owned firms additional incentives to improve their productivity.

Output per worker in state-owned industry rose 52 per cent (in constant prices) during the reform years 1980 to 1989.[6] China proves, then, that it is possible for state-owned firms to be induced to improve their productivity by measures that fall short of privatization.

(iii) The state-owned sector acts as safety net

The transition process in Eastern Europe has imposed large costs on workers, as inefficient state-owned firms suddenly exposed to competition have been forced to lay off workers and national income has plummeted. China, by contrast, has managed its reforms with little overt unemployment. There has been slot of disguised unemployment, as firms maintain bloated labour forces. If these firms had been privatized, many workers would probably have been dismissed. State-owned firms, even if they face increased competition, can avoid laying off workers by relying on government subsidies, as China's state-owned firms have in fact done. Conceivably the inefficiencies this causes have been justified by their cushioning effects, spreading the costs of transition among the population. Workers in state-run firms undoubtedly have low productivity. However, unless there are alternative high-productivity occupations available for them, it is unclear that the economy benefits from dismissing such workers, particularly if society must then support them through a new safety net. The creation of such a safety net is costly in terms of scarce administrative and economic expertise. By keeping firms in state hands, such measures may be delayed until several years into the reform process. This was the case in China, where by the late 1980s rudimentary unemployment compensation measures were in place and gradual workforce rationalization had begun.

State-owned firms produce goods that are of notoriously low quality. For the delayed-privatization policy to work, consumers must want to purchase these firms' outputs; this implies some degree of protection from imports. Thus this approach requires that any reduction in pre-existing barriers to international trade proceed no faster than the internal liberalization. This occurred in China, and could occur in other liberalizing countries. It was not possible, however, when the former East Germany became part of the united Germany: East German firms immediately had to compete with West German firms.

IV. THE STATE MUST MONITOR FIRMS DURING THE TRANSITION

Financial markets in modern market economies imposes variety of disciplines on firms, prodding managers to ensure firms operate efficiently. In the United States and the United Kingdom managers know that poor performance is likely to cost them their jobs: they will be dismissed by the board of directors; or their firm will be taken over and a new managerial team installed; or the firm will fall into bankruptcy, with blame attached to the manager. Further incentives come from the fact that their pay is linked to the firm's stockmarket performance. (Anecdotal evidence sometimes raises doubts about whether US managers do face genuine incentives; but the data show that they do. A correlation, small but statistically significant, exists between poor firm performance and the manager's loss of job; and a correlation, also small but statistically significant, exists between a firm's stockmarket value and its top manager's pay: see Jensen and Murphy, 1990.) In Japan and Germany the source of managers' incentives is different but the incentives are no weaker: banks with large stakes in the firm, both as creditors and as equity holders, monitor the managers' decisions (Hoshi *et al.*, 1991).

An economy in the process of transition lacks financial markets. Fully operating financial markets will take years to develop (Tirole, 1991). In the transforming economy, therefore, the usual capitalist managerial disciplines are absent. The only available substitute is the state. Government officials in a reforming economy must oversee the managers of state-owned firms, as they did when the economy was centrally planned. The incentives of the monitors thus become important (especially since, in the planned economy, government supervision used to produce grossly inefficient firms). Is it in the interest of officials in the reforming economy to maintain the right sort of supervision? Can the bureaucracy be relied on to induce managers to make their firms efficient?

China shows that officials' oversight of managers can generate managerial incentives that, while undoubtedly far from perfect, work in the right direction. State-imposed incentives have replaced state-imposed controls; and, as noted, these incentives have dramatically improved state firms' productivity. What induced China's bureaucrats to regulate for firm efficiency? The increased competition squeezed state-owned firms' profits; this meant that state firms' remittances to the government fell. State firms were the main source of government revenue (as we discuss below). To slow the drop in government revenue, the state was impelled to the mid-to-late 1980s to spur the state firms to become more profitable. Firms had been given some profit incentives at the beginning of the 1980s. But during the late 1980s, driven by their need for revenue, state officials increasingly made profit remittances the primary obligation of firms. Financial discipline was tightened, so that firms faced greater financial risk but also steeper compensation schedules and stronger incentives. The need for increased financial discipline was created by the increased product-market discipline that resulted from entry and competition; financial discipline then reinforced the effects of the product-market discipline.

'Spontaneous privatization' is a problem that has arisen in Eastern Europe and the Soviet Union: with the breakdown of centralized control, some managers have extracted value from the firms for their own benefit (Johnson, 1991). Preventing such plundering is an additional reason why state oversight of state-owned firms must continue during the transition. China's reforms replaced direct controls on firms with incentives. This relaxation of oversight resulted, as noted, in the firms' increasing their productivity; but much of this increase in productivity stayed within the firm. When a firm was granted increased autonomy, the incomes of managers and workers rose significantly, as did the firms' welfare funds. Despite the improved productivity, the amount of profits remitted to the state fell and the subsidies given to the firms by the state rose following the increases in autonomy. Perhaps this is evidence of some plundering; but it was not simply a transfer from the state to the employees of state firms, because other effects worked in the same direction. First, the lower profits were at least in part attributable to the increased competition that the firms were facing as a result of the reforms; and second, the increase in employees' pay reflected the improvements in productivity that followed the reforms. Evidence that autonomy did not lead to severe plundering comes from the fact that state-owned firms significantly increased their productive investments following increases in their autonomy (Groves *et at.*, 1992*a*).

V. PRICE REFORM CAN BE DONE GRADUALLY

One of the most discussed distortions in planned economies is the irrationality of prices: prices bear little relation to either production costs or demand, resulting in a severe misallocation of resources. China is often criticized for having neglected to reform its price system. This criticism is misplaced. Prices have been reformed: not by grand policy, but by stealth.

China did not undertake comprehensive price reform. But gradual marketization accompanied by sustained entry of new producers caused a realignment of prices. Before the reforms, state-owned enterprises were required to sell all their output to the state at state-fixed prices. Under the reforms, these firms have been allowed to sell some of their output on free markets: in 1989, on average 38 per cent of a state-owned firm's outputs were directly sold on markets, and for some state firms market sales were 100 per cent of output. Similarly, an increasingly large fraction of state firms' inputs have been purchased on free markets, rather than being allocated by the state: in 1989, on average 56 percent of a state-owned firm's inputs were procured through market purchases, and for some state firms, 100 per cent of inputs were market-procured.[7] There is a dual price system, with the market price usually being substantially above the official price. From the viewpoint of economic incentives the key point is that, at the margin, decisions are made in the face of market prices. The fact that the price received from the state is less than the price received from the market merely means that the firm is paying a lump-sum tax. For a firm's decisions on how much to produce, what inputs to use, and what kind of investment to undertake, the state-imposed output quota is irrelevant, as long as that quota is smaller than total output.

What matters for such decisions is the price that will he received for any extra output, which is the free-market price (Byrd, 1987).

Evidence that most industries' prices have been effectively reformed comes from data on profit rates. With the erratic pricing of the centrally planned economy, prices bear little relation to costs. In 1980 this was the case: profit rates in industry ranged from 7 per cent to 98 per cent. By 1989 prices had become more uniformly related to costs: in most industries profit rates were between 8 per cent and 23 per cent (Naughton, 1992*b*). Further evidence on China's progressive marketization comes from calculation of marginal products. In a textbook-perfect market economy, the free operation of the price system would ensure that the marginal product of labour became the same in all firms; and similarly for the marginal product of capital. Wide variations among marginal products indicate, on the other hand, that the economy is using its valuable resources of labour and capital inefficiently. Recent research finds that the variation in marginal products of both capital and labour has shrunk as China's reforms have progressed (Jefferson and Xu, 1991; Jefferson *et al.*, 1992).

Dual pricing forced state-owned firms to compete, both with other state-owned firms and with non-state firms. In order to sell on free markets, state-owned firms had to please their customers; they were forced to produce to a higher quality than when they had the governments guaranteed buyer.

The dual-price system is, of course, not ideal. It has enabled illicit profits to be made by obtaining goods at planned prices and selling them at market prices. Buying low and selling high is a normal market activity; but the dual-price system has meant that certain well-connected people can buy at artificially low prices. Anger at such corrupt practices was one of the sparks that ignited Tiananmen. Dual pricing is a temporary expedient to smooth the reform process, and it should be replaced by full market pricing as soon as is feasible. This should have occurred in China (as is obvious with the benefit of hindsight) by the late 1980s.[8]

VI. AGRICULTURE BOOMS WITH REFORM

Agriculture was the first area in which China implemented reforms. The commune system was replaced by the 'household responsibility system'. Under the commune system, peasants were organized into production teams. Each team member was assigned work points, which attempted to measure both how many hours and how effectively he or she had worked. Income depended on the number of work points accumulated. Income was not perfectly related to effort, however, because it was impossible to observe how conscientiously each individual worked: this would have required each peasant to be continually monitored. Moreover, there was a tendency to spread the commune's earnings across the individual commune members: those with larger families were given more income, regardless of effort. Thus the link between individual effort and reward was weak. Under the responsibility system, in contrast, each peasant family is given a long-term lease of a plot of land. The household must deliver a certain quota of produce to the government each year, and may keep anything it produces beyond that quota. The household members consume it themselves, sell it to the government, or sell it in the newly instituted rural markets. With the exception of the special ease of grain, they may decide for themselves what crops to sow and what animals to raise.

In 1978 and 1979 the government increased the prices paid for agricultural outputs, while leaving the structure of the commune system unchanged. Then, from 1980 to 1984, the commune system was gradually replaced by the responsibility system. The results were clear. Agricultural output increased by 67 per cent between 1978 and 1985. In part this was caused by an increase in inputs. But mainly it was due to the strengthened incentives: productivity (measured as the amount of output for a given amount of inputs) increased by nearly 50 per cent, compared with no increase in productivity over the previous two and a half decades (Lin, 1992; McMillan *et al.*, 1989). Over the second half of the decade, agricultural growth was slower but still respectable, averaging 4.5 per cent annually. While land remains state-owned, each peasant family essentially has its own plot of land, and sells any output in excess of the fixed state quota on free markets. A household's income therefore depends on that household's efforts; this linking of effort and rewards has resulted in spectacular increases in the production of food.

The increase in agricultural productivity in turn spurred the growth of rural industry, by generating a pool of savings and excess labour (Byrd and Lin, 1990; Jefferson *et al.*, 1992). Beginning from a small base, rural industry was allowed to grow with few of the restrictions that hobbled state-run industry. Rural industry expanded rapidly. The entry of these profit-seeking firms provided, as we have argued, the main ingredient in China's transition. Thus the transformation of agriculture was crucial to the overall success of the reforms.

VII. REFORM ENTAILS REDESIGNING THE TAX SYSTEM

Centrally planned economies do not have regularized taxation systems. Instead, taxation is implicit in government control of the price system. As a result, price reform in the absence of fiscal restructuring causes an erosion in government revenues; rapid price reform, by itself, entails rapid fiscal collapse. Some contraction in the government's financial resources is, of course, highly desirable. But in the centrally planned economy the government's fiscal revenues include virtually all of national saving. Rapid fiscal collapse thus implies a collapse in national saving and investment; and what economist would advise a country undertaking a difficult restructuring process to begin by reducing investment to zero? By contrast, the Chinese experience shows that gradual marketization can steadily undermine the government's fiscal resources without leading to total collapse. This provides time for the government to build a modern taxation system. It also provides (as discussed in the next section) a favourable environment for the growth of private saving and the financial intermediaries that channel such saving into productive investment.

Instead of clearly codified tax systems, socialist economies rely on governmental control of the price system to concentrate revenues in a relatively small number of state-run industrial firms. The government then relies on a variety of formal and informal means to draw industrial surpluses into the state budget. In China in 1978, industrial enterprises turned over an enormous 25 per cent of GNP to the budgetary authorities in the form of both profits and taxes. Such revenue deliveries were not explicitly regulated by tax codes, but rather reflected the state's roles as both taxation authority and owner of the bulk of industrial firms. The fiscal system was implicit (McKinnon, 1991; Naughton, 1992*b*). In 1980 state-firm profits and taxes accounted for 85 per cent of China's fiscal revenues.

The well-known distortions in the socialist price system are not random. They systematically increase profitability in manufacturing, while maintaining profitability low in a range of agricultural and extractive industries. Moreover, accounting procedures in manufacturing systematically understate capital costs (both depreciation and interest rates are low), also creating a large (and illusory) volume of profits. Finally, wage payments are low, because a portion of worker income is provided by the state in the form of subsidies. Thus, manufacturing costs are severely understated—materials, capital, and labour are all undervalued—and manufacturing paper profits correspondingly high.

Big-bang price liberalization will cause a rapid decline in the relative price of manufactures, and a collapse in fiscal revenues. Since the fiscal system is only implicit in government control of the price system, abandonment of that control will result in fiscal collapse. Implementing an effective big-bang conversion is made substantially more difficult because a newly designed fiscal system must be implemented simultaneously with price liberalization. Moreover, the existing distortions in the price system imply that state industrial enterprises are highly liquid in the initial phases of reform. This liquidity provides firms with resources to deflect stabilization measures, permitting them, for instance, to increase worker non-wage incomes and maintain their own investment programmes. This was quite apparent during the Polish stabilization in 1990.

By contrast, with evolutionary reform this problem is less pressing. On the one hand, entry-driven marketization will gradually push price relationships towards something closer to relative scarcities. State-run industry will be placed under continuous cost pressure as it struggles to meet new competition for underpriced inputs and in output markets. Such pressure is all to the good, as it makes it easier to monitor state enterprise performance. On the other hand, the government can stretch scarce administrative resources by successively implementing reforms that make enterprise accounting more realistic. Capital costs can be increased by raising depreciation charges and interest rates. Such a process can greatly reduce the massive uncertainty which is recognized as a major difficulty of the transition (Tirole, 1991). Constant pressure on inefficient state firms will be the greatest challenge they face, instead of high and non-stationary uncertainty. Fiscal pressure will also be expressed as steady erosion of fiscal revenues, rather than sudden collapse. This is also preferable, since it provides greater scope both for reduction in expenditures, and for gradual creation of an explicit taxation system as a substitute for the former implicit revenue system.

The development of a modern tax system for China has undoubtedly proceeded more slowly than would be desirable. But fiscal authorities now operate a rudimentary value-added tax (with rebates for exporters), urban land-use fees, and a system of social-security contributions; meanwhile, taxes collected on international trade and petty commerce have increased substantially. These are not trivial accomplishments for a developing country.

VIII. MONETARY POLICY MUST ACCOMMODATE RISING DEMAND FOR MONEY

As the government surrenders its control over saving and investment flows, households and private businesses must assume the dominant role in accumulating saving and channelling it into productive investment. This calls for dramatic changes in household behaviour, but the Chinese experience shows that these changes will be forthcoming if appropriate economic policies are followed. An increasing role for households in saving and investment generally leads to an increased demand for money balances. Monetization (or remonetization) occurs, and monetary policy must accommodate a sustained increase in money demand.

In the pre-reform economy, household choice is severely restricted. Money incomes are low and a substantial share of total income is received in non-monetary form as subsidies or benefits over which households have little discretion. As a result, money demand is limited and households hold relatively small amounts of both currency and savings deposits. Money holdings are lower in a socialist economy than in a market economy at a comparable level of development, for an obvious reason: money's value as a bearer of options is greatly restricted under traditional socialism; since money's value is less, households naturally hold less of it.[9]

When reform begins, the range of options open to households expands enormously. On the consumption side, they have access to expensive consumption goods that require preparatory saving. On the production side, households become business units, and their demand for monetary assets for both consumption and investment increases. In China, the most striking transformation was the rapid creation of over 200 million family (farm) businesses that replaced a few hundred thousand collectives. Demand for money increased rapidly. Narrow money increased from 6 per cent of GNP in 1978 to 15 per cent in 1988, then stabilized. Broad money increased much more rapidly.

Reformers must accommodate this increased demand for money; otherwise, an unplanned macroeconomic tightness could suffocate the microeconomic reforms at birth. Generally, the Chinese succeeded in accommodating a money demand curve that was steadily shifting upwards. While there were periods of macroeconomic imbalance and even an incipient inflationary crisis in 1988, overall this monetization was accomplished fairly smoothly. Between 1980 and 1991, the consumer price index increased at an average annual rate of 7 per cent, not a high inflation rate by comparative standards.

In a big-bang transition, it is much more difficult to cope with large and unpredictable shifts in the money demand schedule. This is a variation on the standard problem of stabilization: in inflationary economies, households reduce their holdings of currency that is depreciating in value. Credible stabilization will cause money demand schedules to shift upward, but a stabilization is unlikely to be credible if it permits rapid growth of the money supply. In the short run, the only feasible intersection of money supply and demand may be at ruinously high interest rates. This dilemma appears to be unavoidable in countries where macroeconomic imbalance have already reached critical levels (including Poland at the end of 1989). But in countries where macroeconomic problems are not at critical levels, the argument is strong for gradual accommodation of increasing money demand, sidestepping the traditional dilemma of stabilization.

A contrast with the Chinese experience is provided by the Czech Stabilization of 1991. There was broad agreement that macroeconomic imbalances and monetary overhang in Czechoslovakia were modest. But Czech policymakers believed that they must clearly transform a sellers' market into a buyers' market in order to signal to state enterprises the need to orient themselves to market competition. A zero monetary growth target was set for 1991, and adhered to at the beginning of the year. But since Czech households were beginning to respond to new economic opportunities, money demand schedules shifted upward. The result was a sharp decline in GNP, and a rapid proliferation of inter-enterprise debts, frustrating an intended tight credit policy. Czech policy was excessively rigid, not taking into account the changed behaviour of households and enterprises who would demand more money. The difficulty of managing monetary policy is, therefore, another argument against attempting to achieve an over-rapid transition.

IX. THE PARADOX OF BIG-BANG REFORM

The paradox of big-bang reform is that the impediments to planning a comprehensive reform strategy are similar to the impediments to planning the economy.[10] Central planning fails because it attempts to control the uncontrollable. The planner needs an impossibly large amount of information; the well-known inefficiencies of socialist economies are, in essence, due to decision-makers' lack of some crucial information. The market system, once it is in place, works because it does not require knowledge to be concentrated in one place: a vast amount of information about how to produce things and what things people want to buy is summarized by prices. The problem confronting designers of a big-bang reform is similar in nature if not in degree to the problem facing the planner of an economy.

The planner of big-bang reforms, like the central planner, needs to know a lot. The reformer must decide in what sequence prices are to be freed, enterprises privatized, trade barriers removed, and the financial system revamped. The reformer must decide how to assign ownership rights for state enterprises; whether to institute a Japanese/German-style or a US/British-style financial system; how to design a law of exchange; what kinds of taxation to introduce; and soon. Such choices must also be made, of course, under evolutionary reform. But it is easier to make such decisions piecemeal than all at once. By a process of institutional tatonnement, a gradual convergence to the set of institutions consistent with the available resources and suitable to the economy's needs is allowed to occur. As Robert Solow said, 'There is not some glorious theoretical synthesis of capitalism that you can write down in a book and follow. You have to grope your way.'[11]

A market is not an abstraction in which a demand curve spontaneously intersects a supply curve. A market is an institution, which needs rules and customs in order to work. Given the disparate goals of the market participants and the uneven distribution of information among them, the rules of exchange must be craftily structured for a market to operate smoothly (Wilson, 1987). In practice the rules and customs differ widely from market to market. In a transition economy, these rules and customs must either be designed or evolve. The liberalization process of the other China, Taiwan, is instructive here. Reflecting on his experience as Taiwan's Minister of Economic Affairs and of Finance during the 1960s and 1970s, K. T. Li said: 'A free market is not a given in the social calculas. It must be constructed, slowly, through a process of changes in policy focus' (Li, 1988, p. 104). Muddling through is a way of economizing on the information needed by the reformers: by trial and error, information is accumulated through the reform process; and since each step is small, errors are not costly.

Lacking clear objectives and having weak administrative capabilities, China began its reforms by permitting entry of non-state firms and state firms to sell outside the plan. Markets then spread, gradually revealing, and putting increasing pressure on, inadequate institutional arrangements. The limited administrative resources were then devoted to 'putting out fires', as the progressive marketization undermined the privileged position of the state enterprises and put pressure on the fiscal and banking systems. The pace of marketization was largely driven not by bureaucratic decisions but by the decisions of individual households on saving and entry into new fields of productive endeavour.

X. THE COHERENCE OF EVOLUTIONARY REFORM

China's jumble of ad hoc reforms can be seen, with hindsight, to have added up to a coherent package. Ironically, certain key features of the old planning system eased the beginning of the reforms; and other key features of the planning system gave the reform process the momentum that made it self-sustaining.

State control of the price system ensured high profitability of manufacturing at the start of the reforms. This high profitability induced rapid entry of new firms once restrictions on non-state firms were removed. The profits earned elicited high levels of household saving, generating still more investment by non-state firms. Entry in turn subjected state enterprises to market discipline and reduced state-sector profitability. As a result, the government faced erosion of its revenue base. In an attempt to slow this erosion, the state intensified its monitoring of state firms, and increasingly provided them with incentive systems based on profitability. State firms responded by increasing their efficiency (which was abysmal to begin with), providing the economy with enough stability to encourage further growth, both inside and outside the state sector, while also providing essential producer goods. Faced with the erosion of its traditional sources of revenue, the state also sought to strengthen newly developing financial systems—the banking system and embryonic capital markets—in order to transfer private saving to productive uses.

Reform proceeds by a series of feedback loops: reform begets further reform. A microeconomic reform (resulting in competition for state firms) creates a macroeconomic problem (a squeeze on government revenue) which impels further microeconomic reforms (increasingly profit-oriented regulation of state firms). This positive feedback presupposes a series of constructive policy responses from government leaders; reform will not proceed without appropriate state action. But the dynamics of the process create opportunities for pro-reform leaders to push the reforms forward.[12]

Gradualist reforms, it is sometimes said, will fail because they are not sustainable. A variant of this argument says that only a totalitarian government is strong enough to maintain its course of gradual change. Credibility ceases to be an issue, however, once evolutionary reform is properly understood. The government must only maintain its commitment to allow entry and competition. Beyond that commitment, there is only trial and error; no further promises are being made. Rather, the government is driven by its own need for revenue to create new fiscal institutions, and impelled by its need for popular support to create additional institutions to foster economic growth. Surely, the new democracies of Eastern Europe are at least as capable of sustaining this approach as is the Chinese gerontocracy.

XI. CONCLUSION

We have given a rosy view of China. Even putting aside the primary issue of the lack of political liberties, there is much that is wrong with the Chinese economy: the financial system misdirects funds, with state banks being unable to refuse loans to state enterprises, however unproductive, and non-state firms having restricted access to credit; agricultural production is distorted by the continuing state regulation of grain output; government policy keeps urban incomes artificially high and rural incomes artificially low; labour markets are inadequate or non-existent; the lack of basic laws of exchange and contract is a hindrance to both state and non-state firms; and property rights are ill-defined. China's reforms have probably been too gradual: it could be argued, without contradicting our case against hasty privatization, that the reforms had progressed far enough by the late 1980s that privatization of state-owned firms, development of a stock market, and full market pricing should have begun. But, in order to derive lessons from China's experience, we have focused on what has worked.

Competition is crucial. This Schumpeterian point is the main lesson from China. Competition, notably absent in the socialist planned economies disciplines firms to operate efficiently. Competition in China was generated by the massive entry of non-state firms. Competition was intensified by having state firms sell on free markets against other producers.

China provides a case for evolutionary reform. China's experience does not prove big-bang reforms cannot work: that would require examination of countries in which sudden, comprehensive reform was tried. (Though a recent remark by Polish President Lech Walesa is apposite: 'We listened to the West, and we made too big a leap.')[13] China's experience does not even conclusively establish that evolutionary reform does work, for China is still far short of an efficiently operating economy. But China's reforms have met with measurable success: entry of entrepreneurial firm's has generated vigorous growth, so much so that by 1990 non-state firms were producing almost a half of industrial output; state-owned firms have become more productive; agricultural output has soared; the price system has been effectively realigned; the fiscal and monetary systems have been changed in ways that reinforce the shift to a market economy; and, as the bottom line, living standards have risen for all.

NOTES

1 We thank William Byrd, Stanley Fischer, Peter Gourevitch, Gary Jefferson, Miles Kahler, Michael Rothschild, and Jeffrey Sachs for comments, and the Ford Foundation for research support.

2 In 'The Science of "Muddling Through"' (1959). Lindblom argued that incremental policy-making—mudding through—works better than grand planning, because the huge amount of information needed to make a comprehensive policy is never fully available; people can agree about a small policy change even if they disagree about ultimate goals; and a comprehensive policy rests heavily on the theory it is built on.

3 GNP data must be treated with some caution. China specialists believe that, because of measurement problems, the official data slightly overstate the true growth rate. The improvement in Chinese living standards is somewhat greater than growth rates indicate, on the other hand, in that the range of available goods and household choice has also expanded dramatically. The standard of living in 1978 was lower than the GNP figures indicate, because many goods were subject to rationing and could not be purchased freely. By 1990, however, virtually all goods were available at market prices (though some rationing persists as a means to distribute subsidies to privileged urban dwellers). There seems to have been little increase in inequality over the decade, so the increases in GNP have been broadly shared.

4 In the United States in 1984, for example, firms with fewer than 100 employees accounted for 39 percent of all jobs (Brock and Evans, 1989, p. 8).

5 Lenin, 1968, pp. 284 and 252, respectively; emphasis in original. Kornai (1990) describes the vigorous entry of private firms in Hungary; he says, 'the development of the private sector is the most important achievement of the reform process so far' (pp. 35–6).

6 Production-function estimates (by Chen *et al.*, 1988, Gordon and Li, 1989, and Jefferson, Rawski, and Zheng, 1992) find significant improvements in state-owned firms' productivity.

7 The input and output market ratios are calculated from a Chinese Academy of Social Sciences survey.

8 Dual pricing pre-empted a difficulty that has been identified as a pitfall of partial reform. If the state-owned firms had remained rigidly planned, then they would have been at a competitive disadvantage *vis-à-vis* the non-state firms, in that the non-state firms would have been able to bid inputs away from the state-owned firms (Murphy, Shleifer, and Vishny, 1991). Allowing the state-owned firms to sell some of their outputs and buy some of their inputs on free markets prevented such a misallocation of inputs in China.

9 This does not contradict the popular wisdom of 'currency overhang', which says that, in planned economies, people hold more money than they need for their transactions. Under socialist conditions, there could be currency overhang relative to the low money demand; but then, as the economy becomes marketized, the demand for money could increase by more than enough to cancel out the currency overhang.

10 This point was made in the mid-1980s by some young economists at the Institute of Economics, Chinese Academy of Social Sciences, including Hua Sheng and Zhang Xuejun.

11 *New York Times*, 29 September 1991, p. E1.

12 This is consistent with Hirschman's view of economic development as a process of unbalanced growth: of 'development as a chain of disequilibria'. Hirschman argued that imbalances can be useful in inducing nor only market reactions but

also appropriate government actions, 'since the desire for political survival is at least as strong a motive force as the desire to realize a profit' (Hirschman, 1958, ch. 4).

13 *New York Times*, 25 October 1991, p. C4. Walesa said this 22 months after the enactment of big-bang reforms intended rapidly to transform Poland into a market economy by extensive privatization and institutional reform. At the time of Walesa's remark, the reforms had achieved some successes, but unemployment was over 10 per cent and rising, and national income had plummeted (although Berg and Sachs, 1991, give some evidence that the costs of Poland's big-bang have been overestimated).

REFERENCES

Berg, A., and Sachs, J. (1991), 'Structural Adjustment and International Trade in Eastern Europe: The Case of Poland', mimeo, Harvard University.

Blanchard, O., Dornbusch, R., Krugman, P., Layard, R., and Summers, L. (1991), *Reform in Eastern Europe*, Cambridge, MIT Press.

Brock, W. A., and Evans, D. S. (1989), 'Small Business Economics', *Small Business Economics*, 1, 7–20.

Byrd, W. A. (1987), 'The Impact of the Two-Tier Plan/Market System in Chinese Industry', *Journal of Comparative Economics*, 11, 295–308.

—— (1991), 'Contractual Responsibility Systems in Chinese State-Owned Industry', *Advances in Chinese Industrial Studies*, Vol. 2, Greenwich, JAI Press, 7–35.

—— Lin, Q. (eds.) (1990), *China's Rural Industry*, Oxford, Oxford University Press.

Chen, K., Jefferson, G., Rawski, T., Wang, H., and Zheng, Y. (1988), 'Productivity Change in Chinese Industry: 1953–1985', *Journal of Comparative Economics*, 12, 570–591.

Gordon, R., and Li, W. (1989), 'The Change in Productivity of Chinese State Enterprises, 1983–1987: Preliminary Results', mimeo, University of Michigan.

Groves, T., Hong, Y., McMillan, J., and Naughton, B. (1992*a*), 'Autonomy and Incentives in Chinese State Enterprises', mimeo, UCSD.

—— (1992*b*), 'Chins's Managerial Labour Market', mimeo, UCSD.

Hirschman. A. O. (1958), *The Strategy of Economic Development*, New Haven, Yale University Press.

Hoshi, T., Kashyap. A., and Scharfstein, D. (1991), 'Corporate Structure, Liquidity, and Investment: Evidence from Japanese Industrial Groups', *Quarterly Journal of Economics*, **106**, 33–60.

Jefferson, G. H., Chen. K., and Singh, I. (1992), 'Lessons from China's Economic Reform', *Journal of Comparative Economics*, 16(2), June.

—— Rawski, T., and Zheng, Y. (1992), 'Growth, Efficiency and Convergence in China's State and Collective Industry', *Economic Development and Cultural Change*, forthcoming.

—— Xu, W. (1991), 'The Impact of Reform on Socialist Enterprises in Transition: Structure, Conduct, and Performance in Chinese Industry', *Journal of Comparative Economics*, 15, 45–64.

Jensen, M. C., and Murphy, K. J. (1990), 'Performance Pay and Top-Management Incentives', *Journal of Political Economy*, **98**, 225–64.

Johnson, S. (1991), 'Spontaneous Privatization in the Soviet Union: How, Why, and for Whom?, mimeo, Duke University.

Kornai, J. (1990), *The Road to a Free Economy*, New York, Norton.

Lenin, V. I. (1968), *Lenin on Politics and Revolution*, ed. by J. E. O'Connor, New York, Pegasus.

Li K. T. (1988), *The Evolution of Policy behind Taiwan's Development Success*, New Haven, Yale University Press.

Lin, Y. (1992), 'Rural Reforms and Agricultural Growth in China', *American Economic Review*, **82**(1), 34–51.

Lindblom. C. E. (1959), 'The Science of "Muddling Through"', *Public Administration Review*, 19, 79–88.

Lipton, D., and Sachs, J. (1990), 'Privatization in Eastern Europe: The Case of Poland', *Brookings Papers on Economic Activity*, 2, 293–333.

McKinnon, R. (1991), 'Financial Control in the Transition from Classical Socialism to a Market Economy', *Journal of Economic Perspectives*, 5, 107–22.

McMillan, J., Whalley, J., and Zhu, L. (1989), 'The Impact of China's Economic Reforms on Agricultural Productivity Growth', *Journal of Political Economy*, 97, 781–807.

Murphy, K. M., Shreifer, A., and Vishny. R. W. (1991), 'The Transition to a Market Economy: Pitfalls of Partial Reform', mimeo, University of Chicago.

Naughton, B. (1992*a*), 'Growing out of the Plan: Chinese Economic Reform, 1978–90', mimeo.

—— (1992*b*), 'Implications of the State Monopoly over Industry and Its Relaxation', *Modern China*, **18**.

Schumpeter, J. A. (1950), *Capitalism, Socialism and Democracy*, New York, Harper, 3rd edn.

Sinn, H-W. (1991), 'Privatization in East Germany', mimeo, University of Munich.

Tirole, J. (1991), 'Privatization in Eastern Europe: Incentives and the Economies of Transition', in O. J. Blanchard and S. S. Fischer (eds.), *NBER Macroeconomics Annual 1991*, Cambridge, MA, MIT Press.

Wilson, R. (1987), 'Game-Theoretic Analyses of Trading Processes', in T. Bewley (ed.), *Advances in Economic Theory*, Cambridge, Cambridge University Press.

2

CHINA'S CHALLENGE TO ECONOMIC ORTHODOXY

Asian Reform as an Evolutionary, Self-organizing Process[1]

Ping Chen

INTRODUCTION

Old beliefs often shatter on the rocks of historical events, and new thinking emerges from the wreckage. The twentieth century offers two such historical events: the Great Depression of the early 1930s, and the collapse of the command economies in the late 1980s. The Great Depression shook classical economics to its foundations, and gave birth to Keynesian economics. The transition from command to market economies in the 1990s, the other transcendent event of the 20th century, and the rise of the East Asian economies, may well have equally profound repercussions for economic dogma.

After the Berlin Wall fell in 1989, most observers predicted that the 21st century would be a European century, led by a unified Germany's financial capital and high technology and a Russia rich in human capital and natural resources. China was seen as a coming source of turbulence because of chronic poverty and population pressure. The big-bang prescription for Eastern Europe and the former Soviet Union—wholesale privatization, rapid liberalization—was hailed as the optimal design for quick conversion from command to market systems, while China's experimental approach—controlled decentralization and gradual liberalization—was criticized as a halfhearted reform full of traps and contradictions.

But historical realities, like rocks beneath the waves, threaten to shatter the theories with which these social scientists and policymakers have embarked. After trying various sorts of shock therapy, and huge injections of Western aid, the economies of Eastern Europe and Russia are still in persistent decline. Consider the following contrast in cost-benefit calculation.

Transfer payments to eastern Germany now amount to about 50 percent of that region's GNP (or eight percent for western Germany). These are huge amounts compared with the Marshall plan, which was barely two percent of

Source: *China Economic Review*, Volume 4, Number 2, 1993, pp. 137–42.

Western European GNP. Yet despite the transfers, GNP in eastern Germany has declined over 40 percent (Schrenk, 1993). Meanwhile, the huge cost of German reunification has prolonged the recession in the Western economies, and delayed European integration (Pohl, 1990; Summers, 1991; Marsh, 1993).

In contrast, China has received little foreign aid during its economic transition. The largest source of foreign capital has come from Hong Kong (and overseas Chinese), but roughly the same amount of *Chinese* capital has flowed outward into Hong Kong. Accumulated foreign investment in China was $33 billion in 1992, or only $28 per capita (Gao, 1993). The Chinese level of foreign aid and foreign capital inflows per capita is minuscule—four percent that of Poland, 0.3 percent that of eastern Germany, despite their higher per capita GNP. And in return for this much a more modest investment, we observe in China over the last 14 years an average growth rate in GNP of nine percent, and in exports of 13 percent

Can we explain the spectacular rise of the Chinese economy, and the mysterious fall of the Russian and Eastern European economies, using neoclassical or endogenous growth theory? Alas, only a few economists recognize the need to fit the Chinese experience into our model (Singh, 1991; Amsden, 1993). Most mainstream economists still set China aside, on the grounds of different initial conditions or cultural traditions (Bogetic, 1991; Hirschler, 1991).

To some extent this may reflect the primacy of political over economic concerns. In the current debate over big bang versus gradualism, both sides accept as the primary goal, not the growth-with-stability at which China excels, but rather the rapid and permanent displacement of the command economy by the western-type market economy, as a political end in itself (Islam, 1993). Within this sort of cost-benefit calculus, China's experience drops out of the equation.

But does East Asia have no lessons to teach us? Alan Blinder once observed that the rise of the Japanese economy posed a serious challenge to the neoclassical model based on the western market economy, since Japan had succeeded by doing everything "wrong" (Blinder, 1990). For example, the Japanese stood on its head the American paradigm of serving the consumer, searching for profit, benefiting stockholders, and seeking free trade. Blinder's observation reminds us that China's experience in development strategy and institutional reform may have lessons for developing and developed countries both

Consider some challenging Chinese paradoxes. How, within the neoclassical model, can we explain the fast growth of township and village enterprises, which have no clearly defined property rights and yet play a dynamic role in economic growth and community development? How will we fit into traditional micro- and macro-analysis the catalytic role played in China by provincial, county and even village government?

Consider China's approach to improving the efficiency of state enterprises.

Privatization in this area is feasible only for small-scale firms; for larger firms, especially in heavy and defense industry, this approach is much more problematic (Sachs, 1992). Here, China improved large-scale state sector efficiency mainly by introducing competitive pressure from the growing nonstate sector and breaking monopoly firms into smaller companies.

The current crisis of the Western economies is deeply rooted in the Western tradition of unchecked individualism, excessive welfare provision, unequal income distribution, and insufficient provision of public infrastructure designed to meet the challenge of global competition and technological change (Bellah et al., 1985; Etzioni, 1988; Daly and Cobb, 1989). Is there a parallel crisis in economic orthodoxy? A careful study of the experience of East Asian economies may stimulate fresh thinking in economic science and public policy.

This paper suggests one such lesson, having to do with the nature of institutional change. Rational design argues that the success of Chinese reform stems not so much from its gradualism as from its decentralized approach. Decentralized social change extends this argument, suggesting that decentralized change is effective because economic institutions must be self-organizing. Non-equilibrium economics suggests even broader implications for the nature of economic growth and the need for paradigmatic change in economics.

RATIONAL DESIGN VERSUS DECENTRALIZED EXPERIMENTATION

To characterize the reform debate as "big bang versus gradualism" is misleading. The important choice posed by competing reform strategies today is between the experimental, decentralized Chinese approach and the top-down, designer approach of Russia and Eastern Europe. Prior to 1989, after all, reform in Hungary, Poland and elsewhere was amply gradual; indeed, it was the failure of that very gradualism which precipitated the radicalism of today (Hirshier, 1991). The constant feature of Eastern European reform efforts, both before and after 1989, was that reform measures were designed centrally and then prescribed in a top-down fashion.

China's reforms have been gradual, but more importantly, they have consistently followed an experimental approach. Examples include the rapid quasi-privatization in rural areas (the family responsibility system), a series of mini-big-bang price and trade liberalizations in the special economic zones (SEZS), the two-tier system for prices and exchange rates, and gradual, diverse institutional reforms in the state sector. Government leaders, including radical reformers, were initially suspicious of many of these non-orthodox practices, such as the family contract system, the "illegal competition" of village enterprise, and even the SEZs. Formal institutional changes typically lagged several years behind successful experiments and widespread imitation.

In this process, the most important contribution of China's reform leadership was that they refrained from making quick judgements and suppressing "illegal" practices; instead, they let time be the judge. This tolerance of heterodoxy fostered innovation in institution-building. The "gradualness" of China's reform, then, was not a conscious design of the central government, but rather the inevitable result of compromises among a myriad of conflicting proposals, through a long process of trial and error. China's success demonstrates the effectiveness of providing time for learning and adaptation, rather than importing foreign systems overnight.

DECENTRALIZED SOCIAL CHANGE AND PARADIGM CONFLICT IN ECONOMIC SCIENCE

Why is it that a decentralized, bottom-up, experimentally based approach to reform brought China institutional change at much lower social cost than reforms elsewhere? This section argues that the sense of urgency felt by other reformers led them to choose imported over home-grown solutions; but that the enormous uncertainties inherent in social change make this approach a high-cost one in the end. The fact that top-down "designer reform" is nonetheless being prescribed by Western economists reflects their failure to recognize the limitations of the neoclassical, "equilibrium" paradigm in our discipline.

The big-bang approach to transition put the highest priority on privatization, liberalization, and macroeconomic stabilization. That is, these reformers sought a rapid "return to Europe" by adopting the legal framework of private property, importing the world trade price structure through liberalization, and imposing harsh stabilization policies softened by huge foreign loans (Sachs, 1992). In all three ways, this approach in effect amounted to importing a whole structure from the outside world, rather than stimulating a gradual development of new institutions and forces within the existing economy.

This approach, which assumes a high degree of transferability of institutions from one society to another, reflects the underlying paradigm of modern economics—an equilibrium-oriented approach which says, "Get the prices right, and the rest will follow". But in reality, social change is a complex, path-dependent, and unpredictable process (Stark, 1992). Great uncertainty exists during the bifurcation and transition stage (Chen, 1987, 1991), particularly for large countries like Poland and Russia. This uncertainty translates to a high risk of expensive errors when coupled with the high cost of any social restructuring (the east German experience makes it clear how very high those costs can be).

Big-bang proponents like to argue that "you cannot leap over a chasm in two steps". But what if you leap and then discover that you're even farther on the wrong side of a chasm? Chinese reformers counsel instead that "you can only walk across a river by feeling first for the stones". This clash of metaphors reflects a difference in the underlying padadigms. The former approach, based on the Newtonian paradigm of classical mechanics, believes that after shock therapy knocks the economic system out of the orbit provided by central planning, the forces which move individual markets toward an equilibrium position can and will steer the entire economic system into a new, stable regime.

Few have questioned the analytic foundations of this belief (Murrel, 1991; Stark, 1992). But the new discovery of chaos in dynamic systems suggests that they are far more unpredictable than this, more complex, and more subject to instability, explosive oscillation, or chaos (Day and Chen, 1993). "Rational designers" are oversimplifying complex, non-linear aspects of social systems, and are also overlooking the bounded rationality of human behavior (Prigogine, 1993).

NON-EQUILIBRIUM ECONOMICS, POSITIVE FEEDBACK, AND GROWTH

The foregoing has argued that equilibrium economics is an inappropriate paradigm for anticipating the path which social institutions will take when they change rapidly; and that policies based on that paradigm may therefore fail. But in what sense does dynamic economics better capture these processes? To answer this question, we must consider the catalytic role of positive feedback mechanisms (Buchanan, 1991).

The traditional theory of equilibrium economics emphasizes the role of negative feedback mechanisms in achieving equilibrium and stability. Excess supply generates rising unsold stocks which leads price to fall, deceasing excess supply. Any positive feedback is viewed as destructive: it will cause increasingly large deviations from equilibrium.

But Pareto equilibrium is a static concept; no growth occurs. Yet growth is a crucial ingredient of rapid but stable social change. It provides the lubricant which reduces social friction, the expanding pie with which to buy off injured constituencies. Growth, in turn, depends on innovation, and the driving force behind innovation is the presence of some positive feedback mechanism.

One classic case of positive feedback generating path-dependent growth is the story of Silicon Valley (Arthur, 1989, 1990). But China's experience abounds in similar examples—the family responsibility system in poor, rural inland areas, the SEZ experiment in rich, urban coastal areas, foreign investment in joint ventures, all interacting with each other through waves of positive feedback: communication, learning, imitation. The tiny absolute size of foreign investment, relative to its large result, strongly suggests that the underlying process is catalytic in nature.

CONCLUSION

A complete picture of the social change and economic development which China is experiencing,must include not just negative but also positive feedbacks. The new science of evolutionary self-organization reveals the constructive role played by positive feedback mechanisms in a world of nonlinearities and instabilities. It sheds new light on the catalytic mechanism and on how order emerges under non-equilibrium conditions (Nicholas and Prigogine, 1977, 1989; Day and Chen, 1993). Endogenous growth theory may add a further dimension: the role of catalytic mechanisms in emerging new technology and new organization through non-optimization dynamics under non-equilibrium conditions. These are the lessons which the historic events of the waning twentieth century will eventually provide to economic science.

REFERENCES

Amsden, A. H. (1993). East Asian cues to post-socialist economies. *Transition* (The World Bank), *4*(4), 9–10.

Arthur, B. (1989). Competing technologies, increasing returns, and lock-in by historical events. *Economic Journal*, *99*, 116–131.

Arthur, B. (1990). Positive feedbacks in the economy. *Scientific American*, 92–99, Feb.

Bellab, R. N., Madsen, R., Sullivan, W. M., Swidler, A., and Tiptor, S. M. (1985). *Habits of the heart, individualism and commitment in American life*. New York: Harper & Row.

Blinder, A. (1990, October 8). There are capitalists, then there are the Japanese. *Business Week.*

Bogetic, Z. (1991). A walk or a rush? *Transition* (World Bank), *2*(9), 6–7.

Buchanan, J. (1991). Economics in the post-socialist century. *Economic Journal*, *101*(404), 15–21.

Chen, P. (1987). Origin of division of labor and a stochastic mechanism of differentiability. *European Journal of Operation Research*, *30*, 246–250.

Chen. P. (1991). Neednam's question and China's evolution: Cases of nonequilibrium social transition. In G. P. Scott (Ed.), *Time, Rhythms, and Chaos in the New Dialogue with Nature*. Iowa State University Press, Ames.

Daly, H. E. and Cobb, J. B. (1989). *For the common good, redirecting the economy toward community, the environment, and a sustainable future*. Boston: Beacon Press.

Day, R. H. and Chen, P. (1993). *Nonlinear dynamics and evolutionary economics*. Oxford.

Etzioni, A. (1988). *The moral dimension, toward a new economics*. New York: Free Press.

Gao, S. Q. (1993). Marketization and gradualism: Basic lessons of institutional reform in China. International Symposium on the Theoretical and Practical Issues of the Transition towards the Market Economy in China, at Hainan, China.

Hirschler, R. (1991). Descending the stem of the J-Curve—interviews from Bangkok. *Transition* (World Bank), *2*(9), 14.

Islam, S. (1993). Moscow's rough road to capitalism. *Foreign Affairs*, *72*(2), 57–66.

Upton, D. and Sachs, J. (1990). Privatization in eastern Europe: The case of Poland. Brookings papers on economic activity, *2*, 293–341.

Marsh, D. (1993). Collapse of communism created a corresponding adjustment crisis in the west. *Transition* (World Bank), *4*(3), 10–11.

Murrel, P. (1991). Can neoclassical economics underpin the reform of centrally planned economies? *Economic Perspectives*, *5*(4), 59–76.

Nicolis, G. and Prigogine, L (1977). Self-organization in nonequilibrium systems, from dissipative structure to order through fluctuations, New York: Wiley.

Nicolis, G. and Prigogine, L (1989). Exploring complexity. New York: Freeman.

Prigogine, L (1993). Bounded Rationality: From dynamical systems to socio-economic models. In R. Day and P. Chen, (Eds.), *Nonlinear dynamics and evolutionary economics*. New York: Oxford University Press.

Sachs, J. D. (1992). Building a market economy in Poland. *Scientific American* (March), 34–40.

Schrenk, M. (1993). Structural changes in eastern Germany. *Transition* (The World Bank), *4*(1), 10–11.

Singh, I. (1991). Is there schizophrenia about socialist reform theory? Some thoughts about the two-track approach. *Transition* (The World Bank), *2*(7), 14.

Stark, D. (1992). Can designer capitalism work in central and eastern Europe? *Transition*, *3*(5).

Summers, L. (1991). If the best way to destroy an economy is to bomb it—and if communism is a close second—rampant populism is third. *Transition* (The World Bank), *2*(10), 9–10.

3

COMPLETING CHINA'S MOVE TO THE MARKET

Dwight Perkins

China's economic reform process officially began with the Communist Party Plenum of December 1978. From the outset, China's reforms differed markedly from those of eastern Europe and the Commonwealth of Independent States. China was exhausted from 20 years of dealing with Mao's messianic visions, but it was in no sense ready for revolution. There was nothing comparable to eastern Europe's desire to be like western Europe, the sooner the better. China faced no economic crisis that required immediate and fundamental change, only dissatisfaction with the pace of existing growth, a dissatisfaction fueled in part by increasing awareness of the far better economic performances of China's immediate neighbors. The Communist Party held all of the important reins of power both in 1978 and 15 years later. Where Deng Xiaoping differed from his predecessors was in the strength of his desire to turn China into a wealthy and powerful state and his lack of interest in Maoist ideas of a new kind of society where such things as material incentives would play little or no role. But Deng and his associates had no economic reform blueprint.

In this context, a gradual approach to economic reform was inevitable. Mao Zedong was the believer in "big bangs." Mao's successor's were willing to try almost anything if it worked. They also had a sense that some sectors, notably agriculture and foreign trade, were more in need of reform than others, such as industry. Mao's bias against foreign technology and foreign products had severely hurt China's modernization, and per capita grain output in 1978 was the same as it was in the mid-1950s. These latter views led to a sequencing of the economic reforms, first agriculture and foreign trade, and only later industry. At no time during the early years of reform did the senior leadership of China think that they were aiming toward a full market system.

It was as much by luck as by design, therefore, that China stumbled on a strategy that has proved remarkably successful in moving the economy from a Soviet-style comnsand system to what by the early 1990s was an economy governed in large part by market forces, however distorted some of those market forces may have been. That the economic reforms initiated in

Source: *Journal of Economic Perspectives*, Vol. 8(2), (1994), pp. 23–46.

December 1978 and continuing thereafter have been successful cannot be seriously doubted. The data in Tables 3.1 and 3.2 tell the basic story. China's gross domestic product grew by over 8 percent a year for 14 years, or roughly 7 percent per capita. The 8.8 percent GDP growth rate figure may overstate the real rate by a small amount (mainly because small-scale industries sometimes only report output figures in current prices which may not always be deflated by the statistical authorities), but there is no question that growth has been rapid. This rate is roughly double the GDP growth rate of the previous two decades, 1957–1978.[1] The foreign trade story is even more impressive. In the 1970s, China's exports grew by a modest 3.4 percent a year

Table 3.1 China's GDP and its components

	1978	*1984*	*1988*	*1990*	*1992*
GDP (billion 1990 yuan)	669.4	1,097.0	1,625.9	1,769.5	2,162.9
– per capita (1990 yuan)	695	1,051	1,464	1,548	1,846
– per capita (index)	100.0	151.2	210.6	225.3	266.6

	Growth rates (in % per year)			
	1984/1978	*1988/1984*	*1992/1988*	*1992/1978*
Agriculture	7.3	3.1	4.3	5.2
Industry	8.9	14.2	10.4	10.8
Services	10.1	13.5	5.8	9.8
GDP	8.6	10.3	7.5	8.8

Note: The Chinese GDP figures were calculated by applying the indexes in 'comparable prices' for 1978, 1984, 1988, and 1992 to the current price estimates of the three components of GDP in 1990. This produces rough constant price GDP figures for these years and an index that differs slightly from the official Chinese GDP index for this period.

Sources: State Statistical Bureau, 1992, p. 6; State Statistical Bureau, 1991, pp. 33, 79; and 'Statistical Communique of the State Statistical Bureau of the PRC on the 1992 National Economic and Social Development,' February 18, 1993, *Beijing Review*, March 8–14, 1993, vol. 36, no. pp. 31–40; and State Statistical Bureau, 1993, 19, 21.

Table 3.2 Growth rate of China's foreign trade (in percent per year)

	Nominal		*Real*	
	Exports	*Imports*	*Exports*	*Imports*
1972/1952	7.4	4.8	—	—
1978/1972	19.0	25.0	3.4	13.0
1988/1978	17.2	17.6	14.1	10.2
1992/1978	16.7	15.4	—	—

Sources: Same as in Table 1 plus, for the real rates, China Foreign Trade Yearbook compiling committee, 1984, p. IV-5; and China Foreign Trade Yearbook Compiling Committee, 1989, p. 303. Appropriate price deflators were not available for the post-1988 period.

if one takes away the impact of OPEC-generated increases in the price of petroleum and related across-the-board inflation. This real growth rate rose to 14.1 percent a year during the first decade of reform and 70 percent of these exports were manufactures (petroleum and mining products by 1988 accounted for under 8 percent of exports, as contrasted to 25 percent in 1980).

China's impressive export performance was partly due to the reforms, but it also reflects the fact that China began its reform period from a more advantageous position than did the reformers of eastern Europe, the C.I.S., and Vietnam. The breakup of the Council for Mutual Economic Assistance (CMEA) forced these latter countries to abandon many of their markets with each other and reorient their trade to the west. China went through a similar process in the early 1960s and it was very disruptive to the economy, but by 1978 China had long since completed this adjustment. China also had no foreign debt to pay off in 1978, unlike the situation in China in 1960 or eastern Europe after 1989. China's other big advantage in 1978 was that it began the reform period with no overt inflation and not much repressed inflationary pressure. Reform did not have to begin with a stabilization program.

The remainder of this essay is devoted to explaining the nature of the reforms introduced by the Chinese, why they worked well or poorly in particular cases, and the problems created by the incomplete nature of many of these reforms.

RURAL REFORM

The two principal components of China's rural reforms were the gradual freeing up of the markets for agricultural commodities and the decollectivization of Chinese rural society.

The market for secondary crops and household products was freed up almost immediately after the December 1978 party plenum. Free markets, or rural trade fairs as they were called, had existed before 1978 but were tightly controlled when they were allowed to function at all. However, the state retained a near monopoly of the trade in major crops such as grain, until 1985, and state contracts for the purchase of grain and other key agricultural commodities were made voluntary, although the word "voluntary" as used in China often retains elements of coercion. By the latter half of the 1980s around 60 percent of agricultural commodities were bought and sold on competitive markets, as compared to only 8 percent in 1978 (Lu and Timmer, 1992). By 1990 this share had risen to about 80 percent; markets supplied 89 percent of all aquatic products, 80 percent of fruits, 76 percent of vegetables, 68 percent of meat and eggs, and about half of all grain (*China Daily*, December 17, 1992). By 1993 there was talk of freeing up agricultural prices altogether over the next three years and perhaps 10 percent of the counties had already freed up all prices including grain. The state, however, was still heavily involved in the grain trade and was having trouble fulfilling its purchase quotas and finding cash to pay for the grain it did purchase. The inability of the state trading companies to get bank credits led them to issue IOU's to farmers that were often not redeemed for months (Zhang, 1993).

Decollectivization happened more or less spontaneously. What began as experiments to help the poorest areas in certain provinces spread quickly to other regions. Only when lower level party officials would try to halt or reverse the process did the center move in with orders to let happen what was happening. By the end of 1983, the system of people's communes and the production teams of 20–30 families that had operated as a collective unit had ceased to exist in most of the country.[2] Household agriculture was the norm and the state soon determined that household contracts for the use of the land would last for 15 years.

The response of agriculture to decollectivization and the freeing up of rural markets was immediate and dramatic. The basic picture can be seen in the data in Table 3.3. Production of all crops including grain grew at an unprecedented rate; from 1978 to 1984, the growth rate for agricultural value-added was five times what it had been over the previous two decades. Farm income and consumption grew even more rapidly, although the data are less reliable than those for output. Improving terms of trade for agriculture, plus non-agricultural sources of income, account for most of the difference between output versus consumption or income growth.

These growth statistics also indicate that the agricultural output spurt was a one-shot affair largely exhausted by the end of 1984, when most crop production returned to its long-term growth rate, in part because farmers

Table 3.3 Agricultural growth rate (in percent per year)

	1978/1957	*1984/1978*	*1988/1984*	*1992/1988*
(1) Agricultural value added	1.4[a]	7.3	3.1	4.3
(2) Gross value of crop output	2.9	6.8	1.0	3.7
(3) Grain output				
(4) Farm household net income	2.1	5.0	–0.8	2.9
per capita (real)	—	15.0[b]	2.3	7.6

Note:
[a] The 1957–1978 figure is the growth rate of agriculture's share of net material product.
[b] The changeover from a production team to a household based accounting system makes it difficult to compare net income figures before and after this changeover. Hence the 1978–1984 figure is particularly unreliable.
— Indicates data not available to the author.

Sources: Rows (1)–(3) were derived from data in 'Communique of the State Statistical Bureau of the PRC on the 1992 National Social and Economic Development, pp. 31–40; State Statistical Bureau, 1989, pp. 742–743; State Statistical Bureau, 1991, pp. 243, 294–295.

The raw data for row (4) are from the same sources. The percentage increases in net income were derived from per capita data in current prices divided by the rural retail price index.

preferred to invest their resources in rural industry (Huang, 1993). Reforms also could not alter the fact that China is attempting to feed 1.1 billion people on less than a tenth of a hectare per capita, and crop yields in the best-endowed provinces are already comparable to those in such advanced agricultural systems as Japan, South Korea or Taiwan. Politically, however, the 1978–1984 spurt gave enormous credibility to market-oriented reforms and to the individuals who designed those reforms. The political lesson for future reformers from China's experience is obvious but often forgotten–try to begin the reform process with a clear winner.

Why did market-oriented reforms work so well and so quickly in agriculture? Five elements are needed to make a market work well, and these five categories also describe the concrete steps that a Soviet-type command economy must take if it is to evolve into a functioning market economy. The five steps are: 1) achieve macro stability, meaning an acceptable level of inflation and a balance of payments not in serious disequilibrium; 2) make inputs and outputs available for purchase and sale on the market, rather than allocated administratively through a state bureaucracy; 3) free up prices to reflect relative scarcities in the economy; 4) remove barriers to market entry so that competition between firms in different localities becomes possible; 5) change key elements of the institutional framework so that decision-makers in the production unit (farms and industrial or service enterprises) have an incentive to maximize profits by cutting their costs or raising sales.[3]

For Chinese agriculture, achieving the first four elements of a market economy was not particularly difficult. Macro instability was not a problem and there were no effective barriers to entry in farm production. Making goods available on the market was accomplished gradually over a period of a decade but many goods became available on the market almost immediately. Because rural markets in some form had existed prior to 1978, few had trouble learning how to take advantage of the opportunities offered by the expanded markets. Prices of secondary products were also quickly freed up. Grain prices proved more difficult to liberalize, partly because of the political dangers inherent in a sharp increase in the cost of food to consumers, partly because of the subsidies required from the government budget if producer prices were raised while consumer prices were kept fixed.[4]

The "household responsibility system" that resulted from decollectivization embodied some elements of the property rights required to generate market-oriented incentives for farm households, and went a long way toward meeting the fifth profit maximization criterion of a functioning market economy. Households are natural profit maximizers (subject to the usual caveats about uncertainty and risk aversion) provided that they have the right to keep the income that is earned. This objective was achieved by dividing up the commune land and allocating it to individual households who kept all income from that land after meeting certain tax obligations to the government.

However, property rights in rural China were not complete either immediately after collectivization in the mid-1980s or in the early 1990s. The property rights were both exclusive and enforceable, in the sense that only one farm household should have the right to use a particular plot of land, and that the government would discipline those who didn't respect that right. But property rights should also be secure and transferable, and here the Chinese reformers had greater problems. They did offer a 15-year guarantee of rights to particular plots, plus vaguer promises concerning an extension beyond those 15 years and the right to inherit. But the many twists and turns in Chinese policy over the three decades of Communist Party rule prior to 1979 meant that such promises were not particularly credible.

The issue of transferring land raised the specter of the old landlord system before 1949, and hence such sales were vigorously opposed by many in the Chinese Communist Party. The distinction was made between the right to use the land for a period of time versus ownership. Not until the early 1990s did the state begin to allow the buying and selling of long-term land leases, but only in the urban areas. Acquiring rural land for factory use, in contrast, typically involved laborious negotiations in which the factory guaranteed jobs and other benefits to displaced farmers in exchange for the use of their land. Land transfer within rural areas typically involved guaranteeing a basic grain ration to those giving up their land use rights.[5]

The incomplete nature of property rights in rural China has had a negative impact on agriculture's performance. Because farmers weren't secure that they would keep their property, even over the 15-year lease, they were reluctant to invest in major capital improvements, particularly land improvements such as irrigation systems. Reservoirs and major feeder canals had been a public good and their maintenance had been the responsibility of the collective teams and brigades that no longer existed. Local governments took over some of the functions of the old commune system but left many to a market that was incapable of generating the necessary effort.[6]

The inability to sell land meant that farmers wishing to migrate to urban areas continued to hold onto their land, farming that land using their spare time or elderly relatives simply to maintain their rights. Below market interest rates made it difficult for farmers and many government departments to compete for rural credit against the preferences of local cadres for investment in township and village enterprises. Because township and village enterprises got most of the available credit, one result (as already mentioned) was the use of IOU's to pay farmers for their grain, in effect further lowering the price paid to farmers for that grain.

By the early 1990s, farmers were emphasizing higher-valued cash crops and spending more time on off-farm activities, so farm household incomes continued to rise, although not at the same pace as during the 1979–1984 spurt. The largest beneficiaries were farmers in rural areas near cities that could take full advantage of the opportunities to meet the needs of urban markets.[7]

THE SERVICE SECTOR

The Chinese, like others following Soviet economic practices, distinguished between productive and non-productive sectors. Most services were in the latter category. Private restaurants and personal services were simply suppressed. Commerce and finance were under state ownership and control but were considered inferior activities in comparison with sectors producing material goods. Where the service sectors in a typical low income developing country constitutes between 35 and 40 percent of GDP (Chenery and Syrquin, 1975, p. 20), the service sector in China in 1978 constituted only 23 percent (in 1990 prices). By 1988, however, the share of services had risen to 28 percent of GDP.

From the perspective of China's leadership, services were considered a partial solution to the problem of a labor force rising by 14 million people per year. In addition, by some crude estimates of the number of work days required by the agricultural sector, there were 100 million in the countryside who were already considered to be underemployed. Hence, many of the rules circumscribing small-scale service activities were abolished or ignored. The response was dramatic. The labor force in the service sector doubled during the first decade of reform from 48.7 million people in 1978 to 99.5 million in 1988 (State Statistical Bureau, 1991, p. 99).

Traders and transport workers were the first to take advantage of the new opportunities. Then, collectively- and individually-owned restaurants and small shops sprung up everywhere. In many cases, state commercial establishments became hollowed-out shells housing private vendors who rented space from the state. Labor contracting services developed in such interior provinces as Sichuan, which provided the construction workers for the job of building millions of new apartments for urban residents. The term "floating population" was coined to classify people who had migrated to the cities to work but were not formally classified as urban residents. Before 1978, these people could not get food ration coupons and public security officials would quickly pack them back to the countryside. By the mid-1980s, these people could buy the food they needed on the market and public security usually ignored them. The floating population nationwide probably numbered in the tens of millions.[8] Some because permanent urban residents, but others moved back and forth between temporary urban jobs and their rural homes.

Small-scale services responded quickly to market forces for many of the same reasons that farmers did. Once these activities were legalized, millions of people were prepared to supply them. Barriers to entry were absent and prices charged for these services, for the most part, could not be controlled. Property rights were not a major problem, because services were embodied in the people supplying them. (Restaurants and shops required a physical location and sometimes a roof and walls, but one did not have to own the roof and walls or hold a long-term lease to make effective use of them.) With some exceptions, the capital investments required to establish a service activity were modest, like tractors with carts to haul goods to market. There was nothing comparable to the pervasive Mafia-style organizations found in Russia that restricted entry to service markets and extorted payments from those allowed in, although low-level government officials did extract informal payments of various kinds. This boom in small-scale services was readily observable in other former Soviet-style economies, as well; the streets of Hanoi, Warsaw, and Moscow were also teeming with small traders and new shops.

The large-scale service sector did not respond so quickly. Some large commercial establishments in China, like department stores, did respond because they faced direct competition from the collective enterprises and petty traders. The major financial and transport enterprises, in contrast, were very slow to change. The problems with market-oriented reform for banks, railroads, and airlines have much in common with those faced by large-stale state industrial enterprises and will he discussed below.

FOREIGN TRADE AND INVESTMENT

In China's Soviet-style foreign trade system, all trade was handled by government corporations that had a monopoly over all purchases and sales in particular sectors. All foreign exchange was turned over to the Bank of China, the foreign exchange bank. There was an "air lock" between all producing enterprises and world markets so that prices on world markets had no influence on the domestic price structure. Foreign firms often did not even know to which industrial enterprise the equipment they were selling was going or from which enterprise the items they were purchasing were coming. In addition to this, throughout the Cultural Revolution period (1966–1976) there was active political hostility toward foreign trade in general and foreign technology in particular. Foreign investment did not exist.

After Mao Zedong's death in 1976, policies began to change. The first move was to encourage domestic enterprises to buy inputs from abroad rather then to discourage such purchases. Enterprises responded with such alacrity that China by 1978 found itself with a growing trade deficit, despite increasing prices for China's petroleum exports. Imports in nominal dollar terms rose 51 percent in 1978 and by 44 percent in 1979. Clearly, new and increasing sources of foreign exchange had to be discovered.

In 1979, reforms were introduced to facilitate exports of manufactures and (for the first time) to allow for foreign investiment (Lardy, 1992). In essence, these efforts involved the breakup of the monopoly on foreign trade held by the state corporations, and transferring this authority to regional corporations (but not to producing enterprises for the most part). Special economic zones (export processing zones) were set up to free foreign investors and other exporters from red tape. Various export subsidies were introduced and China's currency was devalued from 1.7 yuan to the U.S. dollar in 1981 to 2.9 yuan to the dollar in 1985 to 4.8 yuan to the dollar in 1990. This 182 percent rise was much more than the 87 percent increase in Chinese retail prices or the 40 percent rise in the ratio of Chinese to U.S. retail prices.

Foreign trade responded to these incentives in dramatic fashion, as indicated by the data in Table 3.2. The response of foreign direct investment was equally dramatic, as the data in Table 3.4 indicate. A Soviet-style economy geared to producing low quality goods for a captive domestic market was suddenly competing head-to-head with its East Asian neighbors, the most dynamic exporters of manufactured goods in the world. What accounts for this extraordinary change?

In the sphere of foreign trade, the challenge for a reforming China was how to plug into the international market system, where goods were freely available at market prices. On the import side, as demonstrated as early as 1977 and 1978, all the government had to do was remove barriers to the purchase of foreign products. Exports of minerals such as petroleum was also straightforward.

The export of manufactures was another matter. Enterprises in China had to acquire the ability to produce what international markets required, and to make a connection with foreign markets. Rather than simply having enterprises fend for themselves, China did not allow many domestic industrial enterprises to deal directly with foreign markets until well into the 1990s. Instead, the foreign trade corporations were decentralized to the provinces and regions, and allowed to compete for business. By 1993, there were 4000 foreign trade companies and manufacturing enterprises allowed to deal directly on foreign markets (Zhang, April 19, 1993, p. 2). The "air lock" between domestic enterprises and foreign markets gradually broke down as the international prices were passed through to a liberalized domestic market, and producing enterprises were allowed to retain larger and larger shares of the foreign exchange they earned.

Table 3.4 Foreign direct investment in China (in billions of U.S. dollars per year)

	1979–1982	*1983–1985*	*1986–1988*	*1989–1990*	*1991*	*1992*
Contracted direct foreign investment	1.50	3.44	3.95	6.10	11.98	58.12
Direct foreign investment actually used	0.29	1.19	2.46	3.44	4.37	11.01

Sources: 'Official Predicts $10 billion more in investment,' *China Daily*, April 26, 1993, Business Supplement, p. 1; 'Foreign Funds hit record $25 billion,' *China Daily*, June 2, 1993, p. 2; State Statistical Bureau, *Zhonguo tongji nianjian, 1991*, p. 629; State Statistical Bureau, *Zhonguo tongji nianjian, 1992*, p. 641; and State Statistical Bureau, *Zhongguo tongji nianjian, 1993*, p. 647.

The market for foreign exchange illustrates how market forces gradually come to dominate. In the early 1980s, foreign exchange was tightly controlled by the Bank of China, although black markets for foreign currency existed. Under pressure from foreign investors, who had trouble obtaining foreign exchange with which to buy imported inputs and repatriate profits, the government created "foreign exchange adjustment centers," swap markets on which those with surplus foreign exchange, notably joint venture hotels, could sell that surplus to foreign firms at a market-determined rate. Eligibility for participation on these swap markets, initially very restricted, became wider with time and included large numbers of domestic firms.

By 1992, partly because of a desire to become eligible to join GATT, China began talking about moving to a single market-determined exchange rate, but a large capital outflow in mid-1993, much of it technically illegal, led to a sharp divergence in the official and swap market rate. The gap had been about 10 percent in 1992; by mid-1993, it was more like 75 percent. However, in March 1993, China for the first time did legally allow individuals to take *renminbi*, the state currency, out of the country and the goal remained full convertibility at some future date (Zhou, February 8, 1993, p. 3). The desire to join GATT also prompted China to reduce import duties and to eliminate many import quotas in favor of tariffs (N. Li, 1993, pp. 13–15).

The primary force leading to the capital outflow and the devaluation of the yuan was probably the desire by individuals and organizations to protect the value of their assets against the rising rate of inflation. Real interest rates on deposits and central government bonds were negative by mid-1993, and moving money to Hong Kong was one way to avoid losses. In July 1993, the Chinese government did intervene heavily in the swap markets by selling off dollars, but controlling inflation and/or raising domestic interest rates was likely to be a more effective solution to maintaining an appropriate exchange rate over the long run.

But the opening of China to trade does not explain its success in foreign markets; after all, other countries more open to international market influences than China have not enjoyed China's surge in the export of manufactures. China's exports of manufactures increased from around $5 billion in 1978 to $68 billion by 1992. One cannot prove the point systematically, but connections with Hong Kong probably account for much of China's success. In 1979, 22.6 percent of Chinese exports went to Hong Kong and 79 percent of those exports stayed in Hong Kong. By 1987, despite the increasing knowledge of foreign markets on the Chinese mainland, Hong Kong's share of all exports rose to 31.1 percent (of a much larger total than in 1979) and 62 percent of these exports to Hong Kung were reexported. Among manufactures, Hong Kong's share was much higher, ranging from 46 percent for textile fabric to 62 percent for clothing and 87 percent for machinery (Sung, 1991). By 1992 Hung Kong's share in total Chinese exports (including re-exports) had risen further to 44 percent (General Administration of Customs,

1993). In the 1990s, a similar process seems to be happening though Taiwan. In effect, the formidable marketing talents of Hong Kong and Taiwan are being grafted onto the manufacturing capacity of the mainland.

Part of this export performance came from joint venture firms and other firms with various kinds of foreign investment—$17.4 billion in 1992, which marked a 44 percent rise over 1991. At first glance, China's success in attracting foreign investment is a puzzle. After all, foreign investors have traditionally had little security in China. China does not have a strong legal tradition; in fact, lawyers and most commercial law were abolished during the Cultural Revolution. The system after 1976 had to be rebuilt from scratch, and the new laws were not very reliable protection against official assaults on foreign property rights. Whatever one's legal rights of ownership, official support was required to gain access to state controlled inputs such as electricity, foreign exchange, or railroad transport. The expansion of the domestic market for many inputs eased this problem but did not eliminate it. After the political crisis caused by the events on Tiananmen on June 4, 1989, there was even reason for foreign investors to expect a reversion to more bureaucratic controls over the economy, not fewer. And yet foreign investment continued to rise.

Investment designed to supply the Chinese domestic market can perhaps be explained by noting that the lure of a billion customers can offset many worries. The rapid growth of export-oriented foreign investment, in the face of insecure property rights, is also easier to understand if one recognizes that most of this foreign investment was coming from Hong Kong, and to a lesser degree other overseas Chinese, and was going into Guangdong Province next door to Hong Kong. In 1990, for example, 55 percent of all realized foreign investment cattle from Hong Kong and Macao and 46 percent of all investment whose regional destination could be identified went to Guangdong Province. Fujian Province, with the closest ties historically and culturally to Taiwan, came next with 9 percent (State Statistical Bureau, 1991, pp. 630–631). The direct investment of Japan and the United States in 1990, in contrast, was 14 and 13 percent of the total respectively and no other country had over 2 percent.

Why did Chinese in Hong Kong and Taiwan move into an area where other investors feared to tread? The primary answer involves at least two components. First, most Hong Kong investments were small in scale and payback periods were short, often three years or less. Property rights don't have to be all that secure if a high rate of return on investment is possible in a short period. The other advantages possessed by the overseas Chinese were their family and other informal ties to their relatives and friends on the mainland. Connections (*guanxi*) are what makes things work in China and connections are based on personal ties. Japanese and American corporations might have better connections at the top of the Chinese pyramid, but nothing comparable to the Hong Kong-Guangdong connections that really counted in day-to-day operations.

Despite the pervasiveness of personal connections, formal rules did matter. The attempt to create rules with which foreign investors could live also had the important side effect of benefitting Chinese investors, too. The special economic zones set up by China illustrate the point. Originally there were only a handful of such zones, all in Guangdong and Fujian provinces, designed to free foreign investors from the various restrictions and red tape of the domestic economy. Rules that made sense for foreigners were increasingly applied to domestic firms, first within the zone and then outside of them. Soon other provinces and coastal cities wanted similar advantages and so more liberal rules spread up the coast. China's interior lagged behind in creating economic rules to attract foreign investors and other exporters, but by the early 1990s they were trying hard to catch up. Foreign investors still got some advantages not available to domestic firms, and vice versa, but these differences were under pressure from such practices as the ability of Chinese firms to launder their money in Hong Kong and bring it back as "foreign investment."

Foreign trade and foreign investment, therefore, has played a central role in moving China toward a market economy. Strong vested interests now know how to take advantage of foreign marketing opportunities and have a stake in removing the barriers to trade that still exist.

INDUSTRY AND STATE-OWNED ENTERPRISES

The task of reforming state-owned and private industrial enterprises is not fully analogous to creating market conditions for farm households and small shops. Not only do industrial enterprises have much larger and more complex internal structures, these enterprises are embedded in external institutions, a banking system, a tax system and much else, that are a product of the old command economy. Reforming all of these institutions together is a complex task, but failure to do so carries with it the danger that partial reforms may not lead to sustained increases in industrial productivity, the central goal of the industrial reform effort.

China began a systematic effort to reform industrial enterprises in 1984. In terms of the five components needed for a functioning market system, the first, macroeconomic stability, wait not a problem in 1984. As for components 2 and 3, China made large quantities of industrial inputs available on the market rather than though the administrative allocation system of the government. Inputs (and outputs) allocated by the state were sold at fixed state-set prices, but inputs distributed through the market were sold at much higher market-determined prices. This dual price system soon provided many with the opportunity to earn easy profits and the resulting corruption contributed to urban discontent in 1989. But the dual price system did mean that market-determined prices governed a large share of enterprise allocated decisions. Component 4, opening up the system to competition, was achieved by abolishing the regional monopolies that until then had determined where almost all industrial enterprises, including small ones, could sell their products. Competition did not result where demand for a product far exceeded its supply at prices that did not allow excessive profits. But where demand was not so strong, as with many consumer goods such as clocks and watches, the more inefficient producers soon found themselves in vigorous competition with efficient high quality producers such as the clock and watch manufacturers of Shanghai.

As for component 5, the enterprise's objective function was changed to emphasize profits rather than gross value output and a myriad of other plan targets. Selling off large state enterprises to private investors was ruled out in both the 1980s and early 1990s, largely on the ideological and political ground that such a move would not be consistent with socialism. The 1988 constitution did include a formal statement allowing private property, and foreign joint ventures and small-scale firms can be private. There was much discussion and numerous experiments with a responsibility system for enterprises which, among other things, was supposed to increase enterprise autonomy vis-a-vis the government ministries.[9] In November 1993, the central Committee of the Party issued a directive that spelled out terms for moving state enterprises even further toward complete autonomy from the central government, at least on paper ("Decision of the CPC Central Committee," Nov. 17, 1993).

The industrial reforms of the mid-1980s had one major success. They led directly to a substained boom in small- and medium-scale industrial enterprises throughout China, particularly along the coast and nearby cities. Because the subject of these enterprises is taken up at length in the essay by Jefferson and Rawski in this symposium, only its relevance to the overall reform effort will be mentioned here.

Making industrial inputs available on a market at market prices was essential to the dynamic growth of what are called the township and village enterprises. Abolition of local monopolies was also important. In 1980, collective and other non-state-owned industries accounted for only 21 percent of the gross value of industrial output. By 1991 this figure had risen to 47 percent. Small- and medium-scale industrial gross output in 1980, however, was 75 percent of total industrial output and by 1991 this share had fallen to 66 percent. Many small- and medium-scale firms were, of course, state-owned (State Statistical Bureau, 1981, p. 212; 1992, p. 70). All but a handful of the really large firms were state-owned.

As work by Jefferson, Rawski, and economists in the Chinese Academy of Social Sciences has shown, total factor productivity after reform rose faster in the non-state sector than in the state sector, but it rose in both (Jefferson, Rawski and Zheng, forthcoming). There is plausible reason to believe that this rise in productivity occurred because the non-state enterprises have solved the problem of getting enterprises to behave according to the rules of the market. Unlike the large-scale state-owned sector, township and village enterprises were not heavily subsidized by the government budget nor by the banking system. They were promoted because they made profits for their workers and for their local governments and, when they made losses, there was little political pressure to keep them open.

How were the property rights defined for small- and medium-scale enterprises, or for township and village enterprises in particular? In souse cases these firms were started by individuals, but often county or township governments also played a central start-up role. County state-owned firms were the property of the whole county, but they were not the property of the provincial government nor the central government. Collective and private firms were partly owned by their workers and managers but they too paid portions of their earnings to the county or township governments, whatever the tax laws might say.[10] County and township governments did not behave exactly like mini private conglomerates, but there were many features in common. Part of the reason, in the case of townships at least, is that they had been run as production units for some time. The township, after all, was basically the old commune which had carried out both production and governmental functions. The county and township governments, unlike the central government, could not print money nor, for the most part, could they readily force the banking system to print money to cover their expenses and the losses of local enterprises. Thus the counties, townships, and their local enterprises faced hard budget constraints. In both a positive and a negative sense, therefore, counties, townships, and their enterprises faced incentives to behave in accordance with the rules of the market. If they made profits, someone or everyone in the country or township could keep them. If they made losses, someone or everyone in the county or township bore the losses.

When one turns to the larger state-owned enterprises and the medium-scale state firms under urban or provincial jurisdiction, however, meaningful autonomy and defined property rights fade away. Ownership by "all of the people" really means a sense of ownership by none of the people. In eastern Europe and Russia, where central governments are weak, the result is often that workers and managers steal state assets and sell them or use them to set up their own firms. Privatization in that situation becomes necessary simply to preserve the assets of the enterprise. China's state apparatus, although much weaker than in the late 1970s, was still strong enough in the early 1990s to limit this kind of predatory behavior. But China's large state enterprises in the early 1990s still found themselves halfway between a bureaucratic command system and a market system. Central planning was gone but government intervention in enterprise operations was common. Managers were loaded down with objectives only partially related to the market's requirement to make profits by cutting costs and raising sales. If managers did what government officials wanted them to do, their losses would be made up with bank loans that didn't have to be repaid. Their budget costraint remained soft.[11]

That large state enterprise budget constraints were soft in 1992 and 1993 was no secret, but changing large enterprise behavior involved many separate but related reforms involving more than just the industrial enterprises themselves. Autonomy and hard budgets could be achieved by simply removing government from the scene and letting enterprises sort the process out on their own at the micro level. But the impact of this approach in eastern Europe, Russia, and Ukraine suggested that the price in human welfare terms could be high. Which institutions must be reformed if large state industrial enterprises are to be brought in line with what the market requires? A partial list would include some of the following factors.

Financial markets

The formal banking system in China used to dominate the financial markets. Formally, commercial banks were separated from the central bank early in the reform period, but in reality, the commercial banks continued to follow the direction of the central bank, and of government policy-makers in general. These banks took for granted that the central bank would bail them out if they got into trouble, which in turn means that the industrial customers of these banks faced soft budgets.

The fiscal system

Before reform, all but a tiny percentage of profits had simply been turned over to the state and then the state reallocated those funds to investment projects determined by the central plan. After reform, in theory, once fixed rate taxes were paid, enterprises retained the remaining profits and did their own investment. In reality, the fixed tax rates were negotiable and a firm with losses or low profits could usually negotiate a lower rate. This flexibility in the tax system also contributed to the soft budget constraint facing state enterprises.

The legal and regulatory framework

The lack of an established legal tradition in China has already been mentioned. Issues such as how to calculate profits lacked clearcut rules making it easier for managers to divert funds toward their own goals and away from the goals of the nominal owners, public or private. Chinese enterprises used several different accounting systems, none of them really designed for a modern market system, and these somehow had to be changed into one appropriate and enforceable set of rules.[12] China also had a bankruptcy law put in place in the latter half of the 1980s, but there were almost no bankruptcies of large firms until the early 1990s and not many then.[13] Politically, it was difficult to bankrupt companies—particularly given the absence of a safety net for those losing their jobs. Practically, it wasn't easy to decide which enterprises really should be closed down, given price distortions and inadequate accounting rules.

The worker welfare system

In China, both before reform and into the early 1990s, the state-owned enterprises were responsible for the housing, health services, day care, and much else for their workers. Getting rid of the many surplus workers in state enterprises, however desirable from an efficiency point of view, meant depriving people laid off of their homes and health care (Ahmad and Hussein, 1989). By the early 1990s, the privatization and marketization of housing (making rents reflect market demand and supply) was underway, but the political/equity constraints on doing this quickly were enormous. The Central Committee directive of November 1993 also called for further steps to separate the dependence of the unemployment insurance and the pension systems on individual enterprises. How quickly these measures will actually be implemented remains to be seen.

Factor markets

After reform, informal capital markets grew rapidly, ranging from inter-enterprise loans (not always voluntary) to the pooling of the funds of friends and relatives. The market for unskilled labor was also freed up when workers were allowed to move freely from one place to another or, at least, were not effectively prevented from doing so. Only in the 1990s, however, did China begin to loosen the tight controls over the allocation of skilled labor such as university graduates. In 1993, for example China began to offer college graduates some choice of job, whereas before they had virtually none (He, 1993, p. 3). Enterprises working to gain access to land had a particularly difficult time. The rapid development of the township and village enterprises was partly the result of the fact that they had much easier access to land than did the large urban enterprises. By the early 1990s, however, the need to find more and more land for the rapidly growing industrial sector was leading China to swallow ideology and set up markets for land. As in the case of markets for foreign exchange, it was the need of foreign investors for long-term leases on land at commercial rates that led the way for domestic firms to have the same possibilities.[14]

Ownership and management

China in the early 1990s in general, and in the Central Committee Directive of November 1993 in particular, still rejected across-the-board privatization.

The question then becomes whether there is a way of simulating the effect of privatization while retaining public ownership. In that context, China's experiments with share ownership and the stock market take on significance. If managers are picked by shareholders, and the shareholders are concerned mainly with the return on their investment, then the career path of enterprise managers is no longer directly determined by the state bureaucracy. Even if the shares are held by other state enterprises, and thus "publicly" owned, if those other state enterprises face hard budget constraints and hence are mainly pursuing profits, they will use their membership on the board of directors of the share-owned enterprise to insist on similar profit-oriented behavior by that enterprise's management.[15] Share ownership is spreading in China and is more widespread than the small number of firms registered on the Shanghai and Shenzhen stock markets. But China's large state enterprises are a long way from a system where most shares are held by other enterprises and private individuals and where management is selected by a board of directors independent of the state bureacracy.[16]

Other analysis might offer a somewhat different list of factors for making large state-owned enterprises responsive to market conditions, but the basic point remains. Getting state enterprise management to behave according to the rules of the market is not just a question of outright privatization or simulated private behavior within a system of some kind of public ownership. The whole economic system must be redesigned to be compatible with a market economy. In mixed economies with a high degree of state intervention, such as Indonesia or South Korea, the move toward a more complete market system has taken a decade or longer—and these economies began the reform process with many elements of a market system in place. A nation does not have to complete all of the changes before it has a functioning market system. It must get far enough down the road from a command to a market system so that mangers are governed more by market forces than by the wishes of government officials. There is no really reliable measure, however, for telling whether a system is governed more by bureaucratic command than market forces.[17] Determining when market forces are sufficiently dominant for the market to function well is even more difficult, at least in practice if not in theory.

MACROECONOMIC STABILITY

Enterprise reform is closely related to the problem of controlling inflation without generating a recession or alternate periods of stop and go growth.[18] Enterprise reform is not really feasible until inflation is brought under control by measures other than direct government allocation of credit quotas. Inflation controlled by state-set quotas on bank loans leads quickly back to state intervention in enterprise behavior in other areas as well. On the other side, without market-oriented enterprise reform, including reform of the institutions such as financial markets, rapid sustained growth tends to lead to bouts of accelerating inflation.

In a market system, inflation is controlled by government actions that determine the amount of high powered money. In turn, the amount of high powered money determines the supply of money, including deposits of the banking system, that are the main source of supply of loans to business. Business demand for credit determines how many loans are actually made.

In a Soviet-style system, this process actually works in reverse. The central plan determines enterprise credit requirements or demand. The banking system then supplies those credits as spelled out in the plan. Because the central bank and the commercial banks were one and the same—both were components of the People's Bank of China—there is not a question of the banking system being unable to supply the necessary credit, usually at zero or way below market rates of interest. The central bank can print whatever is required.

In the partially reformed Chinese banking system of the 1980s and early 1990s, the form of a market system existed, but not the reality. In form, China broke the connection between the central bank and the commercial banks by setting up separate commercial banks and confining the role of the People's Bank of China to central banking. The central planning of credit was abolished and interest rates were raised, although not to market-determined levels. But the process that determined the money supply still worked in reverse from what would be the case in a market system. Enterprises first determined their credit needs. The commercial banks were then expected to supply those needs at below-market interest rates and, in some cases, without much expectation of repayment. The People's Bank of China then created as much high-powered money as was needed to provide commercial banks with the necessary funds.

In such a partially reformed system, controlling high powered money is possible but inefficient. If the People's Bank tightens up the supply of money, enterprises fight to get as large a share as possible, particularly when interest rates, administratively determined, are kept low. Who actually ends up with credit depends as much on political power as profitability of the proposed investment. Raising interest rates in this context will lead to a reduction in the demand for credit from some enterprises, but the queue for loans is likely to remain long. Too many firms know they won't have to repay the loans if the enterprise makes losses.

Inflation in the context of this kind of system is even more difficult to control when price reform is being carried out simultaneously with partial financial reform. Freeing up prices for previously underpriced inputs such as energy leads to higher costs for enterprises. The enterprises, in the usual cost-push way, pass these costs along in the form of higher prices for their products, and the banking system, where necessary, accommodates increased demand for credit.

The impact of an anti-inflation program with only partially reformed state enterprises was apparent in 1989–1990. With the freeing up of many prices together with a rapid increase in the supply of money, inflation began to accelerate to politically unacceptable levels at the end of 1988, reaching an annual rate by the end of the year of around 30 percent. In 1989 and 1990, the government instituted a tight money policy by directly setting quotas on credit given by the commercial banks. Inflation fell quickly and in 1990 the retail price index rose by only 2.1 percent. But output growth in the economy in late 1989 and early 1990 also gound to a halt and unemployment in the cities rose. To avoid the political consequences of rising unemployment, credit was loosened in the latter part of 1990 and the economy resumed growth. In 1991 real GNP rose by 7.3 percent and then skyrocketed to 12.8 percent in 1992 and continued at that pace in 1993. But by mid-1993, prices were again increasing at a high and rising pace and another credit crunch was anticipated. No country has shown that it can eliminate cycles in economic activity, but the current wide fluctuations in China's performance could be damped by reform.

In July 1993, the head of the central bank was fired and replaced by Deputy Prime Minister Zhu Rongji. Immediately following the firing, China announced a whole new set of anti-inflation measures. Some of these, such as the raising of bank deposit interest rates, used market methods to damp down demand. Others involved more administrative interventions to rein in bank lending. But slowing the investment boom in 1993 was more difficult than in 1988–1989. The banks were no longer the main source of enterprise capital. Foreign funds, domestic privately held funds, and bonds issued by provincial governments were alternative sources of investment finance by 1993. Simply ordering the banks to lend less and monitoring their performance would not have had the same impact on investment as it did earlier. As in the case of the foreign exchange market. China was being forced to move away from administrative means of controlling prices toward market instruments because the administrative measures no longer worked well in an increasingly liberalized financial setting. In addition, fear of the political consequences of a major slowdown in economic activity made Chinese leaders reluctant to make full use of the anti-inflationary measures that did work. Until the financial system is fully reformed, however, even real GNP growth of 9 or 10 percent is likely to trigger accelerating inflation followed by retrenchment. Stop and go growth in output and prices appears to be a characteristic of an economy in the twilight zone between command and the market.

CONCLUSION

China has gone a long way toward a market system, especially in agriculture, foreign trade, and small-scale firms. Most of the problems that stand between the partially reformed Chinese economy of the early 1990s and a full market system reside in the large-scale state enterprise sector, and in the partial nature of the reform of the banking system. Together, these account for the inflation and the stop-go nature of Chinese growth in the 1988–1993 period. There are these who believe that the state sector will eventually wither away under competition from the nimble township and village enterprises and locally owned state firms, but this doesn't seem likely. Economies of scale in steel, automobiles, petrochemicals, railroad transport, and electric power grids will ensure the continuance of large firms.

In eastern Europe, the path to reforming large industrial enterprises includes political revolution and across-the-board privatization. But China is not eastern Europe. The decollectivization of agriculture substantially reduced the power of local cadres, but it had the full support of the central authorities. The township and village enterprises reduced the power of the central government, but enhanced the resources available to local governments. The center, after a feeble attempt to rein in the township and village enterprises in 1989–1990, gave up. China's State Planning Commission, never as powerful as its counterpart in the Soviet Union, is a shadow of its former self and is increasingly turning to indirect levers of control. Real political power in China, in any case, rests not so much in the economic bureaucracy as in the army, the public security forces, and a party that still has many elements from its revolutionary and rural beginnings.

China has now had 15 years of experience that demonstrates that those who move most quickly toward a market economy will reap the most benefits. Guangdong province has done better than the others and the coastal provinces have done better than those in the interior. The laggards are now scrambling to catch up. Government no longer controls much of the process even where it might like to do so. The dual price system for industrial inputs will disappear because firms don't want to sell their products at below market prices and the state's ability to force them to is dwindling. Foreign exchange will become convertible because the firms earning foreign currency can easily find ways to hold onto it, whatever the wishes of the Bank of China.

What will be left, once the reform of large state enterprises is well along, is a market economy with all kinds of governmental interventions at both the local and central level, perhaps on the pattern of South Korea or Taiwan in the 1970s. The question is whether these continuing state interventions in an essentially market-oriented economy will slow the growth markedly, or whether growth will continue at the torrid pace of the first 15 years of reform.

NOTES

1 The Chinese net material product indexes for the pre-1978 years are based mainly on 1950s price calculations that give much too heavy a weight to the fast grow-

ing industrial sector and hence exaggerate real NMP growth. Following methods similar to those used in Table 1, I recalculated Chinese NMP for the 1952–1978 period using 1978 prices as the base. This recalculation produced NMP growth rates of 4.8 percent for 1952–1978 or 4.2 percent per year for 1957–1978 (Perkins, 1981).

2 Disscussion of this process from a village viewpoint is in the essays by a variety of people who spent time in Chinese villages in the early 1980s (Parish, 1985, Zweig, 1989).

3 Categories 2–5 are discussed at greater length in Perkins (1988, pp. 602–21).

4 Subsidies required for grain alone rose from 3.9 billion yuan in 1978 to 8.4 billion yuan when grain purchase prices were raised for the 1979 harvest and peaked at 23.4 billion yuan in 1984 (Qiao, p. 28). See also the discussion in Lardy (1983). In the early 1980s, one U.S. dollar exchanged for 1.7–1.9 Chinese yuan.

5 I am indebted to Mr. Mai Lu for this information.

6 Public health and education were two other public goods that may have suffered because of the abolition of the collective system, although the evidence is far from clear. Barefoot doctors or rural paramedics, the backbone of the rural public health system, for example, declined in number and many became pharmacists selling herbs and other medicines for profit. Whether morbidity or mortality actually increased as a result, however, is unknown.

7 Data on income inequality of a systematic kind for China is beginning to become available, and that data indicates that overall inequality in China fell in the early 1980s and then began to rise in the latter half of the decade. There were, however, significant levels of inequality within rural China, about the same degree of inequality as found in India or South Korea. See Rham, Griffin, Riskin and Zhao (unpublished manuscript).

8 I am not aware of any official estimate of the floating (*liudong*) population, but Chinese sources frequently publish estimates of the share of the rural labor force that they consider underemployed. These estimates are based on crude calculations of the number of days needed to till a given amount of arable land and the underemployment estimate that results ranges from 100 million to 210 million people, out of a rural labor force 400 million. See the interview with Chen Xiwen reported by Chen Xiao and Zhang Xiaogang, "Surplus workers in the spotlight," *China Daily*, June 21, 1991, p. 4. A large fraction of this surplus probably "floated" on at least a part-time basis.

9 There are a number of major studies of industrial enterprise reform and the changing behavior of industrial enterprises in the 1980s based on in depth enterprise surveys. They include Tidrick and Chen (1987), Byrd (1992), and Granick (1990).

10 For a good discussion of the way in which township and village enterprises related to country governments in four regions of China, see Byrd and Lin (1990).

11 There is a growing literature on various aspects of the behavior of state enterprises under partial reform in the late 1980s and early 1990s. Among the many recent works are Groves, Hong, McMillan, and Naughton (June 1991) and Chao-nan Liu (1992, pp. 69–81).

12 China in the early 1990s had 70 or more different accounting systems, making it difficult to know whether a firm was profitable or not. On July 1, 1993, the country's first Business Accounting Standards was due to come into effect in an effort to establish a uniform system (X. Wang, 1993, p. 4).

13 Transferring the assets of a failing company to another company was a common way of dealing with failing firms in the early 1990s. Guangdong, as in so many

other areas, was ahead of much of the countty. In 1993 it introduced its own bankruptcy law to cover companies not covered by the national bankruptcy law. By the end of 1992, 14 companies had applied for bankruptcy in Guangdong presumably under the old law. See "Annexation best solution to some failed state firms" (1992, p. 4) and Zheng (1993, p. 1).

14 In 1992–1993, China began to experiment in a serious way with bidding for long-term land leases and other similar market devices but much land, probably most, was still allocated by administrative means and national rules for governing the real estate market were still in the pilot project stage (Liang, 1993, p. 3).

15 The person who is most associated with the debate over the role of share ownership of state owned enterprises is Professor Li Yining of Beijing University. Li's views, along with those of many other Chinese economists are ably discussed by Hsu (1991). A recent article discussing the relationship between shareholders and state enterprise reform is by Lin and Shen (1992, pp. 48–55).

16 By the end of 1992, only 120 state enterprises had been authorized to sell their shares to the public although a much larger number were making less formal arrangements for shared ownership between state enterprises. See "Momentum up for reform measures" (1992, p. 4).

17 There have been a few attempts to come up with a measure that would indicate whether a country was dominated more by market forces than bureaucratic commands, including the Kornai index that uses the ratio of input inventories to output inventories. But none of these measures provide a very reliable guide to where a country stands along the market-command spectrum. For a discussion, see Perkins and Roemer (1991).

18 There is considerable literature on the nature and causes of inflation in China and its relation to enterprise reform or lack thereof: for examples, see Sicular (1992), Naughton (1992), Hussein and Stern (1991), and L. Wang (unpublished 1993). The first three articles deal with the particular relationship between the reform of enterprise prices and the government's fiscal deficit. There is also considerable literature on the sources and nature of inflation in China in Chinese, much of it published during the periods of inflationary buildup such as 1988–1989 and 1992–1993. Some of the different views on whether China was or was not overheating in 1992–1993 are in articles by J. Li (1992, pp. 135–45), D. Wang and Z. Wang (1992, pp. 135–45), and State Planning Commission Investment Research Institute (1992, pp. 161–172).

REFERENCES

Ahmad, Ehtisham, and Athar Hussein, "Social Security in China: A Historical Perspective," The Development Economics Research Program, London School of Economics, CP No. 4, September 1989.

"Annexation best solution to some failed state firms," *China Daily*, October 26, 1992, p. 4.

Byrd, William A., ed., *Chinese Industrial Firms under Reform*. Oxford: Oxford University Press, 1992.

Byrd, William A., and Qingsong Lin, eds., *China's Rural Industry: Structure, Development and Reform*. Oxford University Press, 1990.

Chenery, Hollis, and Moshe Syrquin, *Patterns of Development, 1950–1970*. Oxford: Oxford University Press, 1975, 20.

China Foreign Trade Yearbook compiling committee, *Zhongguo duiwai jingi maoi nianjian 1984*. Beijing: China Foreign and Economic Trade Publishers, 1984.

China Foreign Trade Yearbook compiling committee, *Zhongguo duiwai jingi maoi nianjian 1989–90*. Beijing: China Foreign and Economic Trade Publishers, 1990.

"Communique of the State Statistical Bureau of the PRC on the 1992 National Social and Economic Development Plan," *Beijing Review*, March 8–14, 1993, *36*:10, 31–40.

"Decision of the CPC Central Committee on issues concerning the establishment of a socialist market economic structure," *China Daily*, November 17, 1993 (Supplement).

General Administration of Customs, *China's Customs Statistics*, Series No. 40, No. 1, 1993.

Granick, David, *Chinese State Enterprises: A Regional Property Rights Analysis*. Chicago: Univeristy of Chicago Press, 1990.

Groves, Theodore, Hong Yongmiao, John McMillan, and Barry Naughton, "Autonomy and incentives in Chinese state enterprises," unpublished paper, University of California, San Diego, June 1991.

He, Jun, "Graduates given more freedom to choose jobs," *China Daily*, April 5, 1993, p. 3.

Hsu, Robert C., *Economic Theories in China, 1979–1988*. Cambridge: Cambridge University Press, 1991.

Huang, Yiping, "Government Intervention and Agricultural Performance in China," unpublished doctoral dissertation, Australian National University, 1993.

Hussein, Athar, and Nicholas Stern, "Effective Demand, Enterprise Reforms and Public Finance," The Development Economics Research Programme, London School of Economics, CP No. 10, March 1991.

Interview with Chen Xiwen reported by Chen Xiao and Zhang Xiaogang, "Surplus workers in the spotlight," *China Daily*, June 21, 1991.

Jefferson, Gary H., Thomas G. Rawski, and Zheng Yuxin, "Growth, Efficiency and Convergence in China's State and Collective Industry," *Economic Development and Cultural Change*, forthcoming.

Lardy, Nicholas, *Agriculture in China's Modern Economic Development*. Cambridge: Cambridge University Press, 1983.

Lardy, Nicholas, *Foreign Trade and Economic Reform in China, 1978–1990*. Cambridge: Cambridge University Press, 1992.

Li, Jingwen, "Several viewpoints on the present economic situation and the 1993 development trend." In Liu, Guoguang, ed., *1993 nian zhonguo jingji xingshi fenxi yu yuce*. Beijing: Chinese Academy of Social Sciences Press, 1992, 40–50.

Li, Ning, "China Moves Closer to GATT, "*Beijing Review*," February 8–14, 1993, *36*:6 13–15.

Liang, Chao, "7 cities chosen as pilot for real estate," *China Daily*, May 4, 1993, p. 3.

Lin, Yifu, and Minggao Shen, "A Discussion of the Shareholding system and the reform of large and medium scale enterprises." *Jingji yanjiu*, September 20, 1992. No. 9, 48–55.

Liu, Chao-nan, "The Incentive Structures of China's Enterprises under the Contract Responsibility System," *The Journal of Contemporary China*, Winter-Spring 1992, 2:1, 69–81.

Lu, Mai, and Peter C. Timmer, "Developing the Chinese Rural Economy: Experience of the 1980s and Prospects of the Future," HIID Development Discussion Paper No. 428.AFP, September 1992.

"Momentum up for reform measures," *China Daily*, December 29, 1992, p. 4.

Naughton, Barry, "Implications of the State Monopoly over Industry and its Relaxation," *Modern China*, January 1992, *18*:1, 14–41.

Parish, William L., ed., *Chinese Rural Development: The Great Transformation*. Armonk: M. E. Sharpe, 1985.

Perkins, Dwight H., "An American View of the Chinese Economy. In Jingji yanjiu compilation group, *Guowai jingji xuezhe lun zhongguo ji fazhanzhong guojia jingji*. Beijing: China Finance and Economic Publishers, 1981, 4–5.

Perkins, Dwight H., "Reforming China's Economic System," *Journal of Economic Literature*, June 1988, *26*:2, 601–45.

Perkins, Dwight H., and Michael Roemer, eds., *Reforming Economic Systems in Developing Countries*. Cambridge: Harvard Institute for International Development, 1991, 13–33.

Qiao, Rongzhang, *Jiage butie*, China Price Publishers, 1990, 28.

Qu, Yingpu, "Drive to up trade to $200 billion in 1995," *China Daily*, April 19, 1993, p. 2.

Rham, Rahman Azizur, Keith Griffin, Carl Riskin, and Renwei Zhao, *Sources of Income Inequality in Post-Reform China*, unpublished manuscript.

"Rural Market Needs Further Strengthening," *China Daily*, December 17, 1992, p. 4.

Sicular, Terry, "Public Finance and China's Economic Reforms," Harvard Institute of Economic Research Discussion Paper No. 1618, November 1992.

State Statistical Bureau, *Statistical Yearbook of China*, 1981.

State Statistical Bureau, *Zhongguo tongji nianjian*, 1989.

State Statistical Bureau, *Zhongguo tongji nianjian*, 1991.

State Statistical Bureau, *Zhongguo tongji nianjian*, 1992.

State Statistical Bureau, *Zhongguo tongji nianjian*, 1993.

State Statistical Bureau, *Zhongguo tongji zhaiyao*, 1992.

State Planning Commission Investment Research Institute, "Analysis and forecast of the 1992–1993 investment situation." In Liu, Guoguang, ed., *1993 nian zhongguo: jingji xingshi fenxi yu yuce*. Beijing: Chinese Academy of Social Sciences Press, 1992, 161–72.

Sung, Yun-Wing, *The China-Hong Kong Connection: The Key to China's Open Door Policy*. Cambridge : Cambridge University Press, 1991, 106–07.

Tidrick, Gene, and Jiyuan Chen, *China's Industrial Reform*. Oxford: Oxford University Press, 1987.

Wang, Liansheng, "China's Inflation in the 1980's." Centre for Research in Economics and Business Administration, University of Oslo, unpublished manuscript, 1993.

Wang, Yijiang, "Economic reform, fixed control investment expansion, and inflation: A behavioral moral based on the Chinese experience," *China Economic Review*, 1991, 2:1, 3–27.

Wang, Dayong, and Zhihong Wang, "Improve macro controls, guarantee a successful reform." In Liu, Guoguang, ed., *1993 nian zhongguo: jingji xingshi fenxi yu yuce*. Beijing: Chinese Academy of Social Sciences Press, 1992, 135–45.

Wang, Xiaozhong, "New accounting system tallies well for enterprises," *China Daily*, May 28, 1993, p. 4.

Zhang, Yuan, "Bank ready to fund grain purchasing," *China Daily*, April 19, 1993, p. 1.

Zheng, Caixiong, "Guangdong Unveils New Bankruptcy Law," *China Daily* (Business Weekly), May 24, 1993, p. 1.

Zhou, Kan, "New rule to allow export, import of RMB," *China Daily* (Business Weekly), February 8, 1993, p. 3.

Zweig, David, *Agrarian Radicalism in China, 1968–1981*. Cambridge: Harvard University Press, 1989.

4

CHINA'S MACROECONOMIC PERFORMANCE AND MANAGEMENT DURING TRANSITION

Shahid Yusuf

Alone among the former socialist economies, China has led a charmed life. It was not by any means the first to experiment seriously with market institutions—that distinction belongs to Hungary. Nor did it attempt to "cross the chasm in a single leap." Nor has China's assimilation of market forms been buffered by a major infusion of resources, as in East Germany. Starting with the agriculture sector (Ash, 1993), the country has transformed itself, a step at a time, always ensuring that each economic initiative passed the test of socio-political acceptability before it was widely implemented. Instead of a risky Big Bang, China's reform can be most aptly described as a series of small controlled explosions, which maintained the momentum of change while minimizing the risk of instability.

On balance, the strategy has paid handsomely. Since 1978, China's macroeconomic performance has rivalled that of Japan, Korea, and Taiwan. When economies are compared using purchasing power parity exchange rates, China is already the third largest economy after the U.S. and Japan (IMF, 1993), and if it remains on the current trajectory, there is every likelihood of it moving into first place within the next three decades.

This paper will describe China's macroeconomic performance since the start of reforms, analyze the forces responsible for growth and the periodic bouts of instability, and explain how China has managed this complex and volatile process. Finally, it will conclude with a reform and policy agenda for China, and some speculation about whether the Chinese experience can serve as a model for other countries.

MACROECONOMIC PERFORMANCE, 1978–93

The process of reforms, first in agriculture and then extending to industry, has been mainly responsible for 9 percent per annum growth in China's GDP

Source: Journal of Economic Perspectives, Vol. 8(2), (1993), pp. 71–92.

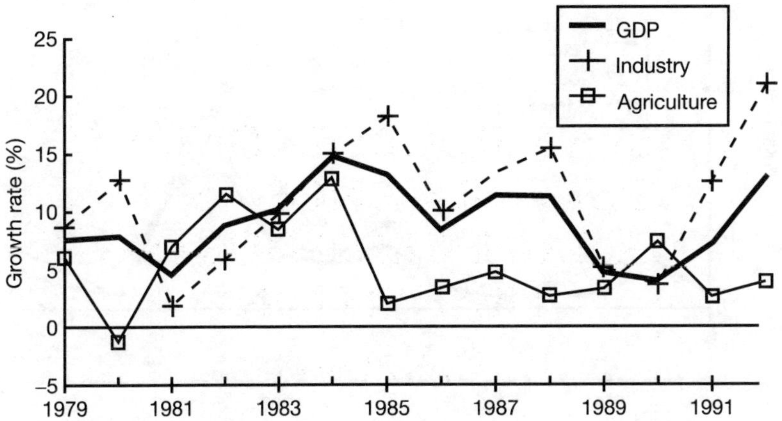

Figure 4.1 GDP, Industry, and Agriculture Growth (1979–1992)
Source: CHINA statistical yearbook, 1991.

since 1979, as shown in Figure 4.1. Agriculture boomed first, increasing at an annual average rate of 8 percent from 1979 to 1984. Agriculture boomed first, increasing at an annual average rate of 8 percent from 1979 to 1984. However, agricultural expansion was slackening by 1984, and as reform efforts widened to embrace manufacturing, the industrial sector moved decisively into the forefront. It has remained the leading sector since then. During this period industry has grown by 12.4 percent per annum and accounted for 66 percent of the increase in national product.

Three aspects of China's performance are especially noteworthy. First, although the pace of expansion was unusually rapid, inflationary pressure was largely absent in the earlier years, only becoming noticeable in the second half of the 1980s. But even making allowance for pervasive price controls, which can lead to underestimation of inflation, all indicators—retail, cost of living, and "market"[1]—show that inflation was in the low single-digit range prior to 1985. Since then, it has approached double-digit levels on the average, though the amplitude of fluctuations have been extremely large, as shown in Figure 4.2.

Second, China's strong export performance and comfortable exchange reserves have smoothed the road to modernization. China's success at exporting, combined with the extensive regulation of imports, has led to current account surpluses in all but four years between 1978–92. Except during 1989–91, when access to the foreign capital market was curtailed by the post-Tianamen political fallout, it is difficult to make the case that development has been hampered by shortages of foreign exchange. In fact, current account surpluses averaging 2.9 percent of GNP in 1990–92 meant that China's debt/GDP ratio at the end of 1992 was a modest 16 percent. It had accumulated

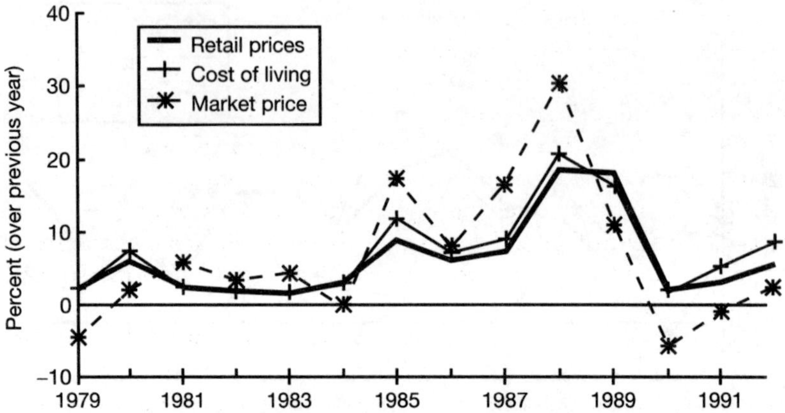

Figure 4.2 Growth Rates of Retail Prices, Cost of Living, and Market Prices[a]
Source: CHINA Statistical Yearbook, 1992. [a]"market prices" are free market prices of consumer goods.

close to $52 billion in reserves—equivalent to 8 months imports—out of a desire to limit vulnerability to external shocks.

Third, a cycle of economic and political reform has become apparent. The scenario, which has been repeated four times since 1978, commences with a series of reform experiments. As their scope is slowly broadened, investment and growth accelerate and are accommodated by credit policy. Soon the economy is expanding at double-digit rates. Once the fear of overheating is widely acknowledged, the government is empowered to contain reform initiatives and to curb growth by deflating demand. After a year's cooling off, the call for a resumption of reforms and faster growth becomes irresistible, as its benefits have been recognized by a wide constituency. Thus, early successes of reforms have generated a self-perpetuating dynamic.[2]

The first round of liberalization in 1978–80 led to a tightening of policy and reduced growth in 1981. When the tempo of reform resumed in 1982, it took only a couple of years before the economy was once again showing signs of strain, with a large current account deficit in 1985 compounding the government's concerns. A dose of deflation in 1986 moderated some of the pressures. However, as enterprise and later price reforms gathered momentum in 1987–88, macro stability was once again at stake in 1988 with sharply rising rates of inflation during mid-year. The subsequent deflation, prolonged by the political aftermath of the events at Tianamen, extended into the second half of 1991. The fourth and most recent cycle of enterprise, price, financial, and trade reforms began in 1991. Together with a relatively permissive monetary environment, they led to a near doubling of GNP growth from 7.2 percent in 1991 to 12.8 percent in 1992 and 13.5 percent in the first three quarters of 1993. Inflation has also rebounded, the urban cost of living index rising from 11 percent in the second half of 1992 to 20 percent during 1993 and China may have entered the high growth phase of a new cycle.

The term "stop-go" has frequently been used to describe China's reform-driven cycles, but downturns have been both short and mild (Hussain and Stern, 1991). In no case has deflation pushed growth much below 4 percent, and when released, the economy has rebounded vigorously, with growth rising by a factor of two or three from trough to peak. This draws attention to the power of growth-inducing forces and to the tremendous elasticity of supply response in this manufacturing-oriented and exceedingly investment-intensive economy.

In sum, the macro scorecard for China is remarkably strong on an absolute as well as on a relative scale. Its growth rate over 15 years is among the highest on record. Growth has been fairly stable, it has been achieved without sacrificing external equilibrium, and inflation has been held in check. No more than a tiny handful of economies can claim as much. Interestingly, this pattern of growth and inflation is broadly comparable to Japanese experience during the 1960–74 period and somewhat superior to that of South Korea from 1965–78 (Ito, 1992). The comparison is particularly striking when account is taken of the relatively benign policy environment confronting Japan and Korea, neither of which had to juggle simultaneously with systemic reform and macromanagement of a complex, weakly integrated, multiprovincial economy.

GROWTH STIMULI AND SOURCES

Economists are still some years from a sophisticated understanding of the factors responsible for China's recent growth, not the least because the economic data base uses a hybrid combination of accounting conventions.[3] However, pieces of the puzzles are beginning to fall into place.

Decentralization

The key factor to understanding the process of economic reform, although it may at first sound like an unlikely candidate, is a far-reaching philosophy of decentralization. Decentralization has a long history in China; traditionally, the nation was governed by an exceedingly small central bureaucracy which depended on gentry managed, local administrative networks to exercise control.[4] In the mid-1960s, the common rationale for decentralization was regional self-sufficiency in the event of war and, more prosaically, because centrally administering such a sprawling country posed insurmountable difficulties. This transfer of power from the center to provincial, municipal, and county governments became more marked after the late-1970s. Once reform had been formally initiated by the Third Plenum of the 11th Party Congress in late 1978, the capabilities of lower level governments were critical for success, chief among them being their close and intimate knowledge of the local economy, their command over the machinery of political mobilization, and the organizational resources to implement policies. In general, reform was to be based on local experimentation, and orchestrated by local political machines, which minimized political risks for the central government and the danger of poorly conceived actions being widely applied.[5]

Decentralization has occurred at three levels. Administrative decentralization has allowed provincial and local authorities substantial latitude in routine decision-making and the conduct of day-to-day government business. These powers have been progressively enhanced. Local governments have taken on the burden of translating broad reform proposals into a workable reality by modifying existing rules or defining new, market conforming institutions.

Second, fiscal decentralization, introduced by degrees after 1981 partly in response to demands from lower levels of government, enables provinces to retain and allocate more of the tax revenues collected instead of passing them on to the center.[6] Local governments can levy surcharges, fees and various duties as well. In addition, they control the budgets of provincially-owned state enterprises and can call upon collective as well as private enterprises for off-budgetary funds. By giving lower level governments a bigger stake in the prosperity of the local economy, fiscal decentralization has been crucial in cementing their support for increasingly more difficult reforms and for promoting development employing heterodox measures that are expanding the ambit of market forces (Shirk, 1993).

Third, industrial policy and supporting investment in infrastructure has been decentralized. In the early 1980s, rural industrialization (a locally managed affair) entered high gear and enterprise reform began significantly dispersing central control over industrial decision-making to provincial bureaus. This reform did not immediately create a multitude of autonomous firms operating in a price-guided milieu; instead, it allowed power to percolate down to thousands of industrial bureaus, who then joined forces with entrepreneurially minded enterprise managers. Local investment in transport and urban infrastructure financed through augmented revenues has buttressed industrial activity, along with generating demand which attracts additional investment (Yusuf, 1993a). For instance, nine-tenths of the intra-provincial road network has been financed locally.

Local entrepreneurship is closely associated with the shift in attitudes towards property rights. Private ownership was formally recognized in 1978, though the so-called "individually-owned" sector only began achieving some significance in the second half of the '80s.[7] Of much greater significance has been the informal acknowledgement by local governments of individual ownership of collectives, which constitute the majority of rural enterprises. On paper these have remained the property of the community. But in an increasing number of instances, "collectives" have either been established by individuals with their own capital or leased to local entrepreneurs. Their ownership claims are tacitly recognized, although in the formal sense rights are fuzzy (Yusuf, 1993b; Freeman, 1993; Pomfret, 1992). In a period of transition, such implicit and uncodified property rights have several advantages: communities can continue to observe ideological norms while implicitly accepting institutions critical for market functioning and resource accumulation; by holding aloft the collective banner, enterprises have gained readier access to credit and other official favors (Young, 1991); and fuzzy rights allow a sharing of risks between individual and community in a time of considerable uncertainty. Should market circumstances or political signals change abruptly, the community shoulders some of the responsibility of seeing the enterprise through difficult times. However, when the enterprise earns profits, community officials can claim some of these. Although fuzzy property rights expose enterprises to "fiscal predation" and might lead to short-sightedness in investment decisions, these have, so far, been outweighed by ownership incentives and risk-sharing.

Decentralization accelerated the demise of central planning and thus indirectly pushed the economy toward the market. Under some circumstances, giving local officials this power to interfere could easily have resulted in a disastrous upsurge of rent-seeking activity. But in China's case, although anecdotes of bureaucratic corruption and high-handedness abound, the overall results have been positive. Entrepreneurially minded local officials have been most active in soliciting ideas, conducting experiments, disseminating those that succeed, and balancing economic possibilities against political sensitivities—ensuring all the while that the pace of change remained broadly acceptable.

Explaining the success of this decentralized but firm management of transition is far beyond the scope of this paper. Suffice it to say that at least three factors might have contributed: local government accountability, enforced by the comprehensive framework of political monitoring and the demands of social responsibility within communities that until recently have been stable and tightly knit; the emergence of competition between provinces (and within these counties) which possess broadly similar industrial structures; and the disciplining effects on Chinese provinces of participating in export markets and seeking to become a focus of foreign direct investment.[8]

Investment and factor productivity

Although decentralization has clearly created a climate for vigorous and effective economic reforms, more conventional economic ingredients like factor supply and total factor productivity have also played their part. Among such factors, capital investment is in the forefront. In common with other socialist economies, China maintained levels of gross investment approaching 30 percent of GNP through the late 1970s. As reforms progressed, the multiplication of profitable opportunities and the difficulty of checking "investment hunger"[9] in a milieu where budget constraints remain fairly soft[10] pushed gross investment to 35–37 percent and fixed investment to over 30 percent. While no precise estimate is available, it seems clear that China's growth from 1978 onwards has been investment-led, and that increased capital investment has probably been responsible for about 40 percent of growth. This is higher than in Japan during 1960–70 (32 percent), but it is in about the same range as South Korea and less than in Singapore.

By improving allocative efficiency, agricultural reforms helped raise efficiency and total factor productivity has accounted for the bulk of the sector's growth. With the spread of reforms, productivity has quickened in industry as well, more so in collective than in state enterprises. In collective enterprises, total factor productivity was rising at an annual rate of 5.3 percent by the second half of the 1980s, contributing a significant share of industrial growth. Table 4.1 offers some data on growth rates in agriculture, state-owned industry, and collectively-owned industry.

New technology has been brought to China in a variety of ways. Investment in equipment has helped speed up embodied technical progress and introduced more efficient work practices, as suggested by DeLong and Summers (1992). Foreign direct investment, especially in manufacturing, has also served as a transmission belt for technology. China has been able to assimilate new practices faster than many other developing countries because of accumulated industrial learning, from the prolonged and single-minded effort at developing heavy manufacturing, starting in the early 1950s.

While the share of total factor productivity in China's industrial growth is on the increase, it does not yet compare with Japan in the 1960s, for a variety of reasons: a sizable share of new fixed investment is in domestically produced equipment of outdated design; managerial techniques are backward; motivation is poor among workers in state enterprises, because of overstaffing and weak incentive mechanisms; market competition is insufficiently strong in many sectors; infrastructure is often weak and the service activities that support manufacturing are sometimes primitive; vertical integration remains

Table 4.1 Sources of growth in China

		Industry	
	Agriculture	*State*	*Collective*
1978–84			
Sector growth	8.0	8.49	14.03
TFP	5.9	3.45	5.2
1984–88			
Sector growth	4.0	10.22	19.86
TFP	3.0	3.01	5.86

Source: Jefferson, Rawski, and Zheng (1992).

very high in medium- and large-scale enterprises and is a source of inefficiency; the industrial workforce, though large and experienced, is short of the skills essential to cope with modern technology; and China's large research establishment still lacks a commercial orientation. These factors slow the pace of technical adaptation and innovation. Production functions estimated for selected industries for iron and steel, coal, textiles and clothing suggest that they are operating well within their production sets, achieving no more than 60 percent of potential output (Wu, 1993b).

The labor market contribution to growth

By a rough accounting, capital and total factor productivity may have contributed close to two-thirds of growth during the 1980s, with the share of total factor productivity beginning to climb significantly since the middle of the decade. The remaining one-third of growth is linked largely to an expansion of labor usage. Increased labor force participation and absorption of the unemployed comes first. In China's case, the natural increase of the labor force averaging 2.8 percent and the vast army of un- or underemployed workers, whose numbers are believed to exceed 100 million, have strongly supported the rapid expansion of manufacturing and service activities.[11] This can be seen most vividly in the spectacular growth of rural industry where employment rose from 70 million in 1985 to 96 million in 1991 (China Statistical Yearbook, 1992; Ody, 1992). Abundant reserves of labor and the growing integration of the national labor market have also had a dampening effect on wage demands, which has sustained competitiveness while enabling firms to generate large investable surpluses.

The quality of the Chinese workforce has had an important bearing on productivity. Three-quarters of all Chinese are literate and close to 90 percent of all new entrants into the labor force have primary education. An increasing proportion now also have secondary schooling together with some vocational skills, although the insufficiency of skilled labor does hamper particular industries. The influence of this human capital on work efficiency is considerable and it is convincingly supported by evidence from cross-country studies that have underscored the role of education in growth.

Along with education, discipline, motivation and "manageability" of the workforce also matter. These traits have been widely observed to matter in East Asia's development success, and are shared by the Chinese workforce, at least in the rapidly expanding non-state sector. In part this is the consequence of a hierarchical culture, which places great stress on obedience. The absence of strikes or rather disruption is also a result of the state's policy toward labor institutions. China's constitution specifically permits unionization, union membership is widespread, and work actions are legal, but pressure from both the government and the Party strongly discourages strikes. Workers' dependence on their unit (*danwei*) for housing and other benefits, the many intersecting bureaucratic controls over an employee's life, and low mobility of urban, state enterprise employees have kept resistance down to very low levels. Overt labor unrest or violence has been minimal and when it has erupted, the authorities have dealt firmly with it. Instead, employee discontent is communicated to managers and bureau supervisors, through both formal and informal channels, in ways which have provided an effective safety valve.

The state has sought to enhance labor discipline and motivation in other ways as well. The urban workforce enjoys many privileges—job security, housing, medical and other benefits generally provided by the enterprise—which serve to accommodate the principal demands of workers. These benefits and the widely-held belief that the Chinese enterprise is there to maximize the utility of its stakeholders, with employees as the dominant group, increase the identification of workers with enterprise. Thus, the institutional elaboration of the internal labor market in a Chinese enterprise has created an environment in many ways similar to Japan or a few of the other east Asian economies, all of which are known for their disciplined workers and the minimum degree of labor unrest. The way in which China differs from these is with respect to the direct involvement of the state in managing labor.

Domestic savings as a source of capital

It was noted above that investment was the principal determinant of growth, and domestic savings have been the main source of finance for this capital accumulation. Gross national savings rose from an already high average of about 33 percent of GDP during 1978–84 to 38 percent in the 1985–92 period, thus matching the level and rise of investment discussed already. In the process, its composition also changed significantly. In 1978, government and enterprise savings dominated the picture, at 15.1 percent and 17 percent of GDP, respectively, while household savings were only 1.1 percent of GDP. Since then, government and household savings have swapped places as fiscal reforms which, among other things, allow enterprises to retain a larger share of their earnings, have steeply reduced government revenues. In 1991, government savings were just 1.8 percent of GDP, while household savings had climbed to 18.7 percent. (Meanwhile, enterprise savings were 19.9 percent in 1991.) With this shift, the pattern of savings in China is coming to resemble other east Asian market economies. The rise in the level of savings, and the shift in its composition, raise critical issues for the future (Ito, 1992).

One factor altering savings behavior has been how long-held patterns interact with the new economic reality. For historical reasons, China's culture is oriented toward production rather than consumption. Because of risk perception or low time preference or dislike of conspicuous consumption, household spending adjusts slowly to changes in income. Likewise, under the influence of decades-old austerity policies, Chinese enterprises are prone to accumulate and acquire assets in preference to current outlay. Hence, the rapid increase of incomes has inevitably led to a piling up of savings.

A second factor at work is the changed perception of ownership. Now that households and enterprises perceive themselves as possessing property rights, the incentive to accumulate has been greatly strengthened. Households feel that they have few wealth assets, in relation to their perceived needs. Many existing enterprises recognize that their plant and equipment is outmoded and in need of replacement. And both household and enterprises have noticed the profitable opportunities created by reforms, especially for small investors.

Demographic trends are also influencing savings behavior and will continue to do so for some time. Average life expectancy in China has risen some 10 years since 1970. It is currently 70 and the trend is upwards. With retirement age still at 55, the middle-aged in particular have every incentive to increase their saving rates to provide for their later years, in the event that pension benefits are either unavailable or prove insufficient. Moreover, fertility has declined sharply since the early 1970s, and with fewer children, households see the need for larger precautionary savings to finance future contingencies.[12]

The emergence of a market economy in China has altered expectations and the structure of wants. Many households are now aspiring to own property, a range of consumer durables and eventually an automobile. Some of the better off expect to send children overseas for education. With financial markets underdeveloped and likely to remain so for the foreseeable future, the vast majority of households expect to have to save in advance of purchase, as was or is the case in Japan, South Korea, and Taiwan. Because the cohorts now entering the labor force and setting up households are so large, the effect on aggregate saving is pronounced.

These are the main reasons behind China's high (but in east Asian terms by no means unprecedented) level of savings. On the east Asian pattern, China's household savings are in a highly liquid form—mostly bank deposits—because of a paucity of financial instruments and the limited sophistication of individual savers. This liquidity and the growing desire of wealthholders for portfolio diversification affects macroeconomic management, a point discussed in the following section.

The role of foreign capital

Although domestic sources of capital have been the dominant source of finance, some mention must be made of foreign direct investment and the resources supplied by multilateral institutions. Until recently, the two combined were a modest addition to China's annual investment during 1985–90—approximately $6.4 billion per year. However, the contribution of foreign investment has been substantial in other ways.

First, these foreign savings have come jointly with a range of expertise. Multilateral institutions have transferred skills on project evaluation, financial analysis, macromanagement and a wide range of technical issues. Industrialists from Hong Kong, Macau, and Taiwan have infused production skills, knowledge of quality control, and background on the logistics of exporting (Sung, 1992). Those from Japan and the United States have introduced China to advanced transport and electronics technology and helped it upgrade key service subsectors such as the hotel industry. These skills, plus China's readiness to assimilate them, have helped push the economy into a higher orbit.

Second, foreign capital has had more concentrated impact on the provinces along the southeastern coast, an area which has been primarily responsible for the surge in China's industrial growth. In particular, Guangdong and Fujian have absorbed the lion's share of foreign direct investment, and derived maximum gains from service industries in Hong Kong as well as "intangible" technology transfers from Southeast Asian economies (Kueh, 1992). These eastern provinces have had annual average growth rates in the 1980s in the 15–20 percent range. Moreover, foreign direct investment along China's southeast rim has stimulated the development of market institutions, and nudged these provincial economies onto the path of export-led growth.

Starting in 1992, foreign direct investment in China moved onto a higher plane. Commitments rose from $7 billion in 1991 to over $100 billion in 1993 and actual disbursements soared from about $3.5 billion in 1991 to nearly $25.76 billion in 1993. This trend appears likely to persist for several years. The main reasons seem to include currency realignments in east Asia, rising labor costs in Japan, Korea and Taiwan, and environmental constraints on industrial expansion. Austerity measures, so long as they are moderate, are unlikely to depress the flow of external capital. Of all the developing southeast Asian countries, China has the largest resource base, technological capability and domestic market.

MACROECONOMIC MANAGEMENT

Despite a record of rapid growth, external balance, and relatively low rates of inflation, China's macroeconomic management has aroused continuing concern. Actual outcomes seem to matter less than the perception, which surfaces with some frequency, that macro trends and institutional changes are pushing the country into economic chaos. The fears voiced both inside China and by the community of China-watchers since the early 1980s focus on four possible problems: soft budget constraints and "investment hunger"; a shrinking tax base; poor monetary management; and a lack of centralized economic power to conduct routine macroeconomic policy. Each of these fears deserves some examination.

Soft budgets and investment hunger

State-owned and collective enterprises in China have long taken "soft budget constraints" for granted. Furthermore, since capital is very cheap to enterprises with soft budget constraints, they have a strong proclivity to investment. The economic reforms, which gave enterprises more autonomy and discretionary control over their earnings, strengthened their desire to expand capacity, start new projects, and add to the factory's social infrastructure.[13] The upward shift in investment after 1984, when enterprise reforms were introduced, indicates how quickly the "produce and build" culture responds to a change in signals. After remaining close to 39 percent of GNP through 1989, investment rates were reduced in 1990–91, but only when the central government used direct administrative controls to regulate the capital spending of state-owned enterprises and limits on credit availability to restrain rural enterprises. Expenditures rose again once checks were eased in 1992 and remained at record levels through 1993.

Soft budget constraints and the associated investment hunger pose risks for macroeconomic stability, but the scale of the problem is diminishing. Provincial action to promote nonstate enterprises has been quite successful. In 1980, state-owned firms produced 75 percent of industrial output, collectively-owned firms another 24 percent, and other individual and private firms the rest. By 1992, however, the state sector produced only 48 percent of industrial output, while the collective sector had risen to 38 percent, and the individual and other to 13 percent. Hence a smaller part of China's economy is now governed by soft budget constraints. In addition, with the progressive unfolding of enterprise reform, the softness of the budget constraint itself has lessened. An increasing number of state enterprises, particularly the provincially-owned medium- and small-sized ones, have had their budget constraints tightened. Since 1992, governments have shown a willingness to use the bankruptcy law that was passed in 1986, and, what is more common, to merge or restructure loss-making enterprises. The blank check is becoming a thing of the past. Perhaps the most important development in this regard is that state enterprises are being forced to compete against one another and against rural industry. The effects of altered market circumstances are evident in the decline and convergence of state enterprise profits (Naughton, 1992; Rawski, 1993b). China's state sector is still a distance from operating according to strictly market rules, but the danger of macro-instability from this quarter is less than it used to be, and declining.

Fiscal trends and policy

China's fiscal situation has been criticized in three areas: the steep fall of the revenue/GNP ratio since 1980 (World Bank, 1990; Chen et al., 1992); inability to narrow or erase budgetary deficits; and the partial nature of tax reforms.

China's revenue/GNP ratio fell from 32 percent in 1980 to 17 percent in 1991. Prior to the reforms, the bulk of government revenues were derived from taxation of enterprise revenues. The latter were deliberately inflated by structuring relative prices so that those of industrial products were biased upwards, allowing enterprises to earn high profits which the government could harvest for the budget. Since the early 1980s, this revenue base has narrowed. Price reforms have diminished the relative price advantages of industrial products. Rising competition has had a further depressing effect on industrial profits. Enterprise reform has given firms latitude to increase compensation for workers and to retain more of their profits (World Bank, 1990). These deliberate reform actions account for virtually all the cut in revenues from profit remittances and enterprise taxes.

Furthermore, since provincial governments know that they must share any tax revenues they collect with the central government, they have instead moved to seeking revenue from extra-budgetary sources,[14] which has further reduced the revenue of the central government. When this effect of fiscal decentralization is factored in, the downward trend in government revenues appears in a very different light. First, the decline inclusive of fiscal extra-budgetary revenues has been moderate—from 32 percent of GNP in 1981 to 24 percent in 1990. Second, the redistribution of revenues from budgetary to extrabudgetary classification reflects a political reality: because of the dynamic generated by reforms, more power resides at lower levels of government and the approach to fiscal policy must be rethought to accommodate this. Third, even for the central government the budget may no longer be the primary tool of macroeconomic management—because of its inflexibility (a common characteristic), and because the central authorities control so many more resources through the financial network. China's use of monetary policy as a primary policy tool will be discussed in a later subsection.

Since 1979, China's budget has continuously shown a deficit; the deficit has averaged about 2.3 percent of GDP between 1987 and 1992, but the size of national debt with respect to GDP is a fairly modest 5 percent. This is largely because of an inability to contain expenditures on subsidies and administrative expenditures, as well as the imbalances caused by unplanned outlays for flood relief and on reflationary capital spending (in 1991). About a quarter of the deficit financing has come from the central bank, and the remainder either from external sources or the bond market.

While budgetary deficits are frequently associated with inflationary pressure and external imbalance, this does not appear to have happened in China, for three main reasons. First, the deficit is relatively small, its level has been stable, and it has been financed in largely noninflationary ways. Second, close to one-fourth of budgetary expenditure (4 percent of GDP) has been on capital construction, which has either built up productive capacity or eased infrastructure constraints. One can argue that an allowance should be made for such outlay in computing the deficit. Third, as in Japan during the latter part of the 1970s, budget deficits helped mop up a very high level of domestic savings, thus helping the economy to realize its growth potential (Lincoln, 1988).

Undoubtedly, the tax system is seriously distorted and coverage of nonstate enterprises is insufficient. The current system of tax contracting does not clearly separate tax payments from profit remittances. It needs to be replaced by uniform tax rates on enterprise income, with dividend payments to the government on the basis of the contract. Further, the tax base is fairly narrow and needs to be gradually expanded through extension of the value-added tax and a phasing in of income taxes. These deficiencies make adjusting the level or type of tax very difficult; thus, when the threat of instability becomes serious, the government's only policy tool is to apply administrative controls over expenditures. Administrative restrictions forcefully applied on capital spending were critical to stabilizing the economy in 1988–89, and the application of administrative brakes will be one of the major stabilizing forces in 1994.

The picture with respect to fiscal policy is decidedly mixed. Through its process of fiscal decentralization, China's budgetary policy has been tremendously effective at stimulating growth, as revenue retention by enterprises and tax-contracting arrangements favoring provincial governments greatly sharpened incentives to develop. As a tool for short-term macroeconomic management, the significance of budgetary policy has been declining for reasons which are by no means peculiar to China. Command over resources exercised through national budgetary policy has declined, although overall control by different levels of the government through various non-budgetary channels has fallen little; tax reforms aimed at raising revenues are proving hard to negotiate. Budget deficits have turned out to be stubborn. On the more positive side, the ongoing attempts at eliminating subsidies promises to reduce claims on the budget over the medium term. These price adjustments will substantially diminish the number of deficit-ridden state enterprises. The most significant loss-making industries are currently coal mining and petroleum extraction, where low administered prices currently lead to some 40 percent of the total state enterprise losses for the nation (Rawski, 1993b).

China's system of planning continues to provide the government with an array of administrative and political levers to regulate spending. When there is a policy consensus, these levers can yield quick results as revealed by the rapidity of adjustment in 1988–90. In 1988, real GDP was growing at 11 percent, the cost of living was rising at 20 percent, investment had reached nearly 40 percent of GDP and the external current account showed a deficit of $3.8 billion. By the second half of 1989, roughly three quarters after deflationary action using predominantly administrative directives was introduced, the situation was reversed. By 1990, growth was down to 3.8 percent, cost of living increased just 1.3 percent, gross domestic investment had fallen by 2.5 percent of GDP, and the current account showed a $12 billion surplus.

Although various steps can be taken to rationalize tax collection, reduce budget deficits, and so on, China is not particularly hamstrung with fiscal disabilities. The main problem lies in the sheer dispersion of fiscal authority, which is making policy coordination exceedingly difficult to achieve, whether for macroeconomic management, infrastructure development or other reform. This issue of coordinating policy between the center and the provinces will be examined in a later subsection.

Monetary management

China's approach to monetary management resembles its mode of fiscal operation in its appearance of centralization, and its reality of substantial de facto decentralization. The People's Bank of China was formally entrusted with central banking functions in 1984 and it has conducted its monetary and regulatory activities through some 2,400 branches located in provinces, counties and major municipalities. Inevitably, in the face of intense demand for financing and the rising power of provincial governments, the expansion of credit has been rapid (an annual average of 23.6 percent in 1987–92) and the control exerted by the central bank has been weak. Figure 4.3 indicates how monetary series have fluctuated relative to price movements and GDP.

A common characterization of monetary policy during the past eight years is that each level of government, together with state enterprises, have aggressively pursued their development objectives and have directed banks to supply the needed financing. By and large, the People's Bank of China is viewed as putting up minimal resistance even when annual credit targets have been breached. Money supply was tightened sharply in 1985 and 1988–89, but these were years of policy consensus when administrative action was also

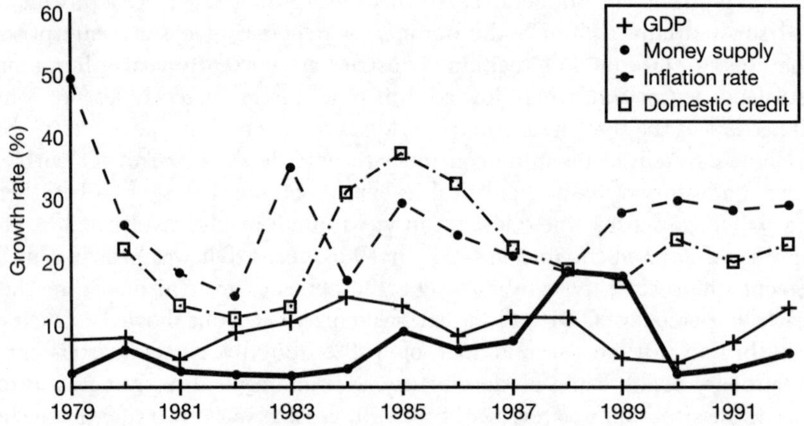

Figure 4.3 GDP and Money Growth Rates, Inflation Rate (1979–1992)
Source: CHINA Statistical Yearbook, 1992.

being used to contain spending, especially on investment. It is highly unlikely that monetary action alone could have achieved such dramatic results without the political agreement between central and provincial governments and the many-layered application of administrative pressure. (For instance, banks and workers in state enterprises were required to buy government bonds.)

Four key factors seem likely to influence the current and future role of monetary policy.

First, as direct subsidies decline, enterprises have become more dependent on financing from banks and financial markets. For instance, state-owned enterprises derive close to half of their funds for fixed capital from banks and an even larger percentage of their working capital. The other side of the coin is that credit allocation is now the major instrument of industrial policy, with approximately two-thirds of all bank loans subject to direction. Thus the role of finance is pivotal.

Second, the very power of credit flows means that their control has become intensely political. As decentralization has proceeded, the management of credit is determined by political bargaining. All players prefer rapid growth of money, and as yet, the central bank has not been given the political mandate to serve as the autonomous and responsible arbitrator. Only a fear of the political damage which rampant inflation might cause has enabled the central government to impose some restraint on monetary increase.

Third, China is becoming a more monetized economy. In the absence of other financial assets, people have had to hold cash or bank deposits. As a result velocity has drifted downwards, from about 2.5 in 1980 to less than 1 in 1992 (Lau, 1992). This downward trend in velocity, which resembles that of Japan in the 1970s and 1980s, implies that if China had heeded the advice to follow a more austere monetary policy, it would have significantly constrained growth and the spread of market activity. The inflationary spikes in 1985 and 1988–89 had little to do with monetary growth; instead, they were tied to sharp changes in expectations following the announcement of reforms. In 1988, for example, anticipations of price adjustment triggered panic buying, which drove up prices. Once the government had retracted earlier statements and expressed a firm commitment to price stability, consumer spending returned to normal.

Fourth, China has promoted a willingness to hold assets in monetary form by adopting a relatively unrepressive interest rate policy (McKinnon, 1993). Except for four years when inflation rose rapidly, those holding half- or one-year deposits have earned positive real interest since the start of the economic reforms.[15] This has encouraged saving, along with financial deepening. Interest rates were indexed against inflation in 1988.

Looking back over the decade of the 1980s, China's monetary management seems to have been surprisingly effective. Chinese policy-makers responded to a steady decline in velocity by permitting higher rates of credit expansion.

They perceived correctly that in an economy in which many prices were set by the state or subject to government guidance, the relationship between money and prices could be manipulated (Peebles, 1992). Through much of the period, deposit rates yielded positive returns. And, when a crisis loomed, the People's Bank of China was able to contract credit (using mainly credit ceilings and forced placement of bonds) as a part of a concerted deflationary strategy.

However, in those aspects which are of special relevance for the future, monetary management needs to be reappraised and strengthened. The conduct of a decentralized monetary policy is likely to be particularly problematic in the 1990s for several reasons: (i) continuing rapid growth and the prevalence of strong demand pressure; (ii) a further dismantling of administrative instruments and increased market orientation; (iii) the liquidity of asset holdings and the quick response of asset holders to changes in real return (Hussain and Stern, 1991); and (iv) the appearance of new financial instruments which will permit wealthholders to diversify portfolios, but which in conjunction with another round of monetization (connected with a reform of real estate) will make it difficult to project movements in velocity and calibrate this with the growth of monetary aggregates. These issues will require both institutional reform and the creation of indirect monetary instruments tailored to a market environment. But first, the issues of decentralization will need to be tackled.

Central-local relations

When igniting reform and achieving an irreversible momentum was a matter of urgency, measures which diluted central control over economic life in China were visibly advantageous. These loosened the bonds of orthodoxy and encouraged experimentation which nudged China marketwards. Now that reform is very much in train, and the economy straining against capacity, the ability to exercise macroeconomic control is taking on a renewed importance. As matters stand, the central government has to build consensus among provincial authorities before deflationary actions can be implemented—fiscal, monetary or administrative.

Persuading the coastal provinces is both crucial and difficult, because they are the ones that must bear the brunt of contractionary policy. Where once the attitude among provincial authorities was unswervingly against inflation, the experience of 1992–93 suggests a certain ambivalence. Faced with the choice of reducing growth by, say, 5 percentage points so as to bring inflation to under 10 percent, provincial leaders from the coastal provinces are finding the tradeoff less attractive. The center's attempts at forging a consensus have also been undermined by a difference of opinion among senior leaders. This division has encouraged provincial leaders to drag their feet and deflect the government's call to administer deflationary medicine.

With urban costs of living increasing by 20 percent on an annualized basis, the process of consensus building seemed to reach agreement (with some backtracking) on a deflationary package in late 1993. But the tortuous course of this package has highlighted some operational implications of the decade-long decentralizing tendencies and the apparent indispensability of administrative controls on credit and spending.[16]

The administrative leverage exercised by the center has only limited effect at the provincial level. However, the center retains considerable power to mobilize support for its views using the Party apparatus, although divisions among the senior leaders can encourage deviance. As a new generation of leaders takes charge, their ability to use the apparatus will depend on their skill at building client networks encompassing the People's Liberation Army and the provincial political machines. If they are unsuccessful in this regard, the center's authority will be further impaired. Differences in provincial performance are widening economic cleavages between the coastal areas and the interior provinces.[17] If this continues, it will become harder for the various parts of the country to agree on a common set of macro policies and the central government's political mediation will become even more important.

In short, as China has decentralized and assimilated market institutions, the approach to policy formulation has come to resemble that in other large market economies—that is, major macroeconomic policy action must be preceded by consensus building. This may become harder to achieve in the future, but at least over the past seven years China has done better than many countries in this regard. Through intense negotiations, together with a tradition of consensual decision-making, officials have been able to agree on an agenda and then to implement it. Equally important is the absence of powerful interest groups—like labor unions and professional bodies—whose demands interfere with attempts at consensus formation in western countries.

CONCLUDING REMARKS

Whether economic achievement is measured by growth rates or stability or macroeconomic management broadly viewed, China's performance appears comparable to that of acknowledged successes like Japan and Korea, if not superior. However, with demand pressures rising in 1993 and provincial authorities resisting the central government's fiscal and monetary discipline, there is little room for equanimity. If China's high rate of saving is sustained, it can both underwrite growth and, within limits, serve as a cushion against demand shocks. Thus, safeguarding household and public sector savings performance through interest rate, financial and fiscal policies must remain at the heart of the government's strategy.

Decentralization has reached a point where its advantages with respect to reform are close to being outweighed by the hurdles it puts in the way of policy-making and consensus building. The political rules and their constitutional underpinnings need to be reappraised in the light of changed economic circumstances. Without a new political contract that brings clarity to the rules of center and provinces, no amount of tinkering with monetary and fiscal instruments will enhance their effectiveness.

Assuming that the central government wins a reaffirmation of its mandate to conduct macroeconomic policy, two kinds of action might yield the greatest long-term results. First, the central bank needs a decent measure of autonomy, which would give it the power to control its branches and the specialized banks. China seems to be edging towards the political agreement which might eventually lead to such autonomy, but these are early days. Second, some rationality needs to be imposed on the budget. In particular, the relevant extra- and off-budgetary items should be brought into the budget, and fiscal responsibilities must be assigned across levels of government in accordance with broadly acceptable rules. Although much work will be required to iron out the details in a way which takes account of international experience and Chinese conditions, such steps are crucial to increasing the center's managerial capacity. But before that stage is reached, the various parties must settle their political differences. Budgetary policy is an exercise in political economy. Without progress in the political sphere, technical solutions will not work.

China's economic strengths are visible to foreign companies who are rushing to invest in the country, to the international banks who are eager to lend, to China's own citizens who express their confidence in the country's future through their high savings propensities, and to all those who seek to draw lessons from China's experience for other countries. However, it is no easy matter to encapsulate China's many-faceted and highly idiosyncratic experience into neat policy formulae (Chen *et al.*, 1992). For example, it is not useful to tell most of the world's countries to make sure that their geographic neighbors should be as economically dynamic as Hong Kong and Taiwan.

Of the lessons which may have general relevance, five would seem to be most pertinent. First, a widely shared political consensus is critical to success. As Fischer (1993) observed in the Russian context, reform cannot get too far ahead of its political base. Second, the entrepreneurial zeal of local officials, the effectiveness of the local administrative apparatus, and the strength of community cohesiveness have provided a disciplined dynamism.[18] Third, China's high rate of saving has not only helped sustain extraordinary rates of investment, but it has also been the key to stability as well as the ability to absorb shocks. Fourth, a socialist economy in transition must assure the power of administrative tools for macroeconomic management until such time that alternative instruments of sufficient potency are in place. A fifth and related point admits that while the development of market institutions is tremendously important, it takes years to actually happen. And even when such institutions are fully in place, there is no guarantee that an economy such as China's can afford to rely wholly on the market.

ACKNOWLEDGMENTS

Shahid Yusuf is Research Administrator, The World Bank, Washington, D.C. The views expressed are those of the author and not of the World Bank or its affiliates. My thanks to Javed Burki, Peter Murrell, Tom Rawski, and the editors of the JEP for their suggestions. They helped me to strengthen and sharpen the arguments made and improve presentation. Yang Li and Xiaofeng Hua assisted me with the research for this paper and Jean Gray Ponchamni was responsible for seamless production. I am indebted to all three. Shortcomings that remain are, of course, my responsibility.

NOTES

1 Initially, "market prices" referred to a small subset of agricultural products and items of daily use sold on "periodic markets." The coverage has widened since the mid-1980s to include a wider range of consumer products, but it is still fairly restricted.

2 This cycle is similar to the demand in several East Asian countries for an outward-oriented development strategy (Krueger, 1993).

3 There are several problems with China's national accounts: (i) conceptual ones related to the partial shift from the Material Product System (MPS) to the System of National Accounts (SNA); (ii) those associated with price deflators; (iii) problems of coverage of services and the real estate sector; and (iv) the accuracy of reporting, especially of rural industry output valued at constant prices. For these and other reasons, the data series, many of which are short and not entirely comparable across periods, must be used with considerable caution (see, for instance, Rawski, 1993; Wu, 1993a).

4 Decentralizing tendencies occurred towards the latter part of each dynastic period in China. For instance, in the twilight years of the Ching dynasty in the mid- and late-nineteenth century, decentralization was on the rise and was particularly notable in the first three decades of the twentieth century (Kuhn, 1970; Pomeranz, 1993).

5 Rural reform in 1978–82 was much more a response to grassroots demand and proposals and not a top-down affair. Later industrial and fiscal and price reforms have been instigated more from the center, though Beijing is continuously absorbing and responding to initiatives proposed by the provinces. China's success with the bottom-up approach has been linked in an interesting way to the M-form organization by Qian and Xu (1993).

6 Tax contracts between the center and provinces are differentiated according to the following characteristics: (i) whether or not the sharing between province and center is fixed, e.g., Tianjin's share is 46.5 percent; (ii) whether sharing is combined with an annual percent increase in the contribution to the center, as with Beijing; (iii) whether the province pays a fixed tax quota; and (iv) whether the fixed quotas are specially favorable. Guangdong has enjoyed (iv) status.

7 In 1985, the share of individually owned enterprises (mostly rural) in total industrial output was 1.8 percent. It rose to 5.7 percent in 1991.

8 These three forms of decentralization did not affect provinces uniformly. Those along the eastern seaboard, and in particular, the provinces along the south-eastern coast were especially favored because of their proximity to the dynamic East Asian economies, the supply of human capital and because this region was

the heir to a strong industrial tradition. The effect on both overall growth and what is perhaps a more sensitive indicator of provincial initiative—growth of non-state industry—was very marked.

9 Because production capacity was critical to meeting and possibly overshooting planned targets (which influences bonuses), socialist enterprises have had a tendency to add plant and equipment wherever possible. The size of production facilities also had a bearing on the allocation of raw material inputs and on the influence of the enterprise managers. Hence, the insatiable demand for investment funding labelled as "investment hunger."

10 State enterprises in China, as in other former socialist economies, are insulated from operational losses because the state is prepared to step in and cover them by way of the budget or directed lending through the state-owned banking system. Janos Kornai coined the term "soft budget constraint" to describe this state of affairs. The hard budget constraint is what one encounters in a market environment, where a firm is responsible for losses incurred and can be driven out of business.

11 The unemployment rate for the formal, urban workforce, whose numbers had reached 152 million in 1991, has ranged from 1.8 percent in 1985 to 2.3 percent in 1991. The total workforce, including rural laborers, was 583.6 million in 1991 (China Statistical Yearbook, 1992).

12 Savings might also be influenced by the strong sense of intergenerational connectedness in Chinese society, which increases the bequest motive. In China as in Japan, households are motivated to save so as to transfer resources which will benefit their progeny (Hayashi, 1986). This desire only reinforces the cautious anti-consumption bent of the average household.

13 Where they can, enterprises have invested heavily in housing for employees and recreational facilities.

14 Local governments derive revenue from surcharges on various taxes and from fees levied on enterprises and particular activities. These revenues are not incorporated in the unified budget but as a side income of the locality.

15 As indicated earlier, the retail price index is a not-entirely-reliable gauge of inflation, especially in the earlier half of the 1980s. However, if that index is applied to the interest rate on one-year deposits, the latter is negative in 1980, 1985, 1988, and 1989. It is zero in 1987.

16 The government's 16-point plan introduced in late July 1993 is aimed at controlling credit by means of ceilings on bank lending and continued placement of bonds. Savings propensities are to be strengthened by raising deposit rates. It seeks to cut public spending by 20 percent through administrative economies and a reduction of capital spending in the state sector. Further price liberalization is suspended and some price controls reintroduced. In addition, curbs were revived on the trading of foreign exchange through the swap market. This program resembles earlier deflationary policy actions in its emphasis on administrative means. Whether it is as effective will depend on the willingness of provincial authorities to implement policies and the degree to which administrative intervention remains effective in China's increasingly complex economy.

17 Widening income differentials have also led to increased interprovincial migration. While much of this is of a temporary nature, the restraints on changing residence have weakened and short-term movements could well become permanent. Migration flows are likely to encourage the richer provinces to agree to more fiscal sharing with interior provinces.

18 The experience of Italy, described by Putnam (1993), nicely buttresses this point.

REFERENCES

Ash, Robert F., "Agricultural Policy Under the Impact of Reform." In Kueh, Y. Y., and R. F. Ash, eds., *Economic Trend in Chinese Agriculture*. Oxford: Clarendon Press, 1993.

Chen, Kuan, Gary H. Jefferson, and Inderjit Singh, "Lessons from China's Economic Reform," *Journal of Comparative Economics*, 1992, *12*, 570–91.

China Statistical Yearbook. State Statistical Bureau. Beijing, 1992.

deLong, J. Bradford, and Lawrence H. Summers, "Equipment Investment and Economic Growth: How Strong is the Nexus," *Brookings Papers on Economic Activity*, 1992, no. 2, 157–211.

Fischer, Stanley, "Socialist Economy Reform: Lessons of the First Three Years," *American Economic Review*, May 1993, *83*:2, 390–95.

Freeman, Richard B., "Labor Markets and Institutions in Economic Development," *American Economic Review*, May 1993, *83*:2, 405.

Hayashi, Fumio, "Why is Japan's Saving Rate so Apparently High?" In Fischer, Stanley, ed., *NBER Macroeconomic Annual*. Cambridge: MIT Press, 1986, 147–234.

Hussain, Athar, and Nicholas Stern, "Effective Demand, Enterprise Reforms and Public Finance in China," *Economic Policy*, April 1991, *6*:1, 142–86.

IMF (International Monetary Fund), *World Economic Outlook*. Washington, D.C., 1993.

Ito, Takatoshi, *The Japanese Economy*. Cambridge: MIT Press, 1992.

Jefferson, Gary H., Tom G. Rawski, and Yuxin X. Zheng, "Growth, Efficiency and Convergence in China's State and Collective Industry," *Economic Development and Cultural Change*, January 1992, *40*:2, 239–66.

Krueger, Anne O., *Political Economy of Policy Reform*. Cambridge: MIT Press, 1993.

Kueh, Y. Y., "Foreign Investment and Economic Change in China," *China Quarterly*, September 1992, no. 131, 637–90.

Kuhn, Philip A., *Rebellion and its Enemies in Late Imperial China*. Cambridge: Harvard University Press, 1970.

Lau, Lawrence J., "Macroeconomic Policies for Short-term Stabilization and Long-term Growth of the Chinese Economy," *Asia Pacific Research Center Working Paper Series No.* 101, Stanford: Stanford University Press, December 1992.

Lincoln, Edward J., *Japan: Facing Economic Maturity*. Washington, D.C.: Brookings Institution, 1988.

McKinnon, Ronald I., "Gradual versus Rapid Liberalization in Socialist Economies: Financial Policies and Macroeconomic Stability in China and Russia Compared." Washington, D.C.: World Bank Annual Conference on Development Economics, 1993.

Naughton, Barry, "Implications of the State Monopoly over Industry and its Relaxation," *Modern China*, January 1992, *18*:1, 14–41.

Ody, Anthony, "Rural Enterprise Development in China, 1986–90," World Bank Discussion Paper No. 162, Washington, D.C., May 1992.

Peebles, Gavin, *Money in the People's Republic of China: A Comparative Study*. Concord: Pauland Company Publishers, 1992.

Pomeranz, Kenneth, *The Making of a Hinterland*. Berkeley: University of California Press, 1993.

Pomfret, Richard, "The Sequencing of Economic Reform," Working Paper No. 93/4, Chinese Economic Research Unit, University of Adelaide, October 1992.

Putnam, Robert D., *Making Democracy Work*. Princeton: Princeton University Press, 1993.

Qian, Yingyi, and Chenggong Xu, "Why China's Economic Reforms Differ," CP, No. 25, STICERD, London School of Economics, London, July 1993.

Rawski, Tom, "How Fast Has Chinese Industry Grown?," World Bank PRE Working Paper Series, No. 1194, World Bank, Washington, D.C., September 1993a.
Rawski, Tom, "Progress Without Privatization." Washington, D.C.: World Bank, mimeo, 1993b.
Shirk, Susan L., *The Political Logic of Economic Reform in China*. Berkeley: University of California Press, 1993.
Sung, Yun-Wing, *The China-Hong Kong Connection*. Australia, New York: Cambridge University Press, 1992.
World Bank, *Between Plan and Market*. Washington, D.C.: World Bank, 1990.
Wu, Harry X., "The 'Real' Chinese Gross Domestic Product for the Pre-Reform Period 1952–77," *Review of Income and Wealth*, March 1993a, *39*:1, 63–86.
Wu, Yonrui, "The Measurement of Efficiency: A Review of the Theory and Empirical Applications to China," Working Paper No. 93/1, Chinese Economy Research Unit, University of Adelaide, April 1993b.
Young, Susan, "Wealth but not Security: Attitudes towards Private Business in China in the 1980s," *Australian Journal of Chinese Affairs*, January 1991, no. 25, 115–37.
Yusuf, Shahid, "The Rise of China's Non-state Sector," World Bank, processed, January 1993a.
Yusuf, Shahid, "Property Rights and Non-state Sector Development in China," mimeo, World Bank, 1993b.

5

CHINA'S MACROECONOMY IN TRANSITION

Barry Naughton

Is macroeconomic stability the Achilles heel of the Chinese economy? Recurrent bouts of inflationary disorder lead some observers to worry that the Chinese government is unable to control the economy. Macroeconomic difficulties show up in a pattern of repeated boom and bust cycles, in which each boom is accompanied by an acute inflationary phase and significant disruption. Moreover, since the reform era began, the peak annual inflation rate of each successive cycle has been higher than that of the preceding one.[1] The most recent attempts to cool off the economy have only led to additional questions. An austerity policy was decreed at the end of June 1993, yet inflation actually accelerated in 1994, and it was not until mid-1995 that it dropped to the levels of mid-1993. The Chinese government was engaged in a quest for an economic "soft landing" for two years without a net reduction in the inflation rate!

Macroeconomic issues also attract attention because of their link to broader questions about the future of Chinese society. For centuries, China has been plagued by the two extremes of dictatorship and chaos. Today, it has thrown off the main institutions of economic dictatorship – the system of central planning – and has created the rudiments of a market economy. But it is possible that the improved economic conditions produced by reform will be threatened by a descent into economic chaos? More broadly, it is obvious that the Chinese political system has not achieved real legitimacy or widespread support among the population. The current government is woefully inadequate to cope with the growing diversity and emergent political demands of Chinese society. In this context, macroeconomic instability often seems to stand in for the spectre of broader social unrest. During the period when the government is temporarily able to maintain direct political control over a changing society, macroeconomic weakness is brought in to demonstrate the paradoxical weakness that shadows this apparently strong government.[2]

Source: The China Quarterly, no. 144 (December 1995), pp. 1082–1104 [Reprinted in Andrew G. Walder (editor), *China's Transitional Economy* (Oxford: Oxford University Press, 1996), pp. 121–42.]

Even on more narrowly economic grounds, it is common to view China as lacking the macroeconomic institutions required to manage a market economy, thus having little protection from economic disorder. Economics-based approaches may stress the relative strength of local governments and their client enterprises[3]; or they may deduce problems from the evolution of macroeconomic magnitudes such as central government budgetary revenues (which are declining) or central bank lending (which fluctuates but is sometimes large).[4] These views are useful in directing attention to a crucial unresolved area in China's economic reform process. It is indeed true that reform of the institutions of macroeconomic control is currently the most urgent need in the reform process, as well as one of the most difficult. However, this article argues that it is simply not the case that the Chinese central government is a feeble state, bereft of effective instruments of macroeconomic control and doomed to a process of economic disintegration. Indeed, anyone who sees the Chinese central government *solely* as a weak government is seriously misperceiving the situation. Instead, the Chinese central government combines paradoxical elements of strength and weakness, and attempts to achieve multiple and sometimes conflicting objectives, including some that require ambitious intervention in the economy.

This combination of conflicting and paradoxical elements often results in inconsistent or destabilizing policies. But there is nothing in the fundamental characteristics of China's macroeconomy that dooms the effort of reformers to establish a stable and consistent policy package. The macroeconomy is *not* the Achilles heel of the reform process. Instead, it is argued that the quest for macroeconomy stability should be seen as an inherently extremely difficult process in a transitional economy. On balance, China has done reasonably well: probably better than anyone had any right to expect. But there are still serious challenges facing policy-makers, and these challenges will become much more formidable if the political process breaks down after the death of Deng Xiaoping.

This article addresses a few of the many issues relating to Chinese macroeconomic policy. The first section details the basic conditions that structure China's macroeconomic problems. Most important is the remarkable shrinkage in the size of the state budget, caused by the rapid entry of new firms that has led to increased competition and the erosion of the previously protected monopoly profits of state-owned enterprises (SOEs) in industry and trade. This process has also led to a distinct division of labour between state and non-state firms across industrial sectors. The second section shows that the retreat of the state from most spheres of the economy has not been accompanied by a similar reduction in state fixed investment. On the contrary, the state has maintained a vigorous and intrusive role in investment, actually growing in the past few years (1992–94). In the third section, the enormous pressures on the banking system created by shrinking state revenues and large state investment are described. The fourth section discusses two other problems that disrupt macroeconomic stability: deficit SOEs and new problems related to the maintenance of external balance. The final section includes a few predictions about future policy and stability.

The article's conclusions can be summarized as follows. First, the overall process of macroeconomic policy-making does not reveal a government bereft of effective instruments. Rather, it shows a government whose policies are clumsy and often delayed, but which eventually responds and achieves results. Secondly, because current problems are difficult and are not about to disappear, continued recurrent inflationary bouts and instability can be expected. This is not because the government is without instruments, but because it is subject to intense, often contradictory, pressures in complex situations, and will inevitably make mistakes. Thirdly, financial reform is a focus of current contradictions and the main area where radical economic reforms are needed. Many of the required measures and institutions have been proclaimed – such as central bank independence – but the point is to make them actually work. When it is considered that the key economic fundamentals are in place – with high domestic saving, rapid growth and the institutional outlines in place – there are some grounds for optimism despite the formidable problems.

THE CONTEXT OF EVOLUTIONARY REFORM

Even in a developed market economy, macroeconomic policy-making is difficult and often surrounded by controversy. In the United States, the Federal Reserve Board possesses abundant sources of information and controls powerful instruments to intervene in sophisticated capital markets. Moreover, the Federal Reserve Board possesses a relatively straight-forward and unitary objective: maintaining price stability. Despite these advantages, hundreds of millions of dollars are spent annually anticipating and placing wagers on policy moves by "the Fed." In a formerly socialist transitional economy, little of the sophisticated institutional apparatus of macroeconomic policy implementation is available. The absence of well-functioning institutions not only makes it more difficult to achieve price stability, it also complicates the overall process by requiring policy-makers to pay attention to multiple objectives. While policy-makers in China or other transitional economies strive for price stability, they must also foster new financial institutions. Fundamentally, financial institutions exist to channel saving into investment, which is necessary for economic growth. Yet in the course of reform, these institutions must undergo massive change. Macroeconomic policy-makers must thus strive for price stability, insure investment finance through existing institutions and reform those institutions. Inevitably, these complex objectives generate conflicts.

The basic context within which the changing role of planners and macroeconomic institutions in China must be placed is the process of marketization and the overall evolutionary reform strategy of "growing out of the plan."[5] In the unreformed economy, planners had direct control over saving and investment. Virtually all national saving was carried out in the state sector, more particularly in state manufacturing enterprises. Those enterprises operated in a protected environment, with prices set at generous levels by the government, and they earned very large profits. They remitted almost all their surpluses to the government budget. Household savings were small, so the allocation of government investment funds by the central planners basically determined the economy-wide balance between saving and investment. What is traditionally thought of as monetary policy (supply of money and credit and establishment of interest rates) was not very important in the planned economy. Prudent fiscal policy was all that was required, and in practice this meant setting the growth of state investment at sustainable levels.

The most crucial step in economic reform was the ending of the government monopoly over the economy, and especially over industrial production and investment. The industrial system was changed by entry of new producers, including township and village enterprises, private firms and new locally-run state firms. Not surprisingly, entry was most rapid in those sectors where profits were high, as was true generally in manufacturing. Competition eroded the huge surpluses that state firms had been accustomed to earning, thus upsetting government budgets and the entire balance of saving and investment in the economy. Many of the government institutional and policy changes that marked the reform era can be seen as responses to this changing environment.

With this came massive change in the role of the government budget. In 1978, government budgetary revenues at all levels came to 35.5 per cent of gross national product (GNP); according to preliminary figures, in 1994 the comparable figure was only 12.7 per cent.[6] Scaled to GNP, budgetary revenues have fallen steadily to about one-third of their 1978 level. Under the pressure of this erosion in revenues, budgetary expenditures have been cut back as well. Overt deficits have been kept to moderate levels: between 2 and 3 per cent of GNP in most years, including 1994. Deficits of this size are not in themselves enough to destabilize an economy, but they are enough largely to eliminate the ability of policy-makers to use "fiscal policy" to affect the macroeconomy. Policy-makers don't have the revenue available to reduce the deficit, and they don't dare run a larger deficit for fear that this would signal economic difficulties. Budgetary authorities have therefore been forced to resign themselves to simply managing the decline in revenues *and* expenditures in an orderly fashion.[7] Previously, only fiscal policy was important; since reform, fiscal policy has been rendered impotent. By contrast, whereas monetary policy used to be fairly trivial, today only monetary policy can really matter for macroeconomic stability.

Since revenues and expenditures are closely related, Figure 5.1 displays only budgetary expenditures. Two facts emerge clearly. First, the reduction in

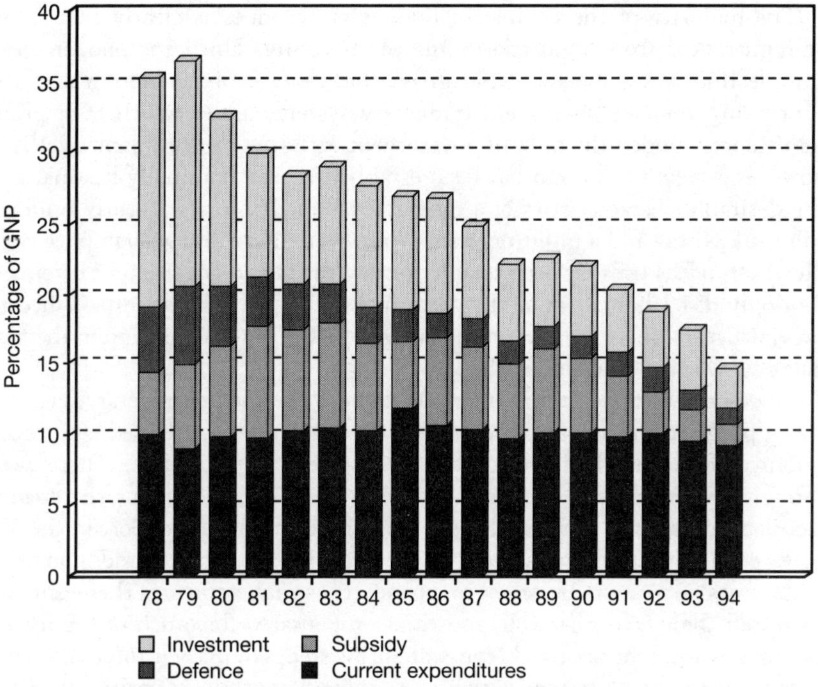

Figure 5.1 Evolution of Budgetary Expenditures (% of GNP)
Source: Zhongguo tongji nianjian (*Statistical Yearbook of China 1994*) (Beijing: Zhongguo tongji chubanshe, 1994), p. 217; Liu Zhongli, "Report on the implementation of the state budget for 1994 and on the draft central and local budgets for 1995," *Beijing Review*, 3–16 April, 1995, pp. VI–VIII.

overall budgetary outlays has been massive and sustained: from 35 per cent to just below 15 per cent of GNP. Secondly, perhaps even more surprisingly, the changes have had very little overall quantitative impact on what might be thought of as "ordinary government," that is, the category of government expenditures labelled "current expenditures" in Figure 5.1. Reductions in expenditures have been concentrated in investment, defence outlays and subsidies. Budgetary outlays for investment were at their highest in 1978 at 16.2 per cent of GNP and have declined steadily since to only 2.7 per cent of GNP in 1994. Military expenditures peaked in 1979 at 5.6 per cent of GNP and generally declined – notwithstanding a blip in 1989–90 – to 1.3 per cent of GNP in 1994. And subsidies – lumping together price subsidies and subventions to loss-making SOEs – peaked in 1981 at 8.2 per cent of GNP and declined to 1.5 per cent of GNP by 1994.[8] By contrast, government current expenditures have been maintained at almost exactly 10 per cent of GNP throughout the entire reform era.[9] Thus, despite the dramatic decline in revenues, the share of GNP going to administration, education and other ordinary government has been sustained.[10]

The majority of the decline in budgetary revenues is clearly as a result of remittances from industrial SOEs plummeting. Until the end of 1993 this decline was understandable given the absence of tax reform and the continuing reliance on the old budgetary system, under which SOE profit remittances funded the bulk of government activities. Since 1 January 1994, however, a new tax system has been established that nominally has many of the desirable characteristics of a modern system. It creates a nearly uniform value-added tax and a profit tax that applies equally to all ownership forms.[11] However, it has thus far been unable to slow the fall in government revenues. Not only did 1994 continue the pattern of declining revenues established in previous years, there are also ominous signs that revenue collection in the first half of 1995 was even slower than in 1994.[12]

As described above, it might appear that the decline in budgetary revenues was a purely negative phenomenon: government saving declined, and fewer resources were available for public investment and services. There was, though, another side to the story. By permitting entry into lucrative manufacturing and trade sectors, the government created new opportunities for private and local interests, and investment by households and non-state enterprises increased. In order to finance those investments, these entities increased their saving as well, and this compensated for much of the reduction in government saving.[13] Non-state firms stepped up their internal saving as SOEs were forced to reduce theirs. As these decentralized entities invested more in the economy, they took over many activities that had previously been dominated by the government. Thus although the government had fewer resources to invest, the need for it to finance all types of investment was eliminated. Moreover, the economy benefited from de-monopolization. It became more diverse and resilient, and developed stronger self-regulating mechanisms, as some decisions were taken out of the hands of central planners.

New division of labour

The result has been the emergence of a *de facto* division of labour between competitive sectors with investment from non-state enterprises, and non-competitive (or not fully competitive) sectors that continue to be dominated by state investment and especially by central government activity. This division of labour began to emerge in the early 1980s, and developed steadily in the 1990s. Figure 5.2 displays one way to look at it. Industrial sectors are arranged in three groups, roughly according to the share of SOEs in gross output.[14] At the top are the non-competitive sectors, in which state output is dominant. Most prominent are the natural resource sectors and utilities, where the government has simply decreed that SOEs will retain a monopoly or near-monopoly position. The remaining sectors are the heavy materials industries that exhibit substantial economies of scale (such as steel and

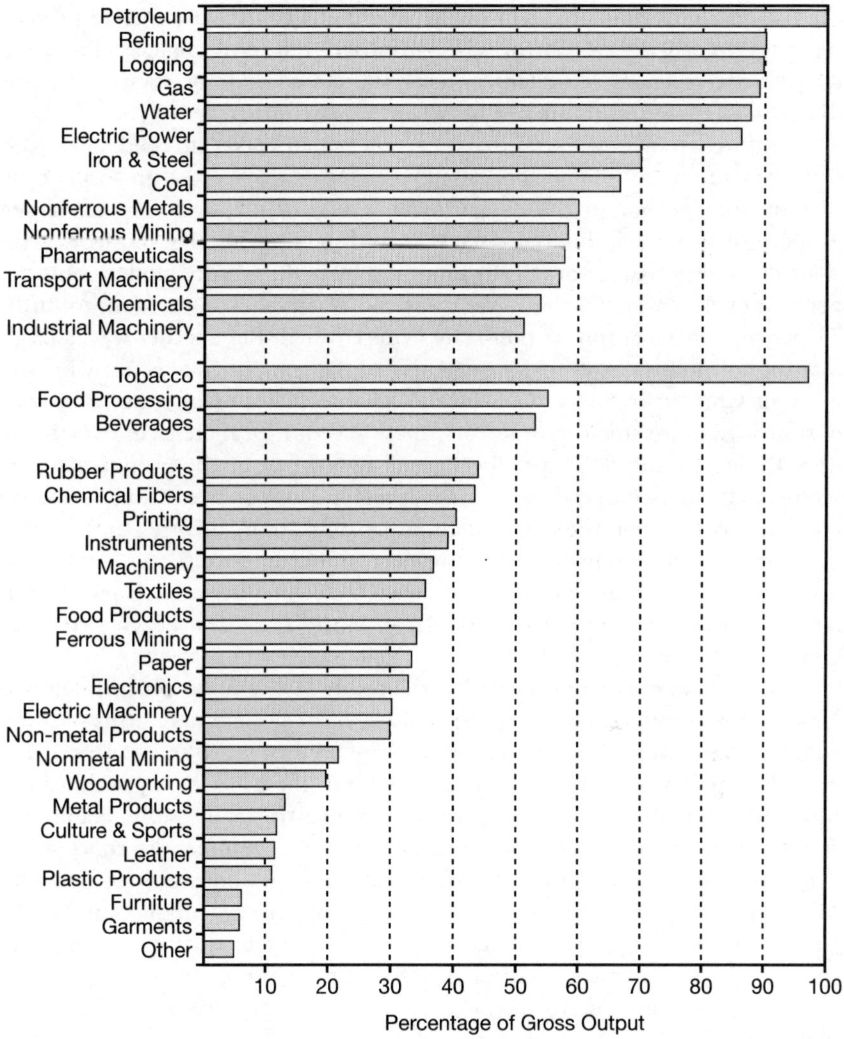

Figure 5.2 Ownership Structure of Industrial Sectors (% of Gross Output Produced by SOEs)

Source: Zhongguo tongji nianjian 1994, pp. 373, 378, 388, 395. See discussion in nn. 14 and 15.

chemicals). In these sectors, the entry of new producers has not fundamentally altered the ownership structure, because of both administrative regulation and economic factors.

A second group comprises three sectors – tobacco, food processing and beverages – in which SOEs are still extremely important. The government continues to control a large part of the agricultural procurements required as inputs, and it reserves these inputs for SOEs. In some cases, such as cigarettes, the national government intentionally maintains control in order to protect revenues. In other cases control is decentralized, but local agencies cling to it to generate revenues for client enterprises. As a result of these lingering distortions, these sectors are not fully competitive either.

The third group is the competitive sector which makes up the largest part of Chinese industry. The sectors classified as competitive make up 53 per cent of industrial output in the data shown in Figure 5.2, and an even larger proportion of total industrial output including very small-scale firms. The share of competitive sector output produced by SOEs is quite modest: only 27 per cent of the covered output. Yet these competitive sectors account for fully 71 per cent of the output of non-state firms covered. Put another way, a large majority of non-state *industrial* output is in the competitive sector, which is most of Chinese industry. Conversely, a large majority of state industrial output is in non-competitive sectors: these account for more than two-thirds of SOE output and SOEs produce about two-thirds of the output of these sectors. The non-competitive sectors represent a minority of Chinese industry, but account for the bulk of resource extraction, utilities and capital intensive materials industry. In this respect, the Chinese state sector is beginning to resemble the state sector in other mixed market economies, with a strong tendency to concentrate on infrastructure and a few heavy industrial sectors.

This division of labour occurred as the result of a complex process. On one hand, new entrants were able successfully to out-compete state firms in some competitive sectors. Output of competitive sectors grew and the need for government investment there was reduced. On the other hand, with robust economic growth, the need for government investment in public goods and infrastructure *increased.* The result was pressure on government to concentrate investment on infrastructure provision and strategic industrial sectors. The initial government response stressed primary energy production (given China's severe energy crisis in the early 1980s), but gradually the emphasis shifted to infrastructure. Central government planning did not cease, but it was focused on a narrower range of activities, the scope of which was determined by the growth of market forces.

INTERVENTION IN INVESTMENT

Does the rapid decline in government (and SOE) saving and state investment financed through the budget, as documented above, mean that overall investment in state-owned units declined as well? In fact, contrary to what might be supposed, overall state investment has remained large and even increased in the 1990s. The contrast between high and rising state investment and low and declining state financing for investment represents the fundamental conflict underlying macroeconomic policy decisions. This section examines overall quantitative trends in government investment, their sectoral impacts and the implication for understanding central and local government roles in the economy.

Quantitative investment trends

From a starting point in 1978 where nearly all fixed investment was in the state sector, the state share of fixed investment first dropped quickly and then declined more slowly until the end of 1988. However, this reduction was not sustained. In 1985, the state accounted for two-thirds of both total fixed investment and total industrial output. After 1989, the state share of industrial output continued to decline, reaching 40 per cent in 1994, but its share of investment remained stubbornly high, and even increased to 69 per cent in 1994.[15] A significant part of this investment, particularly during the 1990s, went to support infrastructure construction. China has experienced extremely rapid rates of overall economic growth, which would have been inconceivable without generally adequate provision of infrastructure. Although bottlenecks have repeatedly re-emerged under the pressure of rapid growth, government investment has generally been sufficient to overcome them and prevent growth from faltering. Adequate provision of infrastructure must be considered the second key element of successful Chinese growth policy, along with vigorous entry and investment in competitive sectors. These have enabled a self-sustaining growth process to become established during the course of transition from a planned to a market economy.

Figure 5.3 provides a general view of government investment in physical infrastructure and social sector fixed capital.[16] Infrastructure investment (physical and social) surpassed 5 per cent of GDP in 1984, and has been maintained at that level since, except in 1989. Since 1992, spending of this type has grown extremely rapidly, and it reached 8 per cent of GDP in 1993. Excluding the social sectors, physical infrastructure expenditure reached 6.5 per cent of GDP in 1993, well above the average of developing countries (4 per cent) and close to the 7 per cent "recommended" by the World Bank.[17] Only in the social sectors has performance seriously lagged: investment eroded from 1.3 per cent of GDP in 1985 to only 0.9 per cent in 1993. Weak social sector investment is attributable to the state's continuing fiscal difficulties and the absence of alternative financing arrangements.

Central and local government investment

The pattern of a continued high level of state investment requires a closer look at the role of central and local governments, since both are included in the general category of state investment. The categories of "central" and "local" are not symmetrical. Central government investment is co-ordinated through the State Planning Commission, generally reflects central government

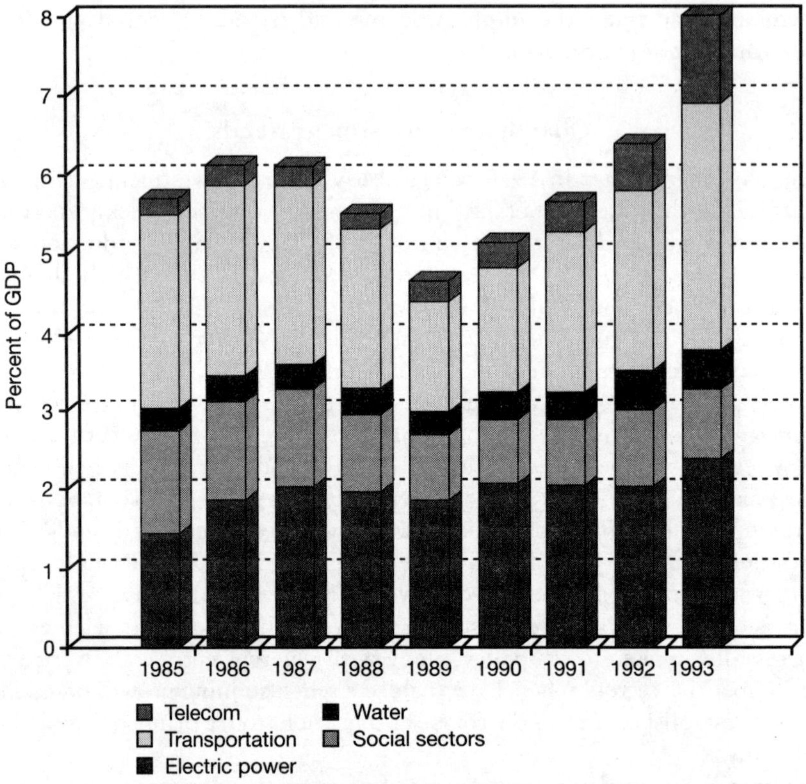

Figure 5.3 Infrastructure Investment
Source: Zhongguo tongji nianjian 1994, pp. 148–49; 16–61. *Zhongguo guding zichan touzi tongji ziliao* (*China Fixed Capital Investment Statistical Materials*) (Beijing: Zhongguo tongji chubanshe, various years).

policy and is roughly equivalent to government investment in other developing countries. By contrast, local investment in state-owned units is the aggregate of investment by local governments as such (for example, urban infrastructure investment), and of state-owned enterprises nominally under the authority of local governments.[18] In practice, many of those state-owned enterprises have gained substantial autonomy in recent years, and their activities correspond to that of parastatals in other developing countries. Moreover, local state-owned unit investment includes investment under the supervision of governments ranging from provinces – which have populations of up to 110 million people – down to counties and even occasionally townships with total populations of only 100,000. It is thus exceptionally difficult to generalize about local state investment in China.

A majority of state investment is local: about 60 per cent in recent years, but slightly higher in 1993–94. Despite ongoing decentralization, central government investment has remained substantial. In 1978, before reform began, investment in central government projects amounted to 8.7 per cent of GDP, and in 1993 it was 8.6 per cent; 1994 preliminary figures indicate a similar 8.3 per cent (see Figure 5.4). Local government investment increased significantly early in the reform era, and it also fluctuates more than that in central government. Before reform, in 1978, investment in local government projects was 9.9 per cent of GDP, and after considerable fluctuation equalled 17.0 per cent of GDP in 1994. Together, central and local governments invested a whopping 25.3 per cent of GDP in state-owned units under their control in 1994 (down slightly from the total in 1993). These state investment rates are higher than any other period of the PRC outside the Great Leap Forward.[19]

The sectoral composition of central and local state investment differ substantially. The Centre devotes 37 per cent of its investment to infrastructure, including the bulk of that in power and telecom; in addition, it provides nearly all of that in primary energy (coal, gas and oil), which accounts for 23

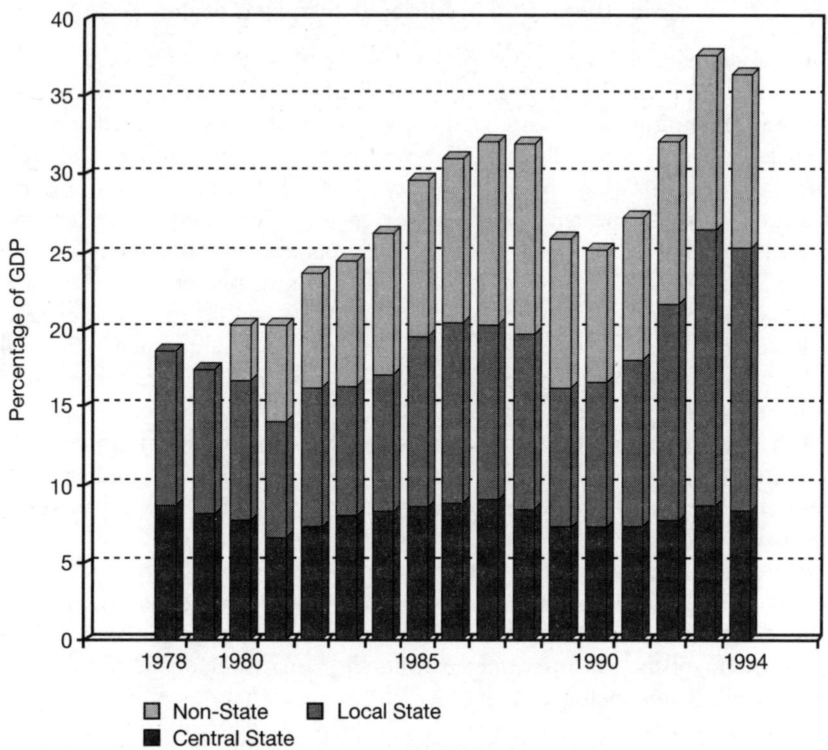

Figure 5.4 Fixed Investment: Total and State Investment
Source: Zhongguo guding zichan touzi tongji ziliao, various years. *China's Latest Economic Statistics* (Hong Kong: China Statistics Information Consultancy Service Centre), January 1995; February 1995.

per cent of its investment. Some 12 per cent of its investment is spent on scientific research and "other," both of which presumably involve national security. As a result, in the central government's investment outlays, infrastructure, primary energy and "science and other" together account for 72 per cent. Only 28 per cent is available for all other uses, and in practice much of this is taken up by investments in industrial sectors characterized by substantial economies of scale: metallurgy, chemicals and transportation equipment. The central government invests almost nothing in the competitive sectors shown in Figure 5.2. By contrast, local governments commit almost nothing to primary energy and "science and other," and about 25 per cent to infrastructure (especially transport, water and social infrastructures). In total, only 30 per cent of state investment under local control goes to infrastructure, energy, and "science and other." Locals have 70 per cent available for other uses, and while they also invest in metallurgy, chemicals and machinery, they have substantial funds available for competitive sectors.

Strengthening of traditional planning organs

One consequence of the increased level of government investment in the 1990s has been a strengthening of the traditional planning organs, especially the State Planning Commission (SPC), where until 1989 the tendency had been for these to lose influence. The traditional plan was frozen and then shrank, greatly limiting the discretionary power of the State Planning Commission. At the same time, alternative centres of economic expertise and forecasting advice developed in the semi-autonomous "think tanks" set up under Zhao Ziyang's auspices. Since 1989, though, planners have become more confident and more interventionist. They have sought to reinvent themselves as guardians of the public interest and agents of a national industrial policy, based on their interpretation of Japanese and Korean experience. Industrial policy has been popular – at least within government – and the SPC has been able to ride a "hot" agenda item back into political influence. In addition, the SPC's renewed influence reflects the weakening, and in some cases elimination, of alternative centres of economic policy-making advice in the wake of June 1989.

Increasing infrastructure investment in the 1990s is thus part of a broader process of increasing central government intervention in the investment process. While traditional allocation of materials is no longer a significant part of SPC power, substantial instruments are used primarily to shape the flows of investment. These include:

- In consultation with the Ministry of Finance, setting the aggregate quantities of budgetary investment; and in consultation with the People's Bank of China, setting the quotas for bank lending for fixed investment.
- Allocation of budgetary grants for capital construction (technical trans-

formation grants are allocated either by the Economics and Trade Commission or by individual ministries).

- Allocation of a large proportion of bank credits for fixed investment projects, the amount of which fluctuates, but has probably been above half of state bank fixed investment lending in the past two years.
- Allocation of that portion of foreign exchange earnings that are under central government control.

Yet the technical capabilities of the SPC are far more limited than their Japanese or Korean counterparts. In practice, the SPC is more like a broker than a steerer. It does not have detailed project planning capabilities, nor does it have great skills in project evaluation or economic analysis. There is a mis-match between capability and ambition at the SPC level.

PRESSURES ON THE BANKING SYSTEM

The preceding sections have shown that there is a fundamental tension between the disappearance of government saving and continued high levels of investment in SOEs. Where does the money come from to fund state investment? Fixed investment is now predominantly funded by a combination of bank loans and various types of retained and earmarked funds. The banking system, in particular, channels financial surpluses (savings) from the household sector to the enterprise sector, a process known as "intermediation." Thus, the Chinese financial system increasingly resembles that in a developing market economy. It is entirely normal that investment be funded through a combination of retained earnings and bank credit derived from household saving balances. However, the financial system is highly distorted by the continuing pressure from the government to provide funds for its priority projects (at both central and local government levels). This is evident both in the banking system and in the disposition of retained funds. Large sums of money are retained within the government sector, either within SOEs or as various types of earmarked funds, and these are intermediated by government bodies outside the formal banking system. Thus both the banking system and the system for using retained funds are influenced to a high degree by government officials at the central and local levels.

An overview of investment financing is provided in Table 5.1. In the investment statistics, various types of retained funds and informal loans are lumped into the category of "own funds" (*zichou zijin*), for which further detailed breakdowns are not available. However, judging from sample surveys and partial statistics, it is possible to estimate roughly the magnitude of some of these flows. Table 5.1 shows that almost a quarter of total investment is financed by bank loans, and half from "own funds." Within the "own funds" category, an estimated 13 per cent of total investment is raised by private firms, households and joint stock companies, that is through formal or informal capital markets. Another 18 per cent is the retained funds of SOEs. An estimated 9 per cent is "fund raising" – various forms of informal borrowing, not approved by the central government, that transfer funds from households and other businesses to SOEs. Finally, another 10 per cent comes in the form of government earmarked funds (*zhuanxiang jijin*). These are really quasi-tax revenues, quite formalized in some cases (such as electricity funds that are levied nation-wide at the rate of 2 *fen* per kilowatt-hour), but in other cases simply extraordinary levies imposed arbitrarily by local governments. (The three biggest formalized levies are those on electricity, railroad freight and vehicles: together they amount to over 1 per cent of GDP in extra-budgetary funds.) Thus, despite the large size of the funds deposited in China's banking system, this is only one part of the huge flow of funds into investment. Roughly the same amount flows into fixed investment outside the banking system – not counting enterprise funds used in the enterprise in which they are retained – as flows into fixed investment through the banking system. However, very little is known about this complex and diverse set of financial institutions.

The formal banking system is subject to multiple forms of government intervention. Earmarked bank loans have long been an important part of bank fixed investment lending, but there may have been a tendency for the proportion of bank lending subject to earmarking to increase in the 1990s, following the reassertion of industrial policy after 1989. The central government thus compels the banking system to provide credit for its priority projects. In this respect, the central government is no different from local governments: both put the banking system under constant pressure to provide funds for their projects. Indeed, the proportion of central and local government projects funded by bank loans is nearly identical, notwithstanding the different sectoral composition of central and local investment.

Table 5.1 Financing of total fixed investment, 1993 (estimated)

Source of finance	*Percentage*
Budgetary	3.7
Bank loans	23.5
Foreign investment	7.3
Own-funds (retained and raised)	50.0
of which: private firms and households	10
joint stock and co-ops	3
state and collective	37
of which: enterprise retained	18
'fund-raising'	9
government earmarked	10
Other	15.6

Sources: *Zhongguo tongji nianjian*, pp. 140–41. Breakdown of own-funds based on sample surveys, see *Zhongguo jinrong nianjian, 1993*. (*Almanac of China's Finance and Banking*, 1993), pp. 268, 277–78. See also *Zhongguo touzi nianjian, 1993 (China Investment Yearbook, 1993)*, pp. 16–17.

In addition, the government generally maintains fairly high levels of central bank (PBC) lending to the specialized (commercial) banks. To a substantial degree, PBC lending is offset by excess deposits maintained at the PBC by the specialized banks. Thus, PBC lending is a way to exercise control over commercial bank deposits, moving funds from one location to another in accord with central government priorities. Finally, and perhaps most important, interest rates are regulated at well below market clearing rates. In effect, the banking system is forced to subsidize government enterprises and investment projects. On balance, these add up to a very substantial reliance on the banking system by the government to substitute for its declining direct budgetary revenues.

The *de facto* tax rate on the banking system is thus extremely high. Depositors get less than they could earn for their funds elsewhere, and borrowers (other than favoured state clients) find their access to funds obstructed. Although the bank system provides a service in intermediating funds from savers to borrowers, the transaction is highly taxed by the government. Indeed, it is remarkable that China's household saving rate has remained as high as it is, given the low return to much of this saving. As a result of this high "tax rate," there is a strong temptation for both savers and borrowers to opt out of the formal state-run banking system and try to make deals through other kinds of institutional arrangements. When this occurs, it is called "disintermediation."

Under the current system, the disintermediation crisis is the most typical kind of financial crisis. When inflation occurs, savers are more highly taxed (because interest rates rise more slowly than does the inflation rate), and they may wish to shift into durable goods that won't depreciate with the currency. When liberalization occurs, both savers and borrowers may find new institutional forms (stocks, bonds, non-bank financial institutions, credit clubs) that allow them to circumvent the banking system with its high tax rates. When both inflation and liberalization occur at the same time (as is usual in China), the effects are particularly severe.

China has experienced two very severe, very obvious disintermediation crises over the past ten years, and probably several smaller ones. The most severe ones occurred in 1988 and 1992–93. They can be clearly seen in Figure 5.5 as the episodes when household saving deposit growth slows or stops while currency in circulation grows rapidly. Households removed funds from the banking system and either hoarded them or put them into other types of investment. Disintermediation can also begin as funds "escape" from the banking system as individuals and organizations seize the opportunity to loan funds into high-return activities. The 1992–93 crisis was particularly interesting in this respect. At the end of 1992, the bank statistics were at their most misleading, since 120 billion *yuan* had been channelled through the inter-bank market and outside the banking system. They were thus "missing," and are listed on the bank balance sheet as a large negative "other" entry.

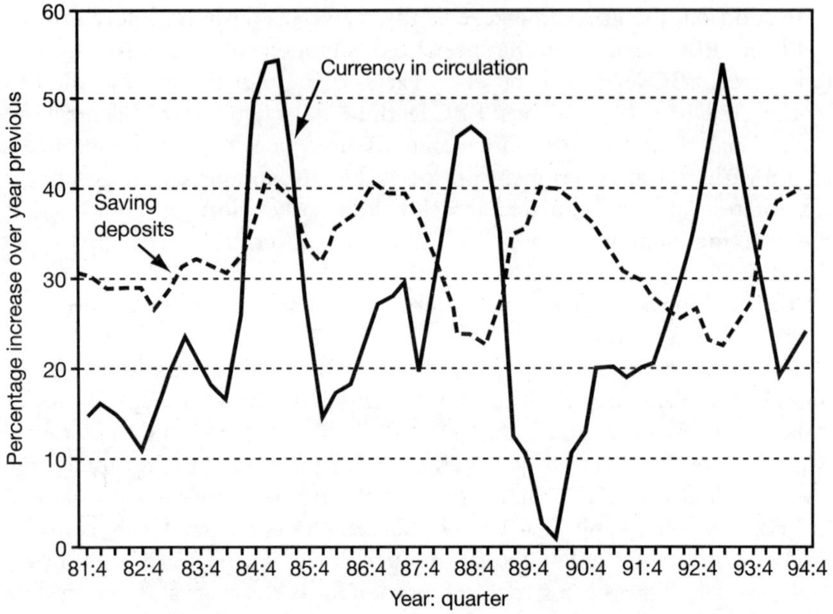

Figure 5.5 Growth of Cash and Savings Deposits
Source: Zhongguo jinrong (*China Banking and Finance*), Beijing periodical, various issues.

Disintermediation crises have interesting effects. They put the banking system into a severe credit squeeze, because suddenly the deposit base drops, despite the rapid growth of the price level and credit. They cannot simply be ignored. The dilemma at that point is whether the central bank should inject additional liquidity into the system. To do so is to threaten higher inflation but not to do so is to put the banking system into an impossible squeeze. In fact, in both 1988 and 1993, the PBC did so, and there was thus a substantial jump in PBC lending precisely in those years.[20] The effect is particularly strong when policy-makers demand a special effort to provide funds for agricultural procurements, which requires additional central bank lending.

The disintermediation crisis is the characteristic form of Chinese macroeconomic imbalance, because it is the stage at which economic accountability finally emerges. Without sensitive signals from interest rates or asset markets, Chinese policy-makers do not get clear messages about the macroeconomic problems they are creating until the disintermediation crisis emerges. Even when economic problems mount, the temptation is enormous to continue to push for additional investment and more growth until the last possible moment. In practice, that moment is generally when a disintermediation crisis emerges. Then and only then are policy-makers forced to adjust their policies.[21]

MACROECONOMIC DYNAMICS AND OTHER PRESSURES

The preceding sections have sketched out a view of China's macroeconomic problems that differs from the popular wisdom both in substance and in emphasis. Instead of seeing macroeconomic difficulties as deriving from a weak central government with inadequate control instruments, it instead portrays difficulties as coming from an activist, interventionist central government with substantial power but immature financial institutions and inadequate capabilities for monitoring the economy. The popular wisdom interprets each episode of loss of macroeconomic control as a symptom of overall weakness, and suggests that it is a harbinger of a coming breakdown of control. The view presented here suggests that the short-term loss of control is due to a competition among government agencies with contradictory objectives (or possibly among competing objectives held by individual leaders). As a result, it suggests that control is likely to be re-established once macroeconomic problems compel temporary agreement that macroeconomic stability is the most important short-term objective. Indeed, that has been precisely the outcome after each inflationary episode in China, including the most recent.

The primary locus of stabilization policy has shifted to monetary policy with the onset of the reform era. However, monetary policy is subject to unrelenting pressure from government officials at both central and local levels. In essence, government officials want the banking system to extend more credit to their priority projects, and they thus create constant pressure for a more rapid growth of credit, and thus of money supply as well. In order to complete the picture, it is necessary briefly to discuss two other sources of macroeconomic instability. The first is deficit SOEs and the second is the problem of instability imported through the foreign trade account.

According to conventional wisdom, China's inflationary tendency results from the government propping up obsolete state-run factories. This amounts to a substantial hidden budget deficit and feeds inflation. While this story is not completely wrong, it is doubtful that it provides much explanatory power. The basic fact is that current subsidies going to state-run enterprises are moderate in size, whereas overall investment flows are very large. It is much more likely that the sources of macroeconomic imbalance lie with investment policy. Macroeconomic imbalances are the flip side of the aggressive infrastructure and industrial policy described above. Total direct government subsidies for prices and to loss-making enterprises have declined steadily during the 1990s, because of the success of price reform. In 1994 they amounted to only 1.5 per cent of GDP, by far the lowest since the beginning of reform. There are without doubt significant hidden subsidies going to state industry, in the form of guaranteed access to relatively cheap credits. But even here caution must be observed. The total increment in credit to industrial enterprises from the state banking system in 1993 was 3.5 per cent of GDP. In addition, there are substantial subsidies in the form of low interest rates – which are very large when inflation is high and real interest rates significantly negative, but moderate when inflation is low and real interest rates poke into the positive range. All together, if current subsidies to the state sector amount to 3 or 4 per cent of GDP (a generous estimate), this is certainly wasteful, but is simply not enough continuously to tip the economy into an inflationary spiral, not when it is generating saving at the rate of over 35 per cent of GDP, as China is.

Nevertheless, SOEs represent a burden on the banking system, and thus are a factor tending to destabilize macroeconomic policy. According to a recent statement by Chen Yuan, vice-head of the PBC, about a fifth of the state banking system's loans are overdue (but still paying interest), and about 3 per cent of loans have been classified non-performing. Most of both categories are loans to SOEs.[22] These numbers represent real challenges to the banking system. Great care must be taken to clean up the bank balance sheets properly, write off non-performing loans and put the banks in a healthy position so they can compete in the new market economy.

Why is the assessment of the SOE problem in this article so different from the popular wisdom? First, the popular wisdom does not adequately distinguish between support for SOEs as a waste or as an obstacle to improving efficiency on the one hand, and support for SOEs as a source of macroeconomic instability on the other. In examining the macroeconomic impact of a government action, the crucial question is not whether the activity is wasteful, but rather whether the action is adequately funded. If a real use of resources is not adequately funded, it will be inflationary to the extent that the government ends up "printing money" to support the activity. Some support for SOEs undoubtedly does come in this form, but although the amount is not really known, it is probably not large. The bigger expenditure is in the form of loss-making enterprises, and most of those losses are fully funded by deductions from profits which would otherwise be remitted to the government. Secondly, the popular wisdom is overly influenced by imprecise statements from Chinese sources. Complaints about SOE losses have been expressed in China for over 15 years, but the nature of the phenomena complained about has changed dramatically. Throughout the 1980s, the overwhelming majority of SOE losses were incurred by commercial units supplying food to urban dwellers. What were then labelled "SOE losses" were in fact policy-determined payments to urbanites. In the 1990s, those losses have been nearly eliminated by price reforms. Meanwhile, industrial SOE losses, which were insignificant in the 1980s, have become substantially more important, though they are only a fraction of the magnitude of the earlier food subsidies. Government officials are naturally concerned because they are used to treating industrial SOEs as their "cash cows." Moreover, as state employees themselves, government officials are understandably somewhat obsessed with the tough problem of how to restructure SOEs without creating mass unemployment. But these very real issues do not necessarily imply that SOEs are a destabilizing factor in the economy.

Finally, the popular wisdom lumps all SOEs into a single category. In fact, as shown in Figure 5.2, SOEs are evolving in different directions in different sectors. In certain sectors in which SOEs are dominant – including electricity generation, steel making and cigarette production – SOEs continue to be highly profitable. In others, including coal and petroleum extraction, losses are substantial partly because of continued government distortions of the price structure. On balance, SOEs are a significant obstacle to further economic reform and improved efficiency. Privatization could begin immediately and be carried out quickly in the competitive sectors. Progress in non-competitive sectors would be slightly slower, since a regulatory framework needs to be created in those areas. But there is no reason not to proceed with privatization and rapid restructuring of SOEs. Conversely, though, there is no reason to believe that the continued presence of SOEs prevents urgently required financial reforms, or makes macroeconomic stability impossible.

A second factor that can destabilize the macroeconomy in today's China is exchange rate policy, which was particularly important in 1994. On 1 January 1994, China devalued and unified the currency at a rate around 8.7 RMB to the dollar. For most purposes this was a substantial devaluation. China's exports responded to the stimulus, and the trade balance swung from a deficit of $12.2 billion to a surplus of $5.35 billion. The magnitude of the change can be better appreciated if only "ordinary" trade is looked at. This is carried out primarily by Chinese foreign trade corporations (FTCs), setting to one side the roughly 30 per cent of China's exports carried out by foreign invested enterprises (FIEs). FIE exports are important, but are not highly sensitive to the exchange rate in the short term because they import a large share of their inputs. By contrast, ordinary exports are highly sensitive to exchange rate fluctuations. During the first eleven months of 1994, ordinary exports increased 42 per cent, while ordinary imports actually declined 5.4 per cent, so the surplus on ordinary trade jumped to $26 billion from a little over $6 billion.[23] This dramatic shift resulted in a huge inflow of income from foreign trade.

In the face of this inflow, the Chinese government had a number of alternatives. It could have allowed the RMB to appreciate (that is, allow its value to increase relative to the dollar, since dollars were less scarce and less valuable), undoing some of the devaluation at the beginning of the year and eventually shrinking the trade surplus. Secondly, it could have encouraged imports, which would have had some benefits: increased import of grain would have moderated inflationary pressures created by the year's poor harvest, and increased imports from the United States would have reduced trade tensions.

The government actually pursued a third option, which was to buy with RMB the dollars earned by exporters, thus increasing foreign exchange reserves and maintaining a stable exchange rate. China's foreign exchange reserves increased 140 per cent during 1994, to reach $51.6 billion, and jumped to $58 billion by the end of March 1995. Thus foreign exchange reserves increased by a total of about $30 billion in 1994, roughly equivalent to the surplus on ordinary trade. At 8.5 RMB to the dollar, this means that the government injected about 250 billion *yuan* RMB into the domestic economy.

With the central bank pumping a substantial amount of money into the economy to purchase foreign exchange reserves, it had little or no leeway to create money by extending new central bank loans. Indeed, on the central bank balance sheets, the increase in new foreign assets (foreign exchange reserves) accounted for 87 per cent of base money creation during the first eleven months of 1994.[24] The central bank made very little money available in new domestic central bank lending. In that sense, monetary policy was quite tight. Total credit (state banks plus rural credit co-operatives) increased at the moderate rate of 20 per cent in 1994. This explains the phenomena of 1994 and 1995. Money supply growth has been fairly rapid – M2 grew 34.4 per cent in 1994 and currency in circulation grew 24 per cent – yet the banks proclaim that they are following a tight monetary policy and enterprises complain about the difficulty in getting bank loans.[25] In fact, the domestic economy faces relatively tight money, while the export sector is awash with liquidity. This helps to resolve the paradox raised in the first paragraph of this article: China's "soft landing" after the July 1993 initiation of austerity policies took so long because it conflicted with the inflationary forces emanating from the export sector.

SOME IMPLICATIONS AND CONCLUSION

There are some clear implications to the preceding analysis. First, the attempt by the government to steer the economy and commandeer resources from the banking system is the ultimate source of macroeconomic imbalance. The imbalances occur not so much because of the continuing cost of propping up a state sector, but rather because the government is committed to maintaining very high rates of new investment in priority sectors, but doesn't have the direct command over resources to pay for it. Moreover, it is currently locked into a difficult set of interactions. It has been "successful" in pumping up large investments in key infrastructure sectors. That has allowed growth to accelerate and insured the profitability of non-infrastructural investments, typically made by decentralized agents. But as inflationary problems increase, the government's investment effort may prove to be unsustainable. With direct control concentrated on infrastructure investment, any cutbacks in central government control will first affect infrastructure investment, and may therefore aggravate bottlenecks and imbalances. There may be a rapid fall from the high-growth path which China has followed for the past few years.

Secondly, given the lack of accountability in the system, the result is likely to be a continued series of macroeconomic crises, as the government continually runs up against the limits of what it can exact from the economy as a whole, and from the financial system in particular. Difficulty in controlling the economy is not caused by an absence of control instruments. Indeed, the Chinese government has repeatedly shown the ability to impose austerity programmes, reduce the growth of bank credit and ultimately bring inflation down, but its resources to those instruments is delayed until after the crisis is full-blown. The real problem is the absence of day-to-day restraint that prevents crises from emerging.

Thirdly, policy-makers in China have already recognized that financial reform is one of the most crucial and most urgent needs of current reform. Indeed, the basic outline of a direction for financial sector reform was passed with the Banking Law of 1995. This set out a vision of independent commercial banks not subject to government intervention. In order to help implement this vision, the State Development Bank and two other government "policy lending" banks were created during 1994 to assume the burden of government-directed loans. Yet it is clear that it will take far more than a simple declaration of principles to implement banking reform effectively. In the first place, the banking system continues to be under pressure from the government's conflicting objectives (indeed, sometimes from the conflicting objectives of different posts of the government). Even if the State Development Bank succeeds in taking over a large portion of the government-directed lending of the commercial banks, it will require a major commitment to prevent central and local government agencies from imposing new lending requirements on the commercial banks. Moreover, banks will inevitably need some facility for restructuring their existing loans, giving them a mechanism to write off bad loans or transfer them to a new facility. Finally, some commitment to liberalize interest rates significantly will be required to make the vision a reality.

Development of capital markets had lagged behind because it is difficult; because there are still ideological obstacles; and because government officials want to retain the power to influence investment and are thus ambivalent about future reform. A foreshadowing of the difficulties of financial sector reform is apparent in the failure of government efforts to shift the investment system to repayable grants. The government has received very little in the form of repayment for past investment in this form.[26] In the financial arena, perhaps more than in other areas, successful reform appears to require a substantial, sustained exertion of political will by a committed central government. In both the banking system and the taxation system, nominal reforms have already been adopted that outline the basic steps required. The question is whether the political system can generate sufficient unity of purpose to make implementation of those reforms a reality.

NOTES

1 Inflation, as measured by the retail price index, peaked at 6.0% in 1980, 8.8% in 1985, 18.5% in 1988 and 21.7% in 1994.

2 Kathleen Hartford, "The political economy behind Beijing Spring," in Tony Saich (ed.), *The Chinese People's Movement: Perspectives on Spring 1989* (Armonk, NY: M. E. Sharpe, 1990), pp. 50–82. Hartford's reasoned arguments become grotesques in Richard Hornik, "Bursting China's bubble: the Muddle Kingdom," *Foreign Affairs*, Vol. 73, No. 3 (1994), pp. 28–42.

3 For example Christine Wong argues, "In the 1990s, the tenuous hold of the central restraints . . . rapidly losing potency, while effective indirect mechanisms are slow in developing. Local governments have led this assault." "China's economy: the limits of gradualist reform," in William A. Joseph (ed.), *China Briefing 1994* (Boulder: Westview Press, 1994), p. 50.

4 A recent World Bank report, *China: Country Economic Memorandum: Macroeconomic Stability in a Decentralized Economy* (26 October 1994), argues that People's Bank of China (PBC) lending represents a hidden budget deficit and attempts to quantify it. PBC lending to state banks has been large since 1988, but soared to 8.5% of GDP in 1993. The World Bank authors guess that 60–80% of this is for "policy loans" (i.e. government ordered spending) and reclassify it as additional deficit spending (see n. 20, below).

5 Barry Naughton, *Growing Out of the Plan: Chinese Economic Reform, 1978–1993* (New York: Cambridge University Press, 1995).

6 Liu Zhongli, "Report on the implementation of the state budget for 1994 and on the draft central and local budgets for 1995," *Beijing Review*, 3–16 April, 1995, pp. VI–VIII. *tongji nianjian 1994* (*China Statistical Yearbook 1994*) (Beijing: Zhongguo tongji chubanshe, 1994), pp. 213–221; Naughton, *Growing Out of the Plan*, pp. 337–39.

7 In this sense, Chinese policy-makers are in the same position as American policy-makers or those of most other countries. Very few countries are currently able to use fiscal policy as a flexible element of overall macroeconomic policy.

8 There are numerous issues relating to budgetary data that cannot be discussed here. Real military outlays are substantially greater than budgetary data reveal, both because the military controls revenue off the books, and because some military expenses are "buried" under other headings. In addition, Chinese budgetary data do not cover social security expenditures by SOEs which are significant. There are many types of "extra-budgetary" funds: the majority are best described as enterprise funds, but some are more like fiscal revenues and ought to be included in budgetary accounts.

9 The different evolution of different functional components of expenditures explains some of the changing relation between central and local government. The central government is responsible for most investment and defence, while local governments are responsible for most current expenditures. Thus a decline in investment and defence relative to current outlays implies a decreasing central government share of expenditures, all else constant.

10 It is true that the share of GNP channelled through the budget to education, health and other expenditures should be increased, and that maintenance of the pre-reform share of GNP is inadequate. The point here is simply to argue that, on

balance, these outlays have been shielded from the worst effects of eroding budgetary resources.

11 Tsang Shu-ki and Cheng Yuk-shing, "China's tax reform of 1994: breakthrough or compromise?" *Asian Survey*, Vol. 34, No. 9 (September 1994), pp. 769–788.

12 "China shows early signs of missing deficit goal," *Reuter*, 13 July 1995, electronically transmitted.

13 Naughton, *Growing Out of the Plan*, pp. 142–44.

14 Chinese authorities do not publish a breakdown of all industrial output. The data in Figure 5.2 are calculated by summing the data on independent accounting enterprises and village run collectives. for which sectoral and ownership breakdowns are available. *Zhongguo tongji nianjian 1994*, pp. 373, 378, 388, 395. The data shown account for 88% of all industrial output. SOEs account for 48% of this output, compared with the 43% of total output they are known to account for. Of the output excluded from Figure 5.2, SOEs account for only 10% and non-state firms, mostly small-scale private firms, account for 90%. Compare Richard F. Garbaccio, *Reform and Structural Change in the Chinese Economy: A CGE Analysis*, Ph.D. dissertation, University of California, Berkeley, May 1994, pp. 102, 106–107.

15 *Zhongguo tongji nianjian, 1994*, pp. 140–41; *China's Latest Economic Statistics* (Hong Kong: China Statistics Information Consultancy Service Centre, January 1995). The shares are not directly comparable, since the investment figures include non-industrial investment and also lump joint-venture investment in with the state sector if an SOE is a joint venture partner. A correction to make the data comparable is possible for 1993 and would reduce the state investment share to 61.5%. The trends are quite robust, however.

16 The following discussion defines infrastructure as consisting of (1) electric power; (2) transportation; (3) telecommunications; (4) urban water supply; and (5) rural water conservation. Social sector investment comprises (6) education construction and (7) health and welfare construction.

17 World Bank, *World Development Report 1994* (Washington, D.C.: International Bank for Reconstruction and Development, 1994).

18 All "state" investment in China is classified according to the level of subordination of the enterprise with the primary responsibility for the investment project, regardless of actual financial participation, which can be more complicated.

19 Central investment is slightly understated since all housing has been deemed local.

20 The disintermediation crisis explanation is superior to the World Bank analysis reported above in n. 4. They interpreted the high level of PBC lending in 1993 as evidence of a chronic, increasing disguised budget deficit. I interpret it as largely a short-term response to a disintermediation crisis. In the following year, 1994, PBC lending dropped almost to zero. This is compatible with the disintermediation crisis explanation, but is either incompatible with the "disguised deficit" interpretation, or else means that the deficit was miraculously closed within a single year.

21 In 1992–93 official recognition of overheating was further delayed by Deng Xiaoping's "bundling" economic reform and rapid growth into a single package. Opposition to expansionary macroeconomic policy was construed as opposition to reform.

22 Associated Press, "China banks to go commercial?" 20 June 1995, over China News Digest.

23 Yao Keping, "An analysis of 1994 balance of payments and a projection for 1995," *Zhongguo jinrong*, No. 4 (1995), pp. 39–40.

24 *Ibid.* p. 40.
25 Monetary data from *Zhongguo jinrong*, No. 3 (1995), pp. 44–45.
26 *Zhongguo jinrong nianjian 1992* (*Almanac of China's Finance and Banking 1992*) (Beijing: Zhongguo jinrong chubanshe, 1993), p. 296.

Part II

THE INDUSTRIAL SECTOR AND ENTERPRISE REFORM

6

ENTERPRISE REFORM IN CHINESE INDUSTRY

Gary H. Jefferson and Thomas G. Rawski

The Chinese economy commands attention because of its immense size, and because China's unique combination of dynamic performance and unusual institutional arrangements challenges many popular notions about the reform of socialist systems. Industry, which by Chinese convention includes mining and utilities as well as manufacturing, exemplifies this arresting mix of scale, dynamism, and unexpected structural features. Industry is the largest sector of China's economy, accounting for 50 percent of total output and 80 percent of exports, and employing 102 million workers in 1992 (Survey, 1993). Its robust growth, amounting to well above 10 percent annually during the 1980s (Table 6.1), undergirds China's standing as the world's fastest-growing economy.[1]

Since China's initial reform efforts began as experimental changes aimed at improving performance rather than, as in eastern Europe, establishing a Western-style market system, it is not surprising that institutional change has been gradual and uneven, with many features of the pre-reform system surviving even today. Rather than attempting a "big bang," China's reform path is more akin to "growing out of the plan" (Naughton, 1994).

Industry stands at the core of China's reform problem. Efforts to revitalize and restructure domestic industry are closely linked to the reform of pricing, banking, public finance, ownership, social welfare, and research and development. If China's recent accomplishments carry distinctive implications for policy design, it is industry, where reform has side-stepped privatization and other standard remedies, that is the most likely source of lessons.

In considering China's experience of enterprise reform, this paper begins by reviewing conditions prior to the reform initiatives of the late 1970s, and then describes the impact of reform policies on structure, conduct, and performance of state-owned industry during the 1980s. Next, we examine the growth of industry outside the state sector, and discuss the problems and prospects for industry in the 1990s. Finally, we consider possible implications of China's recent industrial experience for broader issues of reform strategy in transitional economies.[2]

Source: *Journal of Economic Perspectives*, Vol. 8(2), (1994), pp. 47–70.

Table 6.1 Overview of Chinese industrial performance, 1980–1992

A. *Real output*

Ownership type	*Index of real output (1980 = 100)*				*Average annual growth, 1980/92 (percent)*
	1980	*1985*	*1990*	*1992*	
State	100	148	210	257	7.8
Collective	100	247	554	914	18.4
Private[a]	100	21,752	126,057	241,455	64.9
Other[b]	100	492	3,530	8,736	37.2
Total	100	176	328	480	13.1

B. *Shares of various types of firms in nominal output*

	Shares of nominal (%)				*Percent share of incremental output 1980/92*
	1980	*1985*	*1990*	*1992*	
State	76.0	64.9	54.6	48.4	43.6
Collective					
Urban	13.7	13.3	10.3	11.8	11.5
Township-Village	9.9	18.8	25.3	26.2	28.8
Private[a]	0.0	1.9	5.4	6.8	7.9
Other[b]	0.5	1.2	4.4	7.2	8.3
Total	100.0	100.0	100.0	100.0	100.0
Total Output (¥ billion)	515.4	971.6	2,392.5	3,706.6	

Note: Percentage totals may not check due to rounding error.
[a] Privately-owned firms employing less than 8 workers.
[b] Includes private firms employing 8 or more workers, joint ventures, foreign-owned firms, and other ownership forms.

Source: Yearbook (1993, pp. 409, 413); Rawski, (1993).

INITIAL CONDITIONS

Studies of Chinese industry during the era of socialist planning reveal many commonalities with the Soviet experience of centrally-directed industrialization. Managers focused on quantitative targets, especially those concerning physical output volume and total output value, rather than financial objectives. Profitability did not influence the incomes of executives and workers nor the growth prospects of firms.

Chinese socialism also developed its own distinctive features. The national planning apparatus in China was far less comprehensive than in the USSR (Granick, 1990). As early as 1979, for instance, 64 percent of cement, 41 percent of coal and 23 percent of steel were allocated outside the plan system (Fan and Schaffer, 1991, p. 9). Although fluctuations in the degree of central control over production and investment decisions date back to the 1950s, broad areas of responsibility were routinely delegated to provinces and localities (Perkins et al., 1977, pp. 272–78). Local authorities acquired custodial and usufruct rights over enterprise assets, which were sometimes transferred to enterprise management.[3]

Furthermore, China's mechanism of central planning often failed to determine outcomes within its intended span of control. Naughton (1994) observes that "the ability of planners to obtain compliance with specific detailed directives had always been limited" by the "extraordinarily weak planning apparatus." Hua, Zhang and Luo (1993, p. 71) trace the specific consequences of this fractured structure: "[T]he planning system was so ineffectual that township enterprises . . . though poorly equipped and funded, developed rapidly from the early 1970's . . . market transaction[s], or the 'relationship outside the plan' between township enterprises and state-owned enterprises was widespread even under the traditional system."

Thus, both administrative design and lapses in plan implementation contributed to the pre-reform development of unplanned, semi-market industrial activity under local government auspices. Since the expansion of inherited patterns is easier than the creation of new modes of production and allocation, these atypical features of China's pre-reform industrial system acted to smooth the path of reform.

Beyond these factors, several aspects of China's broader economic environment strongly affected the outcome of partial and gradual industrial reforms. These include the financial, commercial, and technical capabilities of Chinese communities in Hong Kong, Taiwan, and throughout the Asia-Pacific region, which magnified the impact of China's "open door" policy (Chen, Jefferson, and Singh, 1992); the broad dispersion of entrepreneurial drive (Cohen, 1993), which transformed hesitant reform initiatives into massive change that repeatedly swamped the expectations of China's political leaders as well as foreign onlookers; and the dramatic surge in rural production and incomes following the abandonment of collective farming, which relaxed the foreign exchange constraint and gave a huge boost to China's nascent rural industries (Sicular, 1991).

CHINA'S STATE INDUSTRY: SYSTEM REFORM IN THE 1980s

State-owned enterprises are the natural focus of any effort to evaluate the progress of China's industrial reform. The problem is complex: the population of state-owned enterprises is large and diverse; the reforms are partial and uneven; they consist of measures that permit (rather than mandate) new courses of action; and outcomes are ambiguous. A full analysis must penetrate to the enterprise level and transcend the evidence available from anecdotes, small samples, and fragile statistical aggregates.

We adopt the structure-conduct-performance paradigm used in the field of industrial organization. In applying this framework to the area of socialist reform, we expand the notion of "structure" to include not just the nature of product and factor markets, but the whole environment surrounding and conditioning enterprise operations (Jefferson and Xu, 1991). Since data are inevitably limited and uncertain, we hope that consistent findings across three analytic dimensions can offer more convincing evidence of progress or stagnation than any single perspective. We begin with structure.

Structure

At the outset of reform, China's state-owned enterprises functioned as passive agents of the state economic bureaucracy. Managers had little authority over research and development, product innovation, investment planning, marketing, or even such routine matters as production scheduling, material purchases, wage structures, and employment levels (Komiya, 1987). Ten years of reform brought dramatic changes in the allocation of industrial products, the procurement of inputs, the character of incentives, and the degree of competition. By the end of the 1980s, enterprise managers had gained control of most business decisions. Even the largest state-owned enterprises were deeply enmeshed in markets driven by decentralized forces of demand and supply. The new structural environment facing China's state-owned enterprises evolved in response to two distinct policy initiatives.[4]

The first reform effort, implemented around 1980, consisted of tentative steps designed to improve performance within a framework dominated by mandatory output planning and administrative allocation of inputs and products. On the domestic side, state-owned enterprises gained the right to retain a modest share of total profits. They also obtained unprecedented control over any output beyond mandatory plan targets. Decentralized, semi-market transactions, long tolerated as a sort of grey market, were now encouraged as a means of stimulating firms to manage their affairs more actively. On the external side, a new "open door policy" dismantled long-standing barriers to international trade and investment, with southern provinces enjoying special incentives to expand foreign economic contacts.

The second set of reforms, dating from 1984, centered on two innovations: dual pricing and the enterprise contract responsibility system. Dual pricing partitioned supplies of industrial products into plan and market components. Under the dual pricing regime, most state enterprises transacted marginal sales and purchases on markets where prices responded increasing to the forces of supply and demand. At the same time, bank loans began to replace budgetary appropriations as the chief source of external funding for industrial enterprises, signalling the emergence of embryonic factor markets.

New forms of contracting gradually supplanted annual plan targets even for the large firms. Under the contract responsibility system, the enterprise manager, a group of managers, or sometimes the firm's entire work force agree to fulfill specific obligations, typically involving targets for total profit, delivery of profit to the state, and productivity increases, in return for extensive control over enterprise operations, including full or substantial retention of excess profits.

The most visible consequence of these reforms was a shift from planning toward the market. Surveys of state-owned enterprises show that between 1980 and 1989, the share of material inputs purchased through the market rose from 32 to 59 percent (Dong, 1992), or from 12 to 66 percent (Zou and Wang, 1993). The same surveys show the share of output sold on the market rising from 49 to 60 percent (Dong, 1992), or from 13 to 66 percent (Zou and Wang, 1993). Surveys also show that enterprise funds and bank loans replaced state budgetary grants as the chief sources of investment finance during the 1980s (Dong, 1992; Fan and Woo, 1992). The overall impact of reform on the structural environment surrounding state-owned enterprise operations emerges from a review of three categories: autonomy, incentives and competition.

Autonomy

As the scope of mandatory planning declined, the managers of state-owned enterprises acquired growing authority over decisions about the quantity and variety of output, production methods, and selling price. A host of market-supporting institutional developments enhanced enterprise autonomy by increasing choice and reducing transaction costs, thereby expanding the capacity of state enterprise managers to restructure business arrangements. These included the creation of markets for industrial materials; the deregulation of trucking and wholesale trade; the erosion of barriers to commercial arrangements involving foreign participants; expanded opportunities to hire consultants and temporary or contract workers; new mechanisms for enforcing contracts and resolving commercial disputes; patent and copyright legislation; the commercialization of scientific and technical research; the growth of trade and professional associations; and the expansion of advertising, insurance, banking, and telecommunications.

Greater enterprise autonomy has not eliminated intrusive regulation. State agencies sometimes refuse to allow enterprises to exercise their new "rights," especially with respect to foreign trade, employment and financial management. Government officials sometimes manipulate remaining controls in ways that effectively nullify the expansion of enterprise autonomy (Enterprise, 1993). There are also complaints that state-owned enterprise managers seek responsibility only for profits and expect the state to cope with financial losses (Liu and Zou, 1992). Despite these limitations, autonomy has expanded. Survey data from the late 1980s show that the decision-making authority of state firms, previously subject to tight government controls, is no different from the autonomy reported by managers of urban and suburban collectives (Jefferson, Rawski and Zheng, 1992b). Groves et al. (forthcoming) use another set of survey data to demonstrate that the grant of autonomy leads enterprises to hire more contract (non-permanent) labor, increase the share of compensation tied to performance, and raise productivity.

Incentives

New incentive mechanisms have reconfigured the relations between effort, financial outcomes, individual reward, and enterprise control over resources. Beginning around 1980, state-owned enterprises were allowed to retain part of their profits. Unlike Hungary and Poland, where similar reforms failed to alter the leveling tendency of tax and subsidy policy (Kornai and Matits, 1984; Farrell, 1991), Chinese data reveal a substantial and growing link between profit and retained earnings. Data from a World Bank survey of over 900 state enterprises, summarized in Table 6.2, show that a 10 percent rise in gross profit led to increases in retained earnings of 7.6 percent during 1980–83, 8.7 percent during 1984–87, and 9.2 percent during 1988–90. Many enterprises now retain 100 percent of earnings in excess of fixed quotas for profit remittance.

Table 6.2 Measures of state enterprise conduct, 1980–1990

Regression results: $\ln Y = \alpha + \beta \ln X = \varepsilon$		*1980–83*	*1984–87*	*1988–90*
An increase of 1% in *gross profit* (*X*) yields a rise in *retained profit* (*Y*) of	$\hat{\beta}$	0.76	0.87	0.92
	t	(71.84)	(110.15)	(137.25)
	R^2	0.67	0.79	0.76
An increase of 1% in *labor productivity* (*X*) yields a rise in the *average wage* (*Y*) of	$\hat{\beta}$	0.04	0.13	0.18
	t	(8.76)	(19.11)	(25.6)
	R^2	0.03	0.11	0.22
An increase of 1% in *labor productivity* (*Y*) yields an increase in per capita bonus (*X*) of	$\hat{\beta}$	0.22	0.37	0.51
	t	(17.02)	(25.38)	(27.75)
	R^2	0.09	0.18	0.26
An increase of 1% in *gross profit* (*X*) yields an increase in the *per capita bonus* (*Y*) of	$\hat{\beta}$	0.97	1.01	0.99
	t	(58.02)	(68.36)	(43.69)
	R^2	0.56	0.62	0.50
An increase of 1% in *current* (X_1) *or lagged value* (X_2) *of retained earnings* yields an increase in *investment* (*Y*) of	$\hat{\beta}_1$		0.23	
	t		(3.72)	
	$\hat{\beta}_2$		0.50	
	t		(7.62)	
	R^2		0.50	

Note: The final set of estimates covers 1984–90; the estimating equation is $\ln Y = \alpha + \beta_1 \ln X_1 + \beta_2 \ln X_2 + \varepsilon$.

Source: World Bank Survey, covering approximately 900 firms.

Despite continuing support of loss-making enterprises and their employees from direct budgetary subsidies, flexible tax rates, and "soft" bank lending, new incentive arrangements began to generate penalties as well as rewards. Morris and Liu (1993) find that while subsidies rose in response to deteriorating profit performance during the late 1980s, there was a considerable reduction in the softness of budget constraints for state firms. The recession initiated by the anti-inflation policies of 1988–90 forced many state-owned enterprises to curtail bonuses, furlough some workers at a fraction of their basic wage, and pay others in kind rather than in cash. Even in the boom year of 1988, one study of the coal industry, where price controls ensure widespread losses, noted that if "enterprises accumulate large losses, this cannot but influence workers' living standards" (Coal Policy, 1988).

Competition

Reform has meant an expansion not only of markets, but also of competition. Naughton (1992) observes sharp reductions in both the level of state enterprise profits and the dispersion of profitability across branches of Chinese industry. He attributes the decline and convergence of profit rates to the continuing erosion of barriers that formerly protected state enterprises against competition from collective firms, from imported products, and from innovative rivals within the state sector. As a result of past efforts to build "complete sets" of industries in every province, eight-firm concentration ratios for Chinese industry tend to fall considerably below comparable figures for the United States and Japan; they also show a declining time trend (Table 6.3). With military industries converting to civilian production, barriers to internal trade in decline, import penetration on the rise, and the prospect

Table 6.3 Eight-firm concentration ratios for industrial products, 1980–1988

Product	*China 1980*	*China 1985*	*China 1988*	*Japan 1980*	*United States 1982*
Beer	16.2	8.1	10.2	98.9	64.0
Cement	5.7	3.8	2.5	46.0	24.0
Cotton yarn	4.1	3.9	2.8	28.0	44.0
Diesel engines	22.6*	15.6*	16.2*	60.1	n.a.
Machine tools	12.5	10.5	n.a.	n.a.	22.0
Nylon	76.0	62.4	51.2	n.a.	78.0
Refrigerators	42.3	35.7	26.1	73.3	82.0
Steel	37.1	34.7	32.5	65.0	n.a.
Structural glass	40.6	33.6	25.6	100.0	90.0
Televisions	35.8	21.2	19.8	59.2	n.a.

Note:
* Three-firm concentration ratios.

Source: Chen *et al.*, 1991, pp. 196–97.

of sweeping reductions in import restrictions if China joins the GATT, we see rivalrous markets as a well-entrenched fixture of China's industrial economy.

Conduct

Changes in the structure of Chinese industry have, in turn, induced changes in conduct. There is little room to doubt that profit has become the dominant objective of managers in China's state industries. Dong Furen (1992, p. 4) summarizes the outcome of one large survey effort by noting that "enterprises arrange production plans according to market conditions with the objective of increasing profit." Many authors echo this view. Some writers accuse state enterprise managers of excessive attention to short-run financial outcomes (Liu and Wang, 1993; Gu and Cao, 1993); the frequent inclusion of investment and product innovation targets in management contracts indicates that supervisory bodies share this concern. But other observers note a tendency for large firms and enterprise groups to sacrifice current profit for longer-term strategic advantage (Jiang et al., 1993).

Changing attitudes toward the planning system offer another perspective on the objectives of state-owned enterprises. Beginning in the late 1980s, state enterprise leaders sought relief from "unfair" competition with collective firms owned by local governments (Investment, 1991). Their complaints had a strange sound, coming from the very firms that had benefited for decades from preferential allocations of funds, equipment, foreign exchange, university graduates, skilled labor, and scarce materials. In our view, these demands reflect the growing conviction among state-owned enterprise managers that the costs of continued participation in the planning system had come to outweigh the benefits.

Some observers, struck by rapid increases in wages and benefits for workers in state enterprises, argue that worker incomes outweigh profits in the minds of state enterprise managers (Woo et al., forthcoming). Indeed, average monetary compensation of state-owned enterprise industrial workers rose by 252 percent between 1980 and 1992. But nominal labor productivity rose by 231 percent over the same period, or nearly as much as wages, so that labor's income share (wages plus bonuses) of gross output rose only slightly, from 7.0 to 7.5 percent (Yearbook, 1993, pp. 107, 130, 412). Even if we assume that a full accounting of labor's share, including housing and other benefits paid in kind, might double the ratio of labor income to total output, labor's effective income share is unlikely to exceed 0.15, the figure around which estimates of labor's (gross) output elasticity appear to cluster.

Hay and Liu (1992) reach a similar conclusion. Working with panel data, they find that standard neoclassical cost functions can successfully model the behavior of state enterprises. Their results indicate that state firms respond to changing factor prices as anticipated by standard theory, that enterprises located near the production frontier conform more closely to cost-minimizing behavior than other firms, and that the widely criticized system of bonus payments "appears to have been highly effective . . . in improving efficiency and keeping costs down."

If the profit motive dominates decision-making in state enterprises, how do managers distribute the fruits of higher profits and productivity? Table 6.2 uses survey data from a World Bank project to illustrate the evolution of several key relationships during the first decade of reform. The first line of the table illustrates the growing link, noted earlier, between gross profits and retained earnings. The next three lines indicate that wage payments (including base wages and bonuses) have become increasingly responsive to changes in profits and productivity.

The last set of results shows that during 1984–90, investment responded significantly to current or lagged profit performance. This critical link between profitability and capacity expansion is a central requirement for long-term economic success. It is precisely this connection that was absent in Kornai and Matits' (1984) investigation of Hungarian firms' investment behavior between 1975 and 1980. Morris and Liu (1993) confirm the link between profitability and capacity expansion among Chinese state enterprises during the 1980s.

Performance

How have these changes in industrial structure and enterprise conduct affected industrial performance? Rapid growth is the most obvious feature of recent industrial activity. Although the share of the state sector in total industrial output has declined, the real product of state industry more than doubled during the 1980s; expansion continues apace. But rapid, high-cost growth at the extensive margin is the hallmark of socialist systems. So rapid growth of state industry alone cannot demonstrate the efficacy of China's unorthodox reforms.

Expansion of overseas sales offers a more convincing test, especially in view of the recent removal of direct export subsidies.[5] Comprehensive information about the exports of state-owned enterprises is available only for 1985. Available data show, however, that the combined exports of state-owned enterprises and urban collectives grew at an annual rate of about 16 percent during 1985–90. Since the output of state-owned enterprises was nearly five times that of urban collectives in 1985 and somewhat higher in 1990 (Table 6.1), it seems evident that the exports of state-owned enterprises grew rapidly during the latter half of the 1980s.

Information about export composition, which shows swift expansion in categories dominated by state-owned firms (power-generating equipment, textile machinery, machine tools), reinforces this impression, as do survey results showing state enterprise exports growing at annual rates of 20 percent during the late 1980s (Machinery, 1991; Rawski, 1993). Data from a World Bank survey indicate that the ratio of state-owned enterprise exports to value-added rose during the 1980s to levels that match comparable aggregates for U.S. manufacturing. Apparently, many of China's state-owned enterprises are gaining ground in the international marketplace.

Trends in total factor productivity offer another perspective on the performance of state-owned enterprises. Using aggregate data, K. Chen et al. (1988) found that total factor productivity in state industry stagnated from the mid-1950s to the late 1970s, but increased during the reform period. We have identified 13 studies of total factor productivity in China's state industry during the 1980s, most based on sample surveys. Nine studies report annual growth of total factor productivity within the range of 2–4 percent. Of the remaining four studies, two show higher rates and two obtain lower rates of productivity change. Table 6.4 summarizes the results of our own work, which is based on aggregate rather than sample data.

Can we corroborate indications of rising total factor productivity with micro-level evidence of increases in static or dynamic efficiency? We can investigate static efficiency by identifying statistical relationships that should exist in a market system and then testing for their emergence during the reform process.

Market forces create a tendency to equalize financial returns to factors employed in different lines of business. Several studies identify measurable improvements of this sort. China has seen sharp reductions in the dispersion of profitability across branches of industry (Naughton, 1992) and across different ownership types (Rawski, 1993). There is also evidence of convergence in financial returns to capital, labor and materials across ownership types

Table 6.4 Estimated rates of annual productivity growth in Chinese industry

	1980–84	*1984–88*	*1988–92*
A. *Total factor productivity*			
State sector	1.8%	3.0%	2.5% [a]
Collective sector			
Urban and township	3.4	5.9	4.9 [a]
Township-Village	7.3 [a]	6.6 [a]	6.9 [a]
B. *Labor productivity (real terms)*			
State sector	3.8	6.2	4.7
Collective sector			
Urban and township	8.6	7.0	13.8
Township-Village	5.8	14.4	17.7

Note:
[a] Preliminary results

Source: Jefferson, Rawski, and Zheng, 1992a; Yearbook, 1993; authors' calculations.

(Jefferson, Rawski, and Zheng, 1992a) and among large- and medium-size state-owned enterprises (Jefferson and Xu, forthcoming). The dispersion of total factor productivity across enterprises has declined during the reform period, with the greatest convergence evident among enterprises with sales fully disengaged from the plan (Jefferson and Xu, forthcoming). A study of province-level total factor productivity trends for state industry finds "a pattern of convergence among measures of provincial efficiency levels both nationally and across . . . the coast, the centre, and the west" (Hsueh, Rawski, and Tsui, 1992).

Total factor productivity can also grow in response to improved dynamic efficiency, by which we mean accelerated expansion of production frontiers through the adoption of new products, new processes, and new organizational arrangements. Although studies of socialist industrial reform devote little attention to the sources of technological change, a variety of evidence indicates that reform has substantially accelerated innovation in China's state enterprises.

Export growth is perhaps the most visible outcome of successful innovation. During the 1970s, visitors agreed that Chinese manufactures seemed unlikely to penetrate markets in the United States, Japan, or other economies where buyers value style, packaging, finish, service, and prompt delivery as well as low cost and functionality. The recent surge of exports from China's state industries, noted above, includes large sales to the United States and Japan. In apparel and other fields, Chinese export producers have begun to move beyond their initial focus on the low end of the quality/price spectrum; some have even begun to adopt features of "just-in-time" production.

Reform has also increased the effectiveness of innovative efforts. China's government has eased the long-standing split between the efforts of state-sponsored research institutes and the commercial needs of industry by the simple expedient of cutting the budgets of research organizations. This has created a powerful stimulus for researchers "to better serve the economy" (Suttmeier, 1992). Enterprise funds have replaced state appropriations as the major source of finance for research and development: the share of state grants in research and development spending by large and medium enterprises dropped to 11 percent in 1987 and only 7 percent in 1991 (S&T, 1990, p. 251; Yearbook, 1992, p. 749).

Survey research confirms the acceleration of innovative activity within state industry. One study found enterprises focusing on "the development of new products and the abolition of old products" (Dong, 1992); another survey found over 90 percent of large and medium enterprises engaged in some form of innovative activity, with 81 percent developing new products (Innovation, 1993); a third showed that the output share of new products rose substantially during the 1980s (Jefferson, Rawski and Zheng, 1992b). Over 90 percent of the state-owned, urban-collective and township-village enterprises in the latter survey cited state-owned enterprises as the principal innovators in their product lines.

This review leads to the conclusion that reform has pushed China's state-owned enterprises in the direction of "intensive" growth based on higher productivity rather than expanded resource consumption. Although the production of unwanted goods and other characteristic socialist flaws persist (Liu, 1993), we observe a consistent picture of improved results—higher output, growing exports, rising total factor productivity, and increased innovative effort—against a background of gains in static and dynamic efficiency that reflect the growing impact of market forces.

Our survey reveals a massive shift from planning toward market coordination, vigorous competition in product markets, substantial gains in performance, and a distinct, albeit gradual and uncoordinated "corporatization" of China's state industries. Despite these achievements, certain dysfunctional aspects of the former planning regime remain more or less intact. In particular, weaknesses in the financial system perpetuate costly resource misallocation and threaten macroeconomic stability, while the continued absence of well-defined property arrangements compromises incentives and autonomy. Although these defects have not prevented China's state-owned enterprises from increasing output, exports, productivity, and efficiency, the cost of failing to grapple with these issues appears large. Before considering these matters, we turn to a survey of developments outside the state sector.

BEYOND THE STATE SECTOR

No review of China's recent industrial experience can overlook the large and beneficial contribution of enterprises outside the state sector. These enterprises have fortified national economic statistics with substantial increases in output, exports, productivity, and employment. The dynamic performance of enterprises outside the state sector has reduced the share of state-owned firms in total industrial output from more than three-fourths at the beginning of the reform to less than half in the early 1990s (Table 6.1).

The entrepreneurial firms that have undercut the dominance of state-owned producers are widely described as "non-state" enterprises. The data in Table 6.1 make it clear that most of the output in the non-state sector comes from collective firms. These collectives, which are typically controlled by local governments, are part of the public sector. Despite the falling output share of state-owned firms,public enterprise continues to dominate China's industrial scene. The contribution of genuinely private firms, although difficult to measure, is in the vicinity of 10 percent. We focus our study of non-state industry on collective firms, particularly rural collectives, widely known as "township and village enterprises."

Rural collectives expanded during the 1980s on foundations established by the earlier efforts of local governments to promote rural industry (Perkins et al., 1977). Like their predecessors, township and village enterprises operate "under close supervision from the township or village industrial departments" which contribute start-up funds, appoint managers, and "are intimately involved in major strategic decisions" (Wong, 1993, ch. 9; Ody, 1991, p. iv). The growth of township and village enterprises benefitted from the success of China's agricultural reforms, which greatly expanded the supply of rural savings, freed millions of workers to seek non-farm employment, and boosted rural demand for consumer goods.

Table 6.5 describes the scale, capital intensity, and labor productivity of firms operating under different ownership regimes: state, collective, private and "other" (a residual category including joint ventures with foreign participation). We focus on data for 1987 because they permit a breakdown of state-owned enterprises based on firm size. The data show a steady downward progression of scale (measured by workers per firm), capital intensity, and labor productivity as we move from large to small state enterprises and then down the administrative ladder to include collectives organized in cities,

Table 6.5 Characteristics of state and non-state industrial enterprises, 1987

Category	*1987 Gross output ¥ billion current prices*	*Workers per firm*	*Fixed assets (yuan per worker) original cost*	*Fixed assets (yuan per worker) net value*	*Labour productivity (thousand yuan per worker)*
I. State-owned enterprises					
All state firms	825	4,110	19,142	13,070	20.6
Firms employing over 5,000	261	9,851	30,080	19,750	21.3
Other large and medium firms	304	1,492	17,620	12,310	24.6
Small state enterprises	263	256	11,760	8,470	16.0
II. Non-state enterprises					
A. Collective ownership					
Urban collectives	167	110	4,670	3,380	11.3
Rural enterprises					
Township	141	61	3,052	2,388	8.9
Village	120	25			6.8
B. Private ownership					
Urban firms[a]	5	2	n.a.	n.a.	5.6
Rural households[a]	80	3	n.a.	n.a.	4.1
C. Other ownership[b]	28	202	n.a.	n.a.	35.3

Note:
[a] Privately owned firms employing less than 8 workers.
[b] Includes private firms employing 8 or more workers, joint ventures, foreign-owned firms, and other ownership forms.

Source: Rawski, 1993; Yearbook, 1989; TVE, 1989; Industry, 1988.

townships (*xiang*), and villages (*cun*). A dynamic perspective would show both the collective and private sectors gaining ground on state-owned enterprises, especially the smaller units, in terms of total output, enterprise scale, capital intensity and labor productivity. Nominal labor productivity in the collective sector (excluding village-level units), for example, jumped from 60 to 76 percent of the average for state enterprises between 1987 and 1992 (Survey, 1993, p. 81).

The achievements of China's non-state enterprises can be summarized briefly. Output has risen explosively, although standard data probably exaggerate real growth (Ody, 1991; Rawski, 1991). Growing production has absorbed tens of millions of workers. The exports of township and village enterprises (including some non-industrial goods) shot up from US$3.9 to US$12.5 billion between 1985 and 1990, the latter figure amounting to over one-fifth of China's total exports for 1990 (Lardy, 1992). Although efforts to measure productivity growth in the collective sector are impeded by inadequate output deflators and inconsistencies between statistical measures of output and employment, it appears that the growth of output per worker, output per unit of capital, and total factor productivity in the collective sector—and especially among township and village enterprises—has outstripped comparable measures for the state sector. Table 4 contains a set of productivity comparisons that includes township-village enterprises.

The expansion of non-state enterprises has served as a lever forcing often reluctant state firms in the direction of market-oriented behavior. Our own calculations and those of Singh, Ratha and Xiao (1993) show that profitability within the state industry is lowest in provinces where the output of non-state industry has grown most rapidly. Singh, Ratha, and Xiao also find that large provincial shares of non-state industrial output are associated with high levels of total factor productivity in state industry, suggesting that robust growth of the non-state sector both squeezes profits and motivates greater efficiency in the state sector.

The impact of competition extends even to industries like steel and petroleum that face little rivalry from collective enterprises. The continuing fall in profit rates throughout industry, coupled with the expansion of enterprise claims on profit flows, has caused government, the chief holder of industrial capital, to suffer a crushing decline in revenue growth. Fear of inflation has left the state with little choice but to restrict the growth of subsidies and push an ever-growing list of industries into the hurly-burly of the marketplace.

The success of China's collectives has sparked growing interest in measuring and explaining their conduct and performance. Recent studies direct attention to several features that distinguish rural collectives from state enterprises: 1) information channels linking (government) principals with (managerial) agents tend to be shorter and simpler for non-state firms than for state-owned units (Groves et al., forthcoming); 2) local officials and non-state enterprise managers focus sharply on financial objectives (profit plus local tax revenues), while managers of state enterprises, burdened with responsibility for housing and other social services[6] as well as industrial operations, face a more complex set of objectives (Byrd and Gelb, 1990); 3) because localities lack the center's borrowing capacity, enterprises under local jurisdiction face harder budget constraints than state-owned enterprises and often fall into bankruptcy (Qian and Xu, 1992).

Several researchers have also suggested that, despite the absence of well-specified private property rights, the demographic stability of China's rural communities promotes the emergence of "invisible institutions" to provide a "moral framework for rights" or a "cooperative culture" that serves to reduce problems of shirking and monitoring found in most public enterprises (Byrd and Lin, 1990; Yusuf 1993a, 1993b; Weitzman and Xu, 1993).

It is not clear that these considerations can explain the vibrancy of the township and village enterprise sector. Ties with the state sector represent an important and widely neglected ingredient in the successful development of non-state firms. Collective units rely on the state sector as a source of capital, materials, equipment, specialized personnel, technology, sub-contracting arrangements, and sales revenues. In southern Jiangsu province (near Shanghai), a center of booming rural enterprise development, "more than two-thirds of township and village enterprises . . . have established various forms of economic and technical cooperation arrangements with industrial enterprises, research units, and higher educational institutions in larger cities" (Xu, Mao, and Yuan 1993). Officials attempting to develop industry in poor localities are encouraged to pursue "joint operations with scientific research organizations or large- and medium-scale enterprises" (Du, Huang, and Chen, 1992). Survey results indicating near-equality of financial returns to the employment of engineers in urban state firms and suburban collectives provide some quantitative measure of the extent to which reform-induced developments have broken longstanding patterns of market segmentation (Jefferson, Rawski, and Zheng, 1992b).

The erosion of entry barriers associated with China's industrial reform has created a domestic product cycle in which new products, materials, and processes introduced by innovative state firms are adopted by non-state enterprises which use their cost advantages to erode state sector profits and force state industry toward fresh innovations. Chinese manufacturers are enmeshed in multi-layered innovation ladders that link international firms and their Chinese branches to small and unsophisticated township and village enterprises through the agency of state-managed factories, laboratories, and universities (Jefferson and Rawski, 1994).

Despite the important contribution of non-state firms to China's recent industrial achievements, it is too soon to conclude that China's collectives represent an enduring organizational innovation. The dependence of non-state enterprises on resources from the state sector, the tendency for non-state enterprise operations to cluster at the low end of the scale and technology spectrum, and the somewhat artificial nature of the domestic cost advantages enjoyed by non-state firms all suggest that their rapid gains owe much to specific circumstances of China's economy in the 1980. Some authors predict that, as underlying economic conditions change, rural industry will lose ground to large domestic firms, enterprise groups, and joint venture companies during the course of the 1990s (Jiang et al., 1993; Pan, 1993).

CHINESE INDUSTRY IN THE 1990s

The 1990s have brought an unprecedented and virtually unrestrained push toward the market. This dynamic draws on the extraordinary success of China's southern regions as well as a new vision, shared even by the Communist party, of a market-dominated system in which the state's contribution is limited to indirect macroeconomic controls, microeconomic regulation, passive ownership of assets, and the enunciation of overall economic priorities.

Regulations on "Transforming the Management Mechanisms of State-Owned Industrial Enterprises" reflects this new attitude, formalizing the autonomy of state-owned enterprises and their responsibility for the financial consequences of independent business decisions and of market-driven economic change (Regulations, 1992). The text allows firms to "reject" or "refuse" official instructions, including mandatory plan directives, that fall outside narrowly defined boundaries. Overzealous officials who encroach upon enterprise autonomy will "bear responsibility for a criminal act" (FBIS, 1992). Enterprises can dismiss managers and technicians or assign them to blue-collar positions. They can "select employees according to their merits" and "dismiss and fire workers and staff" (Regulations, 1992).

Official foot-dragging has effectively denied these "rights" to some units, especially large firms in the state sector. Even so, managers have begun to address the difficult and politically sensitive issue of redundant workers in state industry. In 1992, China's coal industry cut its work force by 4 percent, while large and medium enterprises in Liaoning province, the heart of China's industrial "rust belt," reduced employment by over 6 percent (Wall Street Journal, December 27, 1993, p. 8; Liaoning, 1993). State industrial enterprises are transferring growing numbers of redundant personnel to newly established units, most engaged in service operations, which will gradually sever their financial ties with the parent units.

The reform of incentives has also expanded the gap between winners and losers. Contrary to the expectations of Chinese managers, who concealed huge profits in advance of negotiations for the renewal of enterprise responsibility contracts in 1990/91 (Wang Haibo, 1992), the new contracts appear to have avoided "ratchet effects" that would have penalized successful firms (Jefferson and Singh, 1993). With state subsidies fixed in nominal terms despite substantial inflation and rising enterprise losses, workers and managers attached to unsuccessful firms face growing financial pressure. While some managers may have expected "virtually unlimited budgetary subsidies" in the past (Ody, 1991, p. 30), financially troubled enterprises now face growing uncertainty about their access even to partial compensation for financial losses, price shocks, or falling profits.

In addition, the central government has expanded the role of market transactions in coal, petroleum, steel, and other sectors formerly regarded as bastions of mandatory planning. By 1993, central plans controlled only 7 percent of industrial output value (Su, 1993). Even these mandatory commodity allocations often "depend on market prices" (Zhang Zhiping, 1993, p. 14). These initiatives, along with a continuing inflow of foreign technology and equipment, have contributed to the continued outward shift of industry's efficiency frontier.

While China's industrial economy is rapidly acquiring many characteristics of a market system, important weaknesses remain. We must differentiate between fundamental issues that could potentially block the path of reform and the myriad distortions and bottlenecks that create difficulties without threatening to derail the reform process. For China, these fundamental issues cluster in two areas: finance and ownership.

The shift from plan to market in the financial sphere has lagged behind parallel changes affecting the markets for industrial materials and products. Official interference in credit decisions, weak control over lending, and insufficient sanctions against insolvent enterprises perpetuate the accumulation of bad debts by major banks. "Policy loans" that are unlikely to be repaid are said to account for 30 percent of new bank credit. Firms often continue to supply non-paying clients in the expectation that the banks will eventually commit funds to eradicate chains of inter-enterprise obligations.

The macroeconomic consequences of these financial arrangements are discussed in a companion paper by Shahid Yusuf. On the microeconomic side, the long-standing policy of maintaining artificially low interest rates encourages excessive investment demand, particularly for mechanization, with three unwanted effects: there are the usual inefficiencies associated with credit rationing; managers devote excessive attention to acquiring new equipment, while neglecting opportunities to improve performance by reorganizing currently available personnel and facilities; low interest rates encourage capital-intensive techniques that aggravate the problem of redundant labor and raise the social cost of labor market reform.

The Chinese government plans to reorganize the banking system during 1994. There will be three types of banks: a central bank, profit-oriented commercial banks, and specialized institutions to finance important projects that may not meet commercial loan standards. There is no guarantee that these changes will halt the accumulation of bad debts in commercial bank portfolios. However, the rapid decline of price controls has reduced one important source of resistance to the imposition of commercial lending standards. This offers some cause for optimism. Success in curtailing the accumulation of unrepayable loans could open the door to liberalization and diversification of domestic capital markets, which would in turn provide new opportunities as well as financial discipline for China's industrial enterprises. At the very least, the most recent reforms will have the desirable effect of consolidating industrial subsidies channeled through the banking system and making them more transparent than in the past.

What of ownership reform? It is essential to recall that 90 percent of Chinese industrial activity, including most of the output from non-state firms, resides in the public sector (Table 6.1). Even joint ventures with foreign firms often include Chinese state enterprises as partners. China's experience of industrial reform suggests that economists tend to overstate the importance of early privatization during the transition process. The strength of government efforts to force enterprises toward financial independence may count for more than the locus of ownership. However, even if this unorthodox view is accepted, we must guard against exaggeration of China's accomplishments. Although reform has reversed a long interlude of productivity stagnation, the scale of recent productivity growth in the state sector is modest at best. No one can doubt that most state enterprises operate well inside their production frontiers. Ownership reform has the potential to unlock further productivity gains in both state and collective industry.

Foreign as well as Chinese economists have expressed misgivings about the incentives created by the current system of responsibility contracts in state industry. These contracts, which typically extend for a term of three to five years, have undoubtedly shifted managerial incentives toward improving financial performance. But they create principal-agent problems that appear more serious than comparable issues arising from corporate management arrangements in the major market economies. Current contracting arrangements provide no opportunity to anticipate the plethora of contingencies associated with rapid institutional change. With a small number of official bodies charged with the supervision of 93,700 state enterprises, monitoring costs are high and information channels clogged. Enforcement costs are magnified by the difficulty of enlarging the current pool of enterprise leaders; the number of people with the specific knowledge and experience required to master the bureaucratic complexities of the state sector environment is very small.[7]

Discussion of ownership reform, temporarily halted following the ouster of Premier Zhao Ziyang in 1989, has resumed with fill vigor (Wood, 1991, 1993; Zhou Shulian, 1993), now accompanied by free-wheeling experimentation. Provincial and local governments have begun to sell loss-making enterprises. Provisions for multi-year tax holidays and expanded autonomy for joint ventures have spurred state enterprise managers to scour the market for offshore investors. Workers, managers and supervisory bodies have converted thousands of collectives and some state-owned firms into locally-held joint-stock companies. In addition to these bottom-up initiatives, the central authorities have (as of late 1993) authorized nearly 150 state enterprises to issue shares on stock exchanges in Shanghai, Shenzhen, Hong Kong, and New York.

As debate and experimentation continue, we see three possible approaches. The government will certainly continue its current policy of expanding managerial autonomy and sharpening the incentive structure of state enterprises. Current reform plans call for intensified efforts to restructure the governance of state enterprises by distributing shares among multiple owners—provincial and local governments, other state firms, banks, newly established asset management companies, and individuals—in the expectation that arm's-length relations between owners and managers will promote better performance. Finally, it is possible that localities, provinces, or even the central government will initiate comprehensive privatization via auction or voucher plans. There is no financial obstacle to selling large numbers of state firms. The bank deposits of China's households, which have grown much faster than the fixed assets of state industry in recent years, amounted to about ¥1.3 trillion at the end of 1992, while year-end 1992 net fixed assets of state industry amounted to ¥1.1 trillion (Yearbook 1993, pp. 419, 664, 667). Seventy firms with assets in excess of ¥1 billion each accounted for ¥225 billion of this total (1991 year-end figures from Industry 1992, p. 416).

CONCLUSIONS

The governments of eastern Europe have clear economic objectives: they hope to build Western-style economic systems that will reward their citizens with income levels comparable to those enjoyed in western Europe and qualify their nations for membership in the European Economic Community. China's leaders initiated industrial reform in the hope of eliciting better performance, but with no specific vision of a desirable post-reform industrial system. Not surprisingly, China's reforms have followed an evolutionary path marked by frequent shifts of direction and ad hoc responses to unanticipated outcomes. Bottom-up initiative, experimentation, learning, and adaptation stand at the core of the reform process in Chinese industry.

We view the implementation of substantive economic reform measures from the perspective of the microeconomic theory of investment (Jefferson and Rawski, 1993). If investment decisions cannot be costlessly reversed, we expect a firm that faces uncertain demand prospects and uncertain returns to changes in technology, product mix, and capital stock to invest more gradually than an enterprise with a sharply delineated vision of demand conditions and project outcomes (Pindyck, 1991). This approach provides a purely economic explanation for China's seeming hesitancy to move decisively toward market-style institutions.

If China's circumstances suggest a theoretical case for a more gradual approach to reform than what we see in nations like Poland or the Czech Republic, China's recent history proves that gradual reform of state industry is a feasible policy alternative that is capable of generating very substantial results. We do not deny that reform is a "seamless web" in which the rate of progress in one direction affects the consequences of reform efforts in other directions (Dhanji, 1991). But this does not imply that every reform component, however desirable in the long run, must be initiated at once. In the reform of socialist economies, as in earlier episodes of industrialization (Gerschenkron, 1962) and development (Hirschman, 1958), a comparative approach demonstrates that there is no unique recipe for successfully managing economic change.

The technique of building a market system is not one of fixed proportions. Temporary recourse to semi-market arrangements like China's systems of dual pricing and management contracts may produce outcomes that dominate the result of immediate efforts to achieve comprehensive price liberalization or rapid privatization of state enterprises. China's industrial gains of the past 15 years are partly attributable to favorable initial conditions. But the contrast between China's trend of buoyant increases in industrial output, real wages, employment, and exports and the performance of industry in states that have attempted to accelerate the pace of institutional change is too large to be explained solely by differences in initial conditions. We cannot avoid speculating that China is not the only venue in which the optimal path from plan to market might involve a lengthy interlude of gradual reform and a succession of transitional structures that deviate widely from standard market institutions.

During the past 15 years, China's industrial economy has achieved important progress toward building a market system. The accumulation of market experience and the confidence inspired by large increases in living standards have created a consensus favoring a market-based economy with a limited role for state ownership, government planning, and bureaucratic regulation of economic activity.

This new sense of purpose, which did not exist ten, five, or even three years ago, is itself a consequence of gradual reform. The emergence of a widely shared vision of China's post-reform economy has broadened the scope of feasible policy alternatives. Both the government and the Communist party have approved a new reform agenda that promises to install many elements typical of a full market system. The new reform push has begun with the creation of a unified exchange rate and a sweeping reduction in price controls for industrial goods. China's leaders now seem intent upon pursuing more complex and difficult industrial reform objectives, including the commercialization of bank lending, the expansion of domestic markets for industrial labor and capital, the creation of genuinely independent business management, and the reduction of government staff in industry-related fields to levels appropriate to the needs of strategic planning rather than micro-management of individual enterprises.

China has deployed an unorthodox strategy of industrial reform to great advantage. An initial round of partial reforms opened the door to growing competition involving old and new forms of public enterprise. During the 1980s, competition emerged as a powerful force for beneficial change in all segments of China's semi-market industrial system. As a result, this episode of partial reform raised the level of industrial output and enhanced the economic welfare of China's factory work force while creating the foundation for a market system.

Starting from the semi-market economy of the early 1990s, the current acceleration in the tempo of industrial reform, with its new focus on establishing conditions similar to standard market economy arrangements, may open the way to harnessing China's potential for further gains in industrial productivity without creating intolerable political tensions or social costs.

ACKNOWLEDGMENTS

We gratefully acknowledge research support from the Woodrow Wilson International Center for Scholars, the John Simon Guggenheim Memorial Foundation, the Henry Luce Foundation, Brandeis University's Mazer Fund, the University of Pittsburgh's University Center for International Studies, and the World Bank. We also thank Joseph Berliner, Alan Gelb, Alan Krueger, Nicholas Lardy, Derek Morris, Peter Murrell, Barry Naughton, Dwight Perkins, Carl Shapiro, Timothy Taylor, Shahid Yusuf, and Yuxin Zheng for detailed comments on our initial drafts.

NOTES

1 We refrain from detailed comment on the accuracy of Chinese economic statistics, except to note that officially compiled data on industrial inputs and outputs typically convey the order of magnitude of relevant levels and rates of change.

2 Other discussions in this vein include Chen, Jefferson, and Singh (1992); Gelb, Jefferson, and Singh (1993); and Singh (1993), and McMillan and Naughton (1993).

3 Yusuf (1993b) decomposes ownership into four basic rights: custody, or deciding how assets are used; usufruct, which entitles the holder to control income streams; alienation, determining the sale or transfer of assets; and destruction, affecting the ultimate disposition of assets.

4 For more detailed accounts, see Hua, Zhang, and Luo (1993); Naughton (1994); and Ten Years (1990).

5 Indirect subsidies remain, including low-interest bank loans to favored exporters (Lardy,1993).

6 Du and Shang (1993) note that state enterprises provide housing for 93 percent of their employees and 51 percent of all urban residents.

7 One experienced manager told us that learning to deal with various administrative superiors, which he regarded as more difficult than the technical issues or intra-firm responsibilities associated with his current executive post, had taken four years.

REFERENCES

Authors of Chinese-language publications are cited in the Chinese fashion, with surnames first.

Byrd, William A., and Alan Gelb, "Why Industrialize? The Incentives for Rural Community Governments." In Byrd, William A., and Qingsong Lin, eds., *China's Rural Industry: Structure, Development, and Reform*. New York: Oxford University Press, 1990, 338–58.

Byrd, William A., and Qingsong Lin, "China's Rural Industry: An Introduction." In Byrd, William A., and Qingsong Lin, eds., *China's Rural Industry: Structure, Development, and Reform*. New York: Oxford University Press, 1990, 3–18.

Chen, Kang, Gary H. Jefferson, and Inderjit Singh, "Lessons from China's Economic Reform," *Journal of Comparative Economics*, 1992, *16*, 201–25.

Chen, Kuan et al., "Productivity Change in Chinese Industry, 1953–1985," *Journal of Comparative Economics*, December 1988, *12*, 570–91.

Chen, Xiaohong, et al., "Preliminary Overview and Analysis of Concentration in Chinese Industry." In Wang Huijiong and Chen Xiaohong, eds., *Chanye zuzhi ji youxiao jingzheng: Zhongguo chanye zuzhi de chubu yanjiu* (Industrial organization and effective competition: a preliminary study of Chinese industrial organization). Beijing: Zhongguo jingji chubanshe, 1991, 191–209.

Coal Policy, "A Study of China's Policy on Coal Prices, Part 1," *Jiage lilun yü shijian* (Price Theory and Practice), 1988, no. 6, 40–46.

Cohen, Myron L., "Cultural and Political Inventions in Modern China: the Case of the Chinese 'Peasant'," *Daedalus,* Spring 1993, 151–70.

Dhanji, Farid, "Transformation Programs: Content and Sequencing," *American Economic Review Papers and Proceedings*, May 1991, *81*:2, 323–28.

Dong Furen, "Behavior of China's State-owned Enterprises Under the Dual System," *Caimao jingji* (Finance and Economics), 1992, no. 9, 3–15.

Du Haiyan, and Shang Lie, "Distribution of Fringe Benefits for Employees of State-owned Enterprises," *Zhongguo gongye jingji yanjiu* (Research on Chinese Industrial Economics), 1993, no. 2, 46–52, 30.

Du Miaodeng, Huang Shiqiu, and Chen Xuewen, "On the Management of 'High Starting Point' Enterprises in Poor Townships and Districts," *Jingji guanli* (Economic Management), 1992, no. 12, 55–57.

Enterprise, "How Has the Self Management Right of Enterprises Been Implemented?" *Jingji cankao* (Economic reference news), February 22, 1993, 1.

Fan, Gang, and Wing Thye Woo, "Decentralized Socialism and Macroeconomic Stability: Lessons from China," Department of Economics, University of California-Davis, Working Paper Series No. 411, 1992.

Fan, Qimiao, and Mark E. Schaffer, *Enterprise Reforms in Chinese and Polish State-owned Industries*. London School of Economics Development Economics Research Programme, STICERD, CP No. 13, 1991.

Farrell, John P., "Monitoring the Great Transition," *Comparative Economic Studies*, 1991, *23*:2, 9–28.

FBIS, "More on [Minister] Chen Jinhua Comments on State Firms Law," U.S. Department of Commerce, Foreign Broadcast Information Service, *Daily Report: China*, July 28, 1992, p. 27.

Gelb, Alan, Gary H. Jefferson, and Inderjit Singh, "Can Communist Economies Transform Incrementally?," *NBER Macroeconomics Annual 1993*, Cambridge: MIT Press, 1993, 87–132.

Gerschenkron, Alexander, *Economic Backwardness in Historical Perspective*. New York: Praeger, 1962.

Granick, David, *Chinese State Enterprises: A Regional Property Rights Analysis*. Chicago: University of Chicago Press, 1990.

Groves, Theodore, Yongmiao Hong, John McMillan, and Barry Naughton, "Autonomy and Incentives in Chinese State Enterprises," *Quarterly Journal of Economics*, forthcoming.

Gu, Shutang, and Cao Xuelin, "Create the Conditions for Surmounting Difficulties: On Enlivening State Enterprises to Escape Contradictions, *Jiage lilun yü shijian* (Price theory and practice), 1993, no. 2, 12–17.

Hay, Donald A., and Guy S. Liu, "Cost Behaviour of Chinese State-owned Manufacturing Enterprises During the Reform Period, 1979–1987," Applied Economics Discussion Paper No. 134, Institute of Economics and Statistics, Oxford University, 1992.

Hirschman, Albert O., *The Strategy of Economic Development*. New Haven: Yale University Press, 1958.

Hsueh, Tien-tung, Thomas G. Rawski, and Kai-yuen Tsui, "The Impact of Reform on China's State Industry: A Regional Perspective." Paper presented to a conference on "Productivity, Efficiency, and Reform in China's Economy," Chinese University of Hong Kong, August 1992.

Hua, Sheng, Xuejun Zhang, and Xiaopeng Luo, *China: From Revolution to Reform*. Houndsmills: Macmillan, 1993.

Industry, 1988, 1991, 1992. *Zhongguo gongye jingji tongji nianjian* [Statistical Yearbook of China's Industrial Economy]. Beijing: Zhongguo tongji chubanshe, annual.

Innovation, "Technical Development in Large and Medium Industrial Firms—Innovative Activity Develops Universally," *Zhongguo tongji* (China's Statistics), 1993, no. 4, 10.

Investment, "Speed Up the Pace of Technical Reform at Large and Medium State Enterprises: Summary of a Meeting on 'Policy Toward Enterprise Technical Reform' Organized by the China Association of Investment Studies." *Touzi yanjiu* (Investment research), 1991, no. 7, 45–48.

Jefferson, Gary H., and Thomas G. Rawski, "A Theory of Economic Reform," University of Pittsburgh, Department of Economics, Working paper No. 273, 1993.

Jefferson, Gary H., Thomas G. Rawski, and Yuxin Zheng, "Institutional Change and Industrial Innovation in Transitional Economies." Paper presented at the Annual Meeting of the Allied Social Science Associations, Boston, 1994.

Jefferson, Gary H., Thomas G. Rawski, and Yuxin Zheng, "Growth, Efficiency, and Convergence in China's State and Collective Industry," *Economic Development and Cultural Change*, 1992a, 40:2, 239–66.

Jefferson, Gary H., Thomas G. Rawski, and Yuxin Zheng, "Innovation and Reform in Chinese Industry: A Preliminary Analysis of Survey Data (1)." Paper delivered at the annual meeting of the Association for Asian Studies, Washington DC, April 1992b.

Jefferson, Gary H., and Inderjit Singh, "China's State-Owned Industrial Enterprises: How Effective Were the Reforms of the 1980s?" Washington, DC: World Bank, 1993.

Jefferson, Gary H., and Wenyi, Xu, "The Impact of Reform on Socialist Enterprises in Transition: Structure, Conduct, and Performance in Chinese Industry," *Journal of Comparative Economics*, 1991, *15*, 45–64.

Jefferson, Gary H., and Wenyi, Xu, "Assessing Gains in Efficient Production Among China's Industrial Enterprises," *Economic Development and Cultural Change*, forthcoming.

Jiang Xiaojuan et al., "New Features of China's Industrial Growth and Structural Change," *Zhongguo gongye jingji yanjiu* (Research on Chinese Industrial Economics), 1993, no. 8, 32–40.

Komiya, Ryutaro, "Japanese Firms, Chinese Firms: Problems of Economic Reform in China, Part 1," *Journal of the Japanese and International Economies*, March 1987, *1*:1, 31–61.

Kornai, Janos, and Agnes Matits, "Softness of the Budget Constraint—An analysis relying on data of firms," *Acta Oeconomica*, 1984, *32*:3–4, 223–49.

Lardy, Nicholas R., "Chinese Foreign Trade," *China Quarterly*, 1992, no. 131, 691–720.

Lardy, Nicholas, R., "China's Foreign Trade Reform in the 1990's." Paper presented to the Association for Asian Studies, Los Angeles, 1993.

Liaoning, "Increase the Developmental Stamina of Large and Medium State-Owned Enterprises," *Shengchanli zhisheng* (Voice of Productive Forces), 1993, no. 5, 6–7, 12.

Liu Li, "Analysis of Industrial Results for 1992 and Thoughts on the Strategy for Industrial Development," *Jingji guanli* (Economic Management), 1993, no. 2, 12–14.

Liu Lili, and Wang Shengjiao, "Strengthen the Management of State-owned Coal Resources, Perfect the Mechanism of Contract Service," *Zhongguo nengyuan* (China Energy), 1993, no. 1, 21–23.

Liu Renxiu, and Zou Bailin, "We Must Smash the Problem of Enterprises Taking Responsibility for Profits and not for Losses," *Jingji yanjiu* (Economic Research), 1992, no. 12, 22–24.

Machinery, *1986–1990 Zhongguo jidian chanpin chukou wunian* (China's exports of machinery and electrical products over five years, 1986–1990). Beijing: Gaige chubanshe, 1991.

McMillan, John, and Barry Naughton, "How to Reform a Planned Economy: Lessons from China," *Oxford Review of Economic Policy*, 1993, *8*:1, 130–43.

Morris, Derek, and Guy Shaojia Liu, "The Soft Budget Constraint in Chinese Industrial Enterprises in the 1980s," unpublished manuscript, Oxford University, January 1993.

Naughton, Barry, "Implications of the State Monopoly Over Industry and its Relaxation," *Modern China*, 1992, *18*:1, 14–41.

Naughton, Barry, *Growing Out of the Plan: Chinese Economic Reform, 1978–1993*. New York: Cambridge University Press, 1994.

Ody, Anthony J., "China: Rural Enterprise, Rural Industry, 1986–1990," unpublished paper. Washington, DC: World Bank, 1991.

Pan Xining, "Development of Rural Industry Confronts Nine Big Issues," *Shengchanli zhisheng* (Voice of Productive Forces), 1993, no. 7, 33–34.

Perkins, Dwight H. et al., *Rural Small-Scale Industry in the People's Republic of China*. Berkeley: University of California Press, 1977.

Pindyck, Robert S., "Irreversibility, Uncertainty, and Investment," *Journal of Economic Literature*, September 1991, *29*:3, 1110–48.

Qian, Yingyi, and Chenggang Xu, "Why China's Economic Reforms Differ: The *M*-form Hierarchy and Entry/Expansion of the Non-State Sector," Stanford University CEPR Publication No. 319, 1992.

Rawski, Thomas G., "How Fast Has Chinese Industry Grown?" Research Paper Series, No. 7, Socialist Economies Reform Unit, Country Economics Department, World Bank, 1991.

Rawski, Thomas G., "An Overview of Chinese Industry in the 1980s," unpublished, University of Pittsburgh, 1993.

Regulations, "Text of Regulations on Transforming State Enterprises," U.S. Department of Commerce, Foreign Broadcast Information Service, *Daily Report: China*, July 28, 1992, 27–36.

S&T, *Zhongguo kexue jishu sishinian (tongji ziliao) 1949–1989* (Statistics on Science and Technology of China 1949–1989). Beijing: Zhongguo tongji chubanshe, 1990.

Sicular, Terry, "China's Agricultural Policy During the Reform Period." In U.S. Congress, Joint Economic Committee. *China: Economic Dilemmas in the 1990s: The Problems of Reforms, Modernization, and Interdependence*. Washington DC: U.S. Government Printing Office, *1*, 340–64.

Singh, Inderjit, Dilip Ratha, and Geng Xiao, "Non-State Enterprises as an Engine of Growth: An Analysis of Provincial Industrial Growth in Post-Reform China," working paper, Transition and Macro Adjustment Division, the World Bank, 1993.

Su, Ning, "China's Industrial Policy During Economic System Transformation." Paper delivered to an International Conference on Macroeconomic Management," Dalian China, 1993.

Survey, *Zhongguo tongji zhaiyao 1993* (A Statistical Survey of China 1993). Beijing: Zhongguo tongji chubanshe, 1993.

Suttmeier, Richard P., "High-Technology Development in China: Some Critical Issues," unpublished paper, University of Oregon, 1992.

Ten Years, *Zhongguo qiye gaige shinian* [Ten Years of Enterprise Reform in China.] Beijing: Gaige chubanshe, 1990.

TVE, *Zhongguo xiangzhen qiye nianjian 1978–1987* [Yearbook of China's village and township enterprises, 1978–1987]. Beijing: Nongye chubanshe, 1989.

Wall Street Journal, "China To Free Coal Prices," December 27, 1993, p. 8.

Wang Haibo, "Now is the Time to Strengthen the Unity Between High Speed Growth and Raising Efficiency," *Zhongguo gongye jingji yanjiu* (Studies in Chinese Industrial Economics), 1992, no. 10, 23–28.

Weitzman, Martin, and Chenggang Xu, "Chinese Township and Village Enterprises as Vaguely Defined Cooperatives," unpublished manuscript, Harvard University, 1993.

Wong, Christine, "Economic Reform in China," unpublished manuscript, University of California, Santa Cruz, 1993.

Woo, Wing Thye, et al., "The Efficiency and Macroeconomic Consequences of Chinese Enterprise Reform," *China Economic Review*, forthcoming.

Wood, Adrian, *Joint Stock Companies with Rearranged Public Ownership: Invigoration of China's State Enterprises Further Considered.* Programme of Research into the Reform of Pricing and Market Structure in China. London: STICERD, 1991.

Wood, Adrian, "Joint Stock Companies with Rearranged Public Ownership: What Can We Learn from Recent Chinese Experience and East European Experience with State Enterprises?" Paper delivered at the International Symposium on Economic Transition in China, Haikou, 1993.

World Bank Survey, "Industrial Reform and Productivity in Chinese Enterprises," a research project administered by the Transition and Macro-Adjustment Division, World Bank.

Xu Fengxian, Mao Zhichong, and Yuan Juying, "New Development a la Sunan," *Jingji yanjiu* (Economic Research), 1993, no. 2, 49–55.

Yearbook 1989, 1992, 1993. *Zhongguo tongji nianjian* (China Statistical Yearbook). Beijing: Zhongguo tongji chubanshe, annual.

Yusuf, Shahid, "The Rise of China's Non-state Sector," unpublished manuscript, World Bank, 1993a.

Yusuf, Shahid, "Property Rights and Non-State Sector Development in China," unpublished manuscript, 1993b.

Zhang Zhiping, "Capital Goods Turn to Free Market," *Beijing Review*, July 5–11, 1993, *36*:27, 13–16.

Zhou Shulian, "Stock-holding is the Way to Transform the Operating Mechanism of State Enterprises," *Zhongguo gongye jingji yanjiu* (Studies in Chinese Industrial Economics), 1993, no. 4, 8–13.

Zou, Gang and Zhigang Wang, "Marketization and Productivity Change," unpublished, University of Southern California, 1993.

7

THE EFFICIENCY AND MACROECONOMIC CONSEQUENCES OF CHINESE ENTERPRISE REFORM IN TRANSITION

Wing Thye Woo, Gang Fan, Wen Hai, and Yibiao Jin

INTRODUCTION

China started the reform of its industrial sector in 1979 by granting state-owned enterprises (SOEs) limited rights in retaining some of the profits for own use and dispensing bonuses to workers. Over time, these "autonomies" were broadened and new ones, like the right to make investment decisions, were added.

The dominant opinion among China specialists until the late 1980s was that the post-1978 reforms had not raised total factor productivity (TFP) growth in the state-owned industrial sector. Typical of that consensus was Lardy (1989) who found that:[1]

> the average annual rate of *decline* in total factor productivity for the period from 1978 through 1985 is 0.3 percent, virtually the same as for the two decades between the end of the First Five-Year Plan (1957) and the onset of the reforms. (pp. 2–3, emphasis added)

Revisionism emerged in late 1980s and early 1990s, notably Chen, Wang, Zhen, Jefferson, and Rawski (1988), henceforth CWZJR; Dollar (1990); Granick (1990); and Jefferson, Rawski, and Zheng (1992), henceforth JRZ. CWZJR, after excluding nonproductive capital and labor and dropping observations that were big negative outliers, found TFP growth in the industrial sector to rise from an annual average of 0.9 percent in the 1957–78 period to 5.5 percent in the 1979–85 period. JRZ estimated *gross* output production function (instead of the usual two-factor value-added production functions) for a sample consisting of industrial SOEs aggregated at the city/

Source: *China Economic Review*, Vol. 14(2) (1993), pp. 153–68

county level at two points in time. JRZ found that annual TFP growth for SOEs averaged 2.4 percent in the 1984–87 period.

Another reason for revisionism on enterprise reforms was the quick growth of technically efficient collectively-owned enterprises (COEs). COEs, unlike SOEs, do not have privileged access to inputs and credits but their operations are subject to much fewer restriction. COEs consist of urban collectives, county collectives, and town and village enterprises (TVEs) in the countryside.[2] The TVEs have registered the most dramatic growth and comprised the bulk of the COEs. Svejnar (1990) found that TVEs had an annual TFP growth rate of about 13 percent in the 1981–86 period.[3] JRZ found that COEs had TFP growth rate of 4.6 percent per year in the 1984–87 period, almost double that of SOEs.

We obtained two new data sets to assess the success of Chinese enterprise reforms. The first dataset contains production and financial information of 300 large and medium industrial SOEs over the 1984–88 period. Our SOE sample is more representative than that of Dollar (1990) which consisted of only 20 SOEs and was biased toward the best performing SOEs.[4]

The second new data set contains production and financial information of 200 TVEs in 10 provinces over the 1984–87 period. Our TVE data set is thus more representative than Svejnar's (1990) which consisted of 122 firms from four counties.[5]

Our paper is organized as follows. The second section reports the regression results for TFP growth in the SOE sample. Our findings contradict those of the revisionist papers that have come to dominate discussion since 1988. We found that TFP growth in SOEs have at best been zero in the 1984–88 period.

The third section reports the results on TFP performance in the TVE sample. Our finding supports the well-known result that TFP growth in TVEs has been positive and higher than in the SOE sector. The fourth section discusses our findings.

The fifth section examines the financial data of the two samples. Our conclusion is that the criteria for judging the success of enterprise reform should be broadened beyond increases in the TFP growth rate to include the financial performance of an enterprise. An increase in technical efficiency means an increase in value added but this does not necessarily mean that government revenue would increase commensurately. We found that not only did a disproportionate amount of the output growth in SOEs but also a larger proportion of their existing output were dispensed, directly and indirectly, to workers and managers. This development has created a fiscal crisis for the government that threatens infrastructure investment and macroeconomic stability. Incorporation of the financial performance criteria will force attention on the linkage between incomplete enterprise reforms and macroeconomic instability.

ESTIMATION RESULTS FROM THE SOE DATA SET

One important criticism by CWZJR of previous empirical studies was their acceptance of Chinese data at face value. Given the obligations of most SOEs to provide social services like housing, the capital and labor not used directly in production should be deducted from the factor input. Table 7.1 estimated the two-input modified translog production function with the adjustments suggested by CWZJR. TFP growth was statistically significant and negative for the food processing and textile industries, and statistically insignificant from zero for the materials and machinery industries. The overall sample yielded a TFP growth rate that was insignificantly different from zero instead of the significant −4 percent when non-productive inputs were included in the estimation.

Both the food and material industries showed unambiguous increasing return to scale, and the materials industry showed economies of scale at the 95 percent significant level but not at the 99 percent level. Only the textile industry exhibited unambiguous constant return to scale. And yet, the overall sample suggested that constant return to scale characterized the industrial sector! This unexpected result was not caused by the preponderance of textile firms in the sample because they formed the smallest industrial cluster.[6] It was more likely caused by the vastly different output parameters across

Table 7.1 Adjusted data with period average capital stock used in modified translog function (two inputs)

1. Managerial and sales personnel excluded from labor input
2. Nonproductive fixed assets excluded from capital stock
3. Capital deflator from Jefferson, Rawski, and Zheng (1992)
4. *t*-statistics in parenthesis

	a_0	a_T	a_K	a_L	$\frac{1}{2}a_{KK}$	*adj.*R^2
Food processing	−1.963	−0.081	0.520	0.807	−0.398	0.466
	(−3.14)	(−2.09)	(6.32)	(7.23)	(−4.23)	
	Test: H0: $a_K + a_L = 1$				F = 13.76	
Textile	−0.020	−0.080	0.733	0.303	0.075	0.653
	(−0.05)	(−2.52)	(3.02)	(1.25)	(0.58)	
	Test: H0: $a_K + a_L = 1$				F = 0.40	
Materials	−0.710	−0.008	0.292	0.791	−0.023	0.739
	(−2.24)	(−0.30)	(4.54)	(9.03)	(−0.44)	
	Test: H0: $a_K + a_L = 1$				F = 4.45	
Machinery	1.000	0.023	0.207	0.613	−0.205	0.496
	(3.11)	(1.20)	(3.26)	(8.44)	(−2.98)	
	Test: H0: $a_K + a_L = 1$				F = 20.58	
Total	0.065	−0.020	0.421	0.576	−0.088	0.608
	(−0.37)	(−1.44)	(13.48)	(14.10)	(−2.87)	
	Test: H0: $a_K + a_L = 1$				F = 0.008	

Notes: *Critical value of* F (1,300):
F = 3.87 at 95%, *F* = 6.73 at 99%, *F* = 11.0 at 99.9%

industries: α_K was 0.8 for food processing but 0.3 for textile, and α_L was 0.7 for textile but 0.2 for machinery. The fact that the overall production function did not look anything like the production functions of the four component industries stresses the importance of being cautious about relying on conclusions from aggregate relationships about economies of scale and TFP growth, until they are confirmed by micro data.

The next step was to extend the analysis to cover the case of three inputs which JRZ had found significant positive TFP growth. Table 7.2 reports the results of the Cobb-Douglas specification where the value of material inputs was deflated with the deflator computed by JRZ. Our results are remarkably similar to those of JRZ. Our overall sample gave an annual TFP growth rate of 2.4 percent during the 1984–88 period compared to JRZ's estimate of 2.4 percent in the 1980–88 period and 3.0 percent in the 1984–88 period.[7] Like JRZ, we also found increasing returns to scale.

We have grounds to believe, however, that the results in Table 7.2 and in JRZ were caused by overdeflation of material inputs. Overdeflation understated the quantity of intermediate inputs used, and forced estimated TFP growth to be higher than actual. The basis of our hunch came from comparing the deflators for value added given in Table 7.3. Table 7.3 reports that the

Table 7.2 Materials inputs deflated by JRZ's deflator, three-input Cobb-Douglas function

1. Capital deflator for JRZ
2. Period average capital stock
3. Unproductive labor and unproductive capital excluded
4. *t*-statistics in parenthesis

	a_0	a_T	a_K	a_L	a_M	$adj.R^2$
Food processing	−0.359	−0.018	0.132	0.048	0.956	0.933
	(−2.00)	(0.19)	(5.61)	(1.46)	(50.00)	
	Test: H0: $a_K + a_L + a_M = 1$				F = 30.27	
Textile	0.205	−0.020	0.069	0.116	0.854	0.970
	(1.60)	(2.07)	(2.26)	(4.14)	(41.96)	
	Test: H0: $a_K + a_L + a_M = 1$				F = 5.53	
Materials	−0.072	−0.025	−0.041	0.162	0.949	0.986
	(−1.02)	(4.05)	(−2.95)	(8.06)	(95.74)	
	Test: H0: $a_K + a_L + a_M = 1$				F = 66.75	
Machinery	1.012	0.034	0.101	0.010	0.834	0.958
	(10.91)	(5.87)	(6.41)	(0.47)	(75.50)	
	Test: H0: $a_K + a_L + a_M = 1$				F = 23.15	
Total	0.358	0.024	0.053	0.086	0.884	0.965
	(6.99)	(6.18)	(6.00)	(7.54)	(128.35)	
	Test: H0: $a_K + a_L + a_M = 1$				F = 14.44	

Notes: *Critical value of F* (1,300):
$F = 3.87$ at 95%, $F = 6.73$ at 99%, $F = 11.0$ at 99.9%

Table 7.3 Overdeflation of intermediate inputs; Jefferson, Rawski, & Zheng (1992) sample in perspective

	Industrial SOE		*Industrial COE*		*For JRZ sample*		*From official GNP*
	value added in current prices	*value added in 1980 prices*	*value added in current prices*	*value added in 1980 prices*	*deflator for value added in industry*		*deflator for value added in industry*
					SOE	*COE*	
	(a)	*(b)*	*(c)*	*(d)*	*(a)/(b) = e*	*(c)/(d) = f*	*(g)*
1980	131.9	131.9	32.2	32.2	100.0	100.0	100.0
1981	131.8	133.2	34.3	34.8	98.9	98.5	100.9
1982	137.3	141.5	36.9	38.8	97.0	95.1	100.7
1983	150.1	158.1	41.5	44.7	94.9	92.9	100.8
1984	172.1	184.6	50.6	62.5	93.2	80.9	103.0
1985	205.8	218.3	67.9	84.4	94.3	80.5	107.8
1986	220.7	240.9	76.3	100.7	91.6	75.8	113.0
1987	252.9	269.4	89.4	124.3	93.9	71.9	115.4
1988	306.3	316.7	113.5	165.3	96.7	68.7	126.1

Note: Because JRZ did not report capital consumption (CC) and major repair funds (MRF) data, we assumed that (CC + MRF) = 0.156* (Gross value – cost of intermediate inputs) to construct column (b). Similar procedure was used to construct column (d). This will equate the 1980 figure for net value added. interdef/ycomp

JRZ procedure for deflating material inputs caused their deflator for value added in industrial SOEs (series (e)) and their deflator for value added in industrial COEs (series (f)) to fall secularly since 1980. But official statistics[8] show that the deflator for value added in the entire industrial sector has been rising since 1980, which means that at least one of the component deflators, SOE or COE, has been rising.

However, the opposite trends in the JRZ and official deflators for value added cannot definitely establish that the former was constructed wrongly. This is because the former was constructed from double deflation (the gross output and intermediate inputs were deflated separately), while the latter was actually the overall deflator for *gross* industrial output (i.e., national gross industrial output in current prices divided by national gross industrial output in base year prices).

We have two reasons to doubt the validity of JRZ's declining deflator for value added in SOEs. The first reason is that its continuous decline over the 1980–84 period even though price liberalization in this period was confined mainly to the prices of final goods. It was only until May 1984 that the "free market" prices of the "liberalized" inputs was permitted to be a maximum of 20 percent above official plan prices. Dual track pricing of intermediate inputs really got started only in February 1985, and even then prices of 23 key intermediate inputs remained controlled.

The second reason to doubt JRZ's deflator is its decline throughout a period of general price increases in the economy. This contradictory movement from 1980 to 1986 for the SOE deflator and from 1980 to 1988 for the COE deflator is highly unusual by international experience, especially in an inflationary environment; see Woo, Hai, Jin, and Fan (1993).

Table 7.4 reestimated the three-input gross output production function, using the firm-specific product price index to deflate material inputs. TFP growth was found to be –4 percent in the food-processing industry, –2 percent in the textile and materials industries, zero in the machinery industry, and –l percent for the overall sample. The only qualitative similarity with JRZ's results is that constant return to scale was rejected.

We still could not obtain positive TFP growth when we used other output price indices to deflate material inputs.

ESTIMATION RESULTS FROM THE TVE DATA SET

Table 7.5 estimated the modified translog specification of the two-factor production function. TFP growth was positive and statistically significant in all cases. Annual TFP growth was eight percent where intermediate inputs were deflated either with the firm-specific product price index or with the

Table 7.4 Materials inputs deflated by deflator of firm-specific product price index, three input Cobb-Douglas function

1. Capital deflator for JRZ
2. Period average capital stock
3. Unproductive labor and unproductive capital excluded
4. *t*-statistics in parenthesis

	a_0	a_T	a_K	a_L	a_M	$adj.R^2$
Food processing	–0.353	–0.040	0.132	0.048	0.956	0.933
	(–1.97)	(–3.62)	(5.62)	(1.46)	(47.04)	
	Test: H0: $a_K + a_L + a_M = 1$				F = 30.33	
Textile	0.210	–0.017	0.069	0.116	0.855	0.970
	(0.64)	(–1.79)	(2.25)	(4.14)	(41.97)	
	Test: H0: $a_K + a_L + a_M = 1$				F = 5.52	
Materials	–0.66	–0.016	–0.041	0.162	0.949	0.986
	(–0.95)	(–0.64)	(–2.97)	(8.09)	(95.02)	
	Test: H0: $a_K + a_L + a_M = 1$				F = 67.21	
Machinery	1.017	–0.02	0.101	0.010	0.834	0.958
	(10.98)	(–0.33)	(6.41)	(0.48)	(75.60)	
	Test: H0: $a_K + a_L + a_M = 1$				F = 23.21	
Total	0.363	–0.014	0.053	0.086	0.884	0.965
	(7.11)	(–3.49)	(6.00)	(7.55)	(128.50)	
	Test: H0: $a_K + a_L + a_M = 1$				F = 14.48	

Notes: *Critical value of F* (1,300):
F = 3.87 at 95%, *F* = 6.73 at 99%, *F* = 11.0 at 99.9%

Table 7.5 Two-input production function: modified translog specification

1. Dependent variable is value added of firm
2. Sample is 200 TVEs, 1984–1987 period
3. Capital deflator is from JRZ
4. Only productive capital and productive labor were used
5. *t*-statistics in parenthesis

Part A: Unconstrained estimation

Equation	*Constant*	a_T	a_K	a_L	$\frac{1}{2}a_{KK}$	*Adj.* R^2
(1)	−1.105	0.077	0.739	0.385	0.105	0.57
	(−4.37)	(2.10)	(8.56)	(4.20)	(4.21)	
(2)	−0.954	0.077	0.756	0.348	0.108	0.58
	(−3.89)	(2.17)	(9.02)	(3.80)	(4.48)	
(3)	−0.640	0.088	0.746	0.351)	0.103	0.66
	(−3.10)	(2.92)	(10.46)	(4.51)	(4.89)	

Part B: Testing for variable return to scale via intensive form

Equation	*Constant*	a_T	a_K	$(a_K + a_L - 1)$	$\frac{1}{2}a_{KK}$	*Adj.* R^2
(4)	−1.105	0.077	0.739	0.134	0.105	0.20
	(−4.37)	(2.10)	(8.56)	(3.00)	(4.21)	
(5)	−0.954	0.077	0.756	0.103	0.108	0.21
	(−3.89)	(2.17)	(9.02)	(2.37)	(4.48)	
(6)	−0.873	0.905	0.747	0.114	0.108	0.25
	(−3.96)	(2.96)	(9.81)	(2.91)	(4.79)	

Part C: Imposing constant return to scale

Equation	*Constant*	a_T	a_K	a_L	$\frac{1}{2}a_{KK}$	*Adj.* R^2
(7)	−0.440	0.095	0.720	0.280	0.108	0.19
	(−3.57)	(2.63)	(8.30)		(4.31)	
(8)	−0.444	0.091	0.741	0.259	0.110	0.20
	(−3.72)	(2.59)	(8.83)		(4.57)	
(9)	−0.312	0.112	0.732	0.269	0.111	0.24
	(−2.90)	(3.51)	(9.57)		(4.91)	

Note:
a. Material inputs in equation (1), (4) and (7) were deflated by firm-specific product price index.
b. Material inputs in equation (2), (5) and (8) were deflated by industry-specific product price index is the average of firm indexes.
c. Material inputs in equation (3), (6) and (p) were deflated by JRZ's intermediate input deflator.

industry-specific product price, to an average of 9.8 percent when JRZ's intermediate deflator was employed, see equations (3), (6), and (9).

Part B of Table 7.5 suggests that the TVE production was characterized by increasing returns to scale. $(\alpha_K + \alpha_L - 1)$ was statistically significant different from zero—see equations (4), (5), and (6).

It was therefore surprising when the positive TFP result from the estimation of the value added production function was not confirmed by the estimation of the gross output production function, see Table 7.6. TFP growth was statistically indistinguishable from zero when intermediate inputs were deflated by the firm-specific product price index and JRZ's capital deflator—equations (2) and (3) respectively. TFP growth was significant only when JRZ's intermediate deflator was used, and it was only six percent per year compared to the 8–11 percent range in Table 7.5.

We note that Svejnar's (1990) TFP growth rate is much higher than our's and JRZ's. We think that Svejnar's result came from the fact that his dependent variable was gross output but he had only two inputs, labor and capital. This assumption of zero intermediate inputs is equivalent to assuming an intermediate deflator of infinity, and we know that overdeflation of material inputs naturally raises the estimated TFP growth rate.

ASSESSING THE DIFFERENT EMPIRICAL FINDINGS

The analysis of our SOE data set suggests that the revisionists might have overstated their case for improved TFP performance in the SOE sector since 1978. CWZJR looked only at data aggregated at the national level, Jefferson (1990) looked only at the iron and steel industry, and Dollar (1990) and Granick (1990) used a sample of 20 high-performance firms. Jefferson and Xu (1991) found that labor productivity in firm-level data was positively

Table 7.6 Three factor inputs production function: Cobb-Douglas specification

1. Dependent variable is gross output of firm
2. Sample is 200 TVEs, 1984–1987 period
3. Capital deflator is from JRZ
4. Only productive capital and productive labor were used
5. *t*-statistics in parenthesis

Equation	*Constant*	α_T	α_K	α_L	α_M	*Adj.* R^2
(1)	0.327	0.005	0.339	0.602	0.206	0.71
	(1.30)	(0.15)	(8.08)	(11.99)	(7.45)	
(2)	0.531	0.004	0.307	0.584	0.245	0.72
	(2.16)	(0.13)	(7.52)	(11.98)	(9.27)	
(3)	0.352	0.018	0.339	0.602	0.206	0.71
	(1.39)	(0.54)	(8.08)	(11.99)	(7.46)	
(4)	–0.085	0.064	0.237	0.557	0.297	0.75
	(–0.50)	(2.54)	(7.00)	(14.87)	(13.33)	

Note:
a. Material inputs in equation (1) were in current prices
b. Material inputs in equation (2) were deflated by firm-specific product price index
c. Material inputs in equation (3) were deflated by JRZ's capital deflator.
d. Material inputs in equation (3) were deflated by JRZ's intermediate input deflator

correlated with various indicators of reforms (e.g., bonus payments), but then they *did not include the firm's capital stock in their regressions.*

In Woo, Hai, Jin, and Fan (1993), we formalized the conditions which would result in a declining value added deflator. We point out that the official method of computing real value added creates two opposite biases: it overcounts gross output and it overcounts intermediate input. Correction of only the second bias in estimation will allow the first bias to ambiguously overstate real value added; and overcorrection of the second bias will accentuate the overstatement of growth, and hence TFP improvement. In our judgment, JRZ's uncritical acceptance of the official real output series, despite Rawski's (1991) warning, and their overdeflation of intermediate inputs are the reasons for their high TFP estimates and their declining value added deflator.

Since our results contradict those of the widely-cited JRZ article, we will discuss it in some detail. JRZ used a cross section sample with values in two years to estimate the frontier production function. They adopted a "novel frontier procedure" (p.250) that dropped outliers upon iterative estimations to "converge" upon the frontier. While most of the observations dropped were those *too far below* the final frontier, points *too far above* the final frontier also had to be dropped to prevent distortion of the curvature of the final frontier. The final frontier was estimated from one-third of the original sample.[9]

There are three major problems with the JRZ paper.

1 The first problem is that it did not discuss the widespread and persistent technical inefficiency that it unearthed. Two-thirds of their observations were still operating *too far* below the production function after seven and a half years of enterprise reform. We have the anomaly of Chinese enterprise reforms being able to raise the production function steadily over time but not being able to push two-thirds of the enterprises to operate at the frontier of the existing production function.
2 The second problem is the attribution of the rise in the production function over time to enterprise reforms (e.g., managerial incentives, bonus to the workers, profit retention). It ignored imported technology as an important source of technological progress was imported technology.[10] The point is that the faster rise in the production function over time could well have been more the result of the opening of the Chinese economy to world trade than the result of the enterprise reforms. If so, the reason for why two-thirds of the Chinese firms were operating below the latest (imported) production function was not just technical inefficiencies but also the shortage of funds and foreign exchange to enable technological upgrading. The quick upward shift in the frontier production function estimated by JRZ should therefore not be taken as evidence of generalized efficiency gains in the SOE sector, but as evidence of privileged access to foreign exchange by favored localities that are being promoted to be inspiration points (as in "Learn from Shenzhen").

3 The third problem with the JRZ paper is its application of their novel frontier procedure to the COE data. As the operations of the COEs are (practically) unregulated by the state, there is no reason to believe that any significant number of them would willingly operate too far below the production function. It is therefore surprising that more observations of COEs were dropped than observations of SOEs.[11] This last fact supports the previous conclusions of that several production functions existed simultaneously and that the usual regression approach is more appropriate than the frontier procedure.

To explore the contribution of China's opening to the world to technical efficiency in SOEs, we added a foreign dummy variable to the regressions. The dummy is unity when the firm has a foreign partner and zero otherwise. The results reported in Table 7.7 shows that the existence of a foreign partner has mixed effects: statistically insignificant effects in the food industry, significant negative effects in the textile industry, and statistically positive effects in the materials and machinery industry. The overall effect was a significant and positive one. It appears that the "foreign partner" has mostly a level effect rather than a growth effect. Only the last equation shows that the foreign partner generates a growth effect. It is important to note that the time trend for TFP remains negative.

The reasons for the positive "foreign" effect could be any combination of the following:

1 the foreign partner brought in foreign exchange which allowed the import of more advanced technology;
2 the foreign manager was a better manager; and
3 the right of joint ventures with foreigners to fire workers more easily resulted in greater work effort by the workers.

Which of the above is responsible for the positive effects will have to await further research.

To sum up the discussion so far, it is reasonable to conclude the TVEs were technically more efficient than the SOEs, and that efficiency gains in SOEs were hard to find. This means that the enterprise reforms have been successful not in the sense of motivating SOEs to produce positive TFP growth but in the sense of allowing the establishment of new enterprises (TVEs) that had positive TFP growth.

BEYOND TECHNICAL EFFICIENCY TO MACROECONOMIC INSTABILITY

The overwhelming focus of the discussions on the enterprise reforms in China has been on their impact on TFP growth. This narrow focus has the unfortunate consequence of pushing to the sideline discussions on enterprise

Table 7.7 Modified translog function with foreign cooperation dummy

1. Unproductive capital and labor excluded
2. *t*-statistics in parentheses

Part A dummy: foreign cooperation

	Constant	a_T	a_K	a_L	$\frac{1}{2}a_{KK}$	a_f	*Adj.* R^2
Food	−1.855	−0.088	0.470	0.842	−0.373	−0.152	0.46
	(−2.85)	(−2.34)	(5.87)	(7.41)	(−4.07)	(−1.26)	
Textile	−0.711	−0.084	0.534	0.600	−0.039	−0.236	0.69
	(−1.60)	(−2.57)	(2.12)	(2.38)	(−0.29)	(−2.33)	
Material	−0.384	−0.014	0.245	0.787	−0.051	0.312	0.71
	(−1.11)	(−0.46)	(3.52)	(8.30)	(−0.89)	(3.39)	
Machinery	1.428	0.054	0.247	0.512	−0.235	0.119	0.48
	(4.26)	(2.64)	(3.72)	(6.76)	(−3.27)	(2.09)	
Total	0.035	−0.011	0.384	0.597	−0.101	0.076	0.59
	(0.19)	(−0.73)	(11.85)	(14.05)	(−3.19)	(1.82)	

Part B dummies: foreign cooperation and (foreign cooperation * time)

	Constant	a_T	a_K	a_L	$\frac{1}{2}a_{KK}$	a_f	a_{f*t}	*Adj.* R^2
Food	−1.724	−0.096	0.443	0.776	−0.316	−0.149	0.036	0.46
	(−2.02)	(−2.20)	(5.80)	(7.15)	(−3.62)	(−0.60)	(0.48)	
Textile	−0.384	−0.105	0.597	0.508	−0.014	−0.412	0.056	0.65
	(−0.80)	(−2.65)	(2.25)	(1.91)	(−0.10)	(−1.67)	(0.76)	
Material	0.252	−0.016	0.371	0.583	−0.015	0.242	0.021	0.74
	(0.74)	(−0.47)	(5.55)	(6.33)	(−0.28)	(1.27)	(0.36)	
Machinery	1.295	0.069	0.243	0.531	−0.231	0.114	0.005	0.47
	(3.62)	(1.91)	(3.55)	(6.74)	(−3.12)	(0.82)	(−0.12)	
Total	0.229	−0.025	0.414	0.546	−0.071	−0.041	0.038	0.60
	(1.22)	(−1.35)	(12.89)	(12.88)	(−2.30)	(−0.44)	(1.37)	

Part C dummy: (foreign cooperation * time)

	Constant	a_T	a_K	a_L	$\frac{1}{2}a_{KK}$	a_f	*Adj.* R^2
Food	−1.247	−0.083	0.443	0.765	−0.314	−0.004	0.46
	(−1.99)	(−2.19)	(5.81)	(7.16)	(−3.61)	(−0.11)	
Textile	−0.458	−0.075	0.625	0.476	0.009	−0.055	0.65
	(−0.95)	(−2.11)	(2.35)	(1.78)	(0.06)	(−1.70)	
Material	0.305	−0.040	0.375	0.583	−0.013	0.086	0.74
	(0.90)	(−1.35)	(5.63)	(6.88)	(−0.25)	(3.25)	
Machinery	1.348	0.042	0.246	0.530	−0.231	0.026	0.47
	(3.83)	(1.84)	(3.60)	(6.73)	(−3.12)	(1.43)	
Total	0.220	−0.020	0.414	0.545	−0.071	0.027	0.61
	(1.18)	(−1.35)	(12.89)	(12.87)	(−2.29)	(2.20)	

reform and macroeconomic stability.[12] The implicit assumption is that greater output from increased efficiency would decrease inflation by increasing the supply of goods and by reducing the government budget deficit.

Greater technical efficiency, it is assumed, would mean greater profits, hence reducing enterprise loss subsidies by the government and increasing the government's revenue from SOEs.

Instead, the state finances have gotten steadily worse since earnest but gradual industrial reforms began in 1984. The combined central and local government budget deficit went from 1.8 percent of GNP in 1984 to 2.5 percent in 1988 and 3.3 percent in 1991, see Table 7.8.[13] The Chinese government had known from the very beginning of reform that state revenue as a proportion of GNP would fall as a consequence of its decentralizing reforms that reduced the responsibilities of the state. But the fall in state revenue has been much faster than anticipated, and hence the growth in the budget deficit.

The size of the budget deficits in Table 7.8 are not very big by international comparison, but it is important to note that they are understatements of the analytically correct budget deficits. The financing of off-budget spending by overdrafts from the central bank should be counted as part of the true deficit. We call the GBR deficits in Table 7.8 the open deficits, and the off-budget spending financed by the central bank the hidden deficits. The hidden deficits are mainly loans to state enterprises to accommodate their investment and to cover their losses. We estimate the "hidden deficit" as the expansion of reserve money in excess of the amount lent to the government for deficit financing. Adding the open and hidden deficit, we find that the true budget deficit has reached 10 percent of GNP in the 1990s.

	Open deficit	*Hidden deficit*	*Consolidated deficit*	*A conservative re-estimate on the assumption that enterprise loans are 70 percent of column (2) deficit*
	(1)	*(2)*	*(3)*	*(4)*
1988	2.49	5.14	7.63	6.09
1989	2.35	5.22	7.57	6.01
1990	2.91	7.55	10.46	8.20
1991	3.34	6.76	10.10	8.07

The reason for the unexpected quick decline in state revenue is the unexpected quick decline in the revenue from industrial SOEs. Naughton (1991) has suggested that the primary reason for the decline in profitability of the SOEs is the expansion of competition by collectively-owned enterprises allowed by the economic reforms. The problem with this explanation is that the fall in profits occurred across the board, even in heavy industries with negligible new entry and in industries where prices have not fallen. Naughton's explanation also cannot explain the large increases in real wages received by SOE workers since 1984. It is puzzling how the SOEs experiencing large decreases in their profits supposedly because of increased competition could have granted large increases in real wages to their workers.

In offering an alternative explanation for the profit decline, we want to first make the point that technical efficiency and financial performance are two separate issues. The former could improve while the latter deteriorates. This is the case where the increase in value added is accompanied by paying enterprise personnel a greater share of the *total* value added. The workers are working harder and the managers are innovating more, and so technical efficiency increases, but then the greater effort is coming about only because the enterprise personnel are allowed to grab the lion's proportion of the increased output.

The ability to effect such a redistribution of the value added between labor and capital is very much determined by how vigorously the firm's management identifies with the capital owners and how vigilantly the firm's management is supervised by the capital owners. With the reduction in state monitoring of SOE activities since 1984, we should thus expect total labor compensation as a proportion of value added to rise faster in SOEs than in TVEs.[14] Table 7.9 supports this hunch.

In our SOE sample, direct wage income increased from 25 percent of value added in 1984 to 36 percent in 1988; and indirect wage income increased from seven percent to 12 percent in this period.[15] Total labor compensation increased by 17 percentage points of value added in the 1984–88 period.

In our TVE sample, on the other hand, total labor compensation was trendless at about 34 percent of value added. This suggests that TVE managers have been much more diligent in defending capital income than SOE managers. This is the reason why in a boom year like 1992 when real GNP increased 12.8 percent, two-thirds of SOEs were running operative losses. The official *China Daily* ("Budgetary deficit will be cut back in '93") reported on January 26, 1993:

> At present, about one-third of State firms are definitely operating at a loss and another one-third suffer hidden losses, according to the State Statistics Bureau.

Hidden losses refers to various methods that allow a firm not to show an accounting loss e.g., the firm being exempted from forwarding sales tax revenue to the state, and a firm's unsold output is valued as income. As long as there is no accounting loss, an SOE can borrow working capital from the banks to pay its employees and supplies.

The conclusions from our two samples are supported by the official aggregate data. The official data on industrial SOEs show that the average annual rates of labor productivity growth and direct real wage[16] growth over the 1978–90 period were 4.4 percent and 4.1 percent respectively. In a recent study, Zhao (1992) estimated that the indirect real wage grew an annual

Table 7.8 The fiscal situation in the reform period

	In billions of yuans				*As percent of GNP*			
	Revenue		*Expenditure*		*Revenue*		*Expenditure*	
	Chinese definition	*'Standard' definition*	*Chinese definition*	*'Standard' definition*	*Chinese definition*	*'Standard' definition*	*Chinese definition*	*'Standard' definition*
1978	112.11	124.75	111.10	123.74	31.24	34.77	30.96	34.49
1979	110.33	126.40	127.39	146.99	27.66	31.69	31.94	36.86
1980	108.52	130.07	121.27	147.12	24.28	29.10	27.13	32.91
1981	108.95	130.22	111.50	140.08	22.83	27.28	23.36	29.35
1982	112.40	140.93	115.33	152.24	21.64	27.14	22.21	29.32
1983	124.90	160.69	129.25	172.97	21.57	27.66	22.25	29.78
1984	150.19	184.28	154.64	196.46	21.57	26.47	22.21	28.22
1985	186.64	229.72	184.48	236.55	21.81	26.84	21.56	27.64
1986	226.03	244.68	233.08	265.56	23.31	25.23	24.04	27.39
1987	236.89	257.58	244.85	282.49	20.96	22.79	21.67	25.00
1988	262.80	280.37	270.66	315.30	18.75	20.00	19.31	22.49
1989	294.79	326.38	304.02	363.91	18.43	20.41	19.01	22.75
1990	331.26	351.60	345.22	403.11	18.72	19.87	19.51	22.78
1991	361.09	365.97	381.36	432.38	18.19	18.43	19.21	21.78

	In billions of yuans budget deficit			*As percent of GNP budget deficit*		
	Chinese definition	*Government borrowing requirement definition*	*Stock definition*	*Chinese definition*	*Government borrowing requirement definition*	*Stock definition*
1978	−1.02	−1.02	−1.02	−0.28	−0.28	−0.28
1979	17.06	20.60	20.60	4.28	5.16	5.16
1980	12.75	17.05	14.68	2.85	3.82	3.28
1981	2.55	9.85	5.59	0.53	2.06	1.17
1982	2.93	11.32	7.33	0.56	2.18	1.41
1983	4.34	12.29	9.54	0.75	2.11	1.64
1984	4.45	12.18	10.48	0.64	1.75	1.51
1985	−2.16	6.82	4.27	−0.25	0.80	0.50
1986	7.05	20.88	17.93	0.73	2.15	1.85
1987	7.96	24.91	19.77	0.70	2.20	1.75
1988	7.86	34.94	30.41	0.56	2.49	2.17
1989	9.23	37.53	33.40	0.58	2.35	2.09
1990	13.96	51.50	38.56	0.79	2.91	2.15
1991	20.27	66.41	NA	1.02	3.34	NA

Notes:
'Standard' definition for revenue means subtracting borrowing from Chinese definition, and adding in the subsidies that were counted as negative revenue.
'Standard' definition for expenditure means adding to the Chinese definition subsidies that were considered negative subsidies.
Government Borrowing Requirement (GBR) definition of deficit is 'Standard' expenditure minus 'Standard' revenue.
'Stock' definition of deficit is GBR definition minus principal repayments.

Table 7.9 Division of net value added (in percent of value added)

	1984	*1985*	*1986*	*1987*	*1988*
S.O.E.					
(a) Taxes & remitted profits	31.5	24.8	20.1	15.3	13.7
(b) Direct wage income	24.8	27.2	40.8	33.1	36.4
(c) Indirect wage income	7.0	10.1	13.7	12.6	12.4
(d) Retained profits	11.3	15.7	15.2	14.7	15.0
(e) Other items (e.g. depreciation)	25.4	22.2	10.2	24.3	22.5
(f) Total labor compensation (b + c)	31.8	37.3	54.5	45.7	48.8
T.V.E.					
(g) Basic wage	16.0	15.3	16.5	15.0	n.a.
(h) Other cash income (e.g. bonus)	23.1	13.8	20.1	15.6	n.a.
(i) Total labor compensation (g + h)	39.1	29.1	36.6	30.6	n.a.

Note: *S.O.E. Sample*
(1) Direct wage income is (basic wage + bonus)
(2) Indirect wage income is (welfare funds + retirement benefits + Training programs + schooling for workers' children)

average of 12.5 percent in the 1978–90 period, raising its share in total (direct plus indirect) real wage from 15 percent in 1978 to 31 percent in 1990.[17] Incorporating Zhao's finding into the official data, the average annual increase in the real wage was 5.4 percent. This finding supports our contention that the higher wage growth caused profitability of SOEs to fall even though technical efficiency (might) have increased.

The official data show that labor productivity growth in the collective sector is much greater than the direct real wage growth there: 8.3 percent and 3.6 percent respectively. Since indirect wages are much lower in the collectively-owned sector, total labor compensation growth could have at most equalled labor productivity growth.

The weak defense of capital income by SOE managers coupled with the "hunger for investment" phenomenon during the reform period meant that the state has been faced with unexpected large decreases in revenue and large increases in loss-subsidies. The heavy subsidy burden of the state in the face of declining revenue meant reductions in infrastructure investment (which could constrain future growth if unchecked), and higher inflation (caused by the need to monetize more of the budget deficit).

It is clear that the criteria for judging the success of enterprise reform should be broadened beyond increases in the TFP growth rate. Incorporation of the financial performance criteria will force attention on the linkage between incomplete enterprise reforms and macroeconomic instability.

CONCLUSIONS

The biggest achievement of enterprise reforms in China is the genesis and explosive growth of industrial TVEs. Their share of gross industrial output leapt from 16 percent in 1984 to 31 percent in 1991.[18] Given the high TFP growth in TVEs, the continued growth of this sector is crucial to the economic development of China.

Our findings of the industrial SOE sector bring the debate back to the original conclusions of Chow (1985) and Dernberger (1988). We found not only negligible TFP growth in industrial SOEs in the high-growth period of 1984–88, but also that excessive compensation paid to SOE personnel has weakened the financial performance of industrial SOEs. The only way which we could generate positive TFP growth for the SOEs in our sample was to understate the amount of intermediate inputs that they used.

Given the contradiction between our findings on SOE performance and those of recent papers, more work in this area is a clear priority for future research.

ACKNOWLEDGMENTS

We are grateful to the Ford Foundation, the Pacific Rim Research Program of the University of California, the World Institute for Development Economic Research, and the Chinese Academy of Social Sciences for supporting our research.

NOTES

1 Earlier studies that had concluded that post-1978 TFP growth was not out of line with poor TFP growth in the previous 30 years are Chow (1985), World Bank (1985), Dernberger (1988) and Perkins (1988).
2 Urban collectives are many times subsidiaries setup by SOEs to evade regulations on operations. County collectives are generally owned and managed by county governments, and in some cases have many of the operating characteristics of SOEs. The official statistics on TVEs now count all enterprises at and below the township level. The ownership rights of TVEs and their supervision by local authorities vary across regions. In many cases, the only tie between TVE managers and local authorities is an agreement on an annual financial contribution by the former.
3 Estimated from the 1981–86 regression in Table 11.2 by dividing the coefficient of the 1986 dummy by five.
4 Granick (1990), who also used Dollar's data set, noted that three of the firms were among the 10 firms that were selected in 1983 to receive "national awards for distinction in management" (p. 13); and "the sample enterprises were throughout (1976–1982) 40–120 percent more profitable than were Chinese state-owned industrial enterprises as a whole" (p. 180).
5 Source is Table 2.2.
6 Our sample consisted of 111 machinery firms, 85 materials firms, 58 food processing firms, 37 textile firms and nine miscellaneous firms.

7 Table 7 in JRZ.
8 Computed from Table 2.12 in *China Statistical Yearbook 1992* (English version, p. 28).
9 See Lau and Brada (1990) for an alternative frontier estimation method that did not require the dropping of observations, and that decomposed TFP into technical efficiency (how far within the existing production frontier) and technological progress (how far the production frontier moved).
10 Most studies on SOE efficiency also share this weakness.
11 Deduction is drawn from the degrees of freedom of the *F*-statistic reported in Table 6.
12 See Fan and Woo (1992) for a study on the relationship between Chinese-style enterprise reforms and macroeconomic instability.
13 Unless otherwise mentioned, we use the government borrowing requirement definition of budget deficit.
14 This point is argued in greater detail in Fan and Woo (1992).
15 Direct wage is defined as total cash income paid to employees, e.g., basic wage, bonus and subsidies. Indirect wage is defined as total non-cash income paid to employees. Non-cash income includes distribution of goods and "training" trips to historical places. Some items of indirect wage (e.g., training trips) were hidden as operating costs, so we added these "hidden wages" to the reported value added.
16 Data are from Tables 4.37 (industry), 7.1 (overall retail price index) and 10.16 in State Statistics Bureau of China, *China Statistical Yearbook 1991*. Direct wage is the sum of basic wage and *some* kinds of bonuses and cash subsidies.
17 Table 9 in Zhao (1992). Indirect wage growth rate computed by assuming a 4.1 percent annual growth rate for direct wage.
18 TVE data before 1984 is incomparable because of definitional changes.

REFERENCES

Chen Kuan, Wang Hongchang, Zheng Yuxin, Jefferson, G., & Rawski, T. (1988). Productivity change in Chinese industry: 1953–1985. *Journal of Comparative Economics, 12*(4), 570–591.

Chow, G. (1985). *The Chinese Economy*. New York: Harper and Row.

Dernberger, R. (1988). Financing China's development: Needs, sources and prospects. In R. Dernberger & R. Eckaus (Eds.), *Financing Asian development 2: China and India*. University Press of America. 12–68.

Dollar, D. (1990). Economic reform and allocative efficiency in China's state-owned industry. *Economic Development and Cultural Change, 39*(1), 89–105.

Fan, Gang, & Wing Thye Woo. (1992). Decentralized socialism and macroeconomic stability: Lessons from China. Working Paper No.411, Economics Department, University of California at Davis.

Granick, D. (1990). *Chinese state enterprises: A regional property rights analysis*. University of Chicago Press.

Jefferson, G. (1990). China's iron and steel industry sources of enterprise efficiency and impact of reform. *Journal of Development Economics, 33*(2), 329–355.

Jefferson, G., Rawski, T., & Yuxin Zheng. (1992). Growth, efficiency, and convergence in China's state and collective industry. *Economic Development and Cultural Change, 40*(2), 239–266.

Jefferson, G., & .Wenyi Xu. (1991). The impact of reform on socialist enterprises in transition: Structure, conduct, and performance in Chinese industry. *Journal of Comparative Economics, 15*(1), 45–64.

Lardy, N. (1989). Technical changes and economic reform in China: a tale of two sectors. Unpublished manuscript.

Naughton, B. (1991). Implications of the state monopoly over industry and its relaxation. Unpublished manuscript.

Perkins, D. (1988). Reforming China's economic system. *Journal of Economic Literature, 26*(2), 601–645.

Rawski, T. (1991). How fast has Chinese industry grown? Unpublished manuscript.

Svejnar, J. (1990). Productive efficiency and employment. In W. Byrd & Lin Qingsong (Eds.), *China's rural industry: Structure, development, and reform*. Oxford. 243–254.

Woo, Wing Thye, Wen Hai, Yibiao Jin, and Gang Fan. (1993). How successful has Chinese enterprise reform been? Pitfalls in opposite biases and focus. Unpublished manuscript.

World Bank. (1985). *China: Long-term development issues and options*. Johns Hopkins, Baltimore.

Zhao, Renwei. (1992). Some special phenomena in income distribution during China's transition period. *Economic Research (Jingji Yanjiu)*, Issue 1 (in Chinese). 53–63.

8

HOW INDUSTRIAL REFORM WORKED IN CHINA

The Role of Innovation, Competition and Property Rights

World Bank

In China early attempts at partial reform unleashed forces that, fifteen years later, have brought China's economy to the brink of a market system. The participation of tens of thousands of enterprises and millions of administrators, managers, and workers over the duration of the reform eventually built a constituency for market-directed change that was far stronger than any official announcement could have produced. Gradual and partial reform shifted the economy toward a market system under a regime of growth, improved productivity, accelerated technical change, and rising exports. Reactions of firms and governments focused increasingly on innovation, cost reduction, and further deregulation, deepening the cumulative impact of reform, rather than on rent-seeking and subsidies. This process of reform is very different from the top-down, centrally planned approach to reform that is widely advocated by international organizations and economic researchers, but it has produced a durable reform constituency that easily rebuffed high-level efforts to roll back reform in the wake of the inflation scare and political repression of 1989.

China's partial and gradual reform has combined rapid economic progress with institutions and policies that deviate widely from standard prescriptions for reform. China's reforms present economists with a puzzle. Why has China "grown so fast when conditions thought to be necessary for growth . . . were absent?" (Blanchard and Fischer 1993, p. 4). How did China's unorthodox reforms spark an economic surge that has far outpaced results in other ex-socialist economies and in many developing nations?

Many economists view the reform of former socialist economies as a process of replacing old institutions with new structures in an organized top-down

Source: Proceedings of the World Bank Annual Conference on Development Economics 1994 (Washington, D.C.: The World Bank, 1995), pp. 129–56.

fashion directed by reformers. The self-interested response of agents within the economy is expected to stimulate profit-seeking behavior and market activity. If progress is inadequate, planners can impose further rounds of reform.

This type of centrally directed reform has undoubtedly played a role in China's economic transition. It was China's central leadership that initiated economic reforms in the late 1970s, expanding the role of prices and market allocation, rolling back long-standing barriers to international trade and investment, transferring authority from central planners to enterprise managers and local governments, creating a system of dual (plan and market) pricing for industrial goods, and so on. But unlike the postcommunist leaders in countries like Poland and the Czech Republic, China's policymakers embarked on a path of reform with no clear vision of what a restructured economy should look like and no consensus about what policy mix or institutional arrangements would best get the economy there (Hus, Luo, and Zhang 1993; Shirk 1993; Naughton 1994).

Not surprisingly, policy announcements from the center were partial and tentative. The center ratified but did not direct the momentous shift from collective to household farming. Central initiatives in industrial reform focused on the incremental relaxation of controls over state-owned enterprises. Even the revolutionary "open door" strategy, reflected in a sequence of central decisions that shattered long-standing barriers to China's participation in the world economy, concentrated on expanding trade and investment activity in a small number of provinces and special zones along China's southeast coast.

From the usual top-down perspective China's recent economic gains seem remarkably large in relation to the central government's modest reform initiatives. In exploring this anomaly, we focus on an analysis of China's reform dynamics that shows how technical innovation, economizing behavior, market-leaning institutional changes, and a multitude of cumulative and mutually reinforcing choices by administrators, managers, and workers reinforced and eventually overshadowed Beijing's partial reform efforts. The focus is on industry, which it both the largest sector of China's economy and the core of its reform problem.

Successive rounds of partial reform have cumulated into significant changes in industrial structure, conduct, and performance affecting every type of firm, including old-line state firms. In this process partial reform initiatives produce unanticipated outcomes in an interplay of action and reaction among changes in economic conditions, ad hoc policy measures by various levels of government, and uncoordinated strategizing by enterprises and individuals. This interaction occurs in an environment of intense competition involving several types of firms, each with its own distinct technical capabilities and institutional constraints. Partial reform expands entry into product markets, and the ensuing intensification of competition erodes enterprise profits and undermines the revenue base at every level of government. These financial strains generate pressures that promote innovation and cost reduction. Government efforts to ease the revenue constraint and enterprise efforts to innovate and reduce costs lead to fresh rounds of market-directed institutional change.

WHAT NEEDS TO BE EXPLAINED ABOUT CHINA'S INDUSTRIAL REFORM

China's recent industrial achievements deviate from the orthodox reform scenarios in the continued dominance of the public sector; its improved performance, despite the absence of any plans for privatization; and the continued presence of important defects in the institutional underpinnings of China's industrial economy.

Rapid growth is amply documented in World Bank reports, which reveal the broad-based nature of industrial expansion. Joint ventures, foreign-owned firms, and private industry contributed only one-sixth of incremental output gains during 1980–92 (Table 8.1). Despite the highly publicized economic boom in China's southern coastal provinces, the region's 36 percent share in aggregate industrial output in 1992 was only modestly above its 30 percent share for 1978—and below the 36.6 percent share in 1952 (Industry 1949–84, p. 145; Survey 1993, p. 72).

The dominance of public enterprise

The output share of state-owned industry (firms "owned by the whole people" and directly or indirectly controlled by agencies of the central government) plunged from three-quarters to less than half between 1980 and 1992 (Table 8.1). This decline reflects dramatic gains by collectives, especially the rural firms known as township and village enterprises (or TVEs). The 1992 output share of public sector industry, however, which includes state firms and urban and rural collectives, exceeds 85 percent. The output share of private domestic firms remains small, at less than 10 percent.[1]

The explosive growth of TVE output has aroused intense interest. TVE firms, although different in many respects from state enterprises, are public enterprises. Calling TVEs "nonstate enterprises" conveys the misleading impression that rural collectives operate independently of officialdom. Some authors have speculated that TVE firms "mimic private enterprises" or operate like "loosely-structured cooperatives" (Singh, Ratha, and Xiao 1993; Weitzman and Xu 1994). TVE operations are closely monitored and often controlled by "local government entrepreneurs" (Zweig 1991, p. 720) who "exhibit characteristics of both de facto owners and senior managers of township corporations" (Whiting 1993, p. 6).[2] The TVE sector is built on the foundation of earlier industrialization efforts undertaken by local

Table 8.1 Overview of industrial performance in China, 1980–92

	Index of real output (1980 = 100)			*Shares in nominal output (percent)*				*1980–92 (percent)*	
Ownership type	*1985*	*1990*	*1992*	*1980*	*1985*	*1990*	*1992*	*Annual average growth*	*Share of incremental output*
State	148	210	257	76.0	64.9	54.6	48.4	7.8	43.6
Collective	247	554	914					18.4	
Urban				13.7	13.3	10.3	11.8		11.5
Township-village				9.9	18.8	25.3	26.2		28.8
Private[a]	21,752	126,057	241,455	0.0	1.9	5.4	6.8	64.9	7.9
Other[b]	492	3,530	8,736	0.5	1.2	4.4	7.2	37.2	8.3
Total	176	328	480	100.0	100.0	100.0	100.0	13.1	100.0
Total output (¥ billion)				515.4	971.6	2,392.5	3,706.6		

Note:
[a] Privately owned firms employing fewer than eight workers.
[b] Includes private firms employing eight or more workers, joint ventures, foreign-owned firms, and other ownership forms.

Source: Yearbook 1993, pp. 409–13; Rawski forthcoming.

governments (Perkins and others 1977). Like their predecessors, the TVE firms of the 1980s and 1990s operate "under close supervision from the township or village industrial departments" (Wong, Heady, and Woo 1993, chap. 9), which contribute start-up funds, appoint managers, and "are intimately involved in major strategic decisions" (Ody 1991, p. iv).[3]

Improved performance in state industry

No one disputes the significance of the contributions that TVEs have made to the growth of production, exports, productivity, employment, incomes, and material welfare. Their success shows the insufficiency of assuming that a full and immediate end to official influence over enterprise management, preferably through privatization, is a necessary step in the reform of socialist systems.

But the inconsistency between recent Chinese industrial experience and free-market orthodoxy runs even deeper. China's old-line state enterprises have responded to ongoing partial reform by behaving less like passive bureaucratic followers and more like profit-seeking commercial businesses. Reform has altered the objectives, incentives, and corporate culture of state firms, bringing substantial improvements in performance. With State industry accounting for nearly half of industrial output and absorbing 35 percent of aggregate fixed investment, China's recent economic gains could hardly have occurred had state industry served only as a drag on economic progress.[4]

This article is not the place for a detailed review of evidence supporting these assertions.[5] The discussion here is limited to the following propositions about state industry, each resting on substantial empirical foundations:

- State enterprises, formerly devoted to plan fulfillment, now take profit as their chief objective. Data on state enterprise performance generate increasingly robust statistical relationships of the kind expected from profit-seeking firms operating in a competitive market setting.
- State enterprises have achieved substantial increases in labor productivity and steady, although modest, increases in total factor productivity.[6]
- State enterprises have sharply increased the pace of research and development, new product development, and process innovation (Jefferson, Rawski, and Zheng 1992a,b).
- Exports of state enterprise manufactures, which increased at an estimated annual rate of 18 percent between 1985 and 1992, reflect the impact of greater attention to quality, variety, customer requirements, and cost control.[7]
- State enterprises constitute an important and often crucial source of technology, equipment, funds, information, expertise, and marketing opportunities essential for the successful development of TVEs.

Persistence of institutional weaknesses

In looking at China's recent achievements, the challenge is to explain dramatic gains in industrial performance in the absence of comprehensive efforts at the center to promote liberalization and institutional change. The key question concerns the process that has moved public sector firms reared under state planning to place unprecedented emphasis on efficiency, quality, and innovation, with no program or even credible threat of privatization, and to explain how China's industrial advances have occurred without the features that many economists regard as core elements of a market system.

Chinese industry continues to operate in an environment of incomplete specification of property rights. Rules of commerce are neither clearly defined nor consistently enforced. Competing firms in the same industry or locality face widely differing legal, fiscal, and regulatory regimes. Government intervention in business affairs extends well beyond the boundaries observed in even heavily regulated market economies (Japan, Republic of Korea), often with the effect of softening budget constraints. These difficulties restrict innovation and productivity growth, particularly, but not exclusively, in the state sector.[8] They have also enabled insolvent and hopelessly inefficient state enterprises to continue to operate, wasting large amounts of productive resources and requiring subsidies large enough to affect macroeconomic stability (Sachs and Woo 1993; Woo and others 1993). The cost of these institutional shortcomings, although difficult to quantify, appears large.

A MODEL FOR ANALYZING INDUCED INDUSTRIAL REFORM

We propose the following model of China's industrial reform, which we see as a cumulative process that begins when partial relaxation of the institutional constraints associated with socialist planning initiates competition in the markets for industrial products. Competition reduces profits, creating financial pressures that induce technical innovations, promote economizing behavior, and stimulate fresh rounds of market-leaning institutional change. This model rests on four key institutional features of China's industrial economy: decentralized supervision, incipient competition, fiscal dependence on industrial profits, and a hierarchy of heterogeneous enterprise types.[9]

Decentralized supervision

Central control of industrial enterprises was never as tight in China as in Eastern Europe and the Soviet Union (Granick 1990). Decentralization increased during the late 1960s and 1970s as the central government transferred supervision of many firms to provincial and municipal governments. This system of decentralized supervision encouraged provinces and localities to create and pursue their own industrial development strategies. When reform began, decentralized decisionmaking also made it possible to introduce piecemeal reforms and to conduct local policy experiments without disrupting the whole economy. Successful local reforms inspired widespread emulation.

Incipient competition

The term "incipient competition" well describes the circumstances of domestic Chinese markets for industrial products on the eve of reform. Actual competition was sharply limited by policies that had the effect of creating strong barriers to entry. Removing these barriers, however, quickly revealed multiple competitors in nearly every product line. In China, unlike Russia and other countries of the former Soviet Union and Eastern Europe, deregulation leads to industrial competition, not to monopoly.

Competitive pressures arose from four sources. Rural industry developed widely in the decades prior to reform but was largely confined to fabricating local materials into goods for local buyers (Perkins and others 1977). Entrepreneurial leaders in hundreds of counties and thousands of production brigades were poised to take advantage of deregulation by bursting into markets that they had coveted for years. China's southern regions, excluded from large-scale industrial investment during three decades of central planning, took advantage of the new open door policy to promote industrial growth with the aid of capital, skill, and commercial contacts from overseas Chinese, most of whom trace their ancestry to the southern coastal provinces. Defense conversion brought strong new entrants into a number of civilian industries; by the early 1990s at least two-thirds of output from defense industries consisted of civilian products (Blasko 1994). Finally, China's long-standing policy of building complete sets of state-owned industries in most provinces provided a ready-made source of competition.

Fiscal dependence on industrial profits

Industrial profits and tax payments are a key component of fiscal revenue at every level of government. State enterprises contributed 80 percent or more of adjusted budgetary revenues in every year during 1978–87; in 1988 state industry accounted for 73 percent of profits and profit taxes from all state enterprises (Sicular 1992, Table 5 and p. 3).

The fiscal reforms of the 1980s created a system in which each level of government collected taxes from enterprises under its jurisdiction, "turned over a contractually specified amount to the next higher level of government, and could keep the residual." The result was "a shift toward local fiscal power at the expense of the center, as the center's proportion of total government revenue fell" from 50 percent in the 1970s to less than 30 percent in the 1980s (Walder 1994, pp. 17, 19).

Chinese industry as a hierarchy of heterogeneous enterprise types

China's industrial sector displays extreme heterogeneity. There is a hierarchy of domestic industrial enterprises ranging from foreign-linked firms to state enterprises, urban and rural (TVE) collectives, and private businesses. These groups of firms exhibit systematic differences in technological capabilities, cost structures, and institutional arrangements. There is an inverse relation between innovative capability and labor costs. Among domestic firms, state enterprises have the greatest technical strength. They also have the highest labor costs and suffer the greatest restriction from institutional constraints. TVEs are least affected by institutional limitations. The interaction of these different enterprise types creates a kind of innovation and competition ladder.

Vernon (1966) and Grossman and Helpman (1991) have developed models of international product cycles and quality ladders that focus on interactions between innovative firms in the "North" and imitators in the "South." Northern firms rely on product innovations to support their high-cost manufacturing operations. Southern firms, with lower production costs, can capture markets from northern rivals by replicating northern products. The North retaliates with fresh rounds of innovation. Rivalry among different types of producers leads to an ongoing evolution of product characteristics, while the locus of manufacturing activity may shift back and forth between firms located in the "industrial" North and those in the "developing" South.

This approach fits nicely with China's recent industrial history once we extend these concepts to encompass the existence of product cycles and quality ladders *within the domestic economy of nations participating in global trade* as well as across high- and low-wage economies. Chinese industrial goods rarely match the quality and characteristics of products manufactured by global leaders. But the most accomplished Chinese firms, on their own or with the cooperation of foreign partners, can produce reasonable substitutes at a low cost. Rapidly growing exports of textiles, garments, footwear, machinery, and consumer durables illustrate China's participation in international quality ladders.

At the top of the international quality ladder are the overseas firms that set the innovative pace in global markets. These firms define technical and quality standards that Chinese firms seek to attain. Chinese industry has its own hierarchy of firms that generates domestic versions of the rivalries, flows, and pressures associated with global product cycles. On the top rung of China's domestic ladder of technological capabilities are foreign-invested firms; below them are state enterprises, urban collectives, TVEs, and privately owned firms. We focus on the three largest categories.

- *Foreign-invested firms*. Close foreign links give these firms better access to foreign capital and technologies than purely domestic competitors. While foreign-linked firms operate under many of the restrictions that apply to state enterprises, they enjoy favorable tax treatment and special autonomy in labor-management relations, wage setting, and foreign trade. China's open door policy has allowed these firms to flourish, with beneficial effects on export growth, technology inflows, and the spread of opportunities for purely domestic firms to explore new approaches to production, management, and sales.

- *State-owned enterprises*. State enterprises were the traditional centerpiece of economic planning. Decades of favorable treatment have endowed them with a legacy of technical capabilities surpassing those of other domestic enterprise types. At the same time, state enterprises bear heavier burdens of social responsibilities and bureaucratic intrusion than any other type of enterprise.
- *Collective enterprises*. Urban and rural collectives are owned by local governments and sometimes by state enterprises. Their operations are generally more labor-intensive than state enterprise production; their products typically cluster at the low end of the price-quality spectrum. Some of these firms have begun to apply modern technologies and sophisticated equipment to produce goods that can compete in national and international markets as well as in local markets.

There is a well-defined hierarchy of domestic technological capabilities extending downward from joint ventures to state enterprises and collectives. Among purely domestic firms state enterprises enjoy superior endowments of equipment, laboratory facilities, and skilled and educated workers, technicians, and managers. This resource differential favoring state firms shows up in the outcomes of quality inspections. In the fourth quarter of 1993, for example, 73.8 percent of goods from a sample of 2,221 firms passed inspection; the success rate was 90 percent for "big state enterprises" but only 62 percent for "township and private manufacturers" (Ma 1994).[10] Managers of urban collectives and TVEs (as well as state enterprises) overwhelmingly identify state firms as the domestic technological leaders in their own industries (Jefferson, Rawski, and Zheng 1992b).

As in the transnational version of the product cycle, technology percolates down China's domestic quality ladder. The example of bar coding illustrates how links with international markets necessitate the mastery of suitable technologies and the achievement of specific quality standards that gradually spread into the domestic economy. Export-oriented firms have learned to use bar codes, which they see as "tickets to foreign supermarkets." Today only a few dozen domestic retail outlets use bar codes. But by the end of 1995 "China aims to have bar codes on all its exported goods and 60 percent of domestic commodities" (Sun 1994, p. 8).

One important and widely overlooked aspect of Chinese quality ladders is the dependence of many TVE producers on funds, equipment, product designs, technical information, management skills, and subcontracting opportunities obtained from state enterprises (Jefferson and Rawski 1994). In southern Jiangsu province (near Shanghai), a center of booming rural enterprise development, "more than two-thirds of township and village enterprises . . . have established various forms of economic and technical cooperation arrangements with industrial enterprises, research units, and higher educational institutions in larger cities" (Xu, Mao, and Yuan 1993). Officials attempting to develop industry in poor localities are encouraged to pursue "joint operations with Scientific research organizations or large- and medium-scale enterprises" (Du, Huang, and Chen 1992).

The domestic quality ladder also resembles its international counterpart in that cost pressures move in the opposite direction from technological capabilities. The manager of a TVE garment firm that had begun with an infusion of cash and used equipment from a much larger state enterprise observed that "in the area of product quality, household producers can't match collectives and collectives can't match state enterprises; but as for costs, state enterprises can't match collectives and the collectives can't match individual households" (interview, June 1993). Wage costs are highest in foreign-invested firms and lowest in TVEs (Table 8.2). The cost advantage of collectives over state firms is a staple topic of discussion in Chinese newspapers and economic journals, which emphasize the extra burden of pensions, taxes, redundant workers, fringe benefits, and welfare responsibilities assigned to state firms, especially compared with TVEs. The extra cost burdens are large and, in some cases, growing rapidly. For example, state enterprises are obliged to pay retirement benefits out of current income. National data (probably excluding the farm populace) show that the ratio of retirees to active workers increased from 1:26 in 1978 to 1:6 in 1990 (Du and Shang 1993). A 1989 sample study showed that enterprises paid about 232 yuan per worker for medical costs (Du and Shang 1993); by 1993 a survey of 100 units in Hebei province found average annual medical costs of 1,201 yuan—equivalent to 37 percent of money wages (Li and Qin 1993).[11]

Table 8.2 Average wages for different classes of enterprise in China's textile industry, 1989–91 (yuan per person-year)

Ownership type	*1989*	*1990*	*1991*
Joint venture	3,663	4,232	5,674
State sector	2,069	2,252	2,377
Urban collective	1,368	1,688	1,862
Township-village	1,132[a]	—	—

— Not available.

a. Average wage for all TVE industries.

Source: Jefferson, Rawski, and Zheng 1994.

Distinct technical and institutional frontiers

Firms occupying different rungs of the quality ladder face different institutional regimes, which implies that domestic competition may take the form of efforts to remake institutions as well as products. Economists think of innovations as changes in technology (a new product) or managerial systems (just-in-time inventory controls) that expand the production frontiers for individual firms or whole industries, while the firm's objectives, behavior, organization, and surrounding institutional environment remain unchanged. Since the task of economic reform consists precisely of altering these basic circumstances, the assumption of institutional stability within and outside the firm is not tenable in transition economies.

Firms in transition economies face separate technical and institutional frontiers: the technical frontier embraces the standard idea (in its neoclassical or evolutionary form) that firms can draw on alternative blueprints or techniques to transform resources (including knowledge and experience) into products. The institutional frontier delineates the set of resource configurations that is attainable under prevailing custom, law, and regulation. In the context of socialist systems and transition economies, institutional restrictions prevent the exploitation of many options that are technically feasible and block choices that would be made in the absence of institutional change.[12]

Chinese authors routinely comment on the long-standing practice of applying separate laws and regulations to firms operating under different ownership arrangements. We have already mentioned differences in taxation and labor costs. Regulatory regimes affecting labor unions, environmental hazards, workplace safety, and the like are applied more vigorously to joint ventures and state firms than to urban or rural collectives. TVEs benefit from short lines of command. Business decisions are often reached through a single telephone conversation or a meeting of two or three people. State firms, by contrast, often report to multiple supervisory agencies whose overlapping jurisdictions and competing agendas complicate even routine business decisions (Byrd 1992). Shorter lines of command make it easier for TVE's to reach decisions and form business coalitions with domestic or foreign partners. TVEs and joint ventures can dismiss workers more easily than can state enterprises. Jefferson, Lu, and Zhao (1994), using a composite indicator of management authority, find a high degree of decisionmaking autonomy at the enterprise level for nearly two-thirds of 300 TVEs surveyed in 1991 but for less than half of 900 state enterprises. Bankruptcy, long a reality for TVEs, is only now emerging as a possibility for state firms.

THE DYNAMICS OF PARTIAL REFORM IN CHINA'S INDUSTRY

We see the dynamics of partial reform in China's industry as a succession of responses to imbalance by both enterprises and governments. Our framework is in the tradition of Hirschman's (1958) analysis of unbalanced growth. The dynamic that transforms partial reform into improved performance is simple and direct:

- The government implements partial reform measures that reduce entry barriers and lower the cost of many types of transactions. These initiatives have different impacts, on the options available to various groups of firms. Partial reform accelerates the domestic product cycle by facilitating the transmission of cost pressures and technologies up and down the hierarchy of industrial enterprises.
- The differential impact of reform efforts destabilizes the existing division of industrial resources and product markets among different types of firms. Competition in industrial product markets intensifies.
- Stronger competition diminishes the flow of quasi-rents derived from the enforcement of entry barriers and market segmentation. Reduced profitability limits the growth of wages and bonuses for some firms and throws others into a position of financial loss. The erosion of profits also limits the growth of revenues accruing to local and provincial authorities and to the central government.
- Firms react to financial pressures by choosing strategies involving one or more of the following components: restructuring operations, lobbying for further deregulation to facilitate profit-seeking initiatives, and lobbying for government subsidies or official intervention to restore the initial financial position.
- Governments also react to financial pressures that reduce their share of total output and destabilize the distribution of fiscal revenue across regions and administrative levels. Officials face conflicting enterprise lobbying efforts, some demanding further autonomy and deregulation, others seeking protection from the effects of earlier reforms.
- These induced responses of firms and governments further erode entry barriers and reduce transaction costs. Beneficial feedback effects accelerate every dimension of the reform process by intensifying competition, further diminishing quasi-rents, and motivating enterprises and governments to undertake new reform efforts. These changes set in motion further rounds of technical development, economizing efforts, and incremental reform.
- This entire process affects the attitudes of enterprise personnel and government officials to the direction and outcome of reform. Changing attitudes affect the objectives and strategies of all participants.

Although this mechanism focuses attention on endogenous or bottom-up aspects of the reform process, not every industrial policy initiative undertaken since the beginning of reform represents an endogenous response to the initial partial reform effort. Many policy changes, such as the partial commercialization of bank lending and the reduction of budgetary appropriations for industrial research and development projects, probably represent a combination of endogenous response and exogenous initiative.

Furthermore, there is no guarantee that partial reform will succeed. If governments act to stifle competition, equalize financial outcomes for winners and losers, or alter regulations to restore the prereform status quo in product markets, the endogenous process linking initial reforms with innovation, economizing, and further institutional change may stall.

We see this cumulative process of endogenous response as the key to explaining how China recorded unexpectedly strong achievements in both growth and institutional change despite modest reform initiatives on the part of its central government. Our discussion focuses on seven propositions about Chinese industrial reform corresponding to each element of the model.

Proposition 1: Partial reform erodes market segmentation, thereby lowering barriers to technology and resource flows

China's reforms of the late 1970s restored household agriculture and reopened rural markets; expanded China's participation in global markets for commodities, capital, and technology; and began to loosen controls in the industrial sector. Each of these policy shifts eroded barriers to competition in industrial factor and product markets.

Agricultural reforms provided a big boost to China's rural industries by increasing the supply of labor and raw materials and, following the quick rise of farm incomes, boosting demand for output. As Sachs and Woo (1994) point out, China's comparatively large rural sector creates possibilities for rapid productivity growth that are not accessible to more urbanized states like the Czech Republic, Poland, and Russia.

The open door policy brought a rapid increase in imports of industrial goods, many of them competing directly with domestic products. Partial liberalization of the external sector sharply reduced the transaction costs associated with international inflows of capital, technology, market information, managerial skills, and equipment. New policies speeded the transfer of capabilities and cost pressures across China's borders and throughout the hierarchy of domestic enterprises. The pace of change was particularly rapid in regions of southern China that benefited from proximity to Hong Kong as well as from accelerated deregulation.

The initial industrial reforms were directed mainly at large-scale, urban-based state enterprises. The objective was to enliven large-scale industry by encouraging firms to shed the passive mentality of plan followers in favor of self-motivated efforts to take full advantage of available resources. Large firms were allowed to retain a portion of their profits. And because discretionary funds cannot stimulate production or innovation unless they can be used to acquire productive inputs, the reforms included measures that diverted industrial resources from planned allocation into market channels.

Although intended to stimulate state enterprises, these measures had their largest impact in the TVE sector. Urban-oriented reform enabled TVEs to obtain inputs formerly reserved for clients of the plan system and to penetrate markets outside their home areas. The relaxation of restrictions on information-sharing, consulting, and technical ties across urban-rural administrative boundaries made it easier for collectives and TVEs to adopt new technologies and to produce substitutes that could compete with state enterprise products. These changes shattered constraints that had previously restricted TVE growth. The result was an unexpected growth explosion in China's rural industries.

These partial and uneven reforms substantially eroded barriers that had long obstructed flows of resources and products across the boundaries separating different types of firms and different administrative and bureaucratic jurisdictions. As old distinctions gradually blurred, resources, products, funds, and information began to circulate in new directions. The new market channels were soon large enough to leave quantitative traces in the form of shrinking divergences in factor returns among different enterprise groups (Table 8.3). The bright growth prospects and high rates of return enjoyed by TVEs at the start of reform attracted a large inflow of funds, which pushed down returns to TVE capital. Naughton (1992) documents a related phenomenon: the convergence of rates of return to capital across different

Table 8.3 Profit/capital ratios in different segments of Chinese industry, selected years, 1980–92 (percent)

	Before taxes			*After taxes*		
Year	*State enterprises*	*Urban collectives*	*TVEs*	*State enterprises*	*Urban collectives*	*TVEs*
1980	24.8	26.6	32.5	16.0	18.5	26.7
1982	23.4	22.0	28.0	14.4	13.8	20.2
1984	24.2	22.3	24.6	14.9	13.9	15.2
1985	23.8	24.5	23.7	13.2	15.3	14.5
1988	20.6	19.7	17.9	10.4	11.3	9.3
1990	12.4	—	13.0	3.2	—	5.9
1992	9.7	—	14.2	2.7	—	7.2

— Not available.

Note: Rate of return is the ratio of the sum of profit figures (positive or negative) for all firms to the sum of net (of depreciation) value of fixed assets plus average amount of working capital in use.

Source: State enterprises, Yearbook 1991, p. 416; yearbook 1992, p. 437, Urban collectives, Industry 1984, p. 85; Industry 1986, p. 87; and State Statistical Bureau. TVEs, Yearbook 1991, pp. 377–79; Yearbook 1993, pp. 396–97.

branches of industry. These changes occurred prior to the creation of organized capital markets, which remain embryonic even today.

Access to high-level technical personnel offers another example of declining market segmentation. Comparing data from China's 1985 industrial census with 1989 survey results reveals a big increase in the availability of engineers and technicians outside the state sector. Using the 1989 survey data, Jefferson, Rawski, and Zheng (1992c) find a surprisingly close correspondence between the marginal profitability of upper-level technicians within state enterprises, TVEs, and urban collective firms in three branches of industry.

Proposition 2: reform intensifies competition in markets for industrial products

On the eve of reform China's industry was in a position of incipient competition, with large numbers of potential entrants poised to intensify product-market competition. Partial reform rapidly turned this potential into reality. Booming imports of manufactures, swift expansion of joint ventures and other foreign-linked enterprises, and rapid erosion of the economic and administrative barriers preventing state enterprises from raiding each other's customers all contributed to the upsurge of competition. The greatest impetus to competition came from the growth of TVE production, which leaped from 10 to 25 percent of total industrial output between 1980 and 1990 (see Table 8.1).

Competition expanded most rapidly in markets directly affected by the growth of TVE output, but competitive pressures extended to other markets as well. By the late 1980s more than half of industrial products were being sold through markets, and that share has since risen to more than 80 percent. Less than 10 percent of industrial output is decided through mandatory plans. Concentration ratios are low and declining (Jefferson and Rawski 1994). With competition from manufactured imports on the rise and barriers to domestic trade increasingly porous, it is clear that partial reform has firmly installed rivalrous produce markets as a regular feature of everyday operations for most of China's industrial enterprises. Few firms remain immune from competition. The experience of the Luoyang Tractor Works, China's largest manufacturer of wheeled tractors and bulldozers, is illustrative. According to an article in *China Daily*, Luoyang "is trying to improve the quality of its products as well as its marketing and publicity techniques in a bid to offset . . . sluggish domestic sales. . . . The Luoyang tractor complex had been forced to sacrifice more than half of its profits in trying discounts, lotteries, and free delivery of goods to boost sales" (Gao 1990).

Proposition 3: competition erodes profits and curtails the growth of fiscal revenues

Reform has brought a large decline in industrial profits. Rates of return for state enterprises and TVEs in 1990–92 are less than half what they were in 1980–82 (see Table 8.3). Rates of return (including taxes) by industry confirm the impression of declining profits (Table 8.4). Growing opportunities for tax evasion have widened the error margins for reported profit totals. Wang (1992) cites studies suggesting that the hidden profits of state industry in 1990 may have surpassed the amounts reported to the statistical authorities. Some observers (Sicular 1992) argue that the decline in profitability is mild, confined mostly to state enterprises, and may reflect cyclical factors (the retrenchment of 1988–90). Despite these qualifications, the data strongly support the hypothesis of secular decline (see Tables 8.3 and 8.4), especially since the boom years of 1992 and 1993 brought no revival in rates of return.

Rates of return shown in Table 8.4 also reflect the powerful impact of TVE competition on industrial profitability. In the early years of reform, profits fell fastest in branches with the greatest TVE activity. During 1980–85 falling profitability was concentrated in industries using agricultural raw materials,

Table 8.4 Rates of return to capital in Chinese industry, 1980–93 (percent)

Sector	*1980*	*1985*	*1991*	*1992*	*1993*
Industry	25.2	23.8	11.9	10.1	10.6
Light industry	49.1	31.8	15.0		
Farm materials	54.7	32.0	15.9		
Nonfarm materials	39.1	31.5	13.0		
Heavy industry	18.5	20.3	10.2		
Sectors with active TVE competition					
Food processing	20.4	17.5	9.7		
Beverage	48.5	28.4	18.6		
Tobacco	326.9	207.4	113.6		
Textile	69.0	26.5	6.6		
Apparel	46.0	26.0	11.7		
Leather, hides	30.3	19.4	5.6		
Handicrafts	43.0	27.4	12.0		
Plastics	31.6	21.2	9.1		
Sectors with limited TVE competition					
Power	20.6	16.0	13.0		
Chemicals	22.0	21.7	14.0		
Ferrous metallurgy	18.3	25.8	15.5		
Machinery	13.0	19.3	7.9		
Electronic	14.0	24.9	8.5		

Note: Rate of return equals taxes plus profits as a percentage of the net (of depreciation) value of fixed assets plus working capital.

Source: Data for 1992 and 1993, communique 1994. Other data, industry 1992, pp. 168–78.

especially beverages, tobacco, textiles, and apparel. During the second half of the 1980s the downward pressure on profitability extended to branches with little direct TVE competition, including power, chemicals, iron and steel, machinery, and electronics, but profitability eroded even more in branches with strong TVE activity. The 1991 rates of return for branches with extensive TVE participation are less than half the 1980 base; none of the branches with limited TVE participation experienced as steep a drop in profitability. Singh, Ratha, and Xiao (1993), using provincial data for 1984–89, also show that faster growth of nonstate industry (collective, foreign-invested, and private firms) is associated with lower profit rates for state industry.

Profit erosion also affected government revenue, which has declined sharply as a share of total output from about 30 percent in the early 1980s (as reform began) to 20 percent at the end of the decade and to 14 percent in 1992 (Wong, Heady, and Woo 1993). Slow growth of revenues from industry, the chief source of government income, was the principal cause.

Proposition 4: Enterprises react to market pressure by searching for financial gain

Enterprises facing competition and declining profit margins have several options for strengthening their financial position. They can improve their performance within existing institutional limits, pressure the government to extend greater autonomy and incentives to the firm, or pursue rent-seeking alternatives (subsidies, soft loans to offset losses, lobbying for restrictions to stifle competition). We examine the firm's opportunities in each of these directions.

Improve performance within existing institutional limits

Chinese state enterprises, particularly firms facing fierce competition and declining profits, have demonstrated a substantial capacity to economize and innovate. As state-owned enterprises came under increasing competitive pressures during the 1980s, total factor productivity improved steadily (Wu 1993). Singh, Ratha, and Xiao (1994) establish an explicit link between competitive pressure and productivity growth by showing that total factor productivity in state industry rose most rapidly in provinces with the largest shares of nonstate production in total industrial output.

We tested this association between competition and state enterprise efficiency using the following regression equation with 1990 enterprise data:

$$\ln(Q/L) = -1.25 + 0.63\ln(K/L) + 0.09\,\text{COMP} + 0.65\,\text{PCOMP} - 0.11\ln(NK/K)$$
$$\quad\quad (3.04)(13.94) \quad\quad (2.55) \quad\quad (4.72) \quad\quad (2.54)$$

$$R^2 = 0.32,\ \text{obs.} = 496, \tag{1}$$

where *Q/L* is labor productivity, *K/L* is the capital-labor ratio, and *NK/K* is the share of nonindustrial capital held by the enterprise.[13] COMP and PCOMP are measures of competition—COMP is an estimate of the elasticity of demand for the firm's major product and PCOMP reflects the firm's assessment of the overall competitive pressure it faces.[14] Using either panels of provincial data or cross-sectional enterprise data, we consistently find that competitive pressures motivate firms to improve overall efficiency.

The partial reforms of the 1980s also brought a distinct acceleration of innovative activity in state enterprises. One survey of eighty state enterprises found that the value of new products as a share of gross output rose from 13.5 percent in 1980 to 18.7 percent in 1985 and to 24.2 percent in 1989 (Jefferson, Rawski and Zheng 1992b). Similarly, in a 1992 survey of 10 percent of China's large and medium-size industrial enterprises, 91.6 percent of the 954 respondents described efforts at product and process innovation. More than half reported major modification to their main products, 80.7 percent had new products in the marketplace, 60.8 percent were engaged in major process innovation, and 65.5 percent were implementing new production technologies (Ma and Zhao 1993).

A second set of panel data covering 249 enterprises in the textile, electronics, and equipment industries provides information on output of new products (but not on the intensity of competition) that allows us to examine the impact of changes in profitability during 1984–86 on new product innovation during 1986–88. We assume a two-year lag between changes in profitability and shifts in the output share of new products. Product innovation is constrained by two factors: diminishing returns to product innovation, captured by NPS86, the initial 1986 share of new products in total output; and financial capacity, represented by PRO86, the 1986 ratio of profit (including tax) to sales. Our estimation yields the following result:

$$\underset{}{\text{NPS8886}} = \underset{(0.617)}{0.005} - \underset{(1.970)}{0.320}\ \text{PRO8684} - \underset{(7.908)}{0.443}\ \text{NPS86} + \underset{(5.921)}{0.371}\ \text{PRO86}$$

$$R^2 = 0.250,\ \text{obs.} = 210. \qquad (2)$$

Here NPS8886 is the change in the share of new products in output value during 1986–88 sod PRO8684 is the change in the profit-sales ratio during 1984–86.[15] These estimation results confirm that declining profitability creates an incentive to innovate, conditional upon the enterprise's financial capability and the diminishing returns to innovation.

Seek greater autonomy and strengthened incentives

Along with efforts to improve performance within existing institutional limits, financially pressed enterprises seek greater autonomy and a larger share of residual earnings. Through the mid-1980s circumstances and opportunities were widely regarded as more favorable for collective or private firms. Toward the late 1980s published materials and interviews with factory managers began to reveal a gradual shift toward the view that the autonomy associated with collective ownership had come to outweigh the privileges available within the state sector, leaving state enterprises at a competitive disadvantage. State firms complain of administrative interference and cost-inflating obligations that TVE firms and joint ventures often escape. Managers in the state sector have gradually emerged as active agents for reform.

Seek rents in the form of direct subsidies and soft loans

A final avenue of response for financially distressed enterprises is to seek rents in the form of direct subsidies, soft loans, and a competition-stifling resumption of regulation. We assume that whenever such assistance is available, enterprises will pursue it as long as the expected payoff exceeds the cost of lobbying. From this perspective the attitude of governments controls the distribution of enterprise resources between economizing and innovation on the one hand and rent-seeking on the other. The following section considers whether reform has reduced the availability of various types of direct and hidden subsidies for enterprises experiencing financial distress.

Proposition 5: On balance, government policy increases industry autonomy and market exposure and hardens budget constraints

The central facts of life for Chinese public finance in the 1980s includes slowdown in revenue growth, a significant hardening of budget constraints for subnational governments (Walder 1994), and repeated episodes of macroeconomic instability attributable to fiscal deficits and excessive monetary expansion.

Subnational governments are generally more able but less willing to subsidize weak firms and industries than their counterparts at the center. The reason is simple: fierce competition among development-conscious subnational jurisdictions. Diverting resources from development spending to subsidies threatens to undercut the ability of provinces, cities, counties, townships, and villages to attract domestic and foreign investment. With local revenues increasingly tied to the growth of profits from local industry, slow growth of investment endangers the revenue prospects of the same bureaus and officials faced with requests for subsidies and protection.

Under these circumstances, how do officials respond to the pleas of firms whose financial interests are damaged by competition? They have two main options: to grant direct or indirect subsidies or to push enterprises toward the market. While subsidies continue, evidence shows that government policy has gradually tilted toward sending enterprises to market.

Subsidies for TVEs are rare. Loss-making firms are closed and their workers are dismissed. At the start of reform, state enterprises typically expected full compensation for losses. By 1986 the ratio of subsidies to losses for state industry had dropped to 0.8 (Table 8.5). Another sharp dropoff in compensation occurred with the retrenchment of 1988 and 1989. Despite some confusion about the exact timing and scope, it is clear that a decade of partial reform has established a declining scale of partial compensation as the general rule for loss-making state industrial firms.

Direct subsidy is not the only avenue of government support for weak enterprises. Public officials can use tax concessions, regulatory protection, and soft bank credits to sustain loss-making firms. Tax concessions are limited by the same constraint as subsidy payments: the high opportunity cost of committing scarce fiscal resources. Regulatory protection runs counter to the general trend of China's domestic and international economic policy. Governments rely on both these tools in specific instances, but large increases in tax concessions or protective trade restrictions are widely viewed as undesirable and unfeasible. In the words of Vice Minister of the State Economic and Trade Commission Chen Qingtai: "In the past enterprises turned to the government when they ran into difficulty because the government could lower taxes and allowed them to retain more profits. This road has now been basically closed" (1994, p. 48).

This leaves the banking system as the primary vehicle for large-scale indirect support of weak firms. China's banks certainly experience strong official pressure to advance funds to weak borrowers. "Policy loans" that are viewed as unrepayable from the start are extended to both large and small industries at the behest of powerful official interests. Finance officials indicate that such loans account for about 30 percent of new lending, with most of the soft credits destined for investment projects (1992 interview).

Table 8.5 Losses and subsidies for Chinese state enterprises, 1986–91 (billions of yuan)

	All public enterprises			*State-owned industries*		
Year	*Loss*	*Subsidy*	*Ratio*[a]	*Loss*	*Subsidy*[b]	*Ratio*[a]
1986	47.71	32.5	0.78	4.71		0.81
1987	48.17	37.5	0.78	5.07		0.72
1988	52.06	44.6	0.86	7.13		0.73
1989	74.96	59.9	0.80	12.80	9.50	0.74 [.53]
1990	93.26	57.9	0.62	27.88	11.80	0.42 [.34]
1991	93.11	50.6	0.54	30.02	14.50	0.48 [.40]

Notes:
[a] Subsidy/loss.
[b] Information provided by the World Bank.

Source: All public enterprises; losses, Hwa 1992; subsidies, World Bank 1992, p. 242. State industries: Wong, Heady, and Woo 1993; World Bank estimates.

Policy lending is an important component of Chinese industrial policy, but it is subject to restrictions. Increases in bank lending have the same inflationary potential as government deficits. Furthermore, the banks, which have developed systems of credit ratings as part of their own profit-seeking agenda (Whiting 1993), have already cut the "policy" component of current lending to less than 10 percent (1993 interview). Banks can be expected to defend their business autonomy with increasing tenacity.

Partly for this reason, China's government has begun to implement financial reforms that will create three layers of financial institutions: a central bank, policy banks to support official priorities, and profit-oriented commercial banks. These reforms will shift the locus of conflict without resolving the problems facing loss-makers. The vice governor of the central bank, reaffirming his determination to "exercise stringent control over the money supply," insists that the new policy-lending banks "must be careful not to run in the red." Yao Zhenyan, president of one of the new policy institutions, makes the same point, emphasizing "the importance of investment efficiency" and insisting that "we must ensure the return of principal, although we are not aiming at profits" (Policy Bank 1994). With highly placed bank officials attacking soft credits even at institutions designed to serve this very need, and with ordinary banks eager to "further commercialize their business" (Wu 1994), executives and workers of loss-making firms can expect only limited relief from their financial predicament unless they improve their performance in the marketplace.

The growing reluctance of government to support weak enterprises is reflected in microeconomic data. Survey data analyzed by Morris and Liu (1993) show that, despite an increase in the absolute level of subsidies, there was considerable hardening of budget constraints for state firms during the late 1980s. Other data support the hypothesis that enterprises facing strong competition move (or are pushed) toward the market in the expectation that greater independence will help them resolve their financial problems.

The following regression, based on 1990 data for state enterprises surveyed in late 1991 and early 1992, evaluates the impact of market conditions on the government's grant of decisionmaking autonomy (DMA) to enterprises:

$$\begin{aligned} \text{DMA} = {} & \underset{(19.40)}{1.73} + \underset{(5.02)}{0.12}\,\text{COMP} + \underset{(3.69)}{0.10}\,\text{PCOMP} - \underset{(2.17)}{0.27}\,\text{PROFIT} + \underset{(0.46)}{0.02}\,\text{IND} \\ & R^2 = 0.10,\ \text{obs.} = 572. \end{aligned} \tag{3}$$

In this regression DMA is a composite measure of enterprise control over production and marketing decisions.[16] COMP and PCOMP are the same measures used in equation 1. PROFIT is the ratio of profit (or loss) to the gross value of output in 1990. To control for differences in autonomy that are specific to the light-heavy industry mix, the equation includes IND, a dummy variable in which 0 represents heavy industry and 1 represents light industry. The regression results show that competition (measured by the firm's estimate of the elasticity of demand for its products and the degree of competitive pressure from rivals) is associated with a relatively high degree of managerial autonomy, which we interpret as synonymous with greater exposure to market forces. Low or negative profits also contribute to a greater transfer of production control and marketing rights to enterprise management.

Recent developments in the woolen textile industry illustrate the government's propensity to assist troubled firms with offers of deregulation rather than direct or indirect subsidies. During 1990–91 the requirement that woolen textile exporters sell through foreign trade corporations insulated them from international market changes and led to large inventories and losses. In response to pressures from producers the government allowed woolen textile companies to export directly to overseas customers. Chinese firms soon began to produce semifinished inventories that could be more quickly transformed into final goods that conformed to the specifications and just-in-time production requirements of overseas customers.

Although government intervention continues to cushion some firms, especially state enterprises, against the consequences of weak performance, limited resources, fear of inflation, and changing attitudes have increased the likelihood that firms and their workers will bear the financial consequences of market outcomes. There is a growing gap between financial outcomes for successful and unsuccessful firms. Loss-making industrial enterprises, formerly eligible for full compensation as part of official administrative routine, face growing difficulties under China's steadily deepening reforms. In the rural sector, losses bring a quick exit for enterprises and dismissal for workers. Subsidies continue, but even for urban state enterprises, subsidies have dropped from full coverage of losses to well below half. Workers associated with loss-making enterprises face a growing probability of sanctions such as slow wage growth, deterioration of bonuses, erosion of health benefits and other nonwage income, layoffs with only partial wage payment, delayed wage payments, compulsory transfers and, most recently, dismissal.

Proposition 6: Feedback mechanisms amplify and extend the reform process

The consequences of reform are not limited to a linear progression in which new policies intensify competition, reduce profits and fiscal revenues, and create pressures for better industrial performance. At every stage we observe feedback mechanisms that reinforce the momentum of beneficial change. The success of some enterprises in reducing costs or developing new products reverberates up and down the domestic quality ladder, escalating the pressure on rival enterprises to follow suit. Every reform that relaxes institutional constraints on market entry, enterprise autonomy, or technological change shortens the distance separating adjacent rungs along the ladders of technology and cost, increases the probability of competition-enhancing innovation, and raises the risks facing enterprises that are slow to reform. Reductions in fiscal resources caused by falling profits or tax evasion (itself an outcome of reform-induced expansion of enterprise autonomy and financial mechanisms) increase pressures on enterprises by reducing the chances of successful rent-seeking, further widening the gap between "winners" and "losers."

Groves and others (1994) provide a quantitative illustration of feedback mechanisms that shows how state enterprises use grants of autonomy to strengthen work incentives and raise productivity. Their analysis of sample data indicates that enterprise autonomy is associated with large shares of discretionary payments in worker compensation and with high shares of untenured contract workers in the labor force. Their statistical analysis confirms the expected positive link between these incentive changes and productivity growth. Thus incremental grants of enterprise autonomy appear to feed back into faster productivity growth, which in turn intensifies competition, and so on.

Proposition 7: China's decision to create a market-based economic system is an endogenous outcome of the partial reform process

China's initial reform efforts sought to improve economic performance; there was no clear picture of what the economy should look like after reform. Partial reform initiated a learning process that expanded the horizons of all participants. Competition among firms organized under heterogeneous institutional arrangements opened the door to a dynamic and interactive reform process in which specific policy initiatives have different effects on the opportunity sets of firms facing different institutional and technological constraints. Enterprises adopted competitive strategies designed to capitalize on the advantages conferred by their institutional as well as technical endowments. Competition forced participants to compare the merits of alternative institutional arrangements in exactly the same way that managers analyze the profit consequences of different product designs, machines, or compensation arrangements. Heterogeneity encouraged a culture of envy in which firms and managers demand access to more attractive institutional possibilities to place them on an equal footing with rivals operating under different institutional arrangements (Liu 1993).

The experience of partial reform created promarket sentiment among former advocates of central planning. Shirk (1993, p. 288; also see Rawski 1994b) shows how managers of large-scale industry changed their views.

> [These leaders] were at first leery of market reforms that threatened to shake them out of their comfortable dependence on the state. But the

> wrenching experience of the 1980–81 readjustment . . . gave them a new appreciation of the opportunities offered by the market, and their envy of the benefits of reform enjoyed by smaller enterprises and non-state enterprises motivated them to demand that these benefits be extended to their own enterprises. . . . Large state factory managers changed from lazy conservatives coddled by the state to active reformers challenging the state.

Government officials and political leaders experienced a similar change of position.

The rise of promarket sentiments among the political and administrative elite represents the biggest feedback of all in China's partial reform process. In the early 1990s these changes coalesced into a stunning reversal of deep-seated attitudes. Ideas that only ten years earlier stood far beyond the limits of permissible discussion now took center stage as the government announced huge staff cuts, ambitious young bureaucrats began leaving the government to pursue private business careers (K. Chen 1994), and China's Communist party formally announced a national goal of creating a decentralized market economy (Decision 1993).

This remarkable change in values, combined with intense fiscal pressures, has sparked a series of policy innovations aimed at relieving governments of the burden of supporting loss-making enterprises. Although official documents rarely use terms like "ownership reform" or "privatization" to describe these changes, recent initiatives amount to a policy of endogenous or induced privatization. Various ministries, provinces, and localities have begun to lease state-owned industrial firms to private agents (including foreign companies). Some loss-making firms have been forced to merge with stronger enterprises, with substantial loss of jobs;[17] others are simply auctioned off to the highest bidder. The government has also begun to encourage organizational innovations designed to restructure state enterprises as limited-liability entities owned by government, corporate, and private shareholders.

CONCLUSION

The contrast between the top-down, centrally planned reforms proposed by international organizations (and endorsed by many economists) and the gradual, cumulative reform process described in this article reminds us of earlier controversies between advocates of "balanced" growth (Rosenstein-Rodan 1943; Nurkse 1953) and proponents of "unbalanced" development (Hirschman 1958).

The balanced growth approach portrays economic growth as an event—a big push or great leap—rather than as a process; it downplays the developmental potential of inherited economic structures and ignores international and domestic linkages. These oversights amplified the surprise attending the subsequent export success of economies such as Japan, the Republic of Korea, and Taiwan [Taiwan (China) is the designation used by the World Bank], wrongly identified as "basket cases" on the basis of low initial capability and unfamiliar institutional arrangements.

Although several years of practical experience have muted the all-or-nothing aspect of initial perspectives on socialist reform, there is still a tendency for discussions of reform issues to repeat the mistakes of the balanced growth approach by underestimating the complexity of imposing market systems from above.

James Buchanan insists that "a market is not competitive by assumption or by construction," but "*becomes* competitive, and competitive rules *come to be* established as institutions emerge" to shape behavior (1979, p. 29, our emphasis). Buchanan thinks that economies should focus on this "process of becoming." This orientation seems highly appropriate for the study of socialist reform. China's gradual and partial path of industrial reform was not determined by a few top officials. Industrial reform evolved from sequences of decisions made by tens of thousands of enterprises and millions of administrators, managers, and workers. The large number of participants and the extended duration of the reform process, which gave people ample time to evaluate alternatives and reconsider their initial views, eventually built a constituency for market-directed change that was far stronger than any official announcement could have achieved. This process is very different from Western parliamentary democracy, but it has produced a durable reform constituency that easily rebuffed high-level efforts to roll back reform in the wake of the inflation scare and political repression of 1989.

Before reform, government officials set the agenda for China's industrial firms. Now everyone has an agenda. Enterprises, managers, and workers design strategies for success. The state finds itself reacting to the outcome of decentralized efforts to implement a multitude of uncoordinated agendas. Enterprises and individuals no longer await the government's announcements, but struggle to shape government involvement in ways that suit their own plans. In short, China's industrial economy, despite its subsidies, soft loans, tenured state enterprise workers, and numerous other divergences from the textbook ideal, looks increasingly like a market system.

ACKNOWLEDGMENT

Gary H. Jefferson is associate professor of economics at Brandeis University. Thomas G. Rawski is professor of economics at the University of Pittsburgh. The authors received support for this research from the Henry Luce Foundation, the John S. Guggenheim Foundation, the University of Pittsburgh's University Center for International Studies, Brandeis University's Mazer Fund, and the World Bank's Project on Industrial Reform and Productivity within Chinese Enterprises. The authors are grateful for the research assistance of John Zhiqiang Zhao and for data and comments from E. C. Hwa, Nicholas R. Lardy, Wei Lo, Penelope Prime, Jeffrey Sachs, Inderjit Singh, Wing T. Woo, and Shahid Yusuf.

NOTES

1 The share of domestic private enterprise is the sum of shares for individual enterprises employing fewer than eight people (*geti gongye*) and larger private firms. Figures for the latter category are obtained as residuals by subtracting the contribution of joint ventures, overseas Chinese firms, and foreign-owned plants from the output share of "other" (*qita*, or other than state or collective) types of ownership (Industry 1992, p. 7). These figures take no account of private firms masquerading as collectives (Walder 1994); including their output would probably raise the 1992 share of private enterprise to more than 10 percent.

2 Similarly, Chang and Wang (1994, p. 2) emphasize that a TVE is "controlled by the township government . . . not by its nominal owners, that is, the local citizens."

3 A 1990 survey of 285 TVEs found that only 16 percent had the authority to appoint their own leaders. In 60 percent of cases the supervisory authority (that is, the local government) appointed enterprise leaders without consultation (Jefferson, Lu, and Zhao 1994). An earlier survey found that more than 80 percent of TVE managers attributed their appointments to the local government (Song 1990). Walder (1994, pp. 15, 34) observes that "the control of top [local] officials over public firms is greatest" in "the smaller rural jurisdictions" where "the party secretaries or other top officials . . . play an active role in the management of their valued industrial assets."

4 Data on fixed investment are for 1992 (Yearbook 1993, pp. 145, 150). It is not easy to specify the share of state firms in industrial fixed investment. The 1992 figure for industrial investment of state enterprises occupies an impossibly large 97.5 percent share of the combined total of industrial investment outlays under the three subheads of basic construction, technical renovation, and "other" (a small category that we assign exclusively to industry even though part should be credited to transport and geology).

5 For extended discussion, including numerous references, see Harrold (1992), Rawski (1994b), and Jefferson and Rawski (1994).

6 Wu (1993) summarizes the literature on productive efficiency. Woo and others (1993) employ sample data to show a declining trend for total factor productivity in several branches of industry, but only by assuming a common trend for product and input prices during a period of rising relative prices for industrial materials. Preliminary calculations by Jefferson, Rawski, and Zheng (1994) suggest that the contribution of total factor productivity to output growth may have risen from 25 to 30 percent during 1980–88 to 50 percent during 1988–92.

7 The estimated annual growth rate of state enterprises' manufactured exports was much lower (7.8 percent) for 1988–92 than for 1984–88 (34.4 percent). However, the figure for 1988–92 probably understates actual growth, which may have surpassed 10 percent (Rawski 1994a). Survey data indicate 20 percent annual export growth for a sample of 244 large state enterprises during 1986–89 (Rawski forthcoming). Lardy (1993) points out that state enterprise exports have benefited from direct subsidies (in the 1980s) and special export credits (in the 1990s).

8 China's state firms have a long history of excessive vertical integration. The

proliferation of customer-conscious behavior should encourage the spread of efficiency-enhancing specialization. But a major study by Chinese economists finds that high transaction costs arising from inadequate contract enforcement and the consequent prevalence of commercial cheating leads to "an obvious tendency toward nonspecialization outside the state sector" (Jiang and others 1993, p. 35). Whiting's (1993) study of TVE behavior comments on "the unwillingness of the courts to enforce loan contracts" and quotes one frustrated enterprise manager as complaining that "contracts here don't mean anything" because there is no practical means of forcing customers to settle overdue accounts.

9 At the conference the discussants noted that factors outside China's industrial sector, including successful agricultural reform, macroeconomic stability, and complementarities with the adjacent economies of Hong Kong and Taiwan [Taiwan (China) is the designation used by the World Bank] have facilitated the reform of domestic industry. We agree (see Gelb, Jefferson, and Singh 1993), but focus here on initial conditions that are specific so domestic industry.

10 For similar reports, see Chou (1992, p. 5) and *China Daily* (August 28, 1993, p. 1 and August 31, 1993, p. 4). Note that the qualification rate for medium-size and small factories in the survey cited in the text was "only 72.9 percent." This and other evidence points to a scale-related hierarchy of technological capabilities within state industry.

11 Data from Du and Shang (1993) include the employer's share of medical expenses incurred by workers and dependants. The Hebei survey covered the first half of 1993 and found average medical expenses of ¥ 600.69 per worker. In 1991 wages for state sector employees in Hebei amounted to 93.4 percent of the national average (Labor 1992, p. 211). We apply this figure to average 1992 state sector wages of ¥ 2,878 (Survey 1993, p. 44) and assume wage growth of 20 percent for 1992–93.

12 Beijing's Capital Steel Works has developed into a multinational conglomerate on the basis of profits accumulated under a long-term agreement that offered exceptional managerial autonomy in exchange for a promise to deliver a steadily rising flow of funds to the national treasury. The firm's own researchers attribute more than half of Capital's large profit increments to the simple fact of autonomy: shifts in the output mix with no major changes in main equipment or in annual supplies of raw materials (Shougang 1986). Lacking Capital's political clout, rival firms found themselves stymied by institutional restrictions that prevented them from raising profits by optimizing their output mix.

13 This variable serves as a proxy for the proportion of nonproduction capital and labor in the enterprise that is devoted to the provision of housing and social services. The formulation implies that capital and labor are used in fixed proportions in the provision of housing and social service.

14 COMP and PCOMP are discrete variables, spanning a range of 1 to 3, from inelastic demand or little competition to highly elastic demand or high competition.

13 In this regression NPS is the ratio of new product output to gross output value and PRO is the ratio of profit and taxes to annual sales. NPS8886 = NPS88/NPS86; also PRO8684 = PRO86/PRO84.

16 DMA ranges from 1 (enterprise has no decisionmaking authority), to 2 (limited authority or authority shared between enterprise and supervisory agency), to 3 (enterprise has full control).

17 The summary of an interview with Li Shuguang, deputy director of the Beijing Siyuan Merger and Bankruptcy Consultancy, noted that "the biggest problem with mergers is the job losses involved in merged firms." Li stated that many

of the enterprises acquiring loss-making firms "are only interested in obtaining the equipment and extra space in a merger," which creates a "problem of redundancies" (Huang 1994).

REFERENCES

Blanchard, Olivier Jean, and Stanley Fischer. 1993. *NBER Macroeconomics Annual 1993*. Cambridge, Mass.: MIT Press.

Blasko, Dennis J. 1994. Review of Paul Folta, "From Swords to Plowshares? Defense Industry Reform in the PRC." *Far Eastern Economic Review*, March 3, p. 37.

Buchanan, James M. 1979, *What Should Economics Do?* Indianapolis: Liberty Press.

Byrd, William A., ed. 1992. *Chinese Industrial Firms Under Reform*. New York: Oxford University Press.

Census 1989. *Zhonghua renmin gongheguo 1985—nian gongye pucha ziliao (jianyaoben)* [People's Republic of China 1985 Industrial Census Materials—abbreviated summary volume]. Beijing: Zhongguo tongii chubanshe.

Chag, Chung, and Yijiang Wang. 1994. "The Nature of the Township Enterprise." Carlson School of Management, University of Minnesota.

Chen, Kathy. 1994. "Chinese Bureaucrats Take Hopes Private." *Wall Street Journal*, January 26, p. A10.

Chen, Qingtai. 1994. "Vice Minister on New Enterprise Reforms." U.S. Department of Commerce, Foreign Broadcast Information Service. *Daily Report: China*, January 27, pp. 48–49.

China Daily. Beijing.

Chou, Yi. 1993. "The Practice beyond Property Right Boundaries: Quality Management in Chinese State-Owned Enterprises and Rural Enterprises." Discussion Paper 9302. Taipei: Chung-Hua Institution for Economic Research.

Communique. 1994. "Communique on the National Economy and Social Development in 1993 by the State Statistics Bureau of the PRC." *Renmin ribao* (People's Daily) March 1, pp 2–3.

Decision. 1993. "China's Central Government Decision on Resolving Several Problems Concerning the Establishment of a Socialist Market Economic System." *Renmin ribao* (People's Daily), November 17, p. 1.

Du Haiyan, and Shang Lie. 1993. "Distribution of Fringe Benefits for Employees of State-owned Enterprises." *Zhongguo gongye jingji yanjiu* (Research on Chinese Industrial Economics) No. 2. 46–52, 30.

Du Miaodeng, Huang Shiqiu, and Chen Xuewen. 1992. "On the Management of 'High Starting Point' Enterprises in Poor Townships and Districts." *Jingji guanli* (Economic Management). No. 12: 55–57.

Gao, Anming. 1990. "Giant Tractor Maker Plagued by Slow Sales." *China Daily*, May 28, p. 4.

Gelb, Alan, Gary H. Jefferson, and Inderjit Singh. 1993. "Can Communist Economies Transform Incrementally?" *NBER Macroeconomics Annual 1993*. Cambridge, Mass.: MIT Press.

Granick, David. 1990. *Chinese State Enterprises: A Regional Property Rights Analysis*. Chicago: University of Chicago Press.

Grossman, Gene M., and Elhanan Helpman. 1991. "Quality Ladders and Product Cycles." *Quarterly Journal of Economics* 106: 557–86.

Groves, Theodore, Yongmiao Hong, John McMillan, and Barry Naughton. 1994. "Autonomy and Incentives in Chinese State Enterprises." *Quarterly Journal of Economics* 109 (1): 183–209.

Harrold, Peter. 1992. "China's Reform Experience to Date.' World Bank Discussion Paper 180, Washington, D.C.
Hirschman, Albert O. 1958. *The Strategy of Economic Development*. New Haven, Conn.: Yale University Press.
Hua, Sheng, Xiaopeng Luo, and Xuejun Zhang. 1993. *China: From Revolution to Reform*. Houndsmills, United Kingdom: Macmillan.
Huang, Zhiling. 1994. "Mergers Revive Loss-making Firms." *China Daily*, April 16, p. 4.
Hwa, Erh-cheng. 1992. "Enterprise Reform in China." Background paper. World Bank, Washington, D.C.
Industry. 1949–54. *Zhongguo gongye jingji tongji ziliao 1949–1984* [Statistical Materials on China's Industrial Economy, 1949–1984]. Beijing: Zhongguo tongji chubanshe.
Industry. 1992. *Zhongguo gongye jingji tongji nianjian 1992* [Statistical Yearbook of China's Industrial Economy 1992]. Beijing: Zhongguo tongji chubanshe.
Jefferson, Gary H., and Thomas G. Rawski. 1994. "Enterprise Reform in Chinese Industry." *Journal of Economic Perspectives* 8(2): 47–70.
Jefferson, Gary H., Mai Lu, and John Zhiqiang Zhao. 1994. "The Reform of Property Rights in China's Industrial Enterprises." Brandeis University, Department of Economics, Waltham. Mass.
Jefferson, Gary H., Thomas G. Rawski, and Yuxin Zheng. 1992a. "Growth, Efficiency, and Convergence in China's State and Collective Industry." *Economic Development and Cultural Change* 40 (2): 239–66.
——. 1992b. "Innovation and Reform in Chinese Industry: A Preliminary Analysis of Survey Data (1)." Paper delivered at the annual meeting of the Association for Asian Studies, Washington, D.C., April.
——. 1992c. "Innovation and Reform in Chinese Industry: A Preliminary Analysis of Survey Data (2)." Research Paper Series 30, Socialist Economies Reform Unit, World Bank, Washington, D.C.
——. 1994. "Institutional Change and Industrial Innovation in Transitional Economies." *Journal of Asian Economics* 5 (4): 585–604.
Jiang Xiaojuan, Zhao Ying, Ren Jijun, Liu Hong, and Xiong Yun. 1993. "New Features of China's Industrial Growth and Structural Change." *Zhongguo gongye jingji yanjiu* (Research on Chinese Industrial Economics) 8: 32–40.
Labor 1992. *Zhongguo laodong tongji nianjian 1992* [Statistical Yearbook of Chinese Labor, 1992]. Beijing: Zhongguo laodong chubanshe.
Lardy, Nicholas R. 1993. "China's Foreign Trade Reform in the 1990s." Paper delivered at the annual meeting of the Association for Asian Studies, April. Los Angeles, Calif.
Li Dianjing, and Qin Chengdiao. 1993. "Survey on Conditions of Reimbursement of Employee Medical Expenses." *Zhongguo wujia* (China Price) 11: 33–34.
Liu, Weiling. 1993. "Enterprise Managers Upset by 'Unfair' Regulations." *China Daily*, September 18, p. 2.
Ma, Zhiping. 1994. "Quality of Chinese Products Improves." *China Daily*, January 20, p. 3.
Ma Ke and Zhao Yuchuan. 1993. "R&D at China's Large and Medium Industrial Enterprises—Innovative Activity Develops Universally." *Zhongguo tongji* (China's Statistics) 4:10.
Morris, Derek, and Guy Shaojia Liu. 1993. "The Soft Budget Constraint in Chinese Industrial Enterprises in the 1980s." Oxford University, Oxford.
Naughton, Barry, 1992. "Implications of the State Monopoly Over Industry and its Relaxation." *Modern China* 18 (1): 14–41.

——. 1994. *Growing Out of the Plan: Chinese Economic Reform, 1978–1993*. New York: Cambridge University Press.

Nurkse, Ragnar. 1953. *Problems of Capital Formation in Underdeveloped Countries*. Oxford: Oxford University Press.

Ody, Anthony J. 1991. "China: Rural Enterprise, Rural Industry, 1986–1990." East Asia and the Pacific Country Department II, Country Operations Division, World Bank, Washington, D.C.

Perkins, Dwight H., and others. 1977. *Rural Small-Scale Industry in the People's Republic of China*. Berkeley: University of California Press.

Policy Bank. 1994. "Policy Bank Opens for Key Projects." *China Daily*, April 14, p. 1.

Rawski, Thomas G. 1994a. "Export Performance of China's State Industries." Department of Economics, University of Pittsburgh.

——. 1994b. "Progress without Privatization: The Reform of China's State Industries." In Vedat Milor, ed., *The Political Economy of Privatization and Public Enterprise in Post-Communist and Reforming Communist States*. Boulder, Colo.: Lynne Rienner.

——. Forthcoming. "An Overview of Chinese Industry in the 1980s." In Gary H. Jefferson and Inderjit Singh, eds, *Reform, Ownership, and Performance in Chinese Industry*.

Regualtions. 1992. "Text of Regulations on Transforming State Enterprises." U.S. Department of Commerce, Foreign Broadcast Information Service. *Daily Report: China*. July 28, pp. 27–36.

Rosenstein-Rodan, P.N. 1943. "Problems of Industrialization of Eastern and Southeastern Europe." *Economic Journal* (June–Sept). Reprinted in A.N. Agarwala and S.P. Singh, eds, *The Economics of Underdevelopment*. New York: Oxford University Press, 1963.

Sachs, Jeffrey, and Wing Thye Woo. 1994. "Reform in China and Russia." *Economic Policy* (April): 101–45.

Shirk, Susan L. 1993. *The Political Logic of Economic Reform in China*. Berkeley: University of California Press.

Shougang R&D Center. 1986. "How Reform Brought Rapid Efficiency Gains at Capital." In *Shougang Chengboazhi* [The System of Enterprise Responsibility Contracts at Capital Steelworks]. Beijing: Jingji guanli chubanshe.

Sicular, Terry. 1992. "Public Finance and China's Economic Reforms." Harvard Institute of Economic Research Discussion Paper 1618. Cambridge, Mass.

Singh, Inderjit, Dilip Ratha, and Geng Xiao. 1994. "Non-State Enterprises as an Engine of Growth: An Analysis of Provincial Industrial Growth in Post-Reform China." Research Paper Series 20, World Bank, Socialist Economies Reform Unit, Washington, D.C.

Song, Lina. 1990. "Convergence: A Comparison of Township Firms and Local State Enterprises." In William A. Byrd and Qingsong Lin, eds, *China's Rural Industry: Structure, Development, and Reform*. New York: Oxford University Press.

Sun, Hong. 1994. "Public, Merchants Learn to Love Bar Codes," *China Daily Business Weekly*, February 21, p. 8.

Survey 1993. *Zhonngguo tongji zhaiyao 1993* [Statistical Survey of China 1993]. Beijing: Zhongguo tongji chabanshe.

Vernon, Raymond. 1966. "International Investment and International Trade in the Product Cycle." *Quarterly Journal of Economics* 80 (2): 190–207.

Walder, Andrew G. 1994. "The Varieties of Public Enterprise in China: An Institutional Analysis." Policy Research Department, World Bank, Washington, D.C.

Wang Haibo. 1992. "Now is the Time to Strengthen the Unity between High Speed

Growth and Raising Efficiency." *Zhongguo gongye jingji yanjiu* [Research on Chinese Industrial Economics] 10: 23–29.

Weitzman, Martin L., and Chenggang Xu. 1994. "Chinese Township and Village Enterprises as Vaguely Defined Cooperatives." *Journal of Comparative Economics* 18 (1): 121–45.

Whiting, Susan H. 1993. "Market Discipline and Rural Enterprise in China: A Principal-Agent Approach." Paper prepared for the conference on The Evolution of Market Institutions in Transition Economies, May 5, 1993.

Wong, Christine, Christopher Heady, and Wing Thye Woo. 1993. "Economic Reform and Fiscal Management in China." Asian Development Bank, Manila.

Woo, Wing Thye, Gang Fan, Wen Hai, and Yibiao Jin. 1993. "The Efficiency and Macroeconomic Consequences of Chinese Enterprise Reform," *China Economic Review* 4 (2): 153–68.

World Bank. 1992. *China: Reform and the Role of the Plan in the 1990s*. Washington, D.C.

Wu, Yanrui. 1993. "Productive Efficiency in Chinese Industry." *Asia-Pacific Economic Literature* 7 (2): 58–66.

Wu, Yunhe. 1994. "Central Bank to Cool Fixed Assets." *China Daily*, March 1, p. 1.

Xu Fengxian, Mao Zhichong, and Yuan Juying. 1993. "New Development à la Sunan." *Jingji yanjiu* [Economic Research] 2: 49–55.

Yearbook. Annual. *Zhongguo tongji nianjian* [China Statistical Yearbook, annual beginning 1981, except for 1982]. Beijing: Zhongguo tongji chubanshe.

Zweig, David 1991. "Internationalizing China's Countryside: The Political Economy of Exports from Rural Industry." *China Quarterly* (128): 716–41.

9

NONSTATE ENTERPRISE REFORM

Christine P. W. Wong
P. B. Rana and N. Hamid (Editors)

INTRODUCTION

It was noted in Chapter 9 (see source) that nonstate enterprises grew rapidly through the 1980s to a 45 per cent share in the gross value of industrial output (GVIO) in 1990. Yet the nonstate sector had been expanding since the mid-1960s. In the period 1965–1980, industry as a whole grew at an average annual rate of nearly 15 per cent, compared with less than 9 per cent for state-owned industry. The share of state-owned enterprises in GVIO peaked in 1965 and dropped steadily thereafter, as collective industry increased its share from 10 per cent in 1965 to 24 per cent in 1980. Private and other types of enterprises have also flourished since the mid-1980s, contributing to the falling share of the state sector.

Was there a Maoist pattern in the expansion of the nonstate sector through the 1980s? How different is the economic behavior of this sector from that of the state sector? This chapter begins by discussing the size structure of Chinese industry. It then examines the official categories of nonstate enterprises and their characteristics. The next two sections deal with the growth and momentum of private and rural enterprises. The chapter winds up with a summary of the findings and a discussion of the degree of autonomy and types of behavior of nonstate enterprises.

SIZE DISTRIBUTION OF CHINESE INDUSTRY

Until 1988, when data from the 1985 industrial census were first published by the State Statistical Bureau (SSB), the size distribution of the country's industrial enterprises was commonly perceived outside the PRC to be markedly skewed toward the low end. According to Chinese statistics, "small" enterprises produced 57 per cent of GVIO in 1978, and "large" enterprises accounted for only 25 per cent (SSB 1981). This finding was difficult to confirm because of the Chinese statistical practice, oriented to production planning, of classifying size according to annual output, productive capacity,

Source: From Centrally Planned to Market Economies: The Asian Approach (Hong Kong: Oxford University Press for the Asian Development Bank, 1996), Chapter 10.

or fixed assets. In the absence of information on the distribution of firm size by employment, the Chinese data could not be subjected to international comparisons. One attempt to estimate the size structure of Chinese industry by employment was made by the World Bank, which reported that, in 1982, 59.2 per cent of the PRC's industrial enterprises had fewer than 33 employees, and only 0.6 per cent had more than 243 employees. These estimates indicate a size structure closer to that of other developing countries than to the size structure of other Soviet-type economies. For example, in India in 1976/77, 51.7 per cent of industrial enterprises had fewer than 33 employees and 4.4 per cent had more than 243; for the Republic of Korea in 1981 the corresponding figures were 80.2 per cent and 2.2 per cent. In contrast, only 2.2 per cent of Hungarian enterprises in 1981 had fewer than 33 employees; 65.1 per cent had more than 243 (World Bank 1985).

Information from the 1985 industrial census and subsequent updates now makes it possible to construct a distribution of enterprises by size of employment. This is done in Table 9.1. A somewhat different picture emerges. The PRC is shown to be suffering from the Soviet disease of "gigantism" after all, albeit in milder form. In 1980, only 5 per cent of enterprises employed 500 or more workers and could therefore be considered "large" by international standards, but these contributed 70 per cent of GVIO and 56 per cent of industrial employment. "Medium" enterprises with 100–499 workers composed 21 per cent of the number of enterprises and provided 24 per cent of GVIO and 33 per cent of employment. Although "small" enterprises employing fewer than 100 made up 74 per cent of all enterprises, they had only a 6 per cent share in GVIO and only 11 per cent in employment (SSB 1985).

The census data cover only enterprises that are independent accounting

Table 9.1 Distribution of enterprises by size of employment, PRC 1980

Number of employees at year-end	*Number of enterprises*[a] *Unit*	*Number of enterprises*[a] *Per cent*	*Share of GVIO (per cent)*	*Share of employment (per cent)*
More than 10,000	271	0.1	17.5	13.5
5,001–10,000	454	0.1	8.9	6.0
3,001–5,000	688	0.2	6.7	5.1
1,001–3,000	5,270	1.5	21.5	16.4
501–1,000	10,755	3.0	15.1	14.5
301–500	16,113	4.5	10.0	12.2
101–300	61,045	17.0	13.8	20.9
100 or less	263,532	73.6	6.4	11.3

Note:
[a] Independent accounting units only.

Source: State Statistical Bureau (1989), vol. 3.

(IA) units, however. These are defined by the State Statistical Bureau as enterprises that have: (i) independent administrative status; (ii) independent accounting, with responsibility for profits and losses and an independent bank account; and (iii) authority to enter into contracts with other units. Unstated criteria for inclusion in independent accounting statistics appear to be ownership and administrative level, as only state-owned enterprises and collective enterprises at the township and higher levels are included.

Nonindependent accounting (NIA) enterprises are those that do not meet the foregoing criteria but are large enough in size and scale of operations to be included in industrial statistics. In this classification are enterprises affiliated with other state-owned or collective enterprises, administrative departments, or schools.

The profile of nonindependent accounting enterprises can be derived from the residuals between the figures for the entire industry sector and the aggregates for independent accounting units. The profile for 1990 in Table 9.2 shows that on the average NIA enterprises are extremely small. This is not surprising since 7.45 million village-owned, individual, and cooperative enterprises are excluded by definition, along with the smallest township and urban collective enterprises.

To give an accurate picture of the size distribution of firms in Chinese

Table 9.2 Profiles of independent and nonindependent accounting enterprises, PRC, 1990 (averages)

	Independent accounting units				*Nonindependent accounting units*
	Work force >10,000	*Work force 10–50*	*Work force <10*	*All units*	
Total number	339	157,039	55,103	417,082	378,700
Annual output (million yuan)	765.9	0.5	0.2	4.5	1.4
Work force	26,500	27	6.3	179	110
Fixed capital (million yuan)	1,131.7	228,000	78,500	3.4	189,000
Working capital at year-end (million yuan)	196.1	121,000	27,000	...	...
Profits and taxes (million yuan)	87.7	31,700	7,700	466,600	76,500
Retained profits (million yuan)	15.0	9,400	3,000	...	...

Source: *Yearbook of Chinese Industrial Economic Statistics* (1990).

industry, nonindependent accounting units should be included. Table 9.3 groups all NIA units under enterprises with fewer than 100 workers, in the process possibly overstating the size of this category slightly and understating the size of the category just above.

Table 9.3 Adjusted size distribution of Chinese industry, 1980 and 1990

Size of work force	*Number of enterprises*		*Share of GVIO*[a]
	Units	*Per cent*	*(per cent)*
1980			
More than 10,000	271	0.1	15.9
5,001–10,000	454	0.1	8.1
3,001–5,000	688	0.2	6.1
1,001–3,000	5,270	1.4	19.6
501–1,000	10,755	2.9	13.8
301–500	16,113	4.3	9.1
101–300	61,045	16.2	12.6
100 or less	282,532	74.9	10.8
1990			
More than 10,000	339	—	10.9
5,001–10,000	642	0.1	5.4
3,001–5,000	1,032	0.1	5.7
1,001–3,000	8,626	1.1	17.3
501–1,000	15,976	2.0	11.6
101–300	106,056	13.3	19.9
100 or less	663,111	83.3	29.3

	Share of GVIO (percent)	
	1980	*1990*
Large	53.7	39.2
Medium	13.8	11.6
Small	21.7	19.9
Very small	10.8	29.3

	Number of enterprises (per cent)	
	1980	*1990*
Large	2	1.4
Medium	3	2.0
Small	20	13.3
Very small	75	83.3

Note:
[a] In current prices.

Source: *Yearbook of Chinese Industrial Economics Statistics* (1990).

The inclusion of NIAs at the bottom end does not significantly alter the lopsided concentration of Chinese firms in the large-size categories in 1980, when the share of small enterprises increased only to 11 per cent of GVIO. For 1990, however, the adjustment is critical in showing the dramatic change in the size distribution of Chinese industry and highlighting the inability of the statistical system to keep pace with the changing economic structure. As private and village enterprises have multiplied, the share of independent accounting enterprises in the gross value of industrial output has plunged, from 91.1 per cent in 1980 to 81.5 per cent in 1985, and to 78.1 per cent in 1990.

In the rest of this chapter, "large" enterprises will refer to those with at least 1,000 workers, "medium" to those with 500–999 workers, "small" to those with 100–499 workers, and "very small" to those with fewer than 100 workers. These ranges vary somewhat from the standard international definitions, but they fit better the realities of labor-rich Chinese industry and the categories used in Chinese statistics.

Enterprises in all size categories, but most especially the smallest ones, grew in absolute terms in the 1980s, both in number and share in GVIO. From a 32.5 per cent combined share in GVIO in 1980, small and very small enterprises accounted for 49.2 per cent in 1990. The "very small" group (called "small" in the discussion above) nearly tripled in size, from 11 per cent of GVIO to 29.3 per cent, largely as a result of the remarkable growth of rural and private enterprises.

TAXONOMY OF NONSTATE ENTERPRISES

"Collectives" are by far the largest category of nonstate enterprises. As defined by the State Statistical Bureau, this category comprises urban and rural collective enterprises, as well as a large number of cooperatives. The 1.74 million collective enterprises in 1990 produced about 36 per cent of GVIO. Their numbers are presented in Table 9.4.

Urban collectives

Official statistics contain few details on the breakdown of urban collective enterprises, despite their importance. In fact, the "urban collectives" category in Table 9.4 is the residual of the entire collective industry minus rural collectives and cooperatives. The report on the industrial census (SSB 1988, 1989) includes a "street/neighborhood factories" category, but no other classifications exist to define urban collectives.

Aside from neighborhood or street factories, two other types of enterprises are classified as urban collectives. "Large collectives" are small and medium-sized enterprises in cities and counties that are affiliated with the vertical systems and local governments. The second type consists of very small enterprises subordinate to or affiliated with SOEs, administrative departments, schools, research institutes, etc. Table 9.5 gives a more detailed breakdown of collective industry excluding cooperatives (which are included in "private

Table 9.4 Structure of collective industry, PRC, 1985–1990

	1985	*1986*	*1987*	*1988*	*1989*	*1990*
Number of enterprises (thousand)	1,742.1	1,823.0	1,819.3	1,853.0	1,747.0	1,742.1
Urban *	150.7	154.1	154.2	157.7	161.6	236.0
Township	217.1	246.0	237.9	237.7	234.3	228.7
Village	632.6	628.1	708.0	733.8	721.6	680.8
Cooperatives	741.7	793.8	719.2	723.8	629.5	596.6
Urban	—	33.3	36.3	37.2	35.4	30.9
Rural	741.7	760.5	682.9	686.6	594.1	565.7
Output value (billion yuan)	311.7	375.2	478.2	658.8	758.8	852.3
Percent of GVIO	32.1	33.5	34.6	36.2	35.7	35.6
Urban *	154.1	168.4	201.6	259.7	305.0	314.9
Township	76.1	98.11	128.4	184.7	219.4	244.1
Village	66.3	83.9	116.5	170.4	211.8	239.4
Cooperatives	15.2	24.8	31.7	44.0	49.6	53.9
Urban	0	2.1	3.0	3.9	5.0	5.5
Rural	15.2	22.7	28.7	40.1	44.6	48.4

Note:
[a] 'Urban' is the residual of all other categories; it does not include urban cooperatives.

Source: *Statistical Yearbook of China* (1991).

Table 9.5 Reclassified composition of "collective" industry, PRC, 1990

	Number of enterprises[a]		*Output value*	
	Units ('000)	*Per cent*	*Billion yuan*	*Per cent*
Total	1,145.5	100.0	798.4	100.0
Urban	236.0	20.6	314.9	39.4
Large collective	90.0	7.9	210.9	26.3
Affiliated	146.0[b]	12.7	105.0	13.2
Rural	909.5	79.4	483.5	60.6
Township	228.7	20.0	244.1	30.6
Village	680.8	59.4	239.4	30.0

Note:
[a] Excludes cooperatives.
[b] Estimated as residual of independent accounting urban collectives.

Source: *Statistical Yearbook of China* (1991).

enterprises" below), based on various reports and interviews of the State Statistical Bureau. In 1990, 21 per cent of all collective enterprises and 39 per cent of collective industry output (or 14 per cent of GVIO) were in the urban sector.

Large collectives

Many large collectives had their origins in the handicraft workshops that were turned into cooperatives during the socialist transformation campaign in the 1950s. Through later decades, as the government widened its control over supply and marketing, the enterprises were gradually incorporated in material allocation and procurement plans and lost their production autonomy. Wong (1986b) showed that by 1978 some three-fourths of all urban collectives were of this type, operating under the supervision of vertical systems. About 60 per cent were under the Ministry of Light Industry, divided between the first and second light industrial bureaus. They produced consumer goods such as bicycles, sewing machines, and arts and crafts, whose production and marketing were often under local planning and management. Another 6,000 enterprises (approximately 6 per cent of all urban collectives) belonged to the Ministry of Textiles. They operated according to strict production plans, with the Ministry exercising tight control over the allocation of raw cotton supplies and the procurement of cotton textiles. By the 1960s these large collectives had lost their financial independence as well, and their workers were put on fixed-wage scales that were parallel to, but lower than, state wage scales. They remitted profits (and losses) to their supervisory departments, and their investments were financed with appropriations from above. In effect, they operated much like state enterprises. In 1990 large collectives composed slightly less than 40 per cent of the 236,000 urban collective enterprises but supplied about two-thirds of output value, with each large collective averaging 2.3 million yuan in annual output value.

Neighborhood collectives

"Neighborhood" collectives were usually very small-scale. Many began as workshops set up during the Great Leap Forward (1958–1961) to bring housewives into the work force. These enterprises experienced another surge in number during the Cultural Revolution decade (1966–1978), when many "neighborhood factories" were set up, usually with minimum capital. In the 1970s these were the only factories without close ties to the state sector, though they were generally supervised and "owned" by neighborhood committees or district governments. There were 36,000 indepentent accounting enterprises listed in this category in 1990, but the actual number was probably much larger.

Affiliated collectives

Statistical information is even more scarce for "sponsored" or "affiliated" collectives, which were usually not independent accounting units. Their precursors were the "May Seventh Factories" (named after a speech by Mao Zedong) that were set up by schools and institutions during the Cultural Revolution so that students and cadres could engage in "productive labor" along with their other activities. By the late 1970s and early 1980s the objective had changed, and many collectives were set up by SOEs and other units primarily to provide jobs to children of employees. Table 9.5 combines neighborhood and affiliated collectives, and their share of total industry output is estimated at 13 per cent (between one-fourth and one-third of the total share of urban collectives).

Rural collectives

Enterprises owned by township and village governments, as well as rural cooperatives, are officially classified under rural collectives, the dominant component of the "collective industry" category, with 85 per cent of the number of enterprises and two-thirds of total output (see Table 9.4). Collectively owned enterprises in townships and villages are the descendants of the "commune and brigade enterprises" of the Cultural Revolution. When the names "people's communes" and "production brigades" were abolished in March 1984, these were renamed "township and village enterprises" (TVEs). In view of the important role of rural enterprises, the next section contains a detailed discussion of their composition and characteristics.

Individual-owned enterprises

"Individual-owned" enterprises are privately owned and employ fewer than eight workers. In this category are the vast majority of private enterprises in the PRC. There were 6.2 million individual-owned enterprises in industry in 1990, producing 129 billion yuan in GVIO. Table 9.6 shows the breakdown of this category into urban and rural segments. Over 90 per cent of individual enterprises are in the rural areas and are also often included under the TVE category in the aggregate statistics for rural or agricultural enterprises.

Other enterprises

Table 9.7 gives the composition of the "others" category of nonstate industry, which had 8,800 listed enterprises and accounted for 4.4 per cent of GVIO in 1990. As is typical in Chinese statistical reporting, the "others" category has swelled and become more heterogeneous in recent years as a result of absorbing all the new ownership forms that do not fit into traditional Soviet-type

Table 9.6 Composition of "individual" industry, PRC, 1985–1990

	1985	*1986*	*1987*	*1988*	*1989*	*1990*
Urban cooperatives						
Number of enterprises (thousand)	330.1	367.4	491.5	452.8	424.9	432.5
Employment (thousand)	1,374.8	675.2	1,076.1	1,024.8	1,088.8	1,010.2
GVIO (million yuan)	3,339	2,913	5,027	6,848	8,970	10,724
Taxes paid (million yuan)	210	161	252	327	435	492
Own capital (million yuan)	908	630	1,118	1,587	2,021	2,085
Rural cooperatives						
Number of enterprises (thousand)	3,017.7	4,417.1	5,061.8	5,695.2	5,699.3	5,743.5
Employment (thousand)	6,943.5	10,272.0	12,460.7	14,826.3	15,399.5	15,843.5
GVIO (million yuan)	14,636	27,941	45,212	72,200	96,796	18,306
Taxes paid (million yuan)	628	976	1,529	2,178	3,031	3,592
Own capital (million yuan)	3,420	5,307	7,579	10,476	13,832	15,215

Source: *Statistical Yearbook of China* (1991).

categories. Lumped together are enterprises totally dissimilar in size and other characteristics. Aside from the various types of foreign investment enterprises, the category also includes very small private enterprises that are too large to be "individual-owned," as well as some large or medium SOEs that have been converted to joint-stock ownership. In these latter cases, even if the state holds a majority of the shares, the enterprise is removed from the state-owned category and reclassified as being of "domestic mixed ownership" in the "others" category. In 1990 foreign joint ventures (JVs) had output of 38.7 billion yuan (37 per cent of the total output of the category), JVs with Hong Kong or Macao (a separate statistical category) 3.3 billion yuan (3.2 per cent), wholly owned foreign enterprises 2.9 billion yuan (2.7 per cent), and domestic mixed enterprises 59.9 billion yuan (57 per cent) (*Almanac of Chinese Industry* 1992).

Table 9.7 Composition of "other" enterprises in industry, PRC, 1985–1990

	1985	*1986*	*1987*	*1988*	*1989*	*1990*
Total number	1,700	2,400	3,900	5,400	7,200	8,800
Foreign JVs	244	391	698	1,084	1,658	2,242
JVs with Hong Kong or Macao	26	28	53	125	185	369
Wholly owned foreign firms	12	34	20	33	89	182
Domestic mixed-ownership firms	1,418	1,947	3,129	4,158	5,268	6,007
Total output value (billion yuan)	11.74	16.31	27.88	49.53	75.84	104.76
As share of GVIO (per cent)	1.2	1.5	2.0	2.7	3.4	4.4

Sources: *Yearbook of Chinese Industrial Economic Statistics* (1990); *Almanac of Chinese Industry* (1992).

RURAL ENTERPRISES

The rural enterprise sector has frequently been hailed as the most dynamic sector in Chinese industry. Its output and employment grew at average annual rates of 28.2 per cent and 11.1 per cent, respectively, in 1979–1990. The basic trends for the sector are presented in Table 9.8, which shows output growth during 1984–1990 to have been especially high, exceeding 30 per cent per annum. This rapid growth has pushed up the share of rural enterprises in the national economy. In 1990 the sector accounted for 39 per cent of nonagricultural employment, 25 per cent of GVIO, and 23.7 per cent of total exports (see Table 9.9). Rural enterprises have dominated the category of collective industry since 1984, when their output surpassed that of urban collective industry.

Through the 1980s, the sectoral and ownership composition of rural enterprises underwent significant change. The distribution of these enterprises across economic sectors is presented in Table 9.10. Agriculture produced 7.3 per cent of total rural enterprise output in 1978 but less than 2 per cent in 1990. Decollectivization and the subsequent disbanding in the early 1980s of most collective enterprises at the brigade and team levels were largely responsible for the decline. The collectives had been heavily concentrated in agricultural sidelines such as chicken raising and pig farming (Wong 1988). Industry's share in total rural enterprise output also fell, from nearly 80 per cent in 1978 to 72 per cent in 1990. This was primarily a reflection of the changing ownership structure of rural enterprises: an ever-larger share of

Table 9.8 Trends in rural enterprises, PRC, 1978–1990

	Number of enterprises ('000)	*Output value (billion yuan)*	*Employment (millions)*
1978	1,524.2	...	28.27
1979	1,480.4	54.84	29.10
1980	1,424.6	65.69	30.00
1981	1,337.5	74.53	29.70
1982	1,361.7	85.31	31.13
1983	1,346.7	101.68	32.35
1984	6,065.2	170.99	52.08
1985	12,224.5	272.84	69.79
1986	15,153.0	354.09	79.37
1987	17,502.4	476.43	88.05
1988	18,881.6	649.57	95.46
1989	18,686.3	742.84	93.67
1990	18,504.0	846.16	92.65
Average annual growth rate (per cent)			
1979–1990	25.8	28.2	11.1
1979–1984	32.6	25.5	12.4
1984–1990	20.4	30.5	10.1

Source: *Statistical Yearbook of China* (1991).

Table 9.9 Share of rural enterprises in the national economy, PRC, 1979–1990 (per cent)

	Employment	*Total output*	*Industrial output*	*Exports*
1979	22.54	7.18	9.05	...
1985	35.27	16.45	18.81	4.8
1990	38.61	22.27	25.29	23.7

Source: *Statistical Yearbook of China* (various years).

output and employment through the decade came from private enterprises (see Table 9.11), which gravitated toward retail trade, transport, and construction.

Decollectivization, which not only returned agricultural production to households but also lifted a host of restrictions on nonagricultural activities, triggered the phenomenal growth of rural enterprises. For the first time in nearly two decades, farmers were free to leave the land; many turned to peddling, handicrafts, transport, and other service trades. After some waffling in official policy through the early 1980s, State Council Document Number 4 (1984) formally endorsed the development of private enterprises in the rural

Table 9.10 Sectoral composition of rural enterprises, PRC, 1978–1990

	Industry	*Agriculture*	*Construction*	*Transport*	*Retail trade and food services*
Shares of output value (%)					
1978	78.1	7.3	7.1	3.8	3.7
1984	72.8	3.1	12.7	2.8	8.6
1999	69.7	1.8	12.7	7.3	8.5
1990	71.5	1.7	11.3	7.7	7.9
Shares of employment (%)					
1978	61.4	21.5	8.3	3.7	5.1
1984	70.2	5.5	13.1	2.5	8.7
1988	59.7	2.6	15.6	7.2	14.9
1990	60.1	2.5	14.5	7.7	15.1

Source: *Chinese Rural Statistical Yearbook* (1992).

Table 9.11 Ownership composition of rural enterprises, PRC, 1984–1990 (per cent shares)

	Number of enterprises		*Employment*		*Total output*	
	Collective	*Private*	*Collective*	*Private*	*Collective*	*Private*
1984	30.72	69.28	76.46	23.54	85.63	14.37
1985	15.13	84.87	62.00	38.00	75.27	24.73
1986	11.40	88.60	57.21	42.79	71.34	28.66
1987	9.04	90.96	53.59	46.41	67.89	32.11
1988	8.42	91.58	51.27	48.73	67.47	32.53
1989	8.22	91.78	50.40	49.60	66.44	33.56
1990	7.86	92.14	49.57	50.43	65.28	34.72

Source: *Statistical Survey of Chinese Rural Enterprises* (1992).

sector, and workers left agriculture in droves (Wong 1988). The share of labor employed in agriculture fell by a remarkable 10 per cent from 1978 to 1986 (from 71 per cent to 61 per cent) as farmers moved into other economic sectors.

These changes created a bustling rural enterprise sector, which benefited not only from the influx of labor and financial resources, but also from huge and growing markets. Liberalization and rising incomes fanned an unprecedented wave of consumerism among rural and urban residents alike in the 1980s, and rural enterprises moved aggressively to meet the new demands.

Private enterprises led the growth. Beginning in 1984, their official numbers increased spectacularly, from 4.2 million to 10.4 million in 1985,

13.4 million in 1986, then to a plateau of around 17 million in 1987–1990. The tripling of private enterprise numbers during 1984–1986, however, reflected in part a one-time adjustment in the reporting system, which had not counted private enterprises before 1984 (Wong 1988). There were few private enterprises during the Cultural Revolution, but by the early 1980s they had reemerged in significant numbers, and the 1984 and 1985 spurts were mostly a catching up in statistical reporting. This aside, the growth of private enterprises *was* in fact spectacular. By 1990, they accounted for 50 per cent of employment and 35 per cent of total output in the rural enterprise sector.

Collective enterprises also grew rapidly through the 1980s to retain a two-thirds share in the GVIO of the rural enterprise sector. Rural collective enterprises are the legacy of the Maoist program of rural industrialization. During the 1960s and 1970s, massive financial and material resources were pumped into the countryside to create a network of enterprises called the "five small industries." The rural sector was thus expected to provide its own basic machinery, fertilizers, building materials, and energy. At the peak of the rural industrialization drive in the late 1970s, more than 700,000 commune and brigade enterprises formed a vast farm machinery repair and manufacturing network in the countries, communes, and brigades (Wong 1982, 1991b).

Through the Cultural Revolution period, rural industry had flourished, with output increasing by an average of 27 per cent yearly during 1971–1978 (Wong 1988). However, this growth was directed from the top, by state policy. Specifically designed to serve the agriculture sector, rural enterprises were overwhelmingly concentrated in heavy industries, replicating state-owned industry in miniature. Like the SOEs they were imitating, these commune and brigade enterprises were also frequently low-profit or loss-making, requiring large state subsidies (Wong 1991b). With the onset of reform and decollectivization, the Maoist drive for agricultural mechanization was quietly abandoned. As subsidies to rural industries began to be phased out in the early 1980s, the network of "five small industries" faced growing financial difficulties.

To help rural collectives make the transition to other lines of production, the government offered an extremely favorable package of policies, by far the most important of which were tax concessions introduced in 1979 under the State Council's "Regulations on Some Questions Concerning the Development of Enterprises Run by People's Communes and Production Brigades." The regulations gave a variety of tax concessions and included a vaguely worded provision urging provinces to grant tax holidays of two to three years to new rural enterprises which "might have difficulty in paying taxes in the initial stage." In local implementation, this was broadly interpreted to mean that local officials could offer three-year tax holidays for both income and turnover taxes to all new enterprises. This provided a great inducement to setting up new enterprises (as well as giving old ones new identities), and it gave rise to a proliferation of rural collective enterprises.

By virtue of their tax-exempt status, rural enterprises enjoyed a significant cost advantage over urban enterprises in many industries (the turnover tax for electric fans, for example, was 25 per cent), and greatly boosted their profits. The many now-defunct farm machinery repair and manufacturing plants were induced to retool and enter the markets for consumer appliances such as electric fans, bicycles, washing machines, and refrigerators, where turnover tax rates and profit rates were extremely high and there was huge excess demand in the early 1980s. Others became suppliers of machinery and equipment for the rapidly growing rural enterprise sector.

At the same time, other new opportunities were opened to the rural collectives by the gradual relaxation of control over agricultural procurement and material allocation. Freed from the Maoist ideological restraint against "going after high profits," rural collectives could enter light industries that used to be monopolized by state-owned enterprises, including food processing and other consumer goods industries based on agricultural raw materials.

Finally, vastly improved access to investment resources in the form of bank credit, especially since 1984, fueled their rapid growth through the 1980s. In this regard, rural enterprises were major (if possibly unintended) beneficiaries of the reform in investment finance. Under the old system, rural enterprises were weak and lowly claimants on budgetary appropriations; the shifting of investment finance to the banking system made them eligible for credit from the Agricultural Bank and the rural credit cooperatives, whose deposits were buoyed as agricultural incomes zoomed. Riding on the wave of credit expansion that swept the nation in 1984 and 1985, rural collectives were able to expand their investment substantially through borrowing.

Table 9.12 shows that total loans to TVEs from the ABC and from RCCs grew from 4.4 billion yuan in 1979 to 29.3 billion yuan in 1984 and to 116.3 billion in 1990. In 1987 the share of bank loans in total investment in fixed assets in TVEs was 48 per cent, higher than for SOEs. This share fell to 35 per cent in 1990, largely as a result of the increase in foreign funds, which financed 21 per cent of investment in TVEs (*China's Township and Village Yearbook*, various issues).

PRIVATE ENTERPRISES

Official statistics place private enterprises in the PRC under "individually operated industrial and commercial households," "private enterprises," or cooperatives. In this discussion, foreign-funded enterprises (including wholly owned foreign firms and foreign joint ventures) will also be counted as private enterprises. Even though foreign joint ventures often have SOEs as domestic partners, their inclusion in the private sector seems appropriate given their profit orientation and their ownership rights over profits.

Table 9.12 Loans to township and village enterprises, PRC, 1979–1990

	Loans from ABC (billion yuan)	*Loans from RCCs (billion yuan)*	*Total*	*Per cent increase*
1979	2.99	1.41	4.40	...
1980	5.30	2.75	8.05	83
1981	6.21	3.55	9.76	21
1982	7.34	4.23	11.57	19
1983	8.00	6.00	14.00	21
1984	15.77	13.50	29.27	109
1985	18.80	16.44	35.24	20
1986	28.79	26.58	55.37	57
1987	35.01	35.93	70.94	28
1988	40.77	44.02	84.79	20
1989	42.06	54.02	96.08	13
1990	46.22	70.07	116.29	21

Source: Whiting (1993).

Size distribution

As noted above, "individual enterprises," many of which are just one-person operations, are by far the most common type of private enterprises. In 1990 there were over 17 million individual enterprises in the rural sector, with nearly 47 million owner/employees and total output valued at 294 billion yuan (see Tables 9.8 and 9.11 above). In the urban sector, there were 432,000 individual enterprises in industry, with 1 million owner/employees, and 2.5–3 million enterprises in services, construction, and transportation. Total employment in the urban individual sector was 6.7 million (see Table 9.13).

There is little information on the official category of "private enterprises" (defined as privately owned firms with eight or more employees), since their statistics cannot be isolated from the rest of the "others" category. According to anecdotal reports, in mid-1988 there were some 225,000 private enterprises employing 3.6 million workers, for an average of 16 per enterprise (*Beijing Review* 31[29], 1988). The recession and retrenchment of 1989–1990 left only 98,000 enterprises by early 1991. These had 1.7 million workers—including 1.47 million employees, for an average of 15 per enterprise—and, on the average, less than 100,000 yuan of capital (*China Business Daily* 9 April 1991).

Sectoral distribution

Private enterprises are found in the service sector in overwhelming numbers. This is not surprising, since the service trades require less initial capital and space, and bristle with unmet demand in view of the notoriously poor supply of public services. Table 9.13 shows the distribution of urban private-sector

Table 9.13 Distribution of urban private-sector employment, PRC, 1978–1990 (10,000 workers)

	Total	*Agriculture, forestry and fishery*	*Industry*	*Construction*	*Transport and telecom-munications*
1978	15.0	—	3.0	1.0	1.0
1979	32.0	—	6.0	1.0	1.0
1980	81.4	0.2	9.5	0.4	0.8
1981	113.3	0.1	11.1	1.0	1.7
1982	146.7	0.1	15.8	0.7	1.9
1983	230.7	0.2	23.7	1.3	3.8
1984	339.4	1.1	37.8	3.5	12.5
1985	450.1	1.9	51.4	5.1	22.3
1986	483.1	1.9	60.0	5.1	24.4
1987	568.8	1.7	74.3	6.5	30.6
1988	659.3	4.2	90.3	9.7	39.5
1989	648.2	2.6	84.5	4.9	34.1
1990	670.5	0.6	91.3	4.6	36.4

	Retail trade and food services	*Residential and neighborhood services*	*Health and social welfare*	*Education, culture, and media*	*Scientific research and consulting services*
1978	9.0	1.0	—	—	—
1979	18.0	6.0	—	—	—
1980	57.1	13.0	0.4	—	—
1981	79.1	20.0	0.4	—	—
1982	105.2	22.0	1.0	—	—
1983	171.0	29.5	1.0	0.2	—
1984	241.7	40.8	1.0	1.0	—
1985	325.0	40.9	2.8	0.7	—
1986	336.7	50.6	3.1	1.2	0.1
1987	390.7	58.6	4.0	2.3	0.1
1988	442.9	65.6	4.1	2.8	0.2
1989	443.1	71.7	3.9	3.1	0.3
1990	431.2	94.3	7.0	3.9	1.2

Source: *Statistical Yearbook of China* (1991).

employment. In 1990, 64 per cent was in retail sales and food services, another 14 per cent in residential and neighborhood services, and 5 per cent in transport. In contrast, only 14 per cent of workers were employed in industry and less than 1 per cent were in agriculture. The share of industry was somewhat higher in the rural sector.

To derive the share of the private sector in Chinese industry, statistics from the different categories of private enterprise are aggregated in Table 9.14, which shows the sector with 9.5 per cent of GVIO and nearly one-fourth of industrial employment in 1990.

Table 9.14 Share of private enterprises in industry, PRC, 1986 and 1990 (unit: 10,000)

	1986		*1990*	
	Urban	*Rural*	*Urban*	*Rural*
Number of enterprises (thousand)[a]	401.2	5,177.6	466.2	6,319.2
GVIO (per cent)	1.2	4.5	2.5	7.0
Employment[b] (per cent)	1.2	17.8	1.6	21.3

Notes:
[a] Private enterprises include 'individual-owned,' cooperative, and foreign investment enterprises.
[b] This figure excludes foreign investment enterprises, slightly understating the employment share.

Sources: Tables 9.6, 9.7, 9.11, and 9.13.

Hidden enterprises

These statistics significantly understate the true size of the private sector. First, weak protection of property rights discourages the full reporting of private activities. Second, private enterprises in the PRC are often registered as collectively owned, with the full concurrence of local officials, who receive management fees and perhaps a share of the profits. This practice began in the early 1980s, when decollectivization in the countryside gave rise to private enterprises with as yet no clear legitimate status. By registering as collectives the enterprises gained access to bank credit and supplies in a system that was extremely biased against private enterprises. Registration also allowed them to bypass strict limits on the number of employees, and conferred a legitimacy that facilitated business transactions. In many localities SOEs and collective enterprises were reportedly forbidden to buy from private enterprises.

Even after 1984, when private enterprises were formally sanctioned, they continued to register as collective enterprises to take advantage of the more favorable tax treatment. At least through the mid-1980s new rural collectives were routinely exempted from income and turnover taxes for three years, as noted in the previous section. Even in the urban areas, enterprises registered as collectives to escape the punitive tax rates levied on private (individual) enterprises, which rose steeply at annual profits in excess of about 2,500 yuan (see Chapter 7). Repeated attempts by the State Tax Bureau to ferret out and reclassify such fake collectives have been futile.

While it is impossible to estimate the number of private enterprises hidden among the ranks of collectives, they are the likely explanation for the relatively small number of "private enterprises" with more than eight employees. The other types of private enterprises are less affected. Foreign enterprises enjoy well-defined legal rights and protection. As for the other domestic private enterprises, the socialist veneer of cooperative status affords them legitimacy and some measure of protection from predatory local officials. At the smaller end, "individual enterprises" may simply find buying official patronage too costly and troublesome for the benefits. The incidence of hiding private enterprises varies widely across localities; whether local officials are willing to go along with the ruse generally depends on whether there are significant collective enterprises under their administration (i.e., whether private enterprises are seen as unwelcome competition).

Private management of collective and state-owned enterprises

In addition, a significant portion of collective enterprises operate under de facto private management. Since the early 1980s, many rural collectives have been contracted out to private operators. In some localities they are run essentially as private businesses, with autonomy over labor recruitment and wage setting; contractors pay rent and sometimes a share of the profits for the use of plant and equipment. Lease arrangements of this type are found in more than 80 per cent of township and village enterprises in Fushan prefecture in Guangdong, and they are also common in Fujian province and in the northern PRC (Nee and Su 1993; Oi 1990).

De facto private management extends to the urban state sector as well. As part of the 1984 reform package designed to improve urban productivity, the government announced a plan to contract or lease to collectives and individuals over a three-year period all small-scale state-owned enterprises with fixed assets under 1.5 million yuan and annual profits of at most 200,000 yuan. By the end of 1984, over 11,000 industrial enterprises and 58,000 service enterprises had been contracted out, with rental agreements running up to five years. If fully implemented, this plan would have turned over to private management approximately half of the 81,000 enterprises in the state sector classified as small-scale. Under the plan, awarding of contracts for enterprises was to be based on some combination of bid prices and the qualifications of bidders. Contractors would pay capital charges and income taxes on profits, and keep a substantial share of the after-tax profits. Since the late 1980s, however, little has been heard about this program, and the degree of implementation is not known. To the extent that the contracting arrangements permit de facto private management, they blur the ownership divisions and render impossible the partition of Chinese industry by ownership shares.

CONCLUSIONS

One of the surprising findings of this examination of the nonstate sector is that, despite the obvious importance the government assigns to ownership, official categories are remarkably unhelpful in deciphering ownership shares in Chinese industry. Not only is the coverage of the categories "collective," "individual," and "others" incomplete or muddled or both, these labels are also applied rather loosely.

A variety of joint-ownership forms have cropped up, further undermining the usefulness of official data. One popular form of joint venture involves cooperation between land-poor urban enterprises and cash-poor rural collectives. State-private joint ventures have resulted from the issuance of equity shares to the public by SOEs to raise capital. Other joint-ownership forms are created when joint-stock companies are formed with shares sold to other state or collective enterprises. These hybrid ownership forms are prevalent to varying degrees in different regions and may be significant in some areas. Nee and Su (1993) report that in 1990, state-private joint-ownership enterprises contributed 31 per cent of GVIO in Xiamen municipality (Fujian), rivaling the share of SOEs (32 per cent). This sort of information has not been reported by the State Statistical Bureau.

Leading role of private enterprises

Even with incomplete data, one can draw the unambiguous conclusion that private enterprises led the growth of the nonstate sector through the 1980s. Rural collectives were second most important. According to SSB figures, collective industry increased its output at an average annual rate of 23.5 per cent during 1980–1990, and "individual" industry at 109 per cent.[1] In the rural enterprise sector, private (including cooperative) output grew by 51.2 per cent yearly during 1984–1990, and the output of collectives by 24.8 per cent. The aggregate data for private industry in Table 9.15 show annual growth of 37.4 per cent during 1986–1990—a decisive break from the Maoist pattern. In addition, the impetus for growth in the nonstate sector during the 1980s has come largely from below, in response to market demands.

The fast growth of private enterprises can be explained by "empirical regularities." Ending more than two decades of official suppression of private enterprise, reform policies opened the floodgates, and entrepreneurs rushed in to fill empty niches in sectors that are occupied everywhere in the world by small-scale private enterprises. With SOEs and large collectives saddled with a surfeit of high-cost labor, opportunities were naturally created for the entry of small nonstate enterprises. Enterprises in rural areas, where opportunity costs of labor are much lower, successfully exploited this advantage.

Another explanation is the beneficial effect on the nonstate sector of gradualist reform and dual pricing, which for a time kept profits high in Chinese industry. Preferential tax policies gave rural collectives a critical boost, with an extra cushion of profits to finance further growth. It comes as no surprise that the smallest enterprises have done so well, given their greater flexibility and relative freedom from bureaucratic restraint.

Table 9.15 Average size of firms by type in the nonstate sector, PRC, 1990 (yuan)

	Annual output
Collective	
Urban	
'Large collectives'	2.3 million
'Neighborhood' or affiliated	720.0 thousand
Rural	
Township	1.1 million
Village	352.0 thousand
Private	
Foreign and joint venture	17.3 million
'Foreign' joint ventures	8.9 million
Joint ventures with Hong Kong	15.9 million
Wholly owned	
Mixed domestic 'other' ownership	10.0 million
Cooperatives	177.0 thousand
Urban	86.0 thousand
Rural	
'Individual'	
Urban	25.0 thousand
Rural	21.0 thousand

Sources: Tables 9.1, 9.4, 9.5, and 9.14.

Degrees of autonomy

The broad range in average annual output of the nonstate sector, from 21,000 yuan in rural private enterprises to 17.3 million yuan in foreign joint ventures (see Table 9.15), attests to its heterogeneous nature. Outside of the foreign sector, which is governed by a completely different set of rules, the average private enterprise is very small, and it operates with very little capital. In 1990 "individual" enterprises in the rural sector had an average of 2.8 owner/employees, capital of 2,650 yuan, and output of 20,600 yuan. Even cooperatives had on the average only 8.5 members and capital of 12,200 yuan (or 1,500 yuan per member), produced annual output of 85,640 yuan, and paid 2,674 yuan in taxes. In the urban sector, the average "individual" enterprise in industry had 2.3 owner/employees, capital of 4,800 yuan, and annual output of 25,000 yuan. Urban cooperatives were much larger, with 17 members and annual output of 177,000 yuan, but still had capital of only 2,500 yuan per member. At the other end of the size spectrum are large collectives, producing annual output of 2.33 million yuan on the average. Rural collectives are in between: township enterprises averaged 1.07 million yuan of output, and village enterprises 350,000 yuan.

The behavior and objectives of nonstate firms are quite variable. Some firms are run purely for profit; others (e.g., large collectives) are also concerned with objectives like job creation and community development. In general, however, nonstate enterprises share a relatively high degree of production autonomy. They are free to make a range of decisions in response to market conditions. This is in stark contrast to the state sector, where state prices still govern a substantial portion of output from large and medium enterprises, along with a portion, albeit diminishing, of inputs.

Virtually all nonstate enterprises, except for those in cotton textiles where pricing constraints continue, have to contend with market prices for both inputs and outputs. This is so because most nonstate enterprises have historically been excluded from production plans. Even prior to reform, only a portion of their input supplies came from planned allocations, and most of their output could be sold outside the plan, at extra-plan prices (Wong 1986b). During the reform period, these enterprises quickly grew out of the plan and led the development of markets and market pricing. Large collectives, which were more tightly incorporated in state plans in the 1970s, have also grown quickly out of the plan, with decontrol of manufactured consumer goods (in which they have specialized) in the mid-1980s.

Foreign enterprises aside, there is a clear inverse correlation between enterprise size and operational autonomy. Private enterprises are the most autonomous, their behavior constrained only by the institutional framework, where the government still controls key supplies such as electricity, plant space, credit, and some raw materials, and where the lack of a strong legal system leaves them vulnerable and in need of official protection. The least autonomous are the large urban collectives, whose progress has been very much similar to the SOEs'. For instance, nominal wages in the collective sector have moved in parallel with those in the state sector through the 1980s, and both are far above the opportunity costs of labor (as measured by wages in the urban neighborhood enterprise sector).

Among rural collectives the picture is mixed. One type of behavior follows the "Jiangnan model," which emphasizes collective ownership and active participation of local governments in promoting economic development. This model originated in and around Wuxi county, a prosperous region south of the Yangzi river where rural enterprises are highly concentrated. Under this model, enterprises are closely supervised by local officials. They have practically no financial autonomy; investments, wages, even loan servicing and tax payments are decided by (or jointly with) township or village officials. Their autonomy is severely constrained in personnel decisions as well. Labor is often allocated by township labor bureaus or industrial companies, which may be more interested in equalizing family income in the locality than in matching the right skills to jobs. As a result, many enterprises are overstaffed.

Managers are also appointed by township or village officials. Whiting found in a recent study that officials in the Wuxi-Shanghai area transfer managerial personnel frequently, to keep them from developing strong ties with their workers and thus to weaken the managers' bargaining position against the officials. In one township in suburban Shanghai, few managers had stayed at the same factory for more than two to three years. Whiting's findings are corroborated as a widespread phenomenon by Qiu (1988). Under the Jiangnan model, wage ceilings are often set to limit income disparities within a locality, and funds are commonly pooled at the township or village level for investment and government finance.

Other development models offer greater enterprise autonomy. The "Wenzhou model" emphasizes private enterprise development. In Wenzhou-type areas, many rural collectives are in fact private enterprises using the collective label as a protective shield. Sometimes they are contracted out to private management, with contractors paying rents or a fixed share of profits to the collective. An intermediate model adopted in some localities allows collective management to coexist with contracting systems. But even in these cases, township or village officials usually engage in unilateral recontracting, a practice that sharply limits the contractors' autonomy. Oi (1990) reported that intervention of local officials is especially common in enterprises that have been unexpectedly profitable.

Like rural collectives, urban "small collectives" operate more or less autonomously, depending on the nature of their relationship with local officials. In some areas, the district governments take an active corporate approach to managing community resources, including enterprises. In other areas their management is more hands-off.

Until more data are available on the relative prevalence of these different models, one can only broadly define the range of behavior among nonstate enterprises. However, provincial data appear to support the hypothesis that private management of rural collectives is increasing. Taking Jiangsu and Shanghai as the bastions of the collectivist Jiangnan model, one may be able to correlate the declining share of their rural enterprises in total rural industrial output (from 27 per cent in 1980 to 22 per cent in 1991) with a loosening of the hold of collective enterprises on the rural enterprise sector. If true, this would be consistent with the overall growth of openly private enterprise in the rural sector.

Toward a model of community enterprises?

It is clear from the discussion in this chapter that nonstate enterprises are, to varying degrees, dependent on local governments for survival and growth. This is because of the embryonic nature of markets, where information is obtained and deals are made often through personal contacts and official support. The dependency is nourished by an incomplete legal system and weak enforcement, making official intervention necessary to guarantee contracts. Local governments, at the same time, depend on enterprises for tax and extrabudgetary revenues. At lower levels of government, the existence of tax-paying industries usually spells the difference between self-supporting jurisdictions and those dependent on subsidies from higher levels.

More importantly, the financial interests of local governments in promoting industrial development increasingly transcend ownership boundaries. All things being equal, local governments might be expected to favor state-owned enterprises over nonstate ones; while they collect taxes from all enterprises, they also reap the net incomes of SOEs as owners. However, given the secular decline in profit rates in Chinese industry through the reform period, the residual incomes of SOEs have rapidly diminished. In many localities, direct taxes produce negative revenues, since loss subsidies to SOEs more than offset the revenues collected. Local budgets are thus overwhelmingly dependent upon indirect tax revenues, and most local governments have been weaned from their wonted partiality to state or collective enterprises. Private enterprises that add to the local tax base are welcomed by cash-starved jurisdictions.

NOTE

1 See Table 9.1 in *From Centrally Planned to Market Economics: The Asian Approach* (Hong Kong: Oxford University Press for the Asian Development Bank, 1996), Chapter 9.

Part III

THE AGRICULTURAL SECTOR

10

THE IMPACT OF CHINA'S ECONOMIC REFORMS ON AGRICULTURAL PRODUCTIVITY GROWTH

John McMillan, John Whalley and Li Jing Zhu

This paper presents a method for assessing the relative importance of price increases and strengthened individual incentives due to the introduction of the responsibility system for the post-1978 increase in China's agricultural productivity. Data on post-1978 Chinese agricultural performance suggest that a little over three-quarters of the measured productivity increase is due to payment system changes and the remainder to price increases. We also use our method to calculate incentive indices, giving an estimate of the fraction of their marginal product that peasants received under the pre-1978 regime.

I INTRODUCTION

Between 1978 and 1984, output in the Chinese agricultural sector increased by over 61 percent (see Table 10.1 below). These impressive output gains followed the adoption of a system stressing individual responsibility in place of a system of communal decision making and rewards. The ongoing economic reforms in China, which began in agriculture and are now slowly spreading to manufacturing and other sectors, have attracted much attention in the West. They represent a major social experiment in the design of institutions in which a system emphasizing social values has been replaced by a system relying on economic incentives.

However, not all the increase in agricultural output since 1978 can be attributed to systemic change because the prices of agricultural outputs and the use of inputs such as chemical fertilizers have increased at the same time.[1] The more responsive is output to individual incentives, the larger is the share of the output growth that can be attributed to the new institutions. And conversely, the more efficient was the communal system, the bigger is the

Source: *Journal of Political Economy*, Vol. 97 (August 1989), pp. 781–807.

fraction of growth attributable to the price increases. Although the Chinese themselves explain the output growth as being mainly due to the introduction of the responsibility system, China experts in the West have expressed skepticism.

Here we present a method for decomposing the productivity increase in Chinese agriculture in the post-1978 period into the part that is attributable to price increases and the part that reflects the effects of strengthened individual incentives. Our method combines standard growth-accounting techniques with a simple optimizing model of peasants' response to the institutional structure within which they work.

Subject to caveats about the special functional forms assumed, excluded factors from our analysis (such as improvements in agricultural techniques), and the shortcomings of available data, our calculations suggest that 78 percent of the increase in agricultural productivity in China between 1978 and 1984 can be attributed to the incentive effects of the new responsibility system and 22 percent to the incentive effects of higher prices. We also obtain a measure of the extent to which individual incentives operated under the pre-1978 communal system. Our calculations suggest that it was as if peasants were paid a little over 30 percent of their marginal value product. As a result, the supply of effort under the communal system was only about 56 percent of that under the responsibility system.

These findings have wider implications than simply improving our understanding of performance in Chinese agriculture. Much of modern microeconomic theory focuses on the design of institutions,[2] and Chinese reforms involve an experiment in institutional design on a large scale (involving around 85 percent of the labor force). In the theorists' analyses, it is individuals' self-interested responses that constrain institutional design. In this paper, we use the results of the Chinese experiment to estimate the force of incentive effects.

Our results suggest that rewarding individual effort yields large benefits. Hence, for other countries in which communal methods have been tried and agricultural performance has been poor (such as in Africa; see Bates [1981]), these results suggest that prices and institutions need to be considered together as explanations of performance. The results also suggest that significant further gains could be achieved by comparable reforms in the Chinese industrial sector, allowing price incentives to operate more freely than has hitherto been the case (although industrial reform faces far greater difficulties than agricultural reform; see Shirk [1985]).

In Section II we briefly describe Chinese agricultural arrangements before and after 1978. Section III presents the theory underlying our decomposition method for estimating the relative importance of institutional changes and price changes for agricultural performance. Section IV presents data on productivity growth, our decomposition calculations, and estimated incentive indices. Section V contains sensitivity analyses on model parameters, data, and assumptions used in our calculations. Section VI offers a conclusion. Our data sources and adjustment procedures are described in the Appendix.

II INSTITUTIONAL ARRANGEMENTS IN CHINESE AGRICULTURE

A typical Chinese rural commune in 1978 consisted of three levels of units: the commune, the production brigade, and the production team. The production team was the basic accounting and production-organizing unit. It owned virtually all the land, draft animals, and farm machinery it used. Each team was given annual production targets (conveyed through the commune and brigade). It then drew up its annual production plan, deciding how to use its land, labor, animals, and farm tools; when to plow and plant; and what types of fertilizer to use for which kinds of crops. All peasants, including women and children, were included in the team's labor plan.

There were two principal methods used to allocate work among team members: assigning work on a daily basis and assigning long-term fixed work. In grain production and other major farm tasks, work was assigned to work groups on a rotating basis. For other tasks, work was given to small groups of peasants who often retained a permanent responsibility for the job.

Each production team distributed income among team members largely according to an estimate of each member's labor contribution to production. Under the "labor day/work payment" system, the quantity of work done was measured in terms of labor days. For each day, those who presented themselves in the field would receive a labor day. The quality of work done was measured by work points received per labor day. Members of teams were classified into different grades according to their technical skills, their capacity for work, and their success in meeting the labor norms set up by the team. Different numbers of work points were attached to each grade. Members periodically assessed each other's work and determined the grade each should be classified at and thus the number of work points each should earn for labor days worked during the period of assessment. In this assessment process, team staff (team leaders and heads of work groups) played the main role.

At the end of the agricultural year, the combined income of the team was divided by the sum of work points credited to all team members to determine the value of one work point. The income of each member was determined by multiplying by the number of work points the individual peasant had accumulated over the agricultural year.

Commune members were also allowed to farm small plots of land for personal use and pastoral areas; they were also allowed to keep a limited number of livestock. In most areas, 5 percent of arable land was allocated for private plots. Peasants used these for fruits, vegetables, tobacco, and produce for feeding chickens and pigs. Peasants were also permitted, although subject to certain restrictions, to engage in sideline production such as weaving, knitting, gathering medicinal herbs, and handicrafts. Peasants could trade their produce from private plots and sideline occupations through a farm market, but this was subject to strict government regulation. Transactions were conducted mainly between commune members, and public agencies and enterprises were not permitted to trade in this market. Peasants were not allowed to go to urban areas and sell their products to urban residents.[3]

At the end of 1978, the Chinese central government decided to introduce major reform in agriculture, in large part because of poor agricultural performance over the preceding 20-year period. A "production responsibility system" was introduced to deal with problems of shirking and mismanagement that were associated with the previous communal system. Under the new system, the individual peasant, rather than the production team, became the basic unit for decision making in Chinese agriculture. Most aspects of collective management have since been abandoned, with only land ownership remaining within the collective (Watson 1984; Lardy 1986*a*, 1986*b*). Introduction of this system began in 1979, and by the end of 1984, 97 percent of farm families operated under the responsibility system (see Table 10.5 below).

The responsibility system involves contracts signed between the production team and each household, which regulate the taxes and delivery quotas payable to the state and the welfare funds and investment funds payable to the team. Any production above the delivery quota is retained by the household, which can sell it and receive the proceeds. Most restrictions on production activities on private plots have been removed, and the size of private plots has increased.

The earlier grain self-sufficiency policy, which required each region to be self-sufficient in grain production, has also been abandoned. Regions are now allowed to specialize in planting crops more suitable to their land, rainfall, temperature, and other environmental characteristics. The number of planned product categories and obligatory targets has been sharply reduced. Furthermore, controls over collective production activities have been relaxed, and production teams have greater freedom to organize nonfarm production.

In addition to these changes, reforms in agricultural prices have occurred. Since 1979, state procurement prices have increased for most major farm products. Grain procurement prices have increased by 20 percent for compulsory delivery quotas, and the additional price premium for above-quota sales has been raised from 30 percent to 50 percent (Kueh 1984*a*). Furthermore, extra grain produced can be sold at prices that reflect conditions in the open market, and procurement prices for other farm products have increased substantially. Comparable procurement and premium prices for cotton have been raised by 15 percent and 30 percent, respectively, and compulsory delivery prices for edible oil and pork have increased by 25 percent (Kueh 1984*a*).

Prices of tobacco, vegetables, and soybeans have also been raised (Walker 1984), and prices of some manufactured goods supplied to the agricultural sector have been reduced.

III DECOMPOSING THE EFFECTS OF PRICE INCREASES AND CHANGES IN THE INCENTIVE SYSTEM

The net effect of all these changes has been a sharp increase in output in Chinese agriculture. However, while the introduction of the responsibility system has attracted the most attention, thus far it has not been clear what portion of the output gain to attribute to it, given the simultaneous price increases. One procedure for making such a decomposition is to use growth-accounting techniques associated with Solow (1957) and Denison (1967), but also to incorporate behavioral responses of agricultural workers to changes in both the incentive system and prices. To empirically implement this procedure here, we assume special functional forms in our analysis.

We assume that a peasant can choose the efficiency with which he or she works. If L represents the total number of peasants and ε is the effort of a typical worker, the contribution of labor to output measured in efficiency units is $L\varepsilon$. This approach to representing the labor input in agricultural production is similar to that underlying Stiglitz's (1976) efficiency-wage hypothesis, but unlike Stiglitz, we model the individual's optimizing choice of effort. Although we describe ε as "effort," it should be interpreted broadly to include everything that determines the effective quality of labor: ε might be increased not only by inducing the workers literally to exert more effort but also by encouraging the use of entrepreneurial talent or by removing restrictions on the kinds of tasks a worker may undertake and thereby allowing labor to flow to its most productive uses.[4]

We assume a Cobb-Douglas agricultural production function,[5] given by

$$Q = \alpha_0(\varepsilon L)^{\alpha_1}K^{1-\alpha_1}, \tag{1}$$

where Q and K represent total output and aggregate nonlabor inputs (capital, land, pesticides, fertilizer, etc.), respectively, and α_1 defines the share parameters on factor inputs ($0 \le \alpha_1 \le 1$). The quantity produced by a representative peasant is thus

$$q = \alpha_0\varepsilon^{\alpha_1}k^{1-\alpha_1}, \tag{2}$$

where q and k represent output per peasant and nonlabor inputs per peasant, respectively.

We suppose that each peasant receives an income that depends on his contribution to production and is given by

$$y = \beta pq + c, \tag{3}$$

where p is the price at which additional output is sold, q is the quantity of output produced by the peasant, β is the fraction of the additional revenue generated that the peasant is allowed to keep, and c is a constant term.

Under the post-1978 responsibility system, c is negative (representing the output quota that the peasant must deliver to the government) and $\beta = 1$ (the peasant keeps the proceeds of sales of output beyond his quota). Under the pre-1978 communal system, c is positive (the payment received by the peasant regardless of his own effort) and $0 \leq \beta \leq 1$ since peasants were typically not fully rewarded for effort at the margin because of the reward structure in the commune. Managerial difficulties in operating the communes gave rise to "the problem that individuals [in the commune] could see little connection between effort expended and what they received as income" (Macrae 1977, p. 371). It was difficult to measure an individual's effort accurately, and to some extent the distribution of rewards within the commune was based on egalitarian criteria (Madsen 1984, pp. 141–44).

While equation (3) does not fully model all the complexities of payment under the work points system, it nonetheless captures its main features. The parameter β is an index of the strength of the incentives offered to peasants: it measures the peasants' perception of what fraction of their marginal value product they would be paid.[6] Our assumptions do not rule out the possibility that the problems of team production were overcome by the commune managers or that exhortations to work for the common good were heeded, so that it was as if β were equal to one.

We assume that peasants receive utility from income but dislike effort. We capture this in the simple utility function

$$U(y, \varepsilon) = y - \frac{\varepsilon^z}{z\delta}, \tag{4}$$

where $\delta > 0$ and $z > 1$ are constants. This function implies that the marginal disutility of effort, ε^{z-1}/δ, increases with effort. The work-disutility coefficient z is such that

$$z - 1 = \frac{\varepsilon \partial^2 u / \partial \varepsilon^2}{\partial u / \partial \varepsilon}. \tag{5}$$

Thus, analogous to the coefficient of relative risk aversion, z measures the curvature of the utility function. The utility function (4) also implies that the disutility of effort is independent of the income level.

We now consider the peasants' optimizing choice of effort. Substitution of (2) and (3) into (4) and optimization with respect to ε imply that the optimal effort ε^* satisfies

$$\varepsilon^* = (\delta \alpha_1 \alpha_0 \beta p k^{1-\alpha_1})^{1/(z-\alpha_1)}. \tag{6}$$

Substitution of this into the per worker production function (2) gives

$$q = \alpha_0 (\delta \alpha_1 \alpha_0 \beta p)^{\alpha_1/(z-\alpha_1)} k^{z(1-\alpha_1)/(z-\alpha_1)}. \tag{7}$$

Finally, multiplication of both sides by L to revert to aggregate variables implies

$$Q = AL^{\gamma_1}K^{1-\gamma_1}, \tag{8}$$

where $\gamma_1 = (z-1)\alpha_1/(z-\alpha_1)$ and

$$A = \alpha_0(\delta\alpha_1\alpha_0\beta p)^{\alpha_1/(z-\alpha_1)}. \tag{9}$$

We label (8) the "institutional" production function to distinguish it from the "technical" production function (1). The difference is that while (1) reflects technical relationships between inputs and outputs (i.e., the laws of biology and physics), (8) in addition incorporates the peasants' response to the institutional arrangements within which they work (i.e., the laws of economics).

We note that the institutional production function (8) is expressed in terms of the observable labor input L rather than the unobservable efficiency measure of labor εL, as in the technical production function. It is (8) rather than (1) that would be estimated by conventional aggregate production function estimation, and the estimated factor shares would be γ_1 and $1-\gamma_1$ rather than those of the technical production relationship, α_1 and $1-\alpha_1$. The parameter A would be estimated as total factor productivity rather than α_0.

The parameters α_0 and α_1 are technologically determined, and δ and z are taste parameters: all are invariant to the institutional form. The two policy variables are the output price, p, and the share of the peasant's marginal output that he retains, β. The sole effect of a change in either or both of these policy variables is to change the total factor productivity coefficient A in the institutional production function (8). We can thus assess the effect of changes in β (as with the introduction of the responsibility system) on agricultural productivity for unchanged agricultural prices and the effect of changes in prices for unchanged β, and in this way we can separate the two effects in which we are interested.

With the subscripts i and j used to denote parameter and policy variables for different years, (9) implies

$$\frac{\beta_i}{\beta_j} = \left(\frac{p_j}{p_i}\right)\left(\frac{A_i}{A_j}\right)^{(z-1)/\gamma_1}. \tag{10}$$

Given price indices p_i and p_j, total factor productivity estimates A_i and A_j, the labor share exponent in production γ_1, and an estimate of the work-disutility parameter z, we can use (10) to compute the ratio of the incentive indices, β_i/β_j. Since $\beta_i = 1$ for marginal production under the responsibility system, we can estimate β_j under the communal system. And having estimated β_i/β_j, we can compute

$$\frac{A_i'}{A_j'} = \left(\frac{\beta_i}{\beta_j}\right)^{\gamma_1/(z-1)}, \tag{11}$$

that is, what the ratio of total factor productivities would have been if there had been no price changes (i.e., if $p_j = p_i$). Equation (11) therefore provides an estimate of the extent to which observed productivity increases were caused by the incentive effect of the institutional changes alone.

Finally, from (6) and the fact that $\alpha_1 = \gamma_1 z/(\gamma_1 + z - 1)$, for a given capital/labor ratio k, we have

$$\frac{\varepsilon_i}{\varepsilon_j} = \left(\frac{\beta_i p_i}{\beta_j p_j}\right)^{(\gamma_1 + z - 1)/(z^2 - z)}, \qquad (12)$$

which shows the effective quality of labor in year i relative to year j, as a function of the institutional arrangements (the β_i and β_j) and prices.

While the foregoing provides a method for allowing this decomposition to be made, it is also important to emphasize that our estimates of the role of incentive effects are determined by residual, and thus other factors excluded from our analysis can affect our results. It is important to note that our model ignores the possibility that the introduction of the responsibility system may have affected not only the quality of labor but also the effective quality of land, especially to the extent that decentralized decision making results in a better matching of crops to land. Also, the opening of new markets, by creating new gains from trade, may have caused productivity growth. And if technical progress occurs, total factor productivity would increase (via a rise in the parameter α_0).[7] To the extent that any of these effects are at work, our procedures will overestimate the relative efficiency of the responsibility system compared with the communal system.

Our approach also ignores the dynamic nature of the reform process. The reforms were introduced gradually between 1978 and 1983, and presumably individual peasants took some time to adapt to the new institutions and higher prices. We have no information on the timing of these lags, but since we use data up to 1984, our implicit assumption is that most of the transitional effects had worked themselves out by 1984.[8]

IV MEASURING INCENTIVE EFFECTS OF AGRICULTURAL REFORMS

Equations (8) and (9) above imply that the effect of a change in the institutional incentive system or a change in prices is to change the measured total factor productivity, A, in agriculture. If we denote the periods during which the responsibility system and the communal system operated by subscripts i and j, respectively, the ratio A_i/A_j equals the ratio of outputs under the two institutional arrangements for any given input vector. This can therefore be used to provide a measure of the productivity gain attributable to the strengthened incentives under the responsibility system and the increases in agricultural prices.

Decomposing agricultural productivity growth into the components due to price increases and strengthened incentives in this way first requires measurements of productivity growth over the period since 1978. There are no estimates currently available, although there are calculations of agricultural productivity growth for the period 1952–77 that indicate either declines or small advances. According to Tang (1980), although agricultural output almost doubled between 1952 and 1977, output increases failed to keep pace with input increases; total factor productivity declined in 1977 to 85 percent of its 1952 level. Similarly, Perkins and Yusuf (1984, chap. 4) calculate that the change in Chinese agricultural productivity from 1957 to 1979 was either negative or modestly positive.

We have computed Chinese agricultural productivity growth for the period 1978–84 using a modified version of the procedures followed by Tang, and we use price data to decompose changes in Chinese agricultural productivity growth into a price component and an incentive component. However, to obtain the data needed for these calculations, a number of adjustments are required to data available from official Chinese sources.

Data on agricultural output and inputs need to exclude rural industry (including handicrafts). Data on inputs, especially fertilizers and capital, require a number of separate series, not all of which are easily available and for which some further modifications are required. Price data, which are used in our subsequent decomposition, present the problem that the appropriate agricultural price for our analysis is the marginal (above-quota) price for output, whereas official price data average procurement and above-quota prices.[9] Because of the volume of manipulations involved, we report the procedures we have followed in the Appendix.

Table 10.1 reports the resulting estimates of Chinese output, inputs, productivity growth, and price changes for the period 1978–84. Because of the assumptions needed to construct some of the current input series (see the Appendix), here we use some central case assumptions and later report some sensitivity analysis on these estimates. These data show that the post-1978 situation has been strikingly different from the pre-1978 period analyzed by Tang. In 1978, agricultural prices began to increase, and during the early 1980s the introduction of the production responsibility system was completed. These changes have resulted in continuous increases in agricultural productivity growth over these years, with the largest increase occurring in 1982 and 1984.

To analyze the relative importance of price increases and payment system changes underlying this increase in agricultural productivity, we note that, from equation (9), changes in β affect the productivity parameter A in exactly the same way as changes in p; that is, changes in the incentive structure and prices act as perfect substitutes. However, information on price changes is available from Table 10.1, whereas information on changes in β is not: the changes in β must be calculated as residuals. Using equation (10), we can

Table 10.1 Chinese agricultural output, inputs, prices, and productivity growth (under central case assumptions), 1978–84

Year	*Index of value of agricultural output (100 million yuan: 1980 prices)*	*Agricultural labor force (10,000)*	*Total sown area of farm crops (10,000 mu)* *	*Value capital inputs (10,000 horsepower equivalents)*	*Total current inputs (thousands of tons)*	*Total factor productivity growth* ($\dot{A}/A$)†	*Index of agricultural prices relative to industrial prices (1950 = 100)*
1978	1,740.6	28,409.6	225,156	20,998	29,889	...	222.7
1979	1,872.4	28,634.4	222,715	23,220	33,954	.0435	267.9
1980	1,964.5	29,808.4	219,569	25,137	33,155	.0173	280.3
1981	2,091.4	30,677.6	217,736	26,790	36,550	.0409	291.4
1982	2,327.6	31,152.7	217,132	28,422	39,259	.0887	292.8
1983	2,508.2	31,645.1	215,990	30,628	11,269	.0556	298.7
1984	2,815.6	31,685.0	216,332	32,912	13,135	.1073	295.4

Notes: – See the appendix for data sources, adjustments involved, and the assumptions involved.
* One mu equals .1647 acres.
† The growth in total factor productivity is computed as

$$\frac{\dot{A}}{A} - \frac{\dot{A}}{Q} \sum_{i=1}^{1} \gamma_i \frac{\dot{N}_i}{N_i}.$$

where N are the factor inputs and the factor shares γ_i are taken from Lang (1980, p. 28). The values used are .50 for labor, .25 for land, .10 for capital inputs, and .15 for current inputs (including fertilizers).

estimate the ratio of incentive indices in different years, β_i/β_j, which we label as an incentive index estimate.

These calculations use the total factor productivity estimates from Table 10.1 along with the price indices, the labor share, and utility function parameters. Agricultural price indices are reported in the last column of Table 10.1. We take the labor share parameter to be 0.50, following Tang (1980).[10] We also need the parameter z, which determines the curvature of the utility function and must satisfy the restriction that it exceed one. Although not directly observable, z can be calculated indirectly. Between 1978 and 1979, there were substantial agricultural price increases (of 22 percent) but little change in the communal system (Watson 1984, p. 90). Assuming that from 1978 to 1979 β was unchanged, we can infer the value of z from (10). We compute this to be 3.1699, and we use this value in our other computations.[11]

Table 10.2 reports our estimates of the incentive index ratio β_i/β_j. If we assume that $\beta = 1$ in 1984 (peasants receive their full marginal value product under the responsibility system), then the 1984 estimate in Table 10.2 implies that in 1978 β was 0.3022. In the communal system as it was organized at the end of the Cultural Revolution, it was as if, on the margin, an individual worker was paid a little over 30 percent of his marginal value product.[12]

Using equation (11) and the β_i/β_j estimates, we can also assess the likely incentive effects had the responsibility system been introduced alone without the agricultural price increases. These results are also reported in Table 10.2, and they show that if there had been no price increase between 1978 and 1984, total factor productivity would have increased by 32 percent, compared with the 41 percent increase that actually occurred. This implies that 78 percent of the productivity gain in Chinese agriculture between 1978 and 1984 can be attributed to the strengthened individual incentives generated by the new institutions and the remaining 22 percent to the price increases.[13] Finally, using equation (12) to compute $\varepsilon_{1981}/\varepsilon_{1978}$, we find that the effective supply of labor in 1978 (taking effort into account) was about 56 percent of what it became in 1984.

V SENSITIVITY ANALYSIS

In our calculations, the least reliable of our parameter estimates is the utility function curvature parameter, z. The greater is z and the marginal disutility of effort, the greater should be the proportion of productivity increase due to reforms of the payment system. In Table 10.3, we report the estimated ratio $\beta_{1984}/\beta_{1978}$ and the percentage of the productivity gain attributable to the incentive scheme change for alternative values of z. Although these estimates are sensitive to changes in the value of z, over a wide range of values the approach still attributes most of the productivity increase to changed incentive structure.

Table 10.2 Incentive indices and total factor productivity change in Chinese agriculture, 1979–84

	1979[*]	*1980*	*1981*	*1982*	*1983*	*1984*
Ratio of incentive indices β_t/β_{1978}[†]	1.000	1.0298	1.1787	1.6962	2.1029	3.3087
Actual total factor productivity *A* (1978 = 100)[‡]	104.35	106.16	110.50	120.30	126.99	140.61
Hypothetical total factor productity *A′*, assuming no price changes (1978 = 100)[§]	104.35	100.68	112.95	118.68	118.68	131.75

Note:
[*] By our choice of z, β_{1979} equals β_{1978}, and so by assumption all the increase in productivity in 1978–79 is due to the price increase.
[†] Computed using eq. (10).
[‡] Computed from table 1.
[§] Computed using eq. (11).

Table 10.3 Impact of changes in the utility function curvature parameter, *z*, on the relative importance of price increases and payments system changes for Chinese agricultural productivity growth

	Case 1: "standard" case (z = 3.1699)	*Case 2 (z = 2)*	*Case 3 (z = 4)*	*Case 4 (z = 5)*
Ratio of incentive indices:				
$\beta_{1984}/\beta_{1978}$	3.3087	1.4901	5.8265	11.5196
Proportion of productivity increase between 1978 and 1984 due to payments system changes	.78	.54	.84	.88

The least reliable data series in our calculations are those that are used to generate the current input series. Strong assumptions are made (see the notes to Table 10.A1, in particular those for river and pond mud and the green manure series), and utilization rates for natural fertilizers such as night soil and hog and large animal manure are assigned somewhat arbitrarily. Utilization of natural fertilizer is also labor- and thus time-intensive, and as a result the increase in prices following the 1978 changes may have caused either increases or decreases in its use, depending on the relative strength of income and substitution effects. The further complication is that because crop stems are usually not recycled back to the field (because of the lack of other kinds of cooking fuel, peasants in many regions of China use them for that purpose), the only way to maintain and improve land quality is through organic fertilizer. Whether peasants have an incentive to undertake investment in land (such as using more organic fertilizer) depends on the term of tenure. Before 1984, the term was limited to 1–3 years, and starting in January 1984, it was extended to 15 years (Kueh 1984*a*, p. 371).

We have carried out sensitivity analysis on the impact of changes in assumed utilization rates for organic fertilizer on A_{1984}/A_{1978}. We reduce utilization rates for night soil and hog and large animal manure by 5 percent per year from 1979 onward and keep the amount of river and pond mud and green manure produced constant (the weights assigned to them are too small to be significant).

As can be seen from Table 10.4 (comparing case 1 with case 2), the impact of these changes on results is quite small, mainly because the factor share on the growth rate of current inputs is only 15 percent, and changing the current inputs series produces only small changes in productivity growth.

To investigate how changes in factor shares affect our results, we use two alternative sets of share parameters. One set is as estimated by Hayami and Ruttan (1985) (.53 for labor .10 for land, .21 for farm capital, and .16 for fertilizer). The other is somewhat arbitrarily chosen, assigning a higher

Table 10.4 Impacts of various sensitivity analysis of measured annual productivity growth and the relative importance of price increases and payments system changes

Annual productivity growth in	*Case 1: "standard" case from tables 1 and 2*	*Case 2: with different measures of current inputs **	*Case 3: with different shares for inputs (labor = .70, land = .15, capital = .05, current imputs = .10)*	*Case 4: with Hayami-Ruttan estimates of shares (labor = .53, land = .10, capital = .21, current inputs = .16)*	*Case 5: with different labor input measurement*
1978–79	.0435	.0498	.0529	.0287	.0435
1979–80	.0173	.0178	.0141	.0045	.0194
1980–81	.0409	.0442	.0391	.0313	.0543
1981–82	.0887	.0914	.0937	.0805	.1018
1982–83	.0556	.0571	.0583	.0453	.0623
1983–84	.1053	.1127	.1132	.0988	.1086
Ratio of incentive indices: $\beta_{1984}/\beta_{1978}$	3.3087	2.9553	2.7147	4.6784	3.8401
Hypothetical total factor productivity A', assuming no price changes (1978 = 100)	1.3186	1.3297	1.3213	1.2665	1.3635
Proportion of productivity increase between 1978 and 1984 due to payments system changes	.78	.76	.75	.83	.80

Note:
* See the Appendix.

weight to labor (.70, .15, .05, and .10, respectively) to reflect higher shares on labor common in OECD countries. Cases 3 and 4 in Table 10.4 show that the impact of using the arbitrarily chosen set is small; for some years the effect is positive, for others negative. With the Hayami-Ruttan estimates, the effect is larger and uniformly negative. The arbitrarily chosen set reduces the contribution of payments system changes to the productivity increase relative to our "standard" case by 3 percent. With the Hayami-Ruttan estimates, the proportion is increased by 5 percent.

Labor inputs are commonly measured using hours worked, but time-series data in this form are not available for the Chinese agricultural sector. Our central case calculations use the number of peasants working in the field as the measure of labor input. After the introduction of the responsibility system, if, as widely reported, peasants worked fewer hours in the field, our measure would overstate labor input.

To investigate how our measurement of labor input affects our results, we use some strong assumptions to estimate the number of hours worked by peasants. A survey study done on a village in Hebei province estimates that hours worked per day by each peasant were 9.55 before the introduction of the responsibility system and 8.80 after (see Dai et al. 1985). We assume that these two estimates apply to all peasants working in the field in China. Because the responsibility system was not introduced until late 1979 or early 1980, measured labor inputs per worker are assumed to be the same for 1978 and 1979; that is, we assume that all peasants worked 9.55 hours per day. Between 1980 and 1984, the percentage of households working under the responsibility system changed in each year (see Table 10.5). Using these to generate estimates of the percentage of peasants working 8.80 hours per day over the period 1980–84, we modify our measures of labor input. Computations done on this basis (case 5, Table 10.4) show that the proportion of agricultural productivity increase between 1978 and 1984 due to incentive scheme changes is 80 percent, 2 percent above our standard case.

Table 10.5 Coverage of the responsibility system in the Chinese agricultural sector

Year	*Total number of households in agricultural sector*	*Percentage of households under the responsibility system* *
1979	17,491.1	...
1980	17,672.2	5†
1981	18,016.2	38†
1982	18,278.6	70†
1983	18,523.2	94‡
1984	18,792.6	97‡

Note:
* The responsibility system referred to here is the contracting-everything-to-household type.
† From Kuch (1981a).
‡ From *Chinese Agricultural Yearbook* (1985).

The last factor we investigate in our sensitivity analysis is the choice of price data. The official agricultural prices are average price data. However, because our calculation requires marginal prices, we have to make strong assumptions in transforming these data into marginal form (see the discussion on the index of relative agricultural to industrial prices in the Appendix, Sec. *F*). To assess the impacts of possible errors in price measurement on our results, we have considered four alternative cases. In these, we change the marginal prices (on which the calculations in the last section were based) for each year from 1979 onward in four cases by +5 percent, +10 percent, −5 percent, and −10 percent, respectively. Table 10.6 presents the results after the price data are altered in this way. As can be seen, they do not significantly change our main conclusion that increases in productivity in Chinese agriculture after 1978 are mainly due to changes in the payments system.

These sensitivity analyses thus seem to suggest that while there is some variation in our results because of data and other assumptions, the size is small, and our results seem to be quite robust. The most important cause of the strong Chinese productivity growth between 1978 and 1984 appears consistently to be payments system changes rather than price increases.

VI CONCLUSION

This paper presents a method for assessing the relative importance of price increases and the introduction of the responsibility system for improved agricultural performance in China following the economic reforms initiated in 1978. We employ a production function approach in which optimizing effort decisions of peasants are captured. Peasant supply of effort expands as either the prices of agricultural products or the fraction of their value marginal product they receive increases. Subject to caveats about the simplifications of our theoretical model, the shortcomings of the data, and the fact that our analysis excludes some other potential sources of productivity growth, our central case results suggest that 22 percent of the increase in productivity in Chinese agriculture between 1978 and 1984 was due to higher prices and 78 percent to changes in the incentive scheme. We estimate that the incentive effects of the change from the pre-1978 communal system to the post-1978 responsibility system resulted in a 32 percent increase in total factor productivity in agriculture. These results seem to be reasonably robust to alternative data and other assumptions.

The approach developed above could also be used to analyze other cases of large-scale institutional change. For example, as Johnson (1985) notes, attempts in the early 1980s to increase agricultural output in the Soviet Union by raising prices were not successful. This is consistent with our finding that in China price increases alone would not have generated large output increases. Also, if a system of large landholdings farmed by sharecroppers is reformed so that the land is put into the hands of the peasants, the

Table 10.6 Sensitivity analysis from different assumed annual agricultural price changes between 1978 and 1984

	Case 1: additional 5% increase each year	*Case 2: additional 10% increase each year*	*Case 3: additional 5% decrease each year*	*Case 4: additional 10% decrease each year*
Ratio of incentive indices:				
$\beta_{1984}/\beta_{1978}$	4.6564	6.4503	2.3102	1.5811
Hypothetical total factor productivity A', assuming no price changes:				
A_{1984}/A_{1978}	1.3237	1.3351	1.3062	1.2787
Proportion of productivity increase between 1978 and 1984 due to payments system changes	.80	.83	.75	.69

parameter β is changed from the contractual share of output retained by the sharecropper (typically 50 percent) to become equal to one. The approach employed in this paper could be used to analyze the effects of such land tenure reforms.

APPENDIX

Data sources and adjustments

This Appendix documents the data sources we have used and describes the various adjustments we have made to produce the series on agricultural inputs, outputs, and prices reported in Table 10.1 in the text. To construct these series we need, in places, to use strong assumptions, and so we have also constructed data under alternative assumptions for the purpose of doing sensitivity analysis. These are also presented in this Appendix.

A. Index of value of gross agricultural output

We use data from the *Chinese Statistical Yearbook 1986* (p. 167). This series includes the value of agricultural output but excludes the value of manufacturing output (including handicrafts) produced in the agricultural sector.

B. Agricultural labor force

This series includes all labor force in the agricultural sector working on planting crops, forestry, herding, fishery, and sideline production but excludes those working on other activities including rural manufacturing. Data for 1980–84 are from the *Chinese Agricultural Yearbook* for 1981–85 (pp. 11, 18, 21, 68, and 122, respectively). Data for 1978 and 1979 are derived using the 1980 ratio of labor force working in the relevant sectors to the total labor force in the whole agricultural sector. The total labor force figures for the two years are from the *Chinese Statistical Yearbook 1985* (p. 213).

C. Total sown area of farm crops

This data series is taken directly from the *Chinese Statistical Yearbook 1986* (p. 174).

D. Total capital inputs

This series is generated by adding together the number of draft animals and the total horsepower of farm machinery (*Chinese Statistical Yearbook 1986*, pp. 188 and 147, respectively). In doing so, we assume that each draft animal is equal to one horsepower. The assumption is based on the observation for Pakistan (see Blomqvist 1986, p. 142) that a bullock-day (a pair of bullock working 8 hours) is paid approximately the same as a tractor-hour, with a typical tractor being between 15 and 25 horsepower. Our capital input series differs from that used by Tang (1980), which is restricted to machinery and other mechanical inputs and excludes draft animals. In a developing country, draft animals provide transportation both in the field and on the road in the countryside. Thus ignoring these as a component of working capital is inappropriate.

E. Total current inputs

Our measures of current inputs for our central case series are reported in Table 10.1 of the text and are based on a number of separate series that are aggregated using a weighting procedure. Each of these series has been separately constructed. Most use procedures similar to those employed in Tang (1980) and, like Tang, also include feed and seed. These series are summarized in Table 10.A1, and the notes to this table summarize their construction. Table 10.A2 lists alternative series on current inputs, constructed under various assumptions on possible changes since the 1978 reforms in the underlying coefficients used by Tang.

F. Index of relative agricultural to industrial prices

Table 10.1 also presents our series on relative agricultural to industrial prices and reflects a number of adjustments to official agricultural price data designed to yield a series based on marginal (above-quota) prices. Official agricultural price data are average price data, averaging above-quota sales and quota deliveries. Since we require a series on marginal (above-quota) sales, we modify these data.

We use data on the percentage of agricultural output purchased at different prices (presented in Table 10.A3). We assume that the above-quota price is the same as both the negotiation price and the free-market price and that the reported average price series (see Table 10.A3) is generated by the weighting scheme, $p^A = \lambda p^{AQ} + (1 - \lambda)p^Q$, where p^A is average price, p^{AQ} is the above-quota price, and p^Q is the quota price; λ is the percentage of output purchased at p^{AQ}. According to Sicular (1985, p. 1061), quota and above-quota procurement price indexes for grains in 1982 (1978 = 100) are 126 and 145, respectively. We make the strong assumption that this ratio applies both for all the agricultural products and for all the years we consider. This yields $p^{AQ} = (145/126)p^Q$ and hence that

$$p^{AQ} = \frac{p^A}{\lambda + (1 - \lambda)(126/145)}.$$

Using this formula, we obtain a value for λ and the marginal price series as reported in Table 10.A3.

Table 10.A1 Series used in calculating total current inputs in table 1 (thousands of metric tons)

Year	*Night soil*[a]	*Hog manure*[b]	*Large animal manure*[c]	*Green manure*[d]	*River and pond mud*[d]	*Oil cake*[f]	*Nutrient content of organic fertilizer*[g]	*Chemical fertilizer*[h]	*Nutrient content of all fertilizer*[i]	*Insecticide*[j]	*Feed*[k]	*Seed*[k]
1978	407,290	542,320	650,650	177,200	152,120	6,266	20,895	8,840	29,735	1,464	38,019	30,477
1979	411,190	575,470	655,500	187,400	152,120	6,809	21,597	10,863	32,269	1,514	46,773	33,212
1980	415,460	549,770	660,080	198,200	152,120	7,659	21,509	12,694	34,203	1,527	53,706	32,056
1981	420,061	528,660	676,640	209,600	152,120	9,572	21,771	13,349	35,120	1,512	56,499	32,502
1982	425,200	541,400	700,830	221,600	152,120	10,215	22,334	15,134	37,468	1,582	61,226	35,450
1983	425,030	537,370	717,250	234,400	152,120	9,952	22,507	16,598	39,105	1,228	64,202	38,728
1984	416,120	552,220	715,140	247,800	152,120	10,589	23,102	17,398	41,500	1,471	64,202	40,712

Notes:

[a] Calculated from the rural and urban population series in the *Chinese Statistical Yearbook 1986* (p. 91) using the same formula as used by Tang (1980, p. 61); i.e. night soil used = .5 × (rural population × (rural utilization rate) + .5 × (urban population) × (urban utilization rate). In our calculation the rural and urban utilization rates are 90 percent and 60 percent, respectively.

[b] Calculated from the hog holding series in the *Chinese Statistical Yearbook 1986* (p. 188) according to Tang's formula (p. 61); hog manure used = 2 × (hog holdings × rural utilization rate = 90 percent).

[c] Calculated from the large animal holding series in the *Chinese Statistical Yearbook 1986* (p. 188) according to Tang's formula (p. 62); draft animal manure used = 7.7 × (draft animal holdings) × (rural utilization rate = 90 percent).

[d] As in Tang (p. 63), we assume that production of green manure increases 5.75 percent annually in the post-1978 reform period.

[e] This is a relatively unimportant nutrient source. The figures are from Tang (pp. 63–64).

[f] Calculated from the soybean output series and cooking oil crops series (including peanut, sesame seed, and rapeseed) in the *Chinese Statistical Yearbook 1985* (p. 255, according to Tang's formula; i.e., oil cake = 49 × (soybean output + cooking oil crops output).

[g] Following Tang (p. 64), we use the formula: nutrient content = .011 × (night soil) + .0141 × (hog manure) + .0087 (large animal manure) + .0091 × (green manure) + .105 × (oil cake) + .0055 × (mud).

[h] This series is from the *Chinese Statistical Yearbook 1986* (p. 194). According to explanators notes for the series, the data reflect effective nutrient content.

[i] This series is obtained by adding together the two previous columns.

[j] Data for 1978–83 are from State Statistical Bureau (1984, p. 251). Figures for 1984 are the average of the figures for 1982–83.

[k] These data are obtained from Sicular (1985). The feed figure for 1984 is assumed to be the same as in 1983. We follow Tang (p. 50) in generating the current input series. The weights assigned to feed, seed, fertilizers, and insecticides are 15.5 percent, 15.5 percent, 64.6 percent, and 4.4 percent, respectively.

Table 10.A2 Series used in calculating total current inputs for sensitivity analyses reported in text (thousands of metric tons)

Year	Night soil	Hog manure	Large animal manure	Green manure	River and pond mud	Oil cake	Nutrient content of organic fertilizer	Chemical fertilizer	Nutrient content of all fertilizer	Insecticide	Feed	Seed	Total current inputs
1978	407,290	542,320	650,650	177,200	152,120	6,266	20,895	8,840	29,735	1,464	38,019	30,477	29,889
1979	386,801	543,500	619,090	177,200	152,120	6,809	20,469	10,863	31,332	1,514	46,773	33,212	32,706
1980	370,895	988,680	586,740	177,200	152,120	7,659	19,329	12,694	32,023	1,527	53,706	32,056	34,047
1981	345,005	440,550	563,870	177,200	152,120	9,572	18,368	13,349	31,717	1,512	56,499	32,502	34,351
1982	323,658	421,090	545,090	177,200	152,120	10,215	17,761	15,154	32,895	1,582	61,226	35,450	36,305
1983	269,911	388,100	518,010	177,200	152,120	9,952	16,748	16.598	33,346	1,228	64,202	38,728	37,550
1984	260,909	368,140	500,760	177,200	152,120	10,589	15,980	17,398	33,378	1,471	64,202	40,712	37,888

Note: —In this table, we report the series used in calculating alternative total current inputs for sensitivity analysis. The method used to generate this table is the same as the one used to generate table A1 (see notes to table A1). However, for the series of night soil, hog manure, and large animal manure, we assume that both rural and urban utilization rates decrease by 5 percent each year from 1979 onward. For the series of green manure, we keep it constant instead of increasing it by 5.75 percent annually as in Tang (p. 63). The rest of the series are the same as those in table A1. The final column is the alternative total current inputs series.

Table 10.A3 Official and constructed price data used in analyzing price and payment system changes in agriculture

	Percentage of agricultural output purchased at different prices				*Retail price index for manufacturing goods sold in agricultural sector*	*Price index for agricultural output purchased*	
Year	*Quota price* *(1)*	*Above-quota price* *(2)*	*Negotiation price* *(3)*	*Market price* *(4)*	*(1950 = 100)* *(5)*	*Average (1950 = 100)* *(6)*	*Marginal (1950 = 100)* *(7)*
1978	84.7	7.9	1.8	5.6	109.8	217.4	244.5
1979	74.5	12.9	5.7	6.9	109.8	265.5	294.2
1980	64.4	17.9	9.5	8.2	110.8	284.4	310.6
1981	58.2	20.9	11.5	9.4	111.9	301.2	326.1
1982	57.5	20.8	11.5	10.2	113.7	307.8	332.9
1983	48.0	28.1	13.4	10.5	114.8	321.3	342.9
1984	33.9	33.6	14.4	18.1	118.4	334.2	349.7

Source: —Cols. 1–4: *Chinese Statistical Yearbook 1985* (p. 479). Cols. 5, 6; *Chinese Statistical Yearbook 1986* (p. 624). Col. 7: Calculated by using the method described in this section.

The relative price series in Table 10.1 is obtained by dividing series *e* in Table 10.A3 by series *b*.

ACKNOWLEDGMENTS

We thank Loren Brandt, Justin Lin, Barry Naughton, Louis Putterman, and Susan Shirk; seminar participants at the World Bank (Washington, D.C.), the Chinese University of Hong Kong, and Chung-Hua Institution for Economic Research, Taiwan; and an exceptionally helpful referee for comments and advice. McMillan's research was supported by a grant from the Academic Senate of the University of California.

NOTES

1 See Hartford (1985, p. 56), Lardy (1986*b*), and Surls (1986, p. 338) for earlier discussions on the difficulties of decomposing output growth into responsibility system and price effects.

2 See the literature on mechanism design (Groves and Ledyard 1987; Hart and Holmstrom 1987; McAfee and McMillan 1987*a*).

3 This description of the communal system closely follows Cheng (1982).

4 This is a Marshallian point of view: "the effective supply of any agent of production at any time depends firstly on the stock of it in existence, and secondly on the willingness of those, in whose charge it is, to apply it in production" (Marshall 1920, p. 437).

5 Brandt (1987) gives some evidence from the 1930s, and Lin (1987*a*) presents evidence for the 1980s.

6 This model of incentives in the commune can be thought of as a reduced form of a more complex reward structure. For a more detailed model of the operation of the work points system, see Lin (1987*b*). Note also that inefficiencies are not inherent in team production. McAfee and McMillan (1987*b*) show that it is possible to devise contracts based on team output that give individuals the appropriate incentives at the margin.

7 Chinese agriculture had already attained a technically advanced state before the period examined here, and thus changes in α_0 during the period in question may have been relatively small. According to Lardy (1983, pp. ix, 47–48), hybrid corn and new rice varieties were introduced from the mid-1960s to the mid-1970s. By 1977, high-yield rice varieties were cultivated on 80 percent of China's rice-growing land (see also Perkins and Yusuf 1984, pp. 54–57).

8 Although 1984 was an unusually productive year, choosing 1984 as our end date affects our results less than might appear at first sight. The large increase in productivity in 1984 was not only sustained but further increased in 1985; total factor productivity in agriculture rose by 4.4 percent from 1984 to 1985.

9 In calculating the marginal (above-quota) price for output, we assume that it is the same as both the negotiation price and the free-market price (see the discussion in the Appendix). A free-market price series is currently available from official sources (State Statistical Bureau 1984, p. 395), but this series shows a fall in price between 1978 and 1980. Besides the issue of how reasonable this is, such a decrease presents problems for us if we use the series in our calculations. In order to calculate the utility function curvature parameter *z*, we assume that the increase in productivity between 1978 and 1979 is due only to the increase in

price (see the discussion about the computation of hypothetical total factor productivity A' in Sec. IV). Clearly, such a calculation cannot be performed if we use this series. As a result, we ignore it in our calculations. The plausibility of such a price fall being recorded in official data, in turn, involves the issue of whether compensating adjustments in transactions costs occurred so that the effective price received by farmers rose. We are grateful to a referee for pointing this out.

10 Tang based his factor share estimates on income shares in 1952, when incomes were determined by competitive market forces. (Brandt [1987] gives some evidence that rural input markets operated reasonably efficiently in prerevolutionary China.) For comparison, the Cobb-Douglas coefficients for the aggregate agricultural production functions estimated by Hayami and Ruttan (1985, chap. 6) from a sample of 22 less developed countries are .53 for labor, .10 for land, .21 for farm capital, and .16 for fertilizer. Thus the Tang estimates for China (respectively, .50, .25, .10, and .15) are much the same as the Hayami-Ruttan estimates for less developed countries generally in the case of labor (the most important coefficient for our calculations) and fertilizer, but they are higher for land and lower for capital.

11 Since differences in weather conditions can cause substantial fluctuations in output, this computation of z presumes that weather was much the same in 1979 as in 1978. Kueh (1984*b*, p. 69) indicates that in 1978, 42.9 percent of grain-growing land was affected by natural disasters, where "affected" means that yields were at least 30 percent below normal; in 1979, the corresponding number was 38.4 percent.

12 Before 1978, between 5 percent and 7 percent of land was cultivated on private plots, producing a disproportionately large share of output (Perkins and Yusuf 1984, p. 83). Presumably $\beta = 1$ on the private plots. This is averaged into our pre-1978 β calculation; as a result, the efficiency of labor on the communes would have been even less than our estimate indicates.

13 Lin (1987*a*) uses the fact that the responsibility system was introduced gradually between 1980 and 1983, at different rates in different provinces, to also estimate these incentive effects. He found that about 60 percent of the output growth between 1980 and 1983 was attributable to the responsibility systems. Our estimate that the responsibility system accounted for 78 percent of the growth in total factor productivity in agriculture between 1978 and 1984 implies that it accounted for about 41 percent of the growth in total output. In comparing Lin's results with ours, note that his results refer to a shorter time interval than ours, and the price increases during 1980–83 were relatively small (see Table 10.1 above), so that one would expect to find a larger responsibility system effect in 1980–83 than in 1978–84.

REFERENCES

Bates, Robert H. *Markets and States in Tropical Africa: The Political Basis of Agricultural Policies*. Berkeley: Univ. California Press, 1981.

Blomqvist, Ake. "The Village and Beyond: Markets and Public Policy (1)." In *Scarp Marden Evaluation Baseline Study*, edited by J. Freedman. Ottawa: Canadian Internat. Development Agency, 1986.

Board of Editors for Chinese Agricultural Yearbook. *Chinese Agricultural Yearbook*. Beijing: Chinese Agricultural Publishing House, various years.

Brandt, Loren. "Farm Household Behavior, Factor Markets, and the Distributive Consequences of Commercialization in Early Twentieth-Century China." *J. Econ. Hist*. 47 (September 1987): 711–37.

Cheng, Chu-yüan. *China's Economic Development: Growth and Structural Change.* Boulder, Colo.: Westview, 1982.

Dai, Xiaojing; Huang, Xiaojing; Jiang, Beichen; and Yang, Guansan. "The Issues of Time Allocation and Household Management in Agricultural Sector." In *Countryside, Economy, Society*, vol. 3, edited by Chinese Rural Development Research Group. Beijing: Knowledge Press, 1985.

Denison, Edward F. *Why Growth Rates Differ: Postwar Experience in Nine Western Countries.* Washington: Brookings Inst., 1967.

Groves, Theodore, and Ledyard, John. "Incentive Compatibility since 1972." In *Information, Incentives and Economic Mechanisms: Essays in Honor of Leonid Hurwicz*, edited by Theodore Groves, Roy Radner, and Stanley Reiter, Minneapolis: Univ. Minnesota Press, 1987.

Hart, Oliver D., and Holmstrom, Bengt. "The Theory of Contracts." In *Advances in Economic Theory: Fifth World Congress*, edited by Truman Bewley. Cambridge: Cambridge Univ. Press, 1987.

Hartford, Kathleen. "Socialist Agriculture Is Dead; Long Live Socialist Agriculture! Organizational Transformation in Rural China." In *The Political Economy of Reform in Post-Mao China*, edited by Elizabeth J. Perry and Christine Wong. Cambridge, Mass.: Harvard Univ. Press, 1985.

Hayami, Yujiro, and Ruttan, Vernon W. *Agricultural Development: An International Perspective.* Rev. ed. Baltimore: Johns Hopkins Univ. Press, 1985.

Johnson, D. Gale. "The Agricultures of the USSR and China: A Contrast in Reform." Manuscript. Chicago: Univ. Chicago, September 1985.

Kueh, Yak-Yeow. "China's New Agricultural-Policy Program: Major Economic Consequences, 1979–1983." *J. Comparative Econ.* 8 (December 1984): 353–75. (*a*)

——. "A Weather Index for Analysing Grain Yield Instability in China, 1952–81." *China Q.*, no. 97 (March 1984), pp. 68–83. (*b*)

Lardy, Nicholas R. *Agriculture in China's Modern Economic Development.* Cambridge: Cambridge Univ. Press, 1983.

——. "Agricultural Reforms in China." *J. Internat. Affairs* 39 (Winter 1986): 91–104. (*a*)

——. "Prospects and Some Policy Problems of Agricultural Development in China." *American J. Agricultural Econ.* 68 (May 1986): 451–57. (*b*)

Lin, Justin. "Household Farm, Cooperative Farm, and Efficiency: Evidence from Rural Decollectivization in China." Discussion Paper no. 533. New Haven, Conn.: Yale Univ., Econ. Growth Center, March 1987. (*a*)

——. "The Household Responsibility System in China's Agricultural Reform: A Theoretical and Empirical Study." Manuscript. New Haven, Conn.: Yale Univ., 1987. (*b*)

McAfee, R. Preston, and McMillan, John. "Auctions and Bidding." *J. Econ. Literature* 25 (June 1987): 699–738. (*a*)

——. "Optimal Contracts for Teams." Manuscript. London: Univ. Western Ontario, 1987. (*b*)

Macrae, John. "Production, Distribution and Economic Organization: Income Distribution and Resource Allocation at the Team Level in Rural China." *J. Development Econ.* 4 (December 1977): 365–85.

Madsen, Richard. *Morality and Power in a Chinese Village.* Berkeley: Univ. California Press, 1984.

Marshall, Alfred. *Principles of Economics.* 8th ed. London: Macmillan, 1920.

Perkins, Dwight H., and Yusuf, Shahid. *Rural Development in China.* Baltimore: Johns Hopkins Univ. Press (for World Bank), 1984.

Shirk, Susan L. "The Politics of Industrial Reform." In *The Political Economy of Reform in Post-Mao China*, edited by Elizabeth J. Perry and Christine Wong. Cambridge, Mass.: Harvard Univ. Press, 1985.

Sicular, Terry. "China's Grain and Meat Economy: Recent Developments and Implications for Trade." *American J. Agricultural Econ.* 67 (December 1985): 1055–62.

Solow, Robert M. "Technical Change and the Aggregate Production Function." *Rev. Econ. and Statis.* 39 (August 1957): 312–20.

State Statistical Bureau. *Zhong guo mao yi wu jia tong ji zi liao, 1952–1983* (Chinese statistical materials on trade and prices). Beijing: Chinese Statis. Publishing House, 1984.

——. *Chinese Statistical Yearbook*. Beijing: Chinese Statis. Publishing House, various years.

Stiglitz, Joseph E. "The Efficiency Wage Hypothesis, Surplus Labour, and the Distribution of Income in L.D.C.s." *Oxford Econ. Papers* 28 (July 1976): 185–207.

Surls, Frederic M. "China's Agriculture in the Eighties." In *China's Economy Looks to the Year 2000*. Washington: U.S. Congress, Joint Econ. Comm., 1986.

Tang, Anthony M. "Food and Agriculture in China: Trends and Projections, 1952–77 and 2000." In *Food Production in the People's Republic of China*, by Anthony M. Tang and Bruce Stone. Research Report no. 15. Washington: Internat. Food Policy Res. Inst., 1980.

Walker, Kenneth R. "Chinese Agriculture during the Period of the Readjustment, 1978–83." *China Q.*, no. 100 (December 1984), pp. 783–812.

Watson, Andrew. "Agriculture Looks for 'Shoes That Fit': The Production Responsibility System and Its Implications." In *China's Changed Road to Development*, edited by Neville Maxwell and Bruce McFarlane. Oxford: Pergamon, 1984.

11

RURAL REFORMS AND AGRICULTURAL GROWTH

Justin Yifu Lin

This paper employs province-level panel data to assess the contributions of decollectivization, price adjustments, and other reforms to China's agricultural growth in the reform period. Decollectivization is found to improve total factor productivity and to account for about half of the output growth during 1978–1984. The adjustment in state procurement prices also contributed positively to output growth. Its impact came mainly from the responses in input use. The effect of other market-related reforms on productivity and output growth was very small. Reasons for slowdown in agricultural growth after 1984 are also analyzed. (JEL O47, P27, Q11).

China's agricultural growth in the socialist period prior to the reforms starting in the late 1970's was sluggish. Despite stress on self-sufficiency, grain production and agricultural output barely kept pace with population growth. This picture changed in 1978, when China began a series of fundamental reforms in the rural sector. Growth rates in all major sectors of agriculture were accelerated to levels several times higher than the long-term averages over the preceding period (see Table 11.1).

The dramatic growth during 1978–1984 was a result of a package of market-oriented reforms. As the rural reforms were so successful, the government was encouraged to take a bolder approach to reforms in both rural and urban sectors in 1985. Although agriculture as a whole still grew at respectable rate of 4.1 percent per year thereafter, rapid growth in the subsector of crops, especially grain and cotton, came to a sudden halt (see Table 11.1). Since most prominent leaders in China have an obsession with the idea of grain self-sufficiency, the disappointing performance of grain production has endangered the future of the market-oriented reforms.

Much has been written about China's economic reform.[1] There are disagreements among students of the Chinese economy about the main reasons behind the remarkable agricultural growth since 1979. The major changes are as follows. The state procurement prices for major crops, on the average,

Source: *American Economic Review*, Vol. 82(1) (1992), pp. 34–51.

Table 11.1 Average annual growth rates of agriculture, 1952–1987

	Annual growth rate (percentage)		
Subsector	*1952–1978*	*1978–1984*	*1984–1987*
Crops	2.5	5.9	1.4
Grain	2.4	4.8	−0.2
Cotton	2.0	17.7	−12.9
Animal husbandry	4.0	10.0	8.5
Fishery	19.9[a]	12.7	18.6
Forestry	9.4	14.9	0
Sidelines	11.2	19.4	18.5
Agriculture (overall)	2.9	7.7	4.1

Notes: In 1952, the weights of the five agriculture subsectors were: crops, 83.1 percent; animal husbandry, 11.5 percent; fishery, 0.3 percent; forestry, 0.7 percent; sidelines, 4.4 percent. In 1987, the weights were: crops, 60.7 percent; animal husbandry, 22.8 percent; fishery, 4.7 percent; forestry, 4.8 percent; sidelines, 7.0 percent. For sidelines, outputs from village-run enterprises were excluded.

[a] The low base level in 1952 is the main reason for fishery's high average annual growth during 1952–1978.

Source: Ministry of Agriculture Planning Bureau (1989 pp. 112–15, 146–9, 189–92) and Ministry of Agriculture (1989 pp. 28, 34).

were raised 22.1 percent in 1979. The change from the collective system to the individual household-based farming system, now called the household-responsibility system (hereafter HRS), began in 1979 and was essentially completed by the end of 1983. The government has also introduced several other changes in its policies of grain procurement and marketing since 1979. Moreover, in addition to the aforementioned reforms, the availability of purchased inputs, particularly chemical fertilizers increased substantially during this period.

Identifying the sources of the rapid agricultural growth during 1978–1984 is important for the future course of rural reforms in China. If the change from the collective system to HRS was the major factor underlying the sudden output growth, then future reforms should be oriented toward strengthening the position of household farms. On the other hand, recollectivization would be the logical course if the shift to HRS was detrimental to production, its harmful impact simply being compensated by rapid output growth arising from rises in price, increases in inputs, and other reforms. The main purpose of this paper is to disentangle the contribution to output growth of the HRS reform from those of other reforms, as well as from that of increased input availability.

Few attempts have been undertaken to assess the effects of particular components of the reforms. Exceptions include Lin (1989), James Guanzhong Wen (1989), and John McMillan et al. (1989). All three studies identify HRS as the main source of the dramatic output growth. However, there are serious drawbacks with each of these three studies.[2]

This paper applies the production-function approach proposed by Zvi Griliches (1963) to evaluate the effects of the various components of reforms on agricultural growth. The data used in this study are the province-level panel data from 1970 to 1987 for 28 of the 29 provinces in mainland China. The novelty of the present study, however, is the inclusion of separate proxies for changes in institution, prices, crop patterns, cropping intensity, and technology in the production function to assess the impacts of these changes.

The organization of the paper is as follows: Section I provides an overview of rural reforms in China. The data used in the empirical evaluation are briefly summarized in Section II. Section III discusses the estimation method and reports the empirical results. The growth accounting for 1978–1984 and 1984–1987 is reported in Section IV. Finally, some concluding remarks are presented in Section V.

I RURAL REFORMS IN CHINA

Broad changes in rural policy began at the end of 1978. The government's original intention was to improve agricultural production through raising the long-depressed state procurement prices for major crops, modifying management methods within the collective system, and increasing budgetary expenditure on agricultural investments. The change from the collective system to the household-based farming system—the most far-reaching change to date in China's economic reforms—was explicitly prohibited in 1978.

A Price reform

Before the reforms, two distinct prices existed in the state commercial system: quota prices and above-quota prices. Quota prices applied to crops sold in fulfillment of procurement obligations; above-quota prices applied to crops sold in excess of the obligation. Effective in 1979, quota prices for grain, oil crops, cotton, sugar crops, and pork were raised an average of 17.1 percent. In addition, the premium paid for above-quota delivery of grain and oil crops was increased from 30 percent to 50 percent of the quota prices, and a 30-percent bonus was instituted for above-quota delivery of cotton.[3] The weighted average increase was 22.1 percent. If only the marginal prices, that is, the above-quota prices, are considered, the increase was 40.7 percent (see column 1 in Table 11.2).

Corresponding to the increase in procurement prices, retail prices for pork, fish, and eggs were raised one-third, but no changes were made in grain and edible-oil prices. To compensate for this, each urban resident received a 5–8-yuan subsidy per month (State Statistical Bureau, 1988a p. 12). As a result, the government's price subsidies increased substantially. The financial

Table 11.2 Price index (1978 = 100)

Year	*State above-quota price index (1)*	*Rural-market consumer price index (2)*	*Rural industrial-product price index (3)*	*Ratio of state above-quota price to industrial-product price index (4)*	*Ratio of market price to industrial-product price index (5)*
1970	97.2	80.4	101.9	95.4	78.9
1971	98.4	87.4	100.4	98.0	87.1
1972	98.4	94.6	99.8	98.6	94.8
1973	98.1	99.6	99.8	98.3	99.8
1974	98.4	101.4	99.8	98.6	101.6
1975	98.7	105.5	99.8	98.9	105.7
1976	99.4	109.7	99.9	93.5	109.8
1977	100.0	107.0	100.0	100.0	107.0
1978	100.0	100.0	100.0	100.0	100.0
1979	140.7	95.5	100.1	140.4	95.4
1980	140.4	97.4	100.9	139.2	96.5
1981	145.1	103.0	101.9	142.3	101.1
1982	144.3	106.5	103.6	139.3	102.8
1983	144.9	110.9	104.6	138.6	106.1
1984	142.5	110.5	107.8	132.1	102.5
1985	129.4	129.5	111.3	116.2	116.3
1986	130.1	140.0	114.9	113.3	121.9
1987	130.2	162.8	120.4	108.1	135.2

Sources: See Appendix.

burden became especially unbearable when an unexpected growth in output began to emerge in 1982. The price subsidies increased from 8.4 percent of the state budget to 24.6 percent of the state budget in 1984 (*China Statistical Yearbook*, 1988 pp. 747, 763). As a way to reduce the state's burden and to increase the role of markets, the mandatory quotas were abolished (for cotton in 1984 and for grain in 1985) and replaced by procurement contracts which were supposed to be negotiated between the government and the farmers. The contract price was a weighted average of the basic quota price and the above-quota price. This change resulted in a 9.2-percent drop in the price margin paid to farmers (see Table 11.2). Following the decline of grain and cotton production in 1985 and stagnation thereafter, however, the contracts were made mandatory again in 1986.

Alongside state commercial channels, market fairs have always existed and played an important role in rural China. Farmers, after fulfilling their quota obligations, could sell their produce in market fairs. With rare exceptions, the market prices are higher than the state procurement prices, even measured with the above-quota premiums. Moreover, as Table 11.2 shows, market prices and state procurement prices do not always move in the same direction. Table 11.2 also reports the time-series of state procurement prices and market prices relative to the prices of manufactured inputs in rural markets, which will be used in Section III to estimate the impact of price changes on agricultural growth.

B Institutional reform

The change in farming institution from the collective system to HRS was not originally intended by the government. Before the reform, agricultural operations were organized in the production-team system. Each team consisted of about 20–30 neighboring households. Because of difficulties in monitoring agricultural work in a team, rewards to individual farmers were not tied directly to their efforts, and incentives to work were thus very low (Lin, 1988).

It was acknowledged in 1978 that the key to improving the farmer's incentives was to solve the managerial problems in the team system. However, the government at that time considered subdivision of collectively owned land into individual household tracts to be opposed to socialist principles, and thus it explicitly prohibited this practice. Nevertheless, toward the end of 1978, a small number of production teams, first secretly and later with the blessing of local authorities, began to try out the system of contracting land, other resources and output quotas to individual households. A year later, these teams brought in yields far larger than those of other teams. The central authorities later conceded the existence of this new form of farming but required that it be restricted to poor regions. However, most teams ignored this restriction. Full official acceptance of HRS was eventually given in late 1981, when 45 percent of the production teams in China had already been dismantled. By the end of 1983, 98 percent of production teams had adopted HRS (see column 1 in Table 11.3). Thus the shift in the institutional structure of Chinese agriculture by and large evolved spontaneously in response to underlying economic forces (Lin, 1987). Under HRS, collectively owned land was assigned to individual households with contracts of up to 15 years.[4]

The government so far still stresses its intention of maintaining the stability of the newly instituted HRS. However, the doctrine of equating advanced technology with big tractors and efficiency with large farm size is still deeply rooted in the minds of many scholars and prominent leaders in China (Robert F. Ash, 1988). Due to increasing discontent with the stagnation of grain production after 1984, the call for recollectivization has emerged, under the guise of enlarging operational size to exploit returns to scale. In some localities, this call has resulted in disruption of contracts before expiration without the consent of farmers (Yaping Jiang, 1988). It is thus possible that farmers may be deprived of the economic independence and greater freedom they have been given in the past 10 years (D. Gale Johnson, 1990 Ch. 8).

Table 11.3 HRS, crop pattern, and cropping intensity

		Sown area (percentage)			
Year	*Household responsibility system (1)*	*Grain crops (2)*	*Cash crops (3)*	*Other (4)*	*Multiple cropping index (percentage) (5)*
1970	0	83.1	8.2	8.7	141.9
1971	0	83.1	8.2	8.7	144.7
1972	0	81.9	8.5	9.6	147.0
1973	0	81.6	8.6	9.8	148.2
1974	0	81.4	8.7	9.9	148.7
1975	0	81.0	9.0	10.0	150.0
1976	0	80.6	9.2	10.2	150.6
1977	0	80.6	9.1	10.3	150.5
1978	0	80.4	9.6	10.0	151.0
1979	0.01	80.3	10.0	9.7	149.2
1980	0.14	80.1	10.9	9.0	147.4
1981	0.45	79.2	12.1	8.7	146.6
1982	0.80	78.4	13.0	8.6	146.7
1983	0.98	79.2	12.3	8.5	146.4
1984	0.99	78.3	13.4	8.3	146.9
1985	0.99	75.8	15.6	8.6	148.4
1986	0.99	76.9	14.1	9.0	150.0
1987	0.99	76.8	14.3	8.9	151.3

Note: Column 1 indicates the proportion of production teams in China that had adopted the household-responsibility system.

Sources: The data for column 1, 1979–1981, are from *Economic Weekly News* [*Jingjixue Zhoubao*] (11 January 1982). Figures for 1982–1984 are taken from *China Agricultural Yearbook* (1984 p. 69, 1985 p. 120). Figures for 1985–1987 are inferred from the fact that no major change has occurred in the farming institution since 1984. Columns 2–5 are taken from Ministry of Agriculture Planning Bureau (1984 p. 132, 1989 pp. 130–1, 335–7) and *China Statistical Yearbook* (1988 pp. 224, 243, 276).

C Market and planning reform

The third most important element of the reforms is the greater role given to markets in guiding agricultural production. The prevalence of planning in agriculture before the reforms was a result of self-sufficiency in grain. Because grain procurement prices were depressed to levels lower than prevailing market prices, the more grain an area sold to the state, in effect, the more tax it paid. Areas with a comparative advantage in grain production were thus reluctant to raise their grain output levels. Consequently, grain deficient areas had to increase grain production themselves if local grain demand increased due to growth in population or income. The national self-sufficiency policy thus degenerated into a policy of local self-sufficiency. To guarantee that each region would produce enough grain for its needs, planning in agricultural production was extensive. Mandatory targets often specified not only acreage for each crop, but also yields, levels of inputs, and so on. As planners gave priority to grain, insufficient consideration was given to profitability and regional comparative advantage. To increase grain output to meet state procurement quotas or local demand, local governments often expanded grain acreage at the expense of cash crops or raised cropping intensity to a level that brought net losses to farmers.

At the beginning of the reforms, the government recognized the losses in allocation efficiency caused by the self-sufficiency policy. The decision to increase grain imports, cut down grain procurement quotas, and reduce the number of products included in agricultural planning reflected an intention to increase the role of markets.[5] Moreover, the government loosened restrictions on private interregional trade in agricultural products. Special measures were also taken to encourage areas with traditional comparative advantage in cotton production to expand cotton acreage.[6]

All the aforementioned reforms reduced the role of state intervention and increased the function of markets in guiding agricultural production. As a result, cropping patterns and cropping intensity changed substantially between 1978 and 1984. The area devoted to cash crops increased from 9.6 percent of total sown acreage in 1978 to 13.4 percent in 1984, a 41.6-percent increase; meanwhile, the multiple cropping index declined from 151 to 146.9 (see Table 11.3).

The climax of the market and planning reform was the declaration at the beginning of 1985 that the state would no longer set any mandatory production plans in agriculture and that obligatory procurement quotas were to be replaced by purchasing contracts between the state and farmers. The restoration of household farming and the increase in market freedom prompted farmers to adjust their production activities in accordance with profit margins. The acreage devoted to cash crops further expanded, while grain acreage declined (see Table 11.3). The expansions in animal husbandry, fishery, and subsidiary production were even faster. As a result of these adjustments, agriculture still grew at a respectable rate of 4.1 percent annually during 1984–1987, although the crop sector stagnated (see Table 11.1).

The market-oriented reforms had aroused anxiety in some sectors of the government from their very beginning. Concerns over "loss of control" were widely reported in the early 1980's (Sicular, 1988). In the wake of unprecedented success between 1978 and 1984, the pro-market group was able to push the reforms further in the market direction. However, when growth rates slowed down and grain output declined in 1985 and thereafter, the government retreated from its position. The voluntary procurement contract was made mandatory again. Throughout the period 1985–1991, administrative intervention in market and production has been increasing.

The above events are the major components of the rural reforms since 1978. As described, the reforms were highly successful up to 1984 but have encountered some problems since then. How much of the output growth during 1978–1984 can be attributed to various components of the reforms and what factors have been responsible for the slowdown since 1984 are the focuses of the following sections.

II DATA

The data used in this study include observations for 28 of the 29 provinces in mainland China for 1970–1987.[7] A number of adjustments were required in order to make the data suitable for this study. Detailed information on sources and adjustments is given in the Appendix. Here, I only report a summary description of the data set.

In this study, agricultural output refers to crop outputs.[8] Values of crop output for each province are calculated from the physical outputs of seven grain crops and 12 cash crops, using official prices of 1980 as weights for aggregation. Nationally, these 19 crops accounted for 92 percent of total acreage and 72.5 percent of the cropping sector's output value in 1980.[9]

Inputs in the data set include four categories: land, labor, capital, and chemical fertilizer. Land refers to cultivated land; cultivated land is used rather than sown acreage because I also want to see how changes in cropping intensity affected outputs. Labor refers to the number of workers in the cropping sector. Capital includes tractors and draft animals, measured in horsepower. Chemical fertilizers refers to the gross weight of nitrogenous, phosphate, and potash fertilizers that each province consumed in each year. The output and input series are summarized in Table 11.4.

In addition to the four conventional inputs, five other factors are included to reflect various components of the reforms. These measures are the ratio of production teams converted to HRS, the index of above-quota prices and market prices relative to manufactured input prices, the percentage of sown acreage for nongrain crops, and the multiple cropping index (the ratio of sown acreage to cultivated acreage). These measures are used to capture, respectively, the impacts of farming institutional change, state procurement price adjustments, and market reforms. The price indexes are the national indexes, and the other three measures are provincial-level observations.[10]

The total number of observations for each variable is 504. However, since information on the number of production teams converted to HRS in each province in 1980 is not available, that year's observations are deleted, and the actual number of observations that will be used in the analysis is 476. This data set presents an unusual opportunity for undertaking a careful analysis of the impacts of reforms on agricultural growth, as well as an opportunity for estimating the Chinese agricultural production function econometrically.[11]

Table 11.4 Index of crop output and inputs (1978 = 100)

Year	Crop output (1)	Farm labor (2)	Labor in cropping sector (3)	Land (3)	Capital (4)	Chemical fertilizers (5)
1970	77.10	99.09	103.04	101.76	51.73	36.30
1971	82.82	101.16	104.00	101.29	58.60	41.55
1972	80.48	100.78	102.04	101.20	64.04	47.94
1973	88.25	102.91	103.76	100.80	69.02	58.52
1974	91.50	102.93	104.21	100.50	75.05	55.08
1975	94.22	100.81	103.35	100.11	79.97	60.87
1976	92.43	100.65	102.46	99.98	85.55	66.06
1977	91.47	100.05	100.41	99.82	93.09	73.09
1978	100.00	100.00	100.00	100.00	100.00	100.00
1979	107.10	102.17	103.66	100.10	104.22	120.15
1980	102.36	104.75	107.63	99.91	122.12	134.29
1981	108.52	107.81	111.58	99.44	131.74	141.44
1982	119.60	109.48	112.82	99.21	141.16	156.00
1983	129.42	111.22	115.34	98.89	153.40	169.06
1984	142.23	111.35	114.69	98.89	165.29	171.62
1985	139.52	106.65	104.56	97.46	176.65	167.38
1986	140.76	107.06	95.79	96.81	191.09	183.10
1987	148.21	108.48	88.70	96.47	209.71	192.10

Source: See Appendix.

III FUNCTIONAL FORM SPECIFICATION AND RESULTS

If production were purely an engineering relationship between inputs and outputs, any variation in inputs, except for those due to random shocks, would be a result of changes in inputs. However, the observed production function in general is an economic relationship, as the intensity with which observed resources are utilized depends on economic decisions made by workers as well as managers in response to institutional arrangements, profitable opportunities, and so on (Harvey Leibenstein, 1966; Michael R. Carter, 1984; McMillan et al., 1989). Therefore, the technical efficiency of production can be altered by economic reforms.

Changes in relative prices are expected to affect not only the level of input use, but also the choice between work and leisure as in standard microeconomic analysis. Adjustments in crop patterns in response to soil temperature, rainfall, and other region-specific characteristics are a major source of productivity growth in agriculture. [12] Changes in the multiple cropping index reflect, in a way, how intensively land and labor inputs are utilized. Finally, any change in farming institution alters the compensation scheme and is expected to affect the level of effort supplied by each farmer.

The agricultural-production function estimated is a Cobb-Douglas function with four conventional inputs: land, labor, capital and chemical fertilizer

(Fert). In addition, six other variables are included in the function: the proportion of teams that have changed to the household responsibility system (HRS), the index of market prices relative to manufactured input prices (MP) the index of above-quota prices relative to manufactured input prices (GP), the percentage of total sown area in nongrain crops (NGCA), the multiple cropping index (MCI), and a time trend (T) (see the Appendix for variable definitions). The non-conventional variables are incorporated to assess the impacts of farming institutional change, price adjustments, market reforms, and technological changes. Because the productivity of conventional inputs also depends on some omitted time-persistent region-specific variables (e.g., soil quality, rainfall, irrigation, temperature, average education level, etc.), 27 provincial dummies are included in the production function in order to obtain consistent estimates. This specification gives rise to the estimation equation

$$\begin{aligned} \ln(\mathrm{Y}_{it}) = \alpha_1 &+ \alpha_2 \ln(\mathrm{Land}_{it}) \\ &+ \alpha_3 \ln(\mathrm{Labor}_{it}) \\ &+ \alpha_4 \ln(\mathrm{Capital}_{it}) + \alpha_5 \ln(\mathrm{Fert}_{it}) \\ &+ \alpha_6 \mathrm{HRS}_{it} + \alpha_7 \mathrm{MP}_{t-1} + \alpha_8 \mathrm{GP}_t \\ &+ \alpha_9 \mathrm{NGCA}_{it} + \alpha_{10} \mathrm{MCI}_{it} + \alpha_{11} T_t \\ &+ \sum_{j=12}^{39} \alpha_j D_j + \varepsilon_{it} \end{aligned} \tag{1}$$

where the α's are the parameters to be estimated, and ε is the error term. The output and the four conventional inputs are in natural-logarithm form. Because size of province varies greatly, to prevent the heteroscedastic problem, the output as well as the conventional input variables are normalized by the number of teams in each province in 1980. Theoretically, the relevant price variables should be the expected prices. For the government procurement price, the current prices at each year are the expected prices at that year, because changes in the state procurement prices are announced prior to the beginning of the production season. However, for the market prices, price expectation is a complicated function of past experience and other information on the economy (John Muth, 1961). Since no information about the structure of market-price expectation in China is available, the market prices are taken simply as the prices in the previous year.

The above specification is in the form of a one-way fixed-effects model. For comparative purposes, a two-way fixed-effects model, which includes both regional dummies and year dummies in the specification, will also be estimated. In the two-way fixed-effects model, the price variables have to be deleted because they are region-invariant national indexes. The coefficients of time dummies capture partly the impacts of year-to-year price changes on productivity. The resulting specification is as follows:

$$\ln(Y_{it}) = \alpha'_1 + \alpha'_2 \ln(\text{Land}_{it}) + \alpha'_3 \ln(\text{Labor}_{it}) + \alpha'_4 \ln(\text{Capital}_{it}) + \alpha'_5 \ln(\text{Fert}_{it}) + \alpha'_6 \text{HRS}_{it} + \alpha'_7 \text{NGCA}_{it} + \alpha'_8 \text{MCI}_{it} + \sum_{j=9}^{36} \alpha'_j D_j + \sum_{k=37}^{52} \alpha'_k T_k + \varepsilon'_{it}. \quad (1')$$

Expression (1) is designed with the intention of estimating the impacts of reforms in institution, price, and the role of markets on *productivity*. However, application levels of conventional inputs, the crop pattern (NGCA), and cropping intensity (MCI) may be endogenous to the shift to HRS and to price changes. If this is so, the impacts of HRS and price changes on *production* may be over- or underestimated in the specification of expression (1). Therefore, to assess their total impacts on agricultural production, I will also estimate a supply-response function in the form

$$\ln(Y_{it}) = \beta_1 + \beta_2 \text{HRS}_{it} + b_3 \text{MP}_{t-1} + b_4 \text{GP}_t + \beta_5 T_t + \sum_{i=6}^{33} \beta_i D_i + \mu_{it}. \quad (2)$$

T in this specification will capture not only the trend in technological change, but also the trend in the availability of inputs.

The appropriate method for obtaining consistent estimates of expressions (1) and (2) depends on the structure of disturbances ε_{it} and μ_{it}. If ε_{it} and μ_{it} are spherical disturbances, the covariance estimator of ordinary least squares (OLS) is the best linear unbiased estimator. If production is inside the efficiency frontier and the disturbance can be specified as the difference of two independent terms, one with a normal distribution and the other one with a positive-half normal distribution, the stochastic-frontier regression developed by Dennis J. Aigner et al. (1977) will produce consistent estimates of parameters. If there exist intertemporal correlations and the covariance matrix is unknown, then the appropriate method for fitting expressions (1) and (2) is estimated generalized least squares (EGLS).

As a first step, I apply both OLS and the stochastic-production-frontier model to estimate expression (1). The results are reported in columns 1 and 2 of Table 11.5. For the sake of simplicity, the estimates for regional dummies are not presented. Except for the index of above-quota prices (GP), all of above-quota prices (GP), and the time trend (T), all other estimates are highly statistically significant. Moreover, the estimates resulting from the stochastic-production-frontier model differ little from the cast-squares estimates.

The last row of columns (1) reports the estimated intertemporal correlation of the disturbance

$$r_{it,it-1} = \left(\sum_{i=1}^{28} \sum_{t=1}^{17} e_{it}, e_{it-1} \right) \Big/ \left(\sum_{i=1}^{28} \sum_{t=1}^{17} e_{it} \right)$$

where e_{it} represents the estimates for ε_{it}. The resulting $r_{it,it-1}$ is −0.15. Under the null hypothesis of no intertemporal or spatial correlation, $r_{it,it-1}$ has a standard error $N^{-1/2}$, where N is the number of observations (George G. Judge et al., 1985 p. 319). There are 476 observations in the sample, and the standard error under the null hypothesis is 0.046. Hence, the evidence suggests that intertemporal correlations exist in the disturbances. Although OLS still produces unbiased estimates for regression coefficients, the significance tests for the estimated coefficients are invalid.

In a one-way fixed-effects model with unknown intertemporal covariance, the individual effects cannot be consistently estimated when the time period is fixed. Nicholas M. Kiefer (1980) suggested that one could first eliminate individual effects by subtracting group means from both regressand and regressor and then estimate regression coefficients and the asymptotic variance-covariance matrix by EGLS. The estimates resulting from applying Kiefer's estimator to expression (1) are reported in column 3 of Table 11.5. As expected, the estimated coefficients differ little from those estimated using OLS, and their associated standard errors are uniformly smaller than those of OLS. While the estimates for market prices (MP), above-quota procurement prices (GP), and time record (T) are still not significantly different from zero, the estimate for capital is statistically significant at the 0.05 level (asymptotic $t = 1.85$.) Column 4 reports the estimates when the insignificant variables MP, GP, and T are dropped. The resulted estimates are basically the same as those in column 3. I shall adopt the estimates in column 4 for growth accounting in the next section.[13]

Column 5 of Table 11.5 reports the results of applying Kiefer's estimator to expression (2). The estimates for HRS are almost identical to those in columns 3 and 4. However, the estimated coefficients for the index of market prices (MP), the index of above-quota prices (GP), and time trend (T) are larger than those in column 3 and, in fact, are highly statistically significant.

The results of fitting the two-way fixed-effects model of expression (1′) are presented in column 6. All the estimated coefficients are in the same range as the estimates in column 4. These results support the use of the estimates in column 4 for growth accounting in the next section.

Table 11.5 Estimates of production and supply response function (dependent variable = Ln(value of crop output in constant prices)

Explanatory variable	*One-way fixed-effects*		*EGLS*			*Two-way fixed-effects*
	OLS	*Stochastic frontier*				
	(1)	*(2)*	*(3)*	*(4)*	*(5)*	*(6)*
ln(Land)	0.65	0.59	0.67	0.67		0.58
	(0.07)	(0.05)	(0.04)	(0.04)		(0.09)
ln(Labor)	0.14	0.11	0.14	0.13		0.15
	(0.03)	(0.03)	(0.02)	(0.01)		(0.03)
ln(Capital)	0.037	0.057	0.050	0.070		0.10
	(0.040)	(0.034)	(0.027)	(0.015)		(0.04)
ln(Fert)	0.18	0.18	0.20	0.19		0.17
	(0.02)	(0.02)	(0.01)	(0.01)		(0.02)
Proportion in household farming (HRS)	0.19	0.22	0.19	0.20	0.18	0.15
	(0.03)	(0.03)	(0.01)	(0.01)	(0.01)	(0.05)
(Market price)/(input price) at time $t-1$ (MP_{t-1})	0.00038	0.0010	0.00051		0.0034	
	(0.00123)	(0.0013)	(0.00061)		(0.0007)	
(Government price)/(input price) at time t (GP_t)	−0.00067	−0.00054	−0.00058		0.0021	
	(0.00055)	(0.00059)	(0.00035)		(0.0004)	
Multiple cropping index (MCI)	0.0020	0.0018	0.0015	0.0020		0.0020
	(0.0009)	(0.0011)	(0.0006)	(0.0006)		(0.0008)
Percentage of nongrain crops (NGCA)	0.0067	0.0093	0.0068	0.0078		0.0078
	(0.0023)	(0.0023)	(0.0015)	(0.0013)		(0.0022)
Time trend (T)	0.0065	0.0005	0.0028		0.021	
	(0.0065)	(0.0068)	(0.0042)		(0.003)	
Regional dummies	yes	yes				yes
Time dummies						yes
Adjusted R^2:	0.961					0.966
Log likelihood:		430.35				
$R_{it,it-1}$:	−0.15					

Notes: Numbers in parentheses are standard errors or estimated asymptotic standard errors. The estimated coefficients of 27 provincial dummies in columns 1, 2 and 6, and of 16 year dummies in column 6 are not reported.

Table 11.6 Accounting for crop output growth: production function

		1978–1984		1984–1987	
Explanatory variable	*Estimated coefficient (1)*	*Change in explanatory variable (2)*	*Contribution to growth (percentage) (3) = (1) × (2)*	*Change in explanatory variable[b] (4)*	*Contribution to growth (percentage) (5) = (1) × (4)*
Inputs			**19.34 (45.79)**		**–0.42 (–9.97)**
Land	0.67	–1.1	–0.74 (–1.75)	–2.4	–1.61 (–38.24)
Labor	0.13	14.7	1.91 (4.52)	–22.7	–2.95 (–70.07)
Capital	0.07	65.3	4.57 (10.82)	26.9	1.88 (44.73)
Fertilizer	0.19	71.6	13.60 (32.20)	11.9	2.26 (53.71)
Productivity			**20.54 (48.64)**		**2.05 (48.69)**
Household-farming reform (HRS)	20.00	0.99	19.80 (46.89)	0	0
Multiple cropping (MCI)	0.20	–4.1	–0.82 (1.94)	4.4	0.88 (20.90)
Ratio of nongrain crops (NGCA)	0.78	2.0	1.56 (3.69)	1.5	1.17 (27.79)
Residual			**2.35 (5.57)**		**2.58 (61.28)**
Total growth:			**42.23 (100.00)**		**4.21** (100.00)

Notes: The estimated coefficients are taken from column 4 of Table 5. HRS, multiple cropping index (MCI), and percentage of nongrain crop area (NGCA) are in a semilog form in expression (1). To calculate the contributions of these variables to output growth in terms of percentage, the estimated coefficients of these variables are multiplied by 100. For land, labor, capital, and fertilizer, "change in explanatory variable" refers to the percentage growth of that variable. For HRS, multiple cropping index (MCI), and percentage of nongrain crop area (NGCA), the change refers to the difference in magnitude of that variable between t_1 and t_2. Changes in output and input are calculated from Table 4; changes in HRS, MCI, and NGCA are from Table 3. The numbers in parentheses are the percentage shares of contribution to total output growth, with total output growth set at 100.

From the evidence presented in columns 3, 4, 5, and 6 of Table 11.5, one can conclude that the shift from the production-team system to HRS had a positive and significant effect on agricultural growth, which came primarily from the change in total factor productivity. The changes in both state procurement prices and market prices also had significant effects on agricultural growth. However, in contrast to the case of institutional reform, these effects derived from impacts on levels of input usage, cropping intensity (MCI), and crop composition (NGCA). The estimated coefficient of the time trend (*T*) is not statistically significant in column 3, but it is positive and highly significant in column 5. This implies that there was no increasing trend in technological change but that there was a positive trend in agricultural output growth during 1970–1987. The latter trend might stem from the increasing availability of inputs such as chemical fertilizers. The positive and significant estimates of cropping intensity (MCI) and crop composition (NGCA) in columns 3, 4, and 6 suggest that, given the inputs and other variables, an increase in the cropping intensity or in the proportion of nongrain crops will also result in an increase in output.

IV SOURCES OF AGRICULTURAL GROWTH DURING 1978–1984 AND 1984–1987

This section attempts to assess the relative contributions of the various components of reforms and changes in inputs to agricultural growth in 1978–1984 and 1984–1987. Table 11.6 reports the growth counting based on the estimate of the agricultural production function in column 4 of Table 11.5, and Table 11.7 reports that based on the supply-response function estimated in column 5. In Table 11.6, the sources of output growth are divided into three categories: change in conventional inputs, productivity change due to reforms, and unexplained residual. The first two categories are in turn subdivided into several items. In Table 11.7, the sources of output growth are divided into the shift to HRS, the changes in market prices and state procurement prices, the time trend, and the residual.

The total output growth during 1978–1984 was 42.23 percent. From the accounting in Table 11.6, it appears that 45.79 percent of this output growth came from increases in inputs. The most important source of growth from inputs was the increase in the application of fertilizer, which alone contributed to about one-third (32.2 per cent) of the output growth during 1978–1984. The growth derived from increases in labor and capital and the adverse impact on growth resulting from reduction in cultivated land were minor. Rural reforms also contributed significantly to output growth during 1978–1984. The productivity change resulting from various reforms made up 48.64 percent of the output growth. Among the various components of reform, the shift from the production-team system to HRS is clearly the most important one. This institutional reform alone produced 48.69 percent

Table 11.7 Accounting for crop output growth: supply-response function

		1978–1984		1984–1987	
Explanatory variable	*Estimated coefficient* (1)	*Change in explanatory variable* (2)	*Contribution to growth (percentage)* (3) = (1) × (2)	*Change in explanatory variable* (4)	*Contribution to growth (percentage)* (5) = (1) × (4)
Household-farming reform (HRS)	18.00	0.99	17.82 (42.20)[c]	0.00	0.00
[Market price]/ [input price] (MP)	0.34	−0.93	−0.32 (−0.76)	15.71	5.36 (127.32)
[State procurement price]/[input price] (GP)	0.21	32.14	6.75 (15.98)	−24.03	−5.04 (−119.72)
Trend (*T*)	2.10	6.00	12.60 (29.74)	3.00	6.30 (149.64)
Residual			5.38 (12.74)		−2.41 (57.24)
Total growth:			42.23 (100.00)		4.21 (100.00)

Notes: The estimated coefficients are taken from column 4 of Table 11.5. HRS, index of market price (MP), index of state procurement price (GP), and time trend (*T*) are in a semilog form in expression (2). To calculate the contributions of these variables to output growth in terms of percentage, the estimated coefficients of these variables are multiplied by 100. The change in explanatory variable refers to the difference in magnitude of that variable between t_1 and t_2. Changes in output and input are calculated from Table 11.4; change in HRS is from Table 11.3; and changes in MP and GP are from Table 11.2. The numbers in parentheses are the percentage shares of contribution to total output growth, with total output growth set at 100.

of the output growth, as much as the combined effects of input increases. The changes in cropping intensity (MCI) and crop pattern (NGCA), which might partially reflect the effect of reforms in the role of planning and markets, had small impacts on growth (one negative and one positive). In this growth accounting, 5.57 percent of the output growth was unexplained residual.

Although the changes in market prices and state procurement prices during 1978–1984 did not affect the total factor productivity, the growth accounting in Table 11.7 indicates that the substantial increase in the state procurement price had a significant impact (probably through input use, cropping intensity, and/or crop mix) on output growth, contributing 15.98 percent of the growth. However, compared to the estimated 42.20 percent that could be attributed to HRS in the supply-response function, the impact of price changes on output growth was not spectacular.[14]

Tables 11.6 and 11.7 also attempt to account for the slowdown in output growth after 1984. Several causes might be responsible for such a change. As Table 11.6 shows, the dominant reasons for the spectacular growth during 1978–1984 were HRS reform and the sharp increase in the use of chemical fertilizers. The HRS reform was completed in 1983–1984. Therefore, even without any other cause, the rate of output growth would have fallen to about half of the previous level. The growth rate of chemical-fertilizer input dropped from 8.9 percent per year during 1978–1984 to 3.7 percent during 1984–1987. If fertilizer use had continued to increase at the previous rate, its contribution to output growth would have been 5.54 percent of the 1984 level, instead of the 2.26 percent that actually occurred. Moreover, there was a swift outflow of the labor force from the cropping sector to other sectors. The growth rate of the labor force dropped from 2.3 percent per year during 1978–1984 to −8.6 percent per year during 1984–1987. This outflow of labor force alone caused output to fall 2.95 percent compared to the 1984 level. Table 11.7 shows that the sharp drop in the state procurement prices relative to input prices was probably the determining factor behind the decrease in the growth rate of chemical-fertilizer usage and the exodus of labor. The change in state procurement prices resulted in a 5.04-percent drop in output in 1987 compared to the 1984 level. The adverse effect of the drop in state procurement prices on output growth, however, was compensated for by the rise in market prices, which lifted the 1987 output level 5.36 percent over that of 1984.

V CONCLUDING REMARKS

This paper attempts to evaluate the impacts of various components of reform on agricultural growth in China. The findings indicate that the dominant source of output growth during 1978–1984 was the change from the production-team system to HRS. It is also found that the change in crop pattern away from grain to nongrain crops had a positive impact and that the decline in cropping intensity had a negative impact on growth during 1978–1984. However, both effects were very small in magnitude. The results also suggest that the changes in state procurement prices and market prices had a significant impact on output growth, probably through their influences on application levels of inputs, cropping intensity and/or crop pattern. However, not all the increases in input use during 1978–1984 could be attributed to the rise in state procurement prices; part of them come from improvements in availability as revealed by the positive time trend in the supply-response function.

It is worth noting that this paper measures only the one-time discrete impact of the HRS reform on productivity and output growth. The shift from the production-team system to HRS, however, also improves farmers' incentives to adopt new technology and may thus be expected to speed the diffusion of new technology (Lin, 1991). Therefore, HRS would also have a long-term, dynamic impact on the growth of agricultural productivity, which is not measured in this paper.

This study also attempts to account for the slowdown in output growth after 1984. In addition to the fact that the one-time discrete effect of the HRS reform had ended in 1984, the evidence suggests that the rapid exodus of the labor force from the cropping sector and the sharp decline in the growth rate of fertilizer usage were responsible for the stagnation. The sharp reduction in state procurement prices is probably the reason for both trends.

The above findings have wider implications than simply improving the understanding of rural reforms in China. An important issue that confronts most developing countries is how to develop agriculture rapidly in order to support industrialization and to meet the ever-increasing food demand brought on by explosive population growth. Small and fragmented holdings, which characterize the landscapes in most densely populated developing countries, are often regarded as a great obstacle for mechanization, irrigation, plant protection, efficient allocation of inputs, and so forth. Consequently, many policymakers and scholars, not only in China but also in many other developing countries, consider collective farming an attractive method for land consolidation and productivity improvement. However, my findings suggest that the household farm has advantages of its own. Since the household farm leads to a more productive use of inputs, it may be a more appropriate institution for the growth of agriculture in developing countries, including China.

Appendix: data sources and adjustments

This appendix documents the data sources and describes the various calculations and adjustments that have been made to make the panel data suitable for econometric analysis.[15]

Gross value of crops

The gross value of each province's crops is calculated from the gross physical outputs of seven grain crops (rice, wheat, corn, potatoes, sorghum, millet, and soybeans) and 12 cash crops (cotton, peanuts, rapeseed, sesame, jute, ramie, sugar cane, sugar beets, tobacco, tussah silk cocoons, mulberry silk cocoons, and tea), using the official 1980 prices as weights for aggregation. The output data for 1970–1978 were taken from State Statistical Bureau (1980a), data for 1979–1987 were from the annual *China Agricultural Yearbook*, and the data on 1980 prices were from State Statistical Bureau (1980b). The indexes are reported in Table 11.4.

Land

The data on cultivated land for 1970–1979 were taken from State Statistical Bureau (1980a), data for 1980–1983 were from State Statistical Bureau (1984a), and data for 1984–1987 were provided by the Agricultural Division of the State Statistical Bureau. The data for 1987 can also be found on page 224 of the 1988 *China Statistical Yearbook.* The summary indexes of national aggregation of land and other input series are reported in Table 11.4.

Labor force in the cropping sector

The data on the labor force in the cropping sector were estimated from the data on the farm labor force. The data on farm labor prior to 1980 were provided by the Agricultural Division of the State Statistical Bureau, and data for 1980–1987 were taken from the 1981–1988 volumes of the *China Agricultural Yearbook.* The farm labor force includes those working in cropping, animal husbandry, forestry, fishery, and sideline production. To obtain an estimate of the labor force in the cropping sector, the farm labor forces were weighted by the value share of crop output in total agricultural output. The gross values of crops are calculated as described above. The gross value of agriculture for each province prior to 1986 was obtained from State Statistical Bureau (1987), while the values for 1986 and 1987 are from the 1987 and 1988 *China Statistical Yearbook.* The reported values were measured at current prices in each year. They are converted to the values at 1980 prices by deflating with the state-procurement price index on page 401 of State Statistical Bureau (1984b), with the index in 1980 being set to 100.[16] Other weighting methods were also tried, and the regression estimations were similar; however, the fits were not as good. Because crop and agricultural output may fluctuate from year to year, the values of three-year averages are used in computing the weights.

Capital

Capital is measured by the horsepower of tractors and draft animals. Data on the numbers of tractors for 1970 and 1975–1978 were taken from State Statistical Bureau (1980a). Data on the number of tractors for 1971–1974 and on draft animals prior to 1979 were provided by the Division of Agriculture of the State Statistical Bureau. Data on the numbers of tractors and draft animals after 1978 were taken from the *China Agricultural Yearbook* (1980–1988). To convert these numbers into horsepower, the following weights are used: 18 hp for big tractors, 12 hp for walking tractors, and 0.7 hp for draft animals. These weights are recommended by the State Statistical Bureau.

Chemical fertilizer

This refers to the gross weight of fertilizer consumed. Data for 1970, 1975, and 1979 were taken from State Statistical Bureau (1980a); data for the rest of years prior to 1980 were provided by the Agricultural Division of the State Statistical Bureau; data for years after 1979 were taken from the *China Agricultural Yearbook* (1981–1988).

Changes in farming institution

These changes were measured by the ratio of teams in each province that had converted to HRS by the end of each year. All households were in the production-team system before 1979; after 1984, over 99 percent of teams had adopted HRS. The ratios for 1981 and 1982 were provided by the Research Center for Rural Development of the State Council, and those for 1983 and 1984 were available in the 1984 and 1985 *China Agricultural Yearbook.* However, detailed information about the change in the farming institution for each province is not available for 1979 and 1980. Since, nationally, only 1.02 percent of all teams converted to HRS in 1979 it should be acceptable to generalize that the farming institution in each province was still the production-team system in 1979. However, in 1980, 14.4 percent of teams had converted. Therefore, I eliminated the 1980 observations from the data. As a result, the data set contains 476 cross-section and time-series observations. Information on the ratio of terms converted to HRS nationally is reported in Table 11.3.

Index of state above-quota prices relative to input prices

The relevant data should be the above-quota prices relative to input prices. However, the price indexes given in State Statistical Bureau (1984b) and State Statistical Bureau (1988b) were quota prices. Quota price indexes were converted to above-quota price indexes by the following adjustments. (i) The above-quota price series for grain was calculated. (ii) The above-quota prices for cash crops were inferred. (iii) The above-quota price index for crop output was calculated as the weighted average of the above two series, using each year's percentage shares of grain and cash crops in the total output as weights. (iv) Finally, the resulting above-quota price indexes were divided by the indexes of manufactured input prices in rural areas to obtain relative price indexes. The original series set the index in 1950 equal to 100. For ease of interpretation, the series is converted by setting the 1978 index to 100, as reported in Table 11.2.

Index of market prices relative to input prices

Table 11.2 also reports the index of market prices and the index of market prices relative to input prices. The market-price index, available in State Statistical Bureau (1988b), was a weighted average of prices for crops, livestock, and other products sold in rural market fairs. Therefore, this series contains some errors in measurement if it is to be used as a proxy for the market prices of crops. This error may reduce the estimated effect of changes in market price on growth in terms of crops.

Percentage of area devoted to nongrain crops

This percentage was obtained by dividing the sown acreage of nongrain crops by total agricultural sown acreage. The data on total sown acreage for 1970, 1975, and 1979 were taken from State Statistical Bureau (1980a); for the rest of years prior to 1979, data were provided by the Agricultural Division of the State Statistical Bureau; and for years after 1979, data were from *China Statistical Yearbook* (1981–1988). Data on nonagricultural sown acreage were obtained from the difference between total agricultural sown acreage and total grain sown acreage. Data on total grain sown acreage prior to 1980 were available in State Statistical Bureau (1980a), and data after 1979 were from *China Agricultural Yearbook* (1981–1988). Table 11.3 reports the percentages of sown area in grain, cash crops, and other crops on the national level, which were taken from Ministry of Agriculture Planning Bureau (1989 pp. 130–1), and *China Statistical Yearbook* (1988 p. 243).

Multiple cropping index

This index was obtained by dividing the total agricultural sown area by the cultivated land in each province. Table 11.3 reports the series for multiple cropping index on the national level. The data for 1970–1986 was from the Ministry of Agriculture Planning Bureau (1984 p. 132). For 1984–1987, figures are calculated from the total sown acreage and total cultivated land in China in the corresponding years.

NOTES

1 For a survey of papers by Western economists, see Dwight H. Perkins (1988). In addition, there are several books and conference proceedings devoted exclusively to the economic reforms: see for example, Elizabeth J. Perry and Christine Wong (1985), *Journal of Comparative Economics* (1987), and *China Quarterly* (1988).

2 Lin (1989) employs a production-function approach. The results are suspect due to strong multi-collinearity in the estimated production function. The multicollinearity problem arises from the fact that the panel data employed only cover the period from 1980 to 1983. Wen (1989) estimates a supply-response function. His estimate, based on only 35 observations, is not very credible. McMillan et al.

(1989) use a Dennison-Solow-type growth-accounting technique to analyze the national aggregated time-series from 1978 to 1984. The customary criticisms against the Dennison-type growth accounting are applicable to their studies (see Zvi Griliches, 1963). In addition, their decomposition of the growth in total factor productivity into a price component and an incentive component requires strong assumptions about the form and parameters of the utility function, and their results are sensitive to these assumptions. Furthermore, the price used in their analysis should, theoretically, be marginal price, but they use instead the state above-quota procurement prices, which in general are lower than the prices prevailing in rural markets. Moreover, these two prices often move in opposite directions.

3 For detailed chronology of the price changes in 1979 and thereafter, see Terry Sicular (1988).

4 For a chronology of the policy evolution, see Robert F. Ash (1988). For a summary of the development from various types of responsiblity systems to HRS, see Yak-Yeow Kueh (1984). For a discussion of some new issues related to HRS, see Reeitsu Kojima (1988).

5 For example, net grain imports increased from 6.9 million tons in 1978 to 14.9 million tons in 1982 (Ministry of Agriculture Planning Bureau, 1989 pp. 522, 535), grain purchase quotas were reduced 2.5 million tons in 1979 (Ash, 1988), and the categories of planned products were reduced from 21 in 1978 to 16 in 1981 and were reduced further to only 13 categories in 1982 (Kueh, 1984).

6 In 1979, the government instituted a policy that awarded above-quota delivery of cotton with low-price grain sale. This policy made a substantial expansion of cotton acreage possible in the traditional cotton-producing regions.

7 Tibet is excluded because the lack of output data.

8 In Chinese statistics, agriculture includes cropping, animal husbandry, forestry, fishery, and sideline production. Forestry, fishery, and sideline production are in general not included in agricultural productivity studies. Animal husbandry is not included, mainly for two reasons. First, data for the relevant output and input series of animal husbandry previous to 1979 are not available. Secondly, most activities of animal husbandry were carried out by individual households even before the HRS reform; therefore, the institutional reform should not have a direct impact, even though there might have been indirect effects.

9 Those crops excluded from the data set are mainly vegetables and fruits, which command higher value than grain and cash crops.

10 Using the national index as a proxy for state procurement prices will not cause any trouble in the estimation, because the prices are set by the state and implemented uniformly in each province. However, market prices vary across provinces, although the general trends are the same. Using the national market-price index thus may reduce the sharpness with which the influence of market prices on output can be estimated.

11 As pointed out by Dwight Perkins and Shahid Yusuf (1984 p. 46), attempts by other scholars to estimate the Chinese agricultural production function empirically have not yielded plausible estimates due to the lack of cross-sectional data. A floppy disk containing my data will be provided to researchers upon request.

12 This factor is especially emphasized by Nicholas R. Lardy (1983). He attributes much of the stagnation in Chinese agriculture before the recent reform as well as the rapid growth after the reforms to the loss and gain of regional comparative advantages.

13 It would have been preferable to perform a test for the joint insignificance of MP, GP, and *T* before dropping them from the regression. However, this was not possible because the test statistic for Kiefer's EGLS estimator has not been developed.

14 If one follows the convention of growth accounting and treats residuals as productivity change, then, based on Table 11.6, the increase in total factor productivity during 1978–1984 was 22.89 percent, and 89.73 percent of this increase was attributable to HRS. McMillan, et al. (1989) estimated the increase in total factor productivity as 41 percent and attributed 78 percent of the increase to HRS. McMillan et al.'s larger estimate for improvement in total factor productivity is mainly due to the fact that output in their study includes not only crops, but also animal husbandry, fishery, and forestry. According to their definition, the output growth during 1978–1984 was 61.76 percent. However, with the exception of livestock feed, they employed only those inputs used for crops to construct the index of current inputs and capital. Animal husbandry, fishery, and forestry all had higher rates of growth than crops. Moreover, animal husbandry and fishery are in general more intensive in current inputs and capital than crops. Therefore, McMillan et al.'s estimate of growth in total factor productivity had an upward bias.

15 Since the page numbers are too numerous to list, detailed information will be provided by the author upon request.

16 Technologically, the labor intensity in the cropping sector is lower than that in animal husbandry, fishery, and sideline production. Therefore, in perfect competitive markets, using the value share of crop output in total agricultural output as a weight may lead to an exaggeration of the labor force in the cropping sector. However, the prices of crop outputs in China in general are suppressed, compared to output prices in other sectors. Therefore, using the value share as a weight may understate the labor force in the cropping sector. These two considerations may cancel each other out, to a certain extent.

REFERENCES

Aigner, Dennis J., Lovell, C. A. Knox and Schmidt, Peter, "Formula and Estimation of Stochastic Frontier Production Function Models," *Journal of Econometrics*, July 1977, *6*, 21–38.

Ash, Robert F., "The Evolution of Agricultural Policy," *China Quarterly*, December 1988, (116), 529–55.

Carter, Michael R., "Resource Allocation and Use Under Collective Rights and Labour Management in Peruvian Coastal Agriculture," *Economic Journal*, December 1984, *94*, 826–46.

Griliches, Zvi, "The Source of Measured Productivity Growth: United States Agriculture, 1940–60," *Journal of Political Economy*, July 1963, *71*, 331–46.

Jiang, Yaping, "All We Want Is To Cultivate Land: An On-The-Spot Report of a Dispute of Land Contract in Shunyi County, Beijing" [in Chinese: "Wo men bu gou yao zhong di: beijing shunyixian yiqi chengbao tudi hetong jiufeng jishi"], *People's Daily* [*Renmin Ribao*], 26 October 1988.

Johnson, D. Gale, *The People's Republic of China: 1978–1990*, San Francisco: ICS Press, 1990.

Judge, George G., Griffiths, W. E., Hill, R. Carter, Lutkepohl, Helmut and Lee, Tsoung-Chao, *The Theory and Practice of Econometrics*, 2nd Ed., New York: Wiley, 1985.

Kiefer, Nicholas M., "Estimation of Fixed Effect Models for Time Series of

Cross-Sections with Arbitrary Intertemporal Covariance," *Journal of Econometrics*, October 1980, *14*, 195–202.
Kojima, Reeitsu, "Agricultural Organization: New Forms, New Contradictions," *China Quarterly*, December 1988, (116), 706–35.
Kueh, Yak-Yeow, "China's New Agricultural-Policy Program: Major Economic Consequences, 1979–1983" *Journal of Comparative Economics*, December 1984, *8*, 353–75.
Lardy, Nicholas R., *Agriculture in China's Modern Economic Development*, Cambridge: Cambridge University Press, 1983.
Leibenstein, Harvey "Allocative Efficiency vs. 'X-Efficiency'," *American Economic Review*, June 1966, *56*, 392–415.
Lin, Justin Yifu, "The Household Responsibility System Reform in China: A Peasant's Institutional Choice," *American Journal of Agricultural Economics*, May 1987, *69*, 410–5.
——, "The Household Responsibility System in China's Agricultural Reform: A Theoretical and Empirical Study," *Economic Development and Cultural Change*, April 1988, *36* (supplement), S199–S224.
——, "The Household Responsibility System in China's Rural Reform," in Allen Mauder and Alberto Valdes, eds., *Agriculture and Governments in an Interdependent World: Proceedings of the XX International Conference of Agricultural Economists*, Aldershot, U.K.: Dartmout, 1989, pp. 453–62.
——, "The Household Responsibility System Reform and the Adoption of Hybrid Rice in China," *Journal of Development Economics*, October 1991, *36*, 353–72.
McMillan, John, Whalley, John and Zhu, Lijing, "The Impact of China's Economic Reforms on Agricultural Productivity Growth," *Journal of Political Economy*, August 1989, *97*, 781–807.
Muth, John, "Rational Expectations and the Theory of Price Movement," *Econometrica*, July 1961, *29*, 315–35.
Perkins, Dwight H., "Reforming China's Economic System," *Journal of Economic Literature*, June 1988, *26*, 601–45.
—— and Yusuf, Shahid, *Rural Development in China*, Baltimore: Johns Hopkins University Press, 1984.
Perry, Elizabeth J. and Wong, Christine, eds., *The Political Economy of Reform in Post-Mao China*, Cambridge, MA: Harvard University Press, 1985.
Sicular, Terry, "Agricultural Planning and Pricing in the Post-Mao Period," *China Quarterly*, December 1988, (116), 671–705.
Wen, Guanzhong James, "The Current Land Tenure and Its Impact on Long Term Performance of the Farming Sector: The Case of Modern China," Ph.D. dissertation, University of Chicago, 1989.
China Agriculture Yearbook [*Zhongguo Tongye Nianjian*], Beijing: Agriculture Press, 1981–1988 (annual).
Economic Weekly News [Jingjixue Zhoubao], 11 January 1982.
Journal of Comparative Economics, September 1987, *11* (3).
Ministry of Agriculture, *China Agriculture Statistical Material, 1987* [in Chinese: *Zhongguo Nongye Tongji Ziliao, 1987*], Beijing: Agriculture Press, 1989.
Ministry of Agriculture Planning Bureau, *A Comprehensive Book of China Rural Economic Statistics, 1949–1986* [in Chinese: *Zhongguo Nongcun Jingji Tongji Ziliao Daquan, 1949–1986*], Beijing: Agriculture Press, 1989.
——, *Agricultural Economic Data 1949–1983* [in Chinese: *Nongye Jingji Ziliao, 1949–1983*], Beijing: Ministry of Agriculture, 1984.
State Statistical Bureau (1980a) *National Agricultural Statistics for the 30 Years Since the Founding of the People's Republic of China, 1949–1979* [in Chinese: *Jianquo 30 Nian*

Quanguo Nongye Tongji Ziliao, 1949–1979], Beijing: State Statistical Bureau, 1980.

——, (1980b) *Scheme for Computing Gross Agricultural Value* [in Chinese: *Nongye Zongchanzhi Jisuan Fangan*], Beijing: State Statistical Bureau, 1980.

——, (1984a) *National Agricultural Statistics (Continuation), 1978–1983* [in Chinese: *Quanguo Nongye Tongji Ziliao (Xubain), 1978–1983*], Beijing: Statistical Bureau, 1984.

——, (1984b) *China Trade and Price Statistics, 1952–1983* [in Chinese: *Zhongguo Maoyi Wujia Tongji Ziliao, 1952–1983*], Beijing: China Statistical Press, 1984.

——, *A Compilation of National Income Statistics, 1949–1985* [in Chinese: *Guominshouru Tongji Ziliao Huibain, 1949–1985*], Beijing: China Statistical Press, 1987.

——, (1988a) *A Compilation of Price Statistics Documents* [in Chinese: *Wujia Tongji Wenjian Huibian*], Beijing: China Statistical Press, 1988.

——, (1988b) *China Price Statistical Yearbook, 1988* [in Chinese: *Zhongguo Wujia Tongji Nianjian, 1988*], Beijing: China Statistical Press, 1988.

12

AGRICULTURAL DEVELOPMENT SINCE 1978

Robert F. Ash

Robert F. Ash and Y. Y. Kueh (Editors)

THE LEGACY OF REFORM

The diversity of China's agricultural experience during the 1980s highlights the challenges and opportunities facing the farm sector during the present decade. Until 1985 agriculture's performance was widely regarded as an unqualified success. Decollectivization and institutional initiatives provided a framework which allowed, for the majority of farmers, an unprecedented degree of independence in decision-making. Farming was once more practised on a household basis, peasants' activities increasingly geared towards the market and their economic relationship with the state defined by legal contracts. Large increases in the purchase prices of major farm products provided the material incentive for the expansion of all branches of the agricultural economy. These same increases were the source of substantial gains in income, which contained the wherewithal for large-scale investment in agricultural production.

But from 1985 the story changes. It is true that in some areas – such as animal husbandry, sidelines and aquatic production – the pattern of expansion continued unchanged. In the crop sector, however, earlier growth gave way to stagnation. Simultaneously, the decline in state and local government support for agriculture (already in evidence in the first half of the 1980s) intensified, but was still unaccompanied by any offsetting rise in indigenous investment from within the farm sector. The improvement in incentives, consequent upon the previous purchase price increases, was also increasingly eroded by much sharper rises in input prices. This discouraged crop farming and in particular led to a disinclination to engage in its least profitable, but most important, branch – grain cultivation.

During the second half of the 1980s peasant worries about the state's commitment to a de-collectivized agriculture mirrored uncertainty amongst Party and government leaders about the future direction of agricultural

Source: *The Chinese Economy Under Deng Xiaoping* (Oxford: Oxford University Press, 1996), pp. 55–87.

strategy. Some looked to more radical reform measures in order to restore peasant confidence, rekindle their enthusiasm for crop production and encourage a more active involvement in long-term investment. In some ways, the logical destination of such thinking was the privatization of land ownership, although ideological retrenchment after 1988 made it difficult to articulate this view publicly. Others, on the pretext of seeking to realize economies of scale (*guimo jingying*), were advocates of a return to a more collectivist system of agriculture. Arguments over the role and extent of further price reform were corollaries of this debate.

Public-ownership of land has remained an ideological shibboleth, which has so far proved unassailable. By contrast, the primacy of planning has weakened, although even in the mid-1990s the central authorities seek to retain a residual role in order to resolve tensions arising out of conflicting priorities of the state and individual peasant. In any case, it bears repeating that the on-going debate over agricultural policy reflects very real *economic* dilemmas confronting the Chinese government. The evolution of a farming system guided by a "household responsibility system with remuneration linked to output" (*lianchan chengbao zerenzhi*) and the demise of collective agriculture no doubt had a profound effect in releasing peasant initiative. But the experience of agriculture after the attempted elimination of the state monopoly procurement system in 1985 demonstrates that the shift from a supply-orientated to a demand-orientated structure of production contained the seeds of a basic conflict between private and public interests. The 1985 policy decision was largely prompted by the appearance of supposedly unmanageable surpluses of grain and other farm products. It is an irony that one of the consequences of that decision was quickly to renew the spectre of a food crisis, as rational income-maximizing principles encouraged peasants to abandon grain production in favour of the cultivation of cash crops (or better still, to take up economic pursuits outside crop farming). Such a response suggests that it would be facile merely to condemn advocacy of more interventionist methods as wholly lacking any rational foundation.

There is evidence too that the demise of the collective system and its replacement by household-based operations have had adverse implications for long-term infrastructural investment in agriculture and left a void which remains unfilled. The summer floods of 1991 were perhaps the most spectacular recent manifestation of the critical role of water control in China. But there is no denying that funding, and implementing, such projects has become more difficult in the new, decentralized framework of farming.[1]

Such tensions were reflected in the *Ten-Year Development Programme* (*10YP*) *and Eighth Five-Year Plan* (*8FYP*) *for National Economic and Social Development*,[2] formally adopted by the National People's Congress (NPC) on 9 April 1991. The drafting process apparently got under way early in 1990, the intention being to bring an initial draft before a plenary session of the CCP Central Committee in October of that year. In the event, differences of opinion over the nature of future economic strategy compelled a postponement of the meeting, which was not convened until December. Indeed Deng Xiaoping was reportedly so discouraged by the excessive centralist thrust of early formulations that he rejected the first draft, drawn up by Yao Yilin under the influence of Chen Yun's economic thinking.

The final document has been described as a compromise between the reformist urge of Deng Xiaoping and the more centralist convictions of Chen Yun. The evidence suggests that the final outline of the *10YP* and *8FYP* was, however, more closely in line with Deng's philosophy. In the earlier version,[3] for example, it was argued that excessive decentralization had come to characterize many areas of production, distribution and finance and that appropriate re-centralization of material and financial resources was necessary in order to obviate current difficulties. This section was omitted from the final, published version. Such differences between the two drafts, as well as ambiguities which remain in the final document,[4] are a reminder of tensions, which have continued to surround the formulation of agricultural policy and to threaten sustained agricultural growth during the 1990s.

GROWTH AND STRUCTURAL CHANGE IN THE AGRICULTURAL SECTOR DURING THE 1980s

Notwithstanding the difficulties which emerged during the second half of the 1980s, the decade as a whole remains a period of impressive growth and unprecedented structural change in China's agricultural sector. The average real rate of increase of agricultural gross value-output (GVAO) during the Sixth (6FYP) and Seventh Five-Year Plan (7FYP) periods (1981–85 and 1986–90) was, for example, 6.4 per cent per annum.[5] This compares with an average annual rate of growth of 4.7 per cent during the immediately preceding decade (1971–80); and 3.05 per cent between 1952 and 1970.[6] Table 12.1 summarizes the growth performance of major branches of agricultural production during the 1980s, as well as showing their previous best performance in a five-year period.

The peculiar role of grain in China's economic development lends its performance a special significance. It is interesting that the growth record of 1981–85 was bettered during the 3FYP period (1966–70), when the average rate of increase of total cereal production exceeded 4.2 per cent p.a. But such a comparison is misleading in one important respect: the increase in total output during 1966–70 was based on a largely unchanged sown area under grain, whereas during 1981–85 some 8.4 million hectares were taken out of cultivation (a decline of over 7 per cent). In short, the more recent growth performance was entirely dependent on improvements in yields.[7]

The less impressive performance of major branches of agriculture during the 7FYP also emerges from the table, although an examination of trends between 1984 and 1989 most dramatically highlights the onset of

Table 12.1 The growth of agricultural production in the 1980s

	Average rate of increase of total output (% p.a.)			
	6FYP 1981–85	*7FYP 1986–90*	*1981–90*	*Previous best five-year record*
Food grains	3.4	3.3	3.4	4.2 (1966–70)
Cotton	8.9	1.6	5.3	4.7 (1953–57)
Oil seeds	15.4	0.4	7.7	1.8 (1971–75)
Sugar	15.8	3.6	9.5	9.4 (1953–57)
Pork	7.9	6.6	7.3	
Pork, beef and mutton	7.9	7.4	7.6	8.6 (1976–80)
Aquatic production	9.4	11.9	10.6	13.3 (1953–57)

Sources: The estimates for pork are derived from data in *TJZY 1991*, p. 59. The remaining figures are available from State Statistical Bureau, *Zhongguo tongji nianjian, 1991 (Chinese Statistical Yearbook, 1991)*, hereafter *TJNJ 1991* (Beijing: Statistical Publishing House, 1991), pp. 346–8, 357 and 363.

stagnation. In 1985, for example, production of grain and cotton fell by 6.92 and 33.73 (*sic*) per cent, although oil crop output continued to rise strongly. By 1989, only grain had reattained its previous peak. In short, the fact that the growth record of the 1980s has no precedent in any previous, comparable ten-year period since 1949 is largely attributable to the extraordinary expansion of production during 1981–84 and the fine harvest of 1990.[8]

The figures for meat and fish production highlight the exceptionally rapid expansion of non-crop farming branches of the agricultural sector. They also demonstrate a more stable pattern of sustained – and in the case of aquatic products, accelerated – growth over the two five-year plan periods. It is not surprising that while average per capita consumption of grain and edible oils has shown little or no increase since 1985, that of meat and fish continued to rise quite strongly.[9]

What Table 12.1 does not show is the extent to which planned targets were fulfilled in the 1980s. The estimates shown in Table 12.2 provide that missing information.

The achievements of the Sixth Five-Year Plan (1981–85) emerge clearly enough. What the figures conceal is that so rapid was agricultural growth in the wake of the early reforms that the targets were over-fulfilled well in advance of the Plan's end-year[10] – and, in the case of cotton and grain, by even larger margins than the 1985 estimates indicate.

If anticipated levels of production in the following (Seventh) plan were based on optimistic expectations engendered by such high rates of growth, it is interesting that despite post-1984 stagnation, so many of the 1990 production targets were also over-fulfilled (although, meat and fish apart, not in advance). The important exception is of course that of oil seeds, which suffered a shortfall of more than 10 per cent.

Table 12.2 Planned and realized levels of total production of major branches of agriculture: achievements of the sixth and seventh five-year plans (1981–85 and 1986–90)

(a) The sixth five-year plan (1981–85)

	1985 Planned output	*1985 Actual output*	*Actual as % planned output*
Food grains	360.0	379.11	105.31
Cotton	3.6	4.15	115.19
Oil seeds	10.5	15.78	150.32
Sugar	46.7	60.47	129.48
Pork		16.54	
All meats	14.6*	17.61	
Aquatic products	5.1	7.05	138.24

(b) The seventh five-year plan (1986–90)

	1990 Planned output	*1990 Actual output*	*Actual as % planned output*
Food grains	425.00–450.00	446.24	99.16–105.0
Cotton	4.25	4.51	106.07
Oil seeds	18.25	16.13	88.39
Sugar	68.75	72.15	104.94
Pork	18.30	22.81	124.65
All meats	22.75	28.00	123.08
Aquatic products	9.00	12.37	137.44

Notes: All figures in million tonnes.
* Pork, beef and mutton only

Sources: Actual output figures from *TJNJ, 1991*, pp. 346–8, 357 and 363; and *TJZY, 1991*, p. 59.

Output targets for 1985 from *Zhonghua renmin gongheguo guomin jingji he hehui fazhan diliuge wunian jihua (1981–85) (The Sixth Five-Year Plan of the PRC for National Economic and Social Development)* (Beijing, People's Publishing House: 1983), pp. 35–6 and 38–9. Output targets for 1990 from State Planning Commission, *Diqige wunian nongcun fazhan zhuanti jihua (Special Topics for the Development of the Rural Economy in the Seventh Five-Year Plan)* (Beijing, Agricultural Publishing House: 1986), pp. 54 and 56.

Associated with the growth record illustrated above was a process of dramatic structural change within the agricultural sector, which is described in Table 12.3.

The emerging pattern is clear. The 1980s witnessed a significant realignment of agricultural activities from crop cultivation towards other farm tasks. In particular, between 1984 and 1988 the share of crop farming – already in decline since 1978 – fell by more than 5 percentage points. The principal beneficiaries were animal husbandry and fisheries, whose combined share in agricultural GVO rose from 19.95 to 24.76 per cent. Admittedly, the cropping sector partially recovered its relative position during 1989–90, but not in such a way as to affect the general trend.[11]

Table 12.3 Structural change in Chinese agriculture, 1980–1990

	GVAO (excluding side-lines)	*Crops*	*Forestry*	*of which: Animal rearing*	*Aquatic products*
1980	100.00	76.73	4.25	17.15	1.88
1981	100.00	75.84	4.65	17.26	2.24
1982	100.00	76.25	4.65	16.82	2.28
1983	100.00	76.01	4.74	16.72	2.52
1984	100.00	75.18	4.87	17.18	2.77
1985	100.00	73.43	5.01	18.37	3.19
1986	100.00	73.96	5.14	17.70	3.20
1987	100.00	72.46	5.17	19.00	3.36
1988	100.00	70.01	5.22	21.15	3.61
1989	100.00	70.96	4.95	20.74	3.35
1990	100.00	72.43	5.06	19.25	3.26

Note: The above percentage estimates reflect the structure of agricultural gross value-output expressed in real terms.

Source: *TJZY 1991*, pp. 52–3.

What is more, within the cropping sector itself profound changes in the pattern of land use were under way. For example, whereas in 1980 grain accounted for 80.1 per cent of China's total sown area, by 1990 it had fallen to 76.5 per cent.[12] The area sown to economic crops meanwhile rose from 10.9 to 14.4 per cent, whilst that under vegetables, green manure, etc. remained unchanged.[13]

It is worth noting that these data take no account of the single most important structural change of all in the countryside during the 1980s: the remarkable expansion of rural township and village enterprises (*xiangzhen qiye*). Its impact on the rural sector is suggested by the finding that in 1990 the contribution of such enterprises to rural social value-output had reached 59.1 per cent.[14]

AGRICULTURAL STRATEGY IN THE 1990s: AN OVERVIEW

The preceding review of agricultural development and structural change defines the context in which the plans for the 1990s have been formulated and are being implemented. Impressive as the economic record of the 1980s may have been, the starting-point of any discussion of these plans must surely be the considerable pessimism which had come to inform official comment on agriculture's situation and prospects at the start of the new decade. The following remarks are typical:

> . . . the overall [agricultural] situation remains quite grim and our tasks in the days to come will be very arduous. . . . This year's [1990] total

> grain output is greater than that of 1984, but the per capita amount . . . is lower than that of 1984. . . . Cotton output . . . is greater than last year, but it still cannot meet state, consumer and export needs. We still need to import some edible oil, sugar, wool and rubber every year to make up for domestic shortages. . . .[15]
>
> . . . Good harvests do not prove that China's overall agricultural production capacity has definitely reached a new level. In fact, the infrastructure and basic conditions have not fundamentally improved: the ability of our agriculture to withstand natural disasters is still very weak and the basis for faster agricultural development remains inefficient.[16]
>
> . . . There is a significant imbalance between the rural economy and social development, and there are still many problems and many constraints. Population growth has been excessive and the contraction in total arable area has still not been brought under effective control. Investment in agriculture is inadequate, its material and technical foundation is weak, its capacity for comprehensive production is not high, and the ability to combat natural disasters is insufficient. . . .[17]

The caution and anxiety contained in such comments were reflected in the quite modest rates of growth targeted in the 10YP and 8FYP outline (see below). No doubt they reflected the disappointing performance of major crops during the second half of the 1980s. But more than that, they appeared to underline an awareness of the technical deficiencies of Chinese agriculture – deficiencies which had not been alleviated, and may have been exacerbated, by post-1978 reforms. They also expressed an awareness of China's continuing vulnerability to the vagaries of the weather.

A striking feature of the "first decade of reform" (1979–88) was the dramatic decline in agriculture's share of total state capital construction investment, as well as other forms of farm support.[18] Recovery was already under way in 1989 and 1990, and – on any rational criteria – ought[19] to have continued through the 1990s. The 10YP/8FYP outline itself was reticent on this aspect, but other authoritative sources made it clear that state support for agriculture – whether through the central budget, from banks and credit cooperatives or through specially created development funds – would be increased.[20]

It was axiomatic that state investment should be reserved for *large-scale* projects, related to water conservancy, infrastructural construction and the establishment of grain and cotton production bases. Irrigation and water conservancy work would be a prime focus of state investment activity, not only in order to reverse infrastructural decline and extend China's irrigated area (by 2 million hectares by 1995),[21] but also to obviate the problems associated with severe flooding, such as occurred during 1991.[22]

Smaller-scale investment projects remained the prerogative of the collective sector and individual peasants. Against the background of the remarkable growth of rural, private savings deposits during the 1980s, Song Ping's statement that "the financial strength of individual [peasant] households is quite weak"[23] seemed disingenuous. It may, however, be that *non-farming* rural residents (especially those working in local enterprises) had accounted for much of those savings – which in any case began to decline after 1984.[24] This would account for the renewed emphasis on labour mobilization as a means of enhancing agricultural investment in the 1990s,[25] as well as on the need for rural industrial subsidies to agriculture.[26]

The *institutional* thrust of agricultural strategy during the 1990s was summed up in the advocacy of the creation a "two-tier operational system" (*shuangceng jingying tizhi*), which would integrate decentralized, household-based farming with a collectively-organized "socialized service system" (*shehuihua fuwu tixi*).[27] Its economic rationale lay in the realization that notwithstanding the success of the system of contracted responsibilities in stimulating peasant initiative during the 1980s, there were many farm tasks, embracing production and distribution, which lay beyond the scope of individual households. The provision of support in these areas – whether to facilitate the development and application of better inputs, encourage infrastructural capital formation or promote the sale of farm produce – would therefore be more effectively (and cheaply) organized on a collective basis.

Even from the perspective of the mid-1990s, it remains questionable to what extent this duality of approach can be transformed into an organic whole, rather than become a divisive force in the countryside. At the beginning of the 1980s it was emphatically denied that advocacy of decentralized agricultural decision-making contained any anti-collectivist hint. Yet within a few years the collective system itself had fallen victim to the new policy. At the beginning of the 1990s there were signs that the emphasis had been reversed. Tian Jiyun was one senior figure who stressed the complementarity between collective and household responsibilities towards contracts,[28] even arguing that the 1980s had seen excessive emphasis on "separate management" to the neglect of "unified management."[29] Hence, no doubt, official encouragement of the expansion of the collective economy.[30]

But these same sources were careful to warn against collective encroachment on household operations. For example, an editorial in *People's Daily* cautioned that ". . . we cannot expand the collective economy by taking back land contracted to the peasants."[31] Significantly, it added that the further development of the collective sector should be achieved on the basis of self-accumulation, not by indiscriminate levies on peasants. In short, the contractually-based household responsibility system was to be retained as a permanent feature of the institutional framework of China's agriculture.

Even allowing for flexible policies, the simultaneous advocacy of individual and collective economic activities seemed decidedly ambiguous. It is true that advocacy of extended collective operations was not incompatible with a continuing emphasis on household-based farm production. But it would be a supreme irony if – paralleling developments in the early 1980s – a revanchist emphasis on the collective economy threatened to undermine the very policies which had made such a positive contribution to increased production during those years.[32]

The conjunction of major agricultural price and output increases between 1979 and 1984 was not of course coincidental. The greater surprise is that despite even larger price rises after 1984,[33] the output of many crops did not continue to respond in the same way. One explanation is that during much of the second half of the decade, the benefits of further purchase price rises were eroded by sharp increases in the cost of inputs (especially chemical fertilizers), which lowered the net return from crop farming.[34] Circumstantial evidence supports this supposition. For example, official data show the purchase price index of farm and sideline products to have risen almost two-and-a-half times faster than that of "agricultural production materials" between 1978 and 1985; by contrast, during 1986–90 the average annual rate of increase was almost the same for both categories.[35] Moreover, from 1985 to 1990 the annual increase in the purchase price of *grain* was less than that of farm and sideline products as a whole in four out of the six years.[36] Not until 1989 did an annual rise in the purchase price of grain exceed that of meat, fish, or fresh vegetables.[37]

During the 1980s *market* prices admittedly came to play an increasingly important role in the purchase of agricultural products. Such liberalization was most apparent in the meat, fish, vegetable and fruit sectors, whose output showed rapid and sustained growth throughout the decade (see Table 12.1 above). But elsewhere, its impact was less. In particular, in the interests of maintaining control over the supply of basic items, the state chose to retain its monopoly over cotton purchases, whilst instituting a "two-track [pricing] system" (*shuangguizhi*) for grain.

That price deregulation contributed to the vitality of the meat, fish, fruit and vegetable sectors seems undeniable. But it is as well to bear in mind that rising demand also kept the prices of these products buoyant. By contrast, in the face of the bumper harvests of 1989 and 1990, grain farmers were unable to find sufficient *state* outlets for their produce and turned to the free market. One consequence was that in 1990 excess supply seems to have been responsible for a sharp fall in the market price which they could command.[38]

Analysis of the movement of market prices for grain during the 1980s confirms the unstable production performance of the cereal sector. Between 1980 and 1985, the market price of grain fell, on average, by about 2 per cent a year; by contrast, during the second half of the decade the trend was sharply reversed, the market price *rising* by an average of 14.5 per cent p.a.[39] It is true that following four years of sharp price rises, 1990 did witness a substantial decline (by 18.6 per cent). No doubt this was partly attendant upon that year's bumper harvest. But it was also the product of other factors, including reduced industrial requirements of grain, falling cereal demand associated with lay-offs of construction workers who returned to their home villages, and the inadequate storage capacity of state warehouses.[40]

In any case, the experience of the 1980s suggested that price rises and price liberalization were powerful instruments of agricultural policy. At the same time, previous experience made it clear that care was needed to ensure that the potential benefits of purchase price adjustments were not eroded by higher input costs. In this respect, it was significant that the large price rise for grain producers in 1989 had been accompanied by efforts to improve farmers' incentives. For example, new rules stipulated that supplies of subsidized chemical fertilizer were to be increased from 3 to 10–15 kilograms for every 50 kilograms of grain delivered under contract to the state.[41]

Development plans for the 1990s in fact provided little detail on pricing policy. They did, however, show an awareness of the lessons of the previous decade in their explicit commitment to raise grain purchase prices and adjust urban retail prices in order to narrow the procurement–retail price differential.[42] There was also a reference to ". . . steadily making grain purchase prices the same as retail prices during the 8FYP period."[43] In this respect, the State Council decision to raise urban retail prices of grain and edible vegetable oil (May 1991 and April 1992) was an important initiative. No doubt the adjustments were primarily designed to reduce the increasingly serious budget deficit suffered by the central government in its grain transaction in circumstances in which the gap between procurement and retail prices had steadily widened during the 1980s. Special wage and pension supplements and other subsidies served to cushion the cost to urban residents and thereby dampened its impact. Neverthelss, the state's willingness to sanction such price increases introduced an added element of flexibility into its pricing policy, which was likely to impringe on urban demand for grain and oilseed products. The subsequent decision to abandon the use of urban grain coupons was another watershed, although their re-introduction during the first half of 1995 raised questions about the sustainability of markets as a means of distributing staple foods to every section of the population.[44]

Maintaining a dual-pricing framework for cereals demanded the creation of extra storage facilities in order to facilitate grain purchases by local granaries. One response to this need was the state's establishment, in the summer of 1990, of a system of "special grain reserves."[45] The impact of this initiative was considerable and by October, the new warehouses had already purchased almost 18 million tonnes of grain.[46] That the new system could not wholly obviate difficulties was, however, made clear in a warning by the Minister of Agriculture, Liu Zhongyi, that storage problems were likely to appear, as well as in appeals to *local* governments to establish their own reserve systems.[47]

The shortage of granary space has exacerbated other difficulties associated with monetary and fiscal constraints. One was the shortage of cash with which to pay farmers for their grain. During the second half of the 1980s, local authorities' use of "IOUs" or "blank slips" (*baitiaozi*) in order to circumvent having to pay cash was the origin of a problem which was eventually to lead to demonstrations and violent protests by peasants in many provinces.[48]

Meanwhile, however, the state's commitment to buy large amounts of grain continued to threaten its fiscal viability. The extent of this threat was ominously suggested in the clear change of emphasis reflected in the following statements dating, respectively, from autumn 1990 and spring 1991:

> . . . All localities . . . [should] . . . procure unlimited quantities of grain at the protected price in order to satisfy the peasants' demand to sell their surplus grain . . .[49]

> . . . We may consider changing procurement under the special grain reserve system from unlimited purchase to fixed quantity purchase, starting this year [1991], the size of purchase being decided by the state. After fulfilling the state procurement target and the special reserve target [the latter at a minimum protected price], excess grain would be channelled into the market.[50]

The prospect of moving from "unlimited" to "fixed quantity" purchase within a mere six months highlights the real fiscal constraints which threatened the state's grain procurement operations. Until the looked-for realignment of wholesale and retail prices had been achieved, there was no guarantee that the budgetary problems of the past would not recur.

Consideration should also be given to the *technical* strategy for agricultural development in the 1990s. China's fundamental scarcity of land and limitations on further increases in multiple cropping made it clear that the main burden of accelerated growth would rest on higher yields and improvements in farm efficiency. This in turn required major increases in the supply of working and fixed capital (fertilizers, insecticides, plastic sheeting and machinery), as well as the popularization of advanced farming techniques.

China's record in these areas during the 1980s had been impressive;[51] Table 12.4 summarizes some of those achievements and also sets out input targets contained in the 8FYP.

The transformation of more than 2.7 million hectares of low- and medium-yielding land between 1988 and 1990 had already been the source of significant increases in the output of grain, cotton, oil seeds and sugar and it was clear that this process was intended to continue.[52] In addition, plans were announced to extend the sown areas of hybrid rice and hybrid maize to 16.7 and 18.7 million hectares by 1995. "Advanced cultivation techniques" would be popularized on a further 6.7 million hectares under rice, wheat and maize.[53]

The development of new hybrid strains and the increased provision of

Table 12.4 Agricultural inputs and 8FYP targets

	Unit	*1980*	*1990*	*1995 plan*
Tractor ploughed area	Mill.ha.	40.99 (a)	48.26 (a)	56.7 (d)
Mechanized sown area	Mill.ha.	14.98 (b)	21.57 (c)	31.1 (d)
Mechanized harvested area	Mill.ha.	4.36 (b)	11.00 (c)	18.7 (d)
Mechanized irrigated area	Mill.ha.	25.32 (a)	27.15 (a)	28.00 (d)
Large/med tractors	Million	0.56 (a)	0.81 (a)	1.1 (d)
Small/hand tractors	Million	1.37 (a)	6.98 (a)	8.0 (d)
Combines	Thousand	27.05 (a)	38.72 (a)	70.0 (d)
Farm trucks	Million	0.14 (a)	0.62 (a)	1.0 (d)
Chemical fertilizer	M. tonnes (standard weight)			100.0 (e)

Note: The figures for tractors, combines and farm trucks show year-end stocks of these items.

Sources:
(a) *TJZY 1991*, p. 63.
(b) He Kang (General Editor), *Zhongguo nongye nianjian 1981 (Chinese Agricultural Yearbook 1981)*, hereafter *NYNJ 1981*, (Beijing: State Statistical Publishing House, 1982), p. 63.
(c) *TJNJ 1991*, p. 329.
(d) Frederick W. Crook, "China's Eighth Five Year Plan: goals and targets for the agricultural sector", p. 42.
(e) *Jihua gangyuao*, p. 110.

chemical fertilizers were likely to play a crucial role in determining future yield increases. Forecasting future trends in the application of fertilizers is always difficult, dependent as it is on the government's willingness to reallocate resources to both the domestic industry and to imports. In this respect, the future performance of agriculture is intimately connected with *industrial* policy. Nevertheless, empirical research had already demonstrated the importance of enlarged supplies of chemical fertilizers and new hybrids in stimulating yield increases during the 1980s.[54] There was no reason to suppose that future yield trends would not continue to be influenced by the availability of such inputs.

The targets summarized in Table 12.4 no doubt reflect a determination to extend the application of science and technology in order to raise agricultural yields. But their fulfilment was dependent on the provision of an appropriate framework for technological research, training and dissemination. In this respect, it was significant that the establishment of "agricultural technical training bases" at provincial and prefectural levels, as well as the formulation of agricultural scientific plans, also emerged as high priorities in development plans at the beginning of the 1990s.[55]

By way of conclusion, it will be useful to comment briefly on the extent to which some of these technical targets have in fact been fulfilled since the beginning of the 1990s. The findings are inconclusive. As of 1993, the effectively irrigated area was some 3 per cent higher than in 1990, while the total area subject to flooding had fallen by a similar proportion.[56] During the same period, however, the total area of water loss and soil erosion had risen markedly (by some 20 per cent) and so, albeit more marginally had that of saline-alkaline land.[57] Chemical fertilizer consumption meanwhile rose by 22 per cent, although it was reported that after adjustment for inflation, real investment in this and other inputs actually declined in 1993. Financial constraints were also evident in reports that about one-sixth of all local-level rural technology centres had been closed because of budget cuts in 1993.[58]

AGRICULTURAL PRODUCTION TARGETS FOR THE 1990s

The 8FYP and 10YP outline followed the precedent of earlier plans in containing virtually no projections of changes in the arable, or sown, area sown under various crops. Specific targets were confined to levels of *total* production of major items for 1955 and, in some cases, 2000. For a few crops, projected five-year average levels of production were also made available.

Table 12.5 provides a summary of these production targets. It also shows total output in 1990 and average production during the 7FYP period (1986–90) in order to facilitate a comparison between recent performance and projected trends.

The average annual rates of growth implied by these figures for the Eighth and Ninth FYP periods are shown in Table 12.6. So, for purposes of comparison, are the average growth rates achieved during the 7FYP (1986–90).

The use of five-year averages eliminates distortions associated with anomalous base and/or end-year conditions and is the more useful basis for comparison.[59] Seen from this perspective and compared with the average rates of increase achieved between 1986 and 1990, the production targets for the 1990s are less modest than they would otherwise appear to be. Indeed, the estimates in Table 12.6(b) show some consistency between performance during the 7FYP and projections for the Eighth and Ninth plans.[60]

Estimates of total agricultural output up to 1993 (and in some cases, preliminary figures for 1994) are available and make it possible to assess extent to which the 8FYP targets are being fulfilled. The quantitative basis of such an assessment is presented in Table 12.7.

There seems little reason to doubt the ability of most branches of agriculture to fulfil their 1995 targets. Indeed, targeted levels of production for oil seeds, meat and fish have been overfulfilled well in advance of that date. The estimates of average realized annual output of grain and cotton (1991–94) would also seem to lend themselves to an optimistic interpretation. But as the data for 1994 suggest, these averages conceal wide annual fluctuations, which undermines such a confident assessment.

The performance of grain gives special cause for concern. Since 1990 the

Table 12.5 Plans for agriculture in the 1990s

(a) Total production of major agricultural products in 1990 and targets for 1995 and 2000

	1990 actual production	*1995 planned production*	*2000 planned production*
Food grains	446.24	455.00	500.00
Cotton	4.51	4.75	5.25
Oil seeds	16.13	18.00	
Sugar	72.15	75.00	
Pork	22.81	23.00	
All meats	25.14	30.00	
Aquatic products	12.37	14.50	

Sources:
1990 data from *TJNJ 1991*, pp. 346–8, 357, 361 and 363.
1995 and 2000 targets from *Jihua gangyao*, pp. 103–4.

(b) Average total production 1986–90 and planned average total production 1991–95 and 1996–2000

	Average total production 1986–90	*Average planned production 1991–95*	*Average planned production 1996–2000*
Food grains	408.47	447.00	478.00
Cotton	4.05	4.64	5.00
Oil seeds	14.46	17.26	
Sugar	61.22	73.72	

Note: All figures in Tables 12.5 (a) and (b) are shown in million tonnes.

Source: As Table 12.5(a)

total production of grain has displayed no clear upward trend.[61] The lack of direction highlights the uncertainty which is bound to characterize any projection of the grain sector's immediate growth prospects. It is worth recording too that the regional dimension of the recent grain performance is noteworthy in that just seven provinces have accounted for three-quarters of the increase in China's production between 1989 and 1993.[62]

The vagaries of agriculture's performance during the 1990s cannot simply be attributed to natural disasters and changing climatic conditions. Other factors were also at work. The differential performances of the various sectors would appear to exemplify the difficulties which have continued to impede the sustained, and above all balanced agricultural growth which the planners have for so long sought. Unless they can be overcome, there is a danger that structural imbalances within the agricultural sector will become even more pronounced. Most serious of all is the situation of the grain sector, which still has to demonstrate its ability to meet the goals set for it in the national plans.

Table 12.6 Average annual rates of growth of total production during the seventh, eighth and ninth five-year plans

(a) Comparison of base and end years only

	Average annual rate of increase (% p.a.):		
	1986–1990 actual	*1991–1995 planned*	*1996–2000 planned*
Food grains	3.3	0.4	1.9
Cotton	1.6	1.1	2.0
Oil seeds	0.4	2.2	
Sugar	3.6	0.8	
Pork	6.6	0.2	
All meats	7.7	3.6	
Fish	11.9	3.2	

(b) Comparison of average 5-year periods

	Average rate of annual increase (% p.a.)		
	1981–85 – 1986–90 actual	*1986–90 – 1991–95 planned*	*1991–95 – 1996–2000 planned*
Food grains	1.9	1.8	1.3
Cotton	−1.3	2.8	1.5
Oil seeds	3.7	3.6	
Sugar	6.0	3.8	

Source: As Table 12.5.

Table 12.7 Planned and realized agricultural production during the eighth five-year plan (1991–95)

	Average annual total output, 1991–94 realized	*Average annual total output 1991–95 planned*	*Total output 1994 realized*	*Total output 1995 planned*
Food grains	444.70	447.00	444.50	455.00
Cotton	4.54	4.64	4.25	5.25
Oil seeds	17.67	17.26	19.84*	18.00
Sugar	82.84**	73.72		
Pork			28.54*	23.00
All meats			36.70	30.00
Aquatic products			20.98	14.50

Notes:
* Estimates for 1993 only.
** Average realized output for 1991–93 only.

Sources: Planned data from Table 12.5.
Estimates of realized output from *TJNJ 1994*, pp. 345–6, 352 and 354 (1991–93); *SWB*, FE/2245 S2/1, 7 March 1995 (1994 preliminary).

If a comparison of the five-year averages shown in Table 12.5 indicates consistency between recent performance and projected trends, there is an area of the plan in which such harmony appears to have been lacking. One of the basic macroeconomic goals is that by the turn of the century, living standards for the majority of the population should have reached a "comfortably well-off" (*xiaokang*) level[63] – a phrase which implies higher consumption of "meat, eggs, milk, fish, vegetables and fruit" for urban and rural residents.[64] Such targets seem to be at variance with the data in Tables 12.5 and 12.6, which indicate a significant planned reduction, during the 8FYP period, in the growth of meat and fish production – precisely the sectors whose performance, unlike that of grain, cotton and oil seeds, was *consistently* buoyant during the second half of the 1980s.

It may be that the cautious assessment of agriculture's sector's capabilities, current at the beginning of the 1990s, explains the apparent contradiction between grain production targets for the 1990s and the objective of securing significant improvements in living standards. Could it be that fears that slow growth of cereal production in the 1990s would generate a serious shortage of *feed* grain[65] led planners to lower their expectations of dietary improvements in the interests of more balanced agricultural development?[66]

The shift from a predominantly grain-based diet has already begun in China's urban sector. In more prosperous rural areas, the same process is under way. But in most parts of the Chinese countryside, direct consumption of grain has probably not yet reached saturation point and rising income is still associated with increased demand for grain for direct human consumption.[67] Continuing rises in per capita income will nevertheless compel a change in the pattern of food consumption and dictate a fundamental transformation of the structure of cereal production and use. Once the demand for "fine" grain (in China, rice, wheat and soya) has been met, a more far-reaching change will occur, as consumers seek to achieve a better diet by increasing their consumption of non-grain – especially animal-based – foods.

This latter shift has serious implications for the grain sector, which can only accommodate the evolving pattern of demand by supplying more grain for feed purposes. Given that about 3.5 kilograms of grain are needed in order to produce 0.5 kilogram of meat,[68] the rapid development of animal husbandry requires an acceleration in the rate of increase of grain production in order to meet rising feed demand. Even allowing for an extension of pasturage on the grasslands of northern China, regional water and climatic constraints mean that plans to increase supplies of meat and dairy produce remain critically dependent upon the accelerated growth of cereal production.

The pressure which increasing demand for animal fodder has already placed upon the grain sector is illustrated in the finding that between 1978 and 1988, China's consumption of feed grain more than doubled, to reach 100 million tonnes (25 per cent of total production).[69] Such pressure is certain to have intensified during the present decade.[70] Realization that the grain sector may be unable to accommodate the change may, however, have delayed the planners' expectation of further qualitative improvements in diet for the majority.

Shortfalls could in theory be offset by imports. There are, however, several factors which militate against the adoption of such a strategy. One is the limited availability of foreign exchange. Another is the perception that dependence on outside supplies of an essential item, such as food, should be avoided. Infrastructural constraints, such as the shortage of port and transport facilities, are further limiting factors. China's trade orientation is in any case towards the import of more obviously developmental goods. Nor is there any guarantee that overseas supplies would be available on the requisite scale: international reserves are after all limited. All these considerations underline the priority requirement of maintaining the fundamental role of the grain sector in the domestic economy.[71]

Yet in the absence of any clear trend in total grain production during the 1990s, there seems to be no secure base for future growth to take total output to the targeted 500 million tonnes by the year 2000.[72] The most gloomy scenario to which such doubts have given rise is that painted by Lester R. Brown, who has predicted that excess demand for food could generate a domestic shortfall of 216 million tonnes (trade weight) of grain by 2030.[73] Such conditions seem unlikely to materialize. Nevertheless, Brown's projections are a salutary reminder that the absence of significant renewed growth could compel greater participation by China in world grain markets.

THE LAND CONSTRAINT AND PROJECTED CHANGES IN SOWN AREA DISTRIBUTION DURING THE 1990s

A notable feature of China's agricultural development in recent years is that increases in output have been achieved against the background of a contraction of cultivated area. Official statistics show that between 1978 and 1990 the total arable area fell by almost 4 per cent (from 99.45 to 95.67 million hectares)[74] – an annual loss of 344,000 hectares. Since 1990, a further 572,000 hectares have disappeared out of cultivation.[75] Even allowing for a deceleration after the mid-1980s, these figures indicate a faster rate of contraction than had taken place before 1978. Despite the potential for land reclamation, it is unlikely that the net decline in cultivated area will be reversed.[76] The scarcity of land remains a fundamental constraint.

A shrinking land base can be offset by higher multiple cropping.[77] Between 1978 and 1990 the total sown area fell from 150.1 to 148.36 million hectares; by 1993, it had fallen to 147.74 million hectares.[78] The decline was smaller than that of arable area, implying that an increase in the multiple cropping index (MCI) from 150.9 (1978) to 155.1 (1990) to 155.4 (1993) had compensated for, but not entirely offset, the loss of cultivated land.

It has been pointed out elsewhere that projections of arable area which indicate a continuing decline from the level of the 1980s have "... powerful implications for the multiple cropping index that would be needed to maintain a desirable total sown area [for China] ...".[79] Throughout the 1980s the pressures for land encroachment were more powerful than the will to reverse the arable decline. If, as suggested earlier, the same pressures are maintained during the 1990s, improvements in land utilization will require the further extension of multiple cropping. The context in which this will have to take place is illustrated by Table 12.8, with the findings summarized in Table 12.9.

Table 12.8 Arable, sown and multiple cropped area in China and its regions: 1978, 1983 and 1990s

	CHINA	*NE*	*N*	*NW*	*C*	*S*	*SW*
AA							
1978	99.49	16.33	29.82	13.50	21.10	7.15	11.54
1983	98.51	16.47	29.41	13.38	20.71	7.05	11.50
1990	95.67	16.23	28.46	12.83	20.15	6.78	11.21
1993	95.10	16.28	28.13	13.16	19.77	6.61	11.16
TSA							
1978	150.96	16.37	42.11	12.77	44.27	15.55	19.89
1983	144.02	16.42	40.63	12.37	42.36	13.35	18.89
1990	148.36	16.22	41.60	12.75	42.66	14.38	20.76
1993	147.74	16.33	41.41	12.95	41.28	14.15	21.62
MCI							
1978	151.7	100.2	141.2	94.6	209.9	217.5	172.4
1983	146.2	99.7	138.2	92.5	204.5	189.4	164.3
1990	155.1	99.9	146.4	98.8	212.1	211.8	185.0
1993	155.4	100.3	147.2	98.4	208.8	214.1	193.7
MCA							
1978	51.47	0.04	12.29	−0.73	23.17	8.4	8.35
1983	45.51	−0.05	11.22	−1.01	21.65	6.30	7.39
1990	52.69	−0.02	13.19	−0.15	22.55	7.59	9.54
1993	52.64	0.05	13.28	−0.21	21.51	7.54	10.52

Abbreviations:
AA Arable area
TSA Total sown area
MCI Multiple cropping index
MCA Multiple cropped area

Notes:
(a) All figures in million hectares, except MCI, which is expressed in percentage terms.
(b) The regional breakdown used here follows *CAAS, 1985*, p. 425. The individual regions comprise the following provinces: *North-east*: Liaoning, Jilin, Heilongjiang: *North:* Shanxi, Hebei, Henan, Shandong, Shaanxi, Beijing, Tianjin; *North-west*: Inner Mongolia, Ningxia, Gansu, Qinghai, Xinjiang; *Centre*: Hunan, Hubei Jiangxi, Jiansu, Anhui, Zhejiang, Shanghai; *South*: Fujian, Guangdong, Guangxi, Hainan; *South-west*: Sichuan, Guizhou, Yunnan, Tibet.

Sources: 1978 and 1983: Walker, "Trends in crop production", pp. 622–3 and 628–9. 1990: *TJNJ 1991*, pp. 314 and 341. 1993: *TJNJ 1994*, pp. 329 and 342.

Table 12.9 Changes in arable, sown and multiple cropped area: 1978–1983 and 1983–1990

	CHINA	*NE*	*N*	*NW*	*C*	*S*	*SW*
Change during 1978–1983:							
AA	–0.98	0.14	–0.41	–0.12	–0.39	–0.10	–0.04
TSA	–6.94	0.05	–1.48	–0.40	–1.91	–2.20	–1.00
MCA	–5.96	0.09	–1.07	–0.28	–1.52	–2.10	–0.96
1983–1990:							
AA	–2.84	–0.23	–1.00	–0.48	–0.60	–0.26	–0.28
TSA	4.34	–0.20	0.97	0.38	0.30	1.03	1.87
MCA	7.18	–0.02	1.97	0.86	0.90	1.29	2.15
1990–1993:							
AA	–0.57	0.05	–0.33	0.33	–0.38	–0.17	–0.05
TSA	–0.62	0.11	–0.19	0.20	–1.38	–0.23	0.86
MCA	–0.05	0.07	0.09	–0.06	–1.06	–0.05	0.90

Note: All figures in million hectares.

Source: As Table 12.8.

The data confirm that in the immediate post-1978 years, the decline in arable area was unrelieved by any offsetting increase in the MCI, so that the total sown area throughout China also contracted (the single, marginal exception was the North-east). Worst affected were the Central and Southern regions, although the loss of multiple cropped area was also serious in the North and South-west. Economic factors are likely to have been mainly responsible for the changes. It was widely accepted that higher costs associated with high MCIs had an adverse effect upon farm incomes and incentives. Accordingly, the search for profit maximization, which guided household operations under the production responsibility systems, dictated that the multiple cropped area should be reduced. This is what occurred.

By 1983 this contraction had attracted critical comment. One view suggested that an optimum MCI for China was between 156 and 158 – significantly higher than the previous peak and well above the then-current level (146). From this time dates a steady recovery in the multiple cropped area – a recovery in which every region, except the North-east, shared. By 1990, a new peak of around 155 had been attained. The fact that the 1993 level showed virtually no change suggests that the MCI may now be close to the putative "optimum".[80]

It is difficult to predict what further changes will take place between now and the end of the century. The stabilization of the cultivated area – especially evident in the 1990s – and the maintenance of a high multiple cropping index does generate a more hopeful picture than the perspective of the mid-1980s offered. This is a significant achievement and one that would have appeared unlikely only a few years ago.

But further increases in the MCI will not readily be achieved in the near future. Natural conditions preclude any significant improvement in the North-east and North-west. In the South-west a sharp decline in the multiple cropped area during 1978–83 has been reversed and since 1983 more than 2 million hectares have been added. The result is that the current index is already higher than the maximum level thought feasible for this region.[81] Central and Southern China have traditionally contributed most to the multiple cropped area and their loss of 3.62 million hectares between 1978 and 1983 accounted for over 60 per cent of the national decline. By 1990 more than 2 million hectares had been recovered and the Centre's MCI had returned to its previous peak. It is unfortunate that this recovery was not maintained during the early 1990s, when both arable and sown area once more contracted. A significant rise in MCI conceals the reality that a parallel decline in arable and sown area has also taken place in the South since 1990. Rapid development and structural change make it unlikely that any significant departure from this pattern will occur in these regions in the future. Perhaps the firmest foundation for sown area expansion lies in the North, where climatic conditions are favourable and the returns from irrigation are high.[82]

Overall it is possible that China's total sown area will remain around 150 million hectares during the 1990s – close to the level of pre-1978 years. If an accelerated decline in arable area were to re-assert itself and/or the multiple cropped area contract, the figure could fall to 145 million hectares by 1995 – and to little more than 140 million by the year 2000. But despite the loss of almost 1.3 million hectares in 1993, earlier progress in easing the land shortage through higher multiple cropping suggests that such estimates are still worst-case scenarios.[83]

The earlier reference to a "desirable sown area" suggests the need for a rational pattern of land use between various crop categories. Before 1978 China's agricultural development was driven by the imperative of grain self-sufficiency. By contrast, agricultural policy in the 1980s encouraged diversification, the previous overwhelming emphasis on grain giving way to a more rational and efficient structure of production, in part dictated by considerations of comparative advantage and geared towards market demand. Price rises after 1978 raised the profitability of all crops, but particularly enhanced the returns available from economic crops, such as cotton, sugar and tobacco. Admittedly, the stagnation of grain production after 1984 introduced a potential new constraint on further shifts in land use. Nevertheless, by the 1990s significant changes in land utilization had taken place, as shown in Table 12.10.

Here is evidence of striking structural change. Between 1978 and 1993, against the background of a tiny contraction in total sown area (less than 1

Table 12.10 The changing distribution of China's sown area: 1978, 1990 and 1992

	Total sown area	*Food grains*	*of which:* *Economic crops*	*Other*
1978	150.10	120.59	14.44	15.08
	[100.00]	[80.34]	[9.62]	[10.05]
1990	148.36	113.47	21.42	13.48
	[100.00]	[76.48]	[14.44]	[9.09]
1992	149.01	110.56	24.28	14.17
	[100.00]	[74.20]	[16.29]	[9.51]

Sources: *Zhongguo nongcun jingji tongji daquan*, p. 131; *TJNJ 1991* p. 341 and *TJNJ 1993*, p. 359.

per cent), the grain sown area fell by some 10 million hectares (more than 6 per cent), whilst that of economic crops expanded by almost the same amount (a 68 per cent rise). In the meantime, the residual area declined by almost one million hectares.[84]

It is of some interest to compare the changes with two CAAS projections for 1990.[85] These anticipated sown areas under grain and economic crops of, respectively, 112–114 million and 19.9–21.6 million hectares (vegetables, leys and other crops meanwhile occupying 14.5–15.9 million hectares). This distribution derived from a projected total sown area of 146.4–151.5 million hectares. The reality is that by 1990 the higher targets for cereals and cash crops had been fulfilled, but with total sown area falling almost exactly halfway between the projected levels, the residual area under vegetables, green fertilizers, etc. had failed to expand.

A NOTE ON GRAIN YIELDS

The earlier analysis of likely arable and sown area trends strongly suggests that the burden of growth of grain production during the 1990s will rest, as it did throughout the 1980s, on rises in sown area yields. How heavy that burden will be is much more difficult to estimate, for it depends on changes in grain sown area and the choice of base year. The estimates in Table 12.11 attempt to quantify that burden by comparing realized yields in the late 1980s and early 1990s with projected planned levels needed to fulfil 8FYP and 10YP targets.

On the basis of the average yield recorded during the 7FYP period, fulfilment of the projected 1995 yield demanded an average increase of 96 kilograms per sown hectare per year during the 8FYP period. The reality is that during 1991–93, grain yields rose, on average, by 67 kilograms p.a. To put such figures into perspective, during 1978–84 increases of more than 300 kilograms per hectare were achieved in four out of six years. Subsequently, however, not until 1990 was the 1984 peak surpassed.

Table 12.11 Estimating the burden on grain yields during the 1990s

	Average grain yield (tonnes per sown hectare)
1986–90	3.66
1991–93	4.00
1995 plan	4.14
2000 plan	4.55

Sources: 1986–89 and 1991–93 averages from *TJNJ 1991*, p. 353; *TJNJ 1993*, p. 371 and SSB, *Zhongguo nongcun tongji nianjian 1994 (Chinese Rural Statistical Yearbook, 1994)* (Beijing, Statistical Publishing House, 1994), p. 183.

1995 and 2000 estimates derived from total output targets shown in Table 12.5 and an assumed grain sown area of 110 million hectares.

Attention has already been drawn to the disappointing performance of grain after 1990. But in one important respect, the experience of the early 1990s differs from that of the second half of the 1980s. During the earlier period, the stagnation of grain production reflected the failure of grain yields to rise.[86] By contrast, as Table 12.11 suggests, post-1990 yields displayed an upward trend, reaching a record level in 1993.[87] The clear inference is that in the 1990s, a contracting sown area has been the major constraint on grain production in China.

CONCLUDING REMARKS

The peculiar combination of factors – natural and technical, economic and institutional – which determines farm performance in any country makes the projection of future trends hazardous. As China has sought to fulfil its recent agricultural plans, it has faced fundamental institutional and economic dilemmas – caught, as it were, ". . . between the plan and the market."[88]

That the government recognizes these difficulties is not in question. Indeed, one of the intriguing features of developments in China in the 1990s has been the reappearance of a slogan, originally conceived in the early 1960s, to the effect that "agriculture is the foundation of the national economy". When this phrase was first used,[89] its rationale was self-evident. China was just emerging from an unprecedented famine, which had resulted in the "excess deaths" of some 30 million people, and the farm sector was in a state of total collapse. In these circumstances, a strategy which sought to prioritize the farm sector – above all, food grain production – made obvious sense.

Against the background of very different conditions in the 1990s, the slogan's continuing currency is more intriguing. In 1962 average per capita grain output was 238 kilograms; by 1993, it had reached 385 kilograms. In the early 1960s, the agricultural sector contributed almost half of China's NDP; some 30 years on, the figure was around 25 per cent. If growth was agriculture-led in the early 1980s, a decade later it was being driven by industry and foreign trade. By the first half of the 1990s, the familiar structural consequences of modern economic growth had already manifested themselves, with the role of primary activities declining in favour of secondary and tertiary sector expansion.

This chapter has sought to highlight some of the factors which have fuelled the concern voiced by senior government and Party officials in the face of agriculture's problems in the first half of the 1990s.[90] No doubt much of that concern reflects the potential social and political implications of such difficulties. The speed of the government's response to problems associated with the issue of "IOUs" to farmers and to reduce illegal exactions amongst peasants is evidence enough of the seriousness with which it regarded the threat which these practices posed to their authority.

There is also a regional dimension to China's agricultural problems. In contrast to coastal regions, where the farm sector accounted for less than a quarter of GDP, the average contribution of agriculture "proper"[91] in the interior provinces remained close to 40 per cent in the early 1990s. And whereas the farm sector's share of employment had fallen to 46 per cent along the coast, the corresponding figure inland was still well over 60 per cent. The structure of coastal and interior *rural* economies had also changed markedly, with agriculture accounting for only a quarter of rural social-value output along the coast, compared with more than half elsewhere.

The lagging performance of crop farming vis-a-vis other agricultural pursuits was another significant factor. Following an almost universal contraction in the output share of the crop sector in the first half of the 1980s, regional patterns diverged. In coastal China, there was a continuing decline, which elsewhere more or less came to a halt. The outcome is that by 1993, crop farming still accounted for almost two-thirds of agricultural output in the interior, compared with some 55 per cent in coastal provinces. The inference is that farmers in China's coastal regions had benefited from rises in income which had increasingly derived from higher-return, non-cropping farm activities.

Even without the benefit of hindsight, one ought not perhaps to be surprised at the intractability of some of the problems confronting China's agriculture and impeding sustained growth in the 1990s. The commitment to preserve contractual arrangements with individual farm households has been a consistent cornerstone of government policy. But the simultaneous advocacy of two-tier management and the maintenance of dual-track pricing have hinted at a more ambiguous attitude by policy-makers towards agricultural development policy. Such tensions no doubt reflect ideological differences within the government. But to explain them in such terms is too simplistic.

Rather, if we are to understand the obstacles to rapid and sustained agricultural growth during the 1990s, it is essential to appreciate the very real underlying *economic* issues that are at stake.

Ironically, the most fundamental of these is still that of grain.[92] Even allowing for accelerated agricultural growth, it is clear that the production and procurement of sufficient grain to meet consumption and other requirements will remain an absolute imperative in the foreseeable future. These issues seem destined to continue to dominate the formulation and implementation of agricultural development policy during the 1990s.[93]

The regional complexion of grain production deserves the final comment. In contrast to the experience of the first three decades of communist rule, the focus of output growth is shifting towards the northern half of the country.[94] By the early 1990s this reversal of the previous pattern was already under way, with significant implications for relative levels of per capita grain output in the various regions, as shown in Table 12.12.

In the early 1980s, when the CAAS investigations were undertaken, Northwest China lacked sufficient grain even to meet basic subsistence requirements, whilst the North had achieved no more than basic self-sufficiency.[95] By contrast, only the provinces of the Centre enjoyed a surplus which allowed significant diversion of grain to animal feed and other

Table 12.12 Per capita grain output in China – a regional perspective

	Average per capita grain output (kg)						
	1982	*1990*	*1993*	*1990A plan*	*1990B plan*	*2000A plan*	*2000B plan*
CHINA	348	390.3	385.2	375.5	388.3	418.1	440.2
NE	362	585.8	584.9	438.8	455.1	533.9	564.0
N	305	363.0	390.9	348.7	361.5	388.2	413.6
NW	269	383.7	337.3	292.4	324.4	347.2	391.0
C	419	429.1	401.7	421.8	433.4	442.3	460.5
S	337	301.2	276.0	340.1	341.2	371.4	399.7
SW	328	338.5	331.2	368.6	383.9	433.0	439.4

Sources: 1982 estimates from *CAAS, 1985*, p. 433.

Note that 1982 was the base year for this part of the CAAS exercise. Hence its inclusion here.

1990 figures from total population data in *TJNJ 1991*, p. 81; and total grain output in *TJNJ 1991*, p. 350. 1993 figures from total population data in *TJNJ 1990*, p. 60; and total grain output in *TJNJ 1994*, p. 345.

1990A, 1990B, 2000A and 2000B are derived from the two sets of projections for total population and total grain output given in *CAAS, 1985*, pp. 379 and 433. In order to obtain the estimates for each region, I have simply assumed that the 1990 regional distribution of total population, as revealed in *TJNJ 1991*, p. 81, remains constant through the 1990s. This is of course unrealistic, although it is hoped that the crude approach will not do violence to the findings.

purposes.[96] The North-east, South and South-west fell somewhere between these positions.

The figures for the 1990s suggest some of the strengths and weaknesses of the grain sector's recent performance. Most spectacular is the extraordinarily high figure already attained by the North-east in 1990 and sustained through 1993.[97] Also impressive was the steady improvement in the position of North China, where a steady increase in per capita output took it into surplus by 1993. The performance of the North-west was more mixed: to have moved out of deficit into comfortable surplus by 1990 was a remarkable achievement, but such progress was not subsequently maintained. In any case, in stark contrast to such successes, marginal improvements registered during the 1980s in the South-west and, in particular, Central China were later reversed. Most disastrous of all, average per capita grain production in the South showed a sustained *decline* (by almost 20 per cent) between 1982 and 1993.

Comparison of realized output in 1990 with the CAAS targets for that year offers a further perspective to developments during the 1980s. It underlines the remarkable achievements of North-east and North-west China and the disappointing performances of the South and South-west.[98] The figures for Central and Northern regions are just about in line with the projected levels.

Looking ahead to 2000, it is telling that the CAAS figures reveal a determination that every region should achieve a level of per capita grain production compatible with the attainment of a "comfortably well-off" living standard. The 1990 estimates of realized output suggested that from the perspective of that year, the provinces of the North-east had already fulfilled that goal and that those of the North-west were well on the way to doing so. Conditions in the North were also apparently moving in a favourable direction. The real problem areas were the South and South-west, where recent trends had made the fulfilment of the 2000 targets less likely.

From the perspective of 1993, the situation was less hopeful. It is true that the North-east and North remained on course. But elsewhere the situation had deteriorated. Not only had conditions in the South and South-west worsened, but the sharp decline in per capita output in Central provinces between 1990 and 1993 had taken it back to a position even below that of 1982.

It is true that the validity of the original CAAS projections has become more questionable in the light of subsequent developments. The comparative perspective which they offer nevertheless remains interesting. First, through the contrasting performances of South and South-west, and North-east and North-west, they suggest the restraining and liberating forces which regional development is likely to play in the continuing search for the basic welfare goal articulated in economic and social development plans for the 1990s. Second, it highlights the gap that now exists between the 8FYP and 10YP targets and production levels needed to fulfil that same goal. Calculations suggest that in order to reach the national average per capita level of grain output originally cited by CAAS, total grain output in 2000 will need to rise to 544–572 million tonnes (9–14 per cent above the official target).[99] Such figures suggest why the optimism of the early 1980s has given way to caution and even pessimism. They are also perhaps a more reliable measure of the burden which rests upon agriculture during the 1990s, as the government continues to search for an appropriate balance between planning and marketization.

NOTES

1 As the evidence of Japan shows, the establishment of cooperative associations in order to promote backward and forward linkages and to guide rural finance may command a strong economic logic.

2 *Zhonghua renmin gongheguo guomin jingji he shehui fazhan shinian guihua he dibage wunian jihua gangyao, (Outline of the 10-Year Programme and Eighth Five-Year Plan for National and Social Development)*, (Beijing: People's Publishing House, 1991), hereafter *Jihua Gangyao*, pp. 75–155. The text can also be found in *Renmin ribao (People's Daily)*, hereafter *RMRB*, 16 April 1991. An English translation is available in British Broadcasting Corporation, *Summary of World Broadcasts, Part 3: The Far East*, hereafter *SWB*, FE/1058, 29 April 1991.

3 This was the document which the Central Committee examined on 30 December 1990. See *SWB*, FE/0958, 31 December 1990.

4 Such ambiguity is suggested by the advocacy of measures, designed simultaneously to "enhance the strength of the collective economy" and establish a "two-tier system combining unified and decentralized management." See also below.

5 State Statistical Bureau, *Zhongguo tongji zhaiyao 1991 (A Statistical Survey of China 1991)*, hereafter *TJZY 1991* (Beijing: Statistical Publishing House, 1991), p. 53.

6 In constant 1970 and 1957 prices, respectively. These figures are derived from data in Ministry of Agriculture (Planning Department), *Zhongguo nongcun jingji tongji daquan, 1949–86 (Compendium of Chinese Rural Economic Statistics, 1949–86)* (Beijing: Agricultural Publishing House, 1989), pp. 106 and 108.

7 The relevant figures are as follows:

	Grain sown area (mill. ha.)	*Av grain yield (tonnes/ha.)*
1965	119.63	1.635
1970	119.27	2.010
1980	117.23	2.745
1985	108.85	3.480

See *TJNJ 1991*, pp. 340 and 353.

8 Increases in total production during 1990 were as follows: grain, 9.5%; oil crops, 24.6%; cotton, 19% (*TJNJ 1994*, p. 347).

9 Compare the following figures:

	Average per capita consumption (kg. p.a.):			
	Grain	*Edible oil*	*Pork*	*Fish*
1980	213.81	2.30	11.16	3.41
1985	251.69	5.08	13.84	4.84
1990	238.80	5.67	16.64	6.53

(*TJNJ 1991*, p. 273).

10 In 1982 for cotton, oil seeds and sugar, and in 1983 for food grains.

11 For a detailed analysis of changes in the structure of agricultural production, as revealed by GVAO estimates, see Robert Michael Field, "Trends in the Value of Agricultural Output" in Y. Y. Kueh and R. F. Ash (eds.), *Economic Trends in Chinese Agriculture: The Impact of Post-Mao Reforms* (Oxford: Clarendon Press, 1993), pp. 123–60.

12 *TJNJ, 1991*, p. 340.

13 *Ibid.* The same source shows that in 1985 grain and economic crops accounted, respectively, for 75.8 and 15.6 per cent of the total sown area.

14 *TJNJ 1991*, p. 65.

15 Vice-Premier Tian Jiyun, the government's most senior spokesman for agricultural affairs, addressing the 16th meeting of the seventh NPC Standing Committee in October 1990. See *SWB*, FE/0908, 30 October 1990.

16 Zou Jiahua (minister of the State Planning Commission) in a written speech to a national meeting on exchanging experience in rural economic work: see *SWB*, FE/1012, 5 March 1991. Zou's views were echoed by Song Ping, addressing the same meeting: *SWB*, FE/1024, 19 March 1991.

17 "Zhonggong zhongyang guanyu jinyibu jiaqiang nongye he nongcun gongzuo de jueding" ("Decision of the CCP Central Committee on further strengthening agriculture and rural work"), hereafter "CCPCC 1991", adopted by the eighth plenary session of the Thirteenth CCP Central Committee on 29 November 1991. The text can be found in *Zhenjiang ribao (Zhenjiang Daily)*, 26 December 1991. It is translated in *SWB*, FE/1268, 3 January 1992.

18 From 11.1% (1979) to 3.0% (1988). *TJNJ 1991*, p. 156. For an analysis of state investment in agriculture and other forms of financial support, see Robert F. Ash, "The Peasant and the State," *The China Quarterly*, No. 127 (September 1991), pp. 493–526.

19 The word is carefully chosen. In 1978 the government gave an undertaking to increase investment allocations to agriculture (from 10 to 15–18 percent) within a few years. A year or two later, it was clear that this commitment had been abandoned (see Nicholas R. Lardy, *Agriculture in China's Modern Economic Development* (Cambridge: Cambridge University Press, 1983), pp. 191–2).

20 "CCPCC 1991" is quite explicit on this. Thus: ". . . During the 8FYP period, state investment in . . . capital construction projects will increase each year, supplemented by the expanded use of foreign funds. Government support funds for agricultural development will also be increased. Counties' non-committed financial reserves should be used mainly for agricultural development. Agricultural development funds and other funds designated for agricultural use must be used for their proper purpose. . . .

State banks should regard loans in support of agriculture as a priority and should ensure that the expansion of such loans is greater than that of the nation's bank loans. . . . Credit cooperatives should appropriately increase deposits and extend more loans in support of agricultural production." (*Zhenjiang ribao*, p. 5.)

21 *Jihua Gangyao*, p. 105. As of 1993, a little over 1.3 million hectares had been added to the 1990 irrigated area (*TJNJ 1994*, p. 335).

22 Acceleration of work designed to control major rivers and lakes did in fact take place in the wake of the publication of the 10YP/8FYP document. It is noteworthy that an entire section was devoted to this issue in "CCPCC 1991."

23 *SWB*, FE/1024, 19 March 1991.

24 Y. Y. Kueh has shown that between 1984 and 1988, the savings ratio of Chinese peasants fell from 22.9 to 12.5 per cent. During the three years from 1985 to 1987, their marginal propensity to save was negative. See "Food consumption

and peasant incomes" in Kueh and Ash (eds.), *Economic Trends in Chinese Agriculture*, especially pp. 239–42.

25 "CCPCC 1991." In the wake of decollectivization, such activities declined greatly in the 1980s. See Ash, "The peasant and the state", p. 499.

26 That is, through the mechanisms of *yigong bunong* ("using industry to assist agriculture") and *yigong jiannong* ("using industry for agricultural construction"): see "CCPCC 1991." Both were used at different times in the 1980s in order to inject funds into the farm sector, but with mixed results. See Robert F. Ash, "Agricultural Policy under the Impact of Reform" and Terry Sicular, "Ten Years of Reform: Progress and Setbacks in Agricultural Planning and Pricing", Kueh and Ash (eds.), *Economic Trends in Chinese Agriculture*.

27 *Jihua Gangyao*, p. 102.

28 Thus: ". . . Ownership of land belongs to the collective. Individuals merely possess the right of operation, but cannot sell or lease the land. . . . Contractors must pay taxes to the state according to law, sell farm produce to the state at prices set by the state, and deliver funds and contract fees to the collective in accordance with the terms of the contract." Tian Jiyun in *Nongmin ribao (Farmers' Daily)*, 9 October 1991, translated in *SWB*, FE/1234, 20 November 1991.

29 *SWB*, FE/1269, 4 January 1992.

30 For example, *Nongmin ribao*, 9 October 1991, which urged that ". . . our attention should be focused on expanded reproduction rather than [on] the few *mou* of peasants' land. . . ." The same source expected that peasants who abandoned farming for industrial or tertiary occupations would release their land "to the collective for unified operation." See also *RMRB*, 22 December 1991, which stated that: ". . . Socialist agriculture should be based on the continuous development of the collective economy. . . ."

31 *Ibid.*

32 *RMRB*, 13 December 1991, "Several issues concerning current rural work," makes the point that in some regions of China agreed fees had been illegally increased and contracted land taken back from the peasants. For more recent evidence of trends towards recollectivization, see *The Asian Wall Street Journal*, 13 March 1995.

33 During 1979–84 the average annual increase in the purchase price of agricultural and sideline products was 7.62% (Hu Bangding (ed.), *Zhongguo wujia nianjian, 1990 (Chinese Price Yearbook, 1990)*, hereafter *ZGWJNJ*, (Beijing, State Price Publishing House, 1990), p. 431). During 1985–89 the corresponding figure was 13% (State Statistical Bureau, *Zhongguo wujia tongji nianjian, 1990 (Chinese Statistical Yearbook of Prices, 1990)*, hereafter *WJTJNJ 1990* (Beijing, State Statistical Publishing House, 1990), p. 113). That this pattern applied to grain is demonstrated by Claude Aubert: see his *Rural China, 1985–90: Are the Reforms Really Bogging Down?* (Chinese University of Hong Kong, Institute of Asia-Pacific Studies: Universities Service Centre Seminar Series, 1991), p. 4. Notice that these figures do not take account of changes in market prices.

34 Aubert (*Rural China*, pp. 6–7) shows this to have been the case for both grain and cotton production.

35 The relevant data can be found in *TJNJ 1991*, pp. 230 and 234. They should, however, be interpreted with some caution, for it seems likely that the category of "agricultural production materials" is narrowly defined and excludes certain critical agricultural inputs – notably, chemical fertilizers. Not until sufficient data are available to facilitate an analysis of price trends for a truly representative range of goods bought by farmers will it be possible to confirm that the price

terms of trade did turn significantly against the farm sector during the second half of the 1980s.

36 *WJTJNJ 1991*, p. 115.

37 See *WJTJNJ 1990*, p. 113. Not since 1979 had there been such a large increase in a single year.

38 See, for example, Tian Jiyun in *SWB*, FE/1026. Official data show that market prices of grain fell by more than 18% in 1990 (*cf.* a decline of 6.8% for grain procurement prices): *TJNJ 1991*, pp. 248 and 254. See also Aubert, *Rural China*, p. 10.

Interestingly, Liu Zhongyi (then Minister of Agriculture) commented in 1990 that sales and storage difficulties affecting grain indicated not a surfeit of production, but "incompatibility in the circulation field" (Robert F. Ash, "Quarterly Chronicle and Documentation", hereafter "QCD", *The China Quarterly*, No. 126 (June 1991), p. 663.

39 Market prices for 1980–88 can be found in State Statistical Bureau, *Zhongguo shangye waijing tongji ziliao, 1952–1988 (Statistical Materials Relating to China's Commerce and External Economic Relations, 1952–1988)* (Beijing: State Statistical Publishing House, 1990), p. 399. Data for 1989 and 1990 are from *WJTJNJ 1991*, p. 93. It is of some interest to compare market price trends for grain with those of fresh vegetables, fish, and meat and dairy produce: the latter three categories all experienced rising prices in both the first and second halves of the 1980s, although in no case was the average annual price increase after 1985 as great as that in the grain sector. Thus:

	Average increase in market price (% p.a.)	
	1981–85	*1986–90*
Grain	− 2.0	+ 14.5
Fresh vegetables	+ 8.6	+ 8.2
Meat, poultry and eggs	+ 6.7	+ 12.2
Fish	+ 13.8	+ 10.5

40 *See ZGWJNJ 1991*, p. 32.

41 Specifically, 10 kilograms of fertilizer for deliveries of wheat and maize; 15 kilograms for husked rice and soyabeans. See *ZGWJNJ* 1990, p. 44.

42 *Jihua gangyao*, p. 139.

43 "CCPCC 1991."

44 The likelihood is that the reintroduction of the coupons was intended to address the inadequacy of food supplies to the most disadvantaged elements of the urban population. Chinese officials meanwhile denied that the reappearance of coupons presaged a partial return to central planning and interventionist methods of food distribution in urban areas.

45 The State Council's decision to build additional warehouses in order to accommodate anticipated additional grain sales was announced by Tian Jiyun in a report to the 16th session of the Seventh NPC Standing Committee on 27 October 1990. See Ash, "QCD", in *The China Quarterly*, No. 125 (March, 1991), pp. 192 and 202. Note that the novelty of the State Council's 1990 decision lay in its proposal to establish the system of special grain reserves, rather than to increase physical storage capacity. As Nicholas Lardy has pointed out, authorization to add 20 million tonnes to the national grain storage capacity was, for example, given by the State Council in 1983 (personal communication).

46 See Aubert, *Rural China*, p. 12.

47 Ash, "QCD", *The China Quarterly*, No. 127 (September 1991), pp. 663–4.

48 One source reported that in the first half of 1993, more than 170 outbreaks of peasant disturbances and rioting had occurred throughout China (Hong Kong, *South China Morning Post*, 27 June 1993). The most notorious case was that of Renshou county in Sichuan province (see *SWB*, FE/1714, B2/1). Resentment was also fuelled by the widespread imposition of illegal exactions (*tanpai*) in order to finance non-budgetary development projects, often unrelated to the needs of agriculture.

49 Tian Jiyun, 27 October 1990, introducing the system of special grain reserves. Quoted in Ash, "QCD", *The China Quarterly*, No. 125 (March 1991), p. 192.

50 Ash, "QCD", *The China Quarterly*, No. 127, p. 664.

51 For a careful analysis, see Bruce Stone, "Developments in agricultural technology", *The China Quarterly*, No. 116 (December 1988), pp. 767–822.

52 *Jihua gangyao*, p. 126.

53 *Ibid.*, p. 103.

54 See Bruce Stone, "Developments in agricultural technology," pp. 790–818. Also Y. Y. Kueh, "Fertilizer supplies and foodgrain production in China, 1952–82", *Food Policy*, August 1984.

55 "CCPCC 1991", p. 5.

56 *TJNJ 1994*, p. 336. Interestingly, the effectively irrigated area in 1993 (2.45 million hectares) was almost identical to the total area susceptible to flooding (2.44 million hectares)!

57 *Ibid.*

58 US Central Intelligence Agency, *China's Economy in 1993 and 1994: The Search for a Soft Landing* (report prepared for submission to the Subcommittee on Technology and National Security of the US Congress, Joint Economic Committee) (22 July 1994).

59 For example, both grain and cotton experienced a sharp fall in total output in 1985, but a sharp increase in 1990. In both cases, these changes were against the previous trends and they lend a spurious impression of growth. The case of oil crops is analogous, but different: total production rose sharply in 1985 and 1990, so that a growth estimate derived from these two years *understates* the "true" trend.

60 It is not of course coincidental that targets for 1995 and 2000 were drawn up against the background of the slower growth of 1986–89, rather than that of the fine 1990 harvest. There may of course be political advantages too in formulating conservative plans: better by far to claim the over-fulfilment of low targets than have to admit the under-fulfilment of high ones! Notice that the 1990 bumper grain harvest owed most to the regional performance of the North and North-east. Together, they contributed two-thirds of the increase in national production during 1990 (half coming from the North-east – i.e. Liaoning, Jilin and Heilongjiang – alone) (*TJNJ 1990*, p. 367 and *TJNJ 1991*, p. 350). We shall return to this regional dimension later.

61 Indeed, on a year-to-year basis, the average rate of growth of total output between 1990 and 1994 was negative (–0.1% p.a.).

62 The seven provinces are Liaoning, Jilin, Heilongjiang, Inner Mongolia, Hebei, Henan and Shandong. Collectively, they achieved an average rate of growth of 6.9% p.a. (1989–93).

63 Tian Jiyun was specific about this: ". . . in the 1990s China's agriculture will be required to meet the demand of over 1.2 billion people at a comfortably well-off standard of living. . ." (addressing a national meeting on rural economic work, March 1991) (*SWB*, FE/1026, 21 March 1991).

64 *Jihua gangyao*, pp. 83 and 146.

65 It may be that China already suffers a feed deficit, which it has accommodated by a combination of imports, running down reserves, cutting rations and using less than efficient grain-meat conversion ratios. See Claude Aubert, "Problems of agricultural diversification: some aspects or animal husbandry and grain utilization in China", in Eduard B. Vermeer (ed.), *From Peasant to Entrepreneur: Growth and Change in Rural China* (Pudoc: Wageningen, March 1992), pp. 105–28. Elsewhere, the same author has pointed out that consumption of grain fodder rose from 13 to 18 per cent of total production between 1978 and 1984 and reached 25 per cent (100 million tonnes) in 1988 (C. Aubert, "The agricultural crisis in China at the end of the 1980s" in Jorgen Delman, Clemens Stubbe Ostergaard and Flemming Christiansen (eds.), *Remaking Peasant China: Problems of Rural Development and Institutions at the Start of the 1990s* (Aarhus: Aarhus University Press, 1990), p. 25.

66 It is worth recording that in July 1990, in an address to a conference on non-staple foodstuffs, Li Peng noted that ". . . with China's limited availability of arable land and low level of grain consumption per head, it would be impossible to raise the animal protein intake by a big margin . . ." (Ash, "QCD", *The China Quarterly*, No. 123 (December 1990), p. 767). Note too that every 1% increase in the animal protein content of human food consumption requires an extra 5 million tonnes of feed grain: see He Kang (principal editor), *Zhongguo liangshi fazhan zhanlue duice (Strategic Measures for the Development of Food Grains in China)*, hereafter *ZGLSFZZL*, (Beijing: Agricultural Publishing House, 1990), p. 31.

67 See Kenneth R. Walker, "Forty Years on: Provincial Contrasts in China's Rural Economic Development", *The China Quarterly*, No. 119 (September 1989), p. 472.

68 This is a rough figure. Conversion ratios differ between individual meats and dairy produce so that the true ratio depends upon the structure of meat production. See Aubert, "Problems of agricultural diversification."

69 Aubert, "The agricultural crisis in China at the end of the 1980s", p. 25.

70 Remember too that demand for grain for *industrial* processing is also likely to increase dramatically in the coming years: see Ash, "Prospects for the Grain Sector: A Chinese Perspective", Wolfgang Klenner (ed.), *Trends of Economic Development in East Asia* (Berlin, Heidelberg, New York, London, Paris, Tokyo: Springer-Verlag, 1989) pp. 419–31. There exists a wide variety of estimates of grain requirements in the year 2000, ranging from 480 to 593 million tonnes! For some of the relevant evidence, see Chinese Academy of Agricultural Sciences (CAAS), Research Group for the Development of Food Grains and Economic Crops, "Woguo liangshi he jingji zuowu de fazhan" ("A study of the development of food grains and economic crops in China"), *Zhongguo nongcun fazhan zhanlue wenti* (*Strategic Issues Relating to China's Rural Development*), hereafter *CAAS, 1985*, (Beijing: Agricultural Scientific Publishing House, 1985), pp. 377–456; Gu Jingde, "2000 nian woguo nongcun fazhan de qige da qushi" ("Seven major trends in China's rural development to the year 2000"), reprinted in *Agricultural Economics*, No. 5 (1985), pp. 20–3; Guo Shiping, "2000 nian woguo heli shiwu jiegouliang de queding ji shengchan nengli de guji" ("Determining a rational food structure and estimating the production capacity of China in the year 2000"), *Nongye Xiandaihua Yanjiu* (*Research on Agricultural Modernization*), No. 3 (1985), pp. 23–6; Cong Anni *et al*, "Lengjing yuce nongye xingshi; shenzhong jueze zhanlue juece" ("A sober projection of the agricultural situation; a careful choice of strategic decisions"), *Caizheng Yanjiu* (*Financial Research*), No. 2 (1989), pp. 34–9; Ma Hong (chief editor), *2000 Nian de Zhongguo* (*China in the Year 2000*)

(Beijing: China – Social Science Publishing House, 1989), pp. 206–29; Chen Liang Yu and Allan Buckwell, *Chinese Grain Economy and Policy* (Wallingford, Oxon: C.A.B. International, 1991).

71 Paradoxically, China has been an exporter of feed products. One Chinese source highlights the irrationality of such exports through the following example: in 1987, 4.3 million tonnes of animal feed were exported. Had these supplies been used domestically, they would have raised 12.28 million pigs. These would, in turn, have yielded 861,000 tonnes of pork, which, if exported, might have earned US $7.83 million *more than* the value of the original feed exports. Meanwhile, the 12.28 million pigs would have generated the equivalent of 890,000 tonnes of chemical fertilizer and so raised domestic grain production by an estimated 1.96 million tonnes. If the additional foreign exchange earned through the sale of the pork were allocated to the grain sector, several extra million tonnes of cereals could have been produced! See *ZGLSFZZL*, p. 35.

72 Fulfilment of this target will require annual rises of 10 million tonnes of grain a year for the rest of the decade.

73 Lester R. Brown, *International Herald Tribune*, 28–9 September 1994.

74 The 1978 figure is from Kenneth R. Walker, "Trends in crop production, 1978–86", *The China Quarterly*, No. 116 (December 1988), Table 1, p. 595. The 1990 figure is given in *TJNJ 1991*, p. 314.

75 Based on arable area data for 1993 in *TJNJ 1994*, p. 329.

76 Most Chinese sources would appear to concede the likelihood of a continuing decline in arable area during the 1990s. See, for example, *CAAS, 1985*, pp. 394–5; and *2000 Nian de Zhongguo*, pp. 230–1. A recent source predicts a loss of 6.67 million hectares by the end of the century, but argues that this figure underestimates the true loss by some 50–100% because so much of the encroachment is likely to affect good-quality land. (See Wu Ziping *et al.*, "Bawu qijian he 2000 nian woguo nongye fazhan de chubu yuce" ("Initial projections of agricultural development during the 8FYP period and in the year 2000"), *Yuce (Projections)*, No. 1 (1991), p. 51. I am grateful to Dr. K. C. Yeh for bringing this article to my attention.

77 Or by increased application of inputs, designed to raise yields per unit area.

78 *TJNJ 1991*, p. 340 and *TJNJ 1994*, p. 342. Differences between sowing and harvesting seasons of crops make it possible to obtain more than one harvest a year from a single piece of land. Sown area differs from arable area by the extent to which such multiple cropping is practised.

79 Walker, "Trends in crop production", p. 594.

80 In its projections for the 1990s, *CAAS, 1985*, p. 395 had looked to the re-establishment of a MCI at the 1977 level of 155.

81 *CAAS, 1985*, p. 446.

82 But the increase in the North's MCI from 138 (1983) to 147 (1993) already constituted an impressive achievement which will be hard to sustain.

83 Projections in *CAAS, 1985*, p. 409 indicate a sown area of 146.4–151.5 million hectares (1990), and 143.3–153.6 million hectares (2000).

84 Under the "other" category, what Table 10 does not reveal is that between 1978 and 1990, there was a major expansion of the area sown to vegetables at the expense of green fertilizers (leys).

85 *CAAS, 1985*, p. 409.

86 By 1989, the grain sown area was some 2.9 million hectares more than in 1985.

87 In only one out of four years during 1990–93 did China's average grain yield decline.

88 Jean C. Oi, *State and Peasant in Contemporary China: The Political Economy of Village*

Government (Berkeley, Los Angeles, Oxford: University of California Press, 1989), p. 235.

89 The strategy of "taking agriculture as the foundation [of] the economy" has its origins in the deliberations of the Ninth Plenum of the Eighth CCP Central Committee (January 1961).

90 There is no lack of evidence of such concern. Cf. Wan Li (1993), arguing that farm problems had ". . . severely undermined the interests of the peasants and damaged relations between them and the Party" and referring to the dangers of ". . . peasant revolt. . . peasants turning against the state . . . agriculture [sliding] into chaos" (*SWB*, FE/1736). Witness Li Peng's warning that rural conditions could become "even more explosive". And see too references to Deng Xiaoping's reported fear that economic problems in the 1990s might come from the farm sector and his belief that such a setback would take a long time to overcome (e.g. in *RMRB*, 8 December 1994).

91 That is, crop farming, forestry, animal husbandry, fishing and sidelines.

92 If agriculture is the "foundation of the national economy," orthodoxy requires us to add that "grain is the basis of that foundation".

93 The same conclusion was reached by Kenneth Walker in 1989: see his "Forty years on", *The China Quarterly*, No. 119 (September 1989), p. 474.

94 The contribution to the increase in total grain output of Centre, South and South-west between the First and Sixth FYP periods was 60%. That of the Northern regions of China was 40%. The CAAS projections anticipated a dramatic reversal of this pattern, the Northern provinces accounting for 52% of the expected rise in total grain production between 1982 and 2000, compared with only 48% from Central and Southern regions. See Ash, "Prospects for China's Grain Sector", p. 427.

95 This statement follows Kenneth R. Walker in assuming that basic self-sufficiency may be defined in terms of levels of per capita grain output between 275 and 309 kilograms. See *Food Grain Procurement and Consumption in China* (Cambridge: Cambridge University Press, 1984), p. 3.

96 An average per capita grain production of 400 kilograms or above is my bench-mark in making this statement. This is a figure which has acquired almost talismanic status in China in recent years – although it is noticeable that 8FYP and 10YP targets imply levels that fall below it. See *ZGLSFZZL*, pp. 30–1. It is worth recording that an average per capita grain output of 400 kg. was achieved in the United States and developed European countries some 50–60 years ago. Current levels in these countries are typically in excess of 750 kg. – and over 1,500 kg. in Canada, Australia and the USA.

97 In 1990 average per capita grain production in the North-east rose by 46% (from 400.1kg). The point has already been made that the fine 1990 harvest owed most by far to the performance of this single region. The region remained a major source of national grain supplies in subsequent years.

98 For the former, overfulfilment of targets by 29.6–34.4% and 17.7–30.6%; for the latter, underfulfilment by 7.1–10.8% and 12.7–20.6%.

99 These figures are obtained by multiplying the projected national average per capita estimates given in CAAS by a projected population of 1.3 billion in the year 2000.

Part IV

THE FINANCIAL SECTOR AND FINANCIAL REFORM

13

THE FINANCIAL SYSTEM

Christine P. W. Wong
P. B. Rana and N. Hamid (Editors)

INSTITUTIONAL STRUCTURE

Under central planning, monetary policy played a passive role subordinate to production planning. Virtually all financial flows were routed through the budget: state-owned enterprises remitted profits to the budget and in turn received investment and working-capital appropriations from the budget. All investment was centrally planned by the State Planning Commission and the State Capital Construction Commission. The role of the state bank was confined to cashiering and auditing functions, to ensure that financial transactions conformed to plan stipulations. In pre-reform PRC, even though the economy was quite decentralized, the strong growth orientation and the aversion to financial dictates that were central to Maoist ideology meant that the banking system was still allowed to play only a supporting role in economic management.

The state banking system began to acquire an important role in financial intermediation when enterprise reforms decentralized the financing of investment and working capital. The reform period saw a proliferation of banks and nonbank financial institutions. In the state-owned sector, reform concentrated first on institution building. In March 1978, the People's Bank of China (PBC) was separated from the Ministry of Finance (MOF) and elevated to the ministry level. In September 1983 it was made the country's central bank. Reforms also led to the revival or creation of four specialized banks. These were the Agricultural Bank of China (ABC), Industrial and Commercial Bank of China (ICBC), People's Construction Bank of China (PCBC), and Bank of China (BOC). In addition, the China Investment Bank (CIB) was created in 1981 to handle World Bank loans to the industry sector. It now functions as a wholesale bank and an intermediary for foreign lending to Chinese industry.

Source: From Centrally Planned to Market Economies: The Asian Approach (Hong Kong: Oxford University Press for the Asian Development Bank, 1996), Chapter 8.

People's Bank of China

As the central bank, the PBC formulates and implements monetary policy, controlling the money supply and setting interest rates and foreign exchange rates. It issues currency and draws up and implements the credit plan. It also acts as prudential regulatory agency in supervising and monitoring the operations of specialized banks. As banker to the government, the PBC manages the state treasury and issues government bonds, manages the country's foreign reserves, and represents the Chinese government in international monetary organizations such as the IMF. As of 1990, the PBC had 2,519 offices and a staff of 158,000. Its network comprises regional branches in all the provinces (including Beijing, Shanghai, and Tianjin), subbranches in all cities, and an office in each of the country's over 2,000 counties. The PBC branches and subbranches perform the same functions as the head office and are accountable to both the PBC hierarchy and the local government (see Figure 13.1). They must coordinate not only with specialized banks in their localities but also with local-government agencies.

Specialized banks

Before 1985 these banks strictly specialized in a given sector or type of operation, and had a monopoly over their respective spheres. Since then, all

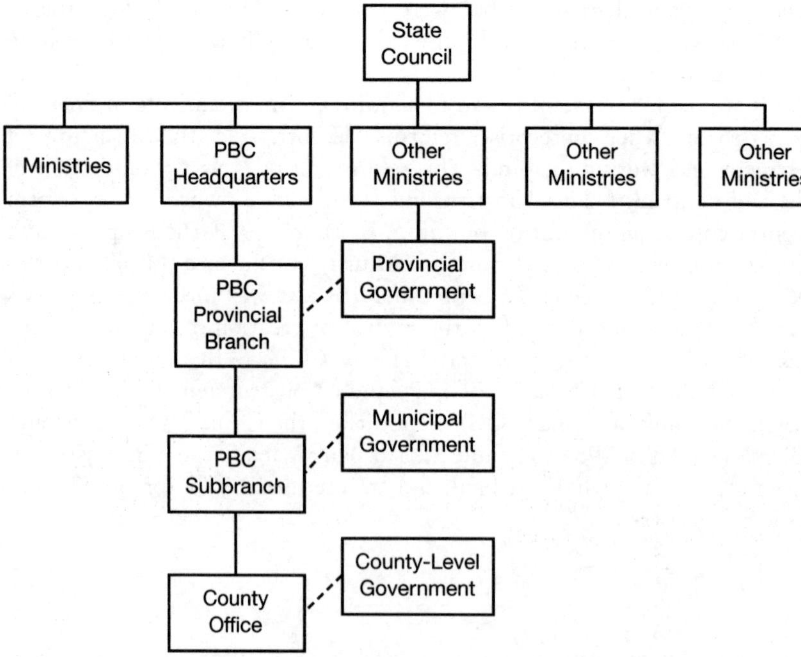

Figure 13.1 People's Bank of China: Organization and Hierarchy

four have been allowed to engage in general banking and to compete for deposits and loans in one another's previously monopolized markets, but all remain highly specialized in their operations. All the specialized banks are organized in the same way as the PBC, with a relatively small head office in Beijing, branches in each province, and subbranches in cities and counties. The local branches and subbranches also come under the "dual leadership" of the head office and local authorities. Table 13.1 shows the size and organizational structure of these banks. Table 13.2 gives the breakdown of offices and staff by administrative level.

Industrial and Commercial Bank of China

The ICBC is the largest specialized bank. It was created in 1983 to take over the commercial operations of the PBC. In 1988 its total assets and liabilities were 561.2 billion yuan—32 per cent of total bank assets and 47 per cent of the domestic operations of the commercial banks (excluding BOC). Its principal functions are mobilization of individual and enterprise deposits in urban areas and provision of working-capital loans to SOEs, collectives, and individual enterprises. It also grants medium-term loans for technical transformation, and engages in trust business directly and in entrusted business through an affiliated trust and investment company. Out of its very large network of more than 30,000 offices with a total staff of nearly 500,000 (see Table 13.2), it provides consulting services and financial leasing services as well.

Agricultural Bank of China

Revived in 1979, ABC had total assets and liabilities of 301.5 billion yuan at the end of 1988. It is the second largest specialized bank, with a market share of 25 per cent in the PRC's domestic banking business. Its main role is to provide working capital to state agricultural supply and marketing units in rural areas. In 1985 it began lending to industrial township enterprises and extending medium-term technical transformation loans. While its deposits come mainly from agricultural marketing and supply units and rural residents, and a major source of its funds is the mandatory redeposits of rural credit cooperatives, ABC has been authorized since 1985 to compete with other banks for urban deposits. The ABC network of offices, branches, and business offices is the largest in the country, comprising more than 55,000 offices and 568,000 employees.

People's Construction Bank of China

The PCBC is the third largest financial institution in the domestic market. It is affiliated with the State Council, but is supervised by the Ministry of

Table 13.1 Structure of the financial system, PRC, 1988

	Number of branches and subsidiaries	*Number of employees*	*Assets (billion yuan)*
Central Bank			
PBC	2,431	131,827	405.0
Specialized banks			
ICBC	29,998	469,805	561.7
ABC	50,777	443,970	301.5
BOC (domestic and foreign)	959	51,986	559.7[a]
PCBC[b]	3,293	172,906	339.4[c]
Universal banks			
BOCOM (incl. Hong Kong)	44	5,620	111.6
CITIC Industrial Bank	2	143	8.8
Development banks			
CIB	28	1,338	6.7
Cooperatives			
RCCs	60,872	471,900	149.0
UCCs	3,274	54,888	20.5
Other deposit takers			
Foreign deposit-taking banks	4	...	...
Foreign joint-venture Banks (19)	29	950	...
Nonbank financial institutions			
TICs	745	16,000	83.9
ITICs	34	–	
PICC (domestic)	2,749	67,645	...
PICC (abroad)	54	750	...
Finance companies	17	400	3.2
Financial leasing companies	9	300	...
Security companies (MOF)	61	–	...
Security companies (PBC)	34	800	...

Notes:
[a] Includes BOC's foreign exchange operations.
[b] PCBC can also be classified as a development bank. These figures, which were taken from its annual report, differed from those provided by PBC (3,511 branches and 141,000 employees).
[c] Includes MOF's trust portfolio.

Sources: People's Bank of China; System Reform Commission; annual reports of the four specialized banks.

Finance. It was created in 1954 to handle disbursements of budgetary funds for capital construction. In 1985 it was given bank status when most budgetary allocations for capital construction were turned into interest-bearing loans. It now also provides banking services to construction enterprises in the state sector.

Table 13.2 Offices and staff in the PRC banking sector, 1990

	Total	*Head-quarters*	*Provincial*	*Municipal*	*Central branch*	*County branch*	*Urban suburbs*	*Township savings branch*	*Business office*
Total									
Offices	125,054	7	195	82	1,905	11,555	4,784	73,149	31,255
Staff	1,507,014	7,406	55,376	21,619	209,005	522,719	149,985	204,622	251,386
PBC									
Offices	2,519	1	30	14	316	2,048	16	2	—
Staff	157,961	2,332	9,710	4,237	37,791	70,269	602	7	—
ICBC									
Offices	30,798	1	29	14	304	2,066	1,159	26,636	...
Staff	491,507	695	7,932	4,937	34,789	142,323	112,044	174,786	...
ABC									
Offices	55,410	1	29	14	305	2,161	474	20,943	30,798
Staff	468,023	677	6,303	2,031	23,225	113,924	20,305	29,379	252,012
PCBC									
Offices	31,595	1	30	14	521	2,429	2,050	25,532	333
Staff	216,601	884	10,364	4,832	73,424	120,743	...	...	...
BOC									
Offices	1,483	1	30	11	110	788	543	...	...
Staff	73,371	1,905	16,932	3,210	17,047	32,630	1,647	...	...
BOCOM									
Offices	189	1	17	...	46	...	89	36	...
Staff	13,839	188	1,763	...	5,601	...	2,837	450	...

Source: People's Bank of China.

Bank of China

Until recently, BOC had the state monopoly over all foreign exchange and international payments. It served as the import-export bank, implemented exchange control regulations, handled international loans, and managed all foreign exchange operations and securities.

The BOC settles trade and other foreign exchange transactions between local and foreign enterprises and banks; extends credit to foreign trade enterprises; mobilizes domestic and foreign currency deposits; finances joint ventures in other countries; issues instruments denominated in foreign currency (including foreign exchange currency certificates); issues bonds in foreign markets; finances the tourist industry; maintains and manages accounts for overseas Chinese; conducts trust business and financial leasing, directly and through a joint-venture leasing company; and provides supervision and consultation for overseas branches of other Chinese banks (e.g., Hong Kong branch of Bank of Communications).

Credit cooperatives

In addition to the four specialized banks, rural credit cooperatives (RCCs) and urban credit cooperatives (UCCs) also engage in commercial banking. RCCs were first set up during the collectivization drive in the 1950s to provide credit to agricultural cooperatives and collectives. They have grown over time into a national network of over 60,000 offices, with 472,000 employees and assets of 149 billion yuan. RCCs accept deposits from rural enterprises and rural households, and make loans to individuals, collectives, and rural enterprises. Until the recent granting of authority to the ABC to compete for deposits in townships, RCCs monopolized rural household deposits. Throughout their history, RCCs have been tightly controlled by the state banks (either the PBC or the ABC), and have been treated as subordinates of those state banks, with little autonomy.

Most UCCs were established after 1987 to supply credit to small-scale urban collectives and private enterprises, a niche that was not well served by the state banks. By 1988 there were 3,300 UCCs with 55,000 employees and assets of 20.5 billion yuan. Just as RCCs are under the purview of the ABC, UCCs are "guided" by specialized banks. About 60 per cent are under the ICBC, about 30 per cent under the BOC, and the rest under the PCBC. The business of UCCs is different from that of state banks and more akin to that of the RCCs. They take deposits from small-scale, nonstate enterprises in the urban areas (including some small state-owned enterprises leased out to individuals). They may also take household savings deposits, but they do so mostly on behalf of the specialized banks in exchange for a fee.

Nonstate banks and nonbank financial institutions

In 1988, aside from the two-tiered state banking system (and its affiliated credit cooperatives), there were 2 national universal banks (Bank of Communications, or BOCOM, and CITIC Industrial Bank), 1 development bank, 17 finance companies, 745 trust and investment companies, 9 leasing companies, 34 security corporations approved by the PBC, 61 security offices under the MOF, and 3 insurance companies (see Table 13.1). Most of the nonbank institutions were set up after 1986. The 1989–1990 retrenchment, however, changed some of these numbers.

The introduction of nonbank financial institutions, along with the entry of foreign banks, has greatly diversified the formal structure of the financial system, vastly expanded the number of financial intermediaries, increased competition, and begun to move financial intermediation away from the traditional sectoral divides. However, the system is still nowhere near being competitive or even market-oriented. Despite the promising trend toward greater participation by nonstate banks (at least through 1988), the four state banks, in which the financial assets of the entire sector are concentrated (87 per cent in 1989), continue to dominate.

Trust and investment companies

Trust and investment companies (TICs) are the most important nonbank financial institutions. TICs grew rapidly in 1986–1988 and by 1989 had assets of 90 billion yuan, accounting for over 6 per cent of total financial assets. However, they drastically decreased in number as a result of the 1989–1990 retrenchment and by early 1991 were down to only 300, with assets of 60–70 billion yuan. Most TICs are owned by state banks, which have turned over to them some of their commercial operations. TICs can invest and grant loans in a broad range of activities, sometimes on their own, and at other times with the "entrusted deposits" of enterprises and governments, which specify the use of their funds. TICs raise funds only in the form of loans and "trust" deposits, either from enterprises or government organizations (with a term of at least one year) or from the PBC, their parent bank, or the interbank money market.

Finance companies

Finance companies are formed by industrial and commercial conglomerates or "enterprise groups" to facilitate intragroup financing. They get their funds mainly from their own capital, time deposits from intragroup or affiliated enterprises, and bank credits and may not receive deposits from nonaffiliated enterprises or households. They lend only to shareholders, for their needs with respect to long-term investment capital or short-term working capital.

FINANCIAL SYSTEM OPERATIONS

In the pre-reform PRC, the PBC supervised the financial transactions of institutions, which were not allowed to use cash, and relied on wage manipulations and controlled supply of consumer goods to keep spending by individuals on an equally tight leash. With decentralization and liberalization, and the consequent increasing monetization of the economy, the currency supply became less easy to manage.

Reforms also replaced direct controls on bank credit with indirect controls, allowing banks to make allocation decisions on their own. Central bank lending nevertheless determined the sectoral focus of bank loans.

The high proportion of "bad" loans became a major sticking point between the government and the banking sector, with each side blaming the other for the problem. Moreover, the convoluted interest rate structure made it difficult for banks to calculate their lending costs.

Monetary circuits

As in other Soviet-type economies, there were separate circuits for enterprise and household money in the pre-reform period. All enterprises and institutions, including government agencies and schools, were required to maintain an account at the PBC, and all transactions worth more than 50 yuan had to go through bank transfers. In this sphere, transactions involved no cash; the transfers passively followed the flow of goods, and money was only an accounting device. Enterprises could hold at most only three days' worth of cash requirements in locations with a bank branch, and two weeks' worth elsewhere. The supervision of these transactions (to verify their consistency with financial and material supply plans) was an important function of the state bank. In contrast, interactions between the state sector and the household sector required cash transfers. Households received their wages in cash, and paid cash for their purchases of consumer goods. Since the cash had to be withdrawn by enterprises, these transactions were also supervised by the PBC. Manipulation of wage policies and the supply of consumer goods made it relatively easy to control currency outstanding.

The economy has become increasingly monetized in the reform period, with decentralization and liberalization, and the much greater volume of currency transactions, especially by farm households and nonstate and private traders, has complicated the control of currency supply. The development of extra-plan trade and the growth of nonstate enterprises have also increased the use of cash in enterprise transactions, weakening the separation between the two monetary circuits. After 1985, when enterprises were allowed to open accounts with more than one bank, the accounting and monitoring functions of the banking system were further eroded. While enterprise transactions must still be done with checks, monitoring has become more difficult.

Controlling bank credit flows

Under central planning, total credit and total allocation of credit was controlled by the credit plan, which was a corollary to the production and investment plans.

Reforms brought some flexibility by replacing some of this direct control with indirect mechanisms. In principle, credit can be controlled by imposing credit ceilings, rationing, central bank lending to specialized banks, reserve requirements, and interest rates. In practice, however, interest rates had little effect on controlling credit through the 1980s. Real rates were low and sometimes even negative, and the cheap credit and continuing softness in enterprise budget constraints fueled "investment hunger" and created excess demand for credit. Rationing was therefore necessary.

During 1984–1988, the increased use of indirect instruments over direct credit rationing gave branch banks greater flexibility to allocate resources on their own. However, given the specialized functions of the banks, central bank lending and credit allocation had substantial impact on sectoral lending and functions. Increased lending and allocation to the ABC directed credit to the rural sector, and increased lending and allocation to the ICBC directed credit to the working-capital needs of urban enterprises. In contrast, the austerity drive of 1989–1990 relied heavily on credit ceilings to rein in total lending. Since 1989, the new industrial policies have also increased the share of "directed" lending. Even nonbank financial institutions were brought under the credit plan and instructed to provide preferential loans to priority sectors such as export industries and the energy sector.

"Bad" or nonrepayable loans

"Bad" loans are not called such in Chinese banks. A loan category called *daizhai* consists of loans that are considered irrecoverable, either because the identity of the borrower has become unclear or because the borrower has gone completely bankrupt. Many loans in the rural sector have had to be reclassified as *daizhai* because the communes or production brigades that signed for them have long since been disbanded and have left insufficient resources to repay the loan. The ABC has had some success in collecting from households that were members of the collectives, but many of the loans were irrecoverable. *Daizhai* is a very small subset of loans that are overdue, however, even for the ABC, the most thoroughly audited among the specialized banks and the one facing the highest risks because of its loans to many rural collectives and small-scale rural enterprises that are now bankrupt. Only about 1.6 per cent of the 400 billion yuan loan portfolio of the ABC in 1991 was considered *daizhai*. Another 13.5 per cent of loans were said to be "sticky," i.e., more than two years in arrears for both principal and interest. The true amount of nonperforming loans may have been much higher; some officials say that the portion of overdue loans could be as high as 33 per cent for the ABC. One estimate placed the proportion of bad loans nationwide at 12 per cent in 1985 (Tam 1986). According to reports from the 1986–1988 period, overdue and nonperforming loans of many local branches of banks ranged from 20 per cent to 80 per cent of their total loan portfolios (Tam 1991). It is likely that the portion of bad loans rose significantly during the 1989–1990 recession.

It is difficult to distinguish between irrecoverable loans and overdue loans partly because of the lack of clear guidelines for identifying and treating defaults on loan payments. The short repayment period for most Chinese loans has made rollovers common. Even for equipment loans, the repayment period is typically 2–3 years. Since the payback for most projects is not as quick, rollovers with small interest penalties are pervasive and widely accepted. Many bankers report that loans are automatically rolled over if a request is made seven days prior to maturity. At the same time, the causes that prompted the rollover are not determined. Banks cannot tell whether a loan had to be rolled over because the repayment term was unrealistically short or because the borrower was in financial straits. Another reason for the low percentage of bad loans is that many industrial loans are guaranteed by supervisory bureaus or corporations, which often cross-subsidize between enterprises, so that outright defaults are rare.

Bureaucratic regulations also discourage write-offs. To write off a loan in excess of 100,000 yuan, a bank has to seek the approval of the State Council, with the support of the PBC head office. Furthermore, the MOF is said to be reluctant to write off bad loans for fear of massive depletion of bank capital and fiscal resources. A small reserve fund has been set aside recently, with money from the MOF, to prepare for the eventual write-off of some loans.

In the view of many economists in the PRC, the problem of bad loans cannot be solved, since many of these were either inherited (e.g., the ICBC inherited both good and bad loans from the PBC when the latter devolved its commercial operations), or had been made under administrative orders in the first place. The MOF and the banking system blame each other for the problem. Bank officials complain of being coerced by the MOF through administrative orders into making bad loans, while MOF officials complain that banks insist on collecting interest from ailing enterprises, thus shifting their investment risk to the budget. The situation deteriorated in 1989–1990, when the government ordered banks to make loans that were clearly problematic to allow enterprises to meet their payroll and to build inventories of unsold goods.

Other losses of State Banks

The financial performance of banks depends on the gross margin between loan rates and deposit rates, as well as on the performance of the loans themselves.

On both counts Chinese banks faced increasing difficulties through the 1980s.

The interest rate structure remains complex. Rates vary according to source, end use, and term. At present there are more than 50 lending rates and about 25 deposit rates. Without detailed information on the balance sheets of banks, it is difficult to calculate the cost and yields of funds; in fact, some Chinese economists question the capability of most banks to calculate their costs under such a complex and nontransparent rate structure. The government worsened matters by introducing "value-preserving" rates for household deposits in September 1988. Not only did the cost of funds go up, banks found it impossible to determine their costs, since the "value-preserving" rates were calculated upon maturity of the term deposits. When inflation slowed in 1991, these notes were eliminated.

Some evidence points to a downward trend in the operating margins of specialized banks through the 1980s. Interest rates have remained administratively fixed in the reform period, and although the government has shown increasing responsiveness to economic conditions, rate adjustments have been consistently biased in favor of preserving or increasing the quantity of deposits over ensuring the profitability of the banks. Over the past few years, deposit rates have gone up ahead of lending rates, while lending rates have gone down ahead of deposit rates. Moreover, increases in deposit rates have not been fully passed on to the lending rates, as the government has attempted to shield enterprises from the full cost increase. The introduction of indexed deposits in 1988 helped reverse the downward trend in household savings, but it also cut gross interest spreads to 0 per cent in 1988 and 1989 for "match fund" one-year deposits and loans, and to –0.36 per cent for three-year deposits and loans (World Bank 1990a). Table 13.3 presents some sample bank rates over the period 1971–1990. It should be noted, however, that deposits from enterprises and government organizations are still paid only 2.88 per cent per annum, significantly pulling down the average cost of funds. At the same time, these low-cost deposits are distributed unequally among the specialized banks, with the ICBC being the biggest beneficiary. In contrast, the ABC has very limited access to enterprise deposits but is obligated to do much of its lending at low, preferential rates. This disadvantage is only partially offset by the ABC's access to large deposits from the RCCs at low interest rates.

Another cause of decline in the gross margin is the shift from low-cost to high-cost deposits, and especially the relative decline in enterprise deposits. These deposits fell from 36 per cent of total deposits in 1979 to only 23 per cent in 1990, while household deposits rose from 9 per cent to 26 per cent of the total during the same period. The share of term deposits in household savings deposits rose from 13 per cent to 22 per cent from 1985 to 1990. The rising cost of funds is clearly cutting profit margins, which are partially offset by low-interest lending by the central bank, but the introduction of reduced-rate "priority loans" in 1990 will further reduce these margins.

Table 13.3 Sample bank rates, PRC, 1971–1990 (per cent per annum)

	Household deposit rates for one-year deposits	*Loan rates for enterprise working capital*
1971–1978	3.24	5.04
1979 (April)	3.96	5.04
1980 (April)	5.40	5.04
1982 (April)	5.76	7.20
1983 (December)	5.76	7.20
1985 (April)	6.84	7.92
1986 (June)	7.20	7.92
1987 (June)	7.20	7.92
1988 (September)	8.64	9.00
1989 (February)	11.34	11.34
1990 (April)	10.08	10.08
1990 (August)	8.64	9.36

Source: State Commission on Restructuring Economic System.

Finally, loan performance directly affects net margins and profitability of bank operations. Data from 1987–1988 indicate increasing principal and interest arrears. The PCBC, for example, had uncollected interest of 9.7 per cent of total interest due in 1987. This share rose to 12.3 per cent in 1988. In the CIB, uncollected interest on local-currency loans reached 31 per cent of total interest due in mid-1989. The recession in 1989–1990 and the deteriorating liquidity of enterprises undoubtedly eroded financial performance further at the banks, although the extent of the problem will not be revealed until more rigorous accounting and audit procedures can be instituted.

CAPITAL MARKETS

The growth and diversification of financial institutions and capital markets has raised the stock of financial assets and brought a relative decline in the share held by the state banking system. Table 13.4 shows the state banks' share of total financial assets falling from 96.5 per cent in 1985 to 86.9 per cent in 1989, and the difference is divided almost equally between the new financial intermediaries (TICs) and the growth in securities outstanding. In the reform period, the range of financial assets available has increased substantially; they now include government bonds, indexed deposits, enterprise bonds and shares, and a variety of short-term financial instruments.

Government bonds

Government bonds have had a checkered history. First issued in 1981, they were sold to individuals and enterprises by administrative allocation.

Table 13.4 PRC's financial assets, 1985–1989

	Commercial banks[a] (1)	Credit coop (2)	Banking system[b] (3)	TICs (4)	PICC (5)	Total Financial intermediaries (6)	Money market: Total (7)	Money market: Interbank (8)	Long-term securities: Gov't bonds (9)	Long-term securities: Corporate bonds (10)	Long-term securities: Equities (11)	Long-term securities: Financial bonds (12)	Total securities outstanding (13)	Total financial assets[c] (14)
(As per cent of total assets)														
1985	86.3	10.2	96.5	0.0	...	96.5	...	...	3.5	...	...	0.1	3.5	100.0
1986	82.8	10.5	93.3	2.8	...	96.1	...	...	3.6	...	...	0.3	3.9	100.0
1987	78.1	11.4	89.5	4.5	...	94.0	...	...	5.5	...	0.1	0.4	6.0	100.0
1988	76.1	11.2	87.2	5.7[d]	...	92.9	...	...	5.7	0.6	0.2	0.6	7.0	100.0
1989 (III)	72.0	14.9	86.9	6.3	...	93.2	...	...	...	...	...	...	6.6	100.0
(As per cent of GNP)														
1985	79.3	9.4	88.7	0.0	1.0[e]	89.7	...	...	3.2	...	...	0.06	3.2	93.0
1986	88.5	11.2	99.7	3.0	...	102.7	...	...	3.8	...	...	0.4	4.2	106.8
1987	87.9	12.9	100.8	5.0	...	105.8	...	...	6.2	...	0.1	0.5	6.8	112.6
1988	83.2	12.2	95.4	6.2[d]	...	101.6	...	...	6.2	0.7	0.3	0.6	7.7	109.3

Notes:

[a] Includes specialized and comprehensive banks.

[b] Includes specialized, comprehensive RCCs and UCCs ([1] + [2]).

[c] Sum of assets of financial intermediaries and all securities outstanding (columns 6 and 13). The figure for 1988 comprises the assets of 16 out of 17 finance companies. PICC is not included. Also, the total asset figures for the second quarter of 1989 excludes securities outstanding.

[d] Includes finance companies. Excluding finance companies figure would be 5.5% of total assets, and 6.0% of GNP.

[e] Finance and investment (1985).

Sources: People's Bank of China; World Bank, *China: Financial Sector Policies*.

Between 1981 and 1984, 4–5 billion yuan worth were sold each year, with a nominal maturity of ten years. (In fact, beginning in the sixth year, 20 per cent were redeemed each year by lot.) Bonds sold to individuals paid a higher interest rate (8 per cent) than those sold to enterprises (4 per cent). Because the rates were calculated at simple interest, with no interim interest payments, the actual rates were lower. For example, a 100-yuan bond would have been sold at par in 1981 and redeemed at maturity in 1991 for 140 yuan, yielding an actual interest of 3.4 per cent per annum compounded. Their compulsory nature and low interest rates accounted for the widespread perception that the bonds were a "tax" rather than a financial asset. An extremely profitable niche thus emerged when a few cities, including Shanghai, were allowed to trade in these securities. Brokers could buy at bargain-basement prices from people who saw the bonds merely as receipts for "donations" to the government.

Over time, interest rates were raised and maturities shortened to make the bonds more attractive, although they still lagged behind bank deposit and other rates. In 1990 treasury bonds were paid higher than bank deposits for the first time. Ironically, this change was a result of bureaucratic bungling. In 1988–1989, when the retail price index was rising at nearly 30 per cent yearly, interest rates on bonds sold to individuals were increased to 14 per cent and a large number of certificates were printed. By 1990 inflation was down to single digits and bank deposit rates had been reduced. (In August 1990 the interest rate on three-year deposits was reduced to 10.08 per cent. In May 1991 it was lowered by another 1 per cent. One-year deposit rates were 7.52 per cent in 1991, having fallen to pre-1988 levels.) Still the certificates were sold as printed, again by administrative allocation. Because of the attractive interest rates, they were extremely popular, and a black market quickly developed.

The growth of a secondary market helped legitimize treasury bonds as a financial asset. Secondary trading has been permitted since 1985, when it was first tried out in a few cities. In April 1988 trading was extended to all bonds and more than 60 cities. Trading volume reached over 2 billion yuan during 1988–1989. By 1990 the volume had exceeded 10 billion yuan. The secondary trading in government bonds established market interest rates that in turn would influence government rate setting by forcing the government to set competitive rates on new issues. In 1991 treasury bonds were being retailed to the public for the first time, with the government hoping to end the practice of compulsory allocation and make the bonds attractive financial assets In April of that year the State Council approved the sale of bonds through syndicates. An initial batch worth 2.5 billion yuan was sold at 10 per cent interest per annum to a few investment companies. These syndicates were to receive a handling fee from the government for retailing the bonds at par value. In early 1993, however, bonds were once again unpopular, as inflationary expectations outpaced the government's interest rate adjustments.

Public enterprise bonds

Public enterprise bonds are government bonds issued by the MOF in behalf of specific enterprises or projects. They are one-time issues, usually at below-market rates of interest, and seen as additional "taxes" to generate funds for public use. Four types have been issued so far: (i) State Key Enterprise Bonds, issued by key enterprises in the electrical, metallurgical, nonferrous metal, and petrochemical industries, guaranteed by the supervisory ministries, and serviced by the PCBC; (ii) Capital Construction Bonds, issued for the State Planning Commission by six TICs and sold to enterprises, banks, and non-bank financial institutions at low interest rates and (in 1989 only) to individuals with indexed rates; (iii) Key Construction Bonds, issued by MOF to raise capital for investment in key infrastructural projects; and (iv) State Construction Bonds, issued in 1988 by the MOF to raise supplementary funds for key investments.

Enterprise securities

Enterprise "shares" began to be issued in the early 1980s in rural areas, to supplement the funds provided by the banking system to the burgeoning rural enterprise sector. By 1984, urban state enterprises were also issuing shares to raise investment funds or simply to circumvent restrictions on wage and bonus payments. The establishment of formal institutions by the state, starting in 1987, to support and regulate the growth in enterprise securities as part of the broader financial reform package, marked the third stage of development of enterprise securities. The deepening of enterprise reforms also saw the introduction of public shares in a few large-scale state enterprises.

Chinese enterprises typically do not distinguish between "shares" and "bonds." What they call shares are often just bonds, with a stipulated interest rate and fixed maturity (mostly one to three years). Some shares are hybrid securities that carry a fixed base interest, plus an excess return based on the profitability of the investment. They are quite different from company stocks, since they confer no voting rights or claims on the liquidated value of the enterprise. Their offerings are also usually limited (e.g., to workers in the enterprise or residents in the locality), and secondary trading is often disallowed or highly restricted (although illegal trading has been reported in many cities).

There are four basic types of enterprise shares: (i) equity shares, which are often used to divide up enterprise ownership during decollectivization, mergers, or acquisitions; (ii) employment shares, which were commonly used to raise investment capital in rural enterprises in the early 1980s, when many enterprises required new workers to contribute hundreds or thousands of yuan (these contributions were often repaid with interest after a designated period); (iii) workers' shares, with which funds can be raised in times of capital shortage, or bonuses paid; and (iv) public shares, which are issued for public subscription. Only public shares are traded.

Official statistics on enterprise shares outstanding include just a fraction of the total. PBC data for 1988 showed only 3.5 billion yuan in enterprise shares outstanding, but a survey of 23 provinces reported 21.4 billion yuan in total share issues by 30 September 1988, including 14.09 billion yuan made available for public subscription (Tam 1991). The difference was partly one of scope; the survey data represented the cumulative total, part of which had already matured and been redeemed. But the discrepancy also points to the lack of uniform national regulations on share issues, and the common failure of local governments to report to higher authorities the issues they have approved. For example, virtually none of the shares issued by rural enterprises were registered or officially approved above the county level; these shares were therefore excluded from the official statistics and probably also from survey statistics. Even in urban enterprises, most issues are informal and limited to workers of the enterprise. In spite of rapid growth in these share issues, especially since 1985, the securities market remains tiny. For example, in Shanghai, 1,255 enterprises issued shares in 1988, but only six were traded on the stock exchange. Nationwide, the volume of trade amounted to only 0.2 billion in 1988 and 2.3 billion yuan in 1989 (Tam 1991). Nonetheless, share issues have contributed significantly to mobilizing household savings for investment, especially in the rural sector.

Other bonds

Other bonds include those issued by the specialized banks, which have used bond issues to raise funds since 1985. "Financial bonds" worth a total of 16 billion yuan were issued in 1985–1989. Enterprise bonds backed by local governments have been issued since 1984. Local governments cannot issue bonds to cover current expenditure, but they can use this method to raise funds for infrastructure or capital investment projects. Through 1989, a total of 16 billion yuan had been issued. Current regulations limit sales to residents of the locality and to overseas Chinese, but this restriction may have been eliminated with the allowance of secondary trading since 1988.

Interbank money markets

Interbank lending and borrowing was first permitted in 1986 in a few major cities to improve liquidity management in the banking system. The market grew rapidly through 1988, with the estimated volume rising from 30 billion yuan in 1986 to 230 billion yuan in 1987 and 520 billion yuan in 1988, but was sharply curtailed in 1989–1991 under charges that the activities were contributing to inflation. By 1989 the volume had fallen to less than 300 billion yuan.

A variety of short-term instruments, including trade bills, commercial papers, bankers' acceptances, and certificates of deposit, have emerged. Trading of these instruments among banks and finance companies has grown swiftly. By June 1988, there were 11.1 billion yuan in bankers' acceptances outstanding. In 1988 an unregulated market for commercial paper was also developing rapidly. In Shanghai, for example, 14 companies issued promissory notes worth 300 million yuan in March 1988 alone; these sold briskly because they offered higher interest than bank deposits. Since 1989, however, tightened standards for credit ratings, under the supervision of a new agency affiliated with the PBC, have caused a sharp drop in the issuance of commercial paper.

By early 1991 the securities issued totaled 220 billion yuan, of which 178 billion yuan were outstanding. Government bonds accounted for 90 billion yuan (40 per cent), financial bonds 30 billion yuan, local government bonds over 20 billion yuan, stocks 4 billion yuan, and transferable notes 60 billion yuan.

RURAL FINANCE

Statistics on the distribution of credit by sector and by end use (Table 13.5) show the acute need for informal credit in the rural sector and private businesses. Agriculture, which produces nearly 30 per cent of GNP, receives less than 7 per cent of total available credit. From 1983 to 1990, output value in the rural collective enterprise sector (comprising township and village enterprises, or TVEs) grew over eightfold, but lending to the sector grew only from 15.7 billion yuan to 93.3 billion yuan, or less than sixfold. Even as private traders and enterprises grew to account for nearly 30 per cent of retail sales and over 5 per cent of total industrial output, credit to the private sector, extended almost entirely by UCCs, remained a minuscule portion of total credit. Unfortunately, little is known about informal credit markets in the urban areas. This section focuses on the demand for informal credit in the rural areas, beginning with a discussion of the ABC and RCCs and highlighting the inadequacy of the state banking institutions in meeting rural needs.

Agricultural Bank of China

The Agricultural Bank of China is the state bank operating in the rural sector. It handles both noncapital budgetary funds for the rural economy and the accounts of state enterprises in rural areas. The primary function of the ABC is to finance the government's agricultural procurement. Loans to the National Federation of Supply and Marketing Cooperatives and the Grain Bureau make up about two-thirds of the bank's loan portfolio. Since 1984 it has also increased lending to rural collective industry and commerce, but its loans to households remain low (3 per cent of its total lending in 1988 and

Table 13.5 Distribution of credit, PRC, 1983–1991 (billion yuan; end of quarter)

	1983	*1984*	*1985*	*1986*	*1987*	*1988*	*1989*	*1990*	*1991*
Total loans	378.8	502.1	618.0	796.0	954.7	1,112.4	1,206.4	1,476.0	1,759.5
Industry	57.0	78.8	98.4	141.7	170.6	208.5	—	—	—
Material suppliers [a]	26.8	31.0	38.0	47.7	49.3	52.1	330.5	421.0	493.0
Commercial sector	197.8	227.2	264.9	308.9	350.6	410.0	476.6	575.7	668.1
TVEs [b]	15.7	28.4	31.0	41.4	53.4	63.6	69.3	81.7	93.3
Private sector	0.1	1.1	1.1	1.0	1.5	1.9	1.5	1.6	2.0
Agriculture	23.1	36.8	41.6	57.0	68.5	81.4	89.5	103.8	120.9
Fixed asset loans	30.7	45.1	70.5	100.5	128.6	155.9	157.0 [c]	198.2	274.4
Construction sector	4.7	18.4	26.7	36.9	46.6	49.4	60.1	67.2	71.5
Other	3.0	9.5	18.0	33.5	33.6	32.0	21.8 [d]	27.1	36.6
MOF borrowing	19.9	26.0	27.5	37.0	51.5	57.6	—	—	—
Per cent distribution									
Industry	15.1	15.7	15.9	17.8	17.9	18.7	—	—	—
Material suppliers [a]	7.1	6.2	6.2	6.0	5.2	4.7	27.4	28.5	28.0
Commercial sector	52.2	45.3	42.9	38.8	36.7	36.9	39.5	39.0	38.0
TVEs [b]	4.2	5.7	5.0	5.2	5.6	5.7	5.7	5.5	5.3
Private sector	0.03	0.2	0.2	0.1	0.2	0.2	0.1	0.1	0.1
Agriculture	6.1	7.3	6.7	7.2	7.2	7.3	7.4	7.0	6.9
Fixed asset loans	8.1	9.0	11.4	12.6	13.5	14.0	13.0	13.4	15.6
Construction sector	1.2	3.7	4.3	4.6	4.9	4.4	5.0	4.5	4.1
Other	0.7	1.9	2.9	3.0	3.5	2.9	1.8	1.8	2.1
MOF borrowing	5.3	5.2	4.5	4.7	5.4	5.2	—	—	—

Notes:
[a] Industry and material suppliers combined for 1989–1991.
[b] Township and village enterprises.
[c] Fixed investment loan after 1989.
[d] Definition of "Other" changed after 1989.

Sources: People's Bank of China; World Bank (1992a).

1989). Few farm households dealt directly with the ABC before 1985. Since then the ABC has been allowed to compete with RCCs for rural household deposits, which constituted 23 per cent of total deposits at the ABC by 1989 (West 1991).

Rural credit cooperatives

Rural credit cooperatives are the principal credit institutions in the countryside. They have an extensive network, with branches in some 80 per cent of the 70,000 townships, suboffices in some 30,000 villages, and nearly 300,000 credit stations scattered throughout the countryside. This huge network enabled the RCCs to adapt quickly when decollectivization increased the number of borrowers from five million production teams to nearly 200 million farm households, over 80 per cent of which have access to credit from the RCCs. But continuing regulation by the ABC has hampered the adjustment to the financial needs of a largely privatized rural sector.

The extractive nature of ABC's control over RCC operations can be seen in Table 13.6, which shows a pattern of very substantial transfers of funds from the RCCs to ABC. Whereas RCC deposits with ABC were nearly 70 per cent of the bank's total assets in 1983, and nearly 40 per cent in 1988–1989, ABC loans to the RCCs accounted for only about 4 per cent of RCC funds in the late 1980s. Through 1985, RCCs were required to redeposit 30 per cent of their total deposits with the ABC. In 1986 this requirement was lowered to a 10 per cent marginal rate on deposits in excess of the 1985 base. However, in December 1987 the reserve requirement was raised to 30 per cent to control credit expansion. It was lowered again, to 12 per cent, at the beginning of 1988, then raised slightly, to 13 per cent later in the year (West 1991).

Aside from this minimum reserve requirement, RCCs place their excess reserves with the ABC and at times have also been required to place "special deposits" with the bank. Not only do these transfers reduce the loanable funds of the RCCs, they also deplete profits, since the interest rates paid by the ABC on RCC deposits are substantially below the RCCs' cost of funds. For example, in 1985 the ABC paid 4.32 per cent on RCC reserve deposits and 4.68 per cent on other RCC deposits, compared with the 6.12 per cent cost of one-year household deposits with the RCCs. In 1989 deposits from farm households composed 85 per cent of all RCC deposits, and an estimated 80 per cent of these were in time deposits, making them a high-cost source of funds. If the inverted rate spread was 2 per cent, the net deposit of 62 billion yuan at the ABC in 1989 would have cost the RCCs 1.24 billion yuan in losses.

This extractive policy originates in the Stalinist model, which calls for the agriculture sector to finance industrialization. Since more than two-thirds of ABC loans go to state procurement agencies, the rural sector not only provides raw materials and food to the urban sector at low prices (sometimes

Table 13.6 Balance sheet of rural credit cooperatives, PRC, 1983–1991 (billion yuan at year-end)

	1983	*1984*	*1985*	*1986*	*1987*	*1988*	*1989*	*1990*	*1991*
Assets	53.2	68.2	80.1	106.2	117.8	148.8	175.3	218.5	272.5
Loans	16.4	35.5	40.0	56.9	77.1	90.9	109.2	141.1	180.8
Rural collective enterprises	2.8	3.8	4.10	4.5	7.2	8.01	10.7	13.4	17.0
Township enterprises	6.0	13.5	16.40	26.6	35.9	45.61	57.0	75.9	100.7
Individuals	7.5	18.1	19.40	25.8	34.0	37.24	41.6	51.8	63.1
Deposits with ABC	36.8	32.7	40.10	49.3	40.7	56.0	65.8	77.4	91.6
(per cent of total)	69.2	48.0	50.1	46.4	34.6	39.0	37.6	35.4	33.6
Liabilities	53.2	68.2	80.1	106.2	117.8	148.8	175.3	218.5	272.5
Deposits	48.7	62.5	72.5	96.2	122.5	140.0	167.1	214.5	270.9
Rural collective enterprises	9.2	9.0	7.2	8.4	8.9	9.2	9.2	10.7	13.6
Township enterprises	6.2	8.1	7.2	9.2	10.5	12.9	12.6	15.0	19.2
Individuals	32.0	43.8	56.5	76.6	100.6	114.2	141.7	184.1	231.7
Demand deposits	10.2	15.3	18.1	22.6	29.7	35.1	33.2	38.7	43.4
Time deposits	21.8	28.5	38.4	54.0	70.8	79.1	108.2	145.4	188.3
Other	1.3	1.6	1.6	2.0	2.5	3.1	3.9	4.7	6.5
Borrowing from ABC	1.6	3.1	3.3	4.2	3.8	3.6	3.8	4.2	5.1
Other liabilities (net)	2.9	2.6	4.3	5.8	–8.5	5.2	4.2	–0.2	–3.6

Sources: People's Bank of China; World Bank (1992a).

below cost) but also largely finances the costs of state procurement with its savings.

The ability of RCCs to expand is also constrained by restrictions on the interest rates they can offer. Despite a 1985 government document calling for increased autonomy for the RCCs and greater flexibility in their operations, the ABC has continued to require RCC interest rates to float within 20 per cent of the state bank rates, although in Guangdong province in 1989 the rates were allowed to differ by 60 per cent (West 1991). Continuing restrictions on lending amounts and targets keep RCCs from responding freely to the new economic conditions in the rural areas. In fact, the high cost of processing the very small-scale loans, the greater riskiness of these unsecured loans, and the extractive policies of the ABC have combined to create many difficulties for RCCs. In 1985, about one-fifth reported losses in their operations (Tam 1988).

Informal finance

The constraints of formal credit have forced the rural sector to rely mostly on self-finance. Informal arrangements are sometimes concluded for extraordinary needs in funds. Total credit to the average household is small, and farmers finance their production and consumption needs mostly with their own savings. Aside from the usual zero-interest loans between relatives and friends, interest-bearing moneylending has reemerged. However, such credit markets have developed unevenly and only in certain localities, and their interest rates vary greatly between localities. In the mid-1980s these rates ranged from 20 per cent to over 100 per cent per annum. In some localities informal lending appears to have grown in scale to rival formal credit, adopting traditional forms such as credit clubs, where members contribute capital and either earn a return on their investment or gain priority right to borrow from the pool. In one county in Guangdong, writes West (1991), 75 "agricultural development fund clubs" with a total capital of 5 million yuan were operating in 1987. (RCCs in the county had deposits of 213 million yuan.) Members contributed a fixed sum to the club; in turn, they received a fixed return on their contribution that was higher than RCC interest rates, plus a share of the profits. One club charged an average interest rate of 22.8 per cent per annum on loans. The higher rates of return offered by such clubs compared with RCC rates may cause a partial displacement of RCCs unless they are freed to respond to this new competition. In some rural areas, however, moneylending at market rates appears not to play a significant role (Feder et al. 1991).

CHRISTINE P. W. WONG

BANKING AND MONETARY REFORMS

Rapid monetization and an impressive household savings rate marked the first decade of reform. But the government's inability to contain money supply and credit pointed to an inadequately managed transition.

Despite the growth in the number of financial intermediaries, resources continued to be concentrated in the state banking system, which still operated under administrative guidance and according to a central plan. Interest rates were administered and consistently low, and so lacked effectiveness as an allocative mechanism. Undue influence on bank branches by local authorities and an incentive structure that countenanced poor lending decisions further limited the success of financial reform.

Overall impact

The first decade of reform in the PRC was accompanied with impressive financial deepening. Household savings increased dramatically in response to economic growth and rising personal incomes. At the same time, the economy was rapidly monetized. The demand for currency rose for several reasons. First, the shift to private household farming increased cash outlays for production inputs. Second, private and small-scale businesses relied on cash transactions rather than bank transfers. As a result, currency in circulation increased rapidly, at rates substantially higher than GNP growth, and the currency-to-GNP ratio rose from 6 per cent in 1978 to 9.4 per cent in 1983, and to 15.2 per cent in 1988. This monetization created opportunities for the development of new financial intermediaries and instruments. During the 1980s, but especially after 1985, the growth and diversification of the financial system made significant progress.

Savings as a percentage of GDP increased during the reform period. Starting at the already high level of 30 per cent, they peaked at 39.6 per cent in 1987 following a period of rapid growth in GDP. Financial savings increased as a result. Bank deposits expanded and a variety of bonds and securities emerged, so that the total stock of financial assets grew from 31.3 billion yuan in 1983 to 133.1 billion yuan in 1988. M2 as a proportion of GDP grew from 37 per cent in 1979 to 71 per cent in 1988, and assets of financial intermediaries grew from 90 per cent of GDP in 1985 to 106 per cent in 1987. The total stock of financial assets (including securities) grew from 93 per cent of GDP to 113 per cent during the same period, before inflation and negative real interest rates caused a reversal in 1988.

It is perhaps premature to judge reforms in the financial sphere at the end of the 1980s, since they began in earnest only in 1984/85, and liberalization had proceeded for only three years before inflation forced a retreat in late 1988. However, it is clear that the monetary authorities did not manage the transition to a new economic environment very well, judging by the wild fluctuations in money supply and credit during the 1984–1988 period, and by their inability to contain money supply and credit growth to within planned targets. Moreover, inflationary problems of the late 1980s appeared to have been directly linked to liberalization of the financial sector.

Structural reforms

The stated goals of financial reform had been: (i) to turn state banks and their branches into commercial banks with responsibility for their own profits and losses; (ii) to diversify banking institutions, by allowing more banks and nonbank financial institutions to be set up, and allowing them to compete in financial markets; (iii) to replace direct instruments with indirect instruments for carrying out monetary policy; and (iv) to develop capital markets and financial assets such as bonds and money markets. These goals would seem to indicate, as one Chinese economist commented, that the PRC has succeeded in achieving the form, but not the substance, of "an integrated financial market" (Wu 1990).

Despite the rapid growth in the number of financial intermediaries, the state banking system continues to dominate. The four specialized banks still held 93–94 per cent of all deposits and loans in 1988 (Zhou 1990), while nonstate banks and nonbank institutions played only a small role in intermediation. The capital market and money markets remained embryonic, accounting for less than 7 per cent of total financial assets. More importantly, the state banks never gained sufficient autonomy or political clout to direct their lending programs independently or to resist pressures to expand credit. Through the 1980s, they continued to operate under administrative guidance, with interest rates set by consultation among superior organizations (State Council, Ministry of Finance, State Planning Commission), and most credit still allocated by plan. Even in the heyday of liberalized banking (1986–1988), various internal and external factors constrained the banking system's ability to control monetary policy with indirect instruments.

Interest rates

Interest rates were never successfully used as an allocative mechanism. Although interest rates were adjusted several times in response to economic conditions, they were never freed to market determination. Since the administered rates were consistently low, excess demand forced dependence on credit rationing. In an environment where enterprises continued to operate with soft budget constraints, and at a time of rapid economic growth, demand for credit tended to be insatiable.

Allocative control

The persistence of price distortions would have made the allocation of credit by market signals problematic, with an allocative pattern that favored profitable manufacturing activities over basic industry, extractive, and agricultural activities. To offset this "twisted" allocation, the PBC intervened to inject budgetary funds, earmarking them as "directed loans" to the low-profit sectors. In the process, these not only helped expand credit but also undermined the banks' autonomy and profit orientation. The problem was that interest rates could not control money supply and at the same time optimize the lending structure.

The internal organization of the banking system, in which local branches of banks are under dual leadership, has rendered the branches susceptible to pressure from local authorities. The credit plan and central bank lending are first distributed among the four specialized banks. Each bank then subdivides its funds among its provincial branches, in consultation with the branches and provincial officials. This process is repeated at the provincial level, where the provincial branches distribute their funds among subbranches, in consultation with subbranch banks and local officials. To insulate the banking system from local influence, managers of provincial branches and subbranches of banks are now appointed by the head office rather than by local authorities. Nevertheless, under the current regulations allowing enterprises to repay loans before income tax payments, local authorities, who control the scheduling of loan repayments, in fact have a good deal of influence over the scale of bank operations. Regardless of the term of the loans, the amount that must be repaid each year by local enterprises is often determined jointly by enterprise managers, local officials (from the fiscal and planning departments), and bank officials. Finally, local officials have a good deal of control over the non-pecuniary benefits of bank staff, including the availability and conditions of housing, schooling, and job prospects for staff offspring. They can also facilitate or block the attempts of the bank branches to open new offices and recruit more workers.

The extent of local bureaucratic control over bank operations is difficult to quantify. A 1986 survey by the ICBC of ten cities where financial reforms were being tested revealed that local authorities routinely imposed mandatory "directed loans" on local branches of banks; these loans composed 50.3 per cent of "technical renovation" loans in 1985 and 73.3 per cent in 1986 (Wu 1990). With local authorities holding so many levers of control over their operations, the bank branches are ill equipped to terminate loan contracts with local enterprises even if the enterprises are performing poorly. Local influence over banking operations creates strong pressure for credit expansion at the local levels. Indeed, in both 1980 and 1984 local expansionism was reined in only after several meetings of governors at which central government officials sought personal guarantees from the governors that they would curb investment in their provinces (Naughton 1985; Zhou 1990). Excessive local influence also results in the fragmentation of the financial market along administrative divisions, with significant regional barriers to capital flows. The Chinese saying "money dies when it reaches the local level" describes this situation. Even in the interbank money market, strong pressures are often brought to bear to prevent the outflow of funds. Finally, since credit allocation by region contains a redistributive element, poor regions have often had excess funds while rich regions have had excess demand for credit; thus the capital flows have generally been west to east, from poorer to richer regions.

The incentive structure of the banking system, where wages and bonuses of bank employees are based on bank revenues rather than financial performance, is also not conducive to efficient behavior. Bank employees will continue lending as long as interest payments can be collected. In an environment of unclear property rights and responsibilities, moral hazard greatly exacerbates bank problems.

Capacity for improvement

Even with all the above structural and incentive problems, it can be argued that the PBC could play a more effective role in controlling monetary policy by developing a strong voice based on technical expertise. It has been suggested that the reversals in monetary policy during 1984–1989 might have been averted if the central bank had held a strong position, instead of bowing to political pressures. For example, when money supply grew by over 40 per cent in 1984 and caused overheating in 1985, the supply was tightened. But after only half a year, political pressures forced a loosening in the spring of 1986, and the bank pumped billions of yuan into credit expansion. As the price index climbed, another tightening was introduced at the end of 1986, again lasting only one quarter. All of this occurred in the absence of any clear policy of the central bank. To improve its effectiveness, the PBC must bolster its technical expertise and develop a core of professional economists to undertake economic analysis and policy design. But the central problem of finance sector reform remains the poorly defined separation between the government and the enterprises. The problems and prospects of the enterprise sector are dealt with in the next two chapters.

14

CONTROLLING MONEY DURING SOCIALIST ECONOMIC REFORM

The Chinese Experience

S. K. Tsang[1]

1 INTRODUCTION

The tragedy surrounding the crackdown of the student movement in China in 1989 highlighted the problems of controlling inflation and containing income inequality during the process of socialist economic reform. The movement was undoubtedly motivated by a genuine and justified quest for more freedom and greater democracy. Nevertheless, deteriorating living standards for some major sectors of the population, particularly the intellectuals, were also an important contributory factor. Surging inflation inevitably enlarges income disparity and academic institutions are bound to suffer when the profit motive suddenly claims priority. The fact that many bureaucrats were able to use their political leverage to reap economic benefits only heightened the sense of injustice among the population and dissatisfaction could easily be transformed into political confrontation.

A paradox in socialist economic reform, which in my view has not been adequately addressed by theorists of all persuasions, is that inflationary pressure invariably increases during the process of change. The same phenomenon has occurred in the Soviet Union, in Eastern Europe and, sadly, also in China recently. It is paradoxical as the reform is supposed to increase supply-side efficiency. It is paradoxical also because one major objective of the reform is to improve the mode of macro-control by the central authority. The traditional system of command was supposed to give way to more indirect, more flexible and therefore more effective methods of monitoring and guiding the economy. Fiscal and monetary policies were expected to play an increasingly important role, at the expense of the shrinking influence of the central plan. That inflation could have escalated and drastically deepened income inequality shows that something terribly wrong must have happened in the macro-control mechanism itself.

The paradox can be analysed from various angles. This paper takes up,

Source: Economy and Society, Vol. 19(2) (1990), pp. 217–41.

unbashedly, the viewpoint of the socialist monetary authority in China. This choice stems from various considerations. Despite the fact that the reform generally results in an increasing degree of monetization of the economy, socialist monetary economics remains a neglected subject. An excursion into uncharted territories hopefully has it own value. Moreover, the publicized advice rendered to China by leading conservative economists in the West is that the country should control the money supply effectively and *then* eliminate all forms of control as soon as possible, if not instantly (e.g. Friedman 1988a; 1988b). The monetarist pre-supposition is heroic. However, we happen not to believe in this form of heroism, and indeed have more sympathy for the scapegoat than for the prophet. An analysis of the dilemma confronting the socialist monetary authority can perhaps serve as an effective objection against this type of 'free-all' programme that conservatives so eagerly want to offer to any socialist economy in crisis.

This paper is organized as follows. Section 2 gives an overview of the Chinese monetary reform and points to some key obstacles to its success. Sections 3 and 4 address the theoretical problems of assessing money demand accurately, paving the way for a summary of the debates among Chinese economists in Section 6. The monetary dilemma is brought into focus from a structural perspective in Section 6. I then move over to the supply side in Sections 7 and 8 and analyse the problems of monitoring and controlling the monetary aggregates, even granting that the central bank knows how to set the targets. Section 9 offers some overall comments.

2 THE CHINESE MONETARY REFORM

One of the key aspects of the Chinese economic reform started in 1989 has been the change in the mode of macroeconomic control by the central authority. As far as reform of the monetary system is concerned, the core problem is the transformation of the mechanism of channelling funds. The way funds are accumulated and distributed exerts a crucial impact on an economy undergoing significant changes in its mode of operation and the direction of reform in China has been to shift from a system based on budgetary allocations to one that is centred around credit. This change aims not only at encouraging savings and promoting the efficiency of enterprises, which are given greater autonomy under the reform, in employing funds, but also at the enhancement of the effectiveness of macroeconomic control.

The central strategy to achieve these goals has been reform in the banking system. After the Third Plenum of the Eleventh Central Committee of the Chinese party in late 1978, the situation whereby the People's Bank of China monopolized the roles of both the Central Bank and the commercial banks has been transformed. A system of 'specialized banks' (*zhuanye yinhang*) was established. Funds among them were divided and monitored through independent accounting. Since 1983, the People's Bank has relinquished all its commercial banking activities and concentrated on its functions as a central bank. Transactions between the central bank and the specialized banks are mainly in the form of credit (re-lending) instead of direct allocations, although various modified forms of the latter have persisted. A reserve system, imposed on deposits of the specialized banks was started in 1985. On the other hand, other non-bank financial institutions and financial markets have also been developed.[2]

On the surface, the results of financial reform have been quite remarkable. In 1979, the ratio of off-budget funds (a good deal of which fell into the hands of enterprises and local authorities) to total budgetary revenue of the central government was 42.4 per cent. It climbed to 89.7 per cent in 1987. Much of these off-budget funds entered the banking and non-bank financial systems in various ways. Another indication is the ratio of total deposits in banks and credit institutions to national income, which rose from 40 per cent in 1979 to 85.2 per cent in 1987.[3] Credit has apparently become a key mechanism of fund allocation.

The real achievement of financial reform cannot of course be judged on these quantative indications alone. If the major objective is to increase the efficiency of fund utilization and the effectiveness of macroeconomic control, the results so far have not been very encouraging. As an example of micro-efficiency, the ratio of profits and taxes to total funds employed for state-owned industrial enterprises under independent accounting stood at 23.86 per cent in 1981. It remained stagnant in the following few years before dropping to 20.65 per cent in 1986 and 20.30 per cent in 1987. The unusually huge credit expansion in late 1984 which accompanied the launching of the second phase of the reform, and the large-scale panic conversion of money into goods under the unprecedented inflationary circumstances of 1988 also throw doubts on the effectiveness of the monetary authority to stabilize the economy. The latter events apparently paved the way for the 'cautious' faction within the leadership to take over the control of economic policy in late 1988.

There are various factors which have prevented a successful realization of the reform objectives. Some of them arise from the fact that the reform has yet to be completed. Perhaps more importantly, the economic system that has emerged from the reform process has not been very conducive to the effective implementation of an indirect and flexible form of control.

In theory, the central principle guiding the Chinese reform is the transformation of the economic system from a barter (or 'natural') economy into a 'commodity economy with planning'. During the process, banks should discard their previous role of serving passively as the cashier or accountant to the State Treasury and assume the more active role of intermediating the complex circuit of funds and regulating their supply and demand. Nevertheless, the whole reform is constrained by developmental factors and institutional legacy. The reform in the monetary subsystem cannot afford to be an exception.

Indeed, it appeared more like one of the main casualties in the setbacks encountered by the reformists in 1988, in that a number of strict administrative measures were re-introduced in the monetary sphere in a bid to clamp down on inflation. The pace was quickened up after the turmoil in 1989.

Chinese economic reform is constrained by the very low level of development of the country itself. Many of the prerequisites for large-scale commodity production and circulation to function properly in a market-like environment, including efficient transportation and communications networks, a stable legal framework for commercial transactions, and relatively high elasticities of supply and demand etc., have not been met. Moreover, the legacy of the pre-reform period of socialist construction also weighs heavily on the economy. The most important of these constraints and legacy are the very low mobility of resources due to underdevelopment and to the state ideology that most production factors and output were not 'commodities' (hence re-trading of any goods was minimal), as well as the special price-quantity system formed by the Stalinist strategy of industrialization, which gave priority to Department I (of means of production) at the expense of Department II (of means of consumption or livelihood). Unfortunately, the Chinese reformists have not paid sufficient attention to these constraints-cum-legacy and the possibility that severe structural imbalance may be generated in the reform if they are not carefully tackled.[4]

Given all these constraints, much more than an exercise in comparative statistics (e.g. that of central planning versus the market mechanism) is needed to provide the reformists with the appropriate perspective and policy framework. The dynamic path leading from the pre-reform system to the new one, which remains unfortunately not well-defined, is a fortuitous and dangerous one. In reality, the economic entity that emerges under the reform is a mixed one where legacy of the past is entangled with half-baked prototypes of the market mechanism, while politics still plays a vital role in many areas of economic activity. In the terminology of the Chinese economists themselves, it is a 'double-track' or 'dual' system (Wu 1986; Wu and Zhao 1987) and is expected by many (Zhang 1988) to last for a very long period of time.

As the operational patterns of such a mixed entity are difficult to grasp, the Chinese monetary authority has been facing a daunting task in trying to estimate with relative accuracy the economy's demand for money, at whatever level of aggregation or disaggregation it chooses. Various factors pull in different directions and it is not easy to come up with a reliable summary view. Moreover, despite the reform, the People's Bank has yet to enjoy the autonomous status commonly assumed for a central bank in the West and the interference into the process of supplying money is still great (some may say that it is even greater than before), its ability to control the magnitudes of credit and monetary aggregates is also manifestly low. All these only make the job of monetary control under the economic reform a very difficult one.

3 FACTORS LEADING TO RISING MONEY DEMAND UNDER THE REFORM

The first major problem confronting the People's Bank is to estimate and forecast the demand for money of the mixed system. This is no easy job. While a number of factors causes the demand for money to increase significantly under the reform, there are also other factors which necessitate the suppression, or at least a very cautious handling, of the desire to cater automatically for the superficial symptoms of such an increase.

The most important factor generating a higher demand for money is the 'commoditization' (or, in Western terminology, monetization) of the economy, which is a consequence of the economic reform. The proportion of direct transfer and allocation of materials, goods and services in overall economic exchanges has dropped markedly. Most transactions are now mediated by money. Failure to cater for such a change may lead to a serious contraction in the real economy.

Second, the rise in the national living standards means that aggregate saving will increase. Since currency in hand and deposits with banks and credit co-operatives are the major form of saving in China, the demand for money under all definitions will rise. This factor is reinforced by the change in government policy to rectify the past Stalinist tendency of emphasizing accumulation at the expense of consumption. To rally the people to the cause of economic reform, the reformists have deliberately carried out measures to raise the income and consumption levels of the population, examples being the large increases in the procurement price for agricultural produce in the first stage of reform (1979–84), and the freedom given to enterprises in the cities to raise wages and consumption funds in the second stage of reform which started in late 1984. Under such circumstances, household income will grow at a higher rate than the economy. As incomes have been largely, if not totally, monetized and higher incomes lead to higher saving in monetary forms, the demand for money will also increase at a higher speed than the growth rate of the economy (Liu 1986).

Moreover, the increasing importance of transactions mediated by cash, due to the fact that banking services in China have not been growing as fast as the economy itself, also implies that the velocity of circulation would fall and demand for money would increase, as cash supposedly changes hands more slowly than transfer across bank accounts.

Given these considerations (see Appendix A for a stylized model using the quantity equation), economists such as Song and Zhang (1986) and Liu (1986) argue strongly that monetary policy must be loose and accommodative during reform, at least in its early stages. Otherwise, severe contractionary forces may be inadvertently imposed on the real economy.

4 THE PRECIPITATION AND RE-EMERGENCE OF MONEY

Nevertheless, the above arguments are implicitly predicated on an assumption of market equilibrium, which may not hold in reality. Other Chinese economists have stressed this possibility and warned against the danger of neglecting the phenomenon of '*huobi chendian*' (monetary precipitation) and consequently over-estimating the demand for money. Further injection of money supply would add to the money stock, part of which is already involuntarily held, and could aggravate the inflation problem.

Monetary precipitation may be caused by at least three different types of factors:

(1) Poor financial services. For example, there are not enough branches of rural credit co-operatives in the countryside. Farmers, irritated by the troubles and unattracted by low interest rates, choose to keep their cash under their pillows.

(2) The problems of the economy being over-heated under the reform. The reform has resulted in an excessive distribution of purchasing power and an aggravated investment thirst. For reasons that we will expound later, various bottle-necks in basic industries, energy and transportation, are formed and effective supplies are severely constrained. As a result, household incomes and funds held by enterprises cannot be smoothly transformed into consumer goods and materials according to ex ante plans. Because of such 'double shortages' in both intermediate goods and final output (Fu *et al.* 1986: 200–7), these parties are forced to store up their money.

(3) The mis-match between supplies and demands. Stockpiling and forced inventory accumulation may occur concurrently with shortages. While speculative stockpiling aims at profiteering, and there is ample evidence that it has been rampant during the reform, forced inventory accumulation is a result of enterprises putting forth 'unsaleable' goods in a market structure dominated by the sellers who are still under a 'soft' budget constraint (Shen 1986). Monetary precipitation will occur when consumers fail to buy goods that they want and enterprises cannot purchase materials that they need.

As things evolve, the first form of precipitation is voluntary saving, the only question is its manner of expression: cash under the pillow instead of deposits in banks or rural credit co-operatives? The second form is however involuntary or forced saving. The intention of the holder of money is not realized. Money is forced to precipitate in the form of withdrawn cash, or to sit immobile in current and fixed deposit accounts. The velocity of any precipitated money will drop significantly, although it may not necessarily be zero. In both cases, anyway, the higher the proportion of precipitated money, the lower the velocity of the monetary aggregate.

The third form of precipitation has aroused some controversy. Inventory accumulation *per se* can be interpreted as a symptom of 'insufficient aggregate demand', *à la* Keynes. It is then meaningless to talk about monetary precipitation. The problem is rather a lack of funds to foster effective demand. The phenomenon could however be a result of mismatch between supply and demand, and monetary precipitation will occur as a result.[5]

The crucial question facing the Chinese monetary authority is to distinguish carefully these forms of monetary precipitation. The first form does not seem to create very serious problems and the major remedial measure is to set up more extensive branching networks and provide better financial services so that the withdrawn cash can be efficiently re-absorbed into the circuit of integrated fund flows. The second and the third forms (the latter interpreted as a corollary of forced inventory accumulation due to mis-match rather than insufficient aggregate demand) however represent the damming up of latent purchasing power, which may re-emerge at any time, making a strong impact on the goods market. Since the economic reform has not removed many of the price controls and restrictions, the phenomenon may as a first approximation be regarded as 'repressed inflation'. The real solution lies in the restoration of the balance in aggregate supply and demand and the match between production and preferences.

A direct consequence of monetary precipitation is that it takes a very long time, if at all, for money holders to pass their money to units which require funds to carry out their normal operations, so that the velocity of monetary circulation drops significantly. These latter constrained units will seek further credit from the banks and other credit institutions to relieve their difficulties. The financial institutions will however be reluctant to respond because their previous loans may already be in jeopardy as enterprises cannot obtain the necessary materials, turn them into profitable sales and repay the principals plus interest. From the macro-perspective, moreover, further monetary injection may lead to another round of precipitation, creating further problems. The situation becomes a real dilemma.

5 RESOURCE CONSTRAINTS AND THE DEBATE ON MONETARY POLICY

For all these reasons, it is no easy task to separate the 'real' from the 'illusory' elements in an apparent increase in money demand in a socialist developing economy under reform. Feltenstein and Farhidian (1987) incorporate disequilibrium specifications, including those of adaptive expectations and partial adjustments, into the money demand function. However, their assumption, which seems to have been forced upon them because of the identification problem in a reduced-form equation over-crowded with parameters, that the 'viral price level' (at which no forced saving occurs) bears a constant log-linear relation to the official price index is objectionable. Portes and Santorum (1987) attempt to tackle the issue of aggregate disequilibrium using Chinese data but their model does not specifically deal with the situation under reform. Naughton (1986; 1987) looks at the problem from the perspective of the saving-investment balance in China and argues that a significant rise in voluntary saving has alleviated the inflationary pressure of the expansionary fiscal policy on the economy during 1979–82. His conclusion contrasts with the findings of Portes and Santorum (1987), who discover evidence of excess consumption demand in 1980–3. It is also not clear whether the same conclusion as his can be drawn about the saving-investment balance under the loose monetary policy generally observed during the second stage of the economic reform launched in late 1984. Moreover, there are serious methodological problems in the ways that Portes and Santorum and Naughton derive their results. I have elsewhere provided detailed criticism (Tsang, 1989).

Rigorous effects to deal with the problem empirically within China have been surprisingly sparse and started to appear only recently. Yang *et al.* (1988), for example, consider the conflicting influence on money demand of only two factors: the monetization of the economy versus price rigidity. Using a modified quantity equation and their own estimates of the ratio of monetization of the economy, which, depending on the definition of income, rose from 78.5 or 82.4 per cent in 1978 to 81.4 or 85.6 per cent in 1986, they come up with estimates of the degree of repressed inflation, which turned out to be about 10 to 12 per cent in 1986. In their conclusion, they criticized both theorists who neglect the trend of increasing monetization under the reform and those who assume price rigidity and repressed inflation away by using equilibrium quantity models.

Efforts of this kind must be regarded as preliminary attempts, and controversy is bound to remain. It has actually aroused heated debates in China. In 1986, economic growth rates nose-dived because of the tightened measures in 1985, which were responses to the overheating of the economy after the launching of the reform in the cities and further liberalization in external trade in late 1984. The pace of industrial expansion slowed markedly, with the year-on-year quarterly real growth rate plunging from over 20 per cent in the first half of 1985 to about 4 per cent in the first quarter of 1986. Chinese economists were split with regard to the diagnosis of the sharp recession. Some (e.g. Song and Zhang (1988)) argued that the tightening was excessive and enterprises were severely constrained in funding. Major pieces of evidence included the decline in the growth rates of currency in circulation and enterprise deposits in the second half of 1985 as well as the rising level of inventories of many enterprises. The economy had thereby in their view become excessively deflated.

Other economists (Wu 1986; Shen 1985), however, countered by pointing out that the very high growth rates prevailing from late 1984 to mid-1985 were far from normal and were stretching the economy to its structural limits. Moreover, there had not been any real monetary contraction, as can be witnessed from Table 14.1.[6] From the first quarter of 1985 to the third

Table 14.1 Growth rates of macro-aggregates in China

Year		*TC*	*TD*	*M1*	*M2*	*M3*	*IP*	*RPI*
1982	Q1	14.9	23.1	3.8	20.9	29.2	12.0	n.a.
	Q2	13.0	21.6	15.1	19.0	28.7	8.0	n.a.
	Q3	12.3	20.0	13.3	16.7	29.0	7.0	n.a.
	Q4	10.9	15.9	10.8	11.7	29.0	3.0	n.a.
1983	Q1	11.2	18.0	28.2	14.6	26.5	7.0	0.7
	Q2	12.8	18.3	19.7	14.0	28.8	11.0	1.2
	Q3	14.5	17.3	23.8	11.5	31.7	11.0	1.4
	Q4	25.7	18.7	20.7	13.8	32.1	12.0	2.7
1984	Q1	13.3	19.6	18.0	14.4	31.6	12.0	1.6
	Q2	13.0	21.0	16.3	16.5	30.6	11.0	2.6
	Q3	17.1	23.1	25.7	18.8	32.0	14.0	2.7
	Q4	32.8	26.8	49.5	22.7	36.1	17.0	4.3
1985	Q1	37.7	30.6	54.1	25.2	41.5	23.0	5.6
	Q2	36.1	23.4	54.3	14.7	40.3	23.0	8.5
	Q3	31.7	21.1	40.9	12.1	38.3	17.0	10.0
	Q4	20.8	15.2	24.7	17.9	33.6	10.0	10.7
1986	Q1	29.9	24.2	14.1	20.1	31.5	4.0	7.5
	Q2	35.9	36.0	17.3	36.3	35.7	5.0	3.5
	Q3	37.5	38.1	18.3	39.2	36.5	8.0	4.0
	Q4	41.5	39.2	23.3	26.2	37.9	16.0	5.5
1987	Q1	29.3	33.7	45.1	29.3	40.7	14.0	5.2
	Q2	27.6	30.5	49.9	25.1	39.1	16.0	7.3
	Q3	28.3	31.1	29.8	25.9	39.4	16.1	8.1
	Q4	20.5	24.2	47.2	16.5	37.2	13.4	8.4
1988	Q1	22.5	22.3	26.2	15.4	33.2	16.9	10.8
	Q2	24.0	23.5	35.9	20.8	30.3	17.3	14.6
	Q3	21.3	17.4	45.7	16.1	23.6	18.0	22.6
	Q4	16.9	13.2	46.7	7.5	23.8	18.9	26.3

Notes: Quarterly growth rates compared with same period in the previous year. TC = total credit; TD = total deposits; M1 = currency in circulation; M2 = total bank deposits minus budgetary deposits and urban savings deposits and plus the deposits of rural credit cooperatives (excluding the deposits of individual farming households); M3 = the total of the urban savings deposits and the deposits of individual farming households; IP = gross industrial production in real terms; RPI = retail price index. From 1985 Q4 onwards, the monetary aggregates included the balance sheet items of the Construction Bank (see note 6). n.a. = not available.

Sources: *China Almanac of Banking and Finance*, 1988; *China Finance, Monthly Bulletin of Statistics – China, China's Latest Economic Statistics*, various issues.

quarter of 1986, the quarterly growth rate of total credit (extended by banks and rural credit co-operatives) stayed without exception above 20 per cent, far above the real growth rate of industrial production and the economy as a whole, as well as the average annual growth rate of total credit in 1981–3 (12.4 per cent). It is highly doubtful whether this large jump could be entirely explained away by factors such as the commoditization of the economy and the increase in the propensity to save.

To these economists, the decline in the growth of currency and short-term deposits was due to various factors such as the over-expansion in fixed investment, the central government's fiscal position, as well as the huge trade deficits incurred under the open-door policy, rather than a result of monetary contraction. The major constraint on the economy was not the shortage in funds or aggregate demand, but the shortage in effective supplies (Wu *et al.* 1986). If most of the enterprises are resource-constrained, the funds they obtained through budgetary allocations or credit cannot be successfully translated into raw materials and intermediate supplies according to their original plans. Production will inevitably be affected adversely. However, part of the money that the enterprises have procured will be turned into wages and other non-productive expenses, widening the gap between effective supply and notional demand. These amounts of money will be forced to precipitate, leading to a fall in the velocity of circulation. Under such a situation, banks and other financial institutions will also feel constrained as many enterprises face difficulties in repaying or even servicing the outstanding loans. They may be reluctant to further expand credit. Subsequently, even enterprises which are operating normally will feel the tension in the whole financial system.

Under such circumstances, further increases in the money supply may lead to even worse problems unless the new funds can eliminate the bottle-necks, rectify the mis-match and remove the blockades in the circuit of money-commodity flows, hence significantly increasing effective supply and re-absorbing large amounts of previously precipitated money. Otherwise, part of the new credit will again precipitate. The time bomb of suppressed buying and the ultimate eruption will be more destructive.

6 ECONOMIC REFORM, STRUCTURAL IMBALANCES AND MONETARY DILEMMA

Rigorous models and conclusive empirical findings[7] that can be used to assess the theoretical positions of the two schools are yet to appear. Nevertheless, prima facie symptoms that resource-constraints have been a serious problem affecting the reform abound. The large-scale withdrawal of deposits (evidenced by the discrepancies among the growth rates of M1, M2 and M3 in Table 14.1) and periodic outbursts of panic buying under escalating inflation rates from late 1987 onwards were the most forceful testimonies to an economy under supply-side strains.

The present debates on centrally planned economies (CPEs) centre around the controversy between the disequilibrium econometricians led by Portes and the 'shortage' theorists under the leadership of Kornai. For a summary view, readers are referred to Kornai (1982; 1986) and Portes (1986). Both schools have however been criticized for neglecting structural problems.

Podkaminer (1986) gives an insightful analysis of the structural disequilibria in the Polish economy and argues that 'it is no longer productive to limit oneself to speculation about the correspondence between traditional macroeconomic aggregates' to determine whether a CPE is in a situation of excess aggregate supply or that of shortage. 'In particular, one should allow for the macroeconomic importance of distortion in relative prices and incomes' (1986: 16). On the other hand, Fforde (1984) stresses the relevance of economic dualism in a 'low-income socialist developing country' such as Vietnam where an 'inside' socialist sector competes with an 'outside' non-socialist sector. Although he assesses Kornai's work favourably, he thinks that the 'crucial element missing from' his work is 'the lack of any integrated treatment of certain *structural* consequences of these problems – in other words, the existence of a substantial "outside" economy' (1984: 12, original emphasis). Fitzgerald (1988) has also emphasized the importance of the need to incorporate inter-sectoral and structural considerations into the Kalecki-Kornai framework in analysing planned economies in the Third World.

These structural perspectives are of great relevance for the study of the Chinese reform. After all, the price-quantity system in the pre-reform regime was widely regarded as 'distorted'. Most 'distortions', however, have not been eliminated in the reform. In fact, there is a lot of evidence that new distortions have emerged, compounding macroeconomic imbalances. Economic dualism is also rampant in the reform: the 'double-track' system is dualistic in nature. The conflicts between the liberalized sectors and the controlled sectors, which have recently become a focus of attention for the Chinese economists (Wu and Zhao 1987; Zhang, 1988), bear resemblance to those between Fforde's 'outside' and 'inside' economies. A deeper understanding of the dilemma facing the central bank hence requires an appreciation of the origins and dynamics of these structural problems.[8]

Under Chinese economic reform, profit incentives and market mechanisms have been introduced into various sectors of the economy with different degrees of vigour. On the whole, basic industries such as iron and steel, raw material, energy and transport have been least affected. The reason is simple. Despite the fact that China, because of her peculiar historical and developmental settings, was forced to deviate somewhat from the mould, the general pre-reform strategy was to implement 'forced industrialization' by speeding up the development of the basic sectors with strong forward and backward linkages (Zhang, 1988). So in general the relative prices of the output of the basic industries were suppressed in order that other industries, especially those producing plant and machinery, could receive cheap input and grow at high speed.[9] This strategy was facilitated by the prevailing ideology that means of production should not be regarded as commodities. The bias in relative prices was also reinforced by the semi-colonial experience of China before 1949 when foreigners and their Chinese accomplices used their political power to exploit Chinese resources at the lowest possible costs (Xu *et al.*

1982; Zhang *et al.* 1988). Even the communist regime found it hard to modify significantly the vector of relative prices. Under the economic reform, efforts to rectify the distorted price system have again been obstructed by various considerations, among which is the fear that significant price increases in the sectors with strong production linkages may touch off inflationary spirals. Hence the 'double-track' price system was instead applied to most of the output of these sectors while the prices of many consumer goods were freed.[10]

Nor is the problem only a matter of relative prices. The expectations of the population have been raised significantly by the economic reform and the open-door policy. In a bid to rectify the past 'Stalinist' mistake of suppressing consumption, the reformists have deliberately facilitated a rapid rise of the living standards of the population. So most Chinese have been keen to raise their income and consumption levels, neglecting whether the strength of the economy could sustain this if everybody goes for it simultaneously. This has been referred to as the phenomenon of 'over-maturing of consumption' (*xiao-fei zaoshu*). As a result, resources have been concentrated on high-profit sectors such as the processing and consumer goods industries, further aggravating the imbalance in the overall economic structure.

The strategy of the reformists to stimulate the economy through decentralizing autonomy and finance to local authorities, captured most succinctly by the motto '*fongquan rangli*' (decentralizing power and conceding material benefits) has also created its own problem, as these units rushed to build up their own newly acquired spheres of power. Liu and Yang (1987) have given a penetrating analysis with a great deal of supporting evidence of the trends of the 'lightening' and 'structural duplication' of industries at the regional levels in the reform period as many local units attempted to do the same things at the same time, on a much smaller scale. Not only were they reluctant to invest in the basic sectors which showed long development and pay-back periods or low profit rates, the potential economies of scale and structural synergy would have been lost anyway even if they had been willing to do so. This affected not just the basic industries but also many sectors producing capital goods and quite a few in the light industries. Given the newly found virtues of self-interest, moreover, the traditional non-mobility of resources, which was not eliminated by the reform, has been compounded by various forms of local protectionism.

Overall, the problem is related to the historical constraints on the Chinese economy and the uneven impact of the reform strategy. Table 14.2 gives some evidence of the seriousness of structural imbalance in the Chinese economy in recent years, using the heavy industries as an example. In the reform period up to 1986, with the exception of 1980–1 when the government implemented adjustment measures to cool the economy, the extraction and raw-material sectors had been relatively neglected, compared with the manufacturing sector. Thus acute structural distortions and bottle-necks were formed.

Table 14.2 Output composition of heavy industries (in percentage)

	1975	*1978*	*1980*	*1981*	*1982*	*1983*	*1985*	*1986*
Extraction (1)	12.1	12.0	11.3	11.7				
(2)				15.2	14.3	13.1	11.4	11.3
Raw material (1)	35.1	35.5	37.8	39.3				
(2)				40.6	39.3	38.3	35.1	35.8
Manufacturing (1)	52.8	52.5	50.9	49.0				
(2)				44.2	46.4	48.6	53.5	52.9

Notes: Series (1) in constant 1970 prices and Series (2) in constant 1980 prices.
Sources: *China Industrial Economic Information Yearbook*, various issues.

Besides material supplies, energy constraints were also very serious. According to the 1986 edition of *Chinese Energy Statistics*, tension in electricity supply heightened during the reform. The elasticity of electrical production (with respect to national income) averaged 1.49 during 1976–80. It dropped to an average of 0.66 in 1981–5 and stood merely at 0.52 in 1985. Comparable figures for the United States, Britain, West Germany and Japan during 1973–82 were 1.53, 1.94, 1.77 and 1.21 respectively.

The problems of structural disequilibria apparently further deteriorated in 1987 and 1988. In 1988, the real growth of industrial production was 17.7 per cent while the output of pig iron, cloth and rolled steel rose in real terms only by 3.8 per cent, 5.5 per cent and 7.0 per cent respectively. Power generated and the volume of railway cargo meanwhile increased by merely 9.3 per cent and 2.7 per cent. No wonder there were signs of structural inflation in 1988.

With regard to monetary policy, the key question is how to prevent forms of structural disequilibria from worsening to such an acute extent. As discussed above, these imbalances have been the results of historical, institutional and strategic factors which the monetary authority may not always be in a position to control or influence. Once caught in the imbalances, however, it could be in a no-win situation. Tightening may push the economy into deep recession, while further injection of money might fuel inflation because the elasticities of production in those bottle-neck sectors are very low, at least in the short term. In the end, inflation, particularly consumer inflation, seems to be the unavoidable cost. Appendix B below, which is adapted from Tsang (1988), gives a stylized presentation of this dilemma.

7 OBSTACLES TO THE EFFECTIVE CONTROL OF THE MONEY SUPPLY

Besides the difficulties of estimating the demand for money, another set of problems troubling the Chinese monetary authority has been its own ability to control the money supply. Due to various institutional and policy factors, that ability has unfortunately been manifestly low.

Firstly, as a central bank, the People's Bank lacks the autonomy of its western counterparts in carrying out an independent and persistent monetary policy. It has been under constant pressures from the state treasury and other ministries to cater for their expansionary ambitions. Its branches at the provincial and city levels face even worse situations under the reform. Local authorities, with their increased power, constantly interfere into the operations of these branches. They even have a say in the appointment of and remuneration to bank officials. So the central bank and its network are often forced to accommodate their high-growth strategy, and plans for credit expansion and issuance of currency have frequently been violated.

Second, as can be inferred from the discussions above, it is very difficult to predict the operational patterns and the twists and turns of the mixed system. Moreover, not enough emphasis has been put on the analysis of monetary precipitation and structural imbalance. Once serious symptoms emerge, monetary tightening may produce adverse effects on production and circulation in the short run, which can be easily observed, while the long-term benefits of the measure remain somewhat uncertain. Given its traditionally inferior status in the bureaucratic hierarchy, the monetary authority is often reluctant to go against the prevailing mood, especially during a boom.

Thirdly, the determinants of the aggregate money supply in the course of the economic reform are very complex, many of which are beyond the control of the central bank. Take the issuance of currency as an example. Table 14.3, which is the equivalent of the money supply formation tables regularly

Table 14.3 Formation table of currency in circulation (unit: RMB 100 million)

Year	*(1) Cash*	*(2) Deposit-loan gap*	*(3) Net fiscal borrowing*	*(4) Reserve*	*(5) International account*	*(6) Capital account*	*(7) Others*
1981	50.14	8.96	−32.92	97.92	−17.08	21.24	−14.50
1982	42.78	−60.65	17.43	128.12	−1.62	35.14	5.36
1983	90.66	1.34	11.41	48.38	18.08	46.17	−57.62
1984	262.33	331.99	93.20	−2.51	2.03	39.43	122.95
1985 (exclude CB)	205.72	556.47	−146.28	−170.46	4.90	34.04	4.87
1985 (include CB)	195.72	801.53	−188.22	−170.46	4.90	209.24	42.79
1986	231.53	519.13	151.92	−15.98	−34.31	91.90	297.33
1987	235.12	247.30	149.38	104.96	16.98	121.56	161.94

Notes: All figures are changed in amount compared with the previous year. The deposit-loan gap refers to the amount by which total loans were greater than total deposits (a negative figure represents the amount by which total deposits were greater than loans).
CB = Construction Bank.

Sources: *Statistical Yearbook of China*, 1988; *China Finance*, various issues. (1) = (2) + (3) + (4) + (5) − (6) − (7).

compiled in the West, presents a quantitative analysis of the 'determinants' of the change in the amount of currency in circulation in 1981–7, using the aggregate statistics of national banking and credit balance.[11] As can be observed, factors leading to an increase in currency circulation include the enlargement of the '*xindai cha'e*' (the deposit-loan gap, see the note of Table 14.3) of the banking sector, the worsening of the government's fiscal position (which results in higher net borrowing from the banking system, other than the issuance of bonds), an improvement in external payments (indicated by the growth in gold and foreign exchange reserve), as well as the accumulation of net external assets (represented by an increase in the net claims to international financial institutions). The decrease in currency circulation, on the other hand, is mainly a result of the growth of the capital account of the banking system.

Among these factors, the People's Bank would find it particularly difficult to control or influence the ones that are related to the fiscal position of the government and the trade balance. Moreover, unlike the situation in the West, their effect on the monetary aggregate is in the same direction. An expansionary policy by a western government through deficit budgeting will usually stimulate imports and lead to a trade deficit. The former result may increase the money supply (if the central bank accommodates) while the latter may reduce it through the drain of reserves. In China, however, a fiscal deficit is typically associated with a trade surplus (or a reduction in trade deficit) and both may lead to a rise in the money supply. A fiscal surplus, on the other hand, normally co-exists with a trade deficit, and both would reduce the size of the money supply. This phenomenon is common among socialist countries which emphasize external trade. The main reason is that because of the lack of flexibility in prices and the exchange rate, government subsidy has become the major tool to improve the trade balance, particularly when a country such as China is displaying 'absolute disadvantage' in nearly all lines of products *vis-à-vis* the advanced industrial countries, with which she is most eager to establish a trade relationship. We have previously given an analysis of this aspect of the Chinese experience in 1979–86 (Woo and Tsang 1988).

The overheating of the economy in 1984, particularly in the fourth quarter, resulted in a significant increase in the amount of currency in circulation, compared with the preceding years. At the same time, the government launched a programme of trade liberalization which decentralized trading authority down to the level of enterprises while requiring them to bear their own profit and loss. The so-called 'agency system' was also pushed through. This enabled the government to cut its fiscal burden. Mainly because of that, 1985 saw the first budget surplus in China since the beginning of reform in 1979. Concurrently, for reasons that Woo and Tsang (1988) have analysed in detail, a trade deficit of historically unprecedented size (US$15.2bn) has resulted. Both these factors exerted strong dampening effects on the issuance of currency. Hence, despite the huge deposit-loan gap of the banking system, the amount of currency in circulation in 1985 was actually *smaller* than in 1984.

In response to the huge deficit unfolding during 1985, the government stared to re-impose centralized measures to control imports and exports. Consequently, the trade deficit shrank but the fiscal deficit reappeared in 1986–7, putting heavy pressure on the central bank to issue money currency again.

In view of such fluctuations in the Chinese government's fiscal and trade policies, which were the result of attempts to wrestle with the mixed system and to push the reform ahead, it would be very difficult for the People's Bank to pursue a stable and persistent monetary policy.

8 INEFFECTIVENESS OF MONETARY TOOLS

Nevertheless, as Table 14.3 shows, the deposit-loan gap of the banking sector is still an important factor affecting the amount of currency in circulation. In this regard, one may argue that the Chinese central bank should be able to exercise more control. The problem however lies in the fact that despite the financial reform, the specialized banks have yet to establish themselves as entities with independent operational status and sufficient resources of their own. In terms of the sources of funds, they are very dependent on the People's Bank because of the fragile nature of their financial balance and the peculiar structure of their assets and liabilities (Wu *et al.* 1987).

Typically, total loans of the banking sector exceeded total deposits by hundreds of billions of Renminbi in the reform years. To maintain balance, the banks had to depend on borrowing from the People's Bank, which often accounted for over 20 per cent of their total funds. As to the uses of funds, the specialized banks turned most of their money into loans. Unlike their commercial counterparts in the West, they did not and could not diversify their funds into a portfolio of assets with different degrees of liquidity, risk and rates of return. Table 14.4 gives in summary form the balance sheet of the Industrial and Commercial Bank, the largest one of the specialized banks, at the end of 1987.

Confronted with such a fragile financial structure of the banking system, it would be very difficult for the People's Bank to implement flexible and effective control of credit expansion and the aggregate money supply. After the system of specialized banks had been set up, the central bank initially used the method of 'gap' control, which failed to produce satisfactory results. Under the system, banks were assigned an approved 'gap' between total deposits and total loans (usually an amount by which loans could exceed deposits). They could further sub-divide the quota among their branches at different levels. As long as the gap was not exceeded, the banks could expand credit by as much as they liked. Abstracting from the effects of fiscal and trade policies and other considerations, the gap between loans and deposits

Table 14.4 Sources and uses of funds of the Industrial and Commercial Bank of China (year-end, 1987) (unit: 100 million RMB)

Sources		*Uses*	
Deposits	3172.38 (64.24)	Loans	4448.17 (90.07)
Capital funds	184.35 (3.73)	Res. dep. at PBC	363.72 (7.36)
Borrowing from PBC	1157.69 (23.44)	Dep. at PBC	98.23 (1.99)
Others	424.24 (8.59)	Vault cash	28.54 (0.58)
Total	4938.66 (100.00)	Total	4938.66 (100.00)

Notes: Numbers in brackets are percentages. PBC – People's Bank of China; Res. dep. – reserve deposits; Dep. – deposits.

Source: *Almanac of China's Finance and Banking*, 1988: 67.

obviously has to be filled by additional cash. Thus the method is equivalent to the control of currency issuance. Since the specialized banks could extend more credit if they were able to procure more deposits, provided that the quota was not exceeded, it was hoped that the banks would have more incentives to solicit deposits (thus encouraging savings and speeding up monetary circulation) and would be more concerned about channelling funds to more efficient units (since deposits had to be financed).

However, due to the segregation between cash circulation and transfer payments through banks, a situation which the economic reform has not changed markedly, such a control mechanism failed to produce notable effects. Chinese households use mainly cash for transactions while exchanges among enterprises are largely settled in the form of cheque payments, and nearly all loans are extended to enterprises and other organizations. Therefore, the cash circuit and the loan-deposit circuit are largely detached from each other. As a result, the money multiplier is very large.[12] Given a 'gap', moreover, the total magnitude of loans and deposits is theoretically indeterminate if the cash drain ratio is unstable unless the monetary authority imposes ceilings on credit, which the central authority actually did most of the time in the reform period. Such credit ceilings, however, are in conflict with the goal of promoting banking efficiency.

To rectify this defect in the control mechanism, the Chinese monetary authority started to introduce reserve requirements on deposits in 1985. Banks have been required to maintain a certain percentage of their deposits as reserve (30 per cent for the Construction Bank and 10 per cent initially for the other banks; the latter ratio has been progressively increased over the past few years). It was apparently hoped that the magnitude of the money multiplier could be lowered without having to resort to administrative control.

Nevertheless, even this new system seems to have done very little to restrain credit and keep a lid on the money supply. In fact, given the fragile financial structure of the banking system, flexible and effective control cannot be achieved through either re-lending policy which makes up for the deposit-loan gap or changing the reserve ratio on deposits. Suppose the monetary authority feels that the economy is overheated and hence reduces re-lending to the specialized banks. With a major source of funds blocked, the specialized banks would find it difficult to open up other sources, particularly in the short run. Since nearly all their funds have been lent out as loans, there is very little liquid asset out of which they can switch. To restore balance they have few alternatives other than limiting new lending and demanding enterprises to repay outstanding loans. This will generate a drastic impact on the operation of enterprises many of which do not have sufficient funds. A lot of ongoing projects will have to stop, touching off chain effects. Hence monetary tightening may lead to severe contraction in the real economy.

Likewise, the effectiveness of raising the reserve ratio is also limited. With the deposit-loan gap amounting to over 20 per cent of the total funds of the banking system, the specialized banks have to rely on the People's Bank to maintain financial balance. An increase in the reserve ratio will put them in the same difficult situation as a tightening in re-lending. The higher ratio may be imposed only on new deposits rather than on total deposits. But there will be the delicate problem of determining the appropriate marginal ratio. During an inflationary boom, new lending may be vital in keeping liquidity in the mixed system.

Because of all these factors, the People's Bank in general has been rather reluctant in taking the initiative to implement monetary contraction, for the fear that it might be blamed for obstructing the high-speed growth of the economy and the progress of the reform (with its 'inevitable' increases in the demand for money). It has been forced to accommodate the ambitious plans of both central and local authorities. Only until evidence of extreme overheating and distortion in the economy comes to everyone's recognition would all the parties of vested interests in power agree to a major clamp-down. Given the institutional reality in China, although such a measure was often linked to the re-imposition of forms of direct control and usually pushed the economy into severe recession, it did perform, to varying degrees of success, the 'positive' functions of curbing demand and redirecting resources to rectify structural imbalances. Hence the sharp fluctuations and cycles in the Chinese economy. It appears that the economic reform has done little to change that, if not actually accentuating the swings.[13]

9 CONCLUDING REMARKS

Under the economic reform, monetary policy is supposed to play a more independent, flexible and effective role in regulating the operation of an increasingly 'commoditized' economy. In reality, however, the objective has yet to be achieved because of the confusing, even chaotic, situations of the mixed system. It is difficult enough to fully grasp the operational dynamics of such a system and accurately predict the net effect on the demand for credit and money of factors that pull in different directions. The fact that the specialized banks as well as the central bank have not established truly autonomous operational status with sufficient resources and capabilities only aggravates the problems of effective monetary control.

The Chinese monetary authority often finds itself in a 'double blind' under the reform, particularly in the heat of an inflationary boom. Monetary tightening may push the economy into a depression. Further accommodation to distorted growth, on the other hand, would only delay the final adjustment and the eventual reckoning may be more painful. This dilemma has largely been a result of severe distortions in the economic structure of a system that as yet lacks flexibility and mobility, and exhibits very low supply and demand elasticities. To be fair, the Chinese central bank is not the leading actor in the play as many of the problems seem to be outside its direct control. To reverse the argument, therefore, monetary policy alone, irrespective of the form it takes, will not be sufficient to correct all the disequilibria built up over a span of many years. It can only be used as one of the levers in a policy package that includes fiscal, monetary, and almost inevitably, administrative measures.

The major lesson of the Chinese economic reform appears to be this: a socialist developing economy under reform must be very careful in handling its own historical, developmental and institutional legacy and pay special attention to the problems of structural disequilibria in formulating its reform strategies. Caution must be exercised to prevent the economy from falling into the trap of serious disproportionality. Otherwise, the costs in terms of the slowing down of economic growth and the progress in reform may be very high, and there is not much the monetary authority can do to alleviate them. Unfortunately, this lesson had apparently not been learnt, and the costs turned out to be huge.

NOTES

1 I wish to thank Michael Artis, Thomas Chan Man-hung, Chen Weishu, Ian Steedman, Bernard Walters, Woo Tun-oy and two anonymous referees for comments and suggestions. Naturally, I remain solely responsible for the opinions and errors in this paper.

2 For more detailed descriptions of the history and the reform in the Chinese banking system, see Zhao (1985) and Li (1987).

3 The statistics quoted in the text, unless otherwise stated, are taken or computed from the Chinese version of the 1988 edition of the *Statistical Yearbook of China*.

4 The intellectual underpinning of this strategy was provided in the 1920s by Fel'dman (1964) and re-presented by Domar (1957). The basic reasoning is simple but forceful enough: in the process of industrialization, characterized by rising capital intensity in all sectors, it is rational to give priority to the sectors producing capital goods (Department I), particularly when factor substitutability and mobility of resources are low, as in the case of developing countries (Fel'dman's basic model assumes fixed technology and total immobility of capital goods once they are assigned to any sector, although the authorities are free to make assignments before hand). Economic growth and improvement in consumption will actually be faster in the long run, despite short-term frustrations, compared with the opposite strategy of promoting Department II first. This type of model can be criticized from various angles: its negligence of the impact of low consumption on productivity, fetters on innovations, as well as the possibility of Department I being self-serving and self-perpetuating, etc. Although this is not the place to dwell on the issue, I should perhaps still state that I doubt whether the relevance and usefulness of such a model for a socialist developing country could be totally discarded. In a way one may even say that many of the problems concerning the Chinese reform have been the result of an over-rapid reversal (consciously or otherwise) of the strategy. The Chinese economists indeed had a little debate on it in 1979–81, the early years of the reform. For a survey, see Liu (1980).

5 Other than forced saving and monetary precipitation, a problem related to both shortage and mis-match is that of forced substitution, whereby users are forced to retreat from their best choices and buy things that they do not really want. As a result, the observed amount of transactions of a good may move outside the range of notional and effective demands. More specifically, the amount of transactions of goods into which people are forced to substitute may be greater than their notional (Walrasian) demand and 'excess demand' may even be observed over these goods. Given forced saving, mis-match and forced substitution, the aggregation of 'excess supply' and 'excess demand' over various markets to form a view about the overall situation in the macro-economy may be problematical. This is actually one of the most contentious points in the debate between the Kornai school and the disequilibrium economists led by Portes that we will refer to in a later section. In this paper, I have to abstract from the problem of forced substitution to make the subject tractable. For an analysis of the problem, see Tsang (1989).

6 The inclusion of the balance sheet items of the Construction Bank into the national banking and credit balance sheet in China from 1985 Q4 onwards creates a problem of consistency. The Construction Bank had some deposits and loans on its balance sheet before 1985 but no systematic quarterly figures on them are available. Only the national table not including the Construction Bank for 1985 Q4 was given. Comparison of the two tables shows that total deposits and total credit of the banking system were increased by about 10 per cent as a result of the inclusion. Fortunately, the comparison also shows that currency in circulation and urban savings deposits remained unchanged. In the context of Table 14.1, therefore, M1 and M3 are not affected, but, as a guestimation, the growth rate of TC, TD, and M2 may have been under-estimated by about 10 per cent before the inclusion. The period affected was apparently not very long, as Chinese reports gave the impression that the Construction Bank picked up its deposit-receiving and lending business rapidly only in 1984–5, and large-scale

conversion of construction allocations into repayable loans ('*bo gui dai*') only took place in 1985. Nevertheless, most Chinese economists did not seem to notice or care about these problems in their debates about the monetary policy. So their arguments should be treated with some caution.

7 The readers are reminded of the problems about the Chinese monetary statistics as explained in note 6.

8 Strictly speaking, imbalance and disequilibrium are two different phenomena. The Fel'dman strategy is a strategy of unbalanced growth, under which the sectors can be in equilibrium in the sense of market-clearing or the lack of a tendency for the proportionalities to change. But not all unbalanced growth patterns are optional (e.g. to Fel'dman, the 'Department II first' strategy is not), so imbalance is still a problem. In the case of the CPEs, it would by very difficult to distinguish between problems generated by imbalance and those by disequilibria. Hence, I am using the two terms interchangeably in this paper.

9 The prices of the output of many of these latter sectors have been very high, resulting in above-average profitability. Hence, as far as relative prices are concerned, the basic sectors which are biased against do not directly correspond to the Department I in the Marxian schema.

10 It may be argued that the double-track system would still be able to clear the market, as the higher prices in the liberalized sectors would do the equilibriating job. This is precisely the point which Nuti (1986) emphasizes in his criticism of the Portes school. Its failure to find evidence of chronic and serious shortage (aggregate excess demand) in the CPEs is to him unsurprising. Although Nuti's arguments add insights to a structural perspective on socialist economies, their implications on supply-demand balance and structural disequilibria need to be dealt with briefly here. In the case of China, there are strong reasons to believe that the higher 'off-plan' prices do not significantly increase effective supplies or drastically curb demands, so as to bring about a final 'equilibrium'. First, even off-plan prices are either subject to some administrative interference, or in those cases that they are not visible, the uncertainty of the government deciding to cancel the newly given freedom by re-imposing control always remains. Examples of this type of reversal abound in all CPEs, whether under reform or not. The restrained sectors are usually those requiring substantial investments and showing relatively long production lags. Hence suppliers would have to face very high risks if they react to the price signal in a way that their Western counterparts do. Second, on the side of demand, the controlled sectors typically produce intermediate output for which there are simply very few alternatives for 'forced substitution' (see note 5), given the developmental and institutional constraints that I have analyzed. No matter how high the unofficial prices are, demands for those output would and could not be markedly reduced. In short, the supply and demand elasticities are probably so low that the intersection of the supply and demand curves may lie far outside the feasibility region of economics and, indeed, politics.

11 It goes without saying that the 'determinants' are not determinants *per se* as these explanatory variables may be correlated with each other in various ways. So the following analysis should only be regarded as a first approximation, just as formation tables like this are normally used.

12 Huang (1988) even argues that the separation is complete. Hence, the multiplier is infinity. This, I think, is exaggerating as a portion of the loans extended to the enterprises is spent as wage payments to workers in the form of cash. So cash drain in the loan-deposit creation process does occur and the cash base is a constraint on deposit creation. The multiplier cannot be infinitive.

13 Due to the limits of space, the question of whether 'high interest rate' experiments can be performed in China to narrow the gap between the actual rates and their equilibrium levels will not be discussed. We have given elsewhere (Tsang and Yu, 1988) an analysis of the difficulties involved.

REFERENCES

I In English

Domar, E. (1957) 'A Soviet model of growth', in E. Domar, *Essay in the Theory of Growth*, Oxford University Press, pp. 223–61.

Fel'dman G. A. (1964) 'On the theory of growth rates of national income – 1', in N. Spulber (ed.), *Foundation of Soviet Strategy for Economic Growth: Selected Soviet Essays, 1924–1930*, Indiana University Press, pp. 174–99.

Feltenstein, A. and Farhidian, Z. (1987) 'Fiscal policy, monetary targets and the price level in a centrally planned economy: an application to the case of China', *Journal of Money, Credit and Banking*, 19 (1): 137–56.

Fforde, Adam, (1984) 'Macroeconomic adjustment and structural change in a low-income socialist developing economy – an analytical model', Birkbeck College Discussion Paper, no. 163.

Fitzgerald, E. V. K. (1988) 'State accumulation and market equilibria: an application of Kalecki-Kornai analysis to planned economies in the Third World', *Journal of Development Studies*, 24 (4): 50–74.

Kornai, J. (1979) 'Resource-constrained versus demand-constrained system', *Econometrica*, 47 (3): 801–20.

Kornai, J. (1980) *Economics of Shortage*, Amsterdam: North-Holland.

Kornai, J. (1982) *Growth, Shortage and Efficiency*, Berkeley: University of California Press.

Kornai, J. (1986) 'The soft budget constraint', *Kyklos*, 39 (1): 3–30.

Naughton, Barry (1986) 'Saving and Investment in China: A Macroeconomic Analysis', Ph. D. thesis, Yale University.

Naughton, Barry (1987) 'Macroeconomic policy and response in the Chinese economy: the impact of the reform process', *Journal of Comparative Economics*, 11 (3): 334–53.

Nuti, D. M. (1986) 'Hidden and repressed inflation in Soviet-type economies: definitions, measurements and stabilization', *Contribution to Political Economy*, 5: 37–82.

Podkaminer, Leon (1986) 'Persistent disequilibrium in Poland's consumer markets: some hypothetical explanations', *Comparative Economic Studies*, 28 (3): 1–16.

Portes, Richard (1986) 'Theory and measurement of macroeconomic disequilibrium in centrally planned economies', Centre for Economic Policy Research, Discussion Paper no. 91.

Portes, Richard and Santorum, Anita (1987) 'Money and the consumption goods market in China', *Journal of Comparative Economics*, 11 (3): 354–71.

Tsang Shu-ki (1989) 'Disequilibrium macroeconometrics and aggregate consumption shortage in China', BRC Working Paper no. CS89003, Hong Kong Baptist College.

Woo Tun-oy and Tsang Shu-ki (1988) 'Comparative advantage and trade liberalization in China' *Economy and Society*, 17, (1): 21–50.

Wu Jinglian and Zhao Renwei (1987) 'The dual price system in China's industry', *Journal of comparative Economics*, 11 (3): 309–18.

II In Chinese

Friedman, Milton (1988a) 'How to use the market mechanism paper presented at the Conference on Chinese Economic Reform, co-sponsored by Fudan University and Cato Institute, Shanghai, September. Chinese version published in *Economic Times*, Hong Kong, 14 September.

Friedman, Milton (1988b) 'Speech in Beijing', 19 September. Chinese version published in N. S. Cheung, *A Moment of Life or Death*, published by Hong Kong Economic Times, pp. 139–58.

Fu Ganzhan et al. (1986) *Macroeconomic Analysis of Socialism*, Xuelin Publishing House.

Huang Xu (1988) 'Supply and demand of money and determination of price level in China', *Jingji Yanjiu* (Economic Research), February, pp. 35–45.

Li Maosheng (1987) *A Study on China's Financial Structure*, Shenxi People's Publishing House and China Social Sciences Publishing House, 1987.

Liu Huiyong (1986) 'Economic reform and the growth of the money supply', *Quantitative and Technical Economics*, (10): 14–19.

Liu Wei and Yang Yuanlung (1987) *An Analysis of Production Economics in China*, China International Broadcasting and Publishing House.

Liu Xun (1980) 'On priority growth of means of production: the debates in the past year', *Jingji Yanjiu*, December, pp. 32–6.

Niu Yenling and Lu Yimin (1987), 'Excessive distribution of national income and the constraints on fiscal issuance of money', *China Industrial Economic Research*, (3): 78–80.

Shen Genwei (1986) 'Relaxation or retrenchment? – Discussion with Song Guoqing and Zhang Weiying', *Jingji Yanjiu*, December: 37–41.

Song Guoqing and Zhang Weiying (1986) 'Several theoretical questions of macroeconomic balance and macroeconomic control', *Jingji Yanjiu*, June: 25–35.

Tsang Shu-ki (1988) 'Models of monetary control under socialist economic reform', paper presented at the International Conference 'The New Stage in China's Economic Reform', Hong Kong, December.

Tsang Shu-ki and Yu Yim-fun (1988) 'Problems of monetary control under economic reform', *China Economic Review*, (4): 1–16.

Wu Jianlian (1986) 'Economic fluctuation and the dual system', *Financial Economics*, June: 1–8.

Wu Ji et al. (1986) 'On effective restoration of economic growth', *Jingji Yanjiu*, June: 19–24.

Wu Jiesi (1987) *Explorations on the Financial Institutional Reform of Our Country*, China Economic Publishing House.

Xu Yi et al. (1982) *Problems of Pricing under Socialism*, China Fiscal Economics Publishing House.

Yang Jongwei et al. (1988) 'Diagnosis on inflation in our country', *Jingji Yanjiu*, April: 19–25.

Zhang Shaojie (1988) 'The transformation in the deep structure of the Chinese economy', paper presented at the International Conference 'The New Stage in China's Economic Reform', Hong Kong, December.

Zhang Shouyi (1986) 'On the theoretical model of the indirect control of the macroeconomy in our country', *Quantitative and Technical Economics*, (9): 24–38.

Zhang Zhuoyuang et al. (1988) *A Study of the Structure of Prices in China*, Shenxi People's Publishing House and China Social Sciences Publishing House.

Zhao Haikuan (1985) *On Money and Banking*, Economic Science Publishing House.

APPENDIX A

Increases in demand for money during economic reform

Let us start with a simple quantity equation:

$$M.V. = P.T \tag{1}$$

where M represents the total demand for money, V velocity, P the price level and T the total amount of transactions of goods and services.

A socialist economy under economic reform witnesses a rising degree of monetization, which we denote as z, and an increased propensity to save, S, which is split between saving in the form of cash, Sc, and that in the form of deposits, Sd. Assume also that because of the relative underdevelopment of financial services compared with the growth of the economy, a rising percentage, q, of all transactions is in cash.

We can divide total demand for money into two components: demand for currency, Mc, and demand for deposits, Md; each with a different velocity, Vc and Vd.

I. Demand for cash

After a portion has been put aside for saving, the amount of currency left must be able to sustain transactions mediated by cash:

$$(Mc - Sc.Mc)Vc = q.z.Y \tag{2}$$

where Y is nominal output, which replaces P. T for simplicity. Denoting $(1 - Sc)Vc = Vc'$, we obtain

$$Mc = (1/Vc')(q.z.Y) \tag{3}$$

II. Demand for deposits

Like-wise, the amount of deposits left after a portion has been set aside for saving should be able to sustain transactions mediated by payments through banks:

$$(Md - Sd.Md)Vd = (1 - q).z.Y \tag{4}$$

Let $(1 - Sd)Vd = Vd'$, then

$$Md = (1/Vd')(1 - q).z.Y \tag{5}$$

III. Total demand for money

Aggregating the two types of demand, we obtain:

$$M = Mc + Md = (1/Vc')q.z.Y + (1/Vd')(1 - q).z.Y \tag{6}$$

and let $V' = (Vc'.Vd')/(Vd'.q + Vc'(1 - q))$, we have finally the modified quantity equation:

$$M = (1/V').z.Y \tag{7}$$

It can easily be checked out that the partial derivatives of M with respect to z, Sc and Sd are all positive, and the partial derivative of M with respect to q is positive if $Vd > Vc$. These results fit the arguments of those reformists advocating accommodative monetary policy.

APPENDIX B

On structural disequilibria, money and inflation under socialist economic reform

The following 'model', inspired by Zhang (1986) and Niu and Lu (1987), is not intended as a general one. It is used only for illustrating what I think is the typical dilemma faced by a socialist economy under reform when it unwittingly reverses the previous strategy in an unbalanced fashion.

Let us start with the basic Marxian two-department equations:

$$I(c + v + m) = W_1 \tag{1}$$

$$II(c + v + m) = W_2 \tag{2}$$

where c is constant capital, v variable capital and m surplus value. Departments I and II have their traditional Marxian meanings and W_1 and W_2 are their gross output respectively. In a growth situation, portions of m are to be distributed to dc and dv, representing increments in the two factors of production, while a remaining portion, i, will be consumed. For simplicity's sake, neglect depreciation and assume i to be the same in both departments.

The following condition for expanded reproduction should then be familiar enough:

$$I(c + v + m) = I(c + dc) + II(c + dc) \tag{3}$$

Equation (3) simply means that the output of Department I must be sufficient for the capital requirements of both departments in the next period for growth to occur. Alternatively, the condition can be expressed from the angle of Department II:

$$II(c + v + m) = I(v + dv + i.m) + II(v + dv + i.m.) \tag{4}$$

Traditionally, the socialist strategy was to give priority to Department I. Under reform, the priority is reversed by design or by default. Since monetization is spreading rapidly and banks are given a freer hand, sectoral equilibrium may be disturbed. Suppose Department II obtains an exceedingly large amount of loans, L, from banks for expansion, which split into A for capital funds and B for wage funds, and sectoral equilibrium is upset:

$$\text{I}(c + v + m) < \text{I}(c + dc) + \text{II}(c + dc + A) \tag{5}$$

$$\text{II}(c + v + m) < \text{I}(v + dv + i.m) + \text{II}(v + dv + i.m. + B) \tag{6}$$

Equations (5) and (6) together constitute the situation of 'double shortages' (Fu *et al.* 1986: 200–7). Although it is not the only possibility, it is probably the prevailing case, at least from a highly aggregated macro-perspective (the co-existence of shortages and slacks in sub-markets being neglected). From a simplistic disequilibrium viewpoint, since there is excess demand, monetary contraction is called for. With such structural disequilibria, however, the matter is more complicated. Department II launches the expansion, but according to equation (5) it is now 'resource-constrained' by insufficient output from Department I. Its ex-ante plans for production hence cannot be realized, as implied by equation (6). As a result, it will have difficulties in repaying L, principal plus interest. If the banks force the enterprises in Department II to cut back production to relieve the pressure in the capital goods market, the degree of excess demand in the consumption goods market may worsen since wage payments have already been made to labourers. During the process, portions of A and B will be forced to precipitate, in bank accounts or under the pillow. If the monetary authority reacts to the drop in velocity by issuing more money or encouraging credit, structural disequilibria may be aggravated.

Other than monetary contraction or administrative measures, equilibria can be restored by price and output increases in both departments:

$$\text{I}(c + v + m)(1 + gP_1)(1 + gQ_1) = \text{I}(c + dc) + \text{II}(c + dc + A) \tag{7}$$

$$\text{II}(c + v + m)(1 + gP_2)(1 + gQ_2) = \text{I}(v + dv + i.m) + \text{II}(v + dv + i.m. + B) \tag{8}$$

where gPs and gQs are rates of increases in prices and output, with the subscript indicating the department where they occur. Now suppose the following: relative prices were biased against the products of I before reform, reformists dare not liberalize their prices for fear of price spirals, production lags are very long in Department I, and enterprises are weary of putting money into it for fear of uncertainty and low profitability due to the loss of economies of scale. As a result, gP_1 and gQ_1 will be very small in value, and equation (7) cannot hold. Rationing and queuing will still have to take place in the capital goods market.

Since enterprises in Department II are constrained with respect to input from Department I, gQ_2 cannot be large either. But then they are given the freedom to raise the prices of their output, due to the reformists' partial belief in the market mechanism, and the temptation to do so is great as they are having problems with the banks. As a result, to fulfil equation (8), gP_2 (i.e. consumer inflation) has to be and will be very large.

15

CAPITAL MARKET REFORM ON THE ROAD TO A MARKET-ORIENTED ECONOMY

The Case of Stock Markets in China

R. Mookerjee and Q. Yu

China is widely seen as a model for successful economic reforms as it attempts to establish a successful "socialist market economy."[1] Indeed, 1994 was labeled a "crucial year" for major restructuring of the Chinese economy in several diverse sectors, with priority given to trade, legal issues, banking, capital markets, reform of state enterprises, and development of a system of market prices.[2] Restructuring efforts in prior years (since 1979) have begun to pay handsome dividends. Overall economic growth was a remarkable 12.8 percent in 1992, approximately 13 percent in 1993, and an estimated 10 percent or more in 1994. Nevertheless, managing the economy with the rudimentary tools available to the government is clearly a problem; it has resulted in an acute escalation in inflation and imposed added pressure on the government to sharply reduce its spending in various sectors of the economy, including funding for a large number of money-losing state-owned enterprises (SOEs).[3]

Much of the growing budget deficit, a significant contributor to inflation pressures, is directly the result of subsidized loans made by the central bank and other sectoral banks to SOEs. To eliminate this source of inflationary pressure on the economy, the authorities have embarked on an aggressive policy to reform the Chinese capital market, both bond and equity. Specifically, the government has attempted to develop the government bond market as a source of funds[4] rather than rely on printing money to finance deficits. The development of the stock market is a direct consequence of the government's efforts to control inflation by weaning inefficient money-losing public enterprises off subsidized loans from the banking sector.

To provide additional sources of funds and to subject SOEs to market discipline, the government has encouraged SOEs to incorporate themselves as joint-stock companies and issue shares. To facilitate this process the

Source: Journal of Developing Areas, Vol. 30 (1995), pp. 23–40.

government has simultaneously encouraged the establishment of stock exchanges. Thus, a well-functioning stock market is key to the government's attempts to successfully transform its public enterprises. Their transformation in turn will allow the Chinese economy to maintain sustained high growth rates[5] with less danger of renewed inflation and social unrest since SOEs are a major source of employment in China. Furthermore, unless SOEs can operate efficiently and raise funds independently by issuing stock,[6] the banking sector in China cannot be successfully reformed since banks will be obligated to continue financing SOEs through subsidized loans and to carry them on their books.

Indeed this is why arguments that downplay the role of stock markets as a source of funds for firms in developing countries and argue in favor of the German or Japanese models emphasizing bank financing as a source of funds are not valid in the current Chinese context, since the banking sector itself is in need of reform. These reforms in turn depend on the ability of SOEs to generate funds independently from both domestic and foreign sources through the issuance of stocks.[7]

It is against this backdrop, which highlights the importance of well-functioning stock markets in China's attempts to restructure its economy, and especially the financial sector, that this paper discusses and examines the historical, institutional, and structural development and characteristics of the Shanghai and Shenzhen stock markets. In addition, the paper considers the shortcomings and problems that must be overcome if the newly established stock market in China is to operate efficiently and thereby play its classical role of channeling funds to the most productive sectors of the economy.[8]

EVOLUTION AND HISTORY OF THE SHANGHAI AND SHENZHEN STOCK MARKETS

The stock system experiment phase

The establishment of organized stock exchanges in China is of recent vintage. The Shanghai stock exchange, the larger and more dominant exchange, began operations on 19 December 1990. The Shenzhen exchange formally opened on 4 July 1991. The origins of China's "stock system," however, can be traced to the early 1980s.

As a result of a growing gap between capital needs and insufficient bank loans,[9] some enterprises sought access to direct finance by issuing bond-type equities that were default free and had a guaranteed yield and repayment of principal. The first such stock company was the Tianqiao Department Store Company of Beijing, which was established in September 1984 and began publicly issuing equities with a three-year maturity. Shortly thereafter Feile Acoustics Company in Shanghai offered nonredeemable equities to the public. In January 1985 Shanghai Yanzhong Industrial Company raised all its capital requirements through the issuance of stocks. Subsequently the practice of direct financing via the issuance of equities swept over all the major Chinese cities.

In 1986 the government permitted SOEs to engage in the stock experiment, a move aimed at restructuring and leveraging the inefficient and money-losing medium- and large-scale SOEs. The first group of SOEs selected for the stock experiment included among others the Vacuum Electron Company and Feile Acoustics Company in Shanghai, Jinbei Auto Company in Shenyang, and Yuzhong Trust and Investment Company in Chongqing. During 1991, some 3,220 enterprises had engaged in the stock experiment across the country (not including joint-venture firms and rural enterprises). Among these stock-experiment enterprises, 55 percent were manufacturing entities, 30 percent were commercial firms, 5 percent were financial firms, 2 percent were construction enterprises, 0.87 percent were transportation enterprises, and approximately 7 percent were other types of firms. Of the 3,220 stock-experiment enterprises, however, only 89—or 3 percent of the total—were permitted to publicly issue equities, which were valued at 5.81 billion yuan.[10] By the end of 1991, there were over 3,600 stock-experiment enterprises in China, and the value of the outstanding stocks of those companies allowed to publicly issue equity amounted to 7.9 billion yuan.[11]

Establishment of regional stock markets

All stock trading was conducted unofficially until the Trust and Investment Company, a subsidiary of the Shanghai Branch of the Industrial and Commercial Bank, opened the first over-the-counter (OTC) market in 1986. In order to check the chaos in the unofficial markets, the State Council authorized the People's Bank of China (PBC) to regulate securities markets in 1987. Simultaneously, the government also permitted Shanghai and Shenzhen to establish stock markets ostensibly to publicize companies and trade stocks. It was not until 4 December 1990 that the PBC authorized such trading.

Thereafter the Shanghai Securities Exchange began trading on 19 December 1990, and the Shenzhen Securities Exchange formally opened in July 1991. In addition, three nationwide securities companies, more than 70 regional securities companies, 400 securities departments in financial institutions, and about 1,500 brokers' offices were organized simultaneously.[12] Functioning primary and secondary stock markets currently exist in Shanghai and Shenzhen. They have gradually blossomed into national markets owing to their accelerated growth and the increasing numbers of nonlocal companies listed by 1993. Table 15.1 reports the basic statistics of both the Shanghai and the Shenzhen exchanges since they began operations. Clearly, both

Table 15.1 Aggregate data for the Shanghai and Shenzhen exchanges

	1990		*1991*		*1992*		*1993*		*1994*	
	SH	*SZ*	*SH*	*SZ*	*SH*	*SZ*	*SH*	*SZ*	*SH*	*SZ*
Number of firms listed	8		8	7	30	19	199	77	169	118
Market value[a]										
All shares	1.23		7.98	2.94	55.84	49.0	245.74	143.36	259.8	109.0
A-shares	—		7.98	—	52.06	45.8	235.34	129.86	248.1	103.2
B-shares	—		—	—	3.78	3.2	10.40	13.50	11.7	5.8
Trading volume[b]										
All shares	0.003		299.6	4.26	1,883.4	1,913.0	—	—	—	—
A-shares	—		—	—	1,570.4	1,766.4	—	—	—	—
B-shares	—		—	—	313.0	146.6	—	—	—	—
Average P/E ratio										
All shares	28.05		81.83	26.71	59.78	—	—	—	—	—
A-shares	—		—	—	72.65	57.52	—	—	—	—
B-shares	—		—	—	17.40	35.56	—	—	—	—
Stock exchange members	—		29	15	171	180	481	426	541	495

Notes: SH = Shanghai exchange; SZ = Shenzhen exchange.
[a] Billion yuan (US $1 = 9 yuan).
[b] Millions of shares.

Sources: *China's Securities Market Annual Report 1993* (in Chinese); and *Securities Market Weekly* (1993 and 1994, various issues) (in Chinese).

exchanges have witnessed significant growth in terms of market capitalization, turnover, and number of listed firms.

The Shanghai stock market

The Primary Market. The primary stock market in Shanghai opened in 1984 with the issuance of stock by the Feile Acoustic Company. There was no clear distinction between equities and bonds, however, until the medium- and large-scale SOEs began to issue stock in 1987. The involvement of the SOEs enhanced the growth of the primary market. In 1990, 11 enterprises issued stock valued at 887.03 million yuan. By 1992, 53 companies had issued stock valued at one billion yuan. By 1993, the number of firms involved in the primary market had grown to 76.[13] To improve the functioning of the primary market, the government introduced a bidding system for initial public offerings that took effect June 1994. Prior to that date, new shares were allocated among securities firms at a fixed price.

The Secondary Market. The development of the secondary market involved three distinct stages—(l) a black-market stage, (2) an OTC stage, and (3) the establishment of the stock exchange.

1 Black-market stage (November 1984–September 1986): As soon as Shanghai Feile Acoustics Company issued shares, individual holders conducted share transactions in the black markets. In order to check black-market trading and fulfill public liquidity needs, the Shanghai branch of the PBC directed sellers and buyers to meet with each other individually to finalize trades and then go to the Shanghai Trust and Investment Company to legalize and record the transactions. The price of a stock, which was set by the Shanghai PBC branch, was equal to the stock's par value plus the prevailing interest rate on demand deposits. The total volume of trades undertaken via this procedure was 11,453 shares. Many more stock transactions, however, were undertaken unofficially in the black markets.
2 OTC stage (September 1986–November 1991): In September 1986, the Shanghai PBC authorized the Shanghai Trust and Investment Company to open the first OTC market and also to set the stock price equal to the par value plus the expected dividends and bonus. The total value of OTC trading amounted to 2.62 million yuan in 1987. In November 1987 the Shanghai PBC abandoned the practice of setting stock prices and approved the establishment of 16 more OTCs. As a result, prices were set through negotiation between buyers and sellers. Not surprisingly, OTC trading value increased to 49.63 million yuan in 1990. Black-market transactions, however, were still conducted on a large scale.
3 Establishment of the stock exchange (December 1990–present): The Shanghai securities market opened on 4 December 1990. During the period from 19 December 1990 to 20 May 1992, the exchange set a daily

price limit, allowing a ±5 percent change for share prices; later the price limit was reduced to ±1 percent associated with a daily ±0.3 percent volume change limit. After 21 May 1992 the exchange lifted both the daily price and the volume limits. The official opening of the Shanghai exchange resulted in the elimination of black-market trading. By the end of 1991, 8 companies were listed on the Shanghai exchange with a market value of 7.98 billion yuan. By the end of 1992, the number of listed companies had increased to 30, of which 2 were located in other cities, and the market value of the shares had reached 55.8 billion yuan. In December 1993, the total number of listed companies was 119 with a total market value of 245.79 billion yuan. By December 1994, the total number of listed companies had grown to 169 with a total market value of 259.8 billion yuan.

The Shenzhen stock market

The Primary Market. In May 1987, six credit cooperatives merged to form the Shenzhen Development Bank (SDB) and issued irrevocable stocks to the public. This was the beginning of the primary stock market in Shenzhen. By the end of 1990, over 200 enterprises had engaged in the experiment, among which 5 companies publicly issued stocks with a total value of 270 million yuan. In 1992 alone an additional 7 companies offered stock valued at 1 billion yuan. As they did with the Shanghai exchange, the authorities have introduced a bidding system to improve the workings of the Shenzhen exchange.

The Secondary Market. As in Shanghai, the evolution of the secondary market in Shenzhen also went through three distinct stages—(1) an early stage, (2) a regulated stage, and (3) the establishment of the stock exchange.

1 Early stage (May 1987–June 1991): Initially there was only lukewarm interest in SDB shares. Although the city government urged its employees "to take the lead in buying stocks" and authorized several securities companies to open OTCs, SDB succeeded in selling only 79 percent of its stock. Similar problems were experienced by other companies in subsequent years. The trend changed, however, as a few companies distributed bonuses to their shareholders in 1989, allowing some shareholders to reap unanticipated gains.
2 Regulated stage (May 1990–June 1991): Early in 1990, the Shenzhen stock market was characterized by bullish expectations. This induced large numbers of people, including government employees and securities firms' staff, to engage actively in stock speculation. Consequently, OTC stock prices surged upward rapidly and black-market prices rose even higher. The resulting increase in volatility owing to large-scale speculation generated concern among both central and local authorities. In May 1990 the

city government curbed stock speculation by banning trades outside of the OTCs, levying capital gains taxes, instituting limits on price changes, opening new OTCs, and prohibiting insider trading. The crackdown resulted in a slump in stock prices beginning in November 1990.

3 Establishment of the exchange (July 1991–present): The Shenzhen securities exchange, which was set up in November 1989, started provisional operations on 1 December 1990 and officially opened on 4 July 1991. The exchange lifted price limits once trading began. In 1991, stock prices rebounded as the public regained interest in equities. In November 1991, for example, around four hundred thousand people queued up for several nights in order to participate in a lottery that was being used to allocate newly issued shares. In 1992, there were 24 companies listed on the exchange, including 5 nonlocal companies, and the market value of shares was 49 billion yuan. In December 1993, 77 companies were listed on the exchange, of which 47 were non-Shenzhen firms from 17 other provinces, and the market value of shares was 143.36 billion yuan. At the end of 1994, 118 companies having a combined market value of 109 billion yuan were listed on the exchange.

STRUCTURAL AND INSTITUTIONAL CHARACTERISTICS

Types of shares traded

In the early years of the stock-experiment period (prior to 1986), firms adopted four major structural forms:[14] (1) the quota stock system—an enterprise did not allow its shares to be sold; instead it divided its assets into quotas that it allocated to its staff; (2) the joint-stock system—the state, institutions, and individuals jointly held an enterprise's assets; (3) the group stock system—state enterprises jointly held each others stock; (4) the factor stock system—an enterprise allocated its shares according to the contributions of various factors in production; thus there was a capital, a technology, and a labor share. Enterprises having one of these four different structural forms issued equities that had the following six characteristics: (1) they were a fund-raising instrument for collectively owned or service-oriented enterprises; (2) they were small scale in terms of both volume and value standards; (3) they were predominantly internal stocks; (4) they were bond-type instruments with redeemable and maturity features; (5) they provided higher yields for individual holders than for institutional holders; and (6) they had no uniformity in their face value.

This confusing situation persisted until May 1992, when the authorities implemented a unified set of rules that applied to all stock-issuing companies.[15] Subsequently, all stock-experiment enterprises have been standardized into two forms: limited liability company by shares and limited liability company by grantee. Four classes of shares were also defined: (1) state share—the state assets in stock-experiment enterprises are converted into state shares; these shares are not traded; (2) legal (institution or enterprise) share—the assets owned by the enterprises are converted into legal shares; these shares are traded only on the Electronic Network System between institutions; (3) individual share—the public holdings of stocks are individual shares, also called A-shares; and (4) foreign investors' share—these shares, also called B-shares, are held by foreign investors via foreign stock exchanges.[16] A- and B-shares are traded on the Shanghai and Shenzhen exchanges.[17]

Moreover, limited liability companies by shares are categorized as (1) companies with all shares owned by institutions; (2) companies with all shares owned by their staffs; (3) nonlisted public companies; and (4) listed public companies.

Equities issued are registered at par value in three forms: (1) a hybrid of stock and bond—this type of equity, which accounts for the majority of existing equities, is redeemable with a guaranteed yield and limited voting rights; (2) common stock—this type, which is particular to SOEs engaged in the stock experiment, comprises shares with no specific yield that have an infinite life and carry voting rights with respect to the firm's decisions; (3) preferred stock—these shares, which constitute only a small proportion of stocks, have an infinite life and fixed yields but no voting rights.

A unique feature of the Chinese stock market is the existence of B-shares. These shares are essentially a vehicle for foreigners who wish to invest in the Chinese economy. In order to attract more foreign investment, a few companies in Shanghai and Shenzhen began in 1991 to issue with PBC approval "special RMB shares," or "B-shares," denominated in yuan, for foreign investors. The first underwriters of new issues of B-shares are domestic securities companies, which in turn underwrite them to their foreign counterparts so as to channel B-shares to foreign investors. B-shares are listed on both the Shanghai and the Shenzhen exchanges, and are purchased and sold in foreign currencies converted into RMB via the exchange rates determined in the respective Shanghai and Shenzhen exchange swap centers. The after-tax yield on B-shares can be remitted abroad. By far the dominant type of share traded on both exchanges, however, is the so-called A-share.[18] A-shares are denominated in domestic currency and can be bought and sold only by Chinese citizens; foreigners are not allowed access to such shares.

Listing of companies

Table 15.2 shows the number of companies by sector listed on the Shanghai and Shenzhen exchanges at the end of December 1994. Clearly manufacturing firms dominate on both exchanges. This reflects deliberate government policy to expose manufacturing firms to market discipline and to provide them with access to additional sources of funds aside from subsidized bank

Table 15.2 Listed companies by sector on the Shanghai and Shenzhen stock exchanges as of December 1994

Sector	*Shanghai*	*Shenzhen*
Manufacturers	98	68
Commerce	33	10
Conglomerates	15	11
Utilities	13	12
Real estate	9	14
Finance	1	3

Sources: *Securities Market Weekly* (1994, various issues) (in Chinese).

loans. In addition to supplying these firms with access to foreign funds and technology, the government has agreed to allow a growing list of firms to list their shares on foreign regional exchanges (Hong Kong, Australia, and Singapore) and more recently has announced its intention to permit a select few firms to list their shares on the New York Stock Exchange.[19]

Table 15.3 lists the requirements that a firm must meet in order to be eligible for listing on the two exchanges. Interestingly both exchanges have different criteria. This is a reflection of the fact that while in theory both exchanges are governed by the same regulatory authority, in reality local (regional) authorities are directly responsible for the formulation and implementation of rules. Clearly the requirements for listing on the Shanghai

Table 15.3 Listing standards on the Shanghai and Shenzhen stock exchanges for firms

Shanghai	*Shenzhen*
• Registration as 'limited company by shares'	• Registration as a 'limited company by shares'
• Paid-up capital greater than or equal to 50 million yuan	• Paid-up capital of at least 10 million yuan
• Ratio of net physical capital to gross physical capital of at least 35 percent	• Ratio of net physical capital to gross physical capital of at least 25 percent
• At least 1,000 shareholders, each with shares of no less than 100 yuan (per value)	• At least 800 shareholders
• No illegal record	• No illegal record
• Public holdings of shares of at least 25 percent	• Necessity for initiators or organizers having at least 35 percent of shares in the new company or at least 5 million yuan worth of shares
• Necessity for having made a profit over the last 3 years with a profit rate of at least 10 percent over the past two years.	

Source: *China's Securities Market Annual Report 1993* (in Chinese).

exchange are stricter than are the requirements for listing on the Shenzhen exchange.

Market microstructure

Trading hours on the Shanghai exchange are five hours a day, Monday through Friday, and there is an additional hour at the end of the day for the exclusive trading of government bonds. The Shenzhen exchange has three and a half hours devoted to trading, Monday through Friday.[20] Before January 1995, the Shanghai exchange allowed investors to buy in and sell out of shares on the same day. In Shenzhen, prior to 27 November 1993 investors who bought shares on one day could only sell out the next day.[21] After this date and until January 1995 same-day trades were in effect for A-shares; however, B-shares traded on the Shenzhen exchange still operated under the old rules. Beginning in January 1995, both exchanges adopted a T + 1 trading rule system (i.e., buy today, sell tomorrow) in place of the T + 0 rule in order to reduce speculation and market volatility. Scripless trading was introduced in Shanghai March 1995 with the establishment of a central depository system for share scrips. The Central Depository is also a clearinghouse that settles individual account transactions. In Shenzhen, however, the clearinghouse settles accounts for securities firms, and then each security firm settles with individual investors who have accounts with them.[22]

Single transaction volume limits are in effect for the Shanghai exchange. Investors can buy a maximum of 100,000 shares per transaction in companies with 30 million or more shares outstanding. A transaction limit of 50 thousand shares is in effect for firms with fewer than 30 million shares outstanding. The Shenzhen exchange is not subject to any volume limits.[23] In 1993, turnover on both exchanges combined was 600 percent, with the value of shares traded amounting to 390 billion yuan, although 1994 saw a decline in turnover and value of shares traded owing to growing market volatility and a decline in share prices.

Market professionals

In 1991, members of the Shanghai exchange consisted of 29 securities firms. In 1992, this number rose to 171, of which nonlocal members (domestic firms but not based in Shanghai) were 76.6 percent. In December 1993, there were 481 members with 90 percent nonlocal members, and the number of trading seats on the exchange was 2,600.[24] By the end of 1994, members had increased to 541, and seats on the exchange amounted to 3000.[25]

By the end of 1992, there were 177 firms on the Shenzhen exchange, of which 157 were nonlocal firms. In December 1993, there were 400 members, including 372 nonlocal members, and 700 trading seats.[26] By the end of 1994, these numbers totaled 419 members and 719 trading seats.[27]

Both exchanges also have foreign securities firms as members. These firms trade in B-shares only. At the end of 1993, Shanghai had 16 such firms and Shenzhen had 10.[28] Seats on both exchanges are tradable. In Shanghai, the price of a seat on the exchange for a domestic trading firm is currently 300,000 yuan, and for foreign and specialist firms the price is 600,000 yuan. In Shenzhen all seats are currently priced at one million yuan.[29] Typically, the demand for seats has tended to exceed the supply on both markets.

Ownership pattern of securities

The stock market has experienced a boom in the number of domestic shareholders in 1995. To put the growth of shareholders in perspective, until mid-1993 the total number of officially reported shareholders on both the Shanghai and Shenzhen exchanges stood at a little over 7 million.[30] Since then the number of shareholders has doubled to approximately 15 million and is estimated to be growing at the rate of approximately ten thousand a day.[31] Foreign holdings of Chinese stocks are also experiencing significant growth judging from the quantum increase in the number of companies issuing B-shares and the trading volume.[32]

Differences in trading patterns

As the largest city in China, Shanghai, with a population of over ten million, is important for its industrial base. Shenzhen, on the other hand, is the first special economic zone set up by the government, is in close proximity to Hong Kong, and is the most market oriented city in China. These characteristics together with the local market regulations have influenced the development of the two equity markets. Initiated by the capital needs of public enterprises, the Shanghai exchange trades both bonds and stocks. While bond trades dominated initially, stock trades are now dominant. In 1991 stocks were only 17.7 percent of the market value of total securities traded, while bond trades accounted for 82.3 percent. In 1994 the market value of stocks traded increased 17.92 times, accounting for 76.3 percent of total market value. The Shenzhen exchange, however, is a stock trade-dominated market. In 1992, stocks sold on the exchange accounted for 99 percent of the market value of total securities traded.[33]

Until recently, individual traders dominated trades on the Shanghai exchange, because institutions were restricted to trading A-shares. This resulted in a few large individual participants' having a substantial degree of market influence. In August 1993 this restriction was lifted, and institutional investors have been actively involved in stock trading on the Shanghai exchange.[34] The Shenzhen exchange permits institutional investors to trade A-shares. Consequently more than ten thousand institutional practitioners—including firms, social welfare entities, and property companies—have become the dominant factor in determining trades on the Shenzhen exchange, rather than individuals.

Although Shanghai's population is ten times larger than Shenzhen's and its household savings five times larger, total investment accounts opened by individuals in the two cities are similar, approximately three and a half million. In addition, the value of the average unit transaction in A-shares in Shanghai is on the order of one thousand yuan, whereas in Shenzhen the average unit trade is about ten thousand yuan, thus indicating that in Shenzhen actual individual purchasing power for stocks is greater than in Shanghai.

The first informal connection between the two markets occurred in June 1990. This resulted in the average stock price of all five public firms listed on the Shenzhen exchange to climb rapidly from 8.68 yuan in April 1990 to 21.82 yuan in June 1990. Stock prices in Shanghai, however, remained stagnant. By June 1991, the Shenzhen market was in a slump, while the Shanghai market was subject to an excess demand for stocks. With the PBC's permission the Shanghai International Securities Company opened up an OTC exchange for individuals in Shanghai to buy stocks listed on the Shenzhen stock market.

Demand and supply of equities

Recent economic growth resulting in increases in household savings, coupled with the fact that few financial investment vehicles except bank accounts are available to the Chinese public, has assured a phenomenal increase in the demand for stocks. In 1992, for example, household deposits in banks amounted to 1,154.54 billion yuan, and household cash holdings were estimated at over 500 billion yuan, with the sum of cash holdings and deposits approximating 60 percent of GNP.[35] With inflation reaching double digits, the public has greater incentives to diversify their cash holdings into securities. Not surprisingly the number of shareholders, at 15 million in 1995, is growing at the rate of ten thousand a day. With additional exchanges slated to open, access to exchanges will become easier, thus spurring demand even higher.[36]

The demand for B-shares by foreign investors is expected to increase as China continues to restructure its economy. In addition, beginning in January 1995, the authorities have allowed domestic institutional investors, such as pension funds, to purchase A-shares, a development that is expected to further boost demand. Thus the demand for stocks will continue to grow in the foreseeable future.

Because the government wishes to retain ownership of SOEs, it has instituted tight controls on the number of firms that are allowed to issue shares. At the same time, a relatively small fraction of shares (about 20 percent) for a listed SOE is made available to the general public in the form of A and B shares. Furthermore, in July 1994, the authorities banned the issuance of all new A-shares until the end of 1994, in the face of continually declining share prices throughout 1994. In 1995 limited new issues of A-shares were being permitted contingent on market conditions. These government actions have resulted in the supply of equities lagging behind demand. Equities account for only 2.5 percent of total financial assets. Indeed China's stock market capitalization as a percentage of GNP was only 0.07 percent in 1990, 0.54 percent in 1991, and 4.36 percent in 1992.[37] It is expected to grow to double that percentage in the next few years, with several large SOEs expected to list their shares on the exchanges.

Nevertheless, even this increased supply will continue to ensure a big gap between the demand and supply for securities in the years to come. Not surprisingly, the shortage of equities has resulted in price-earnings ratios being bid up to unrealistic levels. For example, the average P/E ratio for A-shares on the Shanghai and Shenzhen exchanges in 1992 was 72.65 and 57.52, respectively.[38] Clearly these P/E ratios are well above those encountered in other emerging markets around the world[39] and may point to a systematic mispricing of stocks relative to fundamentals by Chinese shareholders.

The regulatory environment

In the early years of the development of the stock market, the PCB was entrusted with formulating and implementing the regulations that would govern the stock exchanges. In reality this function was usurped by local authorities (provincial governments), who applied a variety of standards resulting in chaos for both the primary and the secondary markets. The first national regulatory organ was the Stock Market Meetings Committee (SMM), which was established in the PBC in April 1991. Its main functions were to (1) set up policies for fostering stock market growth, (2) approve regulatory rules, (3) plan the size of stock issues, (4) supervise the Shanghai and Shenzhen exchanges, and (5) coordinate actions of different government branches. In June 1992, the SMM was expanded to become the State Council's Meetings for Securities Regulations (SCMSR).

In October 1992, the SCMSR in turn was replaced by the State Council Commission for Securities (SCCS). As the formal national authority for conducting macromanagement of securities markets, including the stock market, its responsibilities include (1) drafting laws for the securities markets; (2) setting up rules and policies; (3) directing and coordinating activities of provinces or government bodies related to the securities markets; (4) administering the China Securities Regulatory Commission (CSRC), the implementing organ of the SCCS, also established in October 1992; and (5) organizing the issuance and trading of other new financial instruments. In addition, the SCCS is also in charge of planning and approving Chinese companies' listings on foreign exchanges; reviewing applications of securities exchanges; examining securities firms and listed companies; drafting annual plans for securities markets in accordance with aggregate national economic development plans; and setting up stock market development strategies.

Fourteen government organizations are participants of the SCCS, including the PBC, State Committee of Structural Reform, State Planning Commission, Ministry of Finance, Supreme Court, Ministry of Foreign Trade, State Administration for Industry and Commerce, State Administration of Taxation, State Administration of National Assets, State Administration of Exchange Control, and other central government organizations. The SCCS secretariat is in charge of daily activities.

The CSRC regulates securities businesses and markets. It is responsible for (1) drawing up regulatory rules for securities markets; (2) regulating security issues, listings, and trades; (3) supervising securities entities; (4) approving lawyers and accounting offices related to the securities industry and granting licenses to securities companies; (5) supervising companies that are listing abroad; (6) investigating violations of regulations; (7) preparing statistical data and market analysis for the SCCS, and providing information to the public; (8) facilitating international cooperations; and (9) conducting other related matters. Within the CSRC there are eight departments in charge of different areas. In addition, the Securities Association of China, a self-regulatory nongovernmental organization with 200 institutional members and 36 individual members, was founded on 28 August 1991. Its main functions are to self-regulate, arbitrate disputes, and provide training and consultation services to members. In July 1994, arbitration was made mandatory in disputes involving securities. The China Council for the Promotion of International Trade (CCPIT) is entrusted with handling securities-related disputes.

SYSTEMIC PROBLEMS AND STRUCTURAL DEFICIENCIES

Stunted growth

The previous sections have emphasized the major structural and institutional characteristics of the Shanghai and Shenzhen stock exchanges. This section underscores the problems plaguing both exchanges that are a result of structural deficiencies. It also highlights the efficiency problems encountered by both exchanges.

The basic reasons for the government to establish and encourage stock markets are to (1) restructure nonprofitable state-owned enterprises, and (2) attract funds from both domestic and foreign sources. The stock-market experiment as outlined earlier, however, was relatively stagnant in the 1980s and gained momentum only in the 1990s after the establishment of the regional stock exchanges. Lack of progress in the development of markets in the 1980s can be attributed to several factors including government concern over possible erosion of state assets as firms become joint-stock companies. Authorities also expressed misgivings over the potential regional distribution of wealth in society as a result of stock market gains. Furthermore, the annual financial planning exercise was detrimental to the development of the stock markets. In spite of recent growth, the stock markets in China are still relatively small and shallow when compared to those in other emerging markets.

Thin trading

The nature of the SOEs listed on the exchanges and government policies regarding the type and trading of shares have resulted in both the Shanghai and the Shenzhen exchanges' being plagued with problems related to thin (low-volume) trading. With respect to the SOEs there are three major problems. First, SOEs by themselves are economically impotent and heavily reliant on government loans. According to one estimate, approximately one-third of all SOEs are explicit money losers, while another one-third are implicit money losers.[40] Second, another problem involves how to relieve SOEs of their social and welfare functions and reform them as pure profit-making enterprises. Third, Soviet techniques of accounting and auditing are still used in many SOEs. These techniques are clearly not suitable for the stock market requirements regarding financial assessments and transparency (i.e., clarity and accountability). SOEs cannot surmount these problems unless the economic environment and government attitudes change. These changes in turn are crucial for improvements in the quality and soundness of equities, which would result in a growing market.

Government regulations regarding the types of and trading rules for equity are also a major contributor to the thin trading problem on both exchanges. According to current regulations, different rules are applied to different equity concepts: state shares cannot be traded, legal share trading is permitted between institutions only, A-shares are available only to Chinese citizens, and B-shares are exclusively for foreign investors and are purchased on foreign exchanges. Furthermore, an A-share holder is not permitted to hold more than 0.5 percent shares of a company. In addition, companies require permission to convert A-shares into B-shares and vice versa.[41] These regulations to a large extent are intended to ensure a leading role for the state in the ownership of assets in the economy and to prevent state properties from auction.[42] In practice, they are unable to check the devaluation of state properties nor do they preserve fairness for the stock markets.[43] Furthermore, these rules have imposed additional constraints on the growth of equity markets. As state and legal shares account for the majority of total outstanding stocks, the nonliquidity of state and legal shares has become an artificial obstacle to improving market thinness. In 1992, the nontradable state and legal shares were 85 percent of listed companies' stocks on the Shanghai and Shenzhen exchanges, while the liquid individual shares were only 15 percent. In 1993 legal shares alone accounted for 26 percent of total stocks of all listed companies in Shanghai and Shenzhen.[44] In addition, the exclusion of state-assets representatives and, until recently, institutional investors from trading activities has eliminated important market stabilizers.

Recently, however, the authorities have started to address this problem by drafting trading rules for legal shares, and A-shares may be opened to foreign investment funds in the near future,[45] which should help by bringing about a more realistic valuation of shares based on fundamentals. To increase trading volume and market liquidity, the government has recently eliminated the tax on share transactions. Furthermore, it has not discouraged the first attempts at hostile takeovers.[46] To improve accounting practices and transparency, the government has recently announced that all managers of potential future exchange-listed companies must complete a six-month training course related to financial and accounting practices.

Overregulation and deficiencies in legal infrastructure

Excessive volatility in the stock markets is a major concern for the authorities owing to its potential impact on the state's annual financial plans. To contain this problem the government is apt to engage in macrolevel control through passage of mandatory directives. These include the planning of new stock issues[47] and quantitative targets for the purchase of government bonds. These traditional directing methods, more often than not, are arbitrary in nature. At the microlevel, the government directly screens stock-experiment enterprises and potential listed companies. Since this procedure is in essence a preferential policy for enterprises, the criteria are quite subjective and the decisions are more likely to be motivated by compromises between the central and local authorities. All these administrative tools, therefore, hinder the growth of a fair and efficient capital market.

The shortage and ineffectiveness of existing legal infrastructure constitute another restriction on the continued development of the Chinese securities market. Corruption and insider trading are not unusual. A notorious example is the 10 August 1992 "Shenzhen stock-tender riot," which resulted from cheating and the manipulation of shares by over four thousand employees in the securities issue board.[48] Government enforcement of market regulations and a weak legal infrastructure will take time to improve.[49]

CONCLUSION

While China's newly established stock markets in Shanghai and Shenzhen have experienced explosive growth,[50] these stock exchanges are nevertheless still in their infancy, and they continue to be plagued by inefficiencies that are traceable to inadequacies in their institutional and structural makeup. Among the reasons for inefficiency in China's equity markets are market thinness; stock supply problems; shortage of expertise; lack of an adequate infrastructure, both physical and legal; and so on.[51] Indeed two recent quantitative studies have documented significant departures from efficiency on both exchanges.[52]

The fact that both exchanges are seriously inefficient has important implications for the government and investors alike. For the government, the existence of inefficient markets that do not reflect fundamentals impedes the market's ability to play its classical role of channeling funds to the most productive sectors of the economy. Second, to the extent that markets are inefficient, listed firms may find it difficult to raise capital, since investors are unsure of a firm's true prospects. In the case of China, this uncertainty in turn has the potential to significantly reduce foreign portfolio inflows,[53] which are crucial to the SOEs if they are to modernize and compete. Third, market inefficiency may slow the listing of an estimated 50 thousand SOEs that are waiting in the wings. An inability by these firms to become listed could prevent their obtaining access to funds for restructuring purposes, and this situation could jeopardize China's attempts to reform its financial and banking sectors, thereby negatively affecting its long-term growth prospects.

Furthermore, inefficient markets that are open to manipulation and insider trading, as is the case in China, have the potential to provide manipulators with excess profits at the expense of other market participants. These stock price distortions will redistribute wealth in favor of those who possess market information, resulting in market unfairness and excess price volatility, both conditions that are detrimental to financial stability and public confidence.[54]

In the final analysis, market inefficiencies resulting from inadequacies in the structural, institutional, and regulatory framework provide an economic rationale for government intervention in the stock markets in the form of new rules and regulations to eradicate inefficiencies. This intervention is crucially important in China's case given the fundamental implications of an efficiently functioning stock market to the overall future growth prospects for the economy.

NOTES

1 Quote attributed to Chinese Premier Li Peng. See "Li Peng: Seeks Faster Reforms for 'Key Year' of Restructuring," *Straits Times*, 6 April 1994. For a discussion of the reasons for successful reform in China, see Gregory Chow, "How and Why China Succeeded in Her Economic Reform," *China Economic Review* 4 (Special Issue 1993): 117–28.

2 See "Chinese May Increase Volume of A-Share Issues This Year." *Straits Times*, 13 January 1994; and "Li Peng: China Needs Help to Build Economy," *Straits Times*, 13 May 1994.

3 It is estimated that two-thirds of China's 11 thousand large public enterprises are essentially bankrupt, surviving on central bank loans borrowed as income to finance operations and payroll. See "Wuhan's State Firms Face Bleak Times," *Straits Times*, 6 May 1994.

4 For a discussion of the history and development of the bond market in China, see D. Bei, A. Koontz, and L. Lu, "The Emerging Securities Market in the PRC," *China Economic Review* 3 (Spring 1992): 149–72.

5 For a discussion of the importance of state-owned enterprises (SOEs) to the overall growth prospects of the Chinese economy, see "Poor Performance by State Sector Slowing Down China's Economy," *Straits Times*, 2 April 1994.

6 Yoon J. Cho, in "Inefficiencies from Financial Liberalization in the Absence of Well-Functioning Equity Markets," *Journal of Money, Credit, and Banking* 18 (May 1986): 191–99, argues that financial reform in the absence of well-functioning equity markets will result in inefficiencies in investment.

7 Ajit Singh, in "The Stock Market and Economic Development: Should Developing Countries Encourage Stock Markets?" *UNCTAD Review* 4 (October 1993): 1–28, makes the case for a bank-financed system rather than a stock-market system as a major source of external funds for firms in developing countries. For a contrary view, see John Mullin, "Emerging Equity Markets in the Global Economy," *Federal Reserve Bank of New York Quarterly Review* 18 (Summer 1993): 54–83.

8 See Stanley Fischer and Robert Merton, "Macroeconomics and Finance: The Role of the Stock Market," Working Paper, No. 1291 (National Bureau of Economic Research, Boston, MA, 1984).

9 See the article by the Department of Production Structure of the State Commission of Structural Reform, "Conduct of Stock Experiment according to Standardization Requirement," *China's Economic Reform* 5 (1992): 20–24 (in Chinese).

10 The 89 stock-experiment enterprises are located in Shanghai (17), Shenzhen (17), Sichuan (13), Zhejiang (8), Shangdong (6), Henan (6), and Yuennan (2). See Shupin, Jin, "The Current Condition and Future Development of China's Stock Market," *Economic Structure Reform* 1 (1993): 34–41 (in Chinese).

11 See publication of the Securities Association of China, *China's Securities Market Annual Report 1993*, p. 13 (in Chinese).

12 See Jingshi Wong, "The Current Situation and Perspective in China's Securities Sector," *Economic Development* 5 (1993): 17–31 (in Chinese).

13 *China's Securities Market Annual Report 1993* (in Chinese); *Securities Market Weekly* 48 (1993–94, various issues) (in Chinese).

14 Lu Manping, "Multi-Forms in China's Stock Experiment," *Economic Development* 5 (1993): 33–37 (in Chinese).

15 The State Council approved the document prepared by the State Commission of Structural Reform as the State Council's 23rd document in 1992. It contained two parts: "On standardization of limited company by shares"; and "On standardization of limited liability by grantee." See *China's Securities Market Annual Report 1993* (in Chinese). Also according to the Xinghua News Agency, the "Company Law of the PBC [People's Bank of China]" was approved by the National Congress in December 1993 and will be enforced on 1 July 1994.

16 Issuance of different classes of shares, with the state portion dominating, has been widely used in other formerly socialist economies of East Europe in their attempts to restructure their respective public sectors. For a discussion and comparison with the Chinese system, see Adrian Wood, "Joint Stock Companies with Rearranged Public Ownership: What Can We Learn from Recent Chinese and East European Experience with State Enterprises," *China Economic Review* 4 (Special Issue 1993): 181–93.

17 Of the 5.81 billion yuan worth of outstanding stock in 89 stock experimental enterprises in 1991, state shares accounted for 47 percent, legal shares 29 percent, individual shares 14 percent, and B-shares 9 percent. See the article by the Department of Production Structure in the State Commission of Structural Reform, "Conduct of Stock Experiment according to Standardization Requirement," pp. 20–24.

18 The value of A-shares traded is over 90 percent of all stocks traded.

19 A total of 11 firms' shares are listed on foreign stock exchanges. (See "World Stock Exchanges Out to Woo Chinese Companies," *Straits Times*, 7 March 1994.) Shares of Chinese firms listed on the Hong Kong Stock exchange are called H-shares. In addition, the Shanghai stock exchange has agreed to list at least two foreign companies' shares by the second half of 1994, one of which is Germany's well-known industrial concern Daimler Benz. See "China to Launch New Sweeping Reforms," *Straits Times*, 21 January 1994.

20 *Securities Market Weekly* 48 (1993) (in Chinese).

21 *Securities Market Weekly* 42 (1993) (in Chinese).

22 *Securities Market Weekly* 48 (1993) (in Chinese).

23 *Securities Market Weekly* 48 (1993) (in Chinese).

24 See Jiangdong Jin, Xiao Shuoji, and Xu Shuxing, in publication of the Securities Association of China, *China's Securities Market Annual Report 1991*, pp. 43–49 (in Chinese); *China's Securities Market Annual Report 1993*, p. 13 (in Chinese); and *Securities Market Weekly* 48, 51 (1993) (in Chinese).

25 *Securities Market Weekly* 56 (1994) (in Chinese).

26 See *China's Securities Market Annual Report 1993* (in Chinese); *Securities Market Weekly* 49, 51 (1993) (in Chinese).

27 *Securities Market Weekly* 56 (1994) (in Chinese).

28 *Securities Market Weekly* 46 (1993) (in Chinese).

29 *Securities Market Weekly* 46 (1993) (in Chinese).

30 *Securities Market Weekly* 45 (1993) (in Chinese).

31 "China Permits 5 Firms to List on NY Bourse," *Straits Times*, 30 April 1994.

32 For instance, in 1994 B-share turnover amounted to US $250 million a month, compared to approximately $50 million a month in 1993. Total number of B-share companies on both exchanges increased fourfold in 1994 to 58 compared to previous years. See "Capitalization of Chinese Stock Market May Top U.S. $1 Trillion," *Straits Times*, 27 February 1994.

33 See *China's Securities Market Annual Report 1993*, pp. 153 and 156–57 (in Chinese).

34 *Securities Market Weekly* 41 (1993) (in Chinese).

35 See the State Commission of Statistics, *Statistical Yearbook of China 1993* (in Chinese); and Shuping Jin, "Current Condition and Future Development of China's Stock Market," pp. 34–41 (in Chinese).

36 The government had announced plans to set up two additional stock exchanges in the near future. With recent volatility in the markets, however, the government has postponed plans to open new exchanges, pending reforms. See "Tianjin May Win Race for New Stock Exchange," *Straits Times*, 24 January 1994.

37 This ratio is significantly below similar ratios in other emerging markets. See Mullin, "Emerging Equity Markets."

38 The P/E ratios for B-shares in 1992 on the Shanghai and Shenzhen exchanges were 17.40 and 35.56. These lower multiples are due to two factors. First, there has been a large increase in the supply of B-shares. This reflects the government's desire to allow SOEs to generate greater amounts of funds from abroad. Second, these P/E ratios reflect a more realistic appraisal of the future prospects of Chinese firms on the part of foreign securities firms that deal in B-shares.

39 See Mullin, "Emerging Equity Markets"; and Michael Papaioannou and Larry Duke, "The Internationalization of Emerging Equity Markets," *Finance and Development* (September 1993): 36–39.

40 See Guandi Liu, "A Few Problems in Developing Stock Markets," *Economic Research* 3 (1993): 12–19 (in Chinese).

41 See "Beijing Rejects Shanghai Firms' Plan to Convert Some A-Shares," *Straits Times*, 1 March 1994.

42 See Hongru Liu, "Risk and Management in the Stock Market," *China's Economic Reform* 5 (1993): 33–37 (in Chinese).

43 Generally yields on individual shares are higher than yields on state and legal shares. See the article by the Bureau of Production Structure of the State Commission of Structural Reform, "Conduct of Stock Experiment according to Standardization Requirement," pp. 20–24.

44 See Fengxiang Fu, "How to Enhance the Healthy Development of the Stock Experiment and Securities Market?" *China's Economic Reform* 4 (1992): 25–27 (in Chinese); and Xiang Dai, "Normalization and Development of Legal Share Market," *Securities Market Weekly* 49 (1993), p. 38 (in Chinese).

45 See Xiang Dai, "Normalization and Development of Legal Share Market," p. 38.

46 See "Shareholders Try to Clip Wings of High-Flying Shenzhen Firm," *Straits Times*, 6 April 1994.

47 For instance, fearing stock price volatility the government has recently announced the postponement of 5.5 billion yuan worth of new issues. See "Beijing to Delay Float of 5.5 Billion Shares till Next Year," *Straits Times*, 11 May 1994.

48 See Guandi Liu, "A Few Problems in Developing Stock Markets," pp. 12–19.

49 In April 1994, the government regulatory authority reported widespread abuses in the form of stock manipulation and insider trading even within the SCCS. See "Trend Threatens China's Bourses, Warns Watchdog," *Straits Times*, 6 May 1994.

50 This growth is expected to continue. By the year 2000, the total market capitalization of the Chinese stock market is expected to grow to one trillion U.S. dollars, rivaling the London stock exchange. See "Capitalization of Chinese Stock Market May Top U.S. $1 Trillion."

51 For a discussion of other factors that cause inefficiencies in the context of emerging equity markets in developing countries, see Peter J. Drake, "Securities Markets in Less Developed Countries," *Journal of Development Studies* 33 (January 1977): 73–91.

52 See Rajen Mookerjee and Qiao Yu, "Seasonality in Stock Returns on the Chinese Stock Markets: The Case of Shanghai and Shenzhen" (Department of Economics, National University of Singapore, 1994, mimeographed); and Qiao Yu and Rajen Mookerjee, "The Emerging Equity Market in China: Structural Analysis and Market Efficiency Tests" (Department of Economics, National University of Singapore, 1994, mimeographed).

53 See "China Firms to Float $158 Million Worth of B-Shares in Shenzhen," *Straits Times*, 8 April 1994. In 1992 alone, China placed US $654 million worth of B-shares with foreign investors. See Dong Zhi, "Issues of B-Shares in Shanghai and the Function of Domestic Securities Companies," in a publication of Swiss Bank Corporation, *Shanghai Securities Market* (February 1993) (in Chinese).

54 Indeed public confidence already appears to have been negatively affected as evidenced by sharp declines in share prices and volume on both the Shanghai and Shenzhen exchanges in 1994. See "Bears in a China Shop," *Economist* (London), 14 May 1994.

Part V

FOREIGN TRADE AND FOREIGN INVESTMENT

16

THE ROLE OF FOREIGN TRADE AND INVESTMENT IN CHINA'S ECONOMIC TRANSFORMATION

Nicholas R. Lardy

In the almost two decades since economic reform began in China the role of the foreign sector has burgeoned in ways that no one anticipated. The volume of foreign trade and the role of foreign capital are both far greater than could have been foreseen based on the modest Chinese economic reforms initiated in the late 1970s. By the mid-1990s China had become one of the world's largest trading nations, the recipient of more foreign direct investment than any other country in the world, the largest borrower from the World Bank, the largest recipient of official development assistance in the form of low-interest, long-term concessionary loans from industrialized countries, and, except for the Czech Republic, the only transition economy with ready access to international capital and equity markets.

This article attempts to analyse how important foreign trade and foreign capital have been to China's growth acceleration in the reform period and to identify those institutions and policies that have been most effective in this process. It then seeks to analyse the extent to which China's experience is relevant to other transition economies.

FOREIGN CAPITAL

China has become a major participant in international capital markets. It has borrowed money from multilateral lending institutions such as the World Bank and the Asian Development Bank; from national development banks such as the Japanese Overseas Economic Co-operation Fund; from national export-import banks such as the United States Export Import Bank; and from commercial banks. In addition China has floated both debt and equity issues on international capital markets. Finally, as noted above, China has become a major recipient of foreign direct investment. Indeed, in 1993 China was the site of more foreign direct investment than any other country.[1] In 1994 gross

Source: The China Quarterly, No. 144 (December 1995), pp. 1065–82. [Reprinted in Andrew G. Walder (Editor), *China's Transitional Economy* (Oxford: Oxford University Press, 1996) pp. 103–20.]

foreign direct investment inflows into China were exceeded only by those into the United States.

Foreign direct investment

Chinese data on foreign direct investment are given in Table 16.1. The data show it grew from modest amounts of a few hundred million dollars annually in the late 1970s and early 1980s to almost four billion dollars annually in the late 1980s. Because many foreign invested projects were delayed in the aftermath of Tiananmen, actual investment showed no growth in 1990. However, beginning in 1991, China attracted greatly increased amounts of foreign direct investment. It more than doubled in both 1993 and 1994 and rose a further one-fifth in 1994 to reach almost $34 billion actual investment.

The dramatic increases in foreign direct investment in the first half of the 1990s appear to be caused by four factors. First, the magnitude of aggregate foreign direct investment flowing to developing countries increased significantly in the 1990s. Average annual flows in 1990–93 were double those of 1987–89.[2]

Table 16.1 Foreign direct investment in China, 1979–94 (millions of US$)

Year	*Contracted*	*Actual*
1979–82 (cumulative)	6,999	1,767
1983	1,917	916
1984	2,875	1,419
1985	6,333	1,959
1986	3,330	2,244
1987	4,319	2,647
1988	6,191	3,739
1989	6,294	3,773
1990	6,987	3,775
1991	12,422	4,666
1992	58,736	11,292
1993	111,435	27,514
1994	81,406	33,787

Note: The data reported above are inclusive of foreign direct investment in equity joint ventures, contractual joint ventures, wholly foreign-owned enterprises and joint exploration as well as foreign investment in leasing, compensation trade, and processing and assembly.

Sources: Ministry of Foreign Trade and Economic Relations, *Zhonghua renmin gongheguo duiwai jingjimaoyibu xinwen gongbao (The Bulletin of the Ministry of Foreign Trade and Economic Relations of the People's Republic of China)*, No. 2 (25 April 1994), p. 10. Xinhua News Service, "Zhongguo qunian liyong waizi 337 yi duo meiyuan" ("Last year China's utilized foreign direct investment exceeded US$33.7 billion"). *Jinrong shibao (Banking Times)*, 26 January 1995, p. 1.

Secondly, China's seeming political stability in the wake of Tiananmen, combined with the explosive growth of the domestic economy after 1992, led to a fundamental reassessment by foreign firms of China's economic and investment potential. China was deemed a less risky political and economic environment by risk assessment organizations such as the Economist Intelligence Unit.[3] Many multinationals decided that they could not afford not to invest in the world's fastest growing emerging market.

Thirdly, China systematically liberalized its foreign investment regime. Some of the special provisions to attract foreign direct investment, which in the late 1970s and early 1980s had only been available in the four special economic zones in South China, were made much more widely available. For example, special tax concessions, liberalized land leasing and other inducements were made available in a growing number of open coastal cities, economic development areas and high technology development zones, increasing the attractiveness of China as a site for foreign investment. China also opened up sectors such as retailing, power generation and port development that previously had been off limits for foreign investors.[4] Liberalization of foreign participation in property development in the early 1990s led to particularly significant foreign capital inflows directed toward the development of residential housing, retail complexes and other projects.

Fourthly, foreign direct investment flows increased in part because of the phenomena of recycled capital of Chinese origin. In order to take advantage of the special tax and other incentives provided to foreign invested enterprises, Chinese firms moved money off-shore and then recycled it back into China disguised as "foreign investment." The World Bank guessed that these might comprise as much as 25 per cent of gross investment inflows in 1992.[5]

Foreign borrowing

China's second largest source of foreign capital, after foreign direct investment, has been borrowing. The cumulative amount of foreign borrowing from all sources is reflected in Table 16.2. The data show China's total external debt rising from well under $1 billion in 1978, as reform was just getting under way, to $93 billion by the end of 1994. To put these numbers in perspective, only Indonesia among low and lower-middle income economies has a larger outstanding debt. China's external debt is only modestly smaller than the two most heavily indebted upper-middle income economies, Mexico and Brazil.

However, China's debt burden remains modest. In part this is because its exports are so much larger, relative to its outstanding debt, than those of Brazil and Mexico, which the World Bank classifies as moderately and severely indebted, respectively.[6] For example, on average in 1991–93 China's total external debt relative to earnings from the export of goods and services was less than half that of Mexico and less than a third that of Brazil.[7]

Table 16.2 China's external debt, 1978–94

Year	*Millions of US$*
1978	623
1979	2,183
1980	4,504
1981	5,797
1982	8,358
1983	9,609
1984	12,082
1985	16,722
1986	23,746
1987	35,296
1988	42,362
1989	33,812
1990	52,554
1991	60,851
1992	69,321
1993	83,573
1994	92,806

Sources: World Bank, *China: Macroeconomic Stability in a Decentralized Economy* (Washington, D.C.: The World Bank, 1994), p. 184. The People's Bank of China, *China Financial Outlook 1994* (Beijing; China Financial Publishing House, 1994), p. 58. Xinhua News Agency, "Woguo waizhai changzhailu he zhaiwulu diyu guoji gongren jingjie xian shuiping" ("China's external debt, debt service ratio, and debt-to-export ratio are lower than the international warning levels"), *Renmin ribao (People's Daily)*, 21 July 1995, p. 1.

In addition, a relatively large share of China's external debt is concessionary with grace periods of up to ten years before repayments of principal must begin and/or carrying below market interest rates. Even its non-concessionary debt carries favourable interest rates since China is the only transition economy, except for the Czech Republic, that enjoys an investment grade rating on its sovereign debt, allowing it to sell its bonds internationally with a lower interest rate than the market would otherwise demand.[8]

These factors reduce China's debt service, including both amortization and interest payments, below what it would otherwise be. For example, at year-end 1993, of China's total external debt of $83.6 billion, a little over $10 billion was owed to the World Bank and other multilateral lending agencies. A large share of this debt is to the World Bank's soft loan window, the International Development Association (IDA). Loans from IDA bear no interest at all and since 1989 even the initial commitment fee borrowers were once charged has been eliminated.[9] Debt from official bilateral creditors stood at almost $23 billion. Thus borrowing from private creditors on commercial terms comprised only about three-fifths of China's total external debt.

Foreign equity investment

In addition to foreign direct investment and borrowing abroad, China has sold equities for hard currency on both domestic and international markets. The market for B shares in Chinese companies, which are priced in domestic currency but paid for in hard currencies, began in 1992. In that year the B shares of nine companies were listed on the Shanghai stock exchange. Thirteen companies were listed in 1993, with ten more in 1994. By the end of 1994 the B shares of 34 Chinese companies were traded on the Shanghai and Shenzhen stock markets.

Sales of Chinese companies on international markets began in the autumn of 1992 when China Brilliance Automotive was listed on the New York Stock Exchange.[10] At about the same time the Chinese Securities Regulatory Commission approved a plan to list nine Chinese state-owned companies on the Hong Kong Stock Exchange beginning in 1993. More issues were sold in New York in 1993 and 1994. Table 16.3 shows that the proceeds from the international sale of equities and debt instruments roughly doubled in 1993 compared to the previous year. Based on sales of bonds and equity on international markets to September 1994, proceeds in 1994 probably increased by about 25 per cent over 1993.

The data summarized above suggest that China was awash in foreign capital in the mid-1990s. In 1994 gross capital inflows exceeded $53 billion, including about $17 billion in borrowing from commercial banks, international organizations, bilateral development banks and international bond

Table 16.3 China's international equity and debt issues, 1991–94 (millions of US$)

	Equity	*Debt*
1991	11	115
1992	1,049	1,289
1993	1,908	3,184
1994*	1,939	3,134

Notes: * To the end of September 1994.

The value of international equity issues is inclusive of listings of Chinese companies in New York and Hong Kong, the value of B share offerings in Shenzhen and Shanghai, and the value of so-called "back door listings" in which China-backed companies obtain a listing on the Hong Kong Stock Exchange by purchasing a relatively dormant existing listed company. The company then injects assets financed by rights issues and placements. The best examples are Citic Pacific, controlled by Beijing-based CITIC, and Guangdong Investment, controlled by the Guangdong provincial government.

Sources: Monetary Fund, *International Capital Markets: Developments, Prospects, and Policy Issues* (Washington, D.C.: International Monetary Fund, 1994), p. 127. World Bank, *World Debt Tables: External Finance for Developing Countries, 1994–95* (Washington, D.C.: The World Bank, 1994), Vol. 1, pp. 103, 116–17.

markets; $34 billion in foreign direct investment; and about $2.5 billion in equity investments. These numbers might suggest that China is heavily dependent on foreign capital to finance investment and thus to generate the rapid economic growth of the 1990s. However, this conclusion would not be warranted. After taking into account outflows of Chinese capital and changes in holdings of foreign exchange, at least to the end of 1994 foreign capital appears to have been an insignificant source of investment in China.

A quick accounting explains the paradox. First, capital inflows may be used to finance a current account deficit (when imports of goods and services exceed exports of goods and services) or may be added to the foreign exchange holdings of the government, enterprises or individuals. Secondly, capital inflows must be measured on a net basis, that is, outflows of capital must be taken into account.

The first adjustment is somewhat easier than the adjustment from gross to net. Official holdings of foreign exchange by the People's Bank of China more than doubled in 1994, from $21.2 billion at year-end 1993 to $51.6 billion at year-end 1994.[11] In addition, individual holdings of foreign exchange in the Bank of China and other banks authorized to accept foreign exchange deposits, which since August 1992 have not been included in China's official foreign exchange holdings, grew by about $6 billion in 1994.[12] Retained foreign exchange earnings of the Bank of China and other financial institutions presumably also rose. Thus, holdings of foreign exchange appear to have increased by at least $36 billion in 1994.

The adjustment from gross to net capital flows is more difficult because of incomplete information. Outflows on the capital account include amortization of previously contracted foreign debt, officially recorded foreign direct investment abroad by Chinese companies and unrecorded capital outflows. Amortization of existing debt was around $7.5 billion in 1994. Official Chinese balance of payments data, which are published with a considerable time lag, show that China's annual foreign direct investment abroad grew steadily from $20 million in 1982 to $913 million by 1991.[13] Most international observers put the actual amount considerably higher. China's foreign direct investment outflows in 1994 may have been about $5–10 billion. This would be roughly consistent with reports of the increases in the stock of Chinese foreign direct investment abroad. Chinese authorities placed cumulative Chinese investment in Hong Kong alone at $19.2 billion by the end of 1994, an amount that is far larger than could be accounted for by China's officially reported capital outflows.[14] Finally, the errors and omissions entry in the balance of payments, presumably largely reflecting unrecorded capital outflows, was $24.9 billion in 1992 and $20.9 billion in 1993.[15] Based on China's current account surplus of $7.7 billion in 1994, the estimated $36 billion increase in foreign exchange holdings, and other known or estimated components of the capital account, unrecorded capital outflows and the net capital inflow can be estimated at $7 to $12 billion and $28.7 billion, respectively.[16] Increases in holdings of foreign reserves more than absorbed net capital inflows. Thus, unless foreign direct investment outflows or unrecorded capital outflows have been overestimated there appears to have been no foreign contribution to capital formation in China in 1994.

Because of the many uncertainties surrounding entries in the capital account in China's balance of payments data, it is instructive to examine China's current account, that is, the balance on trade in goods and services. Ignoring for the moment changes in reserve holdings, any current account deficit (surplus) must be financed with a capital inflow (outflow). In short, net capital inflows must be used either to finance a current account deficit or be added to foreign exchange holdings. Thus, after adjusting for changes in holding of foreign reserves, China's net capital inflows over time can be measured by its cumulative current account deficit.

Two points emerge from an analysis of the data on China's current account deficit in Table 16.4. First, on a year-by-year basis China's current account position, whether deficit or surplus, has been relatively small. For example, even China's record current account surplus of about $13 billion in 1991 was only 3.7 per cent of GNP.[17] Moreover, the average current account deficit or

Table 16.4 China's current account, 1978–94 (millions of US$)

1978	–932
1979	–2,489
1980	–3,281
1981	1,319
1982	5,748
1983	4,487
1984	2,509
1985	–11,810
1986	–7,334
1987	300
1988	–3,802
1989	–4,316
1990	11,997
1991	13,273
1992	6,401
1993	–11,609
1994	7,669

Sources: World Bank, *China: Macroeconomic Stability in a Decentralized Economy* (Washington, D.C.: The World Bank, 1994), p. 177. International Monetary Fund, *International Financial Statistics*, June 1995), p. 166. Xinhua News Agency, "Woguo qinian guoji shouzhi zhuangkuang haozhuan" ("China's balance of payments situation improved last year"), *Renmin ribao* 18 July 1995, p. 1.

surplus over the 12-year period was less than half that of 1991. Thus, China's average annual current account position has been quite modest.

More importantly, over time China's cumulative current account position is insignificant. From the beginning of 1982 to the end of 1993 it was actually a positive $5.846 billion. This does not mean that China experienced a net outflow of capital, for changes in China's foreign exchange reserves have been ignored.

Over the same period China's total foreign exchange reserves rose by $44.2 billion.[18] Thus China's cumulative capital inflow over the period is the difference between the increase in reserves and the current account surplus or about $38.4 billion. This is a very modest amount, regardless of one's view of the degree to which using the official exchange rate to convert *yuan* to dollars understates the size of China's real GNP. Even using the official exchange rate, which results in the lowest estimate of aggregate output, China's cumulative gross domestic product from 1982 to the end of 1993 was $4,100 billion. Thus cumulative net foreign capital inflows would amount to less than one per cent of cumulative output. Purchasing power parity estimates of Chinese output in 1990 place GDP at from 3.5 to 8 times the level calculated on the exchange rate.[19] If the same relationship holds over the entire period, China's cumulative net capital inflow over 12 years could have been as low as one-tenth of one per cent of Chinese GDP. In short, cumulative net foreign capital inflow relative to cumulative output of the Chinese economy over the 12 years was less than one per cent and may have been vanishingly small.

The same point is borne out by examining data on the relative importance of net foreign savings and gross national saving in financing gross domestic investment. Data for selective years are shown in Table 16.5. They show that the contribution of net foreign savings to gross domestic investment varies; in some years it is positive and in others negative. Thus, contrary to what one might believe from observing the flood of foreign capital flowing into China, on a net basis such inflows have not contributed to domestic capital formation in China.

Although foreign capital has not made a major impact on China's savings-investment balance, it has contributed significantly to the transfer to China of advanced technology and managerial practices in many industries; to the expansion of China's trade; and indirectly to the supply of foreign exchange.

Table 16.5 Investment and savings, selected years (% gross domestic product)

	1980	*1990*	*1991*	*1992*	*1993*
Gross domestic investment	30	35	35	38	43
Gross national savings	28	38	39	39	40
Net foreign savings	2	–3	–4	–2	2

Source: World Bank, *China: Macroeconomic Stability in a Decentralized Economy*, p. 8.

Effect on foreign trade

The transforming effect of foreign investment on China's economy is revealed in Table 16.6, which shows exports generated by foreign invested enterprises. The small amounts of foreign direct investment in the late 1970s and early 1980s initially made a negligible contribution to China's total exports. As late as 1985, six years after the passage of China's foreign investment law and five years after the establishment of special economic zones, the exports of foreign invested enterprises were only $320 million, barely over one per cent of China's total exports. From that modest base they expanded dramatically, reaching about $35 billion by 1994, almost 30 per cent of China's total exports.

Exports produced by foreign invested firms are predominantly products assembled from imported parts and components. In addition, many Chinese firms also produce processed exports using parts and components supplied by or purchased from foreign firms. Total processed exports grew to $57 billion in 1994, almost half of China's exports.[20] They comprised about 60 per cent of $100 billion in manufactured goods exports that year. In recent years about half of these exports have been produced by foreign-funded firms.

Effect on the supply of foreign exchange

Under the provisions of China's foreign exchange control system, foreign-funded enterprises have had full control of their foreign exchange earnings

Table 16.6 Exports of foreign invested enterprises, 1985–94

Year	*Millions of US$*	*Percentage of total exports*
1985	320	1.1
1986	480	1.6
1987	1,200	3.0
1988	2,460	5.2
1989	4,920	8.3
1990	7,800	12.5
1991	12,100	16.8
1992	17,400	20.4
1993	25,240	27.5
1994	34,710	28.7

Note: Exports are inclusive of those produced by equity joint ventures, contractual joint ventures, and wholly foreign-owned firms.

Sources: Nicholas R. Lardy, "Chinese foreign trade," *The China Quarterly*, No. 131 (September 1992), p. 711. New China News Agency, "Zhongguo duiwai maoyi zongjhine qunian zengzhi 1957 yi meiyuan" ("China's foreign trade increases to reach $195.7 billion"), *Renmin ribao*, 10 January 1994. Li Xiaolei, "Sanzi qiye waimao jinchukou zengjia" ("foreign trade imports and exports of foreign invested enterprises increase"), *Renmin ribao*, 18 January 1995, p. 1.

from exports throughout the reform period. Most importantly, a very large share of the exports of foreign-funded enterprises are processed products such as machinery, electronics and garments. Export earnings are largely used to pay for imported components and assemblies used in the production of these goods. For example, in 1994 foreign-funded firms exported $30.58 billion in processed products but imports of parts, components and the equipment needed to carry out the processing amounted to $28.09 billion.[21]

Despite their heavy expenditures on imported parts and components, foreign-funded firms generally have been net sellers of foreign exchange, first through informal markets and, since 1985, in the swap markets for foreign exchange. Their net sales of foreign exchange rose from $442 million in 1988 to more than $3 billion in 1994.[22]

FOREIGN TRADE

More outwardly oriented economies usually achieve higher rates of savings and investment, and greater efficiency in the use of investment resources, both of which contribute to higher rates of growth. Efficiency gains may accrue not only from economies of scale but, more importantly, from the stimulus that international competition provides for technical change and managerial efficiencies.[23] The World Bank in particular believes that success in the promotion of manufactured exports provides a powerful mechanism for technological upgrading and thus a source of rapid productivity growth in the high performing economies of East Asia.[24]

The pace of growth of Chinese exports shown in Table 16.7, particularly manufactured exports, compares quite favourably with the countries the World Bank has identified as the high performing economies of East Asia. Not only have China's exports grown more rapidly than those of any other country, the commodity composition has shifted decisively toward manufactured goods. By 1994 China exported manufactured goods worth more than $100 billion and was probably the eighth largest such exporter in the world. At growth rates observed in recent years, by the year 2000 China's exports of manufactured goods will surpass those of the United Kingdom.

What is less clear is whether this growth has stimulated the postulated improvement in productivity in manufacturing that was characteristic of the other high performing economies in East Asia. If enhanced productivity had spread to the state-owned industrial sector, this presumably would be reflected in evidence of increasing ability to compete with foreign firms either in international or domestic markets.

As already suggested, the most impressive export performance in China has been by foreign-funded enterprises and Chinese firms engaged in export processing. For the most part the latter appear to be township and village enterprises rather than state-owned enterprises. Although exports of state-owned manufacturing firms have grown significantly, their contribution to export

Table 16.7 Chinese exports, 1978–94

Year	*Exports billions of $*	*Of which manufactured exports*	
		Billions of $	*% of total exports*
1978	9.8	—	—
1979	13.7	—	—
1980	18.2	9,005	49.7
1981	22.0	11,756	53.4
1982	22.3	12,271	55.0
1983	22.2	12,606	56.7
1984	26.1	14,205	54.3
1985	27.4	13,552	49.4
1986	30.9	19,670	63.6
1987	39.4	26,206	66.5
1988	47.5	33,110	69.7
1989	52.5	37,460	71.3
1990	62.1	46,205	74.4
1991	71.8	55,698	77.5
1992	85.0	67,948	79.9
1993	91.8	75,090	81.8
1994	121.0	101,330	83.7

Note: Data for 1978 and 1979 were compiled by the Ministry of Foreign Economic Relations and Trade. A breakdown of manufactured goods for these years is not available since the Ministry combined data on exports of manufactures and mineral products in a single category.

Sources: State Statistical Bureau, *Zhongguo tongji nianjian 1993 (Chinese Statistical Yearbook 1993)* (Beijing: State Statistical Publishing House, 1993), p. 634. "Wo waimao jinchukou zaichuang jiaji" ("China's foreign trade again achieves fine results"), *Renmin ribao*, 14 January 1995, p. 1.

growth looks quite modest when measured against the share of manufactured goods that they produce. State-owned firms, which produced two-thirds of all manufactured goods in 1985, have contributed a rapidly declining share of annual incremental exports. In 1986 and 1987 they accounted for more than four-fifths of the growth of exports; in 1991–92, when they still accounted for fully half of all manufactured goods production, their contribution was only a fifth.[25]

Foreign invested enterprises contribute such a small share of total manufactured goods output that they are not even listed as a separate category in the industrial output data published by the State Statistical Bureau in its annual *Statistical Yearbook of China*. The output of foreign-funded enterprises, along with that produced by firms with a variety of less important forms of ownership, is included in the category "other," which expanded from about one per cent of output in 1985 to 7 per cent by 1992.[26] Yet the contribution of foreign-funded enterprises to annual incremental exports rose from 4 per cent in 1986 to an average of three-fifths in 1992–94. By 1994 foreign-funded enterprises accounted for 15 times more exports than would have been expected on the basis of their contribution to output.[27] In short, it is not easy to make the case that state-owned firms have become increasingly successful competitors in the international market.

What about in domestic markets? To what extent are state-owned manufacturing firms successfully competing with foreign firms in the Chinese market? A fully satisfactory answer to this question lies well beyond the scope of this article. However, some important evidence, such as the structure of tariff and non-tariff protection that insulates Chinese industry from international competition, does exist.

A World Bank study of China's trade regime showed that Chinese import tariffs in 1992 were relatively high by international standards, particularly for manufactured consumer goods.[28] In addition, China imposes a variety of non-tariff barriers including a mandatory import plan, canalization of imports and import licensing. The sectors with the highest concentration of these non-tariff barriers are iron and steel products, textile yarns and machinery.[29]

An evaluation that takes into account the high degree of dispersion of China's nominal import tariff levels is even more revealing. Economists have long noted that if tariffs are below average on primary and intermediate goods then the effective rate of protection afforded to the final good will be substantially above the nominal tariff rate applied to that good. The World Bank's analysis of effective rates of protection showed that value added at international prices was negative in 10 of 19 sectors examined, including petroleum refining, machinery, building materials, wood and pulp, food processing, textiles, apparel, paper, and miscellaneous manufactures. This means that under the assumptions of the model "none of these activities would appear to be able to survive under full trade liberalization."[30] The study quickly adds that, because the analysis is based on quite aggregate categories, it would be incorrect to assume that the production of every good in each of these sectors would wither if subject to the full force of international competition. But the results are "indicative of the highly distorted nature of the Chinese trade regime."[31]

Moreover, even some major industries that have positive value added at international prices are heavily insulated from international competition. For example the chemical industry, China's fourth largest, receives an effective rate of protection from imports of more than 110 per cent.[32] It is difficult to envisage that this industry has begun to feel the effects of international competition.

Chinese assessments of the challenge that would be presented by the reduction of tariff and non-tariff protection that presumably would accompany its participation in the General Agreement on Tariffs and Trade (GATT) generally confirms the analysis of the World Bank. An authoritative analysis of the State Planning Commission's Economic Research Institute reported that if China were to accede to the GATT, "the branches of industry that would take the greatest pounding, in order, are the electronics industry (computers, video cameras, xerographic copiers, colour television tubes, cameras, and broadcast and communications equipment), motor vehicles and trucks, petroleum refining, numerically controlled machine tools, and instruments."[33]

In short, the partial evidence that is available suggests that state-owned industries have not participated proportionately in the growth of China's exports. Since they are heavily insulated from international competition, they also appear ill-prepared to compete with foreign firms in China's domestic market. Thus if productivity has been rising in the state-owned sector in China, it would appear to be stimulated by processes that are quite different from those that were important in other high performing economies in East Asia.

CHINA'S TRADE REFORM STRATEGY IN COMPARATIVE PERSPECTIVE

Any comparative assessment of China's foreign trade and investment reform strategy needs to take into account two respects in which China differed fundamentally from many other transition economies. First, China was never a formal member of the Council of Mutual Economic Assistance (CMEA) and at the time economic reform began in China it had been trading predominantly with Western market economies for almost two decades. Thus it avoided the major disruption of trade associated with the collapse of intra-CMEA trade in the early 1990s, which followed the formal introduction of convertible currency settlements in world prices on 1 January 1991 and the decision to dissolve CMEA in June 1991.[34] In the case of Russia, exports to former CMEA countries fell by more than three-quarters between 1990 and 1992 and imports fell by five-sixths.[35] The collapse of intra-CMEA trade, in turn, was one of the most important factors leading to declining real output in Russia and Eastern Europe.

Secondly, China began its economic reform with virtually no external debt. It had imposed a policy of extreme financial self-reliance, right up until the time economic reform began. Its trade with the rest of the world was small and imports were all financed by export earnings. Thus China had not borrowed significant amounts on international markets.[36]

By contrast the former Soviet Union under Gorbachev between 1987 and 1991 had borrowed heavily from the West to finance its budget deficit. External debt shot up from $14.2 billion at the end of 1984 to $56.5 billion by the end of 1991.[37] However, this borrowing was utilized largely to finance current consumption rather than investment that would contribute to Soviet export earnings. As a result, as early as 1989 the USSR began to delay repayment of some external obligations. By the end of 1991, when Russia had become an independent sovereign entity, its unpaid international obligations were around $6 billion.[38] Although it was already in default on its debt, Russia assumed responsibility for almost all the debts of the former Soviet

Union which, it was revealed in late 1994, meant year-end 1991 total external indebtedness was $103.9 billion. As a result of IMF and World Bank lending and modest amounts of official commodity credits from Western governments, by mid-1995 Russian external debt amounted to $130 billion.[39] Since this was more than twice the value of its exports outside the FSU, Russia sought to reach an agreement on rescheduling payments on outstanding debts from the Soviet era, which would presumably facilitate its return to international debt markets. In short, Russia was handicapped in its transition since its huge existing prior debt plus falling exports meant that debt rescheduling, if not default, was almost inevitable. That in turn deprived Russia of access to commercial credit in the early years of its economic transition.

China's strategy of external reform was quite gradual. Key institutional reforms, such as ending the monopoly powers of state-owned trading companies, were phased in over more than a decade.[40] Even as late as 1993 only 839 Chinese manufacturing companies had been granted the right to trade directly in the international market.[41] By contrast in Russia all firms were given the right of direct international trade almost from the outset of reform in January 1992.[42] Similarly the process of convergence of Chinese domestic with international prices for traded goods lasted well into the 1990s whereas, with a few exceptions, prices were liberalized in Russia within a year or so of the break-up of the Soviet Union. The story is similar on import subsidies. As a percentage of gross domestic product they were initially much larger in Russia, but they were abolished in 1994. In China they persisted well beyond the first decade of reform.

China's comparatively gradualistic approach in the external sector was appropriate, given its initial economic conditions and the slow pace of reform in the domestic economy, particularly in the state-owned manufacturing sector. The immediate freeing of all prices in an environment in which state-owned enterprises were still not subject to hard budget constraints would have led, as it did in Russia, to skyrocketing prices for industrial goods. For the same reason moving rapidly to current account convertibility would have caused massive excessive devaluation of the *renminbi*. In short, application of the Russian model in China probably would have created severe macroeconomic imbalances.[43]

The challenge China faces now is to co-ordinate the further liberalization of its trade regime, particularly reducing various barriers to imports, with the reform of the state-owned sector, especially in manufacturing. Subsidies to state-owned enterprises, increasingly in the form of bank loans that are not repaid, absorbed about 10 per cent of gross domestic product in 1993, "an unsustainable structural situation" according to the World Bank.[44] Reform in the state-owned sector will require a substantial degree of industrial restructuring, a process that has been largely postponed.[45] Liberalization of China's import regime, which would subject Chinese firms to increasing international competition, should be an important tool to facilitate industrial restructuring.

CONCLUSION

Despite the impressive expansion of exports, large inflows of foreign direct investment and access to international capital markets that is unparalleled among transition economies, it is still premature to judge that China's external sector reforms have been a stunning success in comparison with others. China has had rapid export growth, but this has depended to an unprecedented degree on foreign invested firms. There is nothing wrong with reliance on foreign-funded enterprises, *per se*. But, combined with the protection provided to state-owned industries, it has inhibited productivity growth, especially in intermediate input industries where prices are still above international levels.[46] Thus rapid export growth from foreign invested firms, a large share of which is export processing, has limited backward linkages and the domestic content of exports is very low. To some extent export industries appear to be enclaves and China's state-owned industries have underparticipated in export growth by a wide margin. Over the longer term it will be difficult for China to sustain the growth of exports at a rate anywhere near that of the past decade unless there is widespread industrial restructuring.

China in recent years has attracted far more foreign direct investment than all the other transition economies combined. But, as already noted above, such investment in China is substantially overstated because of the recycling phenomenon. Moreover, the real difference that remains after correcting for this factor may reflect primarily the relatively early stage of the economic transitions of the former Soviet Union and Eastern Europe. As the data in Table 16.1 reflect, foreign direct investment in China in the first decade of reform was quite modest compared to the inflows recorded in the early 1990s. Foreign direct investment in the six countries of Eastern Europe was $2.4 billion, $3.3 billion and $5.0 billion in 1991–93, amounts that compare quite favourably with direct foreign investment in China at a comparable stage of its transition a decade earlier.[47]

Finally, China's better access to international capital markets was at least partially due to its lack of pre-reform borrowing. At the outset of their reforms Russia, Bulgaria and Poland struggled to generate trade surpluses in order to service debts accrued under old regimes. Ultimately they defaulted and so access to international capital markets was limited to debt restructurings, lending by international organizations and credits extended by Western governments to promote their own exports. By contrast China, with ready access to international borrowing, enjoyed the luxury of running relatively large trade deficits in the first three years of economic reform.[48]

Moreover, China's access to international capital has improved over time. The sale of equities on international markets, for example, did not start until

1992 and bond sales were relatively modest until the same year.[49] Again that suggests, as in the case of foreign direct investment, that the access to international capital markets of other transition economies may compare more favourably to China after their reforms are a decade and a half old.

NOTES

1 World Bank, *World Debt Tables: External Finance for Developing Countries, 1994–95* (Washington, D.C.: The World Bank, 1994), Vol. 1, p. 16.

2 *Ibid.* p. 159.

3 On a scale in which 100 is the riskiest rating, China rated 15 in 1988, one of the EIU's lowest risk ratings. This jumped to 35 in 1989 but by 1992 had fallen back to 25. *The Economist*, 21 May 1994, p. 120.

4 Nicholas R. Lardy, *China in the World Economy* (Washington, D.C.: Institute for International Economics, 1994), pp. 63–71.

5 Peter Harrold and Rajiv Lall, *China. Reform and Development in 1992–93*, World Bank Discussion Paper No. 215 (Washington, D.C.: The World Bank, August 1993), p. 24.

6 Severely indebted countries are those for which either the ratio of the present value of debt service to GNP exceeds 80% or the ratio of the present value of debt service to exports of goods and services exceeds 220%. For moderately indebted countries the ranges of the values of these variables is from 48 to 80% and from 132 to 220% respectively.

7 World Bank, *World Debt Tables 1994–95*, Vol. 1, pp. 55–56.

8 Moody's rates China's long-term sovereign debt at A3 while Standard and Poor's gives a rating of BBB. Both are investment grade ratings. Other transition economies that have rated sovereign debt, but which have been assigned below investment grade ratings, are Hungary and Slovakia. *Transition*, Vol. 5, No. 9 (November-December) 1994, p. 13. Both agencies initially assigned ratings to the Bank of China, the Industrial and Commercial Bank, the People's Construction Bank of China, the Bank of Communications, China International Trust and Investment Company (CITIC), and the Guangdong International Trust and Investment Company (GITIC) that were identical to those they gave to China's sovereign debt. However, in April 1995 Moody's downgraded the first four of these to Baa. Prior to that it had watchlisted CITIC for a potential downgrade. Although Baa is still an investment grade rating, the downgrade led the Bank of China to cancel a HK$5 billion floating rate certificate of deposit issue.

9 Technically the fee is still set annually by the Executive Directors of the World Bank. But it has been set at zero from fiscal year 1989 to fiscal year 1995.

10 Technically China Brilliance Automotive Holdings Limited is a Bermuda-based holding company, not a Chinese company. However, since the holding company's only asset is a 51% ownership in the Shenyang Jinbei Passenger Vehicle Manufacturing Company, Ltd., for practical purposes it may be regarded as a Chinese company. The holding company was established in 1992, only a few months before the initial public offering of the stock on the New York Stock Exchange. According to some sources the Bermuda holding company was created simply to escape the approvals required by China's Securities Regulatory Commission for overseas listings of Chinese firms.

11 Zhu Baihua and Ou Yangwei, "Zhongguo waihui chubei yu wubai yi meiyuan" ("China's foreign exchange reserves exceed $US50 billion"), *Renmin ribao* (*People's Daily*), 28 January 1995, p. 1.

12 Personal savings in foreign exchange denominated accounts amounted to some $20 billion at the end of 1994. "BOC says $20b saved in foreign currency," *China Daily*, 11 January 1995, p. 7.

13 State Statistical Bureau, *1979–1991 Zhongguo duiwai jingji tongji daquan* (*1979–1991 China Foreign Economic Statistics*) (Beijing: Chinese Statistical Publishing House, 1993), pp. 9–11.

14 New China News Agency, Hong Kong Branch quoted in Hong Kong Economic and Trade Office, *Hong Kong Digest Issue No. 1/95*, pp. 5–6.

15 World Bank, *China: Macroeconomic Stability in a Decentralized Economy* (Washington, D.C.: The World Bank, 1994), p. 14.

16 Net capital inflow equals changes in reserves ($36.4 billion) minus current account surplus ($7.7 billion). Unrecorded capital outflows estimated from: gross capital inflow ($53.2 billion) minus gross capital outflow equals net capital inflow ($28.7 billion) where gross capital outflow is the sum of amortization ($7.5 billion), Chinese foreign direct investment abroad ($5–10 billion) and unrecorded capital outflows.

17 World Bank, *China: Macroeconomic Stability in a Decentralized Economy*, p. 14. Even this calculation, since it utilizes the official exchange rate to convert China's GNP in *yuan* into U.S. dollars, overstates the magnitude of the surplus. Taking into account the real purchasing power of the Chinese currency, China's estimated GNP would be at least three times higher and the current account surplus as a percentage of GNP only one-third, or even less, than the 3.7% estimate.

18 Based on estimated total reserves of $49 billion at year-end 1993 and the official figure of $4.773 billion for year-end 1981. Chinese Finance and Banking Society, *1993 Zhongguo jinrong nianjian* (*Almanac of China's Finance and Banking 1993*) (Beijing: Zhongguo jinrong nianjian bianjibu (Chinese Finance and Banking Compilation Department), 1993), p. 368.

19 Lardy, *China in the World Economy*, p. 15.

20 "Wo jiagong maoyi jinchukou qunian tupo qianyi meiyuan" ("China's import and export processing trade broke through the level of US$100 billion last year"), *Renmin ribao*, 23 January 1995, p. 1.

21 "Processed goods lead exports to new high," *China Daily*, 24 January 1995, p. 5.

22 Nicholas R. Lardy, *Foreign Trade and Economic Reform in China, 1978–1990* (New York: Cambridge University Press, 1992), p. 61. Zhu Baihua, "Wo waihui tizhi gaige qujian chengxiao" ("A preliminary view of the results of China's foreign exchange system reform"), *Renmin ribao*, 20 January 1995, p. 1.

23 Gershon Feder, "On exports and economic growth," *Journal of Development Economics*, No. 1–2 (1983), pp. 60–61.

24 World Bank, *The East Asian Miracle: Economic Growth and Public Policy* (Oxford: Oxford University Press, 1993), pp. 22–23.

25 Thomas G. Rawski, "Export performance of China's state industries." unpublished manuscript, March 1994, Table 3.

26 State Statistical Bureau, *Zhongguo tongji nianjian 1993* (*Statistical Yearbook of China 1993*) (Beijing: Chinese Statistical Publishing House, 1993), p. 409. The note defining the scope of the category "other" is at p. 471.

27 Based on the estimate that they account for 2% of manufactured goods output.

28 World Bank, *China: Foreign Trade Reform* (Washington, D.C.: The World Bank, 1994), pp. 55–56.

29 *Ibid.* p. 67.

30 *Ibid.* p. 75.

31 *Ibid.* p. 75.

32 *Ibid.* p. 74.

33 State Planning Commission Economics Research Institute Task Force, "Dui huifu guanmao zongxieding diwei hou de xiaoyi fenxi he duice" ("An effective analysis and countermeasures after China resumes its place in the General Agreement on Tariffs and Trade"), *Guoji maoyi* (*International Trade*), No. 2 (1993), p. 10.

34 Harriet Matejka, "Post-CMEA trade and payments arrangements in the East," in Jozef M. van Brabant (ed.), *The New Eastern Europe and the World Economy* (Boulder, CO: Westview, 1993), p. 63.

35 Anders Aslund, *How Russia Became a Market Economy* (Washington, D.C.: The Brookings Institution, 1995), p. 46.

36 China's borrowing in the pre-reform period was limited to short-term trade financing.

37 Aslund, *How Russia Became a Market Economy*, p. 49.

38 *Ibid.* p. 50.

39 John Thornhill and Andrew Fisher, "Russia pleads for easier payment of Soviet debts," *The Financial Times*, 6 July 1995, p. 2.

40 Lardy, *Foreign Trade and Economic Reform*, pp. 39–41.

41 "The Ministry of Foreign Economic Relations and Trade quickens the approval of foreign trading rights of production enterprises," *Guoji shangbao* (*International Business*), 9 February 1993, p. 1. At the end of 1992 China had 8.61 million industrial enterprises of which 1.03 million were state-owned.

42 Aslund, *How Russia Became a Market Economy*, p. 147.

43 Ronald I. McKinnon, *The Order of Economic Liberalization: Financial Control in the Transition to a Market Economy* (Baltimore: The Johns Hopkins University Press, 1993), pp. 217–225.

44 Harry Broadman, *Meeting the Challenge of Chinese Enterprise Reform*, World Bank Discussion Paper No. 283 (Washington, D.C.: The World Bank, 1995), pp. 15–16.

45 Nicholas R. Lardy, "Trade expansion and domestic structural adjustment in China, Japan, and the United States," paper presented at the Trilateral Workshop, Beijing, October 1995.

46 World Bank, *China: Foreign Trade Reform*, p. 77. Vinod Thomas, "China: assuming its role in global trading," unpublished manuscript, 1994, p. 8. World Bank, *China Updating Economic Memorandum: Managing Rapid Growth and Transition* (Washington, D.C.: The World Bank, 1993), p. 55.

47 Barry P. Bosworth and Gur Ofer, *Reforming Planned Economies in an Integrating World Economy* (Washington, D.C.: The Brookings Institution, 1995), p. 140.

48 Lardy, *China in the World Economy*, p. 30.

49 *Ibid.* pp. 60–62.

17

UNRAVELLING THE MYSTERIES OF CHINA'S FOREIGN TRADE REGIME

A. Panagariya

1 INTRODUCTION

This paper provides an analytic discussion of trade policy reforms undertaken by China during 1978–90 and describes the country's trade policy regime at the end of that period. Special attention is paid to the implementation of national trade policies at provincial and city levels. This is important for understanding developments in China's external sector because, during the 1980s, provinces came to enjoy a high degree of autonomy. Specific examples at provincial and city levels are drawn from Jiangsu province and Wuxi city. Jiangsu is one of the fastest growing provinces in China; it also experienced a rapid growth in exports during the 1980s.

Four themes emerge from the paper. First, during the 1980s, China's trade policy underwent dramatic changes. Chinese authorities were persistent in initiating reforms. Moreover, once the decisions had been made at the top level, they were implemented vigorously at national, provincial, and city levels, at least in dynamic provinces such as Jiangsu. Second, China has aggressively adopted a pro-export policy on the one hand and kept a relatively tight control on imports on the other.[1] Starting in the late 1970s, Chinese authorities began to send very clear signals in favour of an export-oriented trade regime. Despite occasional reversals and incoherence in strategy, there was rarely any doubt about the long-term direction of trade policy. Export-promotion policies included, *inter alia*, geographical and sectoral targeting. The former involved the creation of Special Economic Zones and Open Cities while the latter consisted of promotion of production network for exports in selected industries. Third, purely in static terms. China's trade regime is characterised hy highly distorted prices and allocative inefficiences. Yet, the country has been highly successful in raising per capita incomes and its share in world exports. This suggests that a dynamic process triggered by an export-oriented regime overwhelmed the static allocative inefficiences. Finally, China's spectacular success in the world markets during the 1980s

Source: The World Economy, Vol. 16(1) (1993), pp. 51–68.

cannot be explained purely by its own policies; it also benefited greatly from an inflow of capital, entrepreneurship, and managerial skills from Hong Kong and Taiwan (China). This inflow brought with it crucial links to the world market. This last theme is not developed in the paper but it is an important part of the overall story.

Although a considerable literature on China's trade regime has appeared in recent years, systematic treatments of it are still limited. An important contribution is a recent book by Lardy (1992) which pulls together information from several disparate sources is Chinese and English to construct a coherent picture of China's trade regime during the 1980's and to evaluate its static efficiency. Other contributions include Hsu (1989), Sung (1990), Zhou (1987) and several papers in a two-volume study published by the Joint Economic Committee of the US Congress (1991).[2]

Unlike Lardy and others, my focus in this paper is primarily on China's export expansion policies and their implementation at the provincial and city levels. A detailed, unified treatment of this topic is still lacking in the literature and is essential if we are to eventually understand the Chinese experience. I begin in Section 2 by providing an overview of trade policy reforms during 1978–90. In Section 3, I describe briefly the major institutions involved in conducting foreign trade and foreign exchange transactions. In Section 4, I discuss policies aimed at influencing exports. In section 5, I conclude the paper by discussing the implications of the Chinese experience for other large developing countries such as India.

2 AN OVERVIEW OF TRADE REFORMS[3]

During the three decades following the founding of the People's Republic of China (PRC) in 1949, China's economic strategy was based on the philosophy of self reliance. Trade was relatively unimportant and grew rather slowly, especially in the 1950s and 1960s. As shown in Table 17.1, total trade in 1955 was $3.15 billion and grew, even in nominal terms, to a mere $4.59 billion in 1970. This compares with a total trade of $14.50 billion in August 1992 alone. During the three decades, trade flows were controlled through a centralised planning system under the Ministry of Foreign Trade (MFT). All trade was conducted by 12 centralised Foreign Trade Corporations (FTCs) organised along product lines and having branch offices in the main provinces producing or utilising their products.

Following the launching of economic reforms in December 1978, China began to open its economy to foreign trade and investment. Three major turning points can be identified. First, in July 1979, the 'Law of the PRC on Joint Ventures Using Chinese and Foreign Investment' was enacted. For the first time since 1949, this law permitted foreign investment in China. To give substance to the new policy, four Special Economic Zones (SEZs) (Shenzhen, Zhuhai, Shantou and Ziamen) were established immediately to attract

Table 17.1 Total value of exports and imports 1955–1989

		Billion US$		
Year	*Total*	*Exports*	*Imports*	*Trade balance*
1955	3.15	1.41	1.73	−0.32
1956	3.21	1.65	1.56	0.09
1957	3.10	1.60	1.51	0.09
1958	3.87	1.98	1.89	0.09
1959	4.38	2.26	2.12	0.14
1960	3.81	1.86	1.95	−0.09
1961	2.94	1.49	1.45	0.04
1962	2.66	1.49	1.17	0.32
1963	2.92	1.65	1.27	0.38
1964	3.46	1.92	1.55	0.37
1965	4.25	2.23	2.02	0.21
1966	4.61	2.37	2.25	0.12
1967	4.16	2.14	2.02	0.12
1968	4.05	2.10	1.95	0.15
1969	4.03	2.20	1.83	0.37
1970	4.59	2.26	2.33	−0.07
1971	4.84	2.64	2.21	0.43
1972	6.30	3.44	2.86	0.58
1973	10.98	5.82	5.16	0.66
1974	14.57	6.95	7.62	−0.67
1975	14.75	7.26	7.49	−0.23
1976	13.43	6.86	6.58	0.28
1977	14.80	7.59	7.21	0.38
1978	20.64	9.75	10.89	−1.14
1979	29.33	13.66	15.68	−2.02
1980	37.82	18.27	19.55	−1.28
1981	40.38	20.89	19.48	1.41
1982	39.30	21.82	17.48	4.34
1983	40.73	22.20	18.53	3.67
1984	49.77	24.42	25.36	−0.94
1985	60.25	25.92	34.33	−8.41
1986	60.10	27.01	33.08	−6.07
1987	68.11	34.71	33.40	1.31
1988	80.49	40.64	39.85	0.79
1989	82.58	43.44	39.14	4.3

Source: Almanac of China's Foreign Economic Relations and Trade 1990/91

foreign investment and boost exports. Five years later, in 1984, fourteen coastal cities and the island of Hainan were opened to foreign investors.

The liberalisation process initiated by trade reforms led to several additional developments during 1979–84. Branch offices of FTCs became relatively independent, provinces created their own FTCs to deal with specific foreign trade needs, and line ministries established their own FTCs to trade in their products. In 1979, a system of foreign exchange retention rights at the provincial and enterprise level was instituted. Import licensing, accompanied by decentralisation of the licensing-authority, was also introduced. These changes reduced the volume of trade handled by the Ministry of Foreign Economic Relations and Trade (MOFERT).[4] Trade conducted by FTCs under MOFERT's control declined from 89 per cent in 1981 to 72 per cent in 1984. The share of FTCs controlled by provinces and the line ministries increased correspondingly.

As is usually the case, the immediate effect of the opening-up strategy on the trade balance was negative. Imports expanded more rapidly than exports and what was a small merchandise trade surplus in 1977 turned into a deficit of $2 billion in 1979 and $1.3 billion in 1980 (see Table 17.1). Alarmed by this, the authorities adopted import compression measures which led to a steady decline in imports in the subsequent three years. By 1983, partly due to import compression and partly due to export expansion, a healthy trade surplus appeared and the way was paved for a new round of reforms.

The second round of reforms began in September 1984 with the approval of MOFERT's Report on Reform of the Foreign Trade System by the State Council. The general thrust of this report was to transfer power from the centre to lower levels of administration. The report recommended that FTCs be made independent of their administrative departments and be given full authority to carry out all day-to-day functions related to trade. Subject to the approval by MOFERT, large production enterprises could be allowed to handle foreign trade themselves. The report also recommended the adoption of an agency system under which FTCs were to become passive agents of enterprises and handle exports and imports for a service charge leaving enterprises responsible for profits and losses.

Changes made as a result of the 1984 report loosened MOFERT's control over imports considerably. As shown in Table 17.1, total imports jumped from $25.36 billion in 1984 to $34.33 billion in 1985. A trade deficit of over $8 billion appeared and authorities reimposed many central controls For example, types of activities in which FTCs could engage and their ability to compete against one another were brought under a more strict control of MOFERT. The system of licensing became more elaborate than before. A large number of export and import items were placed under direct control of MOFERT.[5] These changes manifest themselves in a quick brake on the growth of imports and an elimination of the deficit.

The reversals in policy did not change the general direction of China's foreign trade policy towards *export expansion*. Indeed, exports continued to expand rapidly and made it relatively easy for the country to stay on the course of liberalisation. Among other things, China targeted certain sectors for lateral economic cooperation among enterprises to boost exports. This cooperation, discussed later in greater detail, took the form of Production Networks for Export (PNEs) and export associations.

The third phase of reforms began in 1988 with the adoption of the Plan for

Restructuring the Foreign Trade System. This round of reforms stressed the implementation of the contract responsibility system, increased regional autonomy, and the deepening of integration of production and trade activities. The plan enhanced further the role of enterprises, trading companies, and provincial and local governments in foreign trade decisions.

More details on this phase will appear later when we discuss China's current export policies. Presently, we may note some additional developments in the area of trade policy. First, since 1980, the Chinese currency, renminbi, has been devalued several times with the result that the exchange rate has changed from 1.5 renminbi per US dollar in 1980 to 5.22 renminbi per US dollar in 1990.

Second, the foreign exchange retention system, introduced in 1979, has evolved considerably. Third, starting in 1988, China began opening swap centres where retained foreign exchange can be bought and sold at market clearing prices. By August 1989, a total of 90 such centres were already in operation. Finally, in recent years, China has encouraged the formation of enterprise groups along the lines of Japanese zaibatsu which combine the functions of production, trading and finance.

3 INSTITUTIONS

From the viewpoint of trade, three institutions are important: the Ministry of Foreign Economic Relations and Trade (MOFERT) which makes the major trade policy decisions, Foreign Trade Corporations (FTCs) which carry out most of the business functions in the area of trade, and the State Administration of Exchange Control (SAEC) which regulates the sources and uses of foreign exchange. Each of these is briefly discussed below.

Among other things, MOFERT decides the country's overall trade policy, formulates national export and import plans, issues licences for exports and imports of commodities under central jurisdiction, initiates trade reforms, and formulates policies with respect to imports of foreign technology and investment. In each province, MOFERT has a branch office. This office, called the provincial commission of MOFERT, is responsible for management and planning of provincial imports and exports, issuing licenses for exports and imports of commodities under provincial jurisdiction, and approval of the range of commodities to be covered by different FTCs under its jurisdiction. The provincial commission also confers the rights to trade directly on individual firms or enterprise groups within the province. There is also a branch office at the city level referred to as the municipal commission of MOFERT. Generally, this branch is under the supervision of the relevant provincial commission of MOFERT.

Foreign Trade Corporations constitute the business arm of MOFERT and, with minor exceptions, handle all of China's exports and imports. They are organised along product lines and exist at national, provincial, municipal and county levels. It is estimated that nationwide there were 5000 FTCs in operation in 1990.[6] National, provincial and municipal FTCs have the right to export directly. They also import goods for enterprises under their jurisdiction. An FTC procures goods for exports on its own and may also ask a lower-level FTC to do the same on its behalf.

The SAEC was created in 1984 to regulate the sources and uses of foreign exchange. It maintains branch offices in provinces as well as many municipalities. In addition to controlling the province's sources and uses of foreign exchange, a provincial branch is responsible for ensuring that the province's foreign exchange contract with the centre is fulfilled. Between May 1986 and March 1988, branch offices of the SAEC in most provinces also administered foreign exchange adjustment involving a transfer of retained foreign exchange of one enterprise to another. Municipal branches of SAEC perform the same functions at the city level as provincial branches at the provincial level.

In 1988. China decided to create a network of Foreign Exchange Adjustment Centres (FEACs) under SAEC.[7] The main function of FEACs, or swap centres as they are called popularly, is to facilitate the purchase and sale of retained foreign exchange at more or less a market clearing rate albeit for specific purposes within the rules laid down by the centre. Progress on establishing these centres was swift. As many as 57 were established immediately with $6.26 billion being traded there in 1988.[8] By August 1989, the number of centres had risen to 90.

4 EXPORT POLICIES

As emphasised in the introduction, a key objective of China's trade policy reform has been export expansion. Several specific policies have been adopted to achieve this objective. These include geographical targeting, sectoral targeting, direct export rights, foreign exchange retention rights, and export quotas. Policy initiatives at the local level also influence exports. Finally, there are some goods whose exports are restricted, rather than encouraged, through a system of licensing. These policies are now discussed in detail.

a. Geographical targeting: special economic zones (SEZs) and open cities

From the beginning, China has targeted coastal regions to attract foreign investment and boost exports. Four SEZs were created in 1979 in Shenzhan, Zhuhai, Shantou and Xiamen. Of these, the first three were in the Guangdong province which faces Hong Kong and the last one in the Fujian province which faces Taiwan (China).[9] Both Taiwan (China) and Hong Kong were major sources of foreign investment into China. In 1984, fourteen coastal cities and the Island of Hainan were also opened to foreign investment.

Special Economic Zones and open cities are broadly in the spirit of Export Processing Zones although they are geographically more spread out than the latter.[10] The zones and open cities offer preferential tax status to foreign investors, lower tariffs, better infrastructure, more flexible labour markets, and less bureaucratic control. The environment in the SEZs is more competitive than in other regions. The zones have also served as the experiment ground for many of China's major reforms. Often reforms that are perceived to work well in SEZs are extended to other parts of China, especially open cities.

Perhaps the most important contribution of SEZs has been to provide a focus to investment activity, both foreign and domestic. The former came mainly from Hong Kong and Taiwan (China). The zones helped China to exploit agglomeration economies resulting from concentration of several economic activities in one place and scale economies associated with the provision of infrastructure. They also helped the country to develop links with the world market, brought, in part, by Hong Kong and Taiwanese entrepreneurs. In the first ten years of operation, the cumulative direct foreign investment (DFI) into the zones has amounted to $4.1 billion. There has been an even larger quantity of domestic investment.

The record of SEZs is not entirely unblemished, however. They are often criticised for not attracting as much DFI as some other regions of the country. They have also received a larger share of domestic investment than the rest of the country. Growth in exports has often been outstripped by growth in imports leading to a deficit in trade balance.

These criticisms notwithstanding, Guangdong and Fujian where the SEZs are located have benefited overall from a relatively free and competitive environment as well as foreign investment. Although growth was slow in the initial years, during 1985–90, industrial output in these provinces has grown faster than anywhere else in China. Compared with annual growth rate of 6.9 per cent in industrial output in the rest of the economy, growth rates in Guangdong and Fujian have been 16 per cent and 14.7 per cent in real terms.

b. Sectoral targeting: production networks for exports

On a modest scale, China has also pursued a strategy of targeting sectors for export promotion. This strategy has been generally broad based and has been spread over virtually the entire industrial sector. That is to say, industry has been promoted at the expense of agriculture. Targeted sectors have included light industrial products, textiles, and machinery and electronic goods. During the late 1980s, these sectors were given higher foreign-exchange retention rights on export earnings (see Section 3*d* below). More directly, the Seventh Five Year Plan (1986–90) provided for the creation of what are called Production Networks for Exports (PNEs) to stimulate the exports of advanced enterprises within these target industries. The networks' objectives were to move into higher value added exports, improve quality, multiply categories and raise competitiveness.

The first industry group to benefit from this scheme was machinery and electronic goods. Plans for a PNE in this industry group were approved by the State Council in October 1985. Several hundred factories producing rather diverse products were selected to participate in the network. It was envisaged that the government will invest $108 million each year for five years on technical upgrading of the chosen factories. In addition, factories in the network were to be given guaranteed supplies of raw materials, power and packaging materials, preferential access to transportation, tax reductions or duty exemptions on imported equipment and materials, attractive purchase prices for their goods, and higher foreign exchange retention rights than other enterprises in the same industry. By the end of 1987, exports of ten products in the network had reached the level of $100 million or more. These products included watches, radio-cassette recorders, radios, hand tools, architectural hardware, telephones, television sets and ships.

Production Networks for Exports have also been created in light industrial products and textiles, and farm and sideline products. Recently, there has been a move to bring the export-oriented rural enterprises within the fold of PNEs.[11] Thus, in May 1990, 193 township enterprises were chosen by the national government to participate in PNEs.

From the available data, it is difficult to judge the impact of sectoral targeting primarily because it was rather broad based. Tables 17.2 and 17.3 show the composition of exports by two different classifications. According to both tables, the share of textiles and light industrial products in total exports, having declined steadily for several years, did expand significantly after 1985.[12] But the effect on the machinery sector is less clear. According to Table 17.3 which shows combined exports of machinery and transportation equipment, these exports lost ground abruptly in 1989. One thing which does come out of the two tables clearly is that the share in total exports of what appear to be labour intensive goods has gone up in the latter half of the 1980s. The share of heavy industry in total exports had shot up to 47.5 per cent and that of light industry had declined to 37.6 per cent in 1982. By 1989, these shares had reversed with the former declining to 31.9 per cent and the latter rising to 52.9 per cent. To the extent that light industry is labour intensive relative to heavy industry, this change was in accordance with China's comparative advantage.

c. Direct export rights

In recent years, China has encouraged the policy of giving direct export and import rights to qualified enterprises and enterprise groups. There were 27 such enterprises and business groups in Jiangsu in 1990. In 1989, exports by enterprises with direct export rights summed to $80 million and constituted 3.28 per cent of total provincial exports.

Table 17.2 Commodity composition of exports, 1977–1989

		Billion US $							
		1. Agricultural and sideline products		*2. Textile products*		*3. Light industrial products*		*4. Heavy industrial products*	
Year	*Total exports*	*Value*	*% of total*	*Value*	*% of total*	*Value*	*% of total*	*Value*	*% of total*
1977	7.59	2.10	27.60	1.52	20.00	1.97	26.00	2.00	26.40
1978	9.75	2.69	27.60	2.14	21.90	2.43	25.00	2.49	25.50
1979	13.66	3.16	23.10	2.88	21.10	3.27	23.90	4.36	31.90
1980	18.27	3.42	18.70	3.27	17.90	4.38	24.00	7.21	39.40
1981	20.89	3.68	17.60	3.49	16.70	4.66	22.30	9.06	43.40
1982	21.82	3.24	14.90	3.66	16.80	4.55	20.80	10.37	47.50
1983	22.20	3.53	15.90	4.18	18.80	4.95	22.30	9.54	43.00
1984	24.42	4.12	16.90	4.93	20.20	4.71	19.30	10.66	43.30
1985	25.92	4.53	17.50	5.10	19.70	5.20	20.00	11.08	42.80
1986	27.01	5.20	19.30	6.52	24.10	6.55	24.30	8.75	32.30
1987	34.71	5.88	16.90	8.20	23.60	8.98	25.90	11.65	33.60
1988	40.64	6.95	17.10	9.32	22.90	11.16	27.50	13.21	32.50
1989	43.44	6.61	15.20	10.78	24.80	12.21	28.10	13.83	31.90

Source: Almanac of China's Foreign Economic Relations and Trade 1990/91.

Table 17.3 Commodity composition of exports, 1977–1989

	Billion US $											
	Manufactured goods		*Heavy industrial and chenical products*		*Chemicals and related products*		*Products classified by materials*		*Machinery and transport equipment*		*Light industrial and textile products*	
Year	*Value*	*% of total*	*Value*	*% of total*	*Value*	*% of total*	*Value*	*% of total*	*Value*	*% of total*	*Value*	*% of total*
1977	3.53	46.4	0.85	11.2	0.18	2.4	0.37	4.89	0.30	3.9	2.67	35.2
1978	4.53	46.5	1.01	10.4	0.23	2.4	0.44	4.55	0.33	3.4	3.52	36.1
1979	6.34	46.4	1.50	11.0	0.42	3.1	0.61	4.46	0.46	3.4	4.85	35.5
1980	8.51	46.6	2.36	12.9	0.63	3.4	0.88	4.79	0.85	4.7	6.15	33.7
1981	10.53	50.4	3.80	18.2	0.70	3.3	1.32	6.33	1.78	8.5	6.74	32.2
1982	11.36	52.0	4.91	22.5	0.62	2.9	1.15	5.28	3.13	14.4	6.45	29.5
1983	11.93	53.7	4.87	21.9	0.65	2.9	0.91	4.09	3.31	14.9	7.06	31.8
1984	12.24	50.1	4.70	19.2	0.77	3.2	0.82	3.34	3.11	12.7	7.54	30.9
1985	11.88	45.8	3.61	13.9	0.60	2.3	0.82	3.15	2.19	8.5	8.28	31.9
1986	15.22	56.4	5.53	20.5	0.83	3.1	1.08	4.00	3.62	13.4	9.69	35.9
1987	21.26	61.2	7.26	20.9	0.99	2.8	1.67	4.82	4.60	13.2	14.00	40.3
1988	26.19	64.4	9.97	24.5	1.32	3.3	2.83	6.96	5.82	14.3	16.22	39.9
1989	28.35	65.3	9.32	21.4	1.53	3.5	2.67	6.16	5.11	11.8	19.04	43.8

Source: World Bank (various sources).

Direct export rights can be granted by a provincial commission of MOFERT for only those goods not subject to export licensing (i.e., goods in category three in Section 3*f*). The main criterion for obtaining these rights is that the annual value of goods exported by the enterprise through FTCs at the time of application be Y10 million or more.[13] In addition, the Commission must be satisfied with the personnel's qualifications in the area of direct trading. Within three years of the granting of export rights, *direct* exports of the enterprise must reach at least Y3 million (revised recently from Y5 million). Otherwise, the right to trade directly can be withdrawn. Exchange retention rights of these enterprises and groups are the same as of other enterprises in the industry.

d. Exchange retention rights

Yet another aspect of China's export promotion policy is an elaborate system of foreign exchange retention rights. Retained foreign exchange can be either used for imports permitted by the State or sold for specific purposes in a FEAC.[14] On the one hand, the system has served to offset partially the negative effect of low procurement prices paid by FTCs and on the other it has complemented targeting policies.

Rights to foreign exchange generated by exports are shared among the central, provincial and municipal governments, FTCs, and the enterprise responsible for exports. Until recently, the general rule was that for within-quota exports, two per cent of the foreign exchange was allocated to the exporting FTC to cover its foreign exchange costs of operation. The remaining foreign exchange was then divided between the centre and the province in the ratio 75:25. Of the province's share, 12.5 per cent went to the exporting enterprise, 7.5 per cent to the municipal commission, and 5 per cent to the provincial commission. For above-quota exports, foreign exchange was shared in the ratio 20:80 between the centre and province. The province's 80 per cent was subdivided further to give 55 per cent points to the relevant FTC, 12.5 per cent to the enterprise, 7.5 per cent to the municipal commission, and 5 per cent to the provincial enterprise. The rational behind a large share to FTCs on above-quota exports was to give them a strong incentive to export beyond their mandatory quota.

For targeted industries, the allocation of retention rights was different. In the case of light industries, arts and craft, and knitwear, the 20:80 sharing rule applied to all exports. Similarly, in machinery and electronic goods, for within quota exports, the split between the centre and provinces was 35:65. Moreover, enterprises received 21 percentage points out of the province's share rather than the 12.5 percentage points under the other two rules. Recall that light industries, machinery and electrical goods sectors have been subject to targeting by the centre.[15]

Recently, the retention rights have been revised. Since the beginning of

1991, for most commodities, 20 per cent of retention rights are allocated to the central government, 10 per cent to provincial and local governments, 10 per cent to enterprises, and 60 per cent to FTCs. This allocation is modified by a second round of transactions according to which the central government can buy up to 10 and 20 percentage points of retention rights from enterprises and FTCs, respectively, *at the exchange rate prevailing in FEACs*. Thus, ultimately, the central government can acquire up to 50 per cent of the foreign exchange generated by exports. Further details on the current sharing system are unavailable but it appears that for priority sectors such as machinery and electronic goods, retention rights are more favourable to enterprises and FTCs. It is interesting that the rights of FTCs have been kept high as an incentive to export.

e. Contracting system and export targets

China has an elaborate system of contracts to achieve its export and foreign exchange targets. All provinces are required to sign annual contracts with MOFERT specifying their export quotas, the basic amount of renminbi subsidy to be received for earning foreign exchange through exports, and foreign exchange earnings to be turned over to the centre. For example, for three years starting in January 1988, Jiangsu was to provide foreign exchange worth $700 million annually to the centre. Any foreign exchange generated by Jiangsu in excess of this amount was to be shared in the 20:80 ratio between the centre and the province.

In order to fulfil their contractual obligations to the centre, provincial commissions sign contracts with their subordinate bodies. For example, Jiangsu Commission of MOFERT signs contracts with provincial FTCs, municipal commissions under its jurisdiction and some city and county FTCs specifying their export and foreign exchange quotas. Municipal commissions sign similar contracts with FTCs both in the city and counties under their jurisdiction. All FTCs, in turn, sign contracts with enterprises, collectives and Town and Village Enterprises (TVEs).

Some provinces subject enterprises to export quotas that go well beyond what is necessitated by their contract with the centre. In Jiangsu, contracts between FTCs on the one hand and enterprises, collectives or TVEs on the other may contain three types of export targets: instructive, indicative, and market adjustable.[16] These targets are generally negotiated between the FTC and the enterprise. Instructive and indicative targets must be met commodity-by-commodity as stated in the contract whereas market adjustable targets allow a change in the mix of goods. It appears that only instructive targets are necessitated by the centre. For these targets, raw material supplies as well as purchase of the product are guaranteed. For the other two types of targets, neither of these guarantees exists. Sometimes the FTC may assist an enterprise in acquiring raw materials if it is facing difficulty in meeting its indicative target. Enterprises are free to choose an FTC for exports beyond their contractual obligation.

It is perhaps important to note that usually mandatory targets apply only to state owned enterprises. Collectives and TVEs are rarely subject to these targets. Indeed, many TVEs export without being subject to export targets. For example, in Wuxi, of approximately 700 exporting TVEs, only 400 are subject to any export targets and much fewer are subject to mandatory targets.

f. Export licensing and taxes

So far we have looked at policies aimed at export expansion. But like other countries, China also restricts exports of a selected group of commodities. This is done through a system of licensing and export taxes. Export licences are divided into three categories. MOFERT decides which commodities are included in which category. Classification of commodities into the three categories is adjusted frequently.

Category one goods are under the direct control of MOFERT. In this category, all aspects of exports including conclusion of contracts, issuing of export licences, and financing are handled by MOFERT. National FTCs have a monopoly over these exports. The list dated June 1988 had 27 commodities including rice, pork, raw silk, raw cotton, cotton yarn, grey cotton fabrics, diamonds, crude oil, coal and tungsten on this list.[17]

Category two goods are also subject to MOFERT's mandatory export plan. The main difference between this category and the previous one is that trade in this category is divided into two parts. Exports contracts are concluded at the national level while export licensing, financing and other functions are handled at local levels. Commodities in this category include items such as frozen pork, wool, toilet paper, live cattle, beef, mutton, ham, edible sugar, timber, groundnut oil, edible salt, carpet, cement, steel products, knitted grey fabrics, and bed sheets.

Category three goods include all goods not included in categories one and two. Here no export licences are required and central government involvement is minimal. Trade in commodities in this category is handled at provincial or local levels. A sizable proportion of exports fall under this category.

Several justifications are provided by authorities for restrictions on exports of the products in categories one and two. For certain commodities such as rice and crude oil, it is argued that they are staple resources and that national livelihood depends on them. For some other commodities including raw silk and raw cotton, it is felt that China has monopoly power in the world market for them. In the case of some raw material exports, the restrictions are intended to encourage exports of higher value added goods. A final possible reason is that certain goods are subject to voluntary export restraints in the world market and have to be allocated by the central government among provinces.

Export duties are levied on relatively few items. In 1985, export duties were assessed on 35 commodities with rates ranging from 10 to 60 per cent. In January 1987, the number of items subject to this tax fell to eight.

g. Export pricing policies

Depending on the good, procurement prices for exports in terms of renminbi are set by the centre, province or city. For goods in category one which are central monopoly, prices are set by the relevant central FTC. Procurement prices of goods in category three which are not subject to export restrictions are set at provincial or city levels. For category two goods, it appears that some prices are set by the centre and some by the provinces. The basis on which prices are set is not clear, however, Authorities usually claim that prices are based on production costs, although how the latter are estimated is a mystery.

Available evidence suggests that on average domestic sales prices exceed export prices paid by FTCs to enterprises for exports. In two specific cases in which we were able to obtain information, the export price was substantially below the corresponding domestic price. In one of these cases, an enterprise with direct export rights received the highest price on domestic sales, followed by direct export price and the price on exports through the FTC, in that order. According to some sources, in Jiangsu, export prices received by enterprises are on average ten per cent below the corresponding domestic prices.

This pricing policy by itself is likely to discourage exports. Presumably this is why enterprises are subject to export contracts; at export prices that are lower than domestic prices, FTCs will be unable to procure goods for exports. In all likelihood, the losses incurred by enterprises on exports are covered partially through higher prices on domestic sales. Put differently, domestic consumers provide a cross-subsidy on exports.

Recently, China has also encouraged the formation of export associations which are authorised, *inter alia*, to 'advise' FTCs on prices. The aim of these associations is to create order in export marketing by bringing competitive entities together but in practice they are likely to have effects similar to those of a cartel. Currently, five such associations exist. They cover electrical goods, electronics and machinery; cereals, oils, and foodstuffs; metals and chemicals; textiles and garments; and light industrial products, arts and crafts. Foreign Trade Corporations and enterprises with the right to export directly are supposed to join the relevant association. An enterprise or FTC which refuses to follow the association's advice can be expelled from it following which MOFERT can cancel their right to export.[18]

h. Local policies influencing exports

Our discussion up to this point may suggest that exports of provinces are more or less governed by the rules laid down by the centre and that provinces have no policy levers to influence trade flows. This is, however, untrue.

At a general level, it must be remembered that the Chinese economic system is highly decentralised now and the implementation of policy is largely under the control of provinces. For example, the centre gives mandatory targets or export quotas for only a limited number of items or in limited volumes. But in Jiangsu, contracts between FTCs and enterprises for indicative and market adjustable targets are also binding. Similarly, in spite of the existence of trade associations, FTCs seem to continue to have a great deal of power in setting export prices. As noted before, taking advantage of their monopsony power, FTCs often set these prices below the corresponding domestic prices.

Provinces and city governments have other policy instruments at their disposal. For example, within the State's guidelines, provincial and city governments decide the allocation of raw materials imported by using locally retained foreign exchange earnings among enterprises, collectives and TVEs and across different sectors. Provinces and cities also provide indirect export subsidies through the provision of critical inputs such as electric power to export oriented enterprises. Further incentives are provided in the form of higher bonuses for managers and employees on the basis of export performance. Within the guidelines laid down by the State, provinces can confer rights to trade directly upon enterprises and enterprise groups.

A further important instrument at the local level is the establishment of joint ventures between FTCs and enterprises. During the Seventh Plan, Wuxi City alone established 160 of these ventures. According to the Eighth Plan the city will establish another 200 such ventures. As Wuxi's plan is to expand TVEs in a big way, 85 per cent of these ventures will be with TVEs. Thus, Wuxi will be able to influence not only the structure of output by choosing joint ventures in priority sectors but will also enhance the role of TVEs in its economy. Capital for these ventures will come largely from bank loans and partly from retained profits of FTCs and the Foreign Trade Development Fund which is in turn funded from profits on sales of retained foreign exchange and from local taxes.

5 CONCLUDING REMARKS

In this paper, I have laid out clearly various aspects of China's export regime at the central, provincial, and city levels. This should be useful for followers of the Chinese economy because China's trading system is very complex and, to my knowledge, an up-to-date, conveniently accessible, comprehensive source describing it is not available.

From the viewpoint of static efficiency, China's trade regime is highly distorted. This is also one of the main messages of Lardy who provides a careful analysis of the available price data and concludes that domestic prices were highly distorted relative to world prices. Despite this fact, Chinese economy has grown very rapidly during the 1980s. This suggests, at least indirectly, that productivity gains from dynamic forces unleashed by the creation of an investment friendly environment and the subsequent inflow of foreign capital, entrepreneurship, technology and market links played an important role. China also benefited from the clarity of signals sent by its policy reforms. Once the reform process began, there was rarely any doubt about its direction. Provinces and cities which implemented policies were convinced that the country was heading towards greater decentralisation and export orientation.

China has come a long way since the beginning of its reform process. Its share in world exports has more than doubled during 1977–89, rising from 0.67 to 1.4 per cent. During this period, China has also experienced unprecedented growth in its real national income. What implications does this experience have for other large developing countries such as India? The most obvious lesson is that even for large developing countries, growth in exports can be an important key to development and that a reliance on domestic competition alone may be insufficient to generate large improvements in productivity. The more difficult question, however, is how countries can become competitive in the world markets.

Our discussion in this paper shows that China's strategy has been multifaceted involving both carrot and stick. On the one hand, Chinese authorities have subjected enterprises to contracts which set export quotas while on the other they have given them incentives to export by offering cheap raw materials, foreign exchange retention rights, and higher prices on domestic sales. The country has also promoted broad groups of industries via creation of production networks for exports. Most importantly, it has created a less bureaucratic and an investment friendly environment in geographically selected areas and taken advantage of Hong Kong and Taiwanese investments which were looking for a haven. These are difficult policies to replicate but at least the last one may hold some promise for countries like India. India's coastal region to the North and South of Bombay could he targeted for attracting foreign investment from East Asia as well as Western nations. Modest investments in ports and other infrastructure facilities complemented by policies which are friendly to foreign investment could turn this region into India's window to the world markets.

ACKNOWLEDGMENTS

ARVIND PANAGARIYA is from the World Bank and the University of Maryland. The findings. interpretations, and conclusions in the paper are entirely those of the author. They do not necessarily represent the views of the World Bank, its Executive Directors or the countries they represent. The author is indebted to Christine Wallich for many helpful discussions and to Jaime de Melo, Peter Harrold, Donald Keesing, Fernando Montes-Negret, Wendy Takacs and an anonymous referee for comments on an earlier draft.

NOTES

1 For instance. imports of inputs, especially for use in exports, are permitted freely but imports of consumer goods are under a very strict control.
2 The reference list in Lardy's book contains several additional contributions but these are mainly in Chinese.
3 In addition to the sources mentioned earlier, this section relies on Denny (1987), Leung (1990), Ross (1987 and 1988), and World Bank (1988 and 1990).
4 MOFERT was created in March 1982 by combining the Ministry of Foreign Trade, Ministry of Economic Relations with Foreign Countries, Import Export Commission and Foreign Investment Control Commission.
5 For further derails, see Denny (1987).
6 See Leung (1990), Ross (1987) put this number at 1,200 in 1987.
7 FEACs have existed in China since 1985. To my knowledge, the first FEAC was established in Shenszhen. See Yowell (1999).
8 See Brahm (1989).
9 In 1988. Hainan Island was also declared an SEZ. Thus, there are currently five SEZs.
10 An excellent detailed analysis of the SEZs can be found in Crane (1991). Early analyses include Falkenheim (1986) and Pepper (1986).
11 For more details on PNEs, see MOFERT (1988) and Ross (1988).
12 The rather large jump in 1986 should not be attributed entirely to the creation of PNEs. What is likely is that a decision at the centre must have led to an expansion of exports at the expense of domestic consumption. What is interesting, however, is that the larger share has been sustained over the subsequent years.
13 Chinese currency is called Renminbi and denominated in Yuan (Y). Currently, the exchange rate is Y5.2 per US dollar.
14 The central government sets priorities for purchase and sales of foreign exchange. According to the criteria prevailing in 1989, the following five items were given priority: (i) materials for agriculture (e.g., fertilizer and pesticides); (ii) necessities (e.g., rice sugar and grain); (iii) raw materials for light industry such as textiles; (iv) key projects which can generate foreign exchange for the country (e.g., central government supported projects for technical updating and renovation); and (v) joint ventures. If additional foreign exchange was available, the following three items were given the next preference: (i) science, technology, cultural exchange, medical equipment, education and sanitation; (ii) parts needed by electronic enterprises approved by the central government; and (iii) raw materials for other industrial enterprises. Six items were prohibited: (i) general consumption items (e.g., cigarettes, cosmetics, soft drinks, and clothes); (ii) luxury goods (e.g., cars, refrigerators and gold); (iii) products made domestically (e.g., machinery, electronic goods); (iv) foreign debt; (v) leasing fees to be paid abroad; and (vi) investment abroad.
15 For above-quota exports, foreign exchange rights in this sector were divided according to the same 20:80 rule applicable to other industries.

16 As far as one can ascertain, these contracts differ across provinces and what holds true for Jiangsu may not hold true for other provinces.
17 See MOFERT (1989) pp. 107–118, for a complete list of items under different categories of exports.
18 See Leung (1990).

REFERENCES

Brahm, L. J. (1989), 'The Swap Service'. *China Trade Report* (November), 8–9.

Chan, I., and M. Levy (1987), 'The New Customs Law', *China Business Review* (November–December), 45–46.

Crane, G. T. (1991), 'Reforms and Retrenchment in China's Special Economic Zones', in US Congress, Joint Economic Committee, 841–857.

Denny, D. L. (1987), 'Provincial Trade Patterns', *China Business Review*, (September–October), 18–22.

Falkenheim, V. (1986), 'China's Special Economic Zones', in US Congress, Joint Economic Committee, *China's Economy Looks to the Year 2000*, II (Washington), 348–370.

Hsu, J. C. (1989), *China's Foreign Trade Reforms: Impact on Growth and Stability* (Cambridge: Cambridge University Press).

Lardy, N. R. (1992), *Foreign Trade and Economic Reforms in China, 1978–91* (Cambridge, New York: Cambridge University Press).

Leung W. (1990), 'Consolidating Decentralization', *China Trade Report* (June) 6–7.

LoPinto, B. M. (1988). 'Fashioning a Successful Silk Industry', *China Business Review* (March–April), 54–56.

Ministry of Foreign Economic Relations and Trade, *Almanac of Foreign Economic Relations and Trade*, 1988, 1989, and 1990/91.

Pepper, S. (1986), 'China's Special Economic Zones', USFI Reports, 14.

Ross, M. C. (1987), 'Foreign Trade Offensive', *China Business Review* (July–August), 30–35.

Ross, M. C. (1988), 'Changing the Foreign Trade System', *China Business Review* (May–June) 34–36.

Sung, Y-W (1990), 'Explaining China's Export Drive: The Only Success Among Command Economies', mimeo.

US Congress, Joint Economic Committee (1991), *China's Economic Dilemmas in the 1990s: The Problems of Reforms, Modernization, and Interdependence* 2, V (Washington GPO), 713–912.

World Bank (1988), *China: External Trade and Capital* (Washington, DC).

World Bank (1990), *China: Between Plan and Market* (Washington, DC).

Yowell, D. (1988), 'Swap Center System to Expand', *China Business Review* (September–October), 10–12.

Zhou, X. (1987), *An Exploration of the Reform of the Foreign Trade System* (Beijing: Outlook Publishing House).

18

FOREIGN INVESTMENT AND ECONOMIC CHANGE IN CHINA

Y. Y. Kueh

THE CHINESE POLICY PERSPECTIVE

Foreign direct investment (FDI) in China is the most dramatic manifestation of China's open-door policy. Together with continuous import and export expansion, FD1 has increasingly exposed the Chinese economy to the western world during the past decade. There are, however, several differences between FDI and foreign trade in terms of their implications for the domestic economy. The most obvious is that FDI directly helps to relieve domestic capital supply bottlenecks and to promote employment and economic growth. By contrast, increased capital formation through imports of machinery and equipment must be financed by extra export earnings.

Within the Chinese economic context, even more important is the fact that FDI may increase interactions between the planned domestic economy and the outside world. For example, to the extent that FDI seeks to promote import substitution (that is, to substitute for direct imports in production for the domestic market), the primacy of central planning may have to give way to accommodation of foreign interests. A further practical question is how to provide for the conversion of FDI-led *Renminbi* earnings into foreign currency without eroding the system of foreign exchange control, an integral part of the economic rationale of any Soviet-style system of economic control. This is the background against which foreign exchange swapping (or regulatory) centres were increasingly established in Chinese cities in order to facilitate limited exchange of *RMB* for foreign currency among FDI ventures and chosen local enterprises, which held excessive volumes of *RMB* or foreign currency.

Such complications need not arise in circumstances in which a country's economic relations are confined to foreign trade alone. Where – as in China – imports and exports are subject to centralized control, the planned domestic economy can be largely insulated from outside interference. The central planners' main concern is that increased reliance on imports to balance critical

Source: The China Quarterly, No. 131 (September 1992), pp. 637–90. [Reprinted in Robert F. Ash and Y. Y. Kueh (Editors), *The Chinese Economy Under Deng Xiaoping* (Oxford: Oxford University Press, 1996) pp. 159–216.]

domestic supply deficits may leave central planning increasingly vulnerable to outside supplies. Any associated relaxation of import policy may eventually threaten the very *raison d'être* of the Soviet-style strategy of creating an independent, self-sufficient industrial system.

It is, however, impossible to speculate when increased dependence on imports will push the Chinese economy across the threshold of planning instability and undermine its search for long-term industrial independence. Thus it is difficult to judge whether the Chinese government's increased "openness" during the past decade in terms of foreign trade expansion means that it has already effectively abandoned the import substitution strategy (replacing imports with domestic production without FDI) in favour of an outwardly-orientated strategy of import liberalization which seeks to "link the domestic economy to the world economy in order to foster industrialization."[1] In fact, despite vigorous efforts to expand trade and court foreign capital and technology, the current Chinese strategy continues to retain many of the former Soviet policy elements: key industrial products are still largely subject to centralized distribution; their prices are officially controlled in order to ensure financial compliance with the planners' physical allocative priorities; pervasive wage, income and consumption controls, commensurate with the required high accumulation rate (currently 34 per cent of national income), remain in place to guarantee investment maximization; and state investment allocation is still strongly skewed towards the preferential growth sector of heavy industry.[2]

A corollary of this conventional Stalinist strategy is that imports are bound to be selective in order to protect central planning against outside interference. The basic elements of the established import-substitution policy have therefore remained intact, its essential hallmarks being reflected in the government's policy towards FDI. For example, foreign investors are generally expected to furnish their own machinery, equipment and – where possible – raw materials, to be combined with cheap Chinese labour to generate an output destined for export, rather than the domestic market. In other words, FDI ventures are expected to seek to balance their own foreign exchange requirements and help generate extra hard foreign currency to finance the desired import programmes.

This FDI strategy, which the former Party Secretary-General, Zhao Ziyang, referred to as "[placing] two heads outside" (*liangtou zaiwai*), that is, relying on the outside world for both input supplies and market outlet, is very different from the policy of most industrializing Asian countries, which solicit manufacturing foreign direct investment for import substitution. The essential feature of the Chinese approach is that it has simultaneously moved away from "import substitution" to "export-orientated" foreign investment, whilst retaining the basic elements of an inwardly-orientated industrialization strategy, the antithesis of opening up the vast domestic market to foreign competition. Stated in these terms, China's FDI strategy has taken the

Stalinist rationale to its ultimate conclusion. By using FDI to bring in new "hardware" and "disembodied technology" (industrial blueprints and managerial-technical know-how), the strategy has also enhanced the conventional Stalinist urge to borrow advanced technology from the west through regular import channels.[3]

Nevertheless, from the outset China apparently found it necessary to accommodate foreign interests by allowing technologically selected joint ventures to target the domestic market. Moreover, the urge to court foreign capital also prompted the Chinese authorities increasingly to compromise their established import-substitution policy, by opening up areas of hitherto strictly-controlled domestic goods and service markets to foreign direct investment.[4] The potential consequences of such opening up are quite different from those resulting from controlled relaxation of import restrictions. In addition to possible implications for foreign exchange control (see above), central planners may be compelled increasingly to accommodate requirements made by FDI ventures for domestic inputs and make price readjustments in order to make the return from privileged domestic sales conform to international levels. Those familiar with Soviet economics will know that this is inherently subversive to the entire system of central planning. Against the background of intensified American pressure on China to liberalize imports and the country's own greater readiness to accommodate GATT's requirements for membership admission,[5] the 1990s may well see the Chinese economy's integration with the western system of free trade and investment flows accelerate.

This is the background against which this study seeks to consider the impact of FDI during the coming years. The focus is primarily on the coastal provinces, which have absorbed the largest share of FDI and which are most directly exposed to western influences. In addition to FDI, consideration is given to indirect foreign investment – foreign capital essentially borrowed through government channels for investment projects. This latter category is similar to FDI to the extent that conditions are normally set down by creditors in order to guarantee an accountable return on investment. It may, however, differ from FDI in terms of capital efficiency in that any misuse of funds may be covered by the borrowing governmental authority.

The first section discusses the economic importance of the "economically opened coastal (*econocoas*) areas"[6] and suggests the reasons for their choice as recipients of foreign investment. The article then examines overall quantitative trends in foreign investment and its distribution amongst *econocoas* areas and economic sectors, before analysing the contribution of foreign investment to overall capital formation and considering its impact on output and income growth. The available statistical evidence is used to investigate the foreign trade performance of foreign-funded enterprises, with particular reference to the central problem of foreign exchange balance requirements. The final substantive section looks at future trends in foreign investment and highlights the major policy issues of the 1990s. Although the scope of the subject matter means that the discussion is frequently brief, every effort has been made to provide a rounded and integrated overview of China's foreign investment strategy.

THE *ECONOCOAS* AREAS

Table 18.1 sets out the major economic indicators of *econocoas* areas in 1987, when the Chinese strategy of seeking foreign capital was already firmly in place. The opened municipalities and counties in the 11 "opened coastal provinces" (OCPs) clearly constitute a considerable concentration of national wealth. With a population of only 19.5 per cent of the national total, they accounted for almost 40 per cent of national gross value of industrial output (GVIO), 33.45 per cent of gross domestic product and 25.91 percent of all local budget revenue. Even more remarkably, these areas absorbed a tiny fraction – 4.38 per cent – of China's land area.

It is interesting that the capital–labour ratio for all the *econocoas* areas was, at best, comparable with the national average. (Note that Table 18.1 shows their combined relative share of industrial employee in capital stock to have been 0.93.) This may reflect an underlying abundance of labour. But it also highlights the fact that these wealthy regions' capacity for capital stock expansion has been squeezed by continuous fiscal extraction by the central authorities. Thus, the percentage share of the 11 OCPs in the national accumulated local budget expenditure (12.57 per cent) was only half the size of their comparable revenue share (25.91 per cent) in 1987. This clearly points to large-scale fiscal transfers from the OCPs to provinces in the interior – and perhaps to non-opened areas within the OCPs themselves. From this point of view, China's strategy of seeking foreign capital may be interpreted as a means of assisting in the industrialization of the Chinese hinterland by diverting the major proportion of hard foreign currency returns earned in the coastal region towards the less inhabited interior provinces. If correct, this would imply a continuation of foreign exchange control and centralized regional allocation – and might pose a limit to any fully-fledged relegation of decision-making powers to local authorities in the management of foreign investment.

Considerable variations exist within *econocoas* areas. Shanghai remains the single most important contributor to budgetary revenue, following years of "extortion" by the central planners. Various per capita indicators show that the municipality is still the most advanced regional entity, in the context of both OCPs and OCCs ("opened coastal cities"). A minor exception is the measure of per worker capital endowment, in which respect Shanghai trailed marginally behind China's heavy-industrial base of Liaoning province (see Table 18.1). The differentiation amongst the 15 OCCs, implied by the above-average per capita performance indicators for the five listed major municipalities (except Qingdao) is equally revealing. Undoubtedly the entire *econocoas*

Table 18.1 Major indicators of the economically opened coastal (*econocoas*) areas in China, 1987 (value in billion *yuan* in current prices)

	No. of *xian* (1)	Land million km^2 (2)	Population (millions) (3)	GDP (4)	Local budget: Revenue (5)	Local budget: Expenditure (6)	GVIO (7)	Industrial capital (k) stock (8)	Industrial employee (millions) (9)	Relative share of: Population in: Land area (2)/(3) (10)	Relative share of: Population in: GDP (4)/(3) (11)	Relative share of: Industrial employment in: GVIO (7)/(9) (12)	Relative share of: Industrial employment in: K stock (8)/(9) (13)
4 SEZs	15	0.013	9.749	15.655	2.868	3.001	16.684	6.141	1.587	—	—	—	—
% share of													
Shenzhen	2	12.84	5.70	32.50	30.51	23.22	33.23	22.96	18.30	2.251	5.698	1.816	1.254
Zhuhai	2	16.90	4.53	10.02	9.46	9.58	7.81	14.63	3.09	3.729	2.211	2.531	4.737
Shantou	9	70.26	89.77	44.82	43.19	55.45	39.90	35.90	69.30	0.783	0.499	0.576	0.518
Xiamen	2	n.a.	n.a.	12.66	16.84	11.76	19.06	26.52	9.31	n.a.	n.a.	2.046	2.847
15 OCCs	91	0.134	87.926	183.668	37.688	16.176	272.074	118.734	19.775	—	—	—	—
% share of													
Dalian	4	9.23	5.59	6.38	5.87	7.84	6.78	10.46	5.26	1.653	1.141	1.288	1.989
Tianjin	6	8.41	9.46	11.98	14.82	19.26	13.42	19.35	11.63	0.888	1.266	1.154	1.663
Qingdao	7	8.58	13.11	9.31	5.09	5.56	8.71	n.a.	10.41	0.654	0.710	0.837	n.a.
Shanghai	11	4.71	14.21	29.70	44.86	33.29	36.01	44.51	23.22	0.332	2.090	1.551	1.917
Guangzhou	5	5.55	6.43	9.40	9.06	9.35	8.61	8.96	5.47	0.864	1.462	1.573	1.638
11 OCPs	286	0.42	210.70	369.88	60.81	30.50	545.22	283.63	39.70	—	—	—	—
% share of													
Liaoning	24	12.56	10.08	12.73	12.55	14.43	14.06	21.26	12.31	1.246	1.263	1.142	1.727
Hebei	15	4.06	3.40	2.63	1.07	1.97	2.06	3.83	3.05	1.194	0.774	0.675	1.256
Tianjin	6	2.71	3.95	5.95	9.19	10.23	6.70	8.10	5.79	0.686	1.506	1.157	1.399
Shandong	32	12.53	12.69	10.43	6.27	7.77	8.78	8.71	10.54	0.987	0.822	0.833	0.826

Table 18.1 (Cont.)

	No. of	Land million	Population		Local budget			Industrial capital (k)	Industrial employee	Relative share of: Population in: Land area	GDP	Industrial employment in: GVIO	K stock
Jiangsu	49	13.94	19.58	18.85	15.00	11.48	20.04	16.88	22.80	0.712	0.963	0.879	0.740
Shanghai	11	1.52	5.93	14.75	27.81	17.67	17.97	18.63	11.57	0.256	2.487	1.553	1.610
Zhejiang	37	10.72	12.31	11.26	10.00	7.54	12.83	7.86	14.98	0.871	0.915	0.856	0.525
Fujian	33	10.48	8.85	4.46	3.24	6.33	3.23	2.58	4.89	1.184	0.504	0.661	0.528
Guangdong	52	18.90	18.08	17.44	13.78	19.05	13.35	10.81	12.78	1.045	0.965	1.045	0.846
Hainian	19	8.13	2.92	1.51	0.49	2.20	0.40	0.80	0.67	2.784	0.517	0.597	1.194
Guangxi	8	4.47	2.22	n.a.	0.60	1.31	0.59	0.55	0.62	2.014	n.a.	0.952	0.887
PRC Total	—	9.50	1080.73	1105.42	234.66	242.69	1381.29	915.82	118.69	—	—	—	—
% share of													
SEZs	—	0.13	0.90	1.42	1.22	1.24	1.21	0.67	1.34	0.148	1.570	0.903	0.502
OCCs	—	1.40	8.14	16.62	16.06	6.67	19.70	12.96	16.66	0.172	2.042	1.182	0.778
OCPs	—	4.38	19.50	33.46	25.91	12.57	39.47	30.97	33.45	0.224	1.716	1.180	0.926

Notes:

SEZs Special Economic Zones

OCCs Opened Coastal Cities (The original list covers 14 cities, but Weihai in Shandong province was later added to give a total of 15. For the complete list see Table 7.)

OCPs Opened Coastal Provinces

GDP Gross Domestic Product

GVIO Gross Value of Industrial Output

Figures for industrial capital stock covers industrial enterprises with independent accounting (*duli hesuan gongye qiye*) only, and refer to original acquisition prices of year-end fixed assets. The 11 OCPs presumably comprise a total of 288 opened municipalities and *xians*, but the figures given for the individual OCPs add up to only 286.

Sources: State Statistical Bureau (SSB), *Yanhai yingji kaifangqu jingji vanjiu he tongji ziliao (Economic Research and Statistical Materials for the Economically Opened Coastal Areas)* (Beijing: Zhongguo tongji chubanshe, 1989), hereafter *KFQTJZL*. The data were generated from a comprehensive survey undertaken by the SSB in 1988 following the official declaration early that year to open the entire coastal region for foreign investment and trade.

complex represents a mix of highly diverse economic entities, ranging from mere rural-town settings to well-known cosmopolitan conglomerates.[7] The only characteristic shared by all 288 *econocoas* localities is their situation on or near the coastline. One may justifiably ask how such varied localities were chosen to join the enlarged group of opened areas early in 1988.

In theory, possible policy considerations ranged from the advantages of surplus labour, raw material supplies, easy transport facilities and existing conglomerate economies to the simple desire to balance regional disparities in income and living standards. In practice, the 1988 decision seems to have been conditioned by euphoria prompted by foreign investors' renewed confidence in South China and their increased interest in the OCCs in 1987–88, following the notorious setbacks of 1986.[8] No doubt it also reflected the belief that China too could emulate the successful export-led growth strategy of the "four little dragons," after the launch of Zhao Ziyang's theory of "great international circulation" in the declaration that the entire coastal strip would be opened up to foreign investment.[9]

This is not the place to examine Zhao's calculus and his perception of the world market potential to be derived from the new strategy. What is apparent is that with a total population (211 million) three times larger than that of the four little dragons, and with some 288 municipalities and *xian* (counties) opening up simultaneously, it was impossible for central or provincial authorities to concentrate domestic investment into selected areas in order to create the infrastructure necessary to attract foreign capital. The result is that many, perhaps most, of the 288 *xian* and cities have never been visited by potential investors since their designation as possible foreign capital recipients.

From this perspective, the much-publicized Pudong project in Shanghai emerges as a strategic initiative. A considerable volume of capital resources has already been committed for basic construction and the area promises to become even more "special" than any of the other five special economic zones (SEZs) and the 13 economic-technological development districts, in terms of tax concessions, tariff treatment and other preferential measures for foreign-funded enterprises.[10]

Deng Xiaoping's tour of South China from January to February 1992 and his associated call to take still bolder steps to open up China to the west have created even greater euphoria than that which existed during 1988. The consequent nation-wide scramble for foreign capital seems to indicate that virtually anyone can enter the race, even without the official endorsement of central or provincial authorities. This is contrary to the selective approach adopted in 1988, although preferential policy provisions for targeted localities, such as the SEZs and Pudong, remain the prerogative of the central government. It is true too that in line with comprehensive opening up, a number of cities along the Russian border in Heilongjiang and Xinjiang, as well as others along the Vietnamese border in Yunnan and

Guangxi, have also recently been declared open for foreign investment and trade.[11]

OVERALL TRENDS IN FOREIGN INVESTMENT

Differentiation between various categories of foreign capital will facilitate the discussion which follows. The first distinction is between foreign direct investment (FDI) and indirect investment financed by foreign borrowing or loans made by foreign governments, the World Bank, Asian Development Bank and major western private banks or bank syndicates. A second is between foreign capital taken up separately by provincial and central authorities, including the Ministries of Finance, Foreign Economic Relations and Trade, Energy and – notably – the Bank of China. The final distinction is between foreign investment or capital borrowing pledged and that actually taken up, or realized, by the investors or borrowers.

The first and third distinctions are probably familiar. But the second has a special significance in any analysis of the *econocoas* areas. This is because capital loans raised by ministries may also be applied to major projects undertaken by provincial authorities, whilst centrally-sponsored FDI projects necessarily have a provincial home base. Unfortunately, no estimates are available of the regional allocation of such central funds to make possible a more comprehensive investigation of the impact of foreign investment. Note too that most of the subsequent analysis focuses on realized foreign investment, rather than what has been contractually pledged (but not necessarily implemented).

The data contained in Table 18.2 provide measures of China's absorption (realized) of foreign capital between 1979 and 1991. They suggest a number of important findings. First, the provincial absorption of FDI has been consistently higher than that of the various central ministries. Indeed, the share of the provinces has increased in both absolute and relative terms, at the expense of the ministries. This trend reflects the delegation of decision-making powers relating to foreign investment accommodation down to the provincial level.

Secondly, similar changes favouring the provinces occurred in the absorption of foreign loans, even though during 1985–90 the ministries consistently enjoyed a substantially higher share of borrowing. It should of course be borne in mind that the ministries are representative of the state and are therefore likely to have better access to foreign governmental loans.

Thirdly, if FDI and foreign borrowing are taken together, it is clear that China's provinces (whose share rose from 36 to 53 per cent between 1985 and 1990) have gained significantly at the expense of the ministries (64 and 47 per cent, respectively). Even so, the central government, as represented by the ministries, has continued to exert important leverage in the allocation of foreign loans, with the amount under its control in 1990 (US$4,477 million) far exceeding that within the purview of the provinces (US$2,058 million).

Table 18.2 Chinese intake of foreign capital, 1979–91 (million US$)

(a) Realized loans and FDI by provincial and ministerial borrowers (percentage shares in brackets)

	Loans		*FDI*		*Total*		
	Provincial (1)	*Ministerial* (2)	*Provincial* (3)	*Ministerial* (4)	*Provincial* (1) + (3) (5)	*Ministerial* (2) + (4) (6)	*PRC total* (5) + (6) (7)
1979–84 average	—	—	476.50 (69.70)	207.16 (30.30)	—	—	—
1983	—	—	—	—	—	—	1,980.64
1984	—	—	—	—	—	—	2,704.52
1985	281.09 (11.22)	2,224.87 (88.78)	1,318.04 (67.38)	638.11 (32.62)	1,599.13 (35.84)	2,862.98 (64.16)	4,462.11 (100.00)
1986	1,033.66 (20.61)	3,980.91 (79.39)	1,741.65 (77.62)	502.08 (22.38)	2,775.31 (38.24)	4,482.99 (61.76)	7,258.30 (100.00)
1987	1,428.42 (24.61)	4,376.53 (75.39)	1,782.73 (67.36)	863.88 (32.64)	3,211.15 (37.99)	5,240.41 (62.01)	8,451.56 (100.00)
1988	2,460.20 (37.93)	4,026.53 (62.07)	3,149.69 (84.22)	589.93 (15.78)	5,609.89 (54.86)	4,616.46 (45.14)	10,226.38 (100.00)
1989	2,410.88 (38.35)	3,874.82 (61.65)	3,437.37 (91.09)	336.12 (8.91)	5,848.21 (58.14)	4,201.94 (41.86)	10,059.15 (100.00)
1990	2,057.63 (31.49)	4,476.89 (68.51)	3,436.15 (91.51)	318.79 (8.49)	5,493.78 (53.39)	4,795.61 (46.61)	10,289.39 (100.00)
1991	—	—	—	—	—	—	11,137.98

Table 18.2 (Cont.)

(b) Realized FDI by types of joint ventures (JV) (percentage shares in brackets)

	FDI total	*Equity JV*	*Contractual JV*	*Joint exploration*	*Wholly-foreign owned ventures*	*Compensation trade*	*Others*
1979–81	373.56	21.77	117.77	106.04	0.33	94.08	33.57
average	(100.00)	(5.83)	(31.53)	(28.39)	(0.09)	(25.18)	(8.99)
1982	649.27	34.29	177.77	178.52	39.31	122.40	96.98
	(100.00)	(5.28)	(27.38)	(27.50)	(6.05)	(18.85)	(14.94)
1983	915.96	73.57	227.38	291.50	42.76	197.28	83.47
	(100.00)	(8.03)	(24.82)	(31.82)	(4.67)	(21.54)	(9.11)
1984	1,418.85	254.73	465.02	522.92	14.94	98.45	62.79
	(100.00)	(17.95)	(32.77)	(36.86)	(1.05)	(6.94)	(4.43)
1985	1,956.15	579.88	585.04	480.61	12.95	168.59	129.08
	(100.00)	(29.64)	(29.91)	(24.57)	(0.66)	(8.62)	(6.60)
1986	2,243.73	804.47	793.79	260.33	16.30	181.10	187.74
	(100.00)	(35.85)	(35.38)	(11.60)	(0.73)	(8.07)	(8.37)
	2,646.61	1,485.82	619.96	183.20	24.55	222.26	110.82
	(100.00)	(56.14)	(23.42)	(6.92)	(0.93)	(8.40)	(4.19)
1988	3,739,.66	1,975.40	779.93	212.19	226.16	316.59	229.39
	(100.00)	(52.82)	(20.86)	(5.67)	(6.05)	(8.47)	(6.13)
1989	3,773.45	2,037.16	751.79	232.20	371.42	261.29	119.19
	(100.00)	(53.99)	(19.92)	(6.15)	(9.84)	(6.92)	(3.16)
1990	3,754.87	1,886.07	673.56	244.31	683.17	158.74	109.02
	(100.00)	(50.23)	(17.94)	(6.51)	(18.19)	(4.23)	(2.90)
1991	4,370.00	—	—	—	—	—	—

Notes: See text and notes to Appendix Tables 18.A1 and 18.A2 for definitions of foreign loans and FDI, and the distinction between provincial and ministerial borrowings. A detailed explanation of the different types of foreign-funded ventures and their possible behavioural implications is given in Y. Y. Kueh and Christopher Howe. "China's international trade: policy and organizational change and their place in the 'Economic Readjustment'," *The China Quarterly*, No. 100 (December 1984), pp. 834–35. The residual category of "others" in section (b) of the table represents the settlement value of equipment provided by foreign partners for purpose of "processing/assembling" (*jiagong zhuangpei*), and that of equipment leased (*guoji zulin*). "Compensation trade" is valued similarly.

Source: Appendix Tables 18.A1 and 18.A2; and *ZGTJNJ* and *JMNJ*, various issues.

Fourthly, within the total FDI intake, equity joint ventures have gained – at an accelerating pace – at the expense of contractual joint ventures to become the most important form of foreign joint venture in China. This development underlines the increasing confidence felt by foreign partners seeking to make long-term commitments, in the wake of improvements in China's legal framework and investment environment.[12]

Finally, the dramatic increases in FDI in the form of wholly foreign-owned ventures particularly reflect added confidence by foreign investors, as does the declining importance of compensation trade. Trial-and-error adjustments have probably allowed many arrangements in this latter category to be upgraded over the years to become equity or contractual joint ventures.

In short, the changes observed in Table 18.1 point in the direction of irreversible decentralization of the decision-making powers of both FDI and foreign loans to local authorities, and to the increased exposure of the Chinese economy to foreign capital.

Other aspects of the changes also indicate increased penetration by foreign capital. Figure 18.1, for example, shows that in the second half of the 1980s, as recipients of foreign capital for fixed asset investment, urban-collective enterprises have gained in importance at the expense of the state-ownership sector. Further, while the bulk of foreign capital has been allocated to new capital construction during the same period, the investment share of existing state industrial enterprises for purposes of "technical innovation and transformation" (i.e. overhaul) of old machinery and equipment has steadily increased.

Table 18.3 shows that for China as a whole, realized FDI stock grew on average by 29.67 per cent per annum during 1985–90 (33.52 per cent, if FDI sponsored by central authorities is excluded).

Notice that the choice of 1985 as base year in this instance reflects the fact that the national experiment with FDI was by this time firmly established. In any case, such growth rates attest to a very impressive performance, even with allowance for inflationary adjustments for the U.S. dollar. The corresponding growth rate for FDI and capital borrowing combined is somewhat lower (26 per cent per annum), but still constitutes a remarkable achievement.[13]

The national FDI rate of growth is overwhelmingly dominated by the performance of the 11 OCPs, which have absorbed the lion's share of the national total. For Guangdong and the four SEZs (but not Fujian) taken together, the performance does not, however, appear to be so impressive. This reflects the fact that by the mid-1980s, these pioneer *econocoas* areas had already enjoyed several years' experience of foreign capital absorption and were well-established destinations for overseas investors; it also suggests the rapid proliferation of FDI ventures into spheres outside these areas.

The data in Table 18.3 do indeed show that almost all the later-established OCPs and OCCs experienced much higher rates of growth of FDI (see in particular Liaoning, Hebei, Shandong, Shanghai, Jiangsu and Hainan). The

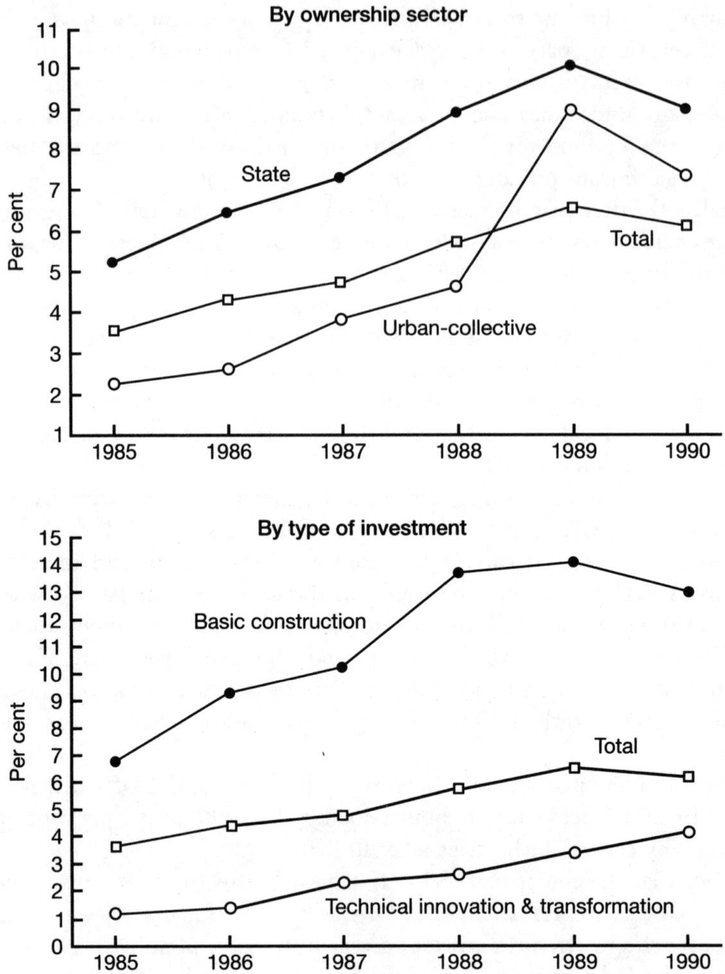

Figure 18.1 Share of Foreign Capital in Fixed Assets Investment in China, 1985–90 (per cent)

Notes: The figures refer to the percentage share in total investment in the respective ownership sectors, or types of investment, as against the shares by the state budget, domestic bank loans, and enterprises' self-raised funds.

Source: ZGTJNJ 1991, pp. 144, 145, 150, 175 and 194.

outcome (see Figure 18.2) is that after the mid-1980s, there was a definite trend towards the equalization of relative FDI shares between such pioneer *econocoas* areas as Shenzhen, and advanced municipalities such as Shanghai and Beijing whose developed economic base initially made them the most obvious destinations for foreign capital.

Following a brief slowing during 1989–90, FDI in China rapidly regained its momentum and in 1991 total realized FDI, sponsored by both provincial

Table 18.3 Growth of foreign direct investment in the *econocoas* areas in China, 1979–90 (cumulative total in million US$)

	1979–84	*1985*	*1986*	*1987*	*1988*	*1989*	*1990*	*Annual growth rate (%) 1985–90*
SEZs	895.87	1,230.64	1,711.43	2,078.89	2,520.86	3,134.04	3,789.68	25.23
Shenzhen	589.05	782.45	1,163.18	1,443.31	1,743.30	2,045.76	2,435.70	25.50
Zhuhai	246.24	299.69	344.87	378.69	426.09	479.37	548.47	12.85
Shantou	9.41	24.05	45.00	80.98	127.60	175.25	299.11	65.56
Xiamen	51.17	124.45	158.38	175.91	223.87	433.67	506.40	32.40
OCCs	472.59	747.71	1,082.06	1,559.73	2,097.10	2,823.53	3,465.69	35.90
	(472.59)	(774.24)	(1,148.38)	(1,665.45)	(2,346.31)	(3,254.93)	(4,116.32)	(39.68)
Dalian	—	14.32	44.81	94.71	169.59	250.16	451.45	99.40
Tianjin	12.87	45.38	88.19	221.32	282.47	313.89	350.82	50.54
Qingdao	—	2.30	13.03	27.03	39.36	97.37	143.25	128.49
Shanghai	123.00	230.54	379.44	593.45	826.62	1,248.74	1,425.93	43.97
Guangzhou	336.72	455.17	556.59	623.22	779.06	913.37	1,094.24	19.18
OCPs	2,120.18	3,050.12	4,161.07	5,290.07	7,221.62	9,555.15	12,266.59	32.09
	(2,256.05)	(3,326.04)	(4,628.70)	(6,104.84)	(8,330.71)	(11,117.78)	(14,043.34)	(33.39)
Liaoning	33.11	57.69	105.87	196.71	327.26	453.40	710.71	65.24

Table 18.3 (Cont.)

	1979–84	*1985*	*1986*	*1987*	*1988*	*1989*	*1990*	*Annual growth rate (%) 1985–90*
Hebei	4.95	13.19	24.46	34.80	53.90	97.63	142.10	60.87
Shandong	16.42	50.62	115.64	180.51	292.06	455.39	641.09	66.16
Jiangsu	—	33.47	67.23	153.58	279.09	406.22	540.19	74.41
Zhejiang	33.62	60.25	85.02	121.32	165.11	219.07	268.21	34.80
Fujian	69.83	188.43	250.93	306.28	451.75	799.78	1,119.67	42.82
Guangdong	1,862.27	2,491.77	3,275.39	4,006.18	5,218.44	6,541.68	8,123.99	26.66
Hainan	19.11	43.10	75.69	84.80	207.25	302.22	405.24	56.55
Guangxi	80.87	111.60	160.84	205.89	226.76	279.76	315.39	23.09
Beijing	350.00	438.82	588.53	694.32	1,197.50	1,517.66	1,796.61	32.57
Province total	2,859.02	4,177.06	5,198.71	7,701.44	10,851.17	14,288.50	17,724.65	33.52
PRC total	4,102.00	6,071.00	8,315.00	10,962.00	14,701.00	18,475.00	22,230.00	29.64

Notes: Figures in brackets for OCCs and OCPs refer respectively to the sum total for all the 15 OCCs and the 11 OCPs (including Tianjin and Shanghai). The PRC total covers FDI sponsored by the various central branch ministries (including notably offshore oil exploration), in addition to the provincial total.

The figures are all book values gross of depreciations. Figures for some areas are incomplete for 1979–84, and the total for the 15 OCCs for the same period is assumed to be the same as that for the five selected cities listed here. This means the estimated growth rate for SEZs, OCCs and OCPs does not match exactly that for their constituent areas. Where the 1979–84 total is an underestimate, especially in the case of the 15 OCCs total, the estimated growth rates for 1985–90 are clearly biased upwards. The same is true for the provincial total to the extent that the cumulative total for 1979–84 may be an underestimate (see notes to Appendix Table 18.A1). Similarly, the growth rates for those areas with incomplete figures for 1979–84 (especially Shantou, Dalian, Qingdao, Hebei, Shandong and Jiangsu) should be interpreted with care.

Source: Appendix Table 18.A1.

and central authorities, reached US$4,370 million (*cf* the low point of US$3,755 in 1990, shown in Table 18.2). If current (1992) exhortations to open up China even more are sustained, the 1990s may well witness a continuing upsurge in FDI.

REGIONAL AND INDUSTRIAL DISTRIBUTION

In terms of FDI stock accumulated since 1979, the U.S. dollar figures presented in Table 18.3 generate the following regional percentage shares in the national FDI total (FDI sponsored by the central ministries is excluded):

	1979–84	*1985*	*1986*	*1987*	*1988*	*1989*	*1990*
11 OCPs	79	80	78	79	77	78	79
of which:							
Guangdong	66	60	55	52	49	46	46
3 SEZs of Guangdong	29	26	26	25	22	19	18
Shenzhen	21	19	20	19	16	14	14

These figures highlight the importance of the 11 OCPs, but also show the special role of Guangdong and its three SEZs as recipients of FDI. It is true that the percentage share for Guangdong during 1979–84 may contain an upward bias,[14] but there is no doubt that the provincial share has declined steadily since the mid-1980s. The same applies to the three SEZs. Thus, to reiterate a point made earlier, the absorption by new *econocoas* areas of any net annual addition to FDI stock has increased at the expense of the pioneer localities.

Even so, Guangdong and its SEZs still account for the largest share of accumulated FDI stock. It is worth emphasizing that the FDI stock estimates are all expressed in terms of original acquisition prices. If adjustments could be made to deflate figures for later years, the shares of Guangdong and Shenzhen would be well in excess of the 46 and 14 per cent shown in the table. The importance of Shenzhen is highlighted by the fact that in almost all the years under investigation, its FDI intake was no less than that of any single province or municipality, including Shanghai and Beijing.[15] The comparison with nearby Guangzhou (Guangdong's provincial capital, only 60 miles north of Shenzhen) is even more telling. The SEZ's receipt of FDI, whether calculated in terms of net annual additions or accumulated total, has consistently been twice as high as that of Guangzhou. It is, however, clear that Shenzhen's prosperity derives overwhelmingly from its propinquity to Hong Kong – which raises the question of whether its example can ever be emulated by other new FDI frontiers within China.

The regional distribution of FDI also reveals that the relative share of the 11 OCPs in the national stock total has remained constant (around 80 per

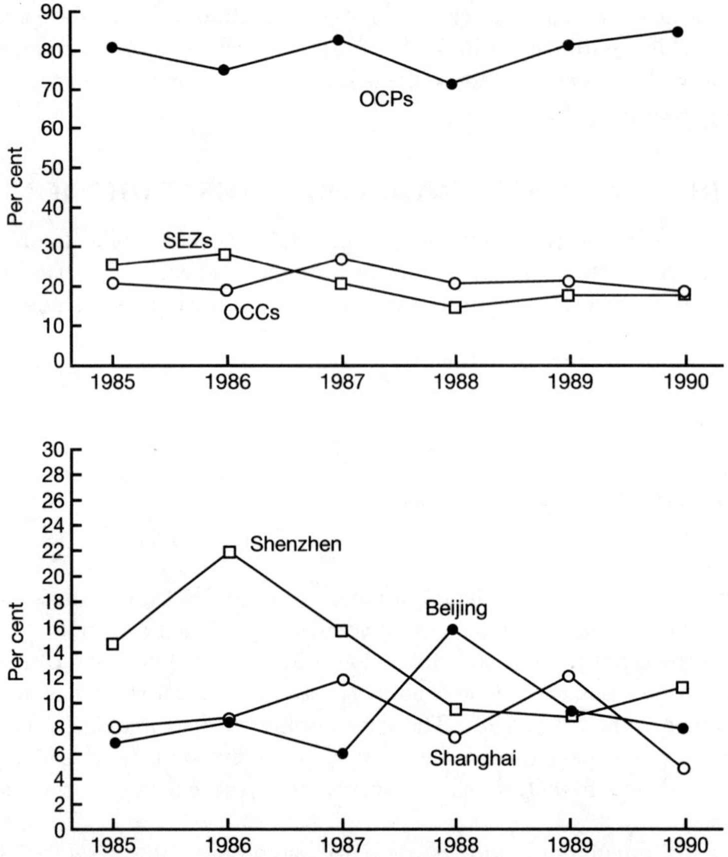

Figure 18.2 Share of Beijing and the *Econocoas* Areas in Foreign Investment in China, 1985–90 (%)

cent) during 1979–90. If adjustments were made for inflationary pressures, this figure would have been even higher by the late 1980s. This suggests that the observed regional redistribution of FDI reflects a shift from the south along the coast to new northern frontiers, rather than from coastal to interior provinces. Such a development has occurred in spite of inland provinces' desire to share in foreign investors' increased enthusiasm for investment in China.

Thus, locational benefits appear to be a prime consideration for foreign investors contemplating participation in any FDI venture in China. In the fierce scramble to secure foreign capital, many municipalities have sought to by-pass central regulations by offering potential overseas investors additional benefits such as concessions on land rentals, labour charges and other local levies, both legal and illegal. Such preferential treatment often outweighs the advantage which the status of being an SEZ confers over other areas

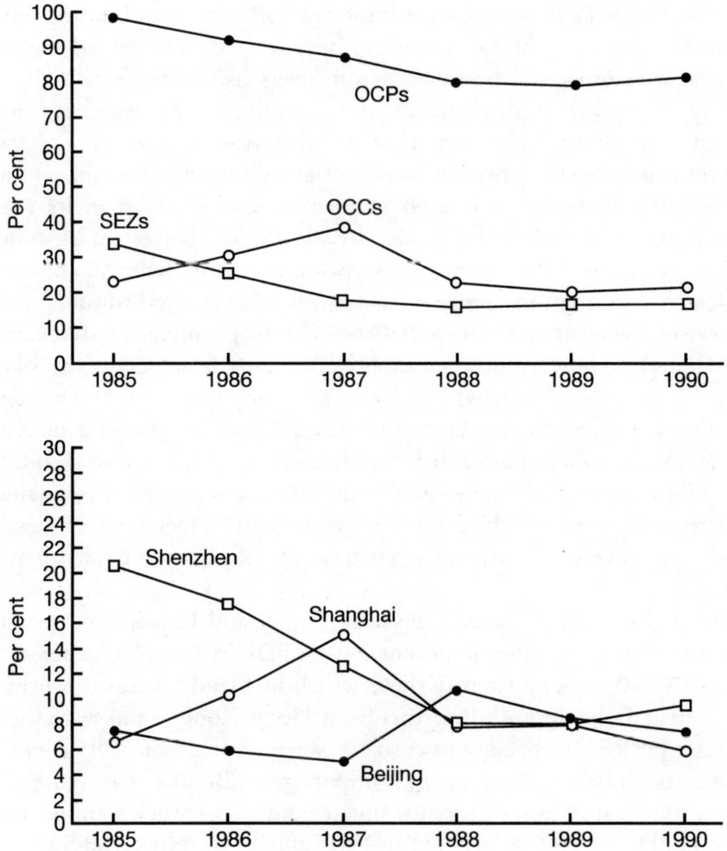

Figure 18.3

Notes:
SEZs Special Economic Zones
OCCs Opened coastal cities (see Tables 18.1 and 18.7)
OCPs Opened coastal provinces (see Table 18.1)
The figures for OCCs cover only Dalian, Tianjin, Qingdao, Shanghai and Guangzhou and those for OCPs include both Tianjin and Shanghai. All the figures exclude capital borrowing and FDI sponsored by various central branch ministries, such as, amongst others, investment in offshore oil exploration.
Sources: Appendix Tables 18.A1 and 18.A2

designated for foreign investment. Shenzhen has, for example, increasingly felt the competitive edge of other regions and recently appealed to the central authorities to be permitted to extend the boundaries of the SEZ to include neighbouring Baoan county.

If *indirect* foreign investment is included in the calculations, it is interesting that total combined volume absorbed by the 11 OCPs declined from 98 to 83 per cent between 1985 and 1990. The corresponding decline for Guangdong province alone is from 58 to 42 per cent.[16] The inference is that whilst the 11 OCPs dominated the intake of both direct and indirect foreign investment flows, the interior provinces have increasingly gained from them as beneficiaries of capital borrowing from overseas. To the extent that such funds are channelled through the central government, this suggests that the powerful centralized fiscal redistribution mechanism amongst the various provinces must also have been at work in the allocation of foreign capital.

Accelerated increases in foreign investment and changes in its regional allocation have also been accompanied by significant changes in its industrial distribution. Table 18.4 shows its absorption by the major economic sectors. It is clear that foreign investment has been heavily skewed towards industry and services, whereas agriculture has received a minimal share (especially of FDI). There has, however, been a pronounced shift from services to industry since 1985 in terms of realized FDI – a trend which holds good for all *econocoas* areas. This development no doubt reflects investors' improved confidence in China as an investment outlet. It is worth recalling that the initial concentration of FDI in tourist industries (hotel and catering services) was explained by the relative ease with which such investment could be recouped, as these areas catered exclusively for overseas visitors in possession of hard foreign currencies.

Most of the *econocoas* areas (especially Fujian and Guangdong provinces) which absorbed a significant proportion of FDI in manufacturing in both 1985 and 1990 were apparently those which had ready access to world markets – particularly through investors from Hong Kong – and were therefore in a better position to balance foreign exchange requirements. By contrast, in spite of its political and cultural importance, Beijing has remained an insignificant destination of foreign investment. The overwhelming proportion of its FDI (90 and 83 per cent in 1985 and 1990 respectively) was in the service sector and dominated by hotel business and the construction of residential blocks for sale to foreign investors (again, especially from Hong Kong).

But notwithstanding the marked shift in favour of manufacturing, at the beginning of the 1990s the service sector continues to be a substantial recipient of foreign capital. This is particularly the case with "late-comers," such as Shanghai, Hainan and even Guangxi. If the current frenzy with which Hong Kong capital is being poured into real estate in South China is any indication,[17] the 1990s may well witness a further rise in the service sector's share of foreign investment.

The accelerated increases in FDI, together with the shift from services towards manufacturing since the mid-1980s, also point to increased industrial dispersal. It is difficult to be both comprehensive and precise, but given that most foreign partners in joint ventures are investors from Hong Kong, there is little doubt that these have mainly involved labour-intensive manufacturing activities driven by soaring local land rentals and labour costs across the border to the Pearl River Delta and other congenial sites in China.[18] The

Table 18.4 Distribution of foreign investment by economic sectors in the *econocoas* areas in China, 1985 and 1990 (%)

	Total (US$ million)		*Agriculture*		*Industry*		*Services*		*Real estate*	
	1985	*1990*	*1985*	*1990*	*1985*	*1990*	*1985*	*1990*	*1985*	*1990*
SEZs										
Shenzhen	206.63(d)(f)	349.20(d)	0.18	—	53.54	80.33	46.27	19.67	7.98	15.97
Zhuhai	110.54(d)(f)	62.19(d)	0.20	1.30	24.39	88.78	75.41	9.92	3.36	7.80
Shantou	7.87(d)(f)	61.25(d)	1.27	0.56	41.80	79.27	56.93	20.18	—	12.33
Xiamen	181.62(d)(e)	—	—	—	39.50	—	60.50	—	11.71	—
OCCs										
Dalian	55.84(d)	—	21.49	—	32.16	—	46.35	—	—	—
Tianjin	—	83.15(d)	—	0.39	—	78.81	—	20.79	—	—
		(351.50)(d)(e)		(0.27)		(65.72)		(32.21)		
Qingdao	n.a.	n.a.	—		—	—	—		—	—
Shanghai	362.82(d)(e)	422.12(c)(f)	—	2.13	64.40	58.57	35.60	41.41	10.43	38.93
	(296.87)(b)(f)				(16.85)		(83.15)		(80.84)	
Guanghzhou	102.16(d)	180.87(d)	4.20	0.21	29.14	77.25	66.66	22.54	45.04	6.79
OCPs										
Lianing	163.53(b)	467.03(b)	0.75	0.71	15.31	82.65	83.94	17.10	81.67	0.46
Hebei	n.a.	n.a.	—	—	—	—	—	—	—	—
Shandong	n.a.	n.a.	—	—	—	—	—	—	—	—
Jiangsu	n.a.	n.a.	—	—	—	—	—	—	—	—
Zhejiang	n.a.	n.a.	—	—	—	—	—	—	—	—
Fujian	376.81(b)	1,161.83(b)	3.25	1.49	45.73	77.65	51.02	18.55	0.77	17.84
Guangdong	515.29(d)	1,459.84(d)	4.46	0.91 *	49.18	86.36	46.36	12.74	31.62	6.28
	(919.10)(c)	(2,023.47)(c)	(2.68)	(1.87)	(66.20)	(77.58)	(31.12)	(20.54)	(22.37)	(4.53)

Table 18.4 (Cont.)

	Total (US$ million)		*Agriculture*		*Industry*		*Services*		*Real estate*	
	1985	*1990*	*1985*	*1990*	*1985*	*1990*	*1985*	*1990*	*1985*	*1990*
Hainan	26.43(c)	189.82(c)	12.64	2.99	33.11	22.39	54.26	74.62	32.12	21.04
		(100.55)(d)		(5.65)		(36.64)		(57.71)		(39.72)
Guangxi	37.00(d)(f)	30.25(d)	—	2.94	3.78	75.07	96.22	21.98	96.22	20.93
Beijing	591.93(d)(e)	276.96(d)	—	—	9.70	16.74	89.50	83.26	76.01	64.64
PRC total		6,596.11(b)		1.85		87.19		10.97		6.86
	(9,867.42)(a)	(12,085.69)(a)	(4.18)	(7.68)	(36.39)	(65.20)	(59.44)	(27.11)	(23.01)	(3.98)

Notes:

(a) pledged total of FDI and capital borrowing
(b) pledged FDI only
(c) realized total of FDI and capital borrowing
(d) realized total of FDI
(e) cumulative total
(f) 1984 or 1986 figures, as 1985 figure is not available.

The standard *JMNJ* classification of branch distribution of foreign investment includes (1) agriculture, forestry, animal husbandry and fishery, (2) industry, (3) construction industry, (4) transport and telecommunication, (5) commerce and catering services, (6) real estate and public utilities, (7) health, sport and social welfare, (8) education, culture and arts, (9) scientific research and integrated technical services. (10) financial and insurance business, and (11) others. There are considerable variations among the provincial and municipal classifications. For our summarized categories, agriculture covers branch (1), industry (2) and (3), and service sector all the remaining branches. The "real estate" sector refers to branch (6) and its percentage figures are shared in the national total.

Considerable discrepancy exists between some of the figures shown here and in Appendix Tables 18.A1 and 18.A2. Some can be explained by the fact that FDI in this table does not include compensation trade investment, international leasing, etc., which are covered in Table 18.A1. Other possible factors include differences in geographic coverage (such as whether the SEZs refer to the zone proper or the greater municipality), and sources and timing of reporting. The main problem is that the standard national yearbooks which are to be preferred to the comparable provincial sources do not give breakdowns by economic sector for the different provincial FDI and capital borrowings. As a result, the table relies on the latter sources which very often give different base figures. Nevertheless the discrepancies are not substantial, except or Dalian (US$55.84 million for 1985) and Tianjin (US$83.15 million for 1990). These figures are much larger than those shown in Table 18.A1 (respectively US$14.32 million and US$36.93 million), and cannot easily be explained. Curiously, the Tianjin figure is given in the original provincial source alongside a cumulative figure for 1979–90 which is virtually identical to the one which may be obtained from Table 18.A1 for the same period.

Sources: As Appendix Table 18.A1.

nature of the exercise dictates that the output is destined, exclusively or overwhelmingly, for re-export through Hong Kong. This is of course consistent with China's strategy of using foreign investment for export purposes.

There have been some FDI projects which were designed and approved by Chinese authorities in line with the policy of import substitution.[19] But these have been the exceptions, not the rule. The more important point is that the relevant FDI ventures, whether export-orientated or import-substitution undertakings, have for the most part involved products at the very end of the relevant product cycle.[20] In other words, they have been internationally well-known products, embodying appropriate technological standards. Bearing in mind the predominant Hong Kong share in FDI ventures, many can probably be described as "sunset" industries in terms of their marketability and technological level.

CONTRIBUTION TO CAPITAL FORMATION

There are various ways in which the impact of foreign investment upon the recipient country's economy can be assessed. The most direct measure is its contribution to capital formation and thereby to output and income growth. Technology transfer is another important potential benefit, although it is difficult to quantify, especially in terms of "disembodied" technology. Likewise it is virtually impossible to verify the competitive impact of import-substituting foreign investment on domestic production and marketing efficiency. The ensuing analysis therefore focuses on the more readily measurable variables.

Estimating the likely contribution of foreign investment to capital formation in China is bedeviled by the need to convert foreign capital into *RMB* equivalent, so that a comparison can be made with the total domestic investment outlay. In the absence of an exchange rate which reflects purchasing-power-parity, any attempt to make the conversion on the basis of the official Chinese exchange rate is potentially hazardous. This is not only because of erratic exchange rate adjustments made by the Chinese authorities during the past decade, but also because no realignment of the administered exchange rate can fully take into account distortions in China's price system which tend to favour industrial, rather than agricultural, products. The data tend to favour industrial, rather than agricultural, products. The data in Table 18.5, showing the relative share of foreign investment in total fixed asset formation in China during 1985–90, should be considered with these caveats in mind.

The high shares shown for 1990 are likely to reflect the effect of the major *RMB* depreciation (by 22 per cent) against the U.S. dollar in December 1989. By contrast, the estimated shares for 1988 probably understate the contribution of foreign investment to domestic capital formation: the *RMB* exchange rate had, after all, not been readjusted since the 17 per cent devaluation of summer 1986. In other words, the high inflation rate experienced in 1988 (by

Table 18.5 Relative contribution of foreign investments to total fixed assets investment in the *econocoas* areas in China, 1985–90 (%)

	FDI only				*FDI and capital borrowing*			
	1985	*1988*	*1990*	*1985–90*	*1985*	*1988*	*1990*	*1985–90*
SEZs	16.01	15.56	33.72	23.66	25.79	32.72	49.30	38.66
Shenzhen	18.37	25.53	34.68	30.53	31.27	37.82	46.11	43.42
Zhuhai	16.14	14.26	34.56	19.43	27.49	65.47	54.16	46.68
Shantou	4.76	4.66	49.21	11.45	10.77	10.35	62.99	22.37
Xiamen	18.31	14.44	19.76	22.83	21.49	49.40	47.03	40.37
OCCs	3.08	3.93	6.61	4.84	4.10	9.46	12.23	9.85
Dalian	1.91	7.15	33.44	10.12	1.98	20.38	65.49	24.84
Tianjin	1.42	2.56	1.99	2.63	3.03	14.41	5.32	10.21
Qingdao	0.63	1.75	7.69	4.66	5.18	5.66	12.61	10.35
Shanghai	2.65	3.28	3.72	4.17	2.68	6.20	6.75	6.80
Guangzhou	7.95	6.41	9.53	7.01	10.43	10.50	15.72	11.27
OCPs	2.90	3.76	6.77	4.30	4.33	7.16	10.12	7.17
	(2.66)	(3.10)	(2.96)	(3.50)	(3.89)	(7.03)	(9.14)	(6.94)
Liaoning	0.52	1.81	4.72	2.10	0.88	4.06	13.33	5.33
Hebei	0.21	0.30	1.17	0.52	0.27	0.44	2.56	1.00
Shandong	0.52	1.12	2.65	1.41	0.94	1.43	3.28	1.92
Jiangsu	0.65	1.24	1.77	1.20	1.00	1.54	3.27	1.82
Zhejiang	0.74	0.71	0.91	0.80	1.72	2.11	2.36	2.14
Fujian	6.32	5.88	14.06	8.60	9.11	11.88	18.77	12.85
Guangdong	9.99	13.57	18.56	14.14	14.59	27.32	23.65	23.17
Hainan	6.64	21.45	12.54	11.94	7.32	22.38	14.24	12.67
Guangxi	2.14	1.00	2.48	2.33	3.13	3.20	4.36	3.83
Beijing	2.75	11.49	6.98	6.64	3.60	13.33	11.93	8.73
PRC total	2.26	3.09	4.03	3.11	5.14	8.44	11.04	8.72

Notes: FDI and capital borrowing in US$ are converted into *RMB* (based on official annual average of exchange rate) to be related to the total fixed assets investment figures (all undeflated) for the years concerned. The OCPs total (in parentheses) covers all the 11 OCPs, including Tianjin and Shanghai.

Sources: Appendix Tables 18.A1, 18.A2 and 18.A3.

18.5 per cent over 1987) reinforced the already-overvalued *RMB* – especially *vis-à-vis* the prices of industrial goods – and led to an understatement of the potential foreign capital shares in this year.

Given that the December 1989 *RMB* devaluation may not have been sufficiently "realistic,"[21] the average contribution of foreign investment to capital formation during 1985–90, as shown in Table 18.5, may well be understated. Nevertheless, with an estimated share close to 9 per cent for FDI and capital borrowing combined for 1985–90, or 11 per cent for 1990 alone, foreign investment can hardly be discarded as being of only marginal significance![22]

Of course, complementary domestic investment (especially for infrastructural purposes, such as the provision of electricity, transport, telecommunications, etc.) is needed in order to realize the potential of FDI. Chinese estimates suggest that for each dollar of foreign capital received, an average of 3 *RMB* must be spent.[23] (This does not include the Chinese capital contribution to Sino-foreign joint ventures.) Application of this 3:1 ratio to total foreign investment indicates that the shares of foreign and related investment in total fixed assets were 16 per cent (the average for 1985–90) and 18 per cent in 1990 alone.[24] These are of course substantial contributions – all the more so, if estimated combined foreign and related investment as a proportion of fixed capital formation in the state-ownership sector alone is considered, this being the pillar of the national economy and the single most important destination for foreign investment.[25]

A more important point to be made in this context is that the foreign investment share has increased across virtually all the *econocoas* areas during the years under investigation, although the regional distribution in 1990 remained highly unequal (see Table 18.5). Not surprisingly, given their economic *raison d'être*, it is the SEZs that enjoyed the highest foreign investment shares in total fixed asset creation: 24 per cent of FDI, or 39 per cent of FDI and capital borrowing combined, during 1985–90. Nevertheless, the difference in the relative contribution of foreign investment to capital formation between pioneer OCPs (for example, Guangdong and Fujian) and other OCPs, or even OCCs, has remained quite striking. The contrast between Guangzhou and Shanghai – both large, cosmopolitan centres – is particularly noteworthy. Despite an accelerated FDI absorption after 1988 (see Table 18.3), the foreign contribution to fixed asset investment in Shanghai was only 6.75 per cent in 1990, compared with 15.72 per cent in Guangzhou (Table 18.5). This suggests the potential that may be available for a late-comer, such as Shanghai, in terms of attracting foreign capital – not least, with Pudong now developing rapidly.

An increased share of foreign capital implies that the rate of increase of foreign capital absorption is outstripping that of domestic fixed investment. The relationship is illustrated in Table 18.6, which presents real rates of growth of foreign investment (with and without capital borrowing) and total fixed capital formation (with and without investment in the non-state-ownership sector). The growth of foreign capital intake during 1985–90 is seen to have been consistently many times higher than the rate of domestic capital formation in all the *econocoas* areas, including Beijing.

Several other points emerge from the table. First, in some areas, notably, Zhuhai, Xiamen, Dalian and possibly Tianjin, high rates of expansion of foreign investment contrast sharply with low rates of growth of total fixed asset creation. This may indicate that foreign funds were increasingly sought as a substitute for local resources. It should be noted that these are areas which exhibited relatively large foreign investment shares during 1985–90 (see Table 18.5).

Secondly, there are, however, areas which have enjoyed high foreign

Table 18.6 Average annual rates of growth of investment (1), industrial output (GVIO) and income (Y) in the *econocoas* areas in China, 1985–90 (%)

	I(A)	*I(b)*	*FI(a)*	*FI(b)*	*GVIO*	*Y(a)*	*Y(b)*
SEZs	6.57	8.29	25.14	20.92	32.68	14.62	15.19
Shenzhen	12.14	11.44	32.29	20.58	44.51	20.75	18.73
Zhuhai	−1.24	−1.74	17.31	23.92	45.92	18.88	18.28
Shantou	9.80	18.94	84.58	52.94	16.31	9.46	12.85
Xiamen	0.15	7.79	63.19	35.18	27.26	15.22	15.45
OCCs	9.12	8.68	27.57	44.68	6.76	3.46	5.03
	(18.06)		(46.62)	(38.32)	(33.27)		
Dalian	4.30	4.22	98.92	185.82	9.61	8.33	9.98
Tianjin	2.27	2.46	46.91	55.16	5.69	2.50	3.88
Qingdao	16.71	17.76	155.74	61.99	14.81	7.91	7.26
Shanghai	11.90	10.77	26.20	47.66	4.40	1.06	1.68
Guangzhou	12.61	13.67	27.66	39.32	12.13	8.54	12.88
OCPs	10.90	12.04	33.33	33.77	12.23	7.84	8.83
	(10.44)	(11.38)	(30.52)	(33.10)	(10.61)	(6.95)	(7.90)
Liaoning	11.66	10.02	84.25	99.64	5.79	5.25	7.00
Hebei	8.95	7.27	54.15	90.79	8.60	7.31	7.93
Shandong	10.47	8.70	52.08	42.43	14.50	7.74	8.41
Jiangsu	9.03	17.15	51.59	70.70	13.15	6.63	6.70
Zhejiang	11.52	17.19	22.24	56.57	12.51	6.89	7.56
Fujian	9.92	12.23	48.35	31.59	15.91	10.65	11.56
Guangdong	13.67	13.59	30.37	28.44	17.55	11.24	13.62
Hainan	18.56	26.43	208.06	218.84	10.75	8.69	9.03
Guangxi	9.27	7.27	30.50	20.31	9.49	9.18	8.94
Beijing	14.19	13.45	68.54	51.59	7.69	5.77	—
PRC total	8.69	8.63	30.05	38.51	9.49	7.53	7.89

Notes: I(a) and I(b): Total fixed assets investments in the state ownership sector (a) and for the country as a whole, including collective and private-individual investment (b), in real terms.

FI(a) and FI(b): Total foreign direct investment (FDI) (FI(a)) and FDI plus foreign capital borrowing (FI(b) in *RMB* and in real terms.

GVIO: Gross value of industrial output in constant 1980 prices.

Y(a): National income (net material product) in comparable prices.

Y(b): GDP/GNP in comparable prices.

See notes to Appendix Table 18.A3 for the conversion of I(a), I(b), FI(a) and FI(b) from nominal to real terms. Figures in parenthesis cover all the 15 OCCs and 11 OCPs, including Tianjin and Shanghai.

Sources: Appendix Tables 18.A1 to 18.A7.

investment growth rates as well as rapid growth of overall fixed capital formation. These include Shenzhen and Guangzhou, the two mature OCPs (Fujian and Guangdong) and, though to a lesser extent, Shanghai. It may be that in these areas initial foreign-induced capital growth subsequently helped promote local investment.

Thirdly, almost all the new *econocoas* frontiers have exhibited exceptionally high rates of growth of foreign investment. The list includes the OCC's shown in Table 18.6 (Guangzhou excepted), as well as such OCP's as

Liaoning, Hebei, Shangdon Jiangsu, Zhejiang and Hainan. The rapid growth was in most cases accompanied by a remarkable implied expansion of domestic capital, compared with the average for China as a whole. The inference is that the substantial complementary domestic investment in infrastructural and other facilities needed to realize the potential available from overseas capital supplies has been forthcoming.

The general picture which emerges of the relationships between foreign investment and domestic outlays cannot be regarded as conclusive. Other factors are, after all, at work. For example, apart from regional policy differences, significant variations in the scale and gestation periods of capital formation from overseas are bound to have affected the nature and pace of foreign investment. The speed of *domestic* investment, especially in major provinces, may also have been triggered by forces other than foreign investment and have generated a momentum of its own. Nevertheless, against the background of the nation-wide campaign to emulate the successful coastal pioneers in attracting foreign capital, the rest of the 1990s may well witness the emergence of coastal provinces, such as Shandong, Jiangsu and Zhejiang (Shanghai too, with its Pudong development project) as important contenders with Guangdong and Fujian for the attention of overseas investors.

To conclude this discussion of the contribution of foreign investment to domestic capital formation, attention may be drawn to the changing relationship between direct and indirect foreign investment. Table 18.6 shows that the rate of growth of total foreign investment (including capital borrowing) for China as a whole during 1985–90 was higher than that of the OCPs (35.51 per cent, as against 33.10 per cent), whereas the OCPs' rate of growth of overall fixed investment was higher than the national figure (11.38 and 8.63 per cent, respectively). The difference in the rate of growth of FDI on its own (30.05 per cent for China, 30.52 per cent for the OCPs) was, however, not nearly so pronounced. These figures suggest once more that central government borrowing has been increasingly – and with some effect – directed to non-OCP areas in order to arrest deteriorating regional imbalances in the receipt of foreign capital. This development reflects the well-established system of centralized redistribution of fiscal resources between regions (see above).

THE IMPACT ON OUTPUT AND INCOME GROWTH

Lack of industry-specific investment and output data make it difficult to make a precise estimate of the impact of foreign investment upon output and income growth in the *econocoas* areas of China. From the highly aggregative figures in Table 18.6, however, some assessment can be made.

First, the shift of FDI from services to the industrial sector, observed after 1985, should *a priori* have been accompanied by accelerated industrial expansion, as measured by the expansion of gross value of industrial output

(GVIO). This is indeed the case in all SEZs, except perhaps Shantou (see below). For the SEZs as a whole, the rate of growth of GVIO during 1985–90 – averaging 33 per cent per annum – is extremely high. This is so no matter whether the basis for comparison is China (9.49 per cent) or such new *econocoas* frontiers as Tianjin (5.69 per cent), Shanghai (4.4 per cent), Liaoning (5.74 per cent), or even Shandong (14.5 per cent), Jiangsu (13.15 per cent) and Zhejiang (12.51 per cent).

Secondly, it is noticeable that the lower GVIO growth rates in the new frontier provinces and the country as a whole (the latter dominated by OCPs) have been associated with high growth rates of foreign investment, compared with those of the SEZs, Guangdong and Fujian. This is readily explained, for unlike the SEZs, provincial output and investment have remained dominated by established sources (see the figures in absolute *yuan* in Table 18.7). In this respect, Shantou, which includes many counties in addition to the area of the SEZ proper, is closer to these provinces – or, more precisely, to such municipalities as Guangzhou and Qingdao – than to the other three geographically more concentrated SEZs.

Thirdly, the short gestation period associated with accelerated additions to the foreign capital stock in the new *econocoas* areas during 1985–90 made it impossible, in many cases, to translate investment into output. But this factor is unlikely to have contributed significantly to the lower rates of growth of GVIO, given the marginal contribution of foreign capital to overall investment in these areas (see column 5 in Table 18.7). By contrast, the higher GVIO rates of growth in the SEZs, and in Guangdong and Fujian, appear to reflect enhanced flows of output from sustained joint-venture investment undertaken in these pioneer *econocoas* regions since the early 1980s. Notice that these areas exhibit a significantly higher marginal foreign capital contribution during 1985–90, compared with other *econocoas* regions. By extension, extrapolating from the experience of the more mature *econocoas* areas and given the accelerated expansion of foreign capital absorption since the mid-1980s, it seems likely that industrial growth in other coastal provinces will come increasingly to deviate from the expansionary trend in foreign investment during the 1990s.

Regional differences in income growth rates relative to those of foreign investment (see Table 18.6) are generally consistent with the observed differences in terms of GVIO. This is the case, no matter whether the narrow measure (net material product), or the broad measure (gross domestic product (GDP) or gross national product (GNP)) is used.[26] There are, however, two minor qualifications to this general finding.

First, for the SEZs, the gap between the average annual rate of growth of GVIO during 1985–90 (32.7 per cent) and that of national income (14.6 per cent for Y(a) in Table 18.6) is wider than for the country taken as a whole (9.5 and 7.5 per cent). This probably reflects the predominance of processing industries, which have relatively low value-added contributions, in areas with heavy concentrations of foreign investment. The same point can be made of Guangdong and Fujian provinces, although not to the same extent as in the SEZs. In any case, the argument should not be pressed too far, for in the case of some major OCPs (notably, Shandong, Jiangsu and – especially – Shanghai) the gap between GVIO and national income growth rates (Y(a) in Table 18.6) turns out to be even wider than for Guangdong and Fujian. Clearly, the structure of domestic industry varies from province to province.

Secondly, using the GNP/GDP measure, the gap between GVIO and income growth rates narrowed significantly during 1985–90 in a number of *econocoas* areas, including Tianjin, Shanghai and Guangzhou. This was not, however, the case in Shenzhen, where the gap apparently grew wider. The explanation may be that tourism led to a more rapid expansion of the tertiary sector in the three municipalities, whilst Shenzhen's expansion was based on what Hong Kong government statistics regard as "outward processing" industrial activities.

Changes in productivity are another important aspect of the economic impact of foreign investment. For want of appropriately disaggregated industrial investment and net output data, we are again compelled to use the aggregate income measures shown in Table 18.7.[27] The observed income multiplier of investment shows the income response per unit of investment outlay. But the estimated "incremental capital-output ratio" cannot without qualification be accepted as a measure of the marginal efficiency of capital.

Take, for example, the SEZs, which consistently exhibit an income multiplier which is greater than the national average, no matter which national income measure is used; or Guangdong and Fujian (even Guangxi), whose multipliers are higher than those of virtually all other *econocoas* regions. Quite apart from the assumed greater efficiency in capital utilization by foreign joint ventures, a number of factors could explain the differences in the value of the multiplier.

One may be that most foreign investment-based projects in the SEZs and the two pioneer provinces have been short-run income-maximizing undertakings. For example, the many thousands of joint ventures (including simple outward processing arrangements) set up in the Pearl River Delta by Hong Kong manufacturers in recent years have almost overnight generated accelerated income and employment opportunities in Guangdong province. Another factor is the erratic nature of the *RMB* devaluation in 1986 and, more especially, 1989. *Ceteris paribus*, to the extent that a large part of joint venture production is exported (see the next section), such devaluations, which help loss-making exporters cover their costs and transform them into profit-making concerns in *RMB* terms, have had the effect of boosting income. What cannot, however, be known is the relative strength of these factors and the possible efficiency implications of foreign involvement to raising the value of the income multiplier.

But by way of contrast, the other major OCPs, which have exhibited

Table 18.7 Income (Y) multiplier of investment (I) in the *econocoas* areas in China, 1985–1990

	100 million yuan					*Multiplier*	
	DY(a) *(1)*	*DY(b)* *(2)*	*DTI* *(3)*	*DFI* *(4)*	*DFI/DTI* *(5)*	*(1)/(3)* *(6)*	*(2)/(3)* *(7)*
SEZs	61.16	87.57	204.95	78.51	0.38	0.30	0.43
Shenzhen	27.47	33.43	100.44	43.95	0.44	0.27	0.33
Zhuhai	7.64	9.49	26.15	11.74	0.45	0.29	0.36
Shantou	15.80	30.66	45.12	9.96	0.22	0.35	0.68
Xiamen	10.24	13.98	33.23	12.86	0.39	0.31	0.42
OCCs	101.27	203.80	1,038.28	101.49	0.10	0.10	0.20
Dalian	23.29	36.87	81.79	19.82	0.24	0.28	0.45
Tianjin	13.54	28.64	211.80	21.40	0.10	0.06	0.14
Qingdao	21.81	27.22	53.72	5.51	0.10	0.41	0.51
Shanghai	14.69	31.27	512.70	34.63	0.07	0.03	0.06
Guangzhou	27.95	79.80	178.27	20.14	0.11	0.16	0.45
OCPs	975.06	1,461.78	4,022.82	283.40	0.07	0.24	0.36
	(1,003.29)	(1,521.69)	(4,966.74)	(339.43)	(0.07)	(0.20)	(0.31)
Liaoning	84.57	151.04	574.81	29.87	0.05	0.15	0.26
Hebei	99.89	143.55	462.35	4.46	0.01	0.22	0.31
Shandong	171.68	243.68	767.54	14.54	0.02	0.22	0.32
Jiangsu	150.57	198.91	769.52	13.83	0.02	0.20	0.26
Zhejiang	98.46	139.47	488.91	10.27	0.02	0.20	0.29
Fujian	74.26	107.89	211.18	26.63	0.13	0.35	0.51
Guangdong	225.09	382.98	748.50	170.77	0.23	0.30	0.51
Hainan	12.56	18.31	55.06	6.79	0.12	0.23	0.33
Guangxi	57.99	75.95	164.36	6.26	0.04	0.35	0.46
Beijing	42.94	—	368.57	30.89	0.08	0.12	—
PRC total	2,126.29	3,096.53	9,769.20	406.89	0.04	0.22	0.32

Notes: DY(a) and DY(b): absolute changes (in real terms) in National Income (Net Material Product) (a) and GDP/GNP (b) between 1985 and 1990.

DTI and DFI: cumulative total (in real terms) of total fixed assets investments for the country as a whole including collective and private individual investments (DTI) and FDI plus capital borrowings (DFI) between 1985 and 1990.

Figures in parenthesis cover all the 11 OCPs (including Tianjin and Shanghai).

Sources: Appendix Tables 18.A2, 18.A3, 18.A6 and 18.A7.

significantly lower income multipliers and enjoyed lower foreign capital shares than Guangdong and Fujian (let alone the SEZs), appear to have been characterized by the conventional Stalinist industrial structure and an investment policy favouring heavy industry or projects with long gestation periods. This pattern has inevitably been reflected in lower income multipliers in areas, such as Shanghai, Tianjin and Beijing (see Table 18.7), which constitute the backbone of the Stalinist development strategy.

Thus the impact of foreign investment can be seen not only in terms of the disparity in income-generating capacity which it has created, but also of the increasing spatial bifurcation of China's industrial structure which has resulted from the government's selective approach to it. It remains to be seen whether the massive effort currently under way to attract foreign investment to other major OCPs will eventually help bring the industrial structure in line with what the competitive international market for foreign capital would dictate – but without compromising China's search for a mix of industrial output appropriate to its modernization goals.

FOREIGN TRADE AND EXPORT PERFORMANCE

The Chinese government's goal of maximizing foreign exchange earnings is to finance its priority import programme. Accordingly, the most important criterion for judging the performance of FDI projects in China is the ability of the foreign-funded enterprises to balance their foreign exchange requirements. It will be useful to preface the analysis of such enterprises' currency balances by considering export production.

Table 18.8 sets out available industrial output and export data for *sanzi* ("three foreign-funded": equity and contractual joint ventures and wholly foreign-owned firms) enterprises in the *econocoas* areas for 1987–91. The figures are expressed as a proportion of total and exported GVIO.

Two major points emerge from the data. First, in virtually all cases, *sanzi* enterprises' share of both output and export increased steadily throughout the period. With the single exception of Shenzhen during 1987–89, for which actual export share data are available, the estimates are based on the assumption that all output from these enterprises was exported. This is of course to overstate the case. But even allowing for domestic sales under the general rule that more than 70 per cent of the output of *sanzi* enterprises should be exported, estimated share of exports for *econocoas* areas remains consistently higher than their share of output.[28] Moreover, a cross-sectional comparison reveals that regions with a higher export share generally also enjoyed a higher output share. These findings imply that most *sanzi* enterprises have targeted their output towards world markets and that China's export-orientated foreign investment strategy has been implemented fairly consistently across the various regions.

What also emerges from Table 18.8 is that *sanzi* enterprises' shares in output and export vary greatly between regions, though in a manner which is consistent with regional differences in average and marginal foreign investment shares in overall fixed capital formation (see the analysis of Tables 18.5 and 18.7, above). For example, in 1991 such enterprises contributed 55 per cent of GVIO, but 76 per cent of exports, in the four SEZs. The corresponding figures for Guangzhou were 21 and 66 per cent. In the same year, the average shares of GVIO and exports accounted for by *sanzi* enterprises in OCCs were only 9 and 37 per cent respectively. Admittedly, Shanghai is excluded from these last calculations. But the predominant industrial and

Table 18.8 Relative contribution of Sanzi Enterprises to total and exported GVIO in the *econocoas* areas in China, 1987–91 (%)

	Total GVIO					*Exported GVIO*				
	1987	*1988*	*1989*	*1990*	*1991*	*1987*	*1988*	*1989*	*1990*	*1991*
SEZs	—	—	52.11	50.03	54.99	—	—	111.22	105.79	109.37
Shenzhen	(61.45)*	(63.25)*	59.04	68.35	68.19	—	(74.36)*	(70.61)	—	113.93
	(63.68)	(61.16)	(59.04)	(66.35)		(75.97)	(73.19)	102.08	112.23	
Zhuhai	—	—	(45.17)*	34.16	47.46	—	—	139.59	105.72	100.24
			31.60							
Shantou	—	—	(30.45)*	22.50	33.31	—	—	—	61.20	83.25
Xiamen	(30.20)	(43.20)	49.30	45.74	53.79	—	—	132.81	170.05	131.16
			(48.54)	(56.37)						
OCCs	2.02	3.52	3.59	3.26	8.68	18.08	19.60	29.76	35.01	53.30
Dalian	—	—	—	2.78	5.00	—	—	—	15.38	21.10
Qinhuangdao	3.39	5.58	5.08	4.15	7.20	—	—	—	41.62	58.89
Tianjin	(1.39)	(2.31)	(3.39)	4.17	4.07	—	—	—	40.71	37.77
				(3.49)						
Yantai	—	0.37	0.30	0.72	17.61	—	2.85	2.04	4.71	18.06
Weihai	—	—	—	1.61	1.82	—	—	—	11.31	10.39
Qingdao	—	—	0.82	1.12	2.53	—	—	5.01	6.73	14.87
Lianyungang	0.58	0.58	2.05	3.24	4.18	8.78	8.28	20.89	37.08	43.59
Nantong	—	1.56	—	4.22	—	—	10.78	—	22.73	—
Shanghai	1.17	2.19	3.50	—	—	—	15.44	24.99	—	—
Ningbo	0.28	0.79	2.40	4.07	6.32	—	—	—	33.52	43.43

Wenzhou	0.01	0.14	0.25	0.98	—	—	—	1.99	8.30	—
Fuzhou	18.22	24.50	26.71	27.30	36.62	—	—	—	115.74	127.49
Guangzhou	3.28	7.52	12.23	15.53	20.96	18.53	36.66	63.75	78.82	94.44
Zhangjiang	—	—	3.93	4.93	4.76	—	—	28.88	54.54	51.01
Beihai	1.41	3.32	4.33	6.62	5.17	—	20.37	24.95	33.08	29.05
OCPs										
Liaoning	—	—	(0.27)	(0.79)	—	—	—	—	—	—
Shandong	—	—	(0.14)*	(0.40)*	—	—	—	—	—	—
Fujian	(9.67)*	(13.96)*	(15.55)*	(21.44)*	—	—	—	—	—	—
	(12.43)	(18.79)	(21.38)	(28.48)						
Hainan	—	6.51	10.03	8.60	14.28	—	127.98	222.07	—	192.41
Beijing	—	—	(4.81)	(6.05)*	—	—	—	—	—	—
				(7.59						
Total (OCCs + SEZs)	2.02	3.52	9.37	11.51	16.71	18.08	19.60	51.37	58.39	75.04

Notes: The GVIO figures cover the greater municipality, not just the city districts or the SEZs proper. The exclude, however, *cunban* (village operated) GVIO, as far as it can be determined. The original absolute figures are in current prices for all the figures with an asterisk and the unbracketed figures for 1990, and in 1980 *RMB yuan* for the rest. The unbracketed figures of *sanzi* share in exported GVIO are derived by assuming that all output from *sanzi* enterprises is exported. However, virtually all the SEZs' shares for 1988–91 exceed 100% which implies that parts of the *sanzi* output were in fact sold to the domestic market. The figures given in parenthesis show therefore the more accurate *sanzi* export shares. None of the figures includes output from "processing activities" which are still quite substantial for the SEZs. The total represents the weighted average of the unbracketed figures for OCCs, SEZs (including Hainan) only, not the national average.

Sources: Appendix Table 18.A1 for all figures in parenthesis: all the others are from *China's Latest Economic Statistics (CLES)*, Part 2, February 1989, pp. 51–5 (for 1987 to 1988); February 1990, pp. 44–7 (for 1989); February 1991, pp. 13–16 (for 1990); and February 1992, pp. 24–7 (for 1991).

trade role of the municipality in China ensured that the implied export share (18 per cent) of its *sanzi* enterprises was already by no means negligible.[29]

At the beginning of the 1990s, *sanzi* enterprises in the SEZs and OCCs taken together probably accounted for about 17 per cent of total GVIO generated in these areas and contributed more than half of exported GVIO. Even more remarkable is the fact that this has been achieved within a decade. More questionable is whether the expansion of exports during the 1980s and into the 1990s could have been sustained without the participation of these enterprises. It is, however, clear enough that foreign joint ventures not only brought China scarce capital, much-needed technology and managerial know-how, but also – and more importantly – provided it with the marketing skills needed for integration in international markets. Furthermore, the competitive pressures which came in the wake of such international involvement encouraged domestic export producers and trading firms to improve the efficiency of their operations.

A proper assessment of the trade performance of foreign-funded enterprises requires an examination of their foreign currency balances of exports and imports. Table 18.9 presents comprehensive data showing the shares of *sanzi* enterprises in total exports and imports of the *econocoas* areas between 1988 and 1991, based on U.S. dollar accounts.

Notice that the export data here differ from those in Table 18.8 not only in terms of currency base, but also of coverage. That is, the figures in Table 18.9 embrace all exports (not only industrial output) from *sanzi* enterprises. They include exports of agricultural products, services and real estate sales, as well as any items which the enterprises may have been permitted to procure from domestic sources for export purposes to help balance foreign exchange requirements.[30]

The export data in Table 18.9 reveal that the *sanzi* shares in total *econocoas* exports increased steadily during 1988–91. The shares for individual regions are found to vary in a manner that is generally consistent with estimates of *sanzi* enterprises' shares in total and exported GVIO, and foreign shares in capital formation. For China as a whole, the *sanzi* share in total exports rose from little more than 5 per cent in 1988 to about 17 per cent in 1991. There is, however, significant variation between different regions: from a high of 46 per cent for the SEZs to 41 per cent (Fujian), 29 per cent (Guangdong) and a low of 11 per cent in both Shanghai and Beijing.

Sanzi exports are, in fact, strongly skewed towards Guangdong, which accounted for 66 per cent of the national total (Shenzhen alone contributed almost 40 per cent of the provincial total in 1991).[31] In absolute U.S. dollar terms, *sanzi* exports in Shenzhen, or Guangdong province, were consistently significantly higher than those of Shanghai or any other *econocoas* area (OCC or OCP). In 1991, for example, the values were US$29.24 million (Shenzhen) and $79.24 million (Guangdong), compared with US$6.59 million for Shanghai, or US$26.52 million for all 15 OCCs (including Guangzhou).[32]

Table 18.9 Percentage share of *sanzi enterprises* in total export and import in the *econocoas* areas in China, 1988–91

	Export				*Import*			
	1988	*1989*	*1990*	*1991*	*1988*	*1989*	*1990*	*1991*
SEZs	22.47	33.31	40.50	45.80	28.91	33.33	54.01	52.74
Shenzhen	26.38	36.99	43.96	50.52	30.67	33.00	51.66	57.24
Zhuhai	15.36	32.53	41.75	44.73	25.85	38.39	90.87	48.52
Shantou	11.66	18.49	23.63	28.38	14.89	2.18	26.57	31.51
Xiamen	18.36	28.02	37.37	41.70	42.83	42.95	56.73	58.50
OCCs	3.11	7.86	11.51	18.87	19.06	26.34	35.53	42.74
	(5.99)	(8.05)	(11.71)	(18.78)	(20.00)	(26.51)	(36.70)	(50.35)
Dalian	6.73	18.70	24.10	40.43	60.77	36.77	50.23	61.64
Tianjin	2.29	3.94	6.00	10.41	13.77	20.91	28.65	33.71
Qingdao	1.39	5.23	7.54	13.07	29.58	37.63	30.83	37.41
Shanghai	1.71	4.65	6.38	10.82	15.81	22.93	29.74	43.87
Guangzhou	7.92	17.61	24.44	33.76	18.64	33.86	46.23	55.26
OCPs	7.61	12.99	17.19	21.97	19.76	25.69	38.35	37.12
	(6.56)	(11.60)	(15.57)	(20.43)	(19.05)	(25.13)	(37.13)	(37.58)
Liaoning	0.99	2.97	4.24	9.26	24.32	17.67	28.89	37.90
Hebei	0.25	0.65	1.25	3.42	37.57	25.79	42.56	33.86
Shandong	0.60	2.34	3.62	6.00	9.72	17.27	25.69	33.89
Jiangsu	2.03	4.37	6.43	12.06	12.25	18.81	36.38	44.53
Zhejiang	2.52	3.73	6.11	9.02	9.52	13.07	19.32	25.24
Fujian	16.97	27.17	36.85	40.95	43.23	47.82	60.59	63.23
Guangdong	12.48	19.56	24.77	29.41	18.56	26.10	38.14	34.82
Hainan	2.10	7.55	7.10	8.48	12.79	17.64	34.89	29.05
Guangxi	1.64	3.40	4.82	7.50	14.72	21.66	26.29	24.50
Beijing	2.68	4.88	7.64	11.47	51.58	65.57	52.87	52.44
Provincial total	5.51	9.62	13.32	17.59	26.05	30.06	36.07	35.61
PRC total	5.15	9.23	12.58	16.76	14.34	19.65	23.56	26.55

Notes: Figures in brackets are sum totals for all the 15 OCCs and 11 OCPs including Tianjin and Shanghai. There is a striking discrepancy in the *sanzi* share in imports between the provincial and PRC totals, compared with the very marginal difference in the *sanzi* share in exports. The implied percentage shares of total PRC import conducted at the central level for the four years amounted to 46.2 (1988), 42.3 (1989), 34.7 (1990) and 29.9 (1991), and that for export only 6.5, 4.2, 5.5 and 4.7 respectively. These figures may understate the real magnitude of centralized control, because in many instances both exports and imports as undertaken by the "provincial-level trading firms" (which make up the shown provincial total) are still subject to various non-tariff restrictions, including export/import licensing, quotas and foreign exchange allocation. Nevertheless, the discrepancy shows that despite the trade decentralization drive imports have remained subject to much greater central control than exports. The situation is thus basically the same as that in the mid-1980s (*cf.* Y. Y. Kueh, "Economic decentralization and foreign trade expansion in China," in J. C. H. Chai and C. K. Leung (eds.), *China's Economic Reforms* (Hong Kong: University of Hong Kong, 1987), pp. 462–6), although the degree of central control over import has tended to decline in recent years.

Sources: Appendix Tables 18.A8 and 18.A9.

But the data in Table 18.9 reveal that regional skewing of *sanzi* export earnings has narrowed over time in favour of the non-pioneer *econocoas* regions.[33] This is entirely consistent with the earlier observation that foreign investment in these regions has grown more rapidly than in the earlier-established areas. The same trends are indeed also reflected in *sanzi* import shares – machinery, equipment and essential raw materials purchased by foreign partners in joint ventures – relative to those of exports (Table 18.9). Thus, the ratio of *sanzi* export to import share for the SEZs (52.74:45.80 per cent 1.15) is much smaller than that of the 15 OCCs (50.35:18.78 per cent = 2.68), or of the 11 OCPs (37.58:20.43 per cent = 1.84). Notice that the OCP figures are dominated by Guangdong and its SEZs.

The implications of the regional variations in import and export shares are clear. If the new *econocoas* frontiers can effectively emulate the success stories of the SEZs, Guangdong or Fujian, assuming that the current scale of imports is translated into exports in accordance with the export-orientated foreign investment strategy, the *sanzi* share in national exports may be expected to increase to around 30 per cent by the middle of the 1990s. Making precise forecasts of such exports is very difficult. But assuming that most *sanzi* enterprises are cautious in their attitude to expected returns on investment and/or have access to established marketing and distribution networks overseas, there is no reason why the new *econocoas* frontiers should not expand their *sanzi* export shares in future. Nor need this be at the expense of the shares already achieved by such regions as Guangdong (30 per cent) and Fujian (41 per cent). Except for Jiangsu province, the *sanzi* export share of all other new OCPs is, after all, no more than 10 per cent.

The most striking finding to emerge from Table 18.10, which shows the trade balance of *sanzi* enterprises, is that throughout 1988–91 virtually no *econocoas* area succeeded in balancing its foreign exchange requirements.[34] It is likely that a number of factors were involved. But the essential explanation is probably to be found in the euphoric confidence which foreign interests have demonstrated in the Chinese investment market. In the new *econocoas* areas, the underlying gestation periods required to translate overseas investment into output and exports would explain the trade imbalances. What is interesting is that the same dynamism appears to have characterized *sanzi* investment in the established *econocoas* regions: the SEZs, Guangdong and Fujian provinces have all continued to exhibit substantial negative *sanzi* trade balances during 1988–91.[35]

The foreign exchange balances of *sanzi* enterprises vary between different industrial destinations of foreign investment. Lack of data makes it difficult to quantify such differences. Nevertheless, foreign exchange surpluses have generally characterized *sanzi* investment in hotels and recreational services, as well as in primary sector activities, especially the extraction of mineral ores, coal and oil for sale in world markets. This suggests that the imbalances suffered by manufacturing and processing enterprises are significantly greater

Table 18.10 Trade balance (export minus import) of *sanzi* enterprises of the *econocoas* areas in China, 1988–91

	(100 million US$)				*As share of export (%)*			
	1988	*1989*	*1990*	*1991*	*1988*	*1989*	*1990*	*1991*
SEZs	−4.01	0.73	−7.63	−6.07	−32.47	3.33	−23.73	−14.11
Shenzhen	−1.88	2.63	−1.70	−3.18	−19.46	15.81	−7.41	−10.88
Zhuhai	−1.11	−0.93	−4.82	−0.98	−130.59	−44.29	−137.32	−19.25
Shantou	−0.18	−0.14	−0.12	−0.57	−20.22	−9.15	−5.29	−16.76
Xiamen	−0.84	−0.82	−0.99	−1.34	−88.42	−41.62	−28.78	−25.28
OCCs	−9.23	−12.72	−11.55	−12.97	−340.59	−173.53	−93.83	−55.76
	(−7.64)	(−13.26)	(−12.28)	(−14.88)	(−137.91)	(−158.61)	(−86.05)	(−56.11)
Dalian	−1.87	−0.39	−0.61	−0.82	−623.33	−36.79	−35.47	−19.11
Tianjin	−0.71	−1.39	−1.04	−1.20	−182.05	−207.46	−97.20	−65.93
Qingdao	−0.30	−0.69	−0.36	−0.44	−1,000.00	−460.00	−128.57	−69.84
Shanghai	−4.23	−7.43	−6.90	−7.00	−503.57	−318.88	−197.14	−106.22
Guangzhou	−2.11	−2.83	−2.65	−3.51	−181.80	−90.71	−46.01	−35.35
OCPs	−20.57	−18.06	−28.96	−20.51	−91.59	−40.43	−40.49	−18.97
	(−25.51)	(−26.88)	(−36.89)	(−28.67)	−107.68)	(−56.59)	(−48.48)	(−24.59)
Liaoning	−2.21	−0.91	−1.10	−1.23	−566.67	−71.09	−49.55	−23.61
Hebei	−1.36	−0.91	−1.32	−0.59	−3,400.00	−758.33	−550.00	−85.51
Shandong	−0.68	−1.12	−0.98	−1.39	−400.00	−157.75	−79.03	−61.78
Jiangsu	−0.77	−1.34	−2.45	−4.22	−157.14	−120.12	−129.63	−102.18
Zhejiang	−0.09	−0.13	0.21	0.25	−23.68	−18.57	15.67	9.54
Fujian	−3.71	−2.61	−2.43	−3.55	−154.17	−52.52	−26.91	−27.54
Guangdong	−10.95	−9.69	−19.57	−8.05	−59.38	−27.43	−35.71	−10.16
Hainan	−0.37	−0.87	−1.14	−1.57	−616.67	−348.00	−300.00	−296.23
Guangxi	−0.42	−0.46	−0.20	−0.16	−466.67	−209.09	−51.28	−27.59
Beijing	−4.72	−5.89	−4.44	−5.37	−1,815.38	−1,178.00	−516.28	−358.00
Provincial total	−54.76	−67.71	−47.55	−38.82	−223.69	−139.69	−60.86	−32.21
PPC total	−77.50	−66.00	87.40	81.19	—	—	—	—

Notes: Figures in brackets refer respectively to the sum total of all 15 OCCs and 11 OCPs including Tianjin and Shanghai.

Sources: Appendix Tables 18.A8 and 18.A9.

than the net balance estimates in Table 18.10 suggest. Of course, it is the latter two categories which have attracted most of the accelerated increase in FDI since the mid-1980s (see Table 18.4). It is impossible to say whether all this indicates excessive optimism by foreign investors or the existence of a real competitive edge for *sanzi* products in western export markets.

Table 18.10 also shows, however, that during 1988–91 the deficits (exports minus imports) of *sanzi* enterprises tended to decline as a proportion of their own exports. Even more remarkable is the fact that for the SEZs, Guangdong and Fujian provinces, the shares were lower than in the other *econocoas* areas. This suggests that as investment generates increased volumes of output and exports, most *sanzi* enterprises in all *econocoas* areas (new and established) can hope to meet the requirements for foreign exchange balance in the years to come.

Finally, there is the redemption of borrowed foreign capital. The issue involved here is similar to that which affects *sanzi* enterprises, except that the redemption of loans undertaken by government depends, so it is argued, on the overall level of the relevant country's export earnings. The outstanding net balance of China's foreign debt was recently said to be "more than US$60 billion," with debt service obligations (amortization plus interest payments) reaching a peak of US$7–8 billion per year during 1992–95,[36] This gives an estimated debt service ratio of 9.7 to 10.8 per cent based on total Chinese exports of US$719.10 million in 1991.[37] This is considerably less than the 12–15 per cent, conventionally regarded as the critical debt service ratio – "critical" in the sense that it threatens to "crowd out" a country's import capacity to promote economic growth.[38]

Even when the 1991 *sanzi* deficit of US$38.82 million (see Table 18.10) has been deducted from total export earnings, China's current debt service ratio will remain below this critical level. In any case, its current foreign exchange reserves (some US$43 billion as of December 1991) constitutes a substantial hedge against unexpected eventualities. In short, for the foreseeable future, China's balance of payments vis-à-vis foreign debt servicing looks healthier than the *sanzi* balances might suggest.

TRENDS AND POLICY DILEMMAS IN THE 1990s

Any attempt to forecast trends in foreign direct investment in China during the rest of the 1990s must confront two, closely related issues. The first concerns the availability of foreign capital; the second, the likely rate of return on investment in China relative to that available elsewhere. Both issues should be viewed against the international perspective of global economic interdependence or the economic evolution of the Asia-Pacific Region. The collapse of the Soviet bloc may, for example, precipitate a reallocation of international capital away from China. By contrast, political upheaval in South-east Asia may cause a reassessment of regional investment risks which favours China. As for established *sanzi* enterprises, plans for further capital injections are likely to be conditioned by the annual decision whether to renew China's Most Favoured Nation (MFN) status, given that a substantial proportion of *sanzi* products are exported to the United States. Similarly, a positive outcome to the ongoing negotiations on China's re-admission to GATT will almost certainly help boost foreign investors' confidence in China.

Above all, the domestic political situation will remain a critical determinant of outside perceptions of China's credit-worthiness and thereby the scale of FDI there. This is evident from the impact of the Tiananmen Square incident. The frenzy with which Hong Kong compatriots and overseas investors responded early in 1992 to Deng Xiaoping's call for an accelerated opening-up of the Chinese economy is another case in point. By the middle of 1992 many of the *econocoas* areas were already recording dramatic rises in both the number of contracts for joint-venture projects which had been signed, and the level of foreign capital that had been pledged and realized.[39] Subsequent support for Deng's policy from "conservative" Chinese leaders and the military had the further effect of boosting the Hong Kong stock market index (the single most important indicator of investors' confidence in China) to an unprecedented degree. The increase in the Hang Seng Index from around 3,500 to 6,000 between March and early June 1992 could hardly have been predicted, not least against the background of a world-wide recession.[40]

The unpredictability of the internal and external factors which impinge upon foreign investment in China may explain the absence of any quantitative targets for such investment or capital borrowing in either the Ten-Year Economic Programme (1991–2000) or the Eighth Five-Year Plan (1991–95). Even so, the role of Hong Kong as a source of FDI during the second half of the 1980s (see Table 18.11) may provide valuable clues for future developments.

Between 1984 and 1990, in only one year did Hong Kong's share in China's total realized FDI fall below 50 per cent – and during 1987–89 the figure was closer to two-thirds. More remarkable still, virtually all the *econocoas* areas shared in the pre-eminent role of Hong Kong.[41] Second in importance was Japan. Its share of the overall FDI intake has, however, never been substantial (in 1989 and 1990, it reached 11 and 13 per cent); nor has that of the United States, which ranks third, closely behind Japan.[42]

Perhaps the most important lesson of Hong Kong's involvement in investment on the Chinese mainland is for Taiwan. Admittedly, Taiwan does not have Hong Kong's benefit of a rail link with China. But the distance across the Taiwan Strait to Fujian is hardly any longer than that between Hong Kong and Guangzhou. Taiwanese capital has made rapid inroads on to the mainland during recent years, although because of strict bans on direct commercial, navigational and postal links with the PRC, such progress has only been possible through cumbersome connections in third countries (above all, Hong Kong). The *Chinese Statistical Yearbook* still does not contain

Table 18.11 Share of Hong Kong in total foreign investment in the *econocoas* areas in China, 1984–90 (%)

	1984	*1985*	*1986*	*1987*	*1988*	*1989*	*1990*
SEZs							
Shenzhen	—	82.74 (d)	91.15 (d)	82.89 (d)	87.21 (d)	78.35 (d)	50.11 (d)
				(63.37) (c)	(63.47) (c)	(61.28) (c)	(46.45) (c)
Zhuhai	—	100.00 (d)	100.00 (d)	79.38 (d)	98.63 (d)	97.25 (d)	84.82 (d)
		(71.69 (b)	(82.84) (b)			(51.22) (c)	(67.94) (c)
Shantou	—	89.20 (d)	81.63 (d)	87.65 (d)	87.69 (d)	90.38 (d)	78.06 (d)
						(91.87) (c)	80.22 (c)
Xiamen	—	80.16 (d)	—	—	64.24 (b)(e)	64.61 (d)	61.98 (d)
OCCs							
Dalian	—	35.66 (d)	20.12 (d)	30.70 (d)	11.97 (d)	—	—
Tianjin	—	—	—	46.83 (b)	—	49.28 (b)	25.03 (d)
						(44.22) (b)(e)	(42.44) (d)(e)
Qingdao	—	—	—	—	—	—	—
Shanghai	—	—	10.95 (b)	64.41 (b)	—	40.63 (c)	—
				(27.16) (b)(e)		(26.03) (c)(e)	
Guangzhou	—	87.97 (b)	67.77 (b)	—	47.24 (b)	77.55 (d)	69.43 (d)
						(43.68) (c)	
OCPs							
Liaoning	—	59.22 (b)	48.32 (b)	34.58 (b)	57.66 (b)	28.25 (b)	68.21 (b)
							(52.28) (b)(e)
Hebei	—	—	—	—	67.85 (c)	49.83 (c)	75.94 (d)
Shandong	—	—	—	—	69.02 (c)	70.87 (c)	53.79 (d)
Jiangsu	—	—	—	—	—	—	—

Zhejiang	—	—	—	19.30 (a)	51.10 (a)	45.60 (a)	52.99 (b) (51.51) (b)(e)
Fujian	—	— (80.16) (d)	35.72 (c)	24.87 (c)	61.43 (c) (61.89) (d)	52.22 (c) (59.39) (d) (68.78) (d)(e)	65.70 (c) (55.48) (d) (43.84) (c)(e) (57.50) (d)(e)
Guangdong	—	87.40 (d) (92.01) (c) (94.06) (a)	92.50 (d) (76.53) (c)	84.63 (d) (72.86) (c)	91.02 (d) (63.04) (c)	82.38 (d) (64.39) (c) (69.81) (a)	69.77 (d) (64.18) (c) (77.71) (a)
Hainan	75.00 (c)	77.56 (c)	64.74 (c)	100.00 (c) (100.00) (d)	82.18 (c) (77.87) (d)	89.53 (c)	49.11 (c) (70.48) (d)
Guangxi	—	100.00 (d)	100.00 (d)	99.89 (d)	97.13 (d)	94.41 (d)	87.73 (d)
Beijing	—	—	42.38 (b)	33.16 (b)	69.56 (b) (41.84) (d)	31.33 (b) (50.49) (d)	29.94 (b) (40.79) (d)
PRC Total	52.69 (d) (27.87) (c)	48.86 (d) (22.78) (c)	59.22 (d) (21.67) (c)	68.35 (d) (24.74) (c)	64.93 (d) (30.40) (c)	62.06 (d) (28.96) (c)	56.42 (d) (23.63) (c)

Notes:
(a) pledged total of FDI and capital borrowing
(b) pledged FDI only
(c) realized total of FDI and capital borrowing
(d) realized total of FDI
(e) cumulative total

All the figures cover Macao where statistics are available. Except for Shenzhen, Zhuhai and Shantou, the figures for all the cities refer to the greater municipality rather than the city district or the SEZ (in the case of Xiamen) proper. However, for 1987 and 1988 for which the related figures are available for both the entire municipality and the SEZs proper, the Hong Kong shares for the three SEZs in Guangdong province show only very marginal differences between the two series. The PRC total for FDI covers the residual category "other investment from foreign investors." This is also widely listed as "commodity credits" to include investments made by way of compensation trade, international leasing and outward processing.

The main problems encountered are similar to those as explained in Table 18.6, as the country breakdowns for foreign investment are very often given alongside the classification by economic sectors.

Sources: As Appendix Table 18.A1; PRC totals are from *ZGTJNJ* (various issues).

a separate entry for Taiwan, but quasi-official accounting now (1992) shows Taiwan to be the fourth largest investor in China.[43]

Looking ahead, political détente between Taiwan and the Chinese mainland is likely soon to be reflected in the establishment of direct links. This would pave the way for the further massive transfer of Taiwanese capital, on a scale similar to the expansion of Hong Kong manufacturing investment in China during the last decade.

In assessing the potential impact of expanded Taiwanese involvement, several factors need to be kept in mind. The first is that Taiwan has for some years enjoyed the highest level of foreign exchange reserves in the world (about US$80 billion, as of December 1991).[44] This provides both the wherewithal and opportunity to seek investment outlets overseas. Secondly, with a population (around 20 million) slightly more than three times that of Hong Kong (5.8 million), and a per capita income that is comparable (US$9,000, compared with US$12,000), Taiwan's foreign trade intensity approaches that of the British Crown Colony. Excluding re-exports, Taiwan's exports in 1991 totalled US$76 billion (*cf.* US$29 billion for Hong Kong; and US$72 billion for the PRC).[45] Given that both the export structure and income level of both regions of "Greater China" are comparable, Taiwan appears to be poised to emulate Hong Kong in relocating its labour-intensive export production to the mainland prior to technological upgrading.[46]

Hong Kong's exports may provide an approximate measure of the potential investment flow from Taiwan. The 1991 estimate of Hong Kong's total exports (US$29 billion), as noted above, took no account of re-exports – essentially involving China – which in the same year totalled US$69 billion, a sum that would have seemed inconceivable before the adoption of the open-door strategy.[47] Most of the exports were output from *sanzi* enterprises, funded by Hong Kong investors.[48] If the Hong Kong re-export ratio (US $69/$29 billion) were applied to Taiwan's domestic export base (US$76 billion), the present level of *sanzi* exports and investment in China deriving from the activities of Hong Kong investors might be doubled. Although crude, this estimate is an indication of the possible direction and magnitude of changes which could be triggered by the normalization of relations across the Taiwan Strait.

South Korea has also shown keen interest in investing in China (especially in Shandong province). The expected normalization of diplomatic relations is therefore another factor which may further contribute to the current "investment fever" in China.[49]

In the end, however, it is Japan which is likely to hold the key to any major breakthrough in foreign investment. It is a curious fact that Japanese involvement in China has been marginal, mainly confining itself to governmental loans.[50] Its FDI contribution (US$1.93 billion during 1988–90) was, for example, little more than that extended to Indonesia between 1983 and 1987 (US$1.65 billion).[51] Indonesia has in fact been the largest Asian recipient of Japanese FDI and virtually the only country to enjoy a trade surplus vis-à-vis Japan. It is difficult to know why Indonesia should have been preferred to China by the Japanese. No less strange is the fact that it was German and French companies (Volkswagen and Peugeot), rather than Toyota, Mazda, Nissan or Honda – all of which have made massive inroads into American and West European markets – which struck the first motor car investment agreements to produce for the Chinese market. What is more, the Volkswagen (Santana) deal was based on China's agreement to obtain the necessary foreign exchange by diverting funds which had originally been earmarked to facilitate car imports from Japan.

What explains this lack of interest in direct investment in China?[52] It may be that Japan perceives its share as already having been represented by Hong Kong and Taiwan investors, whose manufacturing investment in China has, after all, been based on the use of Japanese machinery and equipment and semi-manufactured materials for "outward processing." Nor is such a "trade-for-investment" substitution as cumbersome as it appears. Nevertheless, Japan would undoubtedly benefit from increased accessibility to the Chinese domestic market. In this respect, it is significant that against the background of pressures from GATT and an increase in the American trade deficit with China in recent years, major service sectors (such as retail commerce, banking, transport and communications) now seem poised to receive direct foreign investment.[53] The lifting of all import regulatory taxes, beginning in April 1992,[54] can also be expected to help boost the inflow of import-substituting FDI, as overseas investors take advantage of the de-control of imports and foreign exchange. Japanese investors are in a stronger position than any of the major western countries to meet Chinese demand for industrial import-substitutes, except perhaps for nuclear, aircraft, satellite communications and advanced defence technologies.

Pudong seems to be a particular focus of China's renewed open-door policy. It was apparently Chen Yun himself (the arch-conservative opponent of Deng's strategy) who coined the term "new zone" (*xinqu*) to apply to this project, to distinguish it from other, well-established "special zones" (*tequ*). In contrast to the SEZs, which have been dominated by small-scale, labour-intensive and export-orientated manufacturing investment from Hong Kong, Pudong is expected to attract large-scale foreign investment, embodying the most advanced western technology. The new zone has also been described as a "dragon head" (*longtou*), designed to effect major economic changes throughout the Yangzi River Basin.

It is not clear in what degree of detail the Pudong strategy has been formulated. But given that another Hong Kong is simply not available to assist in creating a second Shenzhen, the core of the project would appear to be one of massive import substitution, designed to ensure that there is no premature collapse to damage public morale. It is also difficult to predict how quickly China's domestic market will be opened to FDI in coming years.

What can be said is that any significant move in this direction will have major implications. These do not merely derive from subjecting domestic large and medium-scale industrial enterprises (the prime focus of central planning) to competitive international pressures. They also arise from potential shifts in the industrial structure and its regional complexion, consequent upon any decontrol of the direction and allocation of FDI in China – shifts which might reflect a fundamental realignment of industrialization strategy.

It is beyond the scope of this study to speculate on whether such a policy shift would be politically acceptable. Certainly, associated economic changes – to wages, incomes, consumption, commodity prices and (not least) foreign exchange rate policy – might prove to be unpalatable. If this were so, the 1990s might well witness a gradualist approach, characteristic of Dengist pragmatism, of controlled economic integration with the west. Adverse political developments might delay this process. But given the strength of current commitment to reform and opening up – and against the background of the collapse of the Soviet bloc – it is unlikely that any new political leadership could wholly reverse it.

CONCLUDING REMARKS

This investigation has shown that following a decade of experimentation foreign direct investment has become a well-established and important part of Chinese economic activity. The strategy of seeking to maximize foreign exchange earnings through export-orientated foreign investment has meant that Sino-foreign joint ventures have been largely isolated from the core of the centrally-planned domestic economy. But there are two respects in which this "alienated" FDI sector has come to assume critical importance. First, it has become a major earner of foreign exchange. Secondly, it has become the bridgehead for the introduction of foreign capital into import-substitution investment in China.

The Chinese leadership is undoubtedly aware that there are limits to the expansion of foreign investment that is exclusively export-orientated. This is not simply because of western countries' limited capacity to absorb associated products. Rather, it reflects the fact that the accumulation of any substantial trade surplus, such as China presently enjoys with western countries, invites political pressures from those countries for a reciprocal opening-up of the domestic market. That said, Chinese authorities do appear to be willing gradually to expose protected domestic industries to competitive international pressures, even if it is difficult to predict how rapidly such controlled relaxation will proceed.

The official position is well summed up in the following extract from a recent textbook compiled by the Central Party School:

> . . . In utilizing foreign capital, [we] should implement a strategy of

> combining import substitution and export promotion. First of all, [we] should make use of foreign capital in order to import advanced technology. As a reward, [we] should open up parts of the domestic market to products for which our country has hitherto relied on imports. The implementation of this strategy will have a positive effect on raising our country's economic capability and technological level, as well as realizing [the goal of] industrialization and building up an independent and integrated industrial system.[55]

If this reads as a cautious statement (perhaps in order to pacify disgruntled hardliners), its rhetoric is certainly very different from that of the Cultural Revolution, when the same goal of industrialization was based exclusively on the principle of "self-reliance." Furthermore, the debt of foreign capital involvement in China is now such that, with or without Deng Xiaoping, the policy of the last decade is most unlikely to be reversed. Against the background of the collapse of the Soviet Union, one could even, in part, interpret the ongoing campaign to accelerate economic opening up as a political act. Hence the underlying political theme of repudiating the "leftists." From this point of view, the possibility of a political backlash seems remote.

Looking ahead, much will hinge on the pace of domestic economic reforms. More specifically, any significant shift in policy towards a genuine import-substitution foreign investment regime will necessarily require the de-regulation of large and medium-scale industrial enterprises. This is because these enterprises constitute the focus of centralized planning and are the focus of modern industrialization in China. Significant decontrol of this sector would encourage integration of the Chinese economy with the west and thereby facilitate the looked-for transfer of advanced technology via direct foreign investment.

This is again an area in which predictions are hazardous. It is, however, interesting that an increasing number of large and medium-scale enterprises, notably in Shanghai, have recently been accorded the kind of managerial flexibility hitherto extended to Sino-foreign joint ventures. In seeking the "invigoration" of this industrial core, policy emphasis has shifted markedly from the "contractual responsibility system" to "pushing [such enterprises] towards the market" (*tuixiang shichang*). Even more significant, the Central Committee's Document No. 4 (June 1992) may presage the regulation of the State Planning Commission – traditionally, the symbol of Soviet-style centralized planning and control in China – to a mere policy centre.[56] If this were to happen, its role would become one of macro-economic regulation, rather than of operational involvement in setting physical input and output targets and balancing material-technical supplies in state industries.

The changes that have taken place (and are still doing so) in China point to an alternative strategy to the "big bang" of the Soviet Union and Soviet bloc countries. Whatever the outcome may be, a host of western investors has already eagerly sought to cash in on the opportunity presented by the "whirlwind" unleashed early in 1992 by Deng Xiaoping.

NOTES

1 Nicholas R. Lardy, *Foreign Trade and Economic Reform in China, 1978–1990* (Cambridge: Cambridge University Press, 1992), p. 5. See also pp. 1–15 for a more detailed discussion of the different foreign trade regimes in relation to the emerging Chinese situation.

2 See *Zhongguo tongji nianjian (Chinese Statistical Yearbook 1991*) (hereinafter *ZGTJNJ* 1991), p. 40 for the accumulation ratio, and p. 150 for investment fund allocation among the major economic sectors.

3 For an elaboration on the implications of the Stalinist legacy on economic reforms in foreign trade and Chinese industry at large, see Y. Y. Kueh, "Growth imperatives, economic recentralization, and China's open-door policy in *Australian Journal of Chinese Affairs*, No 24 (July 1990), pp. 93–119; and "The Maoist legacy and China's new industrialization strategy," *The China Quarterly*, No. 119 (September 1989) pp. 441–4

4 Good examples of FDI ventures being allowed wholly or partly to target output for domestic sales include Schindler Elevators (Switzerland), Pilkington Glass (England), Bell Telephone (Belgium), and Volkswagen Santana (Germany). For an earlier survey of representative joint ventures in China see Samuel P. S. Ho and Ralph Huenemann, *China's Open-Door Policy: The Quest for Foreign Technology and Capital* (Vancouver: University of British Columbia Press, 1984). The Trade Development Council of Hong Kong has recently become highly optimistic that the vast Chinese market is poised to open up to its wide variety of consumer goods; see *South China Morning Post* (hereafter *SCMP*), 20 March 1992 (Business Post, p. 5), and *Ta-kung pao* (Hong Kong) (hereafter *TKP*), 17 June 1992, p. 15.

5 The American government successfully negotiated with the Chinese an agreement on 16 January 1992 relating to protection of intellectual property rights, and moved swiftly afterwards to press for the lifting of essential import barriers by October 1992, under Section 301 of the American Trade Act.

6 Reference is to the summary terms "Yanhai jingji kaifanqu" as used by the State Statistical Bureau for its 1988 survey (see notes and sources to Table 18.1). The *econocoas* areas cover, in the order that they were declared open for foreign investment (and as in Table 18.1): (1) the four Special Economic Zones (SEZs) set up in 1979/1980 in Guangdong and Fujian provinces, (2) the 14 opened coastal cities (OCCs), from Dalian in Liaoning province in the North to Beihai in Guangxi province in the South, made available in 1984, and (3) the opened coastal provinces (OCPs), from Liaoning to Guangxi and Hainan provinces, comprising a total of 288 *xian* (counties), which were all covered by a single government decree for opening up in early 1988. Between 1984 and 1988 smaller pockets of coastal areas (notably the Pearl River Delta, the Yangzi River Delta, and the Liaoning peninsula) were similarly opened, and earlier both Guangdong and Fujian were given special privileges to shape their own external economic relations. Likewise, Hainan Island was converted into an independent province in 1988 and made a Special Economic Zone at the same time. Both the centrally-controlled municipalities of Tianjin and Shanghai were included in the list of the 14 OCCs, but they also form part of the 11 OCPs, with all their subordinated municipals and *xians*. For simplicity, this study merely distinguishes between the three major categories of area, i.e. SEZs, OCCs and OCPs, ignoring, for example, distinctions

within the major opened cities between the city proper and the districts designated as economic-technological development areas (*jingji jishu kaifaqu*). However, while initially the different areas represented different schemes of tax and money incentive, the distinction has become increasingly blurred over the years amidst increased Chinese efforts to court foreign capital.

7 The disparity can indeed be easily confirmed if one probes into the detailed *xian* data for the 11 OCPs as given in *KFQTJZL* (cited under Table 18.1).

8 FDI pledged declined sharply from US$5,931 million in 1985 to US$2,834 million in 1986, and the growth rate of FDI realized was also reduced substantially in 1986. See *ZGTJNJ* 1991, p. 629. Nicholas Lardy, in his *China's Entry into the World Economy* (Lanham: University Press of America, 1987) attributed the decline to the Chinese "requirement that each joint-venture project be self sufficient in terms of foreign exchange" (p. 36) and rising office rental and labour costs (pp. 36–7). The World Bank's *China: External Trade and Capital* (Washington, D.C.: The World Bank, 1988) has similar explanations (pp. 256–7). But these problems have always been encountered by foreign investors, and cannot fully explain the abrupt downturn in 1986.

9 Essentially, Zhao's theory is that by requesting FDI ventures to "[place] two heads outside" (see Introduction), China could follow the path of South Korea, Taiwan, Hong Kong and Singapore in order to benefit from the international investment and commodity flows and generate extra foreign earnings for domestic finances, without exposing the centralized industrial core to the outside world.

10 For the Eighth Five-Year Plan (1991–95), the Shanghai government planned to inject 20 billion *yuan* into Pudong, at an estimated total of 50 billion *yuan* needed for infrastructure investment. See *TKP*, 24 March 1992, p. 3. The 40% share is equal to Shanghai's total fixed asset investment for 1991. For a comprehensive report on the Pudong project against the background of Greater Shanghai, see CERD Consultants Ltd., *Shanghai-Pudong baogao (Report)*, Hong Kong, September 1991.

11 *TKP*, 18 June 1992, p. 2.

12 This is quite different from earlier observations when most of the FDI went to contractual joint ventures as a safeguard against possible investment risks. See Y. Y. Kueh and Christopher Howe, "China's international trade: policy and organizational change and their place in the 'Economic Readjustment'," *The China Quarterly*, No. 100, (December 1984). pp. 813–48.

13 The figure can be obtained from Appendix Table 18.A2.

14 See notes to Table 18.3 and Appendix Table 18.Al.

15 This is revealed in Appendix Table 18.Al.

16 The figures for the intervening years 1986–89 for the 11 OCPs and Guangdong are respectively 94, 91, 86 and 84, and 54, 47, 46 and 44%. These figures refer to the changes in the cumulative total, but they are not exactly comparable to those given in Table 18.3, because for the base years 1979–84, the categories FDI and foreign borrowings have different missing figures. See Appendix Tables 18.A1 and 18.A2.

17 Because of exorbitant property prices in Hong Kong in 1991/1992 many real estate developers from Hong Kong have recently turned to Guangdong province across the border, aimed both at commuting Hong Kong residents and foreign investors in China. Hong Kong newspapers contain advertisements for sales of such properties almost on a daily basis, although it is difficult to estimate the possible volume of FDI made by this.

18 This is confirmed by a recent comprehensive survey conducted by the Federation

of Hong Kong Industries, entitled *Hong Kong's Industrial Investment in the Pearl River Delta*, Hong Kong, 1992.

19 See n. 4, above.

20 See Jean-Francois Hennart, *A Theory of Multinational Enterprise* (Ann Arbor: The University of Michigan Press, 1982), pp. 19–20, for an elaboration of the product cycle model initially developed by Raymond Vernon in 1966, to explain the expansion of FDI by American overseas multinationals.

21 A United States government report maintains, however, that after adjusting for China–U.S. inflation differentials, the *RMB* exchange rate against the U.S. dollar has depreciated in real terms since 1989, although "from 1984 through 1988, nominal devaluation of the *yuan* against the dollar was not sufficient to offset the impact of rising prices in China," resulting in a real appreciation of *RMB*. See U.S. Information Services. EPF413, 16 May 1991, p. 40. The discrepancy evidently depends on what inflation rates are used for the estimates.

22 The foreign capital shares as estimated in Table 18.5 are not exactly comparable to those shown in Figure 18.1. It is not known how the lower *ZGTJNJ* 1991 figures (for Figure 18.1) are calculated, especially with respect to the possible U.S. dollar conversion rate used. But the slightly higher shares obtained here (for Table 18.5) may be partly because these figures relate the whole of any FDI to the fixed assets investment base. although part of the FDI may not have constituted such investment.

23 Wu Zhenkun and Song Zihe (eds.). *Duiwai kaifang jingji fazhan zhanlu bijiao yanjiu (A Comparative Study of the Development Strategies of Opening up the Economy)* (Beijing: Zhonggong zhongyang dangxiao chubanshe, 1991), p. 45. The estimate seems to cover both FDI and foreign borrowing.

24 The estimated average 1985–90 share was obtained by applying the same ratio separately to each of the years concerned. This therefore ignores the possible implications of changes in the *RMB*'s exchange rate.

25 The shares would be 24.44% for 1985–90 combined and 27.40% for 1990, based on fixed assets investment of the state sector alone.

26 The Chinese GNP/GDP measures as adopted since the mid-1980s are still not exactly comparable to the familiar western counterparts because of incomplete coverage of the service sector, but the discrepancy has been very much narrowed from the conventional measure of "net material product" (*guomin shouru*) which excludes a large part of the tertiary sector.

27 Related value-added data are rarely available, with the notable exception of Shenzhen: see *Shenzhenshi guomin jingji tongji ziliao 1989 (National Economic-Statistical Material for Shenzhen Municipality)* (hereafter *SZGMJJTJZL* 1989).

28 See *TKP*, 16 March 1982 for the 70% rule. Nevertheless, it appears that many Sino-foreign joint ventures cannot meet this requirement for export. The average for Shenzhen is 65% in 1987–88 (in 1980 prices) and 58% for 1988 (in current prices), but 73.4% for 1989 (current prices): see *SZGMJJTJZL* 1989, pp. 44, 50, 68, 74, 76 and 120. The last percentage should not however be taken as an accurate measure, because it is obtained by relating total *sanzi* export to GVIO of those *sanzi* enterprises with "independent accounting" only. But as virtually all *sanzi* GVIO is produced by enterprises operating as independent economic entities the discrepancy should be minimal.

29 One of the representative FDI ventures in Shanghai is the Yaohua-Pilkington Glass Corporation which had a total sales volume of 270 million *yuan*, including 160 million *yuan* (i.e. 59%) in 1991 for export sales: see *TKP*, 22 May 1992, p. 4, and *Zhongguo duiwai maoyi (China's Foreign Trade)*, No. 3 (1992), p. 18 for a more comprehensive survey of the joint venture.

30 As a means to mitigate the strict requirements for foreign exchange balance, a number of new policy provisions were given in 1986, including "Guanyu waishang touzi qiye goumai guonei chanpin chukou jiejue waihui shouzhi pingheng de banfa" ("Measures concerning the purchases of domestic products by foreign-funded enterprises for export for balancing foreign exchange requirements), 20 January 1990.

31 See Appendix Table 18.A8.

32 *Ibid.*

33 This can be shown by relating for example the given share of the SEZs to that of Shanghai. The ratio declines over the years.

34 For details about the various components of *sanzi* enterprises' foreign exchange expenditure and receipts see Huang Xunpin, "Shilun Zhongwai heyin qiye de waihui pinheng wenti," in *Guangdong shehui kexue (Guangdong Social Sciences)*, No. 2 (1987), pp. 85–8.

35 Other factors accounting for the continued imbalances may include illicit sales of imported *sanzi* machinery and equipment to domestic buyers, "over-invoicing" of import bills, and depressed export quotations for tax evasion purposes. This seems to be a real and widespread practice among the *sanzi* enterprises, but it is impossible to estimate to what extent it accounts for the estimated *sanzi* deficit.

36 These are the figures given by Li Guixian at a press interview during the 25th Annual Meeting of Asian Development Bank, held in Hong Kong; see *TKP*, 6 May 1992, p. 2.

37 Li Guixian (*ibid.*) gives a debt service ratio of 8%. *TKP*, 24 April 1992 cited a MOFERT source to give a net foreign debt balance of US$52.58 billion, with a debt service ratio of 8.5% up to the end of June 1991.

38 See World Bank, *China's External Trade and Capital* (Washington D.C.: The World Bank, 1988), p. 28.

39 This has been prominently reported in the Hong Kong press. See for example *TKP*, 6 June 1992 about the FDI intake in Shenzhen (p. 18), Fujian (p. 4); and *TKP*, 28 May 1992 about Shanghai. *Cf.* also *SCMP* (Hong Kong), 3 April 1992 (Business Post, p. 2) for a similar report.

40 Moreover the frenetic buying even extended to the "B shares" issued by Chinese enterprises; see *SCMP*, 7 June 1992 (Money Post. p. 6). These stock shares are backed by strong foreign exchange earnings and can only be bought with foreign currency, in contrast to the "A shares" which cater to domestic Chinese subscribers. Note that the Hong Kong Stock Exchange is still pondering whether the major Chinese companies with B shares could he allowed to be publicly listed in Hong Kong without complying with the strict local legal and accounting requirements for listing.

41 An increased share seems to have been taken by mainland Chinese interests based in Hong Kong, but it appears unlikely that such ventures will overrule the importance of genuine Hong Kong investors. For a comprehensive study of Hong Kong's involvement in China see Y. W. Sung, *The China–Hong Kong Connection: the Key to China's Open Door Policy* (Cambridge: Cambridge University Press, 1991).

42 See *ZGTJNJ* 1991, p. 630 for the country-wise distribution of FDI in China.

43 See for example *Wen hui pao* (Hong Kong), 5 June 1992, p. 2; and *TKP*, 13 February 1992, p. 23. A number of Chinese provincial statistical yearbooks do have a separate entry for Taiwanese FDI in recent years. *TKP (ibid.)* reports that Guangdong had the largest FDI intake from Taiwan in 1991, with 410 new Taiwanese enterprises with a pledge of investment of US$490 million. Fujian ranked second, with 329 enterprises and US$400 million. The same sources show that compared with 1990, pledged Taiwanese investment increased by 190%

in Hainan, 50% in Shanghai. 34% in Liaoning, 30% in Beijing and 60% in Nanjing.

44 See C. J. Lee, "An analysis of the international factors that influence the development of small and medium enterprises: the case of Taiwan," paper presented at the conference on "Global Interdependence and Asia-Pacific Co-operation," Hong Kong, 8–10 June 1992.

45 GATT statistics as cited in *SCMP*, 30 March 1992 (Business Post, p. 2).

46 Compared with Hong Kong, Taiwan certainly has a stronger industrial base and demand for technological upgrading of its industrial structure.

47 See n. 45, above.

48 The export of *sanzi* enterprises through Hong Kong has indeed become so substantial that in the last couple of years it has been the focal point of a China–U.S. trade dispute, with the Chinese arguing that its trade surplus with the U.S. should essentially be accounted for by "outward processing" from Hong Kong for which the Chinese partners earn only a minimal share of processing fees.

49 Note that South Korea's export (virtually the same as China) ranks with Taiwan as the world's thirteenth (or fourteenth) largest exporter; see n. 45, above.

50 *ZGTJNJ* 1991, p. 630 shows that for 1989 and 1990 Chinese foreign borrowings from Japan amounted to US$2,595 and 2,500 million respectively, compared with US$1,027 and 1,011 million from the second-largest lender, the World Bank.

51 *Cf. ZGTJNJ* 1990, p. 654, *ZGTJNJ* 1991, p. 630 and Christopher Howe, "China, Japan and economic interdependence in the Asia Pacific region," in *The China Quarterly*, No. 124 (December 1991), pp. 662–93.

52 Christopher Howe, "China, Japan and economic interdependence," attributes the Japanese disinterest partly to the cancellation by the Chinese of the Long-term Trade Agreement in the early 1980s and the souring of Sino-Japanese relations that followed. "Political frictions in the mid 1980s and the failure of the Chinese to satisfy Japanese demands for a stable and non-discriminatory investment environment have [also] led in recent years to an investment 'strike' by Japanese companies and a major mismatch of intentions and expectations" (p. 683).

53 Yaohan, a Hong Kong-based multinational of Japanese origin has recently completed a major deal to open in Shanghai the largest department store in China. This was closely followed by plans for Sun Hung Kai, a giant multi-purpose holding company from Hong Kong, to develop the largest commercial complex in Beijing, just to the east of the Forbidden City.

54 See *TKP*, 3 March 1992, p. 2. The regulatory import taxes are primarily for marking up prices of imported producer foods to levels comparable to that produced domestically. The measure is designed partly to protect domestic industries from outside competition, and partly to balance the discrepancy between internal and external prices caused by the distorted Chinese price system.

55 Wu Zhenkun and Song Zihe, *Development Strategies of Opening up the Economy*, pp. 45–6.

56 The document has not yet been publicly made available, but *TKP*, 15 June 1992, p. 2 disclosed considerable details.

Appendix

Table 18.A1. Foreign Direct Investment (FDI) in the economically opened coastal (*econocoas*) areas in China, 1979–91 (million US$)

	1979	*1980*	*1981*	*1982*	*1983*	*1984*	*1985*	*1986*	*1987*	*1988*	*1989*	*1990*	*1991*
SWZs	—	—	—	—	—	385.75	334.77	480.79	367.46	441.97	613.19	655.63	721.78
Shenzhen	15.37	32.64	112.82	73.79	143.93	210.50	193.40	380.73	280.13	299.99	302.46	389.94	398.75
Zhuhai	4.15	15.75	13.67	56.33	29.39	126.94	53.45	45.18	33.82	47.40	53.28	69.10	134.33
Shantou	—	—	—	—	1.54	7.87	14.64	20.95	35.98	46.62	47.65	123.86	56.14
Xiamen	← [1979–83] 10.73 →					40.44	73.28	33.93	17.53	47.96	209.80	72.73	132.56
OCCs	—	—	—	—	—	—	275.12	334.35	477.67	537.37	726.43	642.16	797.27
							(301.65)	(374.14)	(517.07)	(680.86)	(908.62)	(861.39)	(1,087.90)
Dalian	—	—	—	—	—	—	14.32	30.49	49.90	74.88	80.57	201.29	261.11
Tianjin	← [1979–84] 12.87 →						32.51	42.81	133.13	61.15	31.42	36.93	93.88
Qingdao	—	—	—	—	—	—	2.30	10.73	14.00	12.33	58.01	45.88	46.47
Shanghai	—	← [1980–83] 87.00 →				36.00	107.54	148.90	214.01	233.17	422.12	177.19	164.20
Guangzhou	9.84	30.13	35.31	52.68	52.89	155.87	118.45	101.42	66.63	155.84	134.31	180.87	231.61
OCPs	—	—	—	—	—	—	929.94	1,110.95	1,129.00	1,931.55	2,333.53	2,711.44	—
							(1,069.99)	(1,302.66)	(1,476.14)	(2,225.87)	(2,787.07)	(2,925.56)	—
Liaoning	1.13	4.57	0.80	4.67	7.20	14.74	24.58	48.18	90.84	130.55	126.14	257.31	—
Hebei	—	—	—	—	—	4.95	8.24	11.27	10.34	19.10	43.73	44.47	—
Shandong	—	—	—	—	—	16.42	34.20	65.02	64.87	111.55	163.33	185.70	—
Jiangsu	—	—	—	—	—	—	33.47	33.76	86.35	125.51	127.13	133.97	—
Zhejiang	← [1979–82] 33.62 →				—	—	26.63	24.77	36.30	43.79	53.96	49.14	—
Fujian	0.83	3.63	1.50	1.21	14.38	48.28	118.60	62.50	55.35	145.47	348.03	319.89	—
Guangdong	91.43	208.29	262.57	271.29	397.23	631.46	629.50	783.62	730.79	1,212.26	1,323.24	1,582.31	1,823.00
Hainan	—	0.10	1.09	0.83	2.38	14.71	23.99	32.59	9.11	122.45	94.97	103.02	106.76
Guangxi	← [1979–84] 80.87 →						30.73	49.24	45.05	20.87	53.00	35.63	—

Table 18.A1. Foreign Direct Investment (FDI) in the economically opened coastal (*econocoas*) areas in China, 1979–91 (million US$)

	1979	*1980*	*1981*	*1982*	*1983*	*1984*	*1985*	*1986*	*1987*	*1988*	*1989*	*1990*	*1991*
Beijing	—	←[1980–84] 350.00→					88.82	149.71	105.79	503.18	320.16	278.95	—
Provincial total	←[1979–84] 2,859.02→						1,318.04	1,741.65	1,782.73	3,149.73	3,437.33	3,436.15	—
PRC total	←[1979–81] 1,118.00→			649.00	916.00	1,419.00	1,959.00	2,244.00	2,647.00	3,739.00	3,774.00	3,755.00	4,370.00

Notes: Foreign direct investment as defined here covers FDI proper plus investment made by way of compensation trade, international leasing and other types of "commodity credits" (*chanpin xindai*). With the exception of the PRC total, the figures do not include FDI sponsored by the various central branch ministries, which include notably the National Offshore Petroleum Corporation, MOFERT and CITIC. It seems quite likely that a major proportion of these centrally-sponsored FDI are also allocated to the *econocoas* areas. However, they amounted to a rather small total of US$336.12 million for 1989 and US$318.72 million for 1990, for example, as compared with the provincial total of US$5.848.21 and 5,493.78 million respectively. The PRC total covers nevertheless both the provincial and central FDI.

Figures in parenthesis for OCCs (opened coastal cities) and OCPs (opened coastal provinces) are sum totals for all the 15 OCCs and 11 OCPs (including Tianjin and Shanghai) respectively. The SEZs figures cover not only the SEZ proper, but the *xian* as well. The same goes for Tianjin and Shanghai, and other OCCs. The OCP figures for Guangdong and Fujian include their SEZs' shares, and that of Guangzhou (in the case of Guangdong), and those for Liaoning and Shandong cover respectively Dalian and Qingdao as well. The provincial total for 1979–84 is estimated from the incomplete figures for the 11 OCPs for the same period by assuming that OCP total makes up 78.91% of the national provincial total. The assumed percentage is derived as the average for 1985–90. The result is clearly an underestimate, because most of the 1979–84 figures are missing for Hebei, Shandong and Jiangsu. Nevertheless the bias is probably not great, as the three provinces seem to have hardly any FDI in this period. No entry means either that FDI is nil or that figures are not available.

All the figures are in US$. Where *RMB* figures are used in this study they are obtained by applying the official annual average of exchange rates for the conversion; where deflated *RMB* figures are used, they are derived by applying the official capital accumulation deflator as explained in Table 18.A3.

Sources: Various standard Chinese statistical and economic yearbooks from central and provincial levels, including *Zhongguo tongji nianjian (Chinese Statistical Yearbook)* (hereafter *ZGTJNJ*), *Zhongguo duiwai jingji maoyi nianjian (Chinese Foreign Economic Relations and Trade Yearbook)* (hereafter *JMNJ*) and *Zhongguo jingji nianjian (Chinese Economic Yearbook)* (hereafter *JJNJ*), and similar provincial, municipal and SEZ yearbooks or special compendia. Figures for Shanghai and Beijing for 1980–84 are from Ulrich Hiemenz, "Foreign direct investment and capital formation in China since 1979," in Dieter Casel and Gunter Heiduk (eds.). *China's Contemporary Economic Reforms as a Development Strategy* (Baden-Baden: Nomos Verlagsgesellschaft, 1990), p. 86. Where figures conflict, the central and latest Statistic Information Consultancy Service Centre (edited by *Zhongguo tongji xinxibao*) and distributed by CERD Consultants Ltd., Hong Kong (part 2) (February 1992), pp. 24–7, I am grateful to Dr Thomas Chan, managing director of CERD for making the information available.

Table 18.A2. Foreign capital borrowing and FDI in the *econocoas* areas in China (million US$)

	1979	*1980*	*1981*	*1982*	*1983*	*1984*	*1985*	*1986*	*1987*	*1988*	*1989*	*1990*	*1991*
SEZs	—	—	—	—	—	417.81	539.43	712.70	590.52	929.64	1,023.19	958.45	1,196.30
Shenzhen	15.37	32.64	112.82	73.79	143.93	230.13	329.25	489.33	404.49	444.29	458.09	518.57	579.88
Zhuhai	4.15	15.75	13.67	56.33	29.39	126.94	91.04	75.68	69.63	217.62	169.47	108.28	168.79
Shantou	—	—	—	—	7.04	16.10	33.14	76.93	63.18	103.64	157.41	158.53	264.78
Xiamen	← [1979–83] 10.73 →					44.64	86.00	70.76	53.22	164.09	238.22	173.07	182.85
OCCs							367.16	840.71	1,247.70	1,292.91	1,163.87	1,187.38	2,200.99
							(458.86)	(928.91)	(1,355.14)	(3,648.54)	(2,336.46)	(1,538.87)	(2,658.48)
Dalian	—	—	—	—	—	—	14.86	43.61	270.11	213.46	193.63	394.17	417.05
Tianjin	← [1979–84] 19.81 →						69.21	281.41	361.79	344.01	167.76	96.56	476.29
Qingdao	—	← [1980–83] 87.00 →				—	18.99	51.53	43.65	39.78	101.72	75.19	78.95
Shanghai	—	—	—	—	—	178.75	108.79	285.84	485.68	440.47	466.49	321.04	851.28
Guanghzhou	9.84	30.13	35.31	52.68	52.89	181.84	155.31	178.32	86.47	255.19	234.27	298.42	377.42
OCPs	—	—	—	—	—	—	1,389.12	1,981.30	1,951.85	3,678.89	3,971.87	4,052.90	—
							(1,567.12)	(2,548.55)	(2,799.32)	(4,463.37)	(4,606.12)	(4,472.50)	
Liaoning	1.13	4.57	0.80	7.50	7.20	15.23	41.92	64.49	174.70	292.47	388.14	727.39	—
Hebei	—	—	—	—	—	5.46	10.50	19.01	10.34	28.51	92.91	97.80	—
Shandong	—	—	—	—	—	16.42	62.31	116.79	102.19	142.31	208.33	230.42	—
Jiangsu	—	—	—	—	—	—	51.11	45.57	143.08	156.70	161.16	247.69	—
Zhejiang	← [1979–82] 33.62 →					—	61.73	29.52	106.94	130.57	165.46	127.77	—
Fujian	42.34	9.18	4.51	2.63	47.93	61.68	171.09	165.51	142.44	293.95	387.92	426.84	—
Guangdong	91.43	214.00	288.00	281.00	407.00	644.00	919.10	1,428.00	1,217.00	2,440.00	2,390.27	2,015.41	2,571.66
Hainan	—	0.28	1.09	0.83	4.38	17.84	26.43	32.59	9.11	127.71	94.97	116.98	176.06
Guangxi	← [1979–84] 80.87 →						44.93	79.82	46.05	66.67	82.71	60.60	—
Beijing	—	← [1980–84] 350.00 →					116.28	162.82	161.74	583.89	477.04	392.02	—
Provincial total	← [1979–84] 2,859.02 →						1,599.13	2,775.31	3,211.15	5.609.93	5,843.21	5,493.78	—
PRC total	←[1979–81] 10,024.66→			2,432.34	1,980.64	2,704.52	4,462.11	7,258.30	8,451.56	10,226.39	10,059.15	10,289.35	11,137.98

Note: None of the figures except for the PRC total includes FDI and capital borrowing (indirect investment) sponsored by the various central branch ministries including, notably, borrowing by the Bank of China. It is not known how capital borrowing by the central authorities may have been allocated to the various provinces, although the amounts concerned (US$3,874.82 million in 1989 and 4,476.89 million in 1990) greatly exceed the comparable provincial totals of US$2,410.63 million and 2,057.63 million respectively. The PRC total covers however both the provincial and central shares.

Figures in parenthesis for the OCCs and OCPs are the sum totals respectively for all the 15 OCCs and 11 OCPs (including Tianjin and Shanghai). For other similar definitions and method of conversion into *RMB* value, see notes to Table 18.A1. Where the figures are the same as those given in Table 18.A1, it implies that capital borrowing is either nil or relevant statistics are not available.

Sources: As Table 18.A1, except for the 1991 figures which are from *TKP*, 17 March 1992 for Guangdong: *CLES* (part 2) (February 1992), pp. 24–7 for the other *econocoas* areas; and *TKP*, 21 April 1992, p. 2 for the PRC total (obtained by subtracting the sum total of the annual figures for 1979–90 from the given cumulative total of US$79,627 million for 1979–91).

Table 18.A3. Total fixed assets investments in the *econocoas* areas in China (100 million *yuan* in current prices)

	1979	*1980*	*1981*	*1982*	*1983*	*1984*	*1985*	*1986*	*1987*	*1988*	*1989*	*1990*	*1991*
SEZs	—	—	—	—	17.04	29.27	61.27	51.33	71.14	105.47	86.10	92.77	—
Shenzhen	0.50	1.25	2.70	6.33	9.11	15.56	30.84	21.84	28.52	43.62	51.75	53.66	70.40
Zhuhai	0.36	0.58	1.15	2.30	2.17	4.78	9.70	8.53	9.65	12.34	9.09	9.54	—
Shantou	1.90	—	—	—	2.93	3.32	9.01	11.07	22.32	37.18	12.53	12.01	—
Xiamen	1.07	1.28	1.78	2.43	2.83	5.61	11.72	9.89	10.65	12.33	12.73	17.56	—
OCCs	—	—	—	—	156.23	191.45	262.06	303.84	366.34	507.51	477.26	463.34	—
Dalian	—	—	—	—	8.56	12.01	22.00	29.60	37.60	38.89	28.25	28.72	—
Tianjin	24.77	23.92	27.60	35.06	41.58	48.66	66.94	72.04	77.75	88.65	85.27	88.48	—
Qingdao	3.50	4.75	3.96	5.30	4.94	6.49	10.74	15.05	17.45	26.11	26.22	28.46	—
Shanghai	—	—	—	71.33	76.01	92.51	118.76	141.16	185.28	263.64	244.19	227.09	—
Guangzhou	7.26	9.96	13.44	16.92	25.14	31.78	43.62	45.99	48.26	90.22	93.33	90.59	—
OCPs	—	—	—	475.41	494.27	680.57	940.54	1,167.77	1,510.16	1,907.25	1,780.15	1,911.52	—
				(580.80)	(637.16)	(855.22)	(1,178.89)	(1,448.97)	(1,852.14)	(2,358.15)	(2,205.36)	(2,334.87)	
Liaoning	—	—	—	69.44	72.94	96.17	139.02	177.71	218.98	267.26	251.03	260.36	—
Hebei	—	—	—	73.45	63.87	86.32	113.11	134.03	178.46	239.34	214.29	182.12	—
Shandong	61.35	69.97	79.60	85.00	94.09	139.27	193.42	223.07	297.76	369.82	336.64	334.79	—
Jiangsu	—	—	—	75.41	104.41	129.12	149.97	236.27	316.68	377.15	324.60	361.10	—
Zhejiang	—	—	—	41.71	43.98	64.89	105.44	130.18	185.47	230.18	212.72	257.90	—
Fujian	10.80	12.99	18.11	23.71	26.27	34.43	54.99	60.01	78.09	91.87	87.88	108.54	—
Guangdong	28.29	38.29	60.40	84.73	88.71	130.37	184.59	206.50	234.72	331.63	352.99	406.71	—
Hainan	—	—	—	3.24	3.21	5.31	10.58	12.77	14.54	21.19	28.99	39.21	—
Guangxi	9.61	12.56	10.98	17.72	22.09	28.17	42.07	55.23	64.41	77.42	66.76	68.57	—
Beijing	—	—	—	38.52	50.68	68.83	94.52	105.17	140.15	162.60	146.24	190.81	—
PRC total	—	910.85	961.01	1,230.40	1,430.06	1,832.87	2,543.19	3,019.62	3,640.86	4,496.54	4,137.73	4,449.29	5,276.82

Notes: The figures cover the most comprehensive measure of fixed assets investments comprising "basic construction," investment in "technical innovation and transformation" and others, as undertaken in both the state and collective ownership sectors, as well as by private individuals. Both "productive" and "non-productive" investments are included. All the figures are in current prices, and the official sources do not provide any investment price index. Where deflated figures are used in this study, they are all derived from the capital accumulation index which may be estimated by resorting to the available official deflators for national income (*guomin shouru*) and its consumption component. (We assumed constant weights based on the 1952 consumption and accumulation shares, and ignore the discrepancy between the production and expenditure sides of national income as the overall index is available only for the former series.) I am grateful to K.C. Yeh for suggesting this method of deflating. For the problems involved with adjusting for inflation in this respect, and for an alternative approach of deflating see G.H. Jefferson, "China's iron and steel industry." *Journal of Development Economics*, No. 33 (1990), pp. 330, 336–7, and 352–3.

The OCP totals in parenthesis include the shares of Tianjin and Shanghai which form part of the OCPs. A number of figures (Shantou 1983; Dalian 1983–84; Hainan 1982–83; Guangzhou 1981–82 and Guangxi 1981) are derived from the growth rates of investment in the state sector (see Table 18.A4).

Sources: *ZGTJNJ* (various issues) supplemented by similar provincial, municipal and SEZ volumes; and *Zhongguo guding zichan touzi tongji ziliao (Chinese Fixed Assets Investment Statistical Materials)*, 1980–85 and 1986–87, various pages. The 1991 figure for Shenzhen is from *TKP*, 17 March 1992 (which appears to cover the SEZ proper only), and the 1991 PRC total from premier Li Peng's government work report delivered at the National People's Congress on 20 March 1992.

Table 18.A4. Fixed assets investments by the state ownership sectors in the *econocoas* areas in China (100 million *yuan* in current prices)

	1979	*1980*	*1981*	*1982*	*1983*	*1984*	*1985*	*1986*	*1987*	*1988*	*1989*	*1990*	*1991*
SEZs	—	—	—	—	15.74	28.46	53.74	46.25	50.41	75.28	76.80	81.73	110.89
Shenzhen	0.50	1.25	2.70	6.33	8.86	16.37	29.19	21.19	22.68	35.37	45.40	52.49	70.02
Zhuhai	0.13	0.34	0.58	1.25	1.49	3.73	8.65	7.47	8.23	10.22	9.09	9.15	15.16
Shantou	—	—	—	—	2.93	3.32	7.06	9.19	10.40	20.98	12.53	10.03	14.00
Xiamen	1.06	1.17	1.38	2.11	2.46	5.04	8.84	8.40	9.10	8.71	9.78	10.06	11.71
OCCs	—	—	—	117.98	129.01	156.04	215.93	263.35	308.63	398.82	377.39	391.44	452.55
							(257.80)	(611.70	(385.20)	(497.30)	(460.84)		(572.98)
Dalian	—	—	—	6.74	7.69	10.79	19.76	27.50	32.40	36.54	29.03	27.24	40.97
Tianjin	—	—	25.28	30.04	33.81	38.56	55.08	61.03	62.28	71.07	68.40	72.18	106.44
Qingdao	3.27	4.21	3.21	4.32	4.39	5.68	9.24	12.70	15.10	22.22	23.05	23.62	31.46
Shanghai	—	—	44.26	61.62	65.08	75.80	95.91	119.00	154.45	198.68	178.81	192.23	195.77
Guangzhou	6.86	8.98	12.12	15.26	18.04	25.21	35.94	43.12	44.40	70.31	78.10	76.17	77.91
OCPs	—	—	218.63	277.20	303.70	392.06	591.21	708.51	862.08	1,089.11	969.10	1,125.27	1,259.14
			(288.17)	(368.86)	(402.59)	(506.42)	(742.20)	(888.54)	(1,078.81)	(1,358.86)	(1,216.31)	(1,389.68)	(1,561.35)
Liaoning	—	46.10	47.94	54.41	56.18	72.76	107.05	137.42	172.13	210.65	201.30	215.44	235.76
Hebei	—	—	30.98	39.25	42.38	48.65	62.59	73.89	86.36	111.34	101.25	110.98	122.87
Shandong	31.62	35.83	30.35	43.06	46.74	66.21	100.42	121.95	155.64	192.20	162.30	184.59	215.06
Jiangsu	—	—	27.55	34.78	45.48	51.59	77.10	93.81	125.07	151.31	119.14	129.78	153.13
Zhejiang	13.06	15.99	15.82	20.74	21.29	27.28	39.46	49.45	59.44	69.73	68.60	78.58	83.13
Fujian	10.51	12.61	12.81	15.12	16.92	21.07	36.99	40.04	48.89	53.69	50.29	64.69	68.84
Guangdong	20.06	25.72	38.99	51.77	55.92	80.65	131.11	148.58	162.27	232.26	201.54	269.46	289.79
Hainan	3.22	3.47	3.58	4.53	4.49	7.42	12.46	12.99	11.45	14.99	23.26	30.59	41.74
Guangxi	9.81	12.18	10.61	13.54	14.30	16.43	24.03	30.38	40.83	52.94	41.42	41.16	48.82
Beijing	—	—	32.21	32.94	39.94	53.31	72.87	87.65	115.83	133.24	116.30	152.03	140.09
PRC total	699.36	745.90	667.51	845.31	851.96	1,185.18	1,680.51	1,978.50	2,297.99	2,762.76	2,535.48	2,918.64	3,558.15

Notes: See notes to Table 18.A3 for explanation and method of deflating. The OCC and OCP figures in brackets cover all the 15 OCCs and the 11 OCPs (including Tianjin and Shanghai) respectively. The 1991 figures should be regarded as preliminary statistics. The same source (as noted below) also provides figures for percentage increases over 1990, but most of the figures differ from what can be estimated from the absolute data given here, except the PRC total for which no inconsistency is detected.

Sources: As Table 18.A3, except for the 1991 figures which are from *CLES*, part 2 (January 1992), p. 37, and (February 1992), pp. 24–7.

Table 18.A5. Gross value of industrial output (GVIO) in the *econocoas* areas in China (100 million *yuan* in current prices)

	1979	*1980*	*1981*	*1982*	*1983*	*1984*	*1985*	*1986*	*1987*	*1988*	*1989*	*1990*
SEZs	—	—	—	—	42.98	63.24	86.18	103.90	153.20	225.73	270.75	346.89
Shenzhen	0.61	0.84	2.43	3.62	7.20	18.15	27.04	35.70	57.60	88.81	116.46	167.55
Zhuhai	0.61	0.75	0.93	1.05	2.84	4.98	5.94	6.80	13.00	25.41	30.20	33.11
Shantou	17.57	21.79	—	—	20.92	25.02	40.14	48.89	68.00	94.28	68.61	74.95
Xiamen	8.05	9.43	10.39	11.32	12.02	15.09	21.85	24.69	32.86	48.16	55.49	71.28
OCCs	—	—	—	1,097.56	1,188.43	1,306.07	1,485.33	1,570.15	1,709.13	1,913.37	1,993.68	2,054.97
							(1,847.45)	(1,986.30)	(2,185.80)	(2,505.30)	(2,694.59)	(7,766.95)
Dalian	—	—	76.44	77.17	84.29	91.85	106.46	116.70	129.50	148.25	162.43	167.98
Tianjin	—	—	199.49	211.86	229.25	251.49	285.80	300.40	325.63	362.56	373.61	375.75
Qingdao	—	—	—	67.28	77.63	85.00	99.37	111.10	129.00	160.01	176.84	197.35
Shanghai	—	—	608.70	636.70	678.55	744.37	832.27	873.55	923.50	996.77	1,021.84	1,030.73
Guangzhou	—	91.23	99.10	104.55	118.71	133.36	161.43	168.40	201.50	245.78	258.96	283.16
OCPs	—	—	2,112,74	2,263.83	2,517.95	2,936.09	3,585.36	3,994.55	4,748.72	5,456.28	5,855.02	6,360.47
			(2,920.93)	(3,112.39)	(3,425.75)	(3,931.95)	(4,703.43)	(5,168.50)	(5,997.85)	(6,815.61)	(7,250.47)	(7,766.95)
Liaoning	—	—	451.36	476.31	516.69	577.66	664.39	709.80	782.20	845.96	876.99	878.01
Hebei	—	—	217.65	229.94	252.61	290.25	333.46	358.95	409.92	452.21	483.19	502.47
Shandong	—	—	343.62	367.58	405.55	456.24	539.98	591.25	699.45	858.75	971.92	1,056.77
Jiangsu	—	—	465.69	503.21	569.62	680.13	863.53	983.26	1,192.69	1,391.27	1,450.47	1,590.88
Zhejiang	—	—	213.67	230.70	268.15	333.85	443.95	515.17	613.57	717.60	746.42	794.60
Fujian	—	—	81.81	87.63	95.83	115.76	140.79	156.01	189.24	233.56	260.90	293.09
Guangdong	—	—	250.36	272.18	306.01	366.90	461.01	527.03	681.98	761.95	858.72	1,027.16
Hainan	—	—	6.97	7.52	8.60	11.11	14.57	15.49	19.24	24.06	25.23	23.54
Guangxi	—	—	81.61	88.76	94.89	104.19	123.68	137.59	160.43	170.92	181.18	193.95
Beijing	—	—	216.61	228.69	250.64	281.72	314.67	322.03	357.45	406.81	432.01	454.10
PRC total	—	—	5,177.67	5 ,577.45	6,166.54	7,029.85	8,294.51	9,028.46	10,364.67	11,577.85	12,294.56	13,023.73

Notes: All the figures exclude *cunban* (village operated) industries. The figure for Shantou for 1979 is assumed the same as for 1978, and for 1990 it is derived by applying its national income growth rate for 1990/89 (see Table 18.A6). The OCC and OCP total (in brackets) cover respectively all the 15 OCCs and 11 OCPs (including Tianjin and Shanghai). The PRC total refers to output from enterprises with "independent accounting" (*duli hesuan*) only. This may or may not be comparable to the other given figures. However, the possible discrepancy should be negligible, as these figures include most enterprises above the village level.

Sources: As Table 18.A3.

Table 18.A6. National income (net material product) in the *econocoas* areas in China, 1979–90 (100 million *yuan* in current prices)

	1979	*1980*	*1981*	*1982*	*1983*	*1984*	*1985*	*1986*	*1987*	*1988*	*1989*	*1990*	*1991*
SEZs	26.86	—	—	—	50.30	68.30	95.45	98.92	130.74	196.31	215.34	262.48	329.21
Shenzhen	1.60	2.21	4.20	6.77	10.75	20.22	26.37	27.29	36.26	56.85	72.16	94.26	—
Zhuhai	1.91	2.32	2.99	3.55	4.80	5.95	8.52	8.75	11.79	18.87	22.18	27.92	—
Shantou	18.51	—	—	—	26.59	31.80	45.54	46.77	62.86	91.90	89.45	97.72	—
Xiamen	4.84	5.86	6.66	7.65	8.16	10.33	15.02	16.11	19.83	28.69	31.55	42.58	—
OCCs	—	—	—	—	593.41	666.55	812.32	872.26	959.73	1,223.40	1,298.89	1,372.02	—
Dalian	—	42.60	42.00	42.80	47.00	56.40	69.79	85.18	100.88	128.10	140.17	147.87	—
Tianjin	84.63	93.10	96.00	101.03	108.37	121.68	150.91	165.95	185.66	221.09	234.41	244.05	—
Qingdao	37.32	41.60	41.28	42.69	50.77	59.92	68.77	76.89	91.66	120.32	132.30	143.36	—
Shanghai	—	—	—	—	311.03	341.20	409.73	425.08	473.61	565.34	586.84	617.22	—
Guangzhou	—	—	—	—	76.24	87.35	113.12	119.16	107.92	188.55	205.17	219.52	—
OCPs	—	—	—	—	2,075.85	2,478.52	3,082.19	3,463.57	4,183.86	5,292.05	5,979.55	6,420.48	—
					(2,495.25)	(2,941.40)	(3,642.83)	(4,054.60)	(4,843.13)	(6,078.48)	(6,800.80)	(7,281.75)	
Liaoning	219.50	249.60	249.40	261.60	298.00	354.15	425.72	481.43	566.39	694.48	770.95	783.79	—
Hebei	175.24	188.36	189.47	211.35	238.61	282.01	340.87	375.70	448.77	558.32	631.37	693.73	—
Shandong	220.02	252.17	298.38	332.35	379.33	447.86	552.29	595.84	735.62	915.26	1,055.98	1,144.22	—
Jiangsu	—	—	—	—	390.54	466.31	578.46	663.90	789.19	969.22	1,055.52	1,138.31	
Zhejiang	139.67	158.34	179.06	204.88	220.18	276.70	365.79	422.10	508.35	638.69	598.41	726.49	—
Fujian	62.91	72.87	89.79	98.54	105.76	128.70	164.79	183.61	226.22	307.59	359.83	388.77	—
Guangdong	180.39	217.61	250.81	285.47	303.26	366.27	467.27	525.53	656.25	894.57	1,034.91	1,132.21	1,279.40
Hainan	13.81	15.17	18.44	23.22	24.94	31.11	35.71	39.42	45.52	62.09	72.30	76.98	—
Guangxi	72.06	81.92	95.30	111.51	115.23	125.41	151.29	176.04	207.55	251.83	300.28	335.98	—
Beijing	—	—	—	—	—	157.30	194.50	206.00	236.20	307.70	336.80	366.95	—
PRC total	3,350.00	3,688.00	3,941.00	4,258.00	4,736.00	5,652.00	7,020.00	7,859.00	9,313.00	11,738.00	13,125.00	14,429.00	16,477.92

Notes: Figures in parenthesis cover Tianjin and Shanghai which are both part of the 11 OCPs. Where deflated figures are used in this study, they are all obtained by applying the official national income deflator, although for quite a number of the *econocoas* areas, local deflators are also available. We ignore therefore the possible regional variations in inflation rates. The 1983 figures for Shantou, Shanghai and Jiangsu are derived from the GVIO growth rates (see Table 18.A5).

Sources: As Table 18.A3, except for the 1991 PRC total which is from *TKP*, 21 March 1992, and the 1991 Shenzhen and Guangdong figures which are derived from reported percentage increases as in *TKP*, 17 March 1992.

Table 18.A7. Gross domestic (national) product in the *econocoas* areas in China, 1979–90 (100 million *yuan* in current prices)

	1979	*1980*	*1981*	*1982*	*1983*	*1984*	*1985*	*1986*	*1987*	*1988*	*1989*	*1990*	*1991*
SEZs	33.12	—	—	—	—	80.44	115.01	121.24	160.96	239.92	269.60	320.33	—
Shenzhen	1.96	2.70	4.96	8.26	13.12	23.42	33.25	35.50	47.48	73.75	97.81	107.20	—
Zhuhai	2.99	3.75	3.98	4.73	5.61	7.38	10.31	11.10	15.55	25.07	32.31	31.67	—
Shantou	22.85	—	—	—	—	37.35	53.49	54.93	73.83	105.61	101.55	130.88	—
Xiamen	5.32	6.40	7.41	8.67	9.44	12.29	17.96	19.71	24.10	35.49	37.93	50.58	—
OCCs	—	—	—	—	—	787.19	949.80	1,029.39	1,181.84	1,464.46	1,588.66	1,711.42	—
Dalian	—	—	—	—	—	68.00	79.30	96.30	114.05	151.24	165.44	178.60	—
Tianjin	93.00	103.52	107.96	114.10	123.40	147.47	175.71	194.67	220.00	259.64	283.34	300.31	—
Qingdao	43.45	48.30	49.40	51.77	61.71	70.95	84.25	94.98	112.60	142.56	155.47	168.24	—
Shanghai	—	—	—	—	—	404.74	486.18	504.39	561.98	670.83	696.54	744.67	—
Guangzhou	43.09	57.55	—	—	—	96.03	124.36	139.55	173.21	240.19	287.87	319.60	—
OCPs	—	—	—	—	—	2,926.53	3,575.77	4,052.24	4,869.57	6,223.28	7,032.84	7,687.33	—
						(3,478.74)	(4,237.66)	(4,751.30)	(5,651.55)	(7,153.75)	(8,012.72)	(8,732.31)	
Liaoning	223.20	266.20	285.80	301.90	347.20	415.60	489.60	567.60	663.70	839.30	922.10	964.89	—
Hebei	183.06	—	—	—	—	328.24	396.75	437.29	522.34	654.23	748.99	819.95	—
Shandong	255.00	294.40	337.90	379.10	428.30	543.60	631.30	689.90	822.30	1,050.79	1,175.07	1,332.13	—
Jiangsu	—	—	—	—	—	544.63	675.62	775.41	921.74	1,132.01	1,232.80	1,314.39	—
Zhejiang	157.64	179.68	203.26	230.57	251.26	314.21	413.84	479.79	575.45	721.73	792.32	836.81	—
Fujian	73.67	85.91	103.60	114.49	123.06	149.98	190.80	210.65	258.90	351.52	413.58	459.48	—
GNP	(73.86)	(86.37)	(104.29)	(114.97)	(123.57)	(151.08)	(191.97)	(212.12)	(260.36)	(354.09)	(416.65)	(465.84)	—
Guangdong	207.07	245.71	284.21	331.27	357.43	441.81	553.05	637.75	807.70	1,098.61	1,311.67	1,471.84	1,670.54
Hainan	—	—	—	—	—	38.19	43.84	48.39	55.88	74.76	86.87	95.01	—
Guangxi	84.59	97.33	113.46	129.15	134.60	150.27	180.97	205.46	241.56	300.33	349.44	392.83	—
Beijing	—	—	—	—	—	—	—	—	—	410.20	455.80	500.72	—
PRC total	3,998.10	4,470.00	4,473.00	5,193.00	5,809.00	6,902.00	8,557.60	9,696.30	11,301.00	14,018.20	15,916.30	17,686.10	18,924.13

Notes: The figures refer generally to GDP, except for the PRC total and the 11 OCPs (including Tianjin and Shanghai) for 1988 to 1990, and for Zhuhai, Dalian and Qingdao. Figures in parenthesis for the OCPs total for 1989 and 1990 refer to the sum total of all the 11 OCPs. For a number of areas (Shantou 1984–86; Dalian 1987; Shanghai 1984–87; Guangzhou 1984; Hebei 1984, 1986–87; Jiangsu 1984; and Hainan 1984–86) the figures are derived from the growth rates of national income as shown in Table 18.A6. Where deflated figures are used in this study, they are all obtained by applying the national GNP deflator, although for quite a number of the *econocoas* areas, the official provincial or municipal deflators are also available. We therefore ignore the possible variations in inflation rates.

Source: As Table 18.A3, except for the 1991 PRC total which is from *TKP*, 21 March 1992, and the Guangdong figure which is derived from reported percentage increase in *TKP*, 17 March 1992.

Table 18.A8. Total export and the *Sanzi* share in the *econocoas* areas in China, 1988–91 (100 million US$)

	Total				Sanzi share			
	1988	*1989*	*1990*	*1991*	*1988*	*1989*	*1990*	*1991*
SEZs	54.99	66.75	79.37	93.95	12.35	22.24	32.15	43.03
Shenzhen	36.64	44.96	52.16	57.88	9.66	16.63	22.93	29.24
Zhuhai	5.56	6.46	8.41	11.38	0.85	2.10	3.51	5.09
Shantou	7.63	8.29	9.61	11.98	0.89	1.53	2.27	3.40
Xiamen	5.16	7.05	9.20	12.71	0.95	1.97	3.44	5.30
OCCs	87.05	93.29	106.94	123.26	2.71	7.53	12.31	23.26
	(92.43)	(103.86)	(121.82)	(141.22)	(5.54)	(8.36)	(14.27)	(26.52)
Dalian	4.48	5.68	7.12	10.61	0.30	1.06	1.72	4.29
Tianjin	17.09	16.92	17.78	17.49	0.39	0.67	1.07	1.82
Qingdao	2.09	2.84	3.68	4.82	0.03	0.15	0.28	0.63
Shanghai	48.80	50.15	54.83	60.93	0.84	2.33	3.50	6.59
Guangzhou	14.59	17.70	23.55	29.41	1.16	3.12	5.76	9.93
OCPs	295.31	343.98	416.16	492.15	22.46	44.67	71.53	108.14
	(361.21)	(411.05)	(488.76)	(570.57)	(23.69)	(47.67)	(76.09)	(116.59)
Liaoning	40.00	43.16	52.49	56.25	0.39	1.28	2.22	5.21
Hebei	17.05	17.99	19.01	20.19	0.04	0.12	0.24	0.69
Shandong	29.11	30.26	34.16	37.51	0.17	0.71	1.24	2.25
Jiangsu	24.16	25.36	29.43	34.24	0.49	1.11	1.89	4.13
Zhejiang	14.97	18.72	21.89	29.06	0.38	0.70	1.34	2.62
Fujian	14.13	18.28	24.49	31.48	2.40	4.97	9.03	12.89
Guangdong	147.74	180.62	221.26	269.44	18.44	35.33	54.80	79.24
Hainan	2.62	3.27	5.37	6.25	0.06	0.25	0.38	0.53
Guangxi	5.53	6.33	8.06	7.73	0.09	0.22	0.39	0.58
Beijing	9.77	10.22	11.21	13.08	0.26	0.50	0.86	1.50
Provincial total	444.20	503.86	586.57	685.17	24.48	48.47	78.13	120.53
PRC total	475.20	525.40	620.90	719.10	—	—	—	—

Notes: The figures refer to exports by the "foreign trading units" of the provinces, opened coastal cities and SEZs *Sanzi* (three-foreign-funded) enterprises cover equity joint ventures, co-operative joint ventures and wholly foreign-owned ventures. Figures in brackets refer to the sum total for all the 15 OCCs and 11 OCPs including Shanghai and Tianjin. PRC total includes centrally controlled exports, in additions to the total provincial exports.

Sources: *CLES* (part 2), (January 1989), pp. 45–51; (January 1990), pp. 52–59; (January 1991), pp. 45–55; and (February 1992), pp. 32–42. PRC total for 1988–90 is from *ZGTJNJ* 1991, p. 615; and for 1991 *CLES* (part 1) (January 1992), p. 21.

19

THE MANY WORLDS OF CHINA'S PROVINCES

Foreign Trade and Diversification

Brantly Womack and Guangzhi Zhao
David S. G. Goodman and Gerald Segal (Editors)

'Contemporary history no longer respects the isolation of China or any other country, by land or sea.'

Owen Lattimore, *Inner Asian Frontiers of China*, 1940

In the 1980s China became the world's fastest growing major economy, but the rate of economic growth is not the most novel feature of China's new economic direction. More impressive is that recent growth is a response to a decentralising tendency of Chinese economic policy, and as a result growth has produced an unprecedented diversification of economic activity. All provinces have benefited from the new policies, but they have thereby become less uniform. In conjunction with increasingly permissive policies concerning international economic activity and different degrees and directions of access to foreign markets on the part of provinces, the diversification of provincial involvement in international trade and in provincial patterns of trade is particularly marked.

Diversification and internationalisation are both widely viewed as desirable policy outcomes, and they are clearly related to a vast increase in China's material wealth. Permission to diversify has been a cornerstone of Deng Xiaoping's modernisation programme. At the household level the blessing was given for some to get rich first, and in the area of provincial trade the natural advantages of a place like Guangdong have been enhanced by preferential treatment by the centre.[1] Although the *avant garde* behaviour of Shenzhen Special Economic Zone has been an occasional bone of contention between conservatives and pragmatists since the early 1980s, in general the progress of advanced areas has been viewed as forging a path for the rest of the country. It could be argued that the progress produced by diversification and internationalisation has been an important contributing factor to the stability of the Chinese regime, even if the emerging civil society that they have encouraged also contributed to the ferment and eventual tragedy of Tiananmen.[2]

Source: China Deconstructs (London: Routledge, 1994), pp. 131–76.

It is also clear, however, that the horn of plenty has some of the characteristics of Pandora's box. Growth has occurred with the permission of the centre, but not under its close supervision, and the direction of growth has been centrifugal. The centre could not regain the control it had just a decade ago without severe economic consequences; indeed, some worry that the centre is in danger of losing its general regulative capacity, and that the centrifugal effects of diversification might lead to national disorder.[3] Such concerns are heightened by the example of the Soviet Union. High rates of change and novel directions of growth inevitably raise questions about deeper consequences. In any case, even committed modernisers like Zhu Rongji have been forced to take strong regulatory action at the centre in order to slow the dizzying pace of growth and to control inflation.

By its nature diversity is hard to describe, and the big question of 'where is all this heading?' is too vast to be dealt with comprehensively. This article concentrates on one facet of these developments, namely, differences in the pattern and magnitude of international exports of China's provinces. The facet is an important one for three reasons. First, provinces are a traditional, stable and powerful level of government in China. Diversification at the provincial level is not only a natural first level of disaggregation, it is also one at which political articulation is possible. At the provincial level the contrast between real provincial discretion and political clout on the one hand and on the other their vulnerability to central interference might give rise to federalistic demands. In turn, diversification also poses internal problems for provincial governments in so far as they face rising demands from localities and citizens. Second, international trade is a major area of provincial diversity and one related to provincial wealth. The dimensions will be described below, but it is abundantly clear to foreign visitors that officials in every province consider foreign trade and investment as vital to modernisation. The third reason is fortunately more hypothetical: namely, if disunity develops in China, provincial differences based on disparities in international relations would undoubtedly play a role in the discord.

The first and most important task of this study is to produce a preliminary overview of the scale and diversity of the foreign trade relations of the various provinces. Because of the complexity of dealing with 30 different units in potential relationship with 160 countries, some basic limits of data have been adopted. The primary data base of this research is the 1990 provincial export data reported in the *Zhongguo Duiwai Jingji Maoyi Nianjian 1991* (Almanac of Chinese Foreign Economy and Trade 1991, hereafter *China Trade Almanac 1991*). The data collected concerns volume of exports, volume of exports to the top five destinations for each province, and rankings of destinations in terms of volume. The data is rather complete, with only two provinces (Sichuan and Tibet) lacking information on specific export destinations. Export data is used rather than import data because it is assumed to be more accurate for asserting a specific link between each province and a country of final destination.[4] However, the data does not report indirect trade, nor does it report unofficial trade, and these are serious limitations. Virtually all trade with Taiwan is reported as trade with Hong Kong, and a significant amount of Hong Kong trade is bound for other markets as well, including the United States. Unofficial trade is also a serious problem. For instance, Guangxi Province does not report trade with Vietnam in 1990, and yet unofficial Chinese estimates would place Vietnam second only to Hong Kong as a target for Guangxi exports. There was presumably an even greater volume of direct unofficial trade in 1990 between Fujian and Taiwan, and between Shandong and South Korea. In general, border trade is probably under-reported. Trend analysis is confined to the national level in this study because only recent provincial-level data on trade partners is available, and in any case the complexity of thirty-unit trends would be enormous.

The basic purpose of this research is to convey an overall sense of provincial diversification and its political implications, because the phenomenon is important and complex enough to require a general recasting of our image of China's political economy. A number of graphic techniques are used to facilitate a re-imagining of China's diversity of international relations in the 1990s, and the historical development of China's trade policy is presented in order to explain the context and novelty of current policies. The questions addressed are the following: How does provincial diversification and internationalisation fit in with China's national political dynamics? What is the general scope and pattern of export diversification? What are the specific characteristics of coastal, inland and border provinces, and of their major partners? What are the political implications of provincial diversification?

The first section describes the development of national trade policy from 1949. It emphasises that the increase of Chinese trade in the 1980s occurred in a context of radically new policies that promoted economic differences among provinces. On the one hand, the general policies promoting market decentralisation and local initiative encouraged a new kind of localism, which we term market localism, to replace the traditional autarkic localism. On the other hand, the specific policies of internationalisation encouraged the inherent differences among provinces to unfold. First, overseas Chinese connections were encouraged, and then places with existing external advantages such as Guangdong and Fujian, and later the coastal provinces, were given special privileges. Even policies promoting more general economic internationalisation, such as those relating to foreign investment, in fact benefited the more developed trading centres more than the inland areas. Lastly, the vast improvement in China's relations with its neighbours in the 1980s has created very specific and localised trading opportunities for its border provinces.

The second section presents the diversity of provincial trading patterns. The patterns analysed include the relationship of provincial exports to provincial economic activity (which indicates how the significance of international openness differs among provinces), the five major export partners of each province (which details the specific trading 'world' of each province), and the index of trade dependence (which measures the concentration of trade with one or a few partners). The data are presented in tabular form, but, because the implications and geographical patterns are hard to grasp from columns of numbers, an attempt has been made to display the data in figures that convey an immediate, clear and accurate image of disparities. We then analyse three general categories of provinces: coastal, border and inland. Coastal provinces have what we term grand advantages of global access, which put them at the forefront of internationalisation and also make their trading patterns similar to national trading patterns. Border provinces have the petty advantage of convenient access to a specific neighbour. If the neighbour is Hong Kong, then the advantage is enormous; if it is Nepal, the advantage is less impressive. In any case, however, the trade of a border province is distorted toward its neighbours, and therefore its trading pattern differs considerably from the national pattern.

The third section on provincial trade dependence goes into more detail concerning the concentration of trade and the trading patterns of China's major trading partners. It is clear that provinces with both border and coastal characteristics (Guangdong is the outstanding example) have the highest volume of trade and also the highest trade dependence. Coastal provinces have high volumes of trade but low rates of dependence. Border provinces have unique trade orientations and are variable in amount of trade and dependence. Trade is relatively insignificant for inland provinces and in general they have low dependence. Looking at this pattern from the point of view of major trading partners, Hong Kong is one of the top five export targets for all provinces and is number one for twenty-three provinces. But its trade is spread unevenly, with the highest concentration in Guangdong and other southern provinces. Trade with Japan has a northern bias, though it is also well distributed. Trade with the United States and Europe fits the national trading pattern by being strongest on the coast. Other countries that are among the top five trading partners of one or more provinces tend to be concentrated in the border areas, because they are the exceptions to the national trading pattern.

The final section speculates on the political implications of provincial economic diversification. First, it is clear that the coastal provinces will be vitally interested in national trade policies. In general they would favour internationalisation, but it should be remembered that their economies are also the ones most exposed to external uncertainties. Border provinces would tend to be more focused in their international interests, and their interest in relations with a neighbour might well diverge from national policy. They are exposed to border difficulties as well as to trading opportunities. Inland provinces have less to gain from internationalisation, but they want the advantages enjoyed by provinces with better access. Secondly, all provinces have some characteristics in common, in that each will be pursuing its own advantages in interprovincial arenas but at home they will be managing similar conflicts based on market localism between localities and groups. Thirdly, all provinces have strong reasons to support the centre, and even stronger reasons not to confront and challenge the centre. Even though China is becoming more diverse domestically and in its international connections, we conclude that China is not about to fly apart.

NATION AND PROVINCE IN INTERNATIONAL TRADE

National trading patterns before 1980

As the controversial Chinese television documentary *River Elegy (He shang)* suggested, China has not been an ocean-oriented, international commercial culture, even though traditional domestic commerce was well-developed. The chaos of the first fifty years of this century in China did open the country to international contacts, but they were not of China's choosing and they were premised on conditions of vulnerability and backwardness. China was unevenly exposed to the advantages and disadvantages of international commercial contact, creating a broad contrast between coastal and hinterland areas. But even the most exposed areas were not modern, and the pattern of trade was dominated by the import of finished and luxury goods and the export of raw materials. Until 1890 opium was the primary import, and for most of the pre-1949 period the value of tobacco imports exceeded that of machinery imports.[5] China ran a chronic export deficit in its balance of trade, counterbalanced by remittances from overseas Chinese. In general, neither trade (amounting to 7 per cent of Gross Domestic Product in 1933) nor foreign investment transformed the Chinese economy; they led instead to a partial and uneven development.[6] Of course, considering the colonial transformation of other underdeveloped economies during this period, partial exposure had some advantages. New forms of opportunity went hand in hand with vulnerability in the non-Western world before 1949, a situation best illustrated in China by Japan's interest in Manchuria and later its occupation of the most developed areas of China in 1937–45.

Figure 19.1 illustrates the overall pattern of Chinese trade from 1949 to 1990. In terms of the total value of trade, the pattern is one of stagnation until the early 1970s, at which point the first of four sharp, multi-year increases occurred. The upper line charts trade as a percentage of Gross Social Product (GSP; *shehui zong chan zhi;* also translated as 'total output value'), and it makes clear that the general economic significance of trade declined in the 1960s, and returned to its earlier level only with the first rise in the early 1970s. The increasingly sharp rises in trade in the 1980s doubled its economic significance by the end of the decade.

The initial effect of the establishment of the People's Republic of China in 1949 was to sever the existing ties to the West, and to develop a new

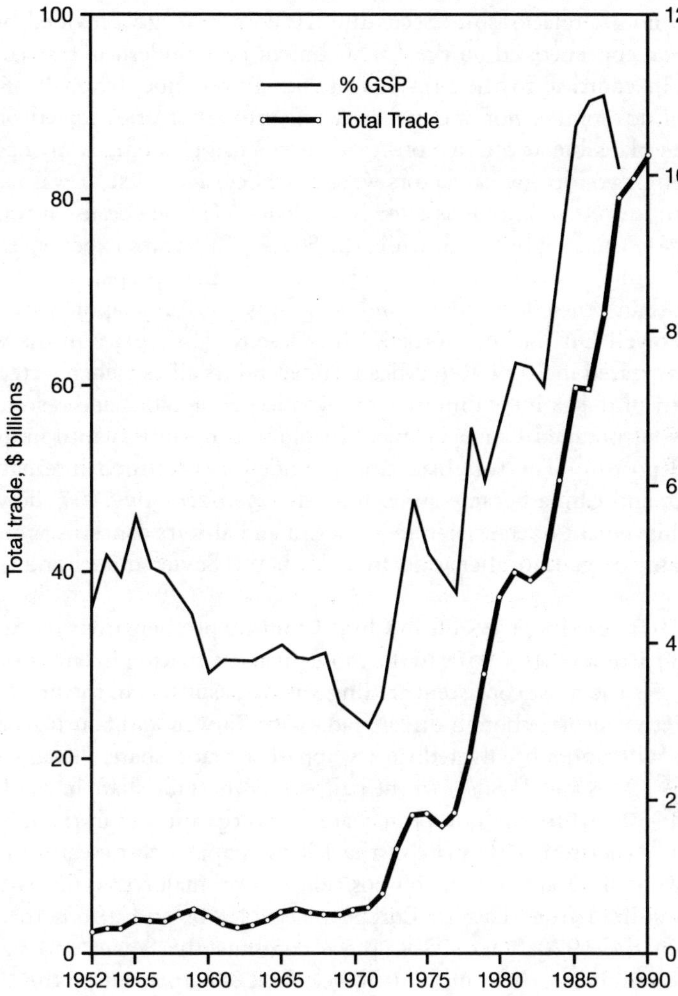

Figure 19.1 China's trade growth

relationship with the Soviet Union based on state-to-state cooperation for development rather than on commercial, market-based trade. The scale of technological and trade dependence on the Soviet Union assumed in the Sino-Soviet Treaty of Friendship, Alliance and Mutual Assistance (signed on 14 February 1950) exceeded any previous bilateral dependence, and it might seem strange that a newly independent country, proud of having finally 'stood up' in the world, would assume such an apparently clientelistic posture.

Four factors modified dependence, two practical and two ideological. First, given the hostility of the West, and especially of the United States, the Soviet Union was the only available major country with which China could pursue a modern economic relationship. Secondly, the economic aid provided by the Soviet Union concentrated on the establishment of a modern industrial base in China. In contrast to the previous period, it was not driven by Soviet commercial advantage, nor was it based on unequal treaties forced on the Chinese. As plausible as the two practical factors might seem, in my opinion the following two ideological factors were more decisive. First, it was natural for China to learn from and be assisted by the Soviet Union because it was just embarking on the socialist road, while the Soviet Union was experienced and successful. China's rural revolutionary experience did not prepare it to build a national, urban-centred economy, and so it was a natural apprentice. Secondly, as Lowell Dittmer has argued, China's sense of its place in the world had to be recreated in 1949. Republican China and its allies were rejected, the old attitudes of the Chinese Empire were even less acceptable, and revolutionary success encouraged China to inject ideological optimism into finding a new world posture. The socialist camp provided a structured international peer group, and China became an enthusiastic member.[7] By 1957, however, China's achievement of transition to socialism and also its concerns about the socialist camp began an alienation from both the Soviet model and Soviet leadership.

Figure 19.2 describes the shift in China's trading partners from the Soviet-dominated pattern of the 1950s to the more diverse situation in later decades. Hong Kong is the most consistent trading partner, as it was in the first half of the twentieth century, though direct trade with Taiwan and South Korea in the 1990s will undoubtedly reduce its apparent trade share. Japan's trade share in the 1970s and 1980s is in the ballpark of its trade share in the 1920s and early 1930s, while the European share is less than it was in the interwar period. The American trade share of the 1980s is approaching earlier levels. Missing from the graph is the composition of non-major trading partners, which has shifted from Eastern Europe in the 1950s and 1960s to Asian countries in the 1970s and 1980s. If we combine the Soviet and Eastern European trade shares, the communist block share is 62 per cent in the 1950s, 21 per cent in the 1960s, 9 per cent in the 1970s and 3 per cent in the 1980s. The larger pie of the 1980s shows that while trade now has greater proportional significance, the distribution of trade has not returned to the lopsided distribution of the 1950s at the national level.

Even before the Soviet Union abruptly withdrew its assistance to China in July 1960, the Great Leap Forward provided an introverted model of modernisation in which the key resource was political mobilisation rather than importable inputs. The failure of the Great Leap Forward and the souring of relations with the Soviet Union led to a certain diversification of trade in the early 1960s, but primarily to meet pressing needs such as the shortage of grain. So, as the figures illustrate, the significance of trade for China's modernisation plans actually declined in the 1960s. Moreover, even internal commerce declined after 1957 as the economy became exclusively state-owned

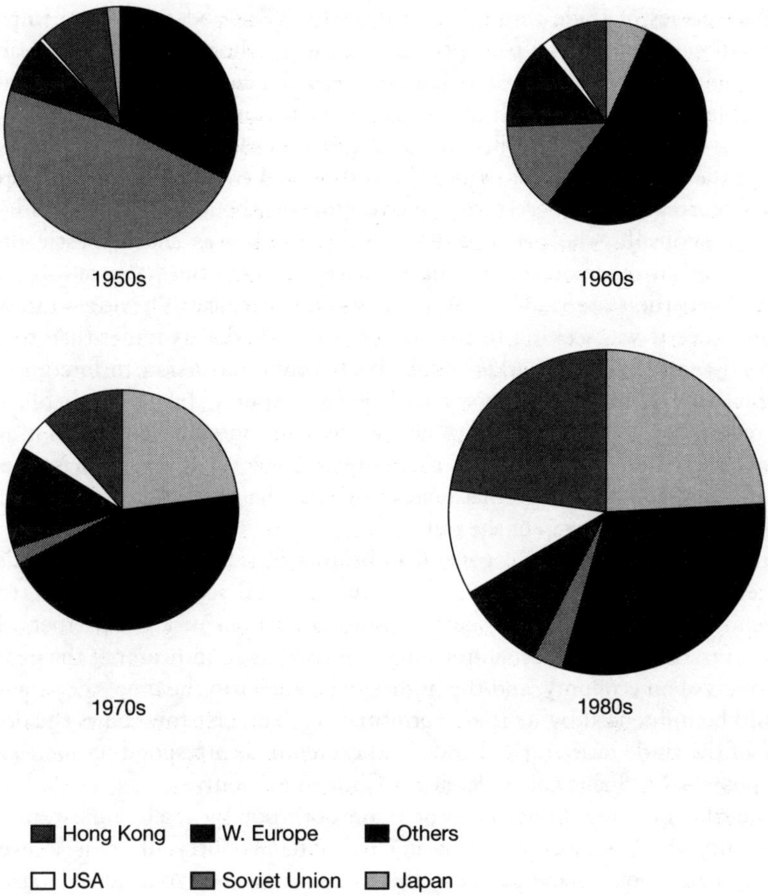

Figure 19.2 China's trading partners

and administered. A wave of trade expansion involving further diversification of partners and products occurred in the early and mid-1970s. This included important capital goods like chemical fertiliser plants, but the increase in trade activity merely returned foreign economic relations to the role in modernisation that they had enjoyed in the 1950s. Hua Guofeng's grandiose but short-lived development plans of 1977–78 were a more fleshed-out hybrid of Western inputs into state-planned central projects. These plans were similar to the role of Soviet aid in Chinese modernisation in the 1950s as well as to the attempts of various Eastern European countries in the 1970s, especially Poland, to jump-start modernisation by importing technological inputs from the West. Although Hua's plans began the growth in foreign trade that continued in the 1980s, the international economic policy that began to develop after 1979 was clearly different in concept.

The species of trade throughout the 1949–79 period was one of imports being directed by central perceptions of domestic shortfalls or modernisation needs, and of exports being arranged to cover the cost of imports. Even after the replacement of the Stalinist modernisation model by a Maoist one, the derivative, centrally-controlled and non-market character of foreign trade retained the generic Stalinist pattern.[8] International trade was a firm monopoly of the centre, and not necessarily an advantage to the localities producing for export. Typically, the price paid to the producer was the domestic price, and any profit made on the international sale went to the state trading company. Even the state trading company was not necessarily trying to make a profit, since it was seeking to cover a specific trade deficit rather than to find as high a price as the market would bear. China's aversion to foreign debt might have encouraged exports to balance imports, but it probably also depressed the general level of trade. In any case, foreign commerce is peripheral and alien in a command economy and the tendency is to isolate its contact and influence. International trade was the small tail of a large dog, and exports were the tip of the tail.

Table 19.1 provides two general indicators of trade dependence: trade as percentage of Gross Social Product; and the Hirschman Index of trade dependence, an index of the skew of trade toward one or a few partners. The ratio of trade to general economic output is used as an indicator of the general openness of an economy, and the higher the trade ratio the more the economy would be influenced by its trade performance.[9] The first row shows the doubling of the trade ratio in the 1980s, and therefore a corresponding increase in the potential influence of trade on the Chinese economy.

But the growing importance of trade does not by itself indicate a vulnerability to the trade policy of any particular country. If trade is evenly distributed among many partners, then general market conditions determine success or failure rather than the behaviour of any one partner. However, the more trade is concentrated with one or a few partners, the more trade is exposed to the decision making of dominant partners. The Hirschman Dependence Index is a measure of concentration of trade. If trade is exclusively with one country the Hirschman Index would be one hundred, if trade is spread evenly it approaches zero.[10] The formula is: $\mathit{Index} = \sqrt{a^{1^2} + a^{2^2} + a^{n^2} + p^2}$ where the a's are percentages of trade of major partners and p is the residual.

Table 19.1 China's national trade dependence

	1951–55	*1956–60*	*1961–65*	*1966–70*	*1971–75*	*1976–80*	*1981–85*	*1986–90*
% GSP	4.71	4.26	3.73	3.41	4.5	5.9	8.36	10.22
Hirschman Dependence Index	54.88	48.98	27.77	30.92	31.87	33.93	39.29	37.02

The table documents the high level of trade dependence on the Soviet Union in the 1950s, and makes clear that, despite the greater significance of trade in the 1980s, the relationship is less concentrated. Considering that Hong Kong is the major trade partner in the late 1980s, the index would be reduced considerably with direct trade between China and Taiwan.

The concept of trade dependence is an important one in this paper, but clearly not in the sense of 'dependency' as it became popular in the 1970s. We can make use of James Caporaso's distinction between 'dependence' as external reliance on other actors, and 'dependency' as incorporation of less developed countries into the capitalist system and the structural distortions resulting therefrom.[11] As the preceding analysis suggests, China's economic structure before 1980 was the opposite of that implied by dependency (and indeed Caporaso refers to China and Albania as models of its opposite, namely, autarkic independence). The concept of trade dependence dates back to concerns about Germany's trade policies in Eastern Europe in the interwar period, and A. O. Hirschman's 1945 work *National Power and the Structure of Foreign Trade*, the source of the index, is the classic study. The index measures the degree of focus in the economy's exposure to trade partners, and since this varies over time in China and, as we shall see, by province, it is a useful analytic tool. A high score is intrinsically neither better nor worse than a low score, but a high score does imply that one or a few trade relationships are very important. At the national level, the present and foreseeable patterns of trade indicate a low and decreasing index of dependence. At the provincial level the situation is quite different, but the differences did not matter until not only the volume but more importantly the structure of foreign trade was transformed in the 1980s.

Clearly provincial trading patterns were not significant in the Stalinist economic framework. The level of foreign trade was low, its salience for local development was negligible, and production for foreign trade was indirect and assigned by the state. Indeed, places relying on comparative advantage experienced relative decline, especially in the 1960s and 1970s.[12] Given that there was no advantage to the producer to produce for export, it could be permitted and encouraged only by the central government's administrative decisions. Even though these decisions did not spread the obligation to produce for export evenly throughout China, the differentiation that occurred was at the behest of the command economy. Centrally-controlled trade was therefore less desirable to the localities and more transparent to the authorities than the market-oriented trade that sprang up in the 1980s.

The transformation of Chinese trade in the 1980s

Foreign trade not only grew along with the expansion of the economy in the 1980s, it was especially benefited by some of the general principles underlying Deng's reforms. Moreover, and central to our concerns here, the transformation in the approach to modernisation unleashed the economic initiative of lower levels of government. If the government had encouraged trade but had not changed its approach to modernisation, much of the diversification described in this paper would not have occurred. Therefore, in addition to the national trade patterns discussed above, the political environment of foreign trade policy must be considered. Three of these new principles of modernisation deserve special attention, namely, the shift from autarkic decentralisation to market decentralisation, the permitting of private and local economic initiatives, and the encouragement to internationalise.

From autarkic to market decentralisation

Decentralisation was an important aspect of the Maoist approach to development, and it would be a mistake to view the 1980 reforms as simply a transition from a centralised Stalinist command economy to a decentralised market. Not only did China lack the material prerequisites of a fully centralised command economy, but already in the mid-1950s Mao had begun questioning the wisdom of a centre-oriented development strategy. Decentralising measures were an important part not only of the leftist economic interventions such as the Great Leap Forward or the Learn from Dazhai campaigns, but also of the more pragmatic policy phases that followed leftist failures.

Under Mao, decentralisation meant autarkic self-sufficiency. Clearly an environment of shortage in basic goods invites such an approach; self-sufficiency is the most complete form of economic security. But Mao made this middle-peasant ideal into a cornerstone of modernisation strategy. Every industrial enterprise should be 'small but complete', every county should develop its own manufacturing capacity for agricultural tools, every province should 'take grain as the key link'. The resulting political economy has been well described as cellular or honeycomb, since horizontal linkages are minimised and even vertical linkages are reduced. The approach encouraged localism, but not necessarily diversity, and certainly not commercial diversity.

Under Deng Xiaoping and Zhao Ziyang decentralisation quietly transformed its meaning, becoming market decentralisation in which each area and unit produces to best advantage within an interdependent market network. By the 1980s the commercialisation of agriculture (percentage of output marketed rather than consumed) became an official measure of modernity. The media now praised fruit-tree and fish-pond millionaires, while earlier they had praised Mongolian communes who with great hardship (and cost to their sheep production) had become self-sufficient in grain. What came to be called socialist commodity production implied an abandonment of the peasant ideal of guaranteed self-sufficiency. It permitted producers to respond to market opportunities not only by investing their surplus, but by reorienting their entire productive capacity, becoming at the same time more profitable and more dependent on the market. Tea villages and button towns reappeared.

The new decentralisation of the 1980s has encouraged a new variety of localism, one with profound implications for Chinese politics. The autarkic localism of cellular decentralisation was primarily concerned with shielding itself from central interference and oversight in order to survive and to pursue relatively modest private opportunities. Market localism has the potential to be more assertive and to be more ambitious in its pursuit of its own interests. Autarkic localism is merely defensive against intrusion, while the interdependence of the market inevitably involves localities in conflicts among themselves of both interests and ambitions. The suppliers of raw materials want to develop their own processing industries; the manufacturing centres want to secure their supplies and markets; the points of transit want to maximise their entrepot advantages. Moreover, the uncertainties and inconveniences created by inadequately controlled market localism give rise in turn to pressures for new dimensions of centralisation, or at least corporatism, in order to secure an orderly national market. Just as economic development has spread unevenly, so market localism makes different demands in different localities: sometimes for market expansion, sometimes for protectionist policies, sometimes for central support. Some of the political symptoms and consequences of market localism will be discussed in the third part of this chapter.

Increased private and local initiative

In theory, China could have pursued commodity modernisation through a more sophisticated central administrative structure, and indeed the central ministries grew and became more sophisticated in their controls in the 1980s. The various attempts at reforming the socialist economic mechanism in European communist countries, from Lieberman and Kosygin in the 1960s and the more ambitious Hungarian policies through Gorbachev's *perestroika*, had such projects. But China historically was less concerned about maintaining central administrative control in new campaigns, and in any case the mechanisms of central administrative control of the domestic economy were less developed.[13]

The encouragement of local initiative in the 1980s involved more than greater slippage in a socialist system, however. The ideological commitment to the elimination of differences between town and country and between mental and manual labour was condemned as ultra-egalitarianism, and everyone was encouraged to pursue individual profit and thereby to advance the common good. The general decriminalisation of material interest was even more important than the numerous new policies permitting local initiative, because it encouraged individuals and units to push at the edge of the permissible. As Ren Zhongyi, First Party Secretary of Guangdong Province in the early 1980s, put it: 'If something is not explicitly prohibited, then move ahead. If something is allowed, then use it to the hilt.'[14]

The quick success and popularity of rural decollectivisation in 1979–82 further encouraged looser reins at all levels of the economy, and different patterns of resources, opportunity and success led to increasing differentiation. The diversification related to foreign trade discussed in this chapter could only occur within the general diversification of society and economy. Otherwise, even if foreign trade had been considered essential to modernisation, its interface with the domestic economy would necessarily have remained under central administration and control. The policies that license and encourage local initiative in foreign trade derive from the general policy context of acknowledging material interest and encouraging initiative; they are unimaginable outside of that context. Foreign trade has merely added another dimension to a general pattern of diversification resulting from local and individual initiative.

International openness

Bold attempts to involve overseas Chinese, capitalist countries, firms and international economic organisations in China's modernization have been a vital part of Deng's reforms from the beginning. Clearly this has been the policy change that has most affected the scale of foreign trade in the 1980s and also its differentiated impact. Foreign trade increased its share of the national GNP from 6 per cent in 1978 to 10 per cent in 1990.[15] The tendency of foreign trade to diversify according to the natural advantages and access of different localities has been exaggerated by a policy pattern exemplified by the creation of the Special Economic Zones (SEZs) in 1980 and the permissions given to Guangdong and Fujian in 1979 to control some levels of foreign trade and to retain income from trade. These are policies that give special advantages of openness to regions and areas that already have better international access in order to encourage even more rapid development. Nevertheless, there have also been general encouragements to foreign trade in conjunction with China's efforts to work with the World Bank and to join the General Agreement on Tariffs and Trade (GATT). Lastly, toward the end of the 1980s border trade has been encouraged between inland provinces and neighbouring countries. Thus four elements of the general policy of international openness may be distinguished: first, openness toward ethnic Chinese; second, special policies toward areas with a trade advantage; third, general efforts to increase access to the world economy and to world economic organisations; and fourth, efforts to expand border trade.

Even before Deng Xiaoping took control in late 1978, policies toward overseas Chinese (primarily targeted at the Nanyang Chinese in Southeast Asia), Hong Kong and Taiwan were becoming more hospitable, and patriotic investment in the ancestral country was encouraged. In 1977 China adopted a more aggressive policy toward promoting the rights of overseas Chinese, reversing a pattern of neglect that had formed in the wake of the Indonesian troubles of 1965. It was intended to encourage a feeling of ethnic community and also investment in China. As luck would have it, the policy was announced just before Vietnam expropriated and expelled a large part of its ethnic Chinese population, and it contributed to the hostile confrontation between the two countries.[16] Restrictions on travel and gifts between Hong Kong and Guangdong were also eased, setting the stage for the special relationship between Hong Kong and Guangdong in the 1980s. Improvement of relations with Taiwan developed more slowly, but the policy of peaceful reunification suggested by the New Year's Message to Taiwan Compatriots in 1979 and developed into a nine-point programme by Ye Jianying in 1981 tended to remove Chinese barriers to indirect trade and investment from Taiwan, thereby increasing the pressure on Taiwan either to bear an increasing cost of enforcement or to moderate its policies.[17] Since Taiwan first relaxed its enforcement of controls of indirect contact and trade, then its policies on indirect trade, and only at the end of the 1980s began to modify controls on direct contact, Hong Kong has been a major conduit and beneficiary of Taiwanese interest in the mainland.

The opening to 'greater China' was not only the first component of international openness, it still plays a central role in external trade and investment, as indicated by Hong Kong's trade share in the 1980s. Indeed, although Hong Kong's trade share will undoubtedly diminish as Taiwan begins direct trade, the share of ethnic Chinese may well increase in the 1990s. Since such trade is grounded in kinship ties, its local impact in China is unevenly distributed. The export trade share of Hong Kong ranges from 8 per cent in Liaoning to 82 per cent in Guangdong. It might be speculated that, given the ethnic and locational specificity of ethnic contacts, such trade and investment would tend to intensify in given locations rather than distribute itself more evenly in pursuit of further locational advantages.

The second aspect of international openness, special treatment to advantaged areas, is closely related to the first. Just as the overseas Chinese were a special part of the international market (and had been so throughout the twentieth century), their places of origin, especially Guangdong and Fujian, were singled out for permissive treatment. Special treatment of Guangdong began in 1979, symbolised by the creation of the SEZs in Shenzhen, Zhuhai, Shantou and Xiamen in 1980.[18] However, unlike the involvement of the overseas Chinese, the permissive policies did have a tendency to spread when they had proven themselves successful. In 1987 special permissiveness was extended to all coastal provinces and since 1989 Shanghai's Pudong development has been the largest focal point of government encouragement. Meanwhile, the rest of the country is attempting to move through the door opened by Guangdong. For example, Hebei Province has announced the establishment of four major economic zones, and it is estimated that there are more than two thousand special zones of various sorts, most at the township level, taking more than 2.4 million hectares out of agricultural production.[19] As permissiveness broadened, it also deepened, allowing rural cooperative enterprises to become involved directly in international trade. In sum, the overall pattern of the spread of permissive policies from advantaged areas has contributed to the rapid growth of these areas, but it has also tended to exacerbate the different rates of development between internationally advantaged and disadvantaged areas. However, permissive policies have tended to expand, so privileges granted to the advanced can be viewed by the envious remainder as the thin edge of a wedge of more general policy reform.

A third frontier of international openness that has directly affected national trade policy was China's responsiveness to the expectations and demands of international economic organisations and of major trading partners. Integration into the world economy has required the development of legal structures and statistics, encouraged movement toward currency convertibility, and has reintroduced large-scale, foreign-funded projects into China for the first time since the 1950s. From the formulation of China's first Joint Venture Law in July 1979 to the decisions in 1992 to publish all tariff rates, rules and regulations, the attempt to involve global investors, traders and economic institutions in modernisation has been a potent force in regularising access and information concerning China's external and internal economic activities. Pressures for global integration have increased general access to foreign markets, as well as foreign access to China, and these pressures continue with China's attempt to enter GATT. Such global openness has uneven effects on foreign and domestic participants because it treats equally those with unequal endowments, but it is an improvement over the previous two categories of openness because it does not give special treatment to the already advantaged.

The last and most neglected aspect of international openness has been the improvement of relations between China and its neighbours and the great increase in overland border trade. In 1978, China had strained or hostile relations along much of its border. The Soviet Union, Mongolia, Afghanistan, India, Burma, Laos, Vietnam – all were sufficiently alienated that mutual trade was minimised. By contrast, relations with every neighbouring country (including some new countries, in the case of the Soviet Union) have improved in the late 1980s, and trade is playing an increasingly important role in the relationship. Moreover, with the relaxation of central control, border provinces are eager to promote trade and cross-border cooperation since it provides an international outlet to these provinces, which are generally inland areas without direct access to a global market. Unfortunately for the purposes of this chapter, border trade is often informal and not well controlled or reported. For instance, in 1990 Guangxi's trade with Vietnam was estimated to be $150 million, making Vietnam Guangxi's major trading partner after Hong Kong, but in national and provincial statistics for that year no trade between the two is reported. Even without the diplomatic problems that existed between Vietnam and China, border trade will tend to be underreported because of the ease of smuggling. Despite such problems the provincial data presented below allow a distinction between inland, neighbouring and coastal trading patterns. Border trade with a neighbouring country is a rather restricted advantage compared to the grand advantage of coastal access to world markets, and one task of this chapter will be to differentiate between what we will call petty and grand advantages in international trade.

The general argument of this section has been that not only has the volume of international trade expanded enormously and its role in national development has been enhanced, but, more importantly for our purposes, the role of the provinces has been transformed by the new policy context of modernisation. The emphasis on commodity trade has allowed market specialisation at every level, replacing the Maoist ideal of self-sufficiency. The new permissiveness toward material incentives has produced a benign attitude toward local initiatives and has encouraged trade by allowing profit retention. Lastly, the four dimensions of international openness – namely, encouragement of overseas Chinese connections; special permissiveness to regions with special endowments; openness to global markets and economic institutions; and border trade – have both encouraged a rapid growth in local involvement in foreign trade and have insured that the impact of trade would differ widely between provinces. In a word, China moved from a policy minimising a relatively uniform and centrally controlled foreign trade to one that encouraged diverse agents to pursue trade according to their endowments. The results of this policy of diversification are the subject of the next section.

THE DIVERSITY OF PROVINCIAL TRADING PATTERNS

It is inevitable that Chinese provinces enjoy a high degree of practical autonomy despite the unitary structure of the national party-state. In most cases they are ancient political units, they administer populations that average 35 million and range above 100 million, and their personnel is fairly stable. As a result, even though the factors influencing trade diversification discussed above affect China down to the village level, the provincial level is a prominent and significant unit of analysis.

In the 1980s, the practical autonomy of the provinces combined with the different advantages of each province to produce significant diversification in many aspects of development, including foreign exports. As a result, the context of provincial autonomy has changed. Vis-à-vis the centre, each province presents a more individuated set of resources and problems than in the past, and each has a greater stake in further central permissiveness, at least in those policy areas that have favoured or might favour that particular province. It is clear that provinces now have more clout against the centre than they did ten years ago, and it can be anticipated that this clout will increase in the event of succession crises in Beijing. Vis-à-vis one another, the interests of the provinces are more divergent, more interdependent, and therefore more likely to conflict, as the concept of market localism discussed above would suggest.

The purpose of this section is to describe provincial diversity of export patterns in order to sketch the range of provincial differences on this important dimension. We will first present the general data, and then discuss their patterns and implications.

Table 19.2 contains the basic provincial export data upon which much of the analysis of this chapter is based. The first data column, percentage of national exports, gives the share of each province in national exports, and directly reflects differences in trade volume. The second data column, exports as a percentage of provincial GSP, indicates the significance of each province's export activity as a percentage of its general economic activity. The country columns indicate amount of exports of each province with their top five trading partners. The provinces differ in their reporting of European trade, some reporting countries separately and some simply as the European Community. For most purposes the data is combined in our statistics. It is important to remember that the data here can be expected to under-report border trade, especially with Vietnam, and that trade with Hong Kong includes trade with Taiwan, South Korea and many other end destinations. It should also be noted that the trade statistics used here do not include the full value of goods involved in export processing, but only the value added in the processing. This method understates Guangdong's gross imports and exports.[20] The aggregate provincial trade for 1990 is $48.01 billion, while the reported national figure is $52.07 billion. The difference appears to consist of direct trade by national ministries.

The data of Table 19.2 and of Table 19.3 below are perhaps more accessible in their general import in Figures 19.3 and 19.4. Figure 19.3 gives a rough idea of the national significance of the exports of various provinces, as well as the shares of the major national trading partners in the trade of each province. Figure 19.4 gives a picture of the relative importance of trade to the economies of each province by setting the size of the pie according to the ratio of exports to provincial production (GSP). The shares of major national trading partners in Figure 19.4 have been adjusted to account for the large amount of indirect trade passing through Hong Kong. Unfortunately it is impossible to make an accurate adjustment because no data are available that would break down Hong Kong's indirect trade by province of origin. So we have taken Hong Kong's overall amounts of re-exports, excluding re-exports to China, and have added Hong Kong's imports from China in order to construct a set of factors of Hong Kong trade which have been used to adjust the shares of the US, Hong Kong, Japan, West Europe and residuals for all provinces.[21] This method undoubtedly understates Guangdong's exports to Hong Kong because many of Guangdong's exports are daily necessities consumed in the colony, but in comparison with Figure 19.3, it indicates in general the

Table 19.2 Provincial trading partners 1990 ($ million)

Province	*% in na ex*	*% in GSP*	*USA*	*Hong Kong*	*Japan*	*W. Germany*	*Singapore*	*USSR*	*N. Korea*	*EEC*	*Burma*	*Saudi Arabia*	*Sri Lanka*	*Thailand*
Beijing	2.75	6.51	164.28	289.06	185.12	82.36		44.24						
Tianjin	3.72	10.31	227.46	351.63	244.93	101.23		62.55						
Hebei	3.62	5.26	120.00	341.00	701.00									
Shanxi	0.95	2.99	22.55	147.74	136.74	19.50		14.81						
Inner-Mongolia	0.68	3.24	12.74	52.34	59.41			98.53		24.69*				
Liaoning	11.66	12.53	1,052.00	471.00	2,255.00		499.00							
Jilin	1.57	4.49	19.74	215.23	180.64		21.06	160.86						
Heilongjiang	2.26	4.24		175.09	172.09			358.95	76.30					
Shanghai	11.07	13.48	745.33	1,029.61	759.08	229.76	182.11							
Jiangsu	6.14	4.07	385.44	653.63	587.91			110.74		463.12				
Zhejiang	4.70	5.57	226.63	659.83	345.19	137.20		94.94						
Anhui	1.36	2.74	51.00	177.00	115.00			94.00		80.00				
Fujian	4.66	12.57	268.00	1,057.00	286.00	105.00	56.00							
Jiangxi	1.17	3.65		208.86	52.50	30.34	27.24	40.32						
Shandong	7.28	5.81	260.00	590.00	920.00			207.00		400.00				
Henan	1.81	2.44	49.46	305.37	96.30			77.68		107.49				

Table 19.2 Provincial trading partners 1990 ($ million)

Province	*% in na ex*	*% in GSP*	*USA*	*Hong Kong*	*Japan*	*W. Germany*	*Singapore*	*USSR*	*N. Korea*	*EEC*	*Burma*	*Saudi Arabia*	*Sri Lanka*	*Thailand*
Hubei	2.23	3.38	61.18	478.20	92.56	34.14		83.83						
Hunan	1.68	3.12	71.55	558.03	68.47	36.69		38.77						
Guangdong	21.99	18.32	403.00	8,709.00	288.00		140.00							
Guangxi	1.52	5.32	61.20	382.41	55.33	24.35						41.48		
Hainan	0.98	15.78		351.80	32.50		9.90						8.35	6.80
Sichuan	2.32	2.62												
Guizhou	0.32	1.79	18.94	43.35	32.09	8.98								
Yunnan	1.17	4.84	22.12	96.28	68.45			19.12			142.73			
Tibet	0.03	2.07												
Shaanxi	0.96	3.24	27.39	140.12	68.92	13.05		11.13						
Gansu	0.39	1.95	14.12	54.28	38.31					29.09				
Qinghai	0.14	3.16		9.01	34.48		3.84	6.46						
Ningxia	0.16	3.43		25.66	8.74			4.24						
Xinjiang	0.70	4.07	13.14	57.68	106.05	13.34		72.81						

Note: The data for this table are mainly from two sources. The provincial GSP is excerpted from the Chinese Statistics Yearbook 1991. The original data are in Renminbi. They are converted into US dollars using the exchange rate of 1990. The rest of the data are expected from the *Almanac of Chinese Foreign Economy and Trade 1991*. West Germany is listed separately because it is one of the largest trading partners. Other West European countries are listed under the heading EEC. * Stands for export to Great Britain. The export partners data are missing for Sichuan and Tibet.

importance of Hong Kong as a final trade destination. It should be recalled that Taiwan and South Korea cannot be displayed because we do not have provincial-level trade data for them. Part of their trade is unofficial and therefore 'off the map', and the official part inflates the Hong Kong share in Figure 19.3 and the residual in Figure 19.4.

In theory, a province could have pies of quite different sizes if its GSP were very much larger or smaller than the national average. The clearest case of this is Hainan Island, whose trade volume is not particularly high but whose GSP is quite low. As a result, Hainan's trade is very important to Hainan itself, but not to the national total, and its pie is small in Figure 19.3 and large in Figure 19.4. But the general similarity of the sizes of the provincial pies in

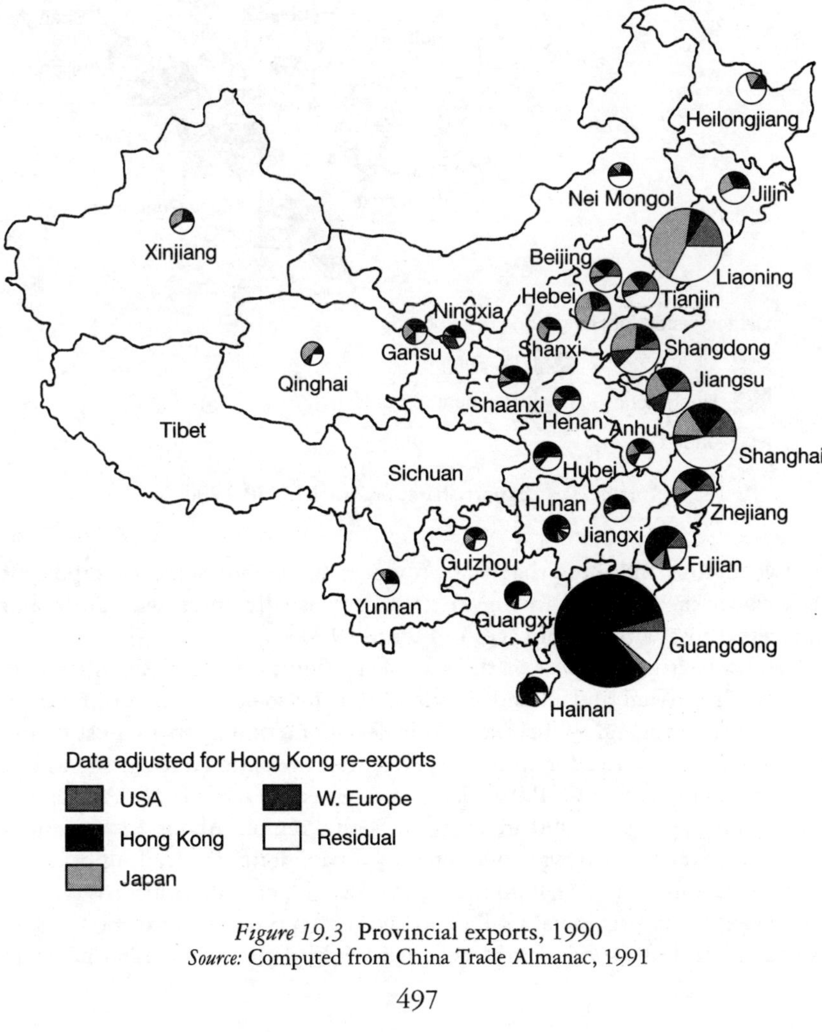

Figure 19.3 Provincial exports, 1990
Source: Computed from China Trade Almanac, 1991

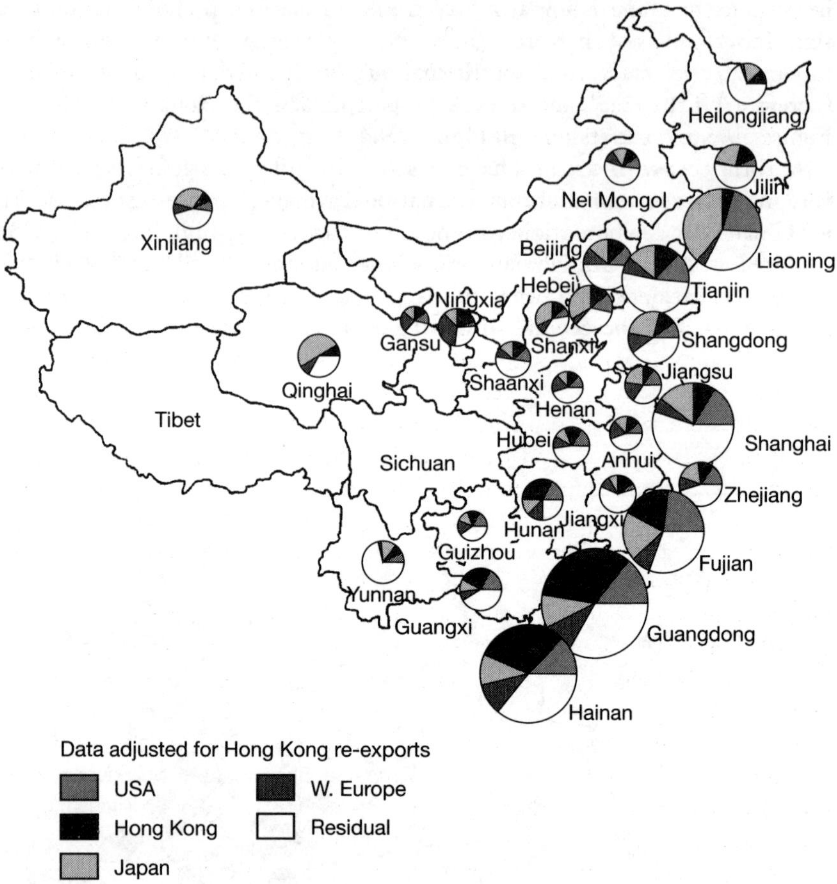

Figure 19.4 Export share, provincial GSP, 1990

the two figures indicates that the provinces for whom trade is important (those with the big pies in Figure 19.4) are usually those who are major exporters (those with the big pies in Figure 19.3).

The most striking aspect of the size of the figures is the great differences between the coastal and inland provinces For most of the inland provinces trade is still peripheral to their economic development. Export in most inland provinces only accounts for around 1 per cent of the national total, and as low as 2–3 per cent of their GSP (the data is presented in Table 19.2). All top ten provinces in exports in 1990 are from the coastal region. About 22 per cent of the total national export was conducted by Guangdong, the leading province in trade. Liaoning and Shanghai account for 11 per cent respectively. The share of export in provincial GSP of all the coastal provinces, except Jiangsu, also rank the highest in comparison with inland provinces, ranging from

18.32 per cent in Guangdong to 5.26 per cent in Hebei. Even if the exports of certain coastal provinces, such as Fujian and Hainan, are less important nationally, they prove to be essential in provincial economic development – exports are 12.57 per cent in Fujian's GSP and 15.78 per cent in Hainan, second only to Guangdong. All in all, for coastal provinces, trade has become central for economic growth, as indicated by the export share of provincial GSP, and these provinces are the primary participants and beneficiaries of the national policy of international openness.

The trading patterns of the various provinces and their partners will be analysed in greater detail below, but some general observations can be made on the basis of the two figures. First, Hong Kong's trade share as final destination (Figure 19.4) is about half of China's total exports to Hong Kong (Figure 19.3)[22] Hong Kong remains a significant export destination in its own right, but beyond southeast China its share is exceeded by the other major trading partners. And the residual, which includes Taiwan and South Korea, has become quite large. In some places, for instance Fujian and Shanghai, Hong Kong's share may be exceeded by trade with Taiwan; in Shandong its share might be smaller than South Korea. But it should be recalled that re-exports are not simply transshipments through the port of Hong Kong. Re-exports involve goods that are bought abroad and then sold abroad, and this can involve significant commercial functions. China in general and Guangdong in particular depends on the commercial expertise of Hong Kong as well as on its consumption.

Secondly, the residual is large because the graphic technique limits the number of 'slices' in the pies. Some components of the residuals for each province cannot be known for certain; for instance, re-export destinations such as Taiwan and South Korea. But the major destination for Hong Kong re-exports (excluding re-exports to China) was the United States; Taiwan and South Korea were only 24 per cent and 14 per cent, respectively, of the US figure in 1990. In some cases, especially in border provinces, major trading partners of particular provinces are only minor trading partners at the national level. Data on the top five export targets of each province will be presented and analysed below.

Thirdly, there are regional patterns of trade, the most obvious being Hong Kong's prominence for Southeast China. There is a less obvious weighting of Japanese trade toward the Northeast, while US and European trade is heaviest on the coast. If we include patterns among minor partners, it is clear that border provinces trade heavily with neighbouring countries. These regional patterns are highlighted more clearly in Figure 19.5.

Although the present analysis cannot venture below the provincial level, the diversifying effects of trade are present at each level of society. The importance of trade to coastal provinces has permeated even the rural areas which used to be the most cellular and autarkic. The rural town and village enterprises are noteworthy examples. They abandoned the old 'self-production and self-consumption' economic model and incorporated themselves into the export-oriented economy. Exports from rural town and village enterprises increased rapidly from about 4 billion dollars in 1985 to more than 12 billion dollars in 1991, constituting more than 20 per cent of total national exports.[23] These export-oriented town and village enterprises are mostly located in the coastal provinces.[24]

Not surprisingly, the greatest intraprovincial regional differences occur in the leading provinces. Guangdong Province has led the national average in GNP and per capita GNP growth by at least three percentage points since 1979, but the Pearl River Delta, the most active area of Guangdong, between Guangzhou and Hong Kong, has led Guangdong by two to four percentage points. In 1990 Guangdong's per capita Gross Domestic Product was 1.5 times the national average, the Pearl River Delta was 1.8 times Guangdong, and Shenzhen Special Economic Zone, the richest part of the Pearl River Delta, was 1.9 times the Delta's average.[25]

The patterns of provincial trade differ between three broad groups of coastal, inland and border provinces. Clearly, coastal provinces are the export leaders in terms of volume and per cent of GSP. But a simple distinction between coastal and inland provinces would miss the distinctive pattern of border provinces. These categories are additive rather than exclusive: a coastal/border province overlays the characteristics of each category. If we rank the provinces according to their export share in GSP, we see that almost all the border/inland provinces have a higher proportion than the other inland provinces (see Table 19.3). Tibet is the exception, but its relatively low export activity can be explained by the physical extremes of its own geography and of its mountain border with India and Nepal. Conversely, if we compare the border/coastal provinces with the coastal provinces, the high volume of trade is shared, but the former show the trade skew characteristic of border provinces.

Border trade existed before the late 1980s, but was small in scale and often discouraged at that time. Starting from the late 1980s, it has become much more lively – more so even than the official data would indicate, since there is much smuggling, gift exchange and informal trade. For example, Heilongjiang's border trade with the Soviet Union has increased 30 times since it started in 1987. Exports to the Soviet Union made up 33 per cent of the total export of Heilongjiang in 1990. The 19 border towns and counties, which used to be among the poorest even in Heilongjiang, have greatly prospered as a result. The GSP of these towns and counties increases at an average rate of 11 per cent annually.[26] They also start to set up 'Border Economic Cooperation Zones' which will no doubt further integrate the economic development of both sides.[27] Border trade in Heilongjiang is but one example. For Xinjiang, the growth rate of total exports in 1989 was 20.8 per cent, but the exports to the former Soviet Union increased by 142.38 per cent. Border trade of Inner Mongolia with the former Soviet Union increased by 28.01 per cent

Table 19.3 Provincial exports by region

Province	*Share in natl. exports %*	*Share in GSP %*	*Top 5 not in natl.*	*Top 5 in natl.*	*Location*
Guangdong	21.99	18.32	2	3	c,b
Liaoning	11.66	12.53	1	3	c,b
Shanghai	11.07	13.48	1	4	c
Shandong	7.28	5.81	1	4	c
Jiangsu	6.14	4.07	0	5	c
Zhejiang	4.70	5.57	0	5	c
Fujian	4.66	12.57	1	4	c
Tianjin	3.72	10.31	0	5	c
Hebei	3.62	5.26	0	3	c
Beijing	2.75	6.51	0	5	c
Sichuan	2.32	2.62	0	5	i
Heilongjiang	2.26	4.24	1	3	i,b
Hubei	2.23	3.38	0	5	i
Henan	1.81	2.44	0	5	i
Hunan	1.68	3.12	0	5	i
Jilin	1.57	4.49	1	4	i,b
Guangxi	1.52	5.32	2	3	c,b
Anhui	1.36	2.74	0	5	i
Yunnan	1.17	4.84	1	4	i,b
Jiangxi	1.17	3.65	1	4	i
Hainan	0.98	15.78	3	2	c
Shaanxi	0.96	3.24	0	5	i
Shanxi	0.95	2.99	0	5	i
Xinjiang	0.70	4.07	0	5	i,b
Inner-Mongolia	0.68	3.24	0	5	i,b
Gansu	0.39	1.95	0	4	i
Guizhou	0.32	1.79	0	4	i
Ningxia	0.16	3.43	0	3	i
Qinghai	0.14	3.16	1	3	i
Tibet	0.03	2.07	3	2	i,b

Note: In the last column of the table, c = 'coastal provinces', b = 'border provinces', i = 'inland provinces'. The differentiation of coastal and inland provinces is determined by the criteria set up by the Chinese State Statistic Bureau in an article named 'Economic Growth in Different Areas' in *Beijing Review*, Vol. 29, No. 49, 8 December, 1986, p. 21.

Source: *Zhongguo Duiwai Jingji Maoyi Tongji Nianjian 1991 (Almanac of Chinese Foreign Economy and Trade 1991): Zhongguo Tongji Nianjian 1991 (China Statistical Yearbook 1991).*

and with Mongolia by 59.62 per cent in 1990. Burma and Nepal are never important in terms of trade nationally, but they are among the top five trading partners to Yunnan and Tibet respectively. Since this is a permanent, geographic advantage, it implies a longer history of international interaction, a more developed commercial and communications infrastructure, and greater familiarity with world markets. Since access to practically every world market is improved by being on the coast, the coastal trading pattern tends to be more diverse, and it reflects global factor advantages. Because their specific location vis-à-vis certain partners is not a factor, trade patterns of coastal provinces tend to be similar to national trading patterns. Moreover, for all of the preceding reasons, coastal provinces tend to act as conduits for the products of inland provinces. Since significant transportation costs are still involved, and smuggling into major ports is risky, the trade tends to be more formal and to be reported in official statistics.

By contrast, the trade advantage of a border province lies in the fact that, assuming normal relations, the communications and transportation costs with a specific foreign partner or partners approaches zero, what we call the 'petty advantage' of border trade. This is also a permanent, geographic advantage, although its historical and infrastructural implications have been obscured by China's hostile relations with many of its neighbours until the last few years. In principle, however, a border province could develop unique contacts and expertise concerning its neighbour. Unlike the coastal provinces, the petty advantage can involve cross-border ethnic and familial ties. In the case of Guangdong and Fujian, the ties are with Han Chinese; in the other cases there exist ethnic minorities that straddle the border.[28] The transportation advantage of a border province is monopolistic at the border and significant for the entire bordering country. It should be noted, however, that border provinces often have poor communications with the rest of China, and it might be more convenient for some other provinces to use coastal avenues to reach a neighbouring country. For instance, it might well be easier to ship goods from Shanghai or Guangdong to Ho Chi Minh City than to transport them overland to Guangxi and then down the length of Vietnam. Distance and 'economic distance' can be different, especially with technological changes in transportation and communication.

The most important difference between the petty advantage of a border province and the grand advantage of a coastal province is that the petty advantage is linked to a specific neighbour. The factor advantages of trade do not necessarily reflect world patterns, and therefore border trade is less likely to be affected by the world economy. If a neighbour is poor, then the border province might serve as a source for manufactured goods or even investment. Again, if the neighbour is poor, there is simply not much potential for trade. The Yunnanese sometimes describe their border trade as '*jiaohua maoyi*', trade among beggars. However, even a poor neighbour expands the market available to local producers and thereby increases economies of scale. Cross-border shopping can be alert to the smallest and most temporary comparative prices. A border provides numerous opportunities for informal trade and for smuggling, and therefore official statistics are likely to under-report border trade.

The trading pattern of a border province is distorted toward its neighbour, and therefore it tends to be quite different from the general national pattern. A change in China's policy toward a neighbour has its greatest effects on bordering provinces, since they might change from being on the military's front line to being first in line for trade in the space of a few years. The fact that Chinese diplomacy is managed in terms of national interest as viewed from Beijing means that the interests of border province are different in both scale and content from national policy making.

The relationship between Guangdong and Hong Kong is a unique combination of grand and petty advantages, because its neighbour is a global entrepot and a major investor in Guangdong. Since most of Guangdong's external trade is investment-related, the availability of Hong Kong capital has been the main engine of its export expansion. Indeed, geographical closeness is not the major dimension of Guangdong's border advantage with Hong Kong; other provinces are not so far away. The ethnic link, reinforced through investment and encouraged by national, provincial and local policies, has been more important.

Fujian's relationship with Taiwan is also developing into a petty advantage of such scale that it embarrasses our terminology. Its success is not well represented in our data because Taiwan investment and trade has expanded only recently. The ethnic link between Taiwan and Fujian is not as strong as that between Guangdong and Hong Kong, and the Taiwan Straight is not as convenient as a land border. Both of these factors reduce the 'border effect' for Fujian of improving relations with Taiwan. An analogous relationship has developed between Shandong and South Korea. South Korea has concentrated half of its China investments in Shandong, reflecting and magnifying trade links.[29] It is important to note that in discussing border provinces each case tends to be unique because the petty advantage is specific. It is a matter of local convenience rather than (or sometimes in addition to) global access.

Geographic location is not the sole reason for the differences in trade development in each province.[30] China is a country where human factors are no less important than natural factors. Moreover, geography is inextricably intertwined with other societal factors, and, as China's earlier policies have demonstrated, it can only display the advantages described above in a favourable political environment. But it is clear that grand and petty advantages with respect to trade are significant and non-transferable, and they contribute to the diversification of China's provinces in the 1980s and beyond.

PROVINCIAL TRADE DEPENDENCE

Trade dependence at the provincial level must be differentiated from national trade dependence in order to avoid misleading inferences. The major difference is that trade policy is made at the national level, and therefore the primary dependence of provincial trade (if one cares to take such a provincial point of view) is on national trade policy. Similarly, the trading partner is usually dealing with China as a unit in determining its policies, and so trade with a particular province is likely to be aggregated with all other provinces as a factor in determining policy, and then weighed with other political factors that lie completely beyond the province.

If one thoroughly analyses a province using national categories, then provincial trade with other provinces should be included along with international trade. The data are not available for such a study, but if they were available they would undoubtedly balance some of the dependencies described below For instance, Guangdong would not look so dependent on Hong Kong if its trade with other provinces were factored in, and Henan would not appear so autarkic if interprovincial trade were included. Guangdong is certainly the most extreme case of external orientation, and yet it is estimated that one-third of its production is oriented toward the rest of China, one-third is consumed within the province, and one-third is exported.[31] Other provinces, especially Hunan, supply 20–30 per cent of Guangdong's food.[32] Guangdong's interprovincial trade reinforces its image as an outward-oriented province, but the outward orientation is bi-directional, towards the rest of China as well as towards Hong Kong.

Even with these reservations in mind, the trade dependence detailed in Table 19.4 is still significant. The economy of a province with a high volume of trade and a high dependence index is vulnerable to fluctuations in trade with one partner; the economy of a province with less trade and less dependence is more buffered. Secondly, the table makes clear that there are significant differences in the direction of provincial trade dependence as well as in level of dependence. In general, four patterns of trade dependence can be distinguished.

First, coastal/border provinces not only rely heavily on foreign trade for their overall economic development, but also tend to have a higher trade dependence rate on their neighbouring countries. They enjoy both the petty advantages of border provinces and grand advantages of coastal provinces. Trade in these provinces constitutes a high proportion in their GSP, and the trade dependence rate of these provinces also ranks at the top. For example, the dependence rate of Guangdong on Hong Kong is 82.66 per cent. The close proximity of Hainan and Fujian with Hong Kong and Taiwan puts them into the category of coastal/border provinces too. Both of them have a high dependence rate on Hong Kong, with Hainan 75.09 per cent and Fujian 50.92 per cent. Since most trade with Taiwan goes through Hong Kong, it is incorporated into the trade with Hong Kong.

The availability of Hong Kong's service industries has allowed Guangdong to depend on Hong Kong for the handling of its trade rather than to develop service industries appropriate to its level of trade. Guangdong's tertiary industry in 1989 was 34 per cent of its gross domestic product, a considerable increase from 25 per cent in 1980 but still lower than India or Pakistan. The national share of tertiary industry in GDP in 1990 was only 27 per cent, placing China in second-to-last place in the World Bank ranking, the last

Table 19.4 Provincial export dependence 1990

Province	*In national export %*	*Dependence rate*	*Location*	*First partner*
Guangdong	18.32	82.66	c,b	HK
Hainan	15.78	75.09	c	HK
Guangxi	5.32	54.41	c,b	HK
Qinghai	3.16	54.14	i	Japan
Fujian	12.57	50.92	c	HK
Hunan	3.12	47.33	i	HK
Liaoning	12.53	47.25	c,b	Japan
Hubei	3.38	47.12	i	HK
Hebei	5.26	46.75	c	HK
Shanxi	2.99	45.05	i	HK
Jilin	4.49	43.59	i,b	HK
Ningxia	3.43	42.91	i	HK
Heilongjiang	4.24	41.89	i,b	USSR
Henan	2.44	41.37	i	HK
Gansu	1.95	41.34	i	HK
Jiangxi	3.65	40.88	i	HK
Inner-Mongolia	3.24	40.49	i,b	USSR
Anhui	2.74	39.28	i	HK
Guizhou	1.79	39.26	i	HK
Xinjiang	4.07	38.94	i,b	Japan
Jiangsu	4.07	37.00	c	HK
Zhejiang	5.57	36.34	c	HK
Shandong	5.81	36.02	c	Japan
Shaanxi	3.24	35.52	i	HK
Yunnan	4.84	34.45	i,b	Burma
Beijing	6.51	30.85	c	HK
Shanghai	13.48	29.81	c	HK
Tianjin	10.31	29.36	c	HK
Tibet	2.07	n.a.	i,b	HK
Sichuan	2.62	n.a.	i	HK

Note: The data for geographic location comes from *Beijing Review* vol. 29, No. 49, 8 December 1986. Other data comes from the *Almanac of Chinese Foreign Economy and Trade 1991*. For Hirschman's Index of trade dependence, see note 8.
i = Inland provinces, c = coastal province, b = bordering province. 1990 National dependence rate 41.68.

place being Uganda.[33] One could say that the high level of re-export trade through Hong Kong is evidence of a dependence of China on Hong Kong for tertiary commercial services.[34]

Second, coastal provinces that are not also border provinces have the least export dependence. They have more diverse trading relations with a greater variety of countries. This is true of provinces like Jiangsu, Zhejiang, Shandong and Shanghai. The trade dependence as well as trade partner patterns of these coastal provinces more or less follow the national patterns.

Third, the trade dependence rate of inland/border provinces seem to vary as suggested by Table 19.4, ranging from 43.59 per cent of Jilin to 34.45 per cent of Yunnan. However, what is unique with these provinces is that, rather than following the national pattern, they tend to have a high trade dependence on their own neighbouring countries. For example, Burma has never been an important trading partner at the national level, but it is the largest partner for Yunnan.

Trade dependence of border provinces is influenced by the level of development of the border provinces and their neighbouring countries. Even though a commodity composition study is not done in this paper, it seems clear that provinces that have a strong economic infrastructure or that are neighboured by an affluent foreign country or region tend to have a high trade proportion in GSP and a high dependence rate. For example, an important reason for Guangdong to become the leading trading province in China is that it borders Hong Kong, which not only provides an export market, but also capital investment. On the other hand, provinces which are relatively less advanced economically and bordered by poor foreign countries or regions tend to have a relatively low trade share in GSP and a low dependence rate. For instance, Yunnan, which is bordered by Burma, has the lowest dependence index of the border provinces. In such situations it can be expected that there will be a small investment outflow from the border provinces to their poorer foreign neighbours rather than incoming capital investment.

Fourth, inland provinces do not have the petty advantages in developing foreign trade discussed above, nor do they have the grand advantages of international openness. Similar to inland/border provinces, the dependence rate of these provinces varies greatly from province to province, but it should be recalled that a high dependence rate is not as significant when the level of trade is low. Unlike inland/border provinces, their number-one trading partners basically follow the national pattern.

Table 19.5 makes clear that Hong Kong is an indispensable partner to all the provinces, not only to those provinces which are geographically close to it. Hong Kong is among the five major export partners for all provinces. It is the largest export partner for 23 provinces, and the second largest for 4 provinces. China is also Hong Kong's dominant partner, because China is not only the market for its import and export, it is also the market for re-export.[35] Hong Kong is an impressive manufacturer and consumer for its size, but its role as an entrepot and as supplier of trade services is essential to its trade role with China. Of course, its role as a re-exporter will diminish as South Korea and Taiwan develop direct trade links. Indeed, since the normalisation of relations with South Korea in 1992, 70 per cent of trade with China is now direct, and Hong Kong has slipped a notch among South Korea's trading partners.[36]

Figure 19.5 is intended to contrast the overall patterns of provincial

Table 19.5 Major provincial export partners 1990

Province	*HK*	*Japan*	*USA*	*W. Germany*	*USSR*	*EEC*	*Singapore*	*Unique partners*
Beijing	1	2	3	4	5			
Tianjin	1	2	3	4	5			
Hebei	1	2	3	4	5			
Shanxi	1	2	3	4	5			
Inner-Mongolia	3	2	5		1	4		
Liaoning	4	1	2					
Jilin	1	2	5		3		4	
Heilongjiang	2	3			1			4[1]
Shanghai	1	2	3	4			5	
Jiangsu	1	2	4		5	3		
Zhejiang	1	2	3	4	5			
Anhui	1	2	5		3	4		
Fujian	1	2	3	4			5	
Jiangxi	1	2		4	3		5	
Shandong	2	1	5			3	4	
Henan	1	2	4		3			
Hubei	1	2	4	5	3			
Hunan	1	3	2	5	4			
Guangdong	1	3	2				4	
Guangxi	1	3	2	5				4[2]
Hainan	1	2		5				3[3],4[4]
Sichuan	1	2	5	3	4			
Guizhou	1	2	3	4		5		
Yunnan	2	3	4		5			1[5]
Tibet	1	2						
Shaanxi	1	2	3	4	5			
Gansu	1	2	4			3		
Qinghai	2	1			3	5	4	
Ningxia	1	3			4	3		
Xinjiang	3	1	5	4	2			

Note: Under the column of 'Unique partners': (1) North Korea: (2) Saudi Arabia; (3) Sri Lanka; (4) Thailand: (5) Burma

Source: *The Almanac of Chinese Foreign Economy and Trade 1991*

exports between the four panels rather than to display detailed information about each province. The first panel of Figure 19.5 displays the southern bias of exports to Hong Kong. While Hong Kong is the dominant trade partner of all but the most remote provinces, with Shandong and Yunnan as the closest exceptions, it is also clear that Hong Kong's relationship to Guangdong Province is unique among China's external relations in terms of its focus and intensity. It would be surprising if the relationship remained as strong as it is at present through the 1990s, because it undoubtedly is a result of the immaturity of Guangdong's direct relations with the global economy as well as the natural geographical advantages of the relationship. The absolute value

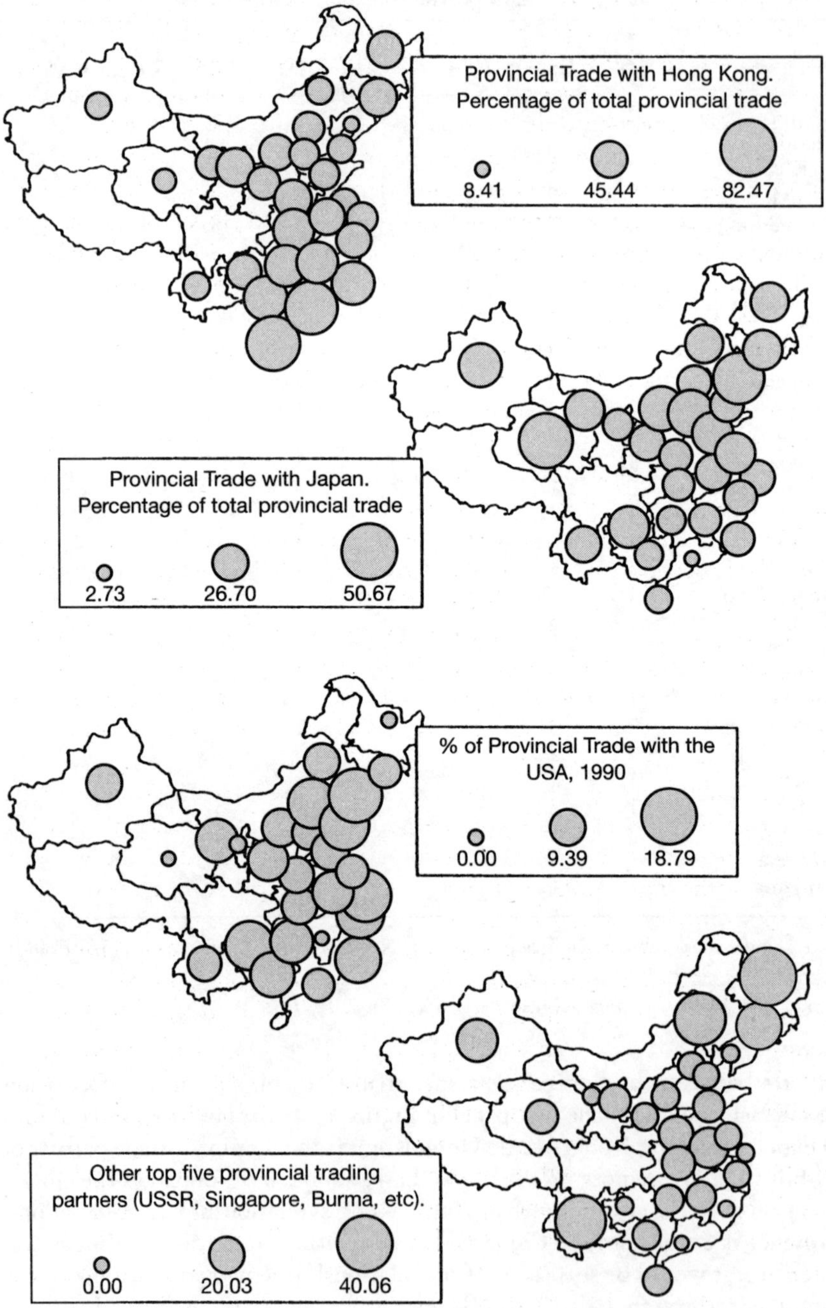

Figure 19.5 Patterns of provincial exports

of Guangdong's Hong Kong trade will undoubtedly increase, but diversification in Guangdong, especially after the establishment of direct trade with Taiwan, will probably increase, and therefore lessen dependence. Nevertheless, even at half the current level of dependence the economic fates of Hong Kong and Guangdong would remain closely and inextricably tied.

Japan is the second-ranked trading partner, both nationally and by number of provinces. Its trade share has expanded steadily since the 1950s, and it has more than kept pace with the trade explosion of the 1980s. The second panel of Figure 19.5 illustrates a northern bias in Japan's provincial trade shares. It is unusually significant not only for close provinces such as Shandong, Hebei and Liaoning, but also for northern border and inland provinces such as Xinjiang, Qinghai and Shanxi. Two factors that may influence Japan's northern reach are that, as distant as Japan is, it is still the closest industrial economy to these regions, and, given the small volumes of trade, a large purchase of a single major export can affect export share. In any case, it is clear that geography affects exports to Japan, but Japan has a large presence throughout China's international economy.

The current dispersion and volume of exports to the United States and Western Europe are roughly similar. However, it should be remembered from Figure 19.2 that Europe has been a much steadier trade partner for China than has the United States, and the uncertainties since 1989 in American trade policy toward China suggest that the volatility in the relationship has not yet disappeared. The third panel of Figure 19.5 shows a relatively even pattern of exports to the United States, and a noticeably larger share with Shanghai and the coastal provinces.

The fourth panel of Figure 19.5 provides a collective illustration of the proclivity of border provinces to trade with their neighbours and their resulting deviance from the national pattern of trade shares. The distinctive trading pattern of the border/inland provinces can be expected to increase rapidly in the 1990s because of its late start in the 1980s, though it certainly does not have the explosive potential of the border/coastal provinces. Nepal can hardly be Tibet's Hong Kong, nor will Tibet be Nepal's Guangdong. Nevertheless, the transformation of China's borders from zones of isolation to zones of commerce is already transforming life in these areas and building new external relations. Moreover, the possibility of entrepot trade over inland borders is not insignificant, especially for Xinjiang (through Kazakhstan) and Yunnan and Guangxi through Vietnam.

Off the maps, and rapidly increasing their trade since 1990, are Taiwan and South Korea. Taiwan's imports from the mainland have increased 27-fold from 1979 to 1992, with an annual growth rate of 27 per cent, while exports have grown 223-fold, or 58 per cent annually.[37] Both countries have been exporting more to China than they have been importing, and in 1993 exports are growing rapidly while imports are stagnant. In terms of total trade, Taiwan and South Korea were China's fourth and fifth largest trading partners in 1992.[38]. Although the export rankings are less impressive, most of Korean and Taiwan investment in China is in export-oriented industry. In 1988 Taiwan's investment was primarily in Fujian Province, but since then it has been shifting towards Guangdong.[39]

THE POLITICAL IMPLICATIONS OF ECONOMIC DIVERSIFICATION

The tea-leaves of provincial diversification are no more decisive about China's political future than the analysis of any number of other major trends, from succession politics to the structural problems of communist regimes. Nevertheless, the diversity of economic situation described above can lead to some plausible hypotheses about perceived economic interests, and while these in turn may not determine who the political actors of the future will be, they might suggest what international interests the leaders at the provincial level might have in mind. We will begin with differences between border, inland and coastal provinces, and then consider generic characteristics of provincial politics of diversity. Lastly we will address the relationships of provinces to the centre.

Looking first at the differentiation between border and inland provinces, it is clear that trade is not an overwhelming interest for either, but it is significantly more important for border provinces. In general, it would seem that inland provinces would have less at stake in international openness, but it must be remembered that the stake of border provinces is quite specific and quite divergent from the national pattern. Thus, a border province like Xinjiang might have much in common with inland provinces on global trade issues. The political leadership of border provinces is likely to become quite involved with the neighbouring country, and it would be likely to favour better relations in its own area, though a bordering province would also be the location of the most acute difficulties in a specific relationship, be they territorial disputes, smuggling, drugs, or ethnic unrest.[40] Inland provinces are less constrained. They might struggle to promote their own international access, or feel free to indulge in heartland nationalism.

Border provinces differ from coastal provinces in the specificity of their international openness. Coastal provinces have the grand advantages of access to the global market, and therefore they are more prosperous, trade is more important for them, and the general environment and structure of trade is a more vital concern. Moreover, the trade pattern of coastal provinces more closely resembles the national pattern, so their concern would focus on the general policy trend. Coastal provinces, and especially cities like Shanghai and Tianjin, would be more concerned about interprovincial barriers to trade. They might therefore have a common interest with the global market in transparency of the national domestic market, although their local economies would be the most exposed to pressures as well as to opportunities. Border provinces have an intense interest in trade with countries of relatively minor national importance, and therefore they might be indifferent to globalisation of trade, but protective and shielding of their own special arrangements. Provinces that are both coastal and border, like Guangdong and Fujian, might be expected to share both characteristics, and be at once intensely interested in specific international relations (with Hong Kong and Taiwan, respectively) and also committed to general policies of openness.

The major difference in internationalisation is between coastal and inland provinces. Clearly coastal provinces have a much more vital interest in the external economy. They would presumably be interested in defending and pushing forward their trading privileges, while the inland provinces would demand the extension of coastal advantages to themselves. This is not necessarily a zero-sum game, but the conflict between inland and coastal provinces over the international marketing of scarce resources can become hostile. The coast has the advantages of money and the national structure of the economy, and the inland areas the advantages of possession and the needs of basic production. These inherent disparities are compounded by national pricing and taxation policies that in the 1980s have been much heavier on the inland provinces. Such conflicts have led to 'wool wars' and 'tobacco wars' between provinces in the 1980s, in which the inland province prohibits the shipment of a specific product.[41] In the late 1980s the conflict advanced to a higher level of sophistication, in which provinces (including coastal provinces) attempted to reserve their local markets for locally produced goods by banning 'imports' from other provinces. But it should be emphasised that such conflicts are premised on the existence of a national market and are therefore expressions of market localism rather than autarkic localism. For instance, Hunan prohibited the sale of rice to Guangdong at one point because it argued that Guangdong should pay more. This action caused the price of Hunan rice to tumble, and as a result the ban was lifted. In a more 'modern' case of market protection, Beijing Municipality forbade the installation of Shunde water heaters from Guangdong in order to protect the local product. Not to be deterred, Shunde began an advertising campaign for its water heaters on Beijing television, and the resulting consumer pressure forced a policy change.[42]

Despite the general interest of coastal areas in global trade, it should be noted that specific problems of openness will be felt there first, leading perhaps to protectionist tendencies against global forces, anti-foreign problems and outbursts, and so forth. Moreover, the familiar societal institutions of the party-state will tend to be weakest in the areas of greatest international exposure and economic development, perhaps encouraging local political as well as economic entrepreneurship.

If we take a more general view of provincial diversity, generic similarities of provincial situations become apparent. First, market localism, the attempt to secure private advantage in an increasingly interdependent and unrestricted context, will condition the general political environment. While this does not necessarily imply a war of all against all, it does imply a connection-building, deal-making, haggling and shielding of all with and against all, and at every level of society. The level of potentially conflictual commotion can rise even if open confrontation is minimised. Like bicyclists and motorists on a crowded road, each can assert their interest and advantage without looking the other in the eye. The provinces themselves will be in the roles of exasperated regulators within their boundaries and at the same time of participants in the national scramble. The provinces are, after all, centres in the eyes of their localities just as they are localities in the eyes of the centre.

Secondly, the provinces will all have to cope with the relative decline of the salience and resources of public institutions. They will have more to do with relatively less fiscal strength, and therefore the effective capacity of the province to provide expected levels of service may well decline. For instance, as economic activity pushes up inflation and life-style expectations, provinces find it increasingly difficult to pay their teachers. Thus the provincial governments of even the most prosperous provinces are likely to have their hands full with their basic governmental responsibilities.

As long as China remains prosperous and growing, it is hard to imagine a serious level of interprovincial hostility resulting from provincial diversification. While the rate of growth in the coastal provinces exceeds that of the inland provinces, all provinces have benefited enormously from Deng Xiaoping's policies. In contrast to development experience in much of the world, the rich are getting richer but the poor are getting richer also, though not necessarily as fast. To take an extreme example, the agricultural production per capita of the minority areas of Guizhou Province was 25.7 per cent of the national average and 52.4 per cent of the provincial average in 1985; by 1988 it had sunk to 17.3 per cent of the national average and 41.2 per cent of the provincial figure. On the other hand, agricultural productivity did increase, GSP increased at 7 per cent per year from 1985–89, and the number of desperately poor people decreased by half.[43] Thus, the poorest regions of one of China's poorest provinces have benefited from reform, and their implicit demands are for more aid from the centre rather than for a reversal of policy direction.

Since the apparent source of wealth is the external connection rather than interprovincial exploitation, the contest is between the haves and the want-to-haves, a competition which sometimes involves conflict, but is basically more of a race than a battle. It is possible to imagine different levels of enthusiasm and commitment to international openness among the provinces, but it is not currently to the detriment of any of them, and it is not likely to become so in the foreseeable future. It is perhaps indicative of a common denominator of provincial interest in diversification that a plan put forward by Li Peng in September 1990 to reform fiscal relations between centre and provinces was defeated by provincial opposition led by Governor Ye

Xuanping of Guangdong.[44] Another difficulty to consider is the possibility of exclusivist or separatist tendencies in the rich coastal provinces. In our opinion it is unlikely for several reasons that a coastal province or provinces would challenge the centre or attempt to establish autonomy. First, outside of Tibet and Xinjiang, there is no tradition of ethno-nationalism that could legitimise separatist tendencies. The chaos of the first half of the twentieth century is a negative memory both for China as a whole and for each of its parts. Secondly, control over military power in China is concentrated at the centre, and this is not likely to change in the foreseeable future.[45] In any confrontation, therefore, the centre holds trump. Thirdly, the nationwide participation in political demonstrations related to the Tiananmen events of May and June 1989 indicated the general importance of the national political arena, the political leadership of Beijing even in unofficial and confrontational politics, and the absence of popular local agendas demanding more autonomy from the centre.[46] Of course changes could occur, but in the meantime the fate of European post-communist regimes has demonstrated the pitfalls of separatism.

We can conclude, then, that even serious tensions between centre and provinces are not likely to eventuate in confrontation or separatism. We can go further and emphasise the basic common interests between centre and provinces. First and most obviously, the centre is responsible for the modernisation policies that have led to the current prosperity and to provincial diversification. The depth of the central leadership's commitment to modernisation and openness can be seen in the steadiness of policy after Tiananmen and the reaffirmation of commitment at the Fourteenth National Party Congress at the end of 1992. Difficulties in international openness are more likely to be bilateral (for instance, with the United States over Most Favored Nation status) rather than general policy reversals. In times of crisis at the centre, it would be clear to all contenders for power that the measure most likely to win support and to diffuse opposition would be a guarantee of continuity in economic modernisation and international openness. Any more progressive central regime would almost certainly remain committed to openness as a matter of principle, while even a more repressive regime might well try to allay international and domestic concerns by reaffirming economic openness.

Second, the provinces need the national ordering provided by the centre. It has become particularly obvious in 1993 that unrestrained investment and growth can lead to an overheating of the economy, and that the centre must intervene and regulate. Zhu Rongji's current attempt to reconstruct the centre as an effective regulator of the national economy may inconvenience the current plans of provinces, but it would be difficult to claim that it is not in their long-term interest. Provincial interest in an effective centre goes beyond controlling inflation. The provincial political and economic structures are modelled on the centre, and any fundamental attack on central institutions would imply a critique of provincial institutions. Relations with other provinces and with foreign countries are regulated by the centre, and no province is in a position to provide these services for itself. Therefore, while provinces might pursue measures that would give them more autonomy from the centre in various areas, a province that threatened to disrupt the central order might well be seen as a threat by other provinces.

The last and most basic common interest between even the most diversified province and the centre is that the internal market of China is essential to prosperity. This is true for Hong Kong as well as for the PRC, and it is rapidly becoming a factor for Taiwan. To be separated from China would mean to cut oneself off from the one-fifth of the world's population that one identifies with ethnically and politically, and that is the major source for trade and resources. To damage the unity of China would put at risk the context of provincial prosperity. At a time when China's neighbours and the rest of the world feel the gravity of the China market, it is difficult to imagine a part breaking free of the surface. And while market localism might be more aggressive and contentious than autarkic localism, commercial development implies a spreading network of interdependence This chapter has described the variety of international interdependence that developed in the 1980s, but these new external orientations are premised on internal unity, they are not centrifugal forces. Great uncertainties remain for China's politics in the 1990s, but the lines differentiating the many worlds of China's provinces probably do not mark fractal patterns.

Although this positive prognostication is not intentionally optimistic, it should be noted that research is usually biased toward rational action by participants and toward the continuation of perceived trends. Events at Tiananmen in 1989 are caution enough that things can happen that no one intends or desires. As long as central succession is uncertain and there is no definition of provincial autonomy, it is impossible to preclude vicious circles leading to national disruption. But diversification, including the dimension of international diversification discussed in this chapter, does not by any means make this possibility either inevitable or desirable.

ACKNOWLEDGMENTS

The authors would like to thank the Miller Center of the University of Virginia for its research support, and the University Service Center of Chinese University of Hong Kong and the University of Binghampton for hosting seminar presentations. Thomas Rawski, Yun-Wing Sun and Herman Schwartz provided helpful comments on earlier drafts.

NOTES

1 See Ezra Vogel, *One Step Ahead in China: Guangdong Under Reform* (Cambridge: Harvard University Press, 1989).

2 The emergence of the term *shimin* (civilians, cityfolk) during the demonstrations and the participation of the *getihu* (individual entrepreneurs) in the 1989 demonstrations are particularly striking signs of the political consequences of societal changes. See Jonathan Unger, ed., *The Pro-Democracy Demonstrations in China: Reports from the Provinces* (Armonk: M.E. Sharpe, 1991).

3 Chen Yuan, the son of Chen Yun, has been a spokesperson for these concerns. See He Pin, Gao Xin, 'Chen Yuan–Taizi dang touhao zhongzi xuan shou', *Minzhu Zhongguo*, no. 8 (February, 1992), pp. 25–32.

4 Further research will be concerned with the differences of export and import patterns, which are considerable.

5 See Albert Feuerwerker, 'Economic Trends, 1912–1949', in John K. Fairbank, ed., *The Cambridge History of China*, volume 12 (Cambridge: Cambridge University Press, 1983), pp. 28–127, esp. pp. 120–127.

6 *Ibid.*, p. 126.

7 Lowell Dittmer, 'China's Search for its Place in the World', in Brantly Womack, ed., *Contemporary Chinese Politics in Historical Perspective* (Cambridge: Cambridge University Press, 1991), pp. 209–61. Its other, unstructured peer group was the third world.

8 For a general treatment see Franklyn Holzman, 'Foreign Trade Behavior in Centrally Planned Economies', in Henry Rosovsky, ed., *Industnalization in Two Systems* (New York: John Wiley, 1966). Nicholas Lardy applies this model to China in the second chapter of *Foreign Trade and Economic Reform in China, 1978–1990* (Cambridge: Cambridge University Press, 1992), and John Kamm gives a more existential account of pre-reform trade practice in Guangdong in his chapter, 'Reforming Foreign Trade', in Ezra Vogel, *One Step Ahead*, pp. 338–94.

9 Ordinarily the ratio of trade to GNP is used as an indicator, but, as Lardy details, cross-national comparisons of China's trade ratio are quite problematic in any case. It happens, however, that the ratio of trade to GSP corresponds quite closely to his preferred estimates of the GNP trade ratio, which would be 5.8 per cent in 1978 and 9.4 per cent in 1988. See Lardy, *Foreign Trade*, Appendix B, pp. 150–55 for a full discussion.

10 See A.O. Hirschman, *National Power and the Structure of Foreign Trade* (Berkeley: University of California Press, 1980, original 1945) for the development of the index, especially Part Two, pp. 85–162. To illustrate the formula: If all trade were with one country, the equation would be: $\text{Index} = \sqrt{100^2 + 0^2 + 0^2 + 0^2} = 100$. If trade were spread evenly among one hundred partners, it would be $\text{Index} = \sqrt{100(1^2)} = 10$. As Hirschman points out in his original formulation (p. 99), the index measures the departure from equal shares of trade, not dependence on one partner. Sometimes the Hirschman Index is given on a scale of one to zero, but we have retained Hirschman's original scale. To convert, divide by 100 (i.e. add a dot in front).

11 James Caporaso, 'Dependence, Dependency and Power in the Global System: A Structural and Behavioral Analysis', *International Organisation*, 32: 1 (Winter, 1978), pp. 13–45.

12 A good illustration would be the sugar cane regions of Fujian Province, which were artificially impoverished in the 1960s and 70s because policies stressed local grain self-sufficiency. With such controls eased and then lifted, sugar production tripled between 1976 and 1981. See Nicholas Lardy, 'State Intervention and Peasant Opportunities', in William Parish, ed., *Chinese Rural Development: The Great Transformation* (Armonk: M.E. Sharpe, 1985), pp. 46–49. According to

Thomas Lyons, 'of the 11 chronic-poverty counties [in Fujian] of 1977–79, one is traditionally the largest fruit producer, two are leading sugar producers, one is the largest tea producer, one is the largest tobacco producer, and three are among the leading producers of seafoods.' Lyons, *China's War on Poverty: A Case Study of Fujian Province, 1985–1990* (Hong Kong Institute of Asia–Pacific Studies, Chinese University of Hong Kong, 1992), p. 27.

13 Alexander Eckstein, *China's Economic Revolution* (New York: Cambridge University Press, 1977). As discussed above, however, the management and role of foreign trade adhered closely to the Stalinist model.

14 Quoted in Vogel, *One Step Ahead*, p. 81.

15 See Lardy, *Foreign Trade*, Appendix B, pp. 150–155.

16 Chang Pao-min, *Beijing, Hanoi and the Overseas Chinese* (Berkeley: Center for Chinese Studies, 1982).

17 See 'Message to Compatriots on Taiwan', *Beijing Review*, 1979. no. 1(5 January), pp. 16–17; 'Chairman Ye's Elaborations of Policy Concerning Return of Taiwan to the Motherland and Peaceful Reunification', *Beijing Review*, 1981, no. 40 (5 October), pp. 10–11.

18 The policy changes toward Guangdong are described in Vogel, *One Step Ahead.*

19 For Hebei see *Dow Jones International*, 9 March, 1993; for overall zone development see Associated Press, 10 February, 1993.

20 See Pak-Wai Liu, Yun-Wing Sun, R. Yue-Chim Wong and Pui-King Lau, *China's Economic Reform and Development Strategy of Pearl River Delta* (Hong Kong: Nanyang Commercial Bank, 1992), pp. 28–31. The statistics used are based on the MOFERT (Ministry of Foreign Economic Relations and Trade) method, the alternative is the Customs method, which is closer to international usage. Using the Customs method, Guangdong's exports would be 30 per cent of national exports in 1990.

21 The Hong Kong data is from *Hong Kong 1993* (Hong Kong, Government Information Services, 1993), p. 430. We have not attempted in Figure 19.4 to separate Taiwan or South Korea from the residual because we lack provincial-level data, but national data is presented in this analysis.

22 Two assumptions of this estimate should be noted. First, our choice of the MOFERT method of calculating exports, discussed above, reduces the apparent role of Guangdong and of Hong Kong. Secondly, our calculations assume that Hong Kong's re-exports to destinations other than China originate in China. Given the pattern of Hong Kong's re-exports this is a plausible assumption. See *Hong Kong 1993*, p. 430.

23 See David Zweig 'Internationalizing China's Countryside: The Political Economy of Exports from Rural Industry', *China Quarterly* No. 128 (December 1991), p. 718. Nicholas R. Lardy 'Chinese Foreign Trade', *China Quarterly*, No. 131 (September 1992) p. 710.

24 Zweig, 'Internationalizing China's Countryside'.

25 Calculated from Pak-Wai Liu, *China's Economic Reform*, pp. 1–3.

26 All the figures concerning trade increase and border trade come from *Zhongguo Duiwai Jingji Maoyi Nianjian (Almanac of Chinese Foreign Economy and Trade)*.

27 Li, Chunlei 'Dakai guomen, bian bu zai qiong' (Opening the Doors, the Border Will No Longer Be Poor), *Liaowang Zhoukan (Outlook Weekly)*, No. 22, 1 June, 1992.

28 The Nung minority on the Vietnam–Guangxi border had the monopoly on border trade until the 1990s, and it is still common for the border porters to be Nung.

29 Xinhua News Agency, 22 February 1993.

30 See Lardy, pp. 711–714, for a very interesting discussion of Guangdong's advantages over Shanghai in coping with the remaining administrative limits on market access and in dealing with interprovincial supply problems.

31 Information supplied by Dr. Yung-Wing Sun of Chinese University of Hong Kong.

32 Pak-Wai Liu *et al., China's Economic Reform*, p. 19.

33 Pak-Wai Liu *et al., China's Economic Reform*, pp. 56–57.

34 Of course, trade with Taiwan and South Korea had to go through intermediaries for political reasons.

35 See Michele Ledic, 'Hong Kong and China: Economic Interdependence' in *China in the Nineties: Crisis Management and Beyond*, David S.G. Goodman and Gerald Segal, eds, Oxford: Clarendon Press, 1991, pp. 201–8.

36 *China Daily*, 21 August 1993.

37 Ricky Tung, 'Economic Interaction Between Taiwan and South China's Fukien and Kwangtung Provinces', *Issues and Studies*, 29: 7 (July 1993), p. 33.

38 The largest trading partners were Hong Kong, the United States and Japan, in that order. Xinhua News Agency 22 February 1993.

39 Ricky Tung, 'Economic Interaction', pp. 29–30.

40 A good example of border province activism would be the grand plans for Mekong development of Wu Guanglan, Party Secretary of Yunnan Province. See *Far Eastern Economic Review*, 16 September 1993, pp. 68–70.

41 There is an excellent analysis of these conflicts in Chen Dongshen and Wei Houkai, 'Some Reflections on Interregional Trade Friction', in *Gaige*, no. 2 (20 March 1989), pp. 79–83. Available in JPRS-CAR-89-077, 24 July 1989, pp. 5–9.

42 Pak-Wai Liu *et al., China's Economic Reform*, p. 21. At last report, Beijing still charges a higher installation fee for Shunde water heaters. See also *Far Eastern Economic Review*, 18 October 1990, p. 89.

43 Li Renshan, 'Guizhou shaoshu minzu zizhi difang jingji shehui fazhan qingkuang cunzai wenti yu jinhoufazhan di jianyi'. (Current problems in the economic and societal developmental situation in Guizhou's autonomous minority localities). In Guizhou sheng shaoshu minzu jingji yanjiu hui, ed, *Guizhou sheng shaoshu minzu jingji yanjiu* [Economic research concerning the national minorities of Guizhou Province] (Guiyang: Guizhou minzu chubanshe, 1991), pp. 1–9. Thomas Lyons describes a similar situation in Fujian, and analyses the effectiveness of a national anti-poverty campaign, in *China's War on Poverty*, but Guizhou is an even more impoverished area.

44 See *Far Eastern Economic Review*, 4 April 1991, p. 26.

45 See Ellis Joffe, 'Regionalism in China: The Role of the PLA', paper presented at the conference *Security Dimensions of Chinese Regionalism*, Hong Kong, June 1993.

46 See Unger, *The Pro-Democracy Demonstrations.*

Part VI

POPULATION AND LABOUR

20

CHINA'S POPULATION CHANGES AND THE ECONOMY

Judith Banister

SUMMARY

This article briefly describes broad demographic trends in China during the 1980s and 1990s, and how they relate to economic trends. The population continued growing during the 1980s because of low mortality, declining age at marriage, fertility slightly above replacement level in most years, and a young age structure. China has achieved rather advanced mortality conditions for a developing country, with apparent further improvement in the 1980s. The death rate is expected to remain low, which will foster continued population growth. During the early 1980s, age at marriage declined in China, which tended to increase the birth rate. But government pressure to postpone marriage may now have arrested this trend.

China's one-child policy is still in effect and has been very successful in urban areas. But in rural areas it has met with continuing resistance. The national and provincial governments have now backed down to the point of allowing some rural couples to have a second child. Couples of the Han Chinese majority ethnic group are forbidden to have more than two children, and the determination of the authorities to stop them has succeeded in continually reducing the proportion of all births that are third and subsequent births. It is expected that fertility levels and population growth rates will remain about the same in the 1990s. If China's Communist government were superseded by a more democratic one, however, compulsory family planning would probably cease, and fertility and the population growth rate would rise.

During the decade of economic reform from 1978 through 1988, China's economic boom facilitated rapid job creation. The employed population increased at 3.0 percent a year while the population of labor force ages grew at 2.5 percent annually. Some of the new jobs were in agriculture, but nonagricultural employment increased at over 6 percent per year. Therefore, the

Source: Congress, Joint Economic Committee, *China's Economic Dilemmas in the 1990s: The Problems of Reforms, Modernization, and interdependence* (Washington, D.C: US Government Printing Office, 1991), Vol. 1, pp. 234–51. [Subsequently reprinted by M. E. Sharpe.]

economic reforms helped to further the transformation of China's economy out of agriculture into industrial and service sector employment. This structural change is much needed because there is a huge surplus labor force in agriculture. But the economic retrenchment policies adopted in late 1988, and the political crackdown of 1989, brought on an economic slump and at least temporarily stopped the economic transformation of China's employment structure.

The economic reform period also saw increased geographical mobility of laborers. While some moved to nearby towns, others flooded into the cities or headed for coastal zones where factories now produce for export. Rural-to-urban migration of workers was one component of China's urbanization trend in the 1980s. Though the current economic slowdown is causing some non-agricultural workers to return to their villages and to farming, it is likely that the urban demand for rural workers will remain important in the 1990s, and that rural-to-urban migration will continue.

China's population will probably continue growing at around 1.4 percent a year in the 1990s, and the total population is expected to be close to 1.3 billion by the year 2000. If the economic slump and political stagnation continue, this population growth could exacerbate problems of food supply, employment, and living standards, but if China's rapid economic development resumes, this rate of population growth would be more manageable.

I INTRODUCTION

China's population size is so huge, and each annual increment to the population so enormous, that we cannot ignore how China's demographic conditions impinge on the country's economic development and quality of life. During the tempestuous years 1957–1977, for example, grain production and population size increased by about the same amount, leaving per capita grain output hardly changed after two decades. Since the beginning of the economic reform period in 1978, the interplay between economic and demographic trends has become much more complex than before. For instance, the sharp increases in agricultural production during 1978–1984 gave China some safety margin in its food supply. Yet the loosening of economic controls over the farmers, which had brought about the surge in agricultural output, also weakened the ability of officials to prevent unauthorized rural births.

The general economic boom of the reform decade 1978–1988 produced a doubling of per capita income accompanied by visible improvement in living standards in both urban and rural areas. Population growth continued, but was so much slower than economic growth that per capita gains in food supply, housing, and consumer goods were impressive, at least for a while. This article briefly traces the interactions between population changes and economic trends in China since 1978, emphasizing the most recent years and prospects for the 1990s. Table 1 includes some available economic and per capita economic indicators for this period.

China, the world's most populous country, counted a total population of about 1.13 billion people in 1990, constituting 21 percent of the world's total population and fully 28 percent of the population in developing countries. Since China's landmark 1982 census, the population has grown 1.47 percent a year on average. This growth rate is very low for a developing country, but in the context of China, it has meant an additional 126 million people in only eight years!

II MORTALITY AND HEALTH

During the 1980s, the rural people's communes were dismantled, and so were the cooperative medical systems that had been organized and highly subsidized by the production brigades under the communes. Now, in most of China's rural areas, health care has shifted to a fee-for-service system in which the former rudimentary arrangements for health and major medical insurance are gone. Some localities have made ad hoc attempts to guarantee minimal health care to everyone regardless of ability to pay. It is unclear how many people are now experiencing reduced access to medical care as a result of the economic transformation of China's rural areas.

Despite some deterioration in China's famous system of preventive and primary health care for the rural population, the data so far available suggest that during the 1980s, survival chances improved for the rural as well as the urban populations at most ages for both sexes.[1] One exception to this generalization is the mortality trend for infants. According to China's 1988 two-per-thousand-population fertility survey, China's infant mortality rate declined sharply through 1977, then stabilized for a full decade through 1987 at approximately 40 deaths in the first year of life per thousand live births.[2] Until death and age data from the 1990 census become available, it is impossible to document mortality trends in China during the most recent years, nor can we even be certain that mortality above infancy did decline during the 1980s as indicated by presently available statistics.

How is it possible to explain the apparent improvement in survival chances for most age groups except infants, in spite of the disarray in the rural medical system during the economic reform decade? The weakening of primary health care may have affected prenatal care and the maternal and child health network the most, which would help explain the lack of further improvement in infant survival. But the doubling of living standards greatly improved food supply, nutrition, and the quality and quantity of housing, all of which may have increased survival chances above infancy. People have chosen to spend some of their higher incomes on medical care and pharmaceuticals, and the numbers of doctors and hospital beds per capita have grown, as shown in Table 1.[3] China worked with the United Nations Children's Fund (UNICEF) and the World Health Organization in the 1980s to immunize over 85 percent of the children in each province against six major diseases, thus greatly reducing child mortality from infectious disease. The government has claimed progress in improving water supply and water quality for most of the rural population in the 1980s decade.[4] Therefore, the economic boom has given people more resources to use for prolonging life and improving health, while the government has continued its emphasis on preventive strategies such as immunization which can significantly reduce mortality.

China's low crude death rate contributes to the continuing population growth. The death rate is low, both because of China's great successes in reduction of mortality, and because the country still has a young age structure due to past high fertility.[5] In a young population, a high proportion of people are in ages with comparatively low mortality.

III MARRIAGE AND THE TIMING OF BIRTHS

Changes in the ages at which women marry and bear children strongly affect annual fertility and population growth by spreading out births or bunching them together. During the 1970s China's government had successfully promoted and required higher ages at marriage in both urban and rural areas. Rising marriage ages significantly reduced the total fertility rates and crude birth rates of the 1970s.[6] But required postponement of marriage was not popular, and this policy was reversed in the revised Marriage Law adopted in 1980. Thereafter, the mean age at first marriage for Chinese women dropped from 23.1 years old in 1979 to 21.7 in 1985; this trend was seen in cities, towns, and rural areas.[7] In addition, there is some evidence that the average time interval between marriage and first birth (known as the "first birth interval") has been reduced in recent years.

Earlier marriage combined with a shorter first birth interval meant that Chinese women in the 1980s bore their children at younger ages than was the case in the late 1970s. The surge of marriages and the shortening of intervals between marriage and first birth caused a bunching of births, especially first births, in the first half of the 1980s. The government has been trying to reverse this trend, and since 1985 marriage age has stabilized or risen slightly.[8]

China's 1980s marriage boom was encouraged by an expansion of available housing space, and simultaneously increased the need for more housing units. The supply of housing escalated rapidly in the reform decade. Rural residents poured much of their newly increased income into expansion and upgrading of their existing dwellings and the building of new houses for family members. In cities, a boom in housing construction helped alleviate a desperate shortage of living quarters. Living space per capita expanded in both urban and rural areas. Escalating demand for housing was driven in part by the surge of marriages, and housing construction in turn made it much easier for young couples to set up a new household.

IV FERTILITY AND FAMILY PLANNING

A The one child policy

Since 1979 China has been in the era of the well-known one-child policy. The rationale for this policy has been that it is unacceptable to allow the population of China to continue growing to 1.4 or 1.5 billion people, which is projected if people bear two children per couple. In 1979, the national government of China boldly presumed that it would be possible under current conditions to educate, cajole, or force urban and rural couples to cease childbearing after the birth of one child. In urban areas, the leadership's confidence was reasonably well-founded. The urban family planning program had been very effective since the early 1960s, and the total fertility rate of the urban nonagricultural population had been reduced to only 1.55 births per woman by 1978.[9] Throughout the 1980s, the urban total fertility rate was around 1.3 births per woman, according to official reports.[10] This is lower fertility than that of almost any country or city in the world, developed or developing, and must be seen as an unqualified success for China's one-child policy.

However, the official goal of one child per couple was severely out of line with rural reality. China's forceful family planning program of the 1970s had already resulted in a steep drop in rural fertility from 6.4 births per woman in 1970 to 3.0 births per woman in 1978, a remarkably rapid shift.[11] But rural couples continued to view it as necessary to have more than one child, including at least one son, to provide farm and household labor for the family. A widespread rural attitude is that sons, after reaching adulthood, are needed to carry on the family name, live with or near their parents, and care for their aging parents because a rural social security system is lacking. In addition to these traditional reasons for desiring several children, the shift from communal to family farming in the 1980s made households into economic production units that could potentially benefit from more children to work the fields, carry out sideline activities, transport and sell output, take jobs in rural enterprises and bring home the earnings, or migrate to a town or city and send money home. During the 1980s, occasional surveys asked rural couples about desired family size, and they almost always answered that two, three, or more children were preferred.[12]

From 1979 through 1983, the Chinese government escalated the pressure on rural couples to stop at one child. This policy applied to the majority Han Chinese population; China's 55 minority groups, who constituted 7 percent of China's total population according to the 1982 census, have been encouraged to limit fertility but not required to abide by the one-child rule. What evolved in the early 1980s was a requirement that Han Chinese women with one child accept the insertion of an IUD which would not be removed on request, and that couples who had managed to bear two children in spite of the one-child policy or before it was implemented were required to have one partner sterilized. In many rural as well as urban areas, family planning workers monitored the menstrual periods and pregnancy status of each married woman of childbearing age, so that an abortion could be required for pregnancies outside the local official birth plan. The coercion level reached its peak in 1983, when family planning surgery teams swooped into villages and carried out mandatory sterilizations, IUD insertions, and abortions on those women deemed "eligible." That year, the number of each kind of birth control operation peaked in China at 21 million sterilizations, 18 million IUD insertions, and 14 million abortions.

B Evolving family planning policies

The strength of the rural backlash against the coercion campaign was never directly reported in China's media and must be indirectly inferred from other evidence. Suddenly in early 1984, previously scheduled family planning campaigns were called off, the director of the family planning program was replaced, and "Document Number 7" was promulgated. This national directive was never published, but was referred to for some years. It counseled that, (in contrast to the 1979–1983 period), "family planning policies must be built on a foundation that is fair and reasonable, supported by the masses, and easy for the cadres to carry out."[13] Document Number 7 directed that rural couples with "real difficulties," thought to constitute no more than 5 or 10 percent of rural couples, might be given permission to have a second child.

Meanwhile, through all this turmoil, rural fertility remained above two births per woman on average. Since 1983, rural couples have continued their struggle to have two, three, or more children in spite of official prohibition. In many places in China, this is very difficult and requires getting an illegal IUD removal, hiding the pregnancy, and leaving the village on some pretense for most of the pregnancy until the baby is born. In other localities, however, the family planning system of regulation has broken down along with the commune system, and women are no longer being constantly monitored.[14] For a few years after 1983, the national government backed down a little and expanded the proportion of rural second parity births that were officially approved.[15] In some provinces now, peasants who have a firstborn girl are allowed a second birth (to try for a boy). In other provinces, all peasants are allowed two births per couple. But in the more developed provinces, the one-child limit is still being applied to many categories of rural couples as well as to urban couples; in Heilongjiang, for example, only a minority of villages may permit second births to couples with a firstborn girl. Now the national and many provincial governments are trying to reduce the proportions of rural couples who are authorized to have a second child.[16]

As of 1990, as far as can be ascertained, China's government is still trying to be as strict as it can get away with in enforcing a one-child limit for most urban couples and a one-child or two-child limit for rural couples. National and provincial governments continually exhort local cadres to hold the line on births; indeed, the harshness of the official rhetoric and the penalties to back up official demands have been escalating since 1986.[17] This policy appears to be successful; actual fertility in China is below desired fertility—that is, both urban and rural couples are bearing fewer children than they would without the compulsory family planning program. Today, family planning workers and "volunteers" for the quasi-official local Family Planning Associations continue to monitor the birth control, menstrual, and pregnancy status of the vast majority of urban women and most rural married women in the reproductive ages.[18] They often achieve their goals of preventing unapproved pregnancies through required IUD use or sterilization, and by securing the induced abortion of fetuses whose births are not authorized.

C Fertility and contraceptive use

As shown in Table 3, China's birth rate has been steady at the low level of 21 births per thousand population annually for four years, according to State Statistical Bureau surveys. Since 1982, 51 or 52 percent of the births each year have been first parity births. This is extraordinarily high for a developing country and attests to the success of the one-child policy. The main parity trend in the 1980s was a steep drop in the proportion of births that were third or subsequent children, a result of China's continuing official insistence that all births above second parity are resolutely forbidden except to members of minority groups. Meanwhile, the proportion of births that were second births rose to one-third, mirroring the slow growth until about 1986 of official tolerance for rural second births.

Today, China's compulsory family planning program is still functioning and keeping fertility low and more or less steady. Each year, there are still 10–13 million IUD insertions, 3–6 million sterilizations, and 10–13 million abortions performed. Of married women in the reproductive ages 15–49, 71 percent are practicing family planning. Such a high contraceptive use rate is typical of developed countries but rare in developing countries. Of these couples practicing contraception, 49 percent have one partner sterilized, 41 percent are using an IUD, 5 percent are using the pill, and 5 percent other methods.[19] This means that a very high proportion of couples in China are using modern effective contraceptive methods which prevent pregnancy. Abortions, voluntary or required, are still heavily used to prevent births when pregnancies occur.

Fertility is very low in China, not far above "replacement level fertility," yet the population continues to grow at over 1.4 percent a year. This is partly because of age structure. China had huge cohorts born in the high-fertility period of the 1960s, who reached their twenties during the 1980s. Births are highly concentrated when Chinese women are ages 21–30, so this bulge in the age structure is tending to drive the birth rate up. This trend will be even more pronounced in the 1990s, when the huge numbers of women in their twenties could cause a "birth peak." As shown in Figure 1, the number of women aged 21–30 increased from 81 million in 1983 to about 106 million in 1990. The peak will come in 1993, with approximately 124 million women in their fertile twenties, and the number will decline only slowly to about 109 million in the year 2000. Therefore, the birth rate could rise in the 1990s if fertility per woman does not drop. China's government is concerned about the coming "birth peak," and therefore is attempting to reduce fertility further.

V LABOR FORCE AND EMPLOYMENT TRENDS

A Economic reform and employment growth

Shifts in China's age structure have also meant that the population of labor force ages has been growing faster than the total population in recent years. For example, from the 1982 census to 1990, the population at ages 15–64 grew 2.5 percent a year while the total population increased 1.5 percent annually. During the decade from the adoption of the reform agenda in 1978 until the implementation of economic retrenchment in late 1988 and the political crisis of 1989, China's booming economy was successful at creating jobs for the growing working age population. The tremendous increase in the size of the employed population was due not only to vigorous economic growth but also to the continuing Chinese government attitude that full employment is essential, even if it comes at the cost of low productivity.

Official Chinese statistics on employment show that at the end of 1978 there were about 402 million people working. The size of the employed population grew 3.0 percent a year to 543 million at the end of 1988, well ahead of the growth of population in labor force ages. In 1989 under economic retrenchment policies, official data still show employment growth of 1.8 percent.[20]

B Surplus labor in agriculture

It is characteristic of China that the employment participation rate of adult men is extremely high; this is also true of Chinese women, which is even more unusual in international perspective.[21] This phenomenon is partly a result of the practice in some localities of classifying those adults not working outside agriculture in the residual category of agricultural workers, even if their contribution to agriculture is marginal or sporadic. Workers in agriculture made up 60 percent of total employed workers in 1989.

The number of agricultural workers is high partly because Chinese agriculture is still at a low level of mechanization. On the whole, farmers make intensive use of the available arable land and water resources in order to feed the huge population, and this requires a lot of labor. Even so, Chinese policymakers recognize that the agricultural sector does not need so many workers. Chinese scholars estimate that approximately one-third of the country's farmers are underemployed, meaning that their efforts are needed only at peak planting and harvesting time. The surplus of adult workers stuck on the land holds down per-worker productivity in agriculture well below what it would be if these workers could be usefully employed elsewhere.[22]

C Employment trends by economic sector

For the last decade, the emphasis in employment policy has been to create jobs for the rising tide of youth entering the work force in urban areas, and in the countryside to absorb some of the excess farm workers into nonagricultural jobs, agricultural sideline occupations, or the production of cash crops. In contrast to the earlier Maoist decades, national policy during the 1980s has allowed self-employment, permitted the reopening of rural and urban markets not run by local governments, encouraged rural enterprises to employ idle agricultural workers, and allowed workers to move in order to find jobs. Until 1989, the results were encouraging. During the period from 1978 through 1988 (based on year-end figures), while employment in agriculture increased at 1.3 percent annually, total nonagricultural jobs grew at a respectable 6.3 percent a year. But the retrenchment policies and upheavals of 1989 stopped the growth of nonagricultural employment; the number of jobs outside agriculture stayed at 220 million from year-end 1988 to year-end 1989.[23]

The growth rate of jobs in the industrial sector of the economy dropped from 7.3 percent in 1986 to 3–4 percent annually in 1987 and 1988. Then, however, urban layoffs and the closing of some rural enterprises in 1989 brought a decline in industrial employment from 97 million at the end of 1988 to 96 million one year later. Employment in the service sector, which had been increasing at 5 or 6 percent a year, grew at a modest 0.9 percent in 1989. Those who lost their nonagricultural jobs, as well as the new entrants to the labor force, either became unemployed, shifted to service sector work, or took up agriculture. The growth rate of employment in agriculture increased gradually from 0.4 percent in 1986 to 3.0 percent in 1989.

The return of workers to agriculture represents a (hopefully temporary) reversal of the long-term transformation of China's economy from poor, rural, and agricultural to a more urban, nonagricultural employment structure accompanied by much higher living standards. The setbacks of 1989, however, do illustrate the wisdom of the millions of rural families who, as a precautionary measure, have hedged their bets on China's economic transformation. Since 1978, rural households have acquired rights to the use of small plots of land in the family land contracting system. While utilizing this land to grow food for the family and for profit, household units have encouraged their members to get jobs in nearby rural enterprises, take up transport work, sell goods in markets, migrate for seasonal employment, or move to a city or town for an urban job.

However, even if all or almost all adult workers in the household took nonagricultural jobs, and most family income came from nonagricultural sources, families have strongly resisted giving up any of their land rights. Instead, such households have shifted to farming the land nonintensively or letting it lie fallow.[24] This system is wasteful of quality agricultural land, a phenomenon decried by both Chinese and Western economists, but makes good sense from the perspective of the household. In an economic recession, if household nonagricultural workers lose their jobs, they can temporarily revert to farming the land. Given the lack of a rural social safety net, land rights act as an insurance policy.

Urban workers who are laid off do not have this option, and many former rural residents who had moved to cities and towns resist moving back to the countryside. Therefore urban unemployment has grown since September 1988 when retrenchment policies, including a severe credit squeeze on collective and private enterprises, began to be implemented. China's unemployment statistics are still poor in quality;[25] rural unemployment is not captured in the statistics at all, and urban unemployment is underreported because it includes only those who have formally registered for work and are officially "waiting for employment." Figures on urban unemployment probably exclude unemployed migrants in urban areas who do not qualify for permanent residence there, and thus are not included in urban statistics. The official urban unemployment rate was 2.0 percent of the urban labor force from 1986 through 1988, then rose to 2.6 percent by the end of 1989.[26] By the end of March 1990, it was reported that 3 percent of the urban labor force in China was completely out of work, and another 3 percent was "partly out of work."[27]

VI LABOR MIGRATION AND URBANIZATION

A Increasing migration of workers

In the Maoist decades, geographical mobility of Chinese families and workers was severely restricted and curtailed by the location-specific permanent population registration and rationing system. Though the vast majority of people did not move at all, there was a trickle of labor migration. Some laborers were required to move to border provinces, some were allowed to move to newly established industrial cities, and some were sent from their city homes to work in rural areas. Often when laborers moved, they were not allowed to bring their families with them.

This system is still in place, but in the economic reform period, restrictions on worker migration have been relaxed.[28] If surplus rural workers could not find nonagricultural work in the vicinity of their homes, the policy that evolved in the 1980s permitted them to travel elsewhere for work. The official guideline was to promote the development of towns and small cities all over the country so that they could absorb rural out-migrants locally. Especially popular with the authorities was allowing peasants to move to a nearby town to take an industrial job or set up a business, and permitting surplus workers from impoverished rural areas to move to a different rural area or leave for seasonal employment part of each year. Gradually, the Chinese government softened its former rigid opposition to allowing migration of rural residents into established urban areas. Workers were allowed to move to cities and towns under certain conditions, for example, if they were responsible for buying their own grain without rations or subsidy, if they brought capital with them to set up shop, if they came alone to work and did not bring a family, and if their legal registration location remained in the rural areas. Different urban localities set up different criteria.[29]

In the 1980s, some migrants were formally allowed to move permanently to urban areas, and their legal household registrations were transferred to the city or town. Urban population statistics are so problematic that it is difficult to estimate the numbers of these formal, legal rural-to-urban migrants. After a complex series of calculations, it was possible to estimate that during 1985, net in-migration accounted for only about 1 percent growth in the total legal permanent resident population of China's cities; only approximately 1.9 million people were granted legal residence that year in the cities that had been established before 1985.[30]

More numerous are the rural-to-urban migrants who have not been granted the coveted city or town permanent household registration. People who are away from their rural legal residence are grouped together under the label "floating population," whether they actually moved permanently to the urban place ten years ago, or they left their village two days ago and are just passing through town. Some cities have periodically tried to count their floating populations, and relatively sophisticated cities like Shanghai distinguish among "temporary" residents who have been there for different lengths of time. For example, an August 1984 survey of Shanghai's estimated 590,000 floating population included 338,000 "temporary" residents living in established households, of whom one-third had been residing there for over five years and a total of almost one-half had been living there for over a year.[31] Yet the city had not granted them permanent residence, so they were not included in the reported population of Shanghai. Fortunately, China's 1982 and 1990 censuses both assumed a anyone who had lived in a certain town or city for a year or more was a resident of that place, so the censuses give more realistic counts of the populations of cities and towns than do city registers.

The floating population of Shanghai Municipality increased from 0.7 million by the end of 1984 to 1.11 million in 1985 and further to 1.25 million in

October 1988, compared to a legal permanent resident population of 12.62 million at the end of 1988. Other cities and many urban towns have also reported floating populations that are large in relation to their legal permanent resident populations. By the end of 1989, a rough estimate of the floating population nationwide was given as 50 million of whom 1.83 million were in Shanghai Municipality, 1.35 million in Beijing Municipality, and 1.1 million in Guangzhou (Canton) Municipality.[32] In February 1990, the floating population was estimated to be between 60 and 80 million people.[33] Statistics on the movement of China's workers and residents are unreliable so far, but Chinese statisticians are trying to remedy this situation using migration surveys and the 1990 census as tools.

B Urbanization

The urbanization of China's population is an important aspect of its economic and social development, but unfortunately the annual official urban statistics have become almost unusable without careful and time-consuming decomposition of the components of urban population growth. For example, the mid-year 1982 census counted an urban population of 206 million, which constituted 21 percent of the civilian population.[34] By year-end 1989, only 7½ years later, official statistics showed a total urban population of 575 million, 52 percent of the national population.[35] Such figures are usually rejected by Chinese and foreign scholars as unrealistic and misleading. The key problem is that in the 1980s hundreds of new cities and thousands of new urban towns were established, and most of these new urban places are seriously "overbounded." While each new city and town may have a genuine urbanized core deserving of urban status, the new urban boundaries are drawn so wide that they encompass large agricultural areas and populations. This problem is caused by the practices of transforming a former xian (county) into a newly established shi (city) and reclassifying a former xiang (township) into a new zhen (urban town) without adjusting the boundary to include only the urbanized area. The latest available statistics show that over half (53 percent) of the total permanent residents living inside the city proper boundaries of China's cities are designated "agricultural" population. Of the total zhen population, 75 percent is "agricultural."[36]

Because China's annual urban population statistics are so problematic, officials of the State Statistical Bureau (SSB) and other leaders of the 1990 census effort decided to define "urban" more narrowly for this census. The enumeration districts in China's censuses are local neighborhood committees in built-up areas and village committees in agricultural areas. The census leadership instructed that village committees, even those inside city and town boundaries, were to be classified "rural" for census purposes. Therefore, the 1990 census seems to have solved the overbounding problem, and the preliminary hand-tabulated result is that only 26 percent of China's population was classified urban in the 1990 census.[37] Comparing this figure with the 1982 census population recorded as 21 percent urban indicates that there has been only moderate urbanization in China during the 1980s. However, this comparison underestimates the speed of urbanization because 1982 census data need to be adjusted downward using the 1990 census definition in order to measure the trend.

VII PROSPECTS FOR THE 1990s

A The cities

A rapid shift is taking place in the age structure of China's urban areas, especially in the built-up city areas, with major short-term and long-term implications. Because the fertility of China's urban nonagricultural population dropped in half from 1963 to 1966, then declined further in the 1970s and 1980s, school enrollments have declined or stabilized in many cities and towns, thus taking the pressure off the urban educational systems to provide more teachers and schools. The small urban cohorts born in the late 1960s and beyond are now beginning to join the childbearing ages and the labor force. The "birth peak" among urban nonagricultural people will be largely over by the mid-1990s. The need to provide greater numbers of entry-level jobs each year to increasingly large cohorts of urban-born youth will soon be history. In fact, without further in-migration from the countryside, China's urban population aged 15–29 would decline precipitously in size between 1990 and the year 2000.[38]

Population aging has also begun in China's cities. During the 1990s, China's urban areas will experience the aging of their labor force as the huge cohorts born in the 1950s and early 1960s begin entering middle age. The proportion of the urban population at ages 65 and above is expected to increase modestly from about 5 percent in 1990 to 8 percent at the turn of the century. This will not be a serious problem in the short run, but if China maintained its urban one-child policy, in the absence of in-migration the elderly proportion of the urban population would rise from 8 percent in the year 2000 to 17 percent in 2020, 33 percent in 2040, and 36 percent in 2060.[39]

Chinese municipal leaders and Chinese demographers advising the authorities are concerned about avoiding such severe aging of China's urban population in the future. They are already discussing reverting to an urban two-child policy at about the turn of the century, which would result in a greater number of working-age adults in the middle of the coming century to provide for the inevitably large numbers of urban elderly.[40]

A continuation of rural-to-urban migration of young adult workers is likely in the 1990s, especially if there is a resumption of China's economic boom and of the transformation into nonagricultural employment. Even with a long period of political stagnation and economic uncertainty, a distinct possibility, China's cities and towns will probably allow millions more peasants to come in to work each year. In the coming decade, there will be a strong urban demand for workers from the countryside, because of the sharp drop in the number of urban-born youth ages 15–29, because those raised in the city are less willing than peasants to do the least desirable jobs, and because there remains a strong unmet demand for all kinds of services in the cities and towns of China.[41]

B The countryside

Age structure shifts in rural areas are a decade behind those in urban areas, and are less pronounced because fertility has not dropped so low in the countryside. School-aged cohorts are no longer increasing rapidly in size, so the provision of basic education is less burdensome now. In the 1990s, couples in their peak childbearing ages will be much more numerous than in the previous decade, a situation which is causing concern about a "birth peak." Yet rural youth who were born in 1977 and later years, after the steep rural fertility decline of the early and mid-1970s, are half as numerous as some of the 1960s cohorts. As they join the work force in the 1990s, there will be a decrease in the number of rural entry-level jobs required. Unfortunately, this incipient beneficial effect of reduced rural fertility will do little to ameliorate the overwhelming need for hundreds of millions of jobs outside agriculture for the rural surplus labor force.

China's rural areas are burdened with a massive backlog of adults who are really not needed in agriculture but have been unable to find other work. During the 1980s, estimates of the number of surplus laborers engaged in crop production ranged from 60 million to 156 million, depending on the technique of estimation.[42] These farmers still need other work, yet the economic and political reversals of late 1988, 1989, and thereafter are crippling China's ability to create employment opportunities outside agriculture. As long as these reversals continue, we can expect very little progress in transforming China's economy into one dominated by nonagricultural work.

C National trends

China has already achieved relatively advanced mortality levels. The death rate is expected to remain low. Further improvements in mortality and health conditions are likely to be slow, because of the intractability of the leading causes of death and illness today. Chronic diseases like heart disease and cancer are everywhere difficult to prevent or cure. In a poor developing country striving for rapid economic growth, cleaning up the polluted air and water has low priority, yet is important for reducing the prevalence of environmental diseases like parasitic and waterborne viral illnesses and respiratory ailments.

It is possible that age at marriage could rise again under official pressure, as happened in the 1970s in both urban and rural areas. But the Chinese people showed in the 1980s that this policy is unpopular, and that they will marry in their early twenties if feasible. A stalemate is the most plausible outcome. Administrative pressure to stop early marriages may already have arrested the decline in marriage age, but popular resistance will probably block full implementation of late marriage policies.

In the 1990s we are most likely to see a continuation of the unstable equilibrium between frequent attempts by couples to have another child and continual pressure from the authorities trying to stop them. Fertility will not drop or rise dramatically under this scenario. With fertility and mortality not much changed, we can expect that China's population growth rate will continue to be around 1.4 percent a year, and that the total population will increase to 1.2 billion by 1995 and reach about 1.3 billion by 2000. This will obviously require further annual increases in food production and availability, which will not be easy given the dearth of arable land and the intensity of agricultural land use already.

If China's democracy movement were to bring about a significant shift in the power structure during the 1990s away from authoritarian Communism, one of the first policies to go would probably be compulsory family planning.[43] This would be followed several months later by a rise in fertility that would be expected to last for many years. Once the policy of required family planning is discredited, subsequent Chinese governments might be hesitant to promote birth control, if the situation in India since the cessation of mandatory sterilization is any guide.

In the 1990s, China's population in the labor force ages (defined as 15–64) will no longer be increasing faster than the total population. Rather, the pool of working-age people will increase at 1.2 percent a year as the population grows about 1.4 percent annually, and the population in the young working ages 15–29 will decline. As long as the economy is in a slump, it will remain very difficult to increase the number of nonagricultural jobs enough to employ the additional numbers of middle-aged workers. If agriculture continues to absorb them, this will exacerbate the already serious problem of the huge agricultural surplus labor force.

For the next couple of decades, China's population structure will be beneficial for economic growth and increased productivity. The population is becoming middle-aged. Because fertility has dropped so low, child dependency has greatly decreased. The population ages 15–29 will peak in 1992, then decline 15 percent in size by the turn of the century only eight years later. The burdens of education and on-the-job training will lighten considerably. Because the process of population aging has only recently begun for the country as a whole, a serious aged dependency burden is several decades away.

With a low dependency ratio, and a bulge in the population in their thirties, forties, and fifties, China is entering its "Golden Age." These age groups tend to be those of highest productivity, reasonably robust health, low crime, and high savings rates. China's age structure of the 1990s and first decades of the next century will be beneficial for promoting economic take-off and social stability.

VIII CONCLUSIONS

The period of rapid population growth that China had experienced since the early 1950s had greatly strained the process of economic development and transformation, the limited supply of arable land, the environment, and the political leadership trying to cope with its effects. Finally in 1978, the government decided to loosen its stranglehold on the rural and town economies, and an economic boom followed. Rapid economic growth far outstripped the reduced rate of population growth, and living standards greatly increased.

But the shift away from a command economy to a market economy slowed in the late 1980s. Government control of the city economies and the elaborate system of subsidies given to urban workers were barely touched. The inflation that accompanied partial price reform was so intolerable to China's population and government that economic retrenchment was introduced to stop it. The reform decade had succeeded in part because of the greater autonomy given to individuals and families in their economic, social, and political lives, but this led to further demands for freedom that the government suppressed in 1989. Economic transformation and political liberalization came to a screeching halt, at least temporarily. China's rapid economic development of the 1980s facilitated great increases in real per capita income and the generation of enough jobs to keep ahead of the growth of population in the labor force ages. But the economic slowdown of 1989 stopped most of this progress, and many nonagricultural workers returned to farming.

Continued population growth in the 1990s will necessitate additional production of food, housing, and consumer goods, as well as more jobs. To further improve living standards will require economic growth well ahead of population growth. Short-term prospects are not promising. By the time China resolves its current drawn-out crisis of political succession, which is weakening its capacity to take bold economic initiatives, perhaps one or more Eastern European countries will have discovered how to transform an urban Communist economic structure like that in China's cities into something workable. China could then adapt whatever has worked elsewhere and resume its shift toward a market economy and its economic takeoff. Population growth will not appear such a formidable problem when that happens.

ACKNOWLEDGMENTS

Chief, China Branch, Center for International Research, U.S. Bureau of the Census. The interpretations and opinions expressed in this article are those of the author alone, and do not represent the policy of the United States Government or the U.S. Bureau of the Census.

NOTES

1 Based on analysis of life tables from the 1982 census and the 1987 one-percent sample census. See Banister, 1990.
2 "China's Infant Mortality Declines in Past Forty Years," *China Population Newsletter*, Vol. 6, No. 2, Apr. 1989, pp. 11, 18; and Banister, 1990, pp. 6–8.
3 China, State Statistical Bureau, Department of Agricultural Statistics, *Woguo nongmin shenghuo de juda bianhua* (Great Changes in the Lives of China's Peasants). Beijing: China Statistics Press, 1984; China, Ministry of Agriculture Planning Bureau, *Zhongguo nongcun jingji tongji daquan* (A Complete Compilation of China's' Rural Economic Statistics), Beijing: Agriculture Press, 1989, p. 563; *Statistical Survey of China 1990*, pp. 46, 109–110.
4 Zhu Baoxia, 'Clean Water Goal Set for Rural Areas," *China Daily*, June 9, 1990, p. 3.
5 With survival chances the same, a country with a young population like China has a lower crude death rate (annual deaths per thousand total population) than a country with an older age structure.
6 Coale, 1984, pp. 48–54. The "total fertility rate" is the average number of children who would be born alive to a woman during her lifetime if she lived through all her childbearing years and conformed to all the age-specific fertility rates of a given year.
7 Wang, Riley, & Lin, 1990, Table l.
8 Wang, Riley, & Lin, 1990, Table 1.
9 China Population Information Centre, 1984, pp. 162–164.
10 Wang Wei, "Guanyu jihua shengyu gongzuo wenti" (Questions about Family Planning Work), *Renkou yu jingji* (Population and Economy), No. 2, Apr. 1986, p. 4; Peng Peiyun, "Why I am Extending the Two-Child Option," *People* (International Planned Parenthood Federation, London), Vol. 16, No. 1, Jan. 1989, p. 12.
11 China Population Information Centre, 1984, pp. 165–167.
12 Karen Hardee-Cleaveland, "Desired Family Size and Sex Preference in Rural China: Evidence from Fujian Province," Ph.D. dissertation, Cornell University. 1988; "The Impact of Rural Family Functions on Fertility Rate," *China Population Research Leads* (Shanghai Population Information Center), No. 2, July 1988, p. 2; *Population and Family Planning*, (Beijing: Foreign Languages Press, 1990), p. 11.
13 Peng Zhiliang, "Tan jihua shengyu zhengce yao heqing heli" (Family Planning Policy Must Be Fair and Reasonable), *Jiankang bao jihua shengyu ban* (Health Gazette, Family Planning Edition), June 29, 1984, p. 3.
14 Greenhalgh, 1990, pp. 204, 216, 222–229.
15 Birth parity means birth order.
16 Details are compiled in Aird, 1900, pp. 59–89.
17 This trend is we11-documented in Aird, 1990, pp. 59–89 and Appendix B.
18 Peng Peiyun. "Guanyu 1989-nian de gongzuo" (On the Work in 1989), *Zhongguo renkou bao* (China Population), Feb. 24, 1989, p. 1.

19 "The Nationwide Fertility and Birth Control Sampling Survey Ended Successfully," *China Population Research Leads* (Shanghai Population Information Center), No. 4, Apr. 1989, p. 3.
20 *Statistical Survey of China 1990*, p. 15.
21 Taylor, 1986, pp. 222–230; Arriaga & Banister, 1985, pp. 170–172.
22 Taylor & Banister, 1989, pp. 43–46.
23 Statistics in this paragraph are from China. State Statistical Bureau, Department of Social Statistics, *Zhongguo laodong gongzi tongji ziliao, 1978–1987* (China's Labor and Wage Statistics, 1978–1987), Beijing: China Statistics Press, 1989, p. 6; *Statistical Yearbook of China 1989*, pp. 106–107; and *Statistical Survey of China 1990*, p. 16.
24 Sun Zhonghua, "A Glimpse of Grain Production from 1984 to 1988—A Survey of the Grain Output of 13,000 Peasant Households in 155 Villages" [In Chinese], *Zhongguo nongcun jingji* (China's Rural Economy), No. 3, Mar. 20, 1990, pp. 16–24, tr. as "5-Year Grain Production Slump Attributed to Peasant Apathy," *Joint Publications Research Service*, No. JPRS–CAR–90–046, June 26, 1990, pp. 78–79.
25 The quality of unemployment data from the 1990 census may be a considerable improvement over currently available figures.
26 *Statistical Survey of China 1990*, p. 18.
27 "Unemployment Increases in First Quarter," *Zhongguo tongxun she* (China News Agency in Hong Kong), May 29, 1990, translated in *Summary of World Broadcasts, Weekly Economic Report*, No. FE/W0131, June 6, 1990, pp. A1–A2.
28 For details on this important policy shift, see Judith Banister, *Urban-Rural Population Projections for China*, Washington, D.C.: U.S. Bureau of the Census, 1986. Center for International Research, Staff Paper No.15.
29 For further information on worker migration from the villages, see Taylor & Banister, 1989, pp. 23–38.
30 In addition, China's city population total grew in 1985 through natural population increase, more city births than deaths) and boundary expansion, and most important, through the establishment of 29 new cities. A similar analysis could be carried out for some more recent years for which the data are now available. Judith Banister, "China: Components of Recent City Growth," presented at the International Conference on Urbanization and Urban Population Problems, Tianjin, Oct. 1987.
31 Zheng Guizhen et al., "A Preliminary Exploration of the Problem of Shanghai Municipality's Floating Population," [in Chinese], *Renkou yanjiu* (Population Research), No. 3, May 29, 1985, pp. 2–7, translated in *Joint Publications Research Service*, No. JPRS–CPS–85–087, Sept. 4, 1985, pp. 33–43.
32 Gu Chu, "Floating Population Puts Strain on Urban Areas," *Joint Publications Research Service*, No. JPRS–CAR–90–026, Apr. 9, 1990, p. 65; "Rapid Increase of China's Floating Population," *China Population Newsletter*, Vol. 1, Feb. 1990, p. 16.
33 "Floating Population Nears 80 Million," *Joint Publications Research Service*, No. JPRS–CAR–90–020, Mar. 14, 1990, p. 58.
34 China 1982 census volume, 1985, p. 26.
35 *Statistical Survey of China 1990*, p. 14.
36 Ministry of Public Security, *Zhonghua renmin gongheguo quanguo fen xian shi renkou tongji ziliao, 1988* (Population Statistics by County and City of the PRC, 1988), Beijing: China Cartographic Press, 1989, pp. 4, 8.
37 "The 1990 Census," *Beijing Review*, Vol. 33, No. 45, Nov. 12–18, 1990, pp. 17–19.
38 Banister, 1989, p. 15.

39 Judith Banister, "The Aging of China's Urban and Rural Populations," presented at the International Academic Conference on China's Population Aging, Beijing, Dec. 1989, p. 11.
40 Judith Banister, "The Aging of China's Population," *Problems of Communism*, Vol. 37, No. 6, Nov.–Dec. 1988, pp. 71–73.
41 This is discussed more fully in Judith Banister and Jeffrey R. Taylor, "China: Surplus Labour and Migration," *Asia-Pacific Population Journal*, Vol. 4, No. 4, Dec. 1989, pp. 17–18; and in Banister, 1989, pp. 12–16.
42 Taylor & Banister, 1989, p. 3.
43 It should be noted that in Romania, the fall of Ceauscescu was followed immediately by cessation of the forced childbearing policy, which had utilized the same policies of harassing women and monitoring their birth control and pregnancy status as China uses, but for opposite goals.

REFERENCES

Aird, John S., *Slaughter of the Innocents; Coercive Birth Control in China*, Washington, D.C.: American Enterprise Institute Press, 1990.

Arriaga, Eduardo E., and Judith Banister, "The Implications of China's Rapid Fertility Decline," in International Union for the Scientific Study of Population, *International Population Conference, Florence 1985, Vol. 2*, Liege, Belgium: IUSSP, pp. 165–180.

Banister, Judith, *China's Changing Population*, Stanford, Cal.: Stanford University Press, 1987.

Banister, Judith, "China: Mortality and Health Under the Economic Reforms," presented at the Seminar on Recent Levels and Trends in Mortality in China, Harvard University, Cambridge, Mass., March 1990.

Banister, Judith, "The Migration of Surplus Laborers in China," presented at the International Academic Conference on China's Internal Migration and Urbanization, Beijing, Dec. 1989.

China 1982 census volume. China, State Council Population Census Office and State Statistical Bureau Department of Population Statistics, *Zhongguo 1982-nian renkou pucha ziliao (dianzi jisuanji huizong)* (Data from China's 1982 Population Census [Results of Computer Tabulation]) Beijing: China Statistical Publishing House, 1985.

China Population Information Center *Analysis on China's National One-per-thousand-population Fertility Sampling Survey*, Beijing, 1984

Coale, Ansley J., *Rapid Population Change in China, 1952–1982*, Washington D.C.: National Academy Press, 1984. Committee on Population and Demography, Report No. 27.

Greenhalgh, Susan, "The Evolution of the One-child Policy in Shaanxi, 1979–88," *China Quarterly*, no. 122, June 1990, pp. 191–229.

Hardee-Cleaveland, Karen, and Judith Banister, 1988a. *Family Planning in China: Recent Trends*, Washington, D.C.: U.S. Bureau of the Census, 1988. Center for International Research, Staff Paper No. 40.

Hardee-Cleaveland, Karen, and Judith Banister, 1988b. "Fertility Policy and Implementation in China, 1986–88," *Population and Development Review*, Vol. 14, No. 2, June 1988, pp. 245–286.

Li Bohua, "Changes in Fertility Rates in China's 28 Provinces Autonomous Regions, and Municipalities Directly Under the Central Authorities [In Chinese], *Renkou yu jingji* (Population and Economics) No. 3, 1990 pp. 3–12.

Statistical Survey of China 1990. China, State Statistical Bureau, *Zhongguo tongji zhaiyao 1990* (Statistical Survey of China 1990), Beijing: China Statistics Press 1990.

Statistical Yearbook of China, annual. China, State Statistical Bureau, *Statistical Yearbook of China*, Hong Kong and Beijing: China Statistical Information and Consultancy Service Centre, annual.

Taylor, Jeffrey R., "Labor Force Developments in the People's Republic of China 1952–1983," in U.S. Congress, Joint Economic Committee, *China's Economy Looks Toward the Year 2000, Vol. 1, The Four Modernizations*, Washington, D.C.: U.S. Government Printing Office, 1986, pp. 222–262.

Taylor, Jeffrey R., and Judith Banister, *China: The Problem of Employing Surplus Rural Labor*, Washington, D.C.: U.S. Bureau of the Census, 1989. Center for International Research, Staff Paper No. 49.

Wang Feng, Nancy Riley, and Lin Fude, "China's Continuing Demographic Transition in the 1980s," presented at the annual meeting of the Population Association of America, Toronto, May 1990.

21

NEW BOSSES IN THE WORKERS' STATE

The Growth of Non-State Sector Employment in China

Lora Sabin

Although the state is still a major economic actor in China's cities, it is widely recognized that the rapid expansion of entities outside the state sphere has already fundamentally altered not just the urban economic landscape but also the forces driving the country's labour markets. The extent and consequences of this expansion are in need of much greater scrutiny, however. A number of analysts have made use of available information to clarify employment growth and changes in employment structure since the early years of the People's Republic and the early period of reform.[1] Recent scholarship has also enhanced understanding of the design, implementation and impact of formal labour reforms, such as the labour contract system, and the nature of worker – management relations in a partially reformed environment.[2] But because of the scarcity of data on the non-state economy, this research has tended to focus on state-owned industrial sector.

In the past few years, several studies have shed light on the growth and character of certain non-state urban sectors, most notably the private economy.[3] While their authors have noted some of the flaws in official data, they have not attempted to measure the degree to which these statistics understate urban private employment. Moreover, research on specific sectors does not allow for a comprehensive analysis of the growth of the non-state sector as a whole and the complex relationships between different economic entities within this sector.

The purpose of this article is to analyse the recent growth of employment outside the state-owned sector and within the private economy in particular. The first section describes the motivation behind the change which occurred after 1978 in official policy toward sectors outside the state economy. Subsequent sections examine, in turn, the Chinese government's promotion of urban collectives, foreign-invested ventures and privately-owned firms, and

Source: The China Quarterly, No. 40 (December 1994), pp. 944–70.

the subsequent employment growth in each of these sectors. Finally, the article seeks to probe behind the government's categorization of urban employment and to construct a picture that more accurately shows the extent to which China's urban workers now move in an essentially private labour market.

MOTIVATION FOR EXPANDING THE NON-STATE SECTORS

In the pre-reform dawn of 1977 China's urban economy was primarily composed of two main socialist sectors, where the quality of a worker's life was closely linked to the sector in which he or she worked. Employees of state-owned enterprises who made up 79 per cent of the urban work force (see Table 21.1), were in the more enviable position. They enjoyed better wages, a full range of benefits, lifetime employment and higher social status. Jobs in collective units were less desirable. Here, wages averaged less than 80 per cent of those in state enterprises, benefits were much less comprehensive where they

Table 21.1 Official figures on urban employment in China, by ownership

Year	*Total urban employment*[a] *(1,000)*	*State-owned units*	*Urban collectives*	*Joint ventures and foreign firms*[b]	*Of which: foreign-invested units*[c]	*Urban individual workers*[d]
1977	91,270	71,960	19,160	n.a.	n.a.	150
1978	95,140	74,510	20,480	n.a.	n.a.	150
1979	99,990	76,930	22,740	n.a.	n.a.	320
1980	105,250	80,190	24,250	n.a.	n.a.	810
1981	110,530	83,720	25,680	n.a.	n.a.	1,130
1982	114,280	86,300	26,510	n.a.	n.a.	1,470
1983	117,460	87,710	27,440	n.a.	n.a.	2,310
1984	122,290	86,370	32,160	370	38	3,390
1985	128,080	89,900	33,240	440	61	4,500
1986	132,920	93,330	34,210	550	125	4,830
1987	137,830	96,540	34,880	720	212	5,690
1988	142,670	99,840	35,270	970	306	6,590
1989	143,900	101,080	35,020	1,320	470	6,480
1990	147,300	103,460	35,490	1,640	659	6,710
1991	152,680	106,640	36,280	2,160	1,178	7,600
1992	156,300	108,890	36,210	2,820	1,539	8,380

Notes:
[a] Year-end figures.
[b] Includes state-collective, state-private, and collective-private domestic joint ventures, Sino-foreign joint ventures and co-operative ventures; ventures operated by overseas Chinese and wholly foreign-owned enterprises.
[c] Includes the latter three types of enterprises listed above.
[d] Includes employment in larger privately-owned enterprises.

Source: *Statistical Yearbook for 1993*, pp. 97, 109; *Statistical Materials on Labour and Wages 1978–1987*, p. 93.

existed at all, and job security was more tenuous. Into small collectives in particular were shunted the least skilled, the young, the old, women, and all others who through circumstance or ill fortune failed to obtain a job higher up the employment ladder. But one could sink deeper still into the remnants of the once-thriving small-scale private sector. China's self-employed faced uncertain wages, enjoyed no benefits or job security, and occupied the very lowest position in urban society[4]

In light of the strong post-1949 bias in favour of the state sector, the government's promotion of non-state enterprises after 1978 represented, a dramatic policy turn-round. The major catalyst for this change was rising urban unemployment which threatened social stability in the late 1970s. While not publicly acknowledging such unemployment, the Chinese government did (and still does) recognize a category of people euphemistically known as "urban people waiting for employment" (*chengzhen daiye renyuan*). After 1977, it was the number of unemployed school graduates in particular that began to swell as the government abandoned its policy of resettling urban youth in the countryside.[5] Adding to their ranks were the previously "rusticated" young Chinese, who, in 1978, began to pour back into cities in unprecedented numbers, threatening to become a source of urban disorder unless productively employed.[6] In numerical terms, government statistics cite a figure of five to six million urban unemployed in 1978–80, yielding an unemployment rate of 4.9–5.3 per cent,[7] but other sources which take into account returnees from the countryside reach much higher estimates ranging from 10 to 25 million.[8]

In order to avoid urban unrest while pushing forward on the reform front, China's leadership had to address the growing clamour for jobs. But relying on the state sector to absorb new entrants into the labour force was no longer a viable option. First, state enterprises were already bloated with excess workers. This problem was compounded by long-standing industrial policies which favoured increasing capital intensity and labour productivity rather than expanding labour utilization.[9] Secondly, creating jobs in the state sector was extremely costly, requiring a public investment of 6,000 to 10,000 *yuan* per worker, compared with roughly 3,000 *yuan* and 100–300 *yuan* per worker (mainly from private investment) in urban collectives and individual ventures, respectively.[10]

The employment motive was reinforced by other economic aims. China's new modernization strategy stressed rapid growth through efficiency-improving reforms. A key aspect of this strategy was opening China's economy to the outside world and encouraging foreign investment. Chinese leaders hoped that increased economic co-operation with more advanced regions, particularly in the form of Sino-foreign joint ventures, would lead to infusions of modern technology and expertise and the refurbishment of antiquated machinery and equipment dating from the era of close collaboration with the Soviet Union in the 1950s.

Moreover, private, collective and foreign-invested ventures, with their more flexible business techniques and ability to adapt to consumer desires, could provide long-ignored urban goods and services. They could also generate taxes for the state and stimulate inefficient state-owned enterprises through head-to-head competition. The pro-privatization stance of influential agencies such as the World Bank, the examples of successful market-oriented reforms in Yugoslavia and Hungary, and the obvious force for rapid development which foreign investment and small family businesses had been throughout East Asia further buttressed internal arguments for expanding the scope of China's non-state economy.

Political factors no doubt affected the decision to expand the non-state economy as well. The chaos and destruction China had suffered during the Cultural Revolution had substantially diminished the legitimacy of the Chinese Communist Party. By loosening controls over the economy and society and allowing a wider range of employment opportunities, the Party stood to improve its public standing. Displaying a more tolerant attitude towards different ownership forms would also send a signal to Hong Kong and Taiwanese leaders that Beijing was sincere in its promises to protect private business activities in Hong Kong and Taiwan upon their reunification with the Mainland.[11]

GROWTH OF THE URBAN COLLECTIVE SECTOR

By 1979, city governments had begun to respond to the challenge of reducing unemployment by encouraging job growth outside the state-owned sector on an experimental basis. In a pattern typical of many reform measures, the success of such trials led to strong endorsement of a liberalized employment policy by well-known economists[12] and then by the Central Committee itself in the summer of 1980, when it convened the first nation-wide work conference on labour. The new policy permitted urban job-seekers to find work in the state, collective or small-scale private sector through three avenues: introductions by labour bureaus, organizing group employment and their own independent efforts.[13] Of the non-state enterprises targeted for growth, collectives had the advantage of being a legitimate, albeit inferior, element of the socialist economy. Promoting their development thus offered policy-makers an ideologically risk-free way of increasing employment opportunties.

In the ensuing years, a series of concrete steps was taken to spur urban collectives. An important 1981 decision urged local governments to set up different types of collectives with investment from individuals as well as from state and collective enterprises.[14] Financial incentives were also provided through the tax system, most notably by granting collectives hiring mainly unemployed youth tax-exempt or tax-reduced status for a fixed period of time[15] and by easing the overall tax burden on the collective sector through an adjustment of marginal tax rates and tax brackets.[16] In addition, the government sought to enhance the efficiency of collective enterprises by implementing regulations (sweeping in language but more limited in actual implementation) allowing collectives a bigger voice in production and sales decisions, labour and wage matters, and asset disposition.[17]

As the pace of reform quickened in 1984, contractual responsibility systems (*chengbao zerenzhi*) similar to those being instituted in the state-owned sector were introduced for sharing profits between collectives and higher-level bodies. After 1986, controls were eased on the use of enterprise-retained profits, particularly for collective units supervised by district-level labour officials or neighbourhood offices.[18] More radical still was a strategy implemented in the mid-1980s of leasing some urban collectives out to individuals. Officially sanctioned by the Central Committee in 1984, this strategy was engineered through contractual arrangements specifying shared profits or rent payments to the state.[19]

The decade-long policy of developing the urban collective sector was given legal form in 1991 when the State Council promulgated the most comprehensive regulations to date on urban collectives. These provide broad definition of "collective ownership" which essentially grants collective status to any enterprise in which private individuals own no more than 49 per cent of total assets. Urban collectives may raise funds from employees or outside individuals and pay dividends on these investments out of enterprise profits.[20] They are also given the right to "engage independently" in production and service activities and to establish their own economic responsibility systems and wage and bonus methods. Thus, in legal terms, urban collectives now enjoy a degree of management autonomy that contrasts sharply with the former top-down central administrative system.

In terms of job creation, efforts to invigorate urban collectives have been a clear success. Official data summarized in Table 21.1 show that employment in urban collective enterprises rose by an impressive 62 per cent between 1978 and 1985, three times the corresponding rate for the state-owned sector, and by 77 per cent over the 1978–92 period as a whole, compared to 46 per cent in state firms. Urban collectives have also absorbed roughly 30 per cent of all new entrants to China's urban labour force since 1978 (see Table 21.2). The impact has been especially dramatic in commerce. Between 1978 and 1992 commercial jobs in urban collectives increased almost five-fold, with the result that the collective share of commerce-related urban employment jumped from 16 to 34 per cent in this period while the state sector share plummeted from 84 to 44 per cent.[21]

While the official data are impressive, they unfortunately do not break down employment by different types of collectives. As a result, they obscure an essential aspect of China's urban collective sector. Despite government efforts to create a comprehensive legal basis for urban collectives and thereby establish a degree of uniformity throughout the sector, from the vantage

Table 21.2 Absorption of new-settled workers, by ownership

Years	*Total new urban employment (1,000 workers)*	*State-owned units*[a]	*Urban collectives*	*Joint ventures and foreign firms*[b]	*Urban individual workers*[c]
1978–85	59,954	37,504	18,096	n.a.	4,354
(%)	(100.0)	(62.6)	(30.2)	n.a.	(7.3)
1986–92	53,423	31,001	16,177	2,065[c]	4,180
(%)	(100.0)	(58.0)	(30.3)	(3.9)	(7.8)

Notes:
[a] Figures for 1978–88 include employees of joint ventures and foreign-invested enterprises.
[b] Includes state collective, state-private, and collective-private domestic joint ventures, Sino-foreign joint ventures and co-operative ventures; ventures operated by overseas Chinese; and wholly foreign-owned enterprises.
[c] Figures and corresponding proportion relate to 1989–92 only.

Sources: *Statistical Yearbook on Labour 1993*, p. 49; *Statistical Yearbook for 1993*, p. 119.

point of the early 1990s, one of the most salient characteristics of urban collectives is in fact their diversity. Whereas large collectives supervised by governments at the district level and above dominated the urban collective sector in the late 1970s, the 1980s and early 1990s witnessed rapid growth in smaller collectives set up by state-owned enterprises or run by lower-level agencies. The latter units span co-operatives originally formed during the 1950s (*shengchan fuwu hezuo lianshe*), service-oriented collectives set up by residents' committees (*jumin weiyuanhui de disan qiye*), as well as reform-era labour service companies (*laodong fuwu gongsi*) and the collectives they operate. Many of these small-scale collectives had by the late 1980s gained significant autonomy with respect to labour and wage matters. Residents' committees in Beijing, for example, claim that the collective enterprise managers under their jurisdiction may hire whomever they wish and lay off workers with advance notification. In addition, performance-linked wage systems have given enterprises with high earnings considerable leeway with respect to wage and bonus distributions.[22]

However, it is the emergence of entirely new forms of collectives which has made the urban collective sector truly multifarious in recent years. One example is firms officially called "collectively-owned enterprises set up from the pooled resources of the urban masses" (*chengzhen qunzhong jizi xingban de jiti suoyouzhi qiye*), but more popularly known as "people-run collectives" (*minban jiti*). Unlike, neighbourhood-run collectives, these units are formed without any assistance from the government and are independent apart from paying a fee to local officials who provide administrative guidance.[23]

By far the most spectacular growth has been achieved by the above-mentioned new type of collective known as labour service companies (LSCs). The first LSCs were established in the late 1970s by official bodies from the provincial down to the neighbourhood level for the purpose of training the jobless and helping them obtain work, especially by setting up small-scale collectives.[24] However, state-owned enterpirses, eager to take advantage of the preferential tax treatment extended to these firms while creating a vehicle to employ their employees' children, soon began to form their own LSCs. In an effort to place the growing number of disparate companies on a common legal footing, the government issued new regulations in 1990 which granted the status of "labour employment service enterprises" (*laodong jiuye fuwu qiye*), as well as continued beneficial tax treatment, to LSCs and subordinate enterprises which drew at least 60 per cent of their members from the urban unemployed.[25] By the end of 1992, official sources estimated that such firms totalled 200,000 and employed nine million workers, representing 25 per cent of overall employment in urban collectives.[26]

Besides failing to capture the full diversity of the urban collective sector, the government's method of basing employment data on enterprise registration means that official statistics actually include a large number of privately-owned firms which have been registered as urban collectives. False registration of private ventures has been common since the early 1980s. Before the legitimacy of large privately-owned firms was belatedly recognized by the government in 1988 (as discussed below), there was an obvious need to register such enterprises under other guises. In more recent years, entrepreneurs have continued to avoid registering their businesses as private because of lower social standing and the relative disadvantages such ventures face with regard to financing, issuance of operating permits, pricing and taxation. The wisdom of this strategy is confirmed by a recent nation-wide survey indicating that the private firms which enjoy the most rapid growth are those which hang a *hong paizi* ("red signboard") by registering as a state or collective enterprise.[27] Many businessmen are also motivated by fears of a future policy backlash against the privately-owned sector.[28]

Securing registration as an urban collective is the most typical method of disguising private businesses. To do so, a private entrepreneur merely reaches a mutually beneficial financial arrangement with a state agency or firm or an urban collective willing to act as a nominal supervisory agency. There is some evidence that local authorities seeking to maintain high employment in their regions collaborate with the owners of such "collectives" to conceal their true nature from higher-level bureaucrats.[29] In fact, recent regulations passed by some district-level agencies have made it quite easy for individuals to establish private firms under the guise of people-run collectives.[30] While the number of such firms is impossible to calculate with any degree of precision, Chinese economists and researchers in Beijing estimate that by 1992 they constituted at least one-half of all urban collectives.[31] Although clearly aware of such widespread deception, China's government has been either unable or unwilling to put a stop to it.

Considering the large numbers of fake collectives, small collectives leased out to individuals since the mid-1980s and collective units given increased administrative latitude after 1987, the official urban collective sector has clearly come to be characterized by significant levels of private management, even where ownership is still nominally "collective." In the early 1990s, several new trends bear witness to the further extension of this autonomy. One is the emergence of shareholding schemes whereby individuals and families pool resources and invest in jointly-held businesses which are privately managed but enjoy the preferential treatment of collectives. The city of Wenzhou, in the south-eastern province of Zhejiang, has pioneered this reform path, claiming a total of 22,000 "shareholding co-operatives" by the summer of 1992.[32] Beijing, too, announced that it would implement a share-capital co-operative system as one means of reforming the city's small-scale state and collective enterprises in 1992–93.[33]

The share-capital co-operative system actually appears to be just one element in a broader push to privatize completely the management of urban collectives supervised by government agencies as well as smaller state firms. Although some cities are achieving this by outright sales of inefficient state and collective shops to private individuals or businesses,[34] more commonly reforms aim to popularize the "state-owned, people-operated" (*guoyou minying*) model introduced when small-scale enterprises were first leased out in 1984–85.[35] By the end of 1992, all the small collectives supervised by one of Beijing's district-level agencies had been leased out on the basis of open bidding, with an expansion of the reform to larger units planned for late 1993.[36] At still lower levels, all collectives are now in the process of being leased or contracted out to individual and other units.[37]

"SANZI" FIRMS: THE EMERGENCE OF THE FOREIGN-FUNDED SECTOR

Having made the dramatic decision to re-open China to Western capitalists, the Chinese government moved quickly to create a legal framework to encourage and regulate incoming foreign capital. In 1979 China enacted a Joint Venture Law, whereby foreign companies or individuals were permitted to join Chinese enterprises to create limited liability corporations.[38] This was followed in 1980 by a joint venture income tax law[39] and a set of labour management regulations.[40] The thrust of these laws was to grant joint ventures favourable tax treatment relative to other enterprises as well as a certain degree of latitude to determine employment conditions, although the latter were still made subject to approval by higher authorities.[41] The labour management regulations also required that salaries in joint ventures be set at 120–150 per cent of the wage level in nearby comparable state firms.

These initial laws and regulations were accompanied by other policy measures which served to underpin the commitment to opening up China's economy to foreign investment. In terms of offering concrete financial incentives, the most significant was the establishment in 1980 of four "special economic zones" (*teshu jingjiqu*) (SEZs) along China's south-east coast where new foreign-funded firms were extended additional preferential treatment, most notably through lower import and income taxes. The SEZs provided a vehicle for attracting large amounts of foreign capital and promoting reform experimentation while in theory preventing any ill-effects of a more open economy from spilling over into the rest of the country.[42]

In later years, a plethora of laws and regulations appeared creating a legal basis for a range of different foreign-invested enterprises and expanding the favourable treatment to which they were entitled. A separate law covering businesses established entirely with foreign capital appeared in 1986.[43] On its heel came the Co-operative Venture Law, which set out more flexible conditions for co-operation between Chinese and foreign firms than those applied to joint ventures.[44] Thereafter, the expression "sanzi enterprises" (*sanzi qiye*, literally "three investment enterprises") became the popular way to refer to the foreign-funded sector, composed primarily of wholly foreign-owned companies, joint ventures and co-operative ventures.[45] In addition to the panoply of local initiatives designed to attract investment to particular areas, national regulations were passed in 1986[46] extending extra preferential treatment to export-oriented and high-technology businesses set up with foreign capital.[47]

Over the course of the development of this overall legal framework, regulations devoted to labour matters have generally granted foreign-funded businesses far more independence than that enjoyed by the state and collective sectors. Although the original 1980 labour management regulations made clear that local labour bureaus were to play a role in approving labour contracts and helping joint ventures obtain workers, they also permitted these ventures to lay off unnecessary employees and to determine their own wage systems. The 1986 regulations extended to foreign-funded enterprises the right to determine the size of their labour force, to hire and fire both managers and regular workers, and to set the form and level of wages.[48] Many of the remaining restrictions relating to labour issues were removed two years later.[49]

In response to the government's promotional efforts, "sanzi" enterprises enjoyed slow but steady growth throughout most of the 1980s. Starting from a negligible base in 1979, annual actual direct foreign investment had topped $2 billion by 1987, double the total amount absorbed between 1979 and 1982.[50] Although the political turmoil in Beijing during the spring and summer of 1989 led many observers to predict a serious decline in foreign investment, both committed and actual foreign investment continued to rise. By 1991, overseas capital was pouring in more rapidly than ever, in part as a result of a headlong rush by local governments to create their own development zones.[51] Actual foreign direct investment exceeded $11 billion in 1992, more than twice the level of the previous year, while committed funds surpassed $57 billion, a six-fold increase over the 1991 figure.[52] Roughly two-thirds of this investment has been concentrated in a small number of sectors, namely telecommunications and transport, chemicals, textiles, equipment, resources, and processing.[53] There are signs, however, that foreign capital may diversify into such areas as banking and tourist resorts in the near future.[54]

Although official employment data for "sanzi" enterprises are only available from 1984, and even then in aggregated terms, they confirm this rapid growth. In fact, the number of jobs in foreign-funded firms expanded more swiftly during the 1980s than in any other sector of China's urban economy, rising at an average annual rate of nearly 60 per cent between 1984 and 1992 (see Table 21.1). As a result of their proximity to Hong Kong, which has contributed well over one-half of total foreign investment, and the location of the four original SEZs within their borders, the two provinces of Guangdong and Fujian alone employed nearly one-half of all workers in this sector in 1992.[55]

However, as in the case of urban collectives, official figures are a poor indicator of the actual growth of the foreign-invested sector. Many "foreign-invested" firms are actually set up by domestic investors – state, collective and private – eager to find ways to register their businesses as "sanzi" enterprises in order to gain tax exemptions, favourable treatment with respect to financing, and import and export autonomy. In resorting to this subterfuge, these investors are also seeking the sales-enhancing reputation, relative ease of worker recruitment and smooth relationships with other work units which tend to flow from designation as a foreign-funded business.[56] The most common way to set up a fake joint venture is to funnel funds to a shell company or agreeable party in Hong Kong and then back to the Mainland in the guise of a "foreign investment." Although figures on the extent of this practice are unavailable, the official Chinese press has openly condemned the "large numbers" of such "sham businesses."[57] One Western source has gone so far as to claim that two-thirds of current foreign investment in China may actually originate from within the country itself.[58]

The phenomenon of disguising domestic investment as foreign capital likewise obfuscates the extent to which the development of the foreign-invested sector has contributed to the expansion of the urban private economy. On first impression, it would seem that ownership is in private hands only in the case of wholly foreign-owned firms and joint ventures in which the Chinese partner is a private enterprise. But when private individuals and firms are providing funds as the "foreign partner," the resulting 'joint ventures" may likewise be totally privately-owned. In these instances, the nominal Chinese partner is a state-owned or collective firm whose role is restricted to simply assisting the new business to obtain designation as a joint venture in return for compensation.[59] As in the case of fake urban collectives, this evasion results in a number of private firms which are hidden from official view.

Whether China is able to sustain high rates of growth in the foreign-funded sector may depend on how much progress is made in further improving the country's business climate. Although foreign firms have encountered a multitude of obstacles, some stemming from China's low level of development and lack of international experience, and others relating to its quasi-socialist, quasi-market economic system, many of the most important ones relate directly to labour matters. The first joint ventures relied on their Chinese partners for their initial work force, which often resulted in inadequate or surplus employees. In recent years, many new joint ventures have sought to recruit their workers from the labour force at large through job fairs, personnel exchange centres and advertisements.[60] Although eager applicants for these jobs are usually plentiful, obtaining personnel with the necessary skills often poses major problems. Sometimes this is due to the need for very particular skills or attributes.[61] More often, recruitment is impeded by general barriers to labour mobility in China, such as difficulties in securing releases from former work units, changing household registration and finding new accommodation. The supply of housing in urban areas is especially tight and firms which do not provide housing for their workers run into problems both employing and retaining skilled staff.[62]

To compensate for the lack of housing as well as reduced job security, these firms generally pay far higher salaries than state enterprises, but keeping wages high enough to guarantee employee loyalty requires constant vigilance.[63] The competition for highly-skilled labour in particular is so keen that firms which do not pay top wages are likely to lose key employees.[64] To avoid letting income taxes cut too deeply into wages, many businesses build up the non-wage portion of total income, especially by investing in housing, contributing to pension funds and medical insurance, and paying out a variety of subsidies. Foreign companies required to hire through a service organization which takes a large cut of employees' salaries may also pay extra wages directly to their staff.[65]

In spite of such problems, on balance the gains accruing to foreign investors have clearly far outweighed the losses. More importantly, the growing numbers of foreign-funded ventures are playing a critical role in the modernization and internationalization of the Chinese economy, especially in the south-east and in areas such as telecommunications and resource development where the foreign presence is greatest. For well-educated and highly-skilled Chinese, jobs in the foreign-funded sector represent an entirely new range of increasingly popular opportunities. Foreign-invested factories in Guangdong and Fujian provinces also provide work for labourers flocking in from poorer regions. Although employment in the foreign sector remains small in relative terms, its impact on certain sectors, regions and segments of China's labour market is already considerable, and if current trends are sustained this impact is certain to be even greater in the years to come.

LORA SABIN

THE RE-EMERGENCE OF CHINA'S PRIVATELY-OWNED SECTOR

Of all the changes affecting China's urban economic structure since the late 1970s, the government's promotion of private businesses represents the most dramatic departure from the past. Since such a major change of policy had to be carried out gingerly or risk sabotage by the many layers of Party and government bureaucracy, the rebirth of China's private economy took place with a noticeable lack of fanfare. Similar to many reforms, private economic activity was initially quietly encouraged in a few regions and by the time public discourse arose on the new policy direction, its positive results were already clear.

The first concrete signs of the new official attitude were revealed when the leadership began to shore up the legal basis of the small-scale individual economy (*geti jingji*). In March 1978, the First Session of the Fifth National People's Congress, China's legislature, reaffirmed the right of such individual businesses to exist.[66] After individually-owned ventures began to mushroom across the country, the 1980 national work conference on employment gave its additional blessing to the changes already afoot. The conference report stated that the individual economy should be "appropriately developed" and called on local officials to battle discrimination against private entrepreneurs.[67] The most delicate issue in the public debate which subsequently ensued, concerning the potentially exploitative nature of the private economy, was officially settled by the publication in July 1981 of the first comprehensive regulations on individual ventures (*getihu*). Declaring that the individual economy was an "essential complement to the state-run economy and collective economy," the State Council regulations granted individual businesses the right to hire two helpers (*bangshou*) and five apprentices (*xuetu*) and codified important aspects of private business operations.[68]

Official support of the individual economy continued throughout the 1980s. In 1982, the rights of *getihu* were granted constitutional status[69] and the next year the State Council broadened the scope of permitted private business activity.[70] Although entrepreneurs came under some pressure during the 1983 drive to wipe out "spiritual pollution" (*jingshen wuran*), as local leaders seized the opportunity to accuse them of dealing in pornography and other contraband, this campaign fizzled out by early 1984.[71] Then, meeting in October 1984, the Third Plenum of the 12th Central Committee raised the reform drive to a new level. The Committee's "Decision on Reform of the Economic Structure" called for deepening economic reforms and offered unqualified support to the "vigorous development" of the individual economy.[72] Reinforcing these high-level actions was a well-orchestrated media campaign designed to encourage people to open their own businesses, calm entrepreneurs' fears of a policy reversal and boost social acceptance of the expanding private sector.[73]

Meanwhile, despite the 1981 regulations limiting individual businesses to seven employees, a small number of larger private firms had been quietly flourishing. While most of these were *getihu* which had expanded beyond seven employees, they also included some collectively-owned firms leased to, and eventually taken over by, private entrepreneurs. In the spring of 1988, the First Session of the Seventh National People's Congress passed an amendment to the 1982 Constitution that finally legitimized the existence of these "private enterprises" (*siying qiye*), which were distinguished from *getihu* solely on the basis of their larger number of registered employees (eight or more).[74]

Statutes outlining the rights of and restrictions on *siying qiye* were published shortly thereafter. In June 1988 a set of provisional regulations were promulgated permitting large private businesses to determine their own wage and profit distribution systems and to enter into contracts with other economic entities.[75] Additional regulations specifically governing labour management were enacted in September 1989. These pointedly urged *siying qiye* to recruit primarily from cities rather than the countryside and required all private enterprise employees to be officially registered. They also included a minimum wage standard that was probably too vague to be enforceable in practice: workers in private enterprises were legally entitled to at least the lowest wage earned in comparable nearby collectives. Benefits were open to mutual negotiation and were to be specified together with other relevant information in a labour contract subject to approval by local government officials.[76]

Like other dynamic segments of China's economy, the private sector suffered serious setbacks toward the end of the decade in the wake of the government's austerity programme and the cautious political atmosphere which followed June 1989. Bank lending to private businessmen tightened considerably in many places and, where funds were available, interest rates soared. An estimated 15 per cent of all private businesses (including *getihu*) were driven out of business in 1989 alone and closures remained high during 1990.[77] Worried by the impact on employment resulting from a collapse of the private sector, by late 1990 the government had launched a major campaign to revive private ventures. In the spring of 1991, the official media gave prominent coverage to new tax incentives for *siying qiye*, efforts to counter malpractice among officials responsible for regulating the private sector, and the communiqué of a regional conference on employment which put special emphasis on the role of self-employment.[78] Moreover, to overcome the popular view of private entrepreneurs as a greedy and dishonest element of society, numerous articles appeared in the official press noting such praiseworthy acts by *getihu* as prompt tax payments and generous donations to flood victims.[79]

Given a major boost by Deng Xiaoping's southern tour and call for additional reforms the following winter, the campaign to expand the private economy reached a fever pitch in the summer of 1992. Cities spanning the length and breadth of China announced special incentives for private businesses and made optimistic forecasts for their future growth.[80] Following the strong endorsement given the private economy by the 14th Communist Party Congress later that autumn, the official press announced that most restrictions on private industrial production and marketing would soon be lifted.[81] Restrictions on wages paid by private firms were also reportedly removed.[82] In their fervour to spur the private sector, some officials simply ignored the limits on the number of workers individual ventures could legally employ and retain *getihu*, as opposed to *siying qiye*, status.[83] The subsequent rise in stature of the private sector was symbolized by the inclusion of 21 entrepreneurs in the March 1993 meeting of the Chinese People's Political Consultative Conference.[84]

The government's campaign has been bolstered by the cumulative effect of socio-economic changes which have given private ventures greater legitimacy than ever before. The impact of reforms has reduced the advantages of the state and collective sectors vis-à-vis the private economy, whose relative independence has become increasingly attractive to many Chinese. Moreover, while many people still find it difficult to accept the argument that some Chinese must be allowed to get rich before others, there is nevertheless considerable admiration for those who do amass personal fortunes. This new-found social acceptance has in turn created an increasingly supportive atmosphere for those who strike out on their own to seek success in the private economy.

The growing importance of the urban private sector is reflected in the rapid expansion of its labour force. According to government data, employment in urban private ventures rose from 200,000 to 8.3 million between 1978 and 1992, an average yearly rate of 33.2 per cent. This compares with annual growth rates of 2.7 and 4.2 per cent for the state and urban collective sectors, respectively (see Table 21.1). Together with changes in the collective sector, the concentration of private firms in commerce has had a major impact on the urban commercial employment structure. The state sector's commanding 84 per cent of total employment in urban commerce in 1978 had fallen to 44 per cent by 1992, while the share of the individual economy had grown to over 20 per cent[85]

As the private economy has expanded, changes in the composition of its work force reveal the higher status attained by this sector. In the early days of reform, *getihu* were drawn almost exclusively from retired workers and "socially idle persons" – including the disabled, former prison and reform-through-labour inmates, and laid-off workers – for whom there were few other alternatives. But by the mid-1980s, school graduates entering the work force for the first time comprised one-quarter of all urban individual workers.[86] Employment in larger private businesses has become even more popular, in some surveys ranking as the favourite job choice of Chinese youth.[87] The highly publicized success of such large private businesses as Beijing's Stone

(*Sitong*) Group and Land (*Nande*) Economic Group has helped fuel the entrepreneurial fever and motivate rising numbers of university graduates to foresake secure employment in the state sector and open their own ventures or take jobs with private firms. The main attractions of the private sector include higher salaries, a freer work environment and more opportunities to use skills. Especially since the mid-1980s, these attributes have also spurred employees in the state and collective sectors to *xia hai*, or "go down to the sea," the popular term for going into private business.[88]

With greater numbers of well-qualified Chinese opening their own businesses, the distinctions separating owners and employees in the private sector have become sharper. Proprietors of both *getihu* and *siying qiye* tend to be older, well-educated and male.[89] Owners of the larger private enterprises represent a particularly privileged class. They often have substantial work experience in state enterprises or government agencies and, in many instances, enjoy connections abroad.[90] By contrast, the typical worker in a private firm is young, of below-average education and female. Although some private enterprises mainly recruit only highly-educated employees,[91] the majority of workers in both large and small private businesses come from China's countryside.[92]

As the appeal of the private economy has extended to include diverse social groups, the distribution of its work force across different regions has also broadened. When the urban individual economy first re-emerged its labour force was highly concentrated in a few regions. In 1980, Guangdong and just four other provinces claimed nearly one-half of all urban *getihu*. But a decade later, the private economy had taken root across the whole of China. By the end of 1992, Guangdong and the next four most heavily represented provinces were home to roughly one-third of total employment in urban *getihu*. Over this same period, nine less developed provinces stretching from Inner Mongolia in the north to Yunnan in the south increased their collective share from 8 per cent to over 14 per cent of the total urban private work force.[93]

Although China's private sector has achieved impressive growth over the last 15 years, the obstacles to its further development have by no means been completely eliminated. Many of the most intractable problems occur at the local level, where private businesses are still constrained by lack of space, poor access to raw materials and a severe scarcity of investment funds.[94] They have also been the targets of harassment by corrupt or staunchly leftist officials in the form of excessive and indiscriminate charges or the arbitrary denial of operating permits.[95] In many areas, such obstructionist tactics have been motivated by concerns that competition from private enterprises could threaten the state and collective sectors.[96] Sometimes state enterprises have taken matters into their own hands and intimidated private ventures.[97] But overshadowing all these problems are persistent fears of policy changes. As recently as 1992, a nation-wide survey found that the government's attitude towards the private sector remained the single greatest worry among owners of large private businesses.[98]

CONCLUSION: URBAN PRIVATE EMPLOYMENT IN CHINA

The three preceding sections have examined the development of urban collective, foreign-invested and private enterprises during the reform period. The discussions of the urban collective and foreign sectors have highlighted the fact that the determined efforts of entrepreneurs to, in the Chinese term, "wear the hat" of a more favoured ownership type means that registered enterprises in these sectors actually include a large number of privately-owned firms. China's system of state enterprise supervision makes "wearing the hat" of a state firm somewhat more difficult. But this form of false registration does occur as well, particularly in China's SEZs, where regulation is comparatively lax.[99] In addition, share-holding schemes introduced in the state sector have often resulted in the concentration of the vast majority of shares and considerable management control in the hands of a small number of private individuals.[100] However, since official statistics are based on enterprise registration, they fail to distinguish the real nature of these firms and therefore vastly understate the recent expansion of employment in the urban private sector.

A second major distortion in official data derives from the lack of a comprehensive and rational system of counting the urban labour force. Official statistics on urban private employment include only registered workers in registered private businesses. Within *getihu*, they only count those persons with urban housing registration. A large number of unregistered urban residents as well as rural owners and employees of individual ventures are therefore excluded from these data.[101] The State Administration for Industry and Commerce (SAIC) in Beijing admitted in 1992 that about one-third of all urban self-employed in large cities are not registered,[102] a percentage which corresponds to the results of earlier city-based surveys of the private economy.[103] Those who do register also frequently employ many more urban residents than are reported with the SAIC, including unpaid family members who are essentially working full-time. Similarly, in order to reduce the various fees which local governments often impose on larger private ventures – usually assessed on a per-worker basis – *siying qiye* chronically under-report their total work force.[104]

Although no one really knows how many rural residence permit holders are engaged in private business in China's cities, the figure is certainly quite high and rising. One comprehensive survey carried out in Beijing in August 1987 found that about one-quarter of the owners of private ventures and a full three-quarters of their employees were from the countryside.[105] When more recent estimates of the urban floating population are compared with published figures on rural workers outside the private sector, the number of rural residents engaged in the urban private economy appears to have far surpassed 10 million by 1992, yet official sources provide a figure for total urban private employment (again comprised mainly of urban residents) of just 8.4 million.[106] A round-up of "street traders" in Beijing in 1989 is suggestive of the degree to which official undercounting of both urban and rural workers obscures the true size of the private labour force. It uncovered an estimated 110,000 unauthorized self-employed workers, nearly twice the number of officially registered urban self-employed.[107]

In order to paint a more accurate picture of the impact of the development of the non-state sector on China's urban employment structure, it is necessary to correct for the distortions resulting from the false registration of privately-owned enterprises and the undercounting of workers in the officially-recognized urban private sector. Table 21.3 presents conservative and liberal estimates of the size of these distortions. As detailed in the notes to the table, these estimates are derived from a wide range of sources, including surveys and the appraisals of Chinese officials and economists.

Having adjusted the official figures on the basis of these estimated distortions, Table 21.4 provides the author's estimates of the true extent of employment in the urban private sector. Not surprisingly, these estimates suggest that employment in privately-owned businesses has grown considerably faster than government data would indicate. Indeed, the private sector's total work force in 1992 appears to have been four to seven times larger than the official figure, depending on which estimates are used to correct for the distortions. Even if only conservative estimates are utilized, the proportion of the overall urban work force employed in the private economy rises from the official 5 per cent to over 21 per cent. This proportion climbs to a full one-third if the more liberal estimates are used.

Although these figures represent only estimates, they underscore the peril of judging the expansion of China's privately-employed urban labour force on the basis of official data alone. In fact, the above analysis is conservative in that it is limited to actual private ownership rather than simply private management. If one includes workers employed in enterprises nominally owned by the state or a collective but whose management is in private hands (such as leased firms and other enterprises which have gained significant management independence), then the "privately-employed" work force would be larger still. But even if the analysis is restricted to formal private ownership, the results suggest that between one-quarter and one-third of the urban labour force is now employed under conditions in which the market forces of supply and demand should be increasingly powerful.

In recent analyses of reforming command economies, some observers have argued that gradualism, as opposed to "big bang" or rapid implementation of a reform package, has been a critical factor in China's strong economic performance since the late 1970s.[108] It is true that the reforms discussed above were instituted gradually, in marked contrast to the much swifter process of collectivization of urban businesses carried out in the mid to late 1950s. Moreover, throughout the reform period, even as the Chinese government has

Table 21.3 Estimates of distortions in official Labour data, 1985–92

A. *Uncounted workers*[a] *(% of official urban private employment)*

Year	Urban workers: Conservative	Urban workers: Liberal	Rural workers: Conservative	Rural workers: Liberal
1985	10.0	30.00	50.0	100.0
1987	10.0	30.00	50.0	100.0
1990	10.0	30.00	100.0	200.0
1992	20.0	40.00	150.0	300.0

B. *Private ownership*[b] *(% of official labour force)*

Year	State-owned units: Conservative	State-owned units: Liberal	Urban collectives: Conservative	Urban collectives: Liberal	State-collective joint ventures: Conservative	State-collective joint ventures: Liberal
1985	0.0	1.0	10.0	30.0	5.0	15.0
1987	0.0	1.0	20.0	40.0	10.0	20.0
1990	1.0	3.0	30.0	50.0	15.0	30.0
1992	1.0	3.0	30.0	50.0	20.0	30.0

Year	State-private joint ventures: Conservative	State-private joint ventures: Liberal	Collective-private joint ventures: Conservative	Collective-private joint ventures: Liberal	Sino-foreign joint ventures: Conservative	Sino-foreign joint ventures: Liberal
1985	10.0	30.0	40.0	60.0	30.0	50.0
1987	10.0	30.0	50.0	70.0	40.0	60.0
1990	20.0	40.0	60.0	90.0	50.0	70.0
1992	40.0	60.0	70.0	90.0	50.0	70.0

Notes:

[a] Refers to all unregistered workers with urban or rural housing registration and all rural workers in urban *getihu*. Estimates are calculated on the basis of numerous survey results, figures provided by officials at the Ministry of Labour and the SAIC, and the informed opinions of prominent economists and professional survey analysts.

(1) Regarding uncounted urban workers, numerous surveys of private activity in different cities from 1985–1987 suggest that the number of unregistered urban workers in large cities is equal to at least 10–40% of registered workers (and even higher in such cities as Nanjing and Wenzhou). Both Beijing and Shanghai, for instance, had about one-third more urban workers in private ventures in 1985 than are listed in official yearbooks. Officials at the SAIC in Beijing in 1992 claimed that for every 100 registered urban *getihu*, another 50 in large cities and 20–30 in smaller cities are unregistered. Some other officials and economists provided slightly lower percentages. In all cases, the estimates used above represent the most conservative ones possible.

(2) Regarding uncounted rural workers, official labour data do not include rural workers in urban *getihu* but, in recent years, they do include rural workers who are employed and registered by larger *siying qiye*. Following this convention, most surveys on *getihu* in the mid-1980s do not include rural workers. However, city-wide data for a number of cities indicate the very large numbers of rural workers who were engaged in the private sector (ranging from at least 100% to 400% of the number of registered urbanites in the private sector). While many of

these people operated in rural counties outside cities, a large number operated within urban districts. For example, surveys conducted in 1985 in Chongqing. Sichuan province, and in 1987 in Beijing indicate that at least 70% of all employees in private ventures were from rural areas. According to the Beijing survey, the total number of uncounted rural *getihu* operators and employees was equal to 61–95% of the number of registered urban workers in *getihu* that year. More recently, surveys of the floating population suggest that in 1990, roughly 25–30 million rural workers were employed in urban areas, of whom 11–12 million were officially registered by non-private firms. Even allowing for under-registration in these firms by up to 50%, the remaining 7–12 million rural workers who must have been engaged in the private sector represent 100–200% of the total official number of workers in the urban private economy (which included a small number of registered rural workers). This estimate is supported by surveys undertaken in seven cities in 1988–89 indicating that 23% of the total urban floating population, or 5.6 million rural workers, were working as pedlars, repairers and domestic helpers alone. By 1992, the number of rural workers among urban transients had increased to an estimated 30–45 million, of whom 12 million were officially registered outside the private sector. Again allowing for 50% under-registration in these sectors, the remaining 12–27 million represent 150–320% of the official number of workers engaged in the urban private economy. All officials, economists and experts consulted concurred with the above final estimates.

(3) Estimates of uncounted urban and rural workers are supported by (a) the above-mentioned 1987 survey in Beijing which found that the number of people engaged in the private economy in the city's urban districts was almost twice the official number; and (b) a reported round-up of "street traders" in Beijing in 1989, during which officials uncovered an estimated 110,000 unauthorized self-employed, as compared to the official number of 57,000 registered self-employed.

[b] Refers to workers in privately-owned firms which are registered as some other type of enterprise, state and collective firms converted to share-holding systems in which most shares are owned by a small number of individuals with considerable management autonomy, and domestic and Sino-foreign joint ventures in which at least 50% of assets are privately held. Because of the illegal and irregular nature of such ownership, there are few relevant data to consult. Estimates are therefore calculated primarily on the basis of the appraisals of officials of the Ministry of Labour and Beijing district-level labour bureaus and the informed opinions of prominent economists and professional survey analysts. However, in the case of urban collectives, the estimates are supported by a 1993 survey in Changchun, Jilin province, which found that about 50% of urban collectives were in fact privately-owned. After conducting extensive surveys on the private economy, a survey company in Beijing likewise estimated that at least half of all urban collectives nation-wide are actually private firms.

Sources: For city-wide surveys on the private economy: *Privately-Hired Labor in Beijing* and *Survey of the Individual Economy*. In the latter, see in particular "Survey of individual industry and commerce in Beijing," p. 13: "Survey of individual industry and commerce in Shanghai," pp. 19, 21, 38: "Survey of individual industry and commerce in Chongqing," pp. 96, 98, 100; Liu Ping, "Guanyu Nanjing getihu qingkuang de diaocha" ("Survey of the conditions of individual ventures"), pp. 86, 94: Shenyang Municipal Administration for Industry and Commerce, "Shenyangshi chengxiang geti gongshangye fazhan ji guanli qingkuang de diaocha" ("Survey of the development and management conditions of urban and rural individual industry and commerce in Shenyang"), pp. 118, 124; and Wenzhou Municipal Administration for Industry and Commerce, "Wenzhoushi geti shangye diaocha" ("Survey of individual commerce in Wenzhou"), pp. 155, 164. For figures on the floating population and the rural workers among them: Shen Yimin and Tong Chengzhu, *Zhongguo renkou qianyi (Chinese Population Migration)* (Beijing: Zhongguo tongji chubanshe, 1992), pp. 207–221: Chinese Academy of Social Sciences and State Statistical Bureau. *1992 nian zhongguo nongcun jingji fazhan niandu baogao jianxi 1993 nian fazhan qushi (Yearly report on China's Rural Economic Development in 1992 and Analysis of Development Trends for 1993)* (Beijing: Zhongguo shehui kexue chubanshe, 1993), pp. 145–46, "Woguo mei ershi ren you yige zai liudong" ("In China, one in every 20 is mobile"), *Renmin ribao*, 26 February 1989, p. 4, and Alan P.L. Liu, "Economic reform, mobility strategies, and national integration," *Asian Survey*, Vol. 31, No. 5 (1991), p. 393. For the number of registered rural workers in non-private enterprises in 1991–92: State Statistical Bureau and Ministry of Labour (comps.), *Zhongguo laodong tongji nianjian 1992 (Statistical Yearbook of Chinese Labour*

1992) (Beijing: Zhongguo laodong chubanshe, 1992), p. 47; *Statistical Yearbook on Labour 1993*, p. 47. For estimates of unauthorized *getihu* in Beijing in 1989, see Sheryl Wudunn, "China taking a harsh line with vendors," *New York Times*, 16 November 1989, p. A6. For estimates of privately-owned "urban collectives": "Zhongdanxia de da taowang; 'jia jiti' ("Fleeing from the great burden: perspectives on the phenomenon of 'fake collective' enterprises"), *Fazhi ribao (Legal Daily)*, 19 November 1993, p. 1; Horizon Market-Research, Inc., "Crisis of your registration," p. 18. See also China Market Survey Group, "The tough problems of 'big money'" and Horizon Market-Research, Inc., "Survey report on private enterprises."

Table 21.4 Employment in China's urban private economy, 1985–92

	Official sources[a]		*Author's estimates*[b]	
Year	*State statistical bureau*	*State administration for industry and commerce*	*Conservative*	*Liberal*
Total labour force (1,000 workers)[c]				
1985	4,500	3,839	10,571	21,252
1987	5,690	4,924	16,240	28,194
1990	6,710	6,592	26,319	43,633
1992	8,380	n.a.	35,914	59,838
Proportion of total urban labour force (%)[d]				
1985	3.51	n.a.	8.25	16.76
1987	4.13	n.a.	11.74	20.50
1990	4.56	n.a.	17.36	28.22
1992	5.36	n.a.	21.47	33.93

Notes:

[a] The State Statistical Bureau (SSB) numbers are compiled from surveys and estimates of the SSB itself and other government agencies. The State Administration for Industry and Commerce (SAIC) figures are based on actual registration data and thus are probably a more accurate reflection of registered private employment. However, only the SSB data are available in published compilations over the entire period since the late 1970s.

[b] Includes *getihu*, *siying qiye*, other privately-owned firms as defined in note b to Table 21.3, and wholly foreign-owned firms.

[c] Year-end figures.

[d] Includes workers in state and urban collective enterprises, domestic and Sino-foreign joint ventures, wholly foreign-owned firms, and urban private businesses. In the author's percentages, the state sector labour force was reduced by 3% (in conservative estimates) or 8% (in liberal estimates) to eliminate the estimated work force employed by state firms operating in rural settings.

Sources: SSB figures: *Statistical Yearbook on Labour 1993*, p. 27. SAIC figures: Information Centre, State Administration for Industry and Commerce (comp.), *Zhongguo gongshang xingzheng guanli tongji sishi nian (Forty Years of Statistics of the State Administration for Industry and Commerce)* (Beijing: Zhongguo tongji chubanshe, 1992), pp. 154, 189, 191, 194.

actively encouraged the expansion of the non-state economy, it has remained steadfast in its ideological commitment to the dominant role of the state sector. But the findings of this study provide striking evidence of just how far China has come in transforming its urban economic and employment structures.

ACKNOWLEDGMENTS

I would like to thank Dwight Perkins, Richard Freeman, Andrew Walder, Dai Yuanchen, Yuan Yue and Jonathan Hecht for their helpful comments and support. This research was supported in part by a fellowship from the Committee on Scholarly Communication with China.

NOTES

1 Two excellent examples are John Philip Emerson. "The labor force of China, 1957–80," in U.S. Congress, *China Under the Four Modernizations, Part 1* (Washington. D.C.: U.S, Government Printing Office, 1982), pp. 224–267 and Jeffrey R. Taylor, *China's Economy Looks Toward the Year 2000, Volume 1* (Washington, D.C.: U.S. Government Printing Office 1986), pp. 222–262.

2 See Hilary K. Josephs, *Labor Low in China: Choice and Responsibility* (Salem, NH: Butterworth Legal Publishers, 1990) and Gordon White, "The politics of economic reform in Chinese industry: the introduction of the labour contract system," *The China Quarterly*, No. 111 (September 1987), pp. 365–389 for in-depth analyses of the labour contract system. Andrew Walder has explored worker and management behaviour through several phases of reforms. Many of his main findings are presented in *Communist Neo-Traditionalism: Work and Authority in Chinese Industry* (Berkeley: University of California Press, 1986).

3 On the urban private economy, see Thomas B. Gold, "Urban private business and social change," in Ezra Vogel and Deborah Davis (eds.), *China on the Eve of Tiananmen* (Cambridge, MA: Harvard University Press, 1990), pp. 157–178 and Susan Young, "Wealth but not security: attitudes towards private business in China in the 1980s," *The Australian Journal of Chinese Affairs*, No. 25 (1991), pp. 115–137. Two interesting studies on the urban collective sector are Jianzhong Tang and Laurence J. C. Ma, "Evolution of urban collective enterprises in China," *The China Quarterly*, No. 104 (Decemher 1985), pp. 614–640 and Martin Lockett, "The urban collective economy," in S. Feuchtwang, A. Hussain and T. Pairault (eds.), *Transforming China's Economy in the Eighties, Volume 2* (Boulder, CO: Westview Press, 1988), pp. 118–137.

4 Most of China's traditional private sector had been collectivized in the mid-1950s, although a small number of street barbers and other licensed artisans continued to operate. In the late 1970s, officially-recognized self-employed urban residents comprised less than 1% of the urban workforce, but if the illegal activities of peasant hawkers, urban returned youth, black marketeers and others are included, the proportion may have been as high as 3%. See Martin King Whyte and William L, Parish, *Urban Life in Contemporary China* (Chicago: University of Chicago Press, 1984), pp. 29–30

5 Less than half a million urban youth were sent to rural areas in 1978, as compared to six million between 1975 and 1977. State Statistical Bureau (comp.), *Zhongguo laodong gongzi tongji ziliao 1949–1985 (Statistical Materials on Chinese Labour and Wages 1949–1985*) (Beijing: Zhongguo laodong chubanshe, 1987), p. 110.

6 The total number of youth leaving the countryside more than doubled between 1977 and 1978 to 2.5 million, of whom 1.3 million were ostensibly "looking for work." *Ibid.* p. 111.

7 *Ibid.* p. 109.

8 These numbers are cited in John Philip Emerson, "Urban school-leavers and

unemployment in China," *The China Quarterly*, No. 93 (March 1983), pp. 1–2, and are for non-agricultural employment.

9 Thomas Rawski estimates that in 1957–74 output growth exceeded labour growth in non-agricultural sectors by a factor of roughly 1.5:1.0. See Thomas G. Rawski, *Economic Growth and Employment in China* (Oxford: Oxford University Press, 1979), pp. 124–25.

10 These figures, which appear to represent the ratio of total fixed and circulating capital to employment, are from Chen Naixing, "Shilun woguo xian jieduan de geti jingji" ("A tentative discussion of China's individual economy at the present stage"), *Jingji wenti* (*Economic Issues*), No. 1 (1983), pp. 8–9.

11 This motive, with respect to the re-establishment of China's private economy, is discussed in Thomas B. Gold, "Urban private business in China," *Studies in Comparative Communism* (Summer/Autumn 1989), p. 200.

12 Particularly strong endorsement came from the one-time director of the State Statistical Bureau, Xue Muqiao. See, for example, Xue's article, "Guanyu chengzhen laodong jiuye wenti de jidian yijian" ("Some opinions on urban labour and employment problems"), in Bao Ji (chief ed.), *Zhongguo dangdai shehui kexue mingjia zixuan xueshu jinghua congshu, 8: Xue Muqiao xueshu jinghua lu* (*A Collection of Selected Scholarly Works by China's Modern Social Science Masters, Volume 8: A Collection of Scholarly Works by Xue Muqiao*) (Beijing: Beijing shifan xueyuan chubanshe, 1988), pp. 405–411.

13 See "Zhonggong zhongyang zhuanfa quanguo jiuye huiyi wenjian 'Jinyibu zuohao chengzhen laodong jiuye gongzuo'" ("The Central Committee of China's Communist Party transmits a document from the National Employment Conference: 'Go a step further in doing labour employment work well'"), in Zhao Dongwan *et al.* (eds.), *Zhongguo laodong renshi nianjian 1949–1987* (*Yearbook on Chinese Labour and Personnel 1949–1987*) (Beijing: Laodong renshi chubanshe, 1989), p. 1603.

14 "Zhonggong zhongyang, guowuyuan guanyu guangkai menlu, gaohuo jingji, jiejue chengzhen jiuye wenti de ruogan jueding" ("Some decisions by the Central Committee of the Chinese Communist Party and the State Council on opening up avenues, invigorating the economy, and solving urban employment problems"), in State Commission for Reform of the Economic Structure (comp.), *Jingji tizhi gaige wenjian huibian 1978–1983* (*Compilation of Documents on Reform of the Economic Structure 1978–1983*) (Beijing: Zhongguo caizheng jingji chubanshe, 1984), pp. 634–38.

15 "Guowuyuan guanyu banfa 'Guanyu chengzhen jiti suoyouzhi jingji ruogan zhengce wenti de zanxing guiding' de tongzhi" ("Notice of the State Council on promulgation of: 'Provisional regulations on certain policy issues with respect to the urban collectively-owned economy'"), in *ibid.* pp. 649–650.

16 A new eight-tiered tax bracket system was introduced for collectives, which formerly had been subject to the same system used by small state-owned enterprises. See "Zhonghua renmin gongheguo jiti qiye suodeshui zanxing tiaoli" ("Provisional regulations on income taxation for collective enterprises of the People's Republic of China"), in Legislative Affairs Bureau, State Council (comp.), *Zhonghua renmin gongheguo fagui huibian 1985* (*Compilation of Laws and Regulations of the People's Republic of China 1985*) (Beijing: Falu chubanshe, 1986), pp. 161–62, 164.

17 See, for example, "Notice of the State Council on regulations on the urban collectively-owned economy," pp. 648–651.

18 Interview with officials at the Labour Service Company of Beijing's Chaoyang District Labour Bureau in March 1993.

19 "Zhonggong zhongyang guanyu jingji tizhi gaige de jueding"("Decision of the Central Committee of the Chinese Communist Party on reform of the economic structure"), in Wang Zhiye and Zhu Yuanzhen (chief eds.), *Jingji tizhi gaige shouce* (*Handbook on Reform of the Economic Structure*) (Beijing: Jingji ribao chubanshe, 1987), p. 12. This strategy is discussed in Lockett, "The urban collective economy," p. 133.

20 "Zhonghua renmin gongheguo chengzhen jiti suoyouzhi qiye tiaoli" ("Regulations for urban collectively-owned enterprises of the People's Republic of China"), in Legislative Affairs Bureau, State Council (comp.), *Zhonghua renmin gongheguo fagui huibian 1991* (*Compilation of Laws and Regulations of the People's Republic of China 1991*) (Beijing: Falu chubanshe, 1992), pp. 593–609.

21 State Statistical Bureau and Ministry of Labour (comps.), *Zhongguo laodong tongji nianjian 1993* (*Statistical Yearbook on Chinese Labour 1993*) (Beijing: Zhongguo laodong chubanshe, 1993), pp. 22–24, 27.

22 Interview with officials at the Balizhuang Neighbourhood Office of Chaoyang District, Beijing in March 1993.

23 For more information on the emergence of this and other types of urban collectives, see Jianzhong Tang and Laurence J. C. Ma, "Evolution of urban collectives" pp. 614–640.

24 In a March 1993 interview, officials at a neighbourhood committee in Chaoyang District, Beijing explained that their labour service company was created by the Ministry of Labour in 1979. Over 50% of the investment in the collective enterprises they established came from borrowed funds, although all of this was eventually repaid. Most of the remainder was contributed by retired local workers.

25 "Laodong jiuye fuwu qiye guanli guiding" ("Regulations on management of labour employment service enterprises"), in Legislative Affairs Bureau, State Council (comp.), *Zhonghua renmin gongheguo fagui huibian 1990* (*Compilation of Laws and Regulations of the People's Republic of China 1990*) (Beijing: Falu chubanshe, 1991), pp. 666–67.

26 *Statistical Yearbook on Labour 1993*, pp. 181, 349.

27 Zhongguo shichang diaochasuo (China Market Survey Group), "'Dakuan' de nanti yu chulu" ("The tough problems of and way out for 'big money'") (unpublished report, 1992), p. 13.

28 Much of this information on the false registration of private enterprises was gained from discussions with researchers in Beijing and with the owners and managers of private businesses in Beijing, Chongqing, Chengdu, Guangzhou and Shenzhen in the summer and autumn of 1992.

29 See Young, "Wealth but not security," pp. 118–19.

30 A new regulation effective in Beijing's Chaoyang District, for example, allows a business with three or more investors and with a minimum of eight employees to qualify for urban collective status. See Administrative Bureau for Industry and Commerce, Chaoyaag District, Beijing Municipality, "Guanyu chengzhen qunzhong jizi xingban de jiti suoyouzhi qiye dengji guanli zanxing guiding (shixing)" ("Temporary regulations on registration and management of collectively-owned enterprises set up from the pooled resources of urban masses (trial implementation)") (unpublished notice, 1992). Previously, such businesses had to produce a scientific or technological product in order to register as a collective. This information was obtained through a small group of private investors who have recently set up a survey and information "collective" under this new regulation.

31 For example, this is the view of a research group in Beijing with considerable experience surveying China's private economy. See Lingdian shichang diaocha yu

fenxi gongsi (Horizon Market-Research and Policy-Analysis, Inc.), "Laoban, ni guakao de weiji" ("Boss, the crisis of your [false] registration"), *Shidian* (*Viewpoint*), No. 4 (1993), p. 18.

32 "A case of get-up-and-go in Wenzhou," *China Daily*, 22 August 1992, p. 4.

33 See "Jingcheng qiqian xiaoqiye guoyou minying" ("Seven thousand small enterprises in the country's capital to be state-owned but people-operated"), *Zhongguo gongshang shibao* (*China Industrial and Commercial Times*) 24 February 1993, p. 1. Besides shareholding systems, the article states that leasing and other private management arrangements, in addition to outright sales of enterprises, will be undertaken to invigorate these units.

34 Shanghai municipal officials recently announced the sale of 43 collectives to private traders in a bid to improve efficiency in the commercial sector. "Inefficient shops sold to private businesses," *China Daily*, 19 July 1993, p. 2. Sales of small state enterprises have picked up as well. See "Hunan to auction off state firms." *China Daily*, 12 July 1993, p. 2 and "Private firm buys state enterprise" *China Daily*, 1 October 1993, p. 2

35 In addition to privatizing the management of urban collectives, a reported one-half of China's small state-owned shops had been leased out by mid-1993. "Leasing of state shops to citizens paying off," *China Daily*, 23 July 1993, p. 3.

36 The agency claimed that financial losses of 310,000 *yuan* had been replaced by rent payments of 690,000 *yuan* from the reform. Interview with officials at the Non-staple Foodstuffs Company of Beijing's Chaoyang District in March 1993.

37 Interviews with officials at the Chaoyang District Labour Service Company and Balizhuang Neighbourhood Office in Beijing in March 1993.

38 See "Zhonghua renmin gongheguo zhongwai hezi jingying qiye fa" ("Sino-Foreign Joint Venture Law of the People's Republic of China"), in *Handbook on Reform*, pp. 423–24. This law stipulated that the foreign partner should generally have at least a 25% stake in the new enterprise and that after-tax profits should be distributed on the basis of equity shares.

39 "Zhonghua renmin gongheguo zhongwai hezi jingying qiye suodeshui fa" ("Sino-Foreign Joint Venture Income Tax Law of the People's Republic of China"), in *ibid.* pp. 433–34.

40 "Zhonghua renmin gongheguo zhongwai hezi jingying qiye laodong guanli guiding" ("Regulations on labour management in Sino-foreign joint ventures of the People's Republic of China"), in *Yearbook on Labour and Personnel 1949–1987*, pp. 1650–51.

41 An authoritative study on Chinese joint ventures is Margaret M. Pearson, *Joint Ventures in the People's Republic of China: The Control of Foreign Direct Investment Under Socialism* (Princeton, NJ: Princeton University Press, 1991).

42 Ezra Vogel, *One Step Ahead in China: Guangdong Under Reform* (Cambridge, MA: Harvard University Press, 1989), pp. 125–29, highlights the political sensitivity of this policy. A good discussion of the development of SEZs is George T. Crane, "Reform and retrenchment in China's special economic zones," in U.S. Congress, *China's Economic Dilemmas in the 1990s: The Problems of Reforms, Modernization, and Interdependence, Volume 2* (Washington, D.C.: U.S. Government Printing Office, 1991), pp. 841–857.

43 "Zhonghua renmin gongheguo waizi qiye fa" (Foreign-Invested Enterprise Law of the People's Republic of China"), in Zhu Yuanzhen and Fan Maofa (chief eds.). *Jingji tizhi gaige shouce* (*xu 2*) (*Handbook on Reform of the Economic Structure (Volume 2)*) (Beijing: Jingji ribao chubanshe, 1989), pp. 319–320.

44 Whereas Sino-foreign co-operative ventures may determine their own profit distribution, profits of joint ventures must be split according to equity shares. Joint

ventures also always have legal person status, but co-operative ventures may be set up as a legal or non-legal person business. See "Zhonghua renmin gongheguo zhongwai hezuo jingying qiye fa" ("Sino-Foreign Co-operative Venture Law of the People's Republic of China") in *ibid.* pp. 441–43. Two articles which help to clarify the differences between the two types of Sino-foreign partnerships are Jerome Alan Cohen, "The long-awaited Co-operative Venture Law," *The China Business Review* (July–August 1988), pp. 14–18 and Laurence W. Bates and Wang Jianping, "The New Co-operative joint Venture Law," *East Asian Executive Reports* (May 1988), pp. 7–10.

45 In addition to "sanzi" enterprises, there are also the representative offices set up by foreign companies and organizations carrying out trade or providing services but not investing in businesses in China.

46 See "Guowuyuan guanyu guli waishang touzi de guiding" ("Regulations of the State Council to encourage foreign investors"), in *Handbook on Reform*, pp. 232–34.

47 In 1991, the various tax regulations were consolidated into one new law specifying unified tax rates for all foreign-funded firms. See "Zhonghua renmin gongheguo waishang touzi qiye he waiguo qiye suodeshui fa" ("Income Tax Law for foreign-invested enterprises and foreign enterprises of the People's Republic of China"), in *Laws and Regulations 1991*, pp. 281–89. Timothy A. Gelatt provides a detailed analysis of the effect of this law and its implementing regulations in "China's new tax law for foreign business," *East Asian Executive Reports* (May 1991), pp.9–14 and "Foreign Business Tax Law: new implementing rules," *ibid.* (September 1991), pp. 9–13. Further tax reforms implemented at the beginning of 1994 unified the tax rates applicable to all foreign and domestic enterprises. Though the effect of these changes remains to be seen, the government has insisted that the overall tax burden on foreign-invested firms will not rise significantly. See "New tax system won't hurt foreign firms," *China Daily*, *Business Weekly*, 23–29 January 1994, p. 1.

48 See Article 15 of "Regulations to encourage foreign investors," p. 233.

49 "Guanyu jinyibu luoshi waishang touzi qiye yongren zizhiquan de yijian" ("Opinion on further implementing the employment autonomy of foreign-invested enterprises"), in Wang Jianxin (chief ed.), *Zhongguo laodong nianjian 1988–1989* (*Yearbook on Chinese Labour 1988–1989*) (Beijing: Zhongguo laodong chubanshe, 1991), p. 375.

50 State Statistical Bureau (comp.), *Zhongguo tongji nianjian 1993* (*Chinese Statistical Yearbook for 1993*) (Beijing: Zhongguo tongji chubanshe, 1993), p. 647.

51 Official sources claim that over 1,800 such zones had been established by October 1992, causing the central authorities to warn of "zone overheating" and to crack down on their further growth. "Zone overheating poses policy woe for state planners," *China Daily*, 2 March 1993, p. 4.

52 *Statistical Yearbook for 1993*, p. 647.

53 "Woguo sanzi qiye huode changzu fazhan"("Our country's foreign-funded enterprises gain rapid development"), *Jingji cankao* (*Economic Reference*), 24 January 1992, p. 1.

54 At the end of 1992, Shanghai became home to China's second joint venture bank and announced approval for another 20 outside-funded financial institutions. "City welcomes its first joint venture bank," *China Daily*, *Shanghai Focus*, 15–21 November 1992, p. 2. Meanwhile, the State Council has offered incentives to attract foreign investment into tourist sites. "Overseas funds OK for resorts," *China Daily*, 26 October 1992, p. 3.

55 *Statistical Yearbook on Labour 1993*, pp. 394–97.

56 See "Joint ventures to come under closer scrutiny," *China Daily*, *Business Weekly*, 6–12 December 1992, p. 1.

57 "Foreign-funded shams work profit magic," *China Daily*, 14 November 1992, p. 4.

58 Sheryl WuDunn, "Booming China is dream market of West," *New York Times*, 15 February 1993, p. A6.

59 This information was obtained through interviews with knowledgeable economists at the Chinese Academy of Social Sciences (CASS) in Beijing.

60 "PRC labor update: China's system makes hiring tough," *Business China*, 16 July 1990, pp. 102–103.

61 One manager of a joint venture in Guangzhou, whose operations require extremely hygienic conditions, explained that his company was uncomfortable hiring workers from the countryside who tended to be less careful and to maintain lower standards of personal cleanliness than urban residents. Interview in November 1992.

62 Foreign managers of "sanzi" businesses now realize how critical the provision of housing is to their ability to retain valued workers. One large joint venture in Beijing found that employees kept leaving despite large salaries. Only after the venture invested in housing facilities did the situation improve. Interview with a joint venture manager in November 1992.

63 Determining just what foreign-funded firms should pay their employees has always been a sensitive matter. Two informative articles explaining the issues involved are: Jamie P. Horseley, "Chinese labor," *The China Business Review* (May–June 1984), pp.16–25 and Jerome Alan Cohen and Charles H. Harris, "Equal pay for equal work," *ibid.* (January–February 1986), pp. 10–13.

64 Most "sanzi" firms have had experiences bearing witness to the stiff competition for skilled workers. One joint venture in Guangzhou lost a valued human resource officer after she happened to see an advertisement for a similar position at McDonalds offering twice her current salary. Once in her new position, she lured many other former colleages over to McDonalds as well. Interview with joint venture manager in November 1992.

65 The representative offices of foreign companies are required to recruit Chinese staff through the Foreign Employee Service Corporation (FESCO), whereas embassies are supposed to hire through the Diplomatic Service Bureau. In both cases, the intermediary organizations keep between 55 and 80% of the wages paid by foreign employers. The extent of extra wages paid to supplement employees' salaries is exemplified by the case of a skilled secretary who left her job at a foreign non-profit organization (where she had earned 800 *yuan* a month) to work for a foreign company. Since FESCO takes 1,800 *yuan* of her now 2,500 *yuan* salary, the company privately pays her an additional 1,800 *yuan.* Interview in October 1992.

66 A translated version of the 1978 Constitution may be found in Joseph En-Pao Wang (ed.), *Selected Legal Documents of the People's Republic of China: Volume II* (Washington, D.C.: University Publications of America, Inc., 1979). Article 5, recognizing the existence of *getihu*, is on p. 134.

67 "Zhonggong zhongyang zhuanfa quanguo jiuye huiyi wenjian 'Jinyibu zuohao chengzhen laodong jiuye gongzuo'" ("The Central Committee of China's Communist Party transmits a document from the national employment conference: 'Go a step further in doing well labour employment work'"), in *Yearbook on Labour and Personnel 1949–1987, pp. 1603–04.*

68 "Guowuyuan guanyu chengzhen feinongye geti jingji ruogan zhengcexing guiding" ("Some policy regulations of the State Council on the urban non-agricultural individual economy"), in *Documents on Reform 1978–83*, pp. 629–630.

69 Legislative Affairs Bureau, State Council (comp.), *Zhonghua renmin gongheguo fagui huibian 1982* (*Compilation of Laws and Regulations of the People's Republic of China 1982*) (Beijing: Falu chubanshe, 1986), pp. 1–42. Article 11, providing that the state "protects the lawful rights and interests of the individual economy," is on p. 8.

70 These changes were outlined in "Guowuyuan 'Guanyu chengzhen feinongye geti jingji ruogan zhengcexing guiding' de buchong guiding" ("Supplemental regulations to the State Council's 'Some policy regulations on the urban non-agricultural individual economy' "), in *Documents on Reform 1978–83*, pp. 645–46.

71 Gold, "Urban private business," p. 164.

72 "Zhonggong zhongyang guanyu jingji tizhi gaige de jueding" ("Decision by the Central Committee of the Chinese Communist Party on reform of the economic structure"), in *Handbook on Reform*, p. 12.

73 For more details on media promotion of the individual economy see Young, "Wealth but not security," pp. 126–28.

74 "Zhonghua renmin gongheguo xianfa xiuzhengan" ("Amendment to the Constitution of the People's Republic of China"), in Legislative Affairs Bureau, State Council (comp.), *Zhonghua renmin gongheguo fagui huibian 1988* (*Compilation of Laws and Regulations of the People's Republic of China 1988*) (Beijing: Falu chubanshe, 1990), p. 1.

75 "Zhonghua renmin gongheguo siying qiye zanxing tiaoli" ("Provisional Regulations of the People's Republic of China on Private Enterprises"). in *ibid*, pp. 911–921.

76 "Siying qiye laodong guanli zanxing guiding" ("Temporary regulations on labour management in private enterprises"), in *Yearbook on Labour 1988–1989*, pp. 384–86.

77 "Protection for private business," *China Daily*, 28 February 1991, p. 4.

78 See "Guojia tiaozheng siying qiye shuishou zhengce" ("The state adjusts tax policy for private enterprises"), *Renmin ribao*, 16 March 1991, p. 2; "New management rules set," *China Daily*, 23 April 1991, p. 1 and "Co-operation needed on jobs in region," *China Daily*, 1 May 1991, p. 4.

79 See, for instance, "Jimo geti shuishou liannian zengzhang" ("Tax revenues from individual [businesses] in Jimo rise for many years running"), *Renmin ribao*, 21 October 1991, p. 2 and "Geti laodongzhe xiang zaiqu juankuan sanqian wan" ("Individual labourers contribute thirty million [*yuan*] to disaster areas"), *Jingji ribao*, 25 September 1991, p. 1.

80 "Beijing encourages more people to run their own business," *China Daily, Business Weekly*, 9–15 August 1992, p. 3; "Policies Set to favour private economies." *China Daily, Shanghai Focus*, 21 June 1992, p. 3; "Guangzhou geti siying qiye shangle 'kuai chedao'" ("Guangzhou's individual and private enterprises get on 'the fast track' "), *Jingji cankao*, 25 June 1992, p. 1.

81 "Private businesses to play a bigger role," *China Daily*, 21 October 1992, p. 1.

82 Earlier, the maximum permitted yearly salary was 10,000 *yuan.* This information came via an interview in November 1992 with a manager at Beijing's *Nande* Economic Group, one of China's largest and most profitable private businesses.

83 In Shenzhen, for example, countless *geti* restaurants clearly hire upwards of ten employees. Shenzhen Labour Bureau officials admitted during interviews in November 1992 that they paid little attention to the number of employees in *geti* businesses as long as they maintained orderly operations.

84 "CPPCC gives voice to private sector of the economy," *China Daily*, 3 March 1993, p. 4.

85 *Statistical Yearbook for 1993*, pp. 22–24, 27.

86 Statistics for Beijing indicate that in 1980, retired workers, idle persons and unemployed youths made up 53.0%, 42.7% and 4.2% of the *getihu* labour force, respectively. In 1985, the relevant proportions nation-wide were 6.3%, 67.0% and 25.7% while In 1991 they were 8.0%, 56.0% and 24.0%. Data for the first two periods are from Chen Jian, "Laodong jiuye youxiao tujing" ("An effective way to increase employment") translated in Stanley Rosen (ed.), "The private economy (Part I), *Chinese Economic Studies*, Vol. 21, No. 1 (Fall 1987), p. 50 and State Administration for Industry and Commerce (SAIC) in Rosen (ed.), "The private economy (Part II)," *ibid.*, Vol. 21, No. 2 (Winter 1987–1988), p. 120. Data on 1991 was obtained in an interview with SAIC officials in September 1992.

87 See the results of a 1991 survey cited in "Job preference," *China Daily*, 21 October 1991, p. 6.

88 Beyond the impressionistic and anecdotal evidence of this trend. a survey carried out in late 1987 in Beijing found that 25% of all private ventures with hired labour were owned by people who had quit or resigned their state sector jobs or had left their former employer while officially retaining their job (through an arrangement known as *tingxin liuzhi*, stopping wages but maintaining the position). See Research Office of the Beijing People's Government and Beijing Municipal Labour Bureau, *Beijing chengzhen de siren gugong* (*Urban Privately-Hired Labour in Beijing*) (Beijing: Beijing jingji xueyuan chubanshe, 1989), p. 5.

89 See *ibid.* pp. 5–9.

90 A major nation-wide survey carried out in spring 1993 found that at least 25% of private firm owners have an above-high school education. This compares with 8.6% of state enterprise employees in industry and construction in 1990 (the only sectors and the last year for which figures are available). Of the 134 entrepreneurs surveyed, 43% had previously been employed in a state enterprise or agency, 29% had come from a collective enterprise, and 5% had retired or been unemployed. At least one-third had overseas ties. Horizon Market-Research. Inc., "Yanjian jingcao bi cangsong: 1993 dalu daibiaoxing siying qiye fazhan zhuangkuang diaocha baogao" ("Pine-like grasses among the rocks: a survey report on the development conditions of representative private enterprises on the [Chinese] mainland in 1993") (unpublished report, May 1993), pp. 5–8. The figure on state enterprise workers is from State Statistical Bureau and Ministry of Labour (comps.), *Zhongguo laodong tongji nianjian 1991* (*Statistical Yearbook on Chinese labour 1991*) (Beijing: Zhongguo laodong chubanshe, 1991), p. 51.

91 Some private firms involved in highly technological areas hire primarily college graduates, but other ventures may have certain requirements as well. One owner of a decorating company in Sichuan province, whose workers were mainly from the countryside, claimed he only hired people with a high school education because they were more capable and reliable. Interview in Chengdu in November 1992.

92 This is indicated by numerous recent surveys. See *Privately-Hired Labour in Beijing*, pp. 3, 193 and 210 and Horizon Market-Research, Inc., "Survey report on private enterprises," p. 30.

93 In 1980, the provinces of Guangdong, Shandong, Henan, Sichuan and Liaoning together accounted for 48.4% of all persons employed in *getihu.* In 1992, Guangdong, Liaoning, Heilongjiang, Anhui and Sichuan provinces together claimed 35.9% of such employment. Neimenggu, Shanxi, Shaanxi, Xizang, Gansu, Qinghai, Ningxia, Xinjiang and Yunnan provinces increased their collective share from 8.2% to 14.4% over this period. Figures for 1980 are from State Statistical Bureau (comp.), *Zhongguo laodong gongzi tongji ziliao 1978–1987*

(*Statistical Materials on Chinese Labour and Wages 1978–1987*) (Beijing: Zhongguo tongji chubanshe, 1989), p. 99. Those for 1992 are from *Statistical Yearbook on Labour 1993*, p. 411.

94 Such problems have been highlighted in numerous surveys and studies. One early example is a 1981 survey analysed in Zhang Hao, Chen Jian and Fang Kuan, "Beijing shi chengqu qingnian congshi geti jingying qingkuang de diaocha" ("Survey of conditions among youth in the individual economy in Beijing's urban districts"), in Youth Labour Research Office, Institute of Youth Research, Chinese Academy of Social Sciences (ed.), *Qingnian jiuyede tansuo yu shixian* (*Exploration and Practice of Youth Employment*) (Beijing: Shehui kexue chubanshe, 1983), pp. 257–269. See in particular pp. 267–69.

95 Continued criticism of such discrimination attests to the severity of this problem. See, for example, "Siying jingji: zhengce goujia youdai wanshan," ("Private economy: policy construction awaits perfecting"), *Jingji ribao*, 18 April 1993, p. 5. Such harassment appears endemic in reforming socialist economies. Private entrepreneurs in Russia complain of very similar treatment. See "The young take off in business," *The Moscow Times*, 18 June 1993, p. 1.

96 Such actions have frequently been justified by the official policy of "appropriate development" of the private economy. One municipal government in Hunan, for example. interpreted "appropriate development" to mean a maximum of four individual enterprises. "Shehui xuyao jiu shi shidang" ("What society needs is appropriate"). *Renmin ribao*, 29 June 1988, p. 2.

97 Many instances of such behaviour are described in "Zijude laoda" ("Posing as Big Brother"), *Renmin ribao*, 10 July 1984, p. 2.

98 China Market Survey Group, "The tough problems of 'big money'," pp. 6–7.

99 A typical example is that of a large company in Shenzhen specializing in real estate speculation. This business is nominally the progeny of two state agencies in Beijing, which in turn receive a share of the company's substantial yearly earnings. Interview with a high-level employee of the company in Shenzhen. December 1992.

100 This phenomenon was described by an economist at CASS who has extensively researched reforms in the state sector.

101. In the past, all rural workers were excluded from urban private employment data, but sources at the State Statistical Bureau and the Ministry of Labour claimed in the summer of 1993 that rural labourers employed by urban *siying qiye* are now included.

102 Interview with SAIC officials in September 1992.

103 See, for instance, Beijing Municipal Government Office, "Beijing shi geti gongshangye fazhan qingkuang de diaocha" ("Survey of the development conditions of individual industry and commerce in Beijing"), in *Survey of the Individual Economy*, p. 13 and Shanghai Municipal Administration for Industry and Commerce, "Shanghai shi geti gongshangye fazhan zhuangkuang de diaocha" ("Survey of the development conditions of individual industry and commerce in Shanghai") in *ibid.* p. 21

104 See Horizon Market-Research, Inc., "Survey report on private enterprises" p. 13. The survey found that *siying qiye* under-report their labour force by 40%.

105 See *Privately-Hired Labor in Beijing*, pp. 3, 193, 210. Another survey conducted in 1985 in Chongqing, Sichuan province, found that approximately 70% of all hired employees in *getihu* and *siying qiye* were from rural areas. Chongqing Municipal Administration for Industry and Commerce, "Chongqing shi geti gongshangye diaocha" ("Survey of Individual Industry and Commerce in Chongqing"), in *Survey of the Individual Economy*, p. 98.

106 See the notes to Table 21.3.

107 See Sheryl WuDunn, "China taking a harsh line with vendors," *New York Times*, 16 November 1989, p. A6.

108 See, for example, John McMillan and Barry Naughton, "How to reform a planned economy" (unpublished mimeo, 1991) and Kang Chen, Gary Jefferson and Inderjit Singh, "Lessons from China's economic reform," *Journal of Comparative Economics*, Vol. 16, No. 2 (1992), pp. 201–225, both cited in Wing Thye Woo, "The art of reforming centrally-planned economies: comparing China, Poland, and Russia" (paper presented at the Conference on the Transition of Centrally-Planned Economies in Pacific Asia, in San Francisco, May 1993).

Part VII

WELFARE AND STANDARD OF LIVING

22

CONSUMPTION AND LIVING STANDARDS IN CHINA

Joseph Chai

The future of the reforms in China ultimately depends on whether, and if so to what extent, reforms introduced in the recent past have improved the consumption and the standard of living of the Chinese people. It also depends on whether any such gains in the standard of living have been widely spread among the whole population. Since 1978 real per capita consumption in China has risen at an average annual rate of 7 per cent which is more than three and a half times that of the preceding 21 years. As a result, the standard of living of the average Chinese citizen in 1990 was more than double that of 1978. However, the growth of consumption and the living standards was rather uneven during the reform period. During the first phase of the reforms (1978–85) the consumption standard increased rapidly without widening existing income disparity. During the second phase (1985–90), however, improvements in consumption standards slowed significantly amidst rising inflation and growing income inequality. The question is whether the recent trend of a relatively slow rise in the standard of living and greater income disparity will continue in the 1990s. The purpose of this article is to examine the recent trends and changes in the level, structure and differentials of Chinese consumption and living standards, and to assess their prospects for the 1990s.

Measurement of a country's living standard is a hazardous undertaking as there is no commonly agreed set of criteria and in any case the criteria are constantly shifting. Measuring the Chinese living standard is even more difficult because of the problematic nature of Chinese consumption and income data[1] as well as the paucity of data on the qualitative aspects of living standards. The following analysis of trends from 1978 to 1990 considers first the quantitative and then the qualitative aspects. In view of the limited data and the lack of objective criteria for measurement of the living standard the work is exploratory in nature and the conclusions should be treated as tentative. They will need empirical confirmation when more data and objective criteria of measurement become available.

Source: The China Quarterly, No. 131 (September 1992), pp. 721–49. [Reprinted in Robert F. Ash and Y. Y. Kueh (Editors), *The Chinese Economy Under Deng Xiaoping* (Oxford: Oxford University Press, 1996), pp. 247–76.]

QUANTITATIVE ASPECTS

The quantitative aspects of consumption and living standard are usually measured in terms of per capita income and consumption. Table 22.1 presents estimates of per capita material consumption for selected years between 1957 and 1990, expressed in 1980 prices. It is worth noting that this statistical series may not accurately reflect the real consumption standard of the Chinese people. This is, first, because material consumption data are derived from the methodology of Chinese national income accounting and include only material components of personal and collective consumption,[2] and secondly, because the price deflator used to derive real consumption is derived from the Chinese linked index of "comparable prices." Table 22.1 shows that, as already mentioned, Chinese material consumption from 1978 to 1990 grew at an annual average rate of 7 per cent which is more than three and a half times that of the previous 21 years, and by 1990 the level of Chinese consumption was more than double that of 1978. However, consumption growth was rather uneven during this period. In the first phase of reforms (1978–85) it was relatively high, averaging 9 per cent, but during the second phase (1985–90) it declined to only 4 per cent, less than half the previous rate.

Table 22.1 Material consumption per capita

Year	*Yuan in 1980 prices*	*Index (1978 = 100)*
1957	141	65
1978	216	100
1979	236	109
1980	256	119
1981	273	126
1982	289	134
1983	310	144
1984	349	162
1985	398	184
1986	422	195
1987	449	208
1988	478	221
1989	475	220
1990	486	225
	Average annual growth (per cent)	
1957–78	2.0	
1978–85	9.1	
1985–90	4.1	
1978–90	7.0	

Note and Sources: Material consumption per capita in 1980 prices are estimated from material consumption per capita in current prices as given in *ZGTJNJ* 1991, pp. 42 and 79, deflated by price deflator derived from Chinese linked index (index in current prices/index in comparable prices) as given in *ZGTJNJ* 1991, pp. 43.

This trend is corroborated by data on the per capita disposable income taken from the household survey sample (see Table 22.2). Disposable income is defined as "income available" for the urban household and "net income" for the rural household. Disposable income of the worker and peasant household are deflated by the cost of living index and rural retail consumer price index, to obtain real disposable income in constant (1980) prices. The estimates of national average disposable income per capita in column 3 are a weighted average of those of worker and peasant households, with the weights being the respective shares of the non-agricultural and agricultural population in the total population. As indicated in the table, the average annual growth of per capita real disposable income in 1978–90 was 7.2 per cent which is four and a half times that achieved in 1957–78. Again, by 1990, Chinese real disposable income per capita was more than double that of 1978. But the rate of growth was also uneven. Most of the growth occurred during the first phase of the reform (1978–85) with a significant slowing-down in the second phase (1985–90).

To discover what caused Chinese per capita consumption to grow so fast during the earlier period and then slow down, its growth can be divided into the growth in the rate of consumption or the share of consumption in NMP and the growth of NMP per capita.[3] Table 22.3 presents estimates of these

Table 22.2 Per capita disposable income (yuan in 1980 prices)

Year	*Urban*	*Rural*	*Nation-wide total*
1957	294	90	129
1978	346	145	181
1979	—	170	—
1980	439	191	238
1981	447	219	261
1982	473	261	300
1983	493	298	335
1984	555	338	380
1985	558	352	394
1986	631	353	411
1987	642	363	420
1988	650	365	424
1989	629	340	401
	Average annual growth (per cent)		
1957–78			1.6
1978–90			7.2
1978–85			11.7
1985–90			1.2

Note: See text for data estimation.

Sources: *ZGTJNJ* 1983, p. 499; 1984, pp. 462 and 471; 1985, p. 551; 1990, pp. 250, 263, 289, 296 and 312; 1991, pp. 230, 243 and 269.

Table 22.3 Sources of growth of material consumption per capita

	Material consumption per capita (1980 yuan)	*NMP per capita (1980 yuan)*	*Rate of accumulation (1980 prices)*	*Rate of consumption (1980 prices)*
1978	216	337	35.9	64.1
1979	236	355	33.4	66.6
1980	256	374	31.4	68.6
1981	273	387	29.3	70.7
1982	289	412	29.8	70.2
1983	310	447	30.6	69.4
1984	349	501	30.3	69.7
1985	398	561	29.0	71.0
1986	422	594	29.0	71.0
1987	449	645	30.4	69.6
1988	478	706	32.3	67.7
1989	475	721	34.1	65.9
1990	486	745	34.8	65.2
		Average annual growth		
1978–80	8.9	5.3		3.5
1981–85	9.9	9.7		0.2
1985–90	4.1	5.8		−1.7

Note: NMP per capita in 1980 prices is estimated according to the procedure in the note to Table 1.

Sources: *ZGTJNJ* 1991, pp. 32, 33 and 79.

together with the rate of accumulation in 1980 prices. It reveals that during the initial years of the reforms (1978–80) the rapid increase of per capita consumption was due to the increase in both the rate of consumption and NMP per capita. The increase in the former was made possible by a significant fall in the rate of accumulation from 35.9 per cent to 31.4 per cent between 1978 and 1980. Between 1981 and 1985 the rate of accumulation changed very little, and hence, most of the rapid increase of per capita consumption was due to the rapid increase of NMP per capita. Finally, during the later period of the reforms in 1985–90, the rate of accumulation rose once again from 29 to 34.8 per cent. Consequently there was a drop in the rate of consumption. This, together with the slowdown of the rate of growth of NMP per capita, contributed to the slower growth of per capita consumption during this period.

QUALITATIVE ASPECTS

The level of welfare of the Chinese people is determined not only by the amount of material consumption but also by qualitative aspects of life which are hard to quantify and very often can be inferred only indirectly. These include changes in consumer satisfaction, access to health and education services, availability of social and economic security, the extent of income inequality and the degree of environmental degradation.

Consumer satisfaction

Consumer satisfaction can be significantly increased, even with a set amount of consumer goods, if means can be found to improve their allocation and distribution.[4] In the past freedom of exchange among consumers was severely limited because of widespread non-price rationing. The reforms brought about a significant reduction in the number of rationed goods and the development of a free market system which has enhanced consumers' freedom of exchange and hence enabled them to achieve a more efficient consumption pattern.

In the past the separation of consumer prices and producer prices and the lack of enterprise autonomy in output decision-making meant that producers either did not know or were not allowed to respond to consumer demand. The introduction of the two-track pricing system brought a greater alignment of producer and consumer prices which, together with the newly-gained greater autonomy in output decisions, helped producers to provide the kinds of goods demanded by consumers. There was also a marked improvement in product design, colour and quality, encouraged by increased competition among producers under marketization.

Finally, Chinese consumer satisfaction was significantly enhanced by improvements in the distribution system. Thanks to the promotion of the service sector in general, and the encouragement of private enterprises in particular, the number of establishments in the retail, catering and service trades per 10,000 population soared from 13 in 1978 to 104 in 1989.[5] This reduced the average shopping time of Chinese consumers and increased their leisure time.

Health and education

Improvement in people's longevity and knowledge depends on the ease of access to health and education services and can be indicated by life expectancy at birth and the adult literacy rate. These, together with per capita income, are considered the basic indicators for human development by the United Nations.[6] As the data in Table 22.4 show, average life expectancy increased only slowly between 1980 and 1989, from 68 to 70 years, compared with a 25-year rise between 1950 and 1975. For the adult literacy rate the figures are even worse. Illiteracy fell from 38.1 to 23.5 per cent during 1962-82, but has suffered a resurgent increase in the more recent period. A plausible explanation of the lack of improvement in health and education is the demise of the

Table 22.4 Human development indicators

	Life expectancy at birth (years)	*Adult illiteracy rate (per cent)*
1950	40[1]	—
1960	47[2]	—
1962	—	38.1[3]
1975	65[2]	—
1981	68[3]	—
1982	—	23.5[3]
1987	70[2]	26.8[3]
1989	70[4]	—

Notes and Source:
[1] Nick Eberstadt, 'Material poverty in the PRC in international perspective,' in U.S. Congress, Joint Economic Committee, *China's Economy Looks Towards the year 2000* (Washington, D.C.: U.S. Government Printing Office, 1986), Vol. I, p. 293.
[2] United Nations, *Human Development Report* (New York: Oxford University Press, 1990), pp. 45 and 134.
[3] SSB, *Zhongguo shehui tongii ziliao (Chinese Social Statistical Materials)*, 1985, pp. 28 and 137; *ZGTJNJ* 1991, p. 852.
[4] World bank, *World Development Report 1991*.

commune system, which, while extremely inefficient in production, did provide wider access to health and education services, especially for the poor and elderly. With the disappearance of communes access has been increasingly unequal because certain services which they previously provided without charge now have to be paid for by the consumer.[7]

Economic security

The well-being of an individual is also affected by the degree of economic security. This can be threatened by inflation and unemployment, both of which lead to a substantial decline in real income. Table 22.5 presents official estimates of annual changes in indexes of Chinese worker and employee cost

Table 22.5 Average annual increases in consumer prices (%)

	1957–78	*1978–90*
Worker cost of living	0.7	6.9
Rural retail prices	0.1	5.9
Free market prices	3.5	6.9

Source: *ZGTJNJ* 1991, pp. 230, 243 and 248.

of living, rural retail prices and free market prices. Such price indicators show that China had little or no open inflation before the reforms. After the introduction of market-orientation the average annual increase in prices was significantly more than that of the pre-reform period. In fact, it is generally agreed that the official price indexes tend to underestimate the true rate of inflation so it may have been even higher in recent years than is suggested by these figures. The greater price instability is a manifestation of the growing difficulties experienced by the government in achieving a balance between aggregate demand and supply under increased decentralization and marketization of the economy.[8]

With the demise of rural communes, the abandonment of guaranteed state jobs and the introduction of a contract worker system in the cities, job insecurity has increased in recent years. Enterprises under pressure to make their operations profitable have informally shed many of their former employees. As previous social aims have to some extent given way to economic considerations, the relatively large amount of disguised unemployment has also diminished and contributed to the growing number of unemployed.

Before the reforms a social security system financed by the communes in rural areas and by urban enterprises in the cities reduced the economic insecurity caused by inflation, unemployment, industrial accidents, illness, old age and so on. With the end of the communes, financial problems have caused access to social security in rural areas to diminish. In the cities, the enterprises still provide social security for tenured workers but not for unemployed migrants from rural areas or contract workers – the latter accounting for an increasing share of the urban workforce.[9] The enterprise-financed system is disintegrating but state-financed social security is still not in place.[10] Thus Chinese workers and peasants are caught in the descending part of the U-curve of economic and social security as observed in other market economies.'[11]

Income differentials

Individuals tend to judge their own level of economic well-being by the standard of living enjoyed by their neighbours. Thus, if income is distributed fairly evenly, people are less likely to feel deprived than if distribution is uneven.

The issue of whether market-oriented reforms are likely to generate increased income inequality cannot be settled by a priori reasoning. On the one hand, income inequality may rise with the re-introduction of the distribution principle "to each according to his/her contribution," as well as the deliberate attempt by government to widen income differentials in order to provide work incentives. On the other hand, the deregulation of economic activities and the reduction in barriers to the movement of production factors under the reforms should enable individuals to gain more equal access to job opportunities and capital, and so encourage specialization in accordance with the principle of comparative advantage. Under such conditions production factor returns would be expected to be much more equal, reducing income inequality. Thus, the net effects of the reforms on income distribution can only be settled empirically. The increased availability of data from China enables us to establish, with some confidence, the trend in income distribution during the reform era. As the survey of these data later in this article shows, there was a slight reduction in income inequality and in the incidence of poverty during the first phase of the reforms, but a rise in both during the second phase.

Environmental degradation

It is reasonable to expect an increase in environmental degradation under the reforms. Its commonly identified indirect causes are rapid economic growth, industrialization and urbanization. China's GDP during the reform era grew almost twice as fast as it had done previously. The annual growth rate of industrial output during 1978–90 was 1.24 times higher than that during 1957–78. Between 1957 and 1978 official data suggest that the proportion of the total population living in cities and towns rose only modestly from 15.4 to 18 per cent, whereas between 1978 and 1990 it jumped from 18 to 26 per cent (see Table 22.13, below). However, these data overestimate the pace of urbanization of China during the reform era due to a change in the definition of "cities and towns" in 1984. A more accurate measure is the share of the non-agricultural population in the total population. As indicated in Table 22.13, while this share declined during 1957–78, it increased from 18 to 21 per cent between 1978 and 1990. Since all three indicators grew much faster during the reform era compared with the earlier period environmental degradation must also have increased at a faster rate under the impact of reforms.

Another commonly identified cause of environmental degradation is inadequate specification of ownership rights. Under the contract responsibility system most resources in China, including land, have been contracted out to individuals, but they are formally still publicly owned and their transferability is normally restricted. Moreover, the responsibility and rights of the contractee over resource use are not clearly delineated, and the contracts are not long or secure enough to encourage private investment and conservation. The reforms have shifted the level of decision-making from the central to local and individual levels, which increasingly rely on price signals as the basis of their decision. Yet most of the common resources, such as air and water, either have no price or are underpriced because of the absence or underdevelopment of markets for them. Insecurity of ownership induces individuals to maximize short-term instead of long-term profit. This behaviour together with the undervaluation of most resources leads to their overuse and lack of maintenance and conservation.

Unfortunately empirical data on the stock of pollutants in air, water, and so on for recent years are patchy. Those for the pre-reform period are virtually non-existent. Hence it is impossible to form a firm judgment on these matters.

To sum up, the quantitative aspects of life in China, as measured in terms of per capita consumption and income, have made significant gains in recent years. Improvements in the qualitative aspects of life, however, have been mixed. On the one hand, consumer satisfaction has increased considerably with greater freedom of consumer choice and more efficiency in the distribution and allocation of consumer goods. On the other hand, there is evidence of growing inequality in access to education and medical care. There is also evidence of increased economic insecurity, income inequality and environmental degradation.

CHANGES IN THE PATTERN OF CONSUMPTION

Changes in the consumption pattern of rural and urban households during the 1980s are presented in Table 22.6. The data are based on the urban and rural household survey. The former covers non-agricultural households such as those of workers and other employees, and the latter covers agricultural or peasant households. "Consumption" in the surveys includes not only commodities or services purchased but also those produced by households.

As Table 22.6 shows, the consumption *structure* has changed markedly because of the rapid rise in the *level* of consumption. Between 1981 and 1990, the nominal share of basic necessities (such as staple food, clothing and fuel) in total expenditure declined for both groups of households, whereas that of non-basic items (non-staple foods, housing, daily goods and others) as well as services, increased. For urban households, the nominal share of expenditure on staple food fell by almost half from 1981 to 1990. A similar pattern is also observable for rural households. The decline in expenditure for clothing for both groups was less dramatic during the same period. The share of fuel appears to have been fairly stable for both groups.

For rural households the nominal share of expenditure on non-staple food increased by more than 30 per cent from 1981 to 1990. The rate of increase was more modest for urban households during the same period. This difference in the rate of increase appears to be related to income differential between the two groups. A similar pattern is discernible for service expenditure. Whereas the nominal share of service expenditure of rural households increased by 208 per cent between 1981 and 1990, it rose by only 39 per cent for urban households. This difference reflects the relatively high level of service consumption already enjoyed by urban households at the beginning of the reform period.

In the case of housing expenditure, a reverse pattern is observable. Deregulation and privatization of the urban housing market was advocated

Table 22.6 Changes in consumption structure (%)

	1981	*1985*		*1990*	
		Current prices	*1981 prices**	*Current prices*	*1981 prices**
Rural households					
Material expenditure	97.6	97.1	97.3	92.6	93.1
Food	59.7	57.8	55.4	54.9	51.7
Staple	32.1	26.2	24.8	18.4	18.0
Non-staple	27.6	31.5	30.6	36.5	32.3
Clothing	12.4	9.9	11.6	8.4	11.0
Housing	9.8	12.4	11.7	12.9	12.0
Fuel	5.6	5.7	6.0	4.5	4.5
Daily goods and others	10.2	11.4	12.5	11.9	14.0
Services expenditure	2.4	2.9	2.8	7.4	6.9
Total (*yuan*)	190.8	317.4	276.0	538.1	282.0
Urban households					
Material expenditure	93.4	93.3	93.5	90.8	91.3
Food	56.7	52.3	46.8	54.2	46.6
Staple	13.0	9.0	10.3	5.6	9.0
Non-staple	43.7	43.3	37.0	47.6	37.6
Clothing	14.8	14.6	17.1	13.4	17.0
Housing	1.4	1.0	1.1	2.3	2.7
Fuel	1.9	1.7	1.9	1.6	1.8
Daily goods and others	18.6	23.8	26.7	19.3	23.2
Services expenditure	6.6	6.7	6.5	9.2	8.8
Total (*yuan*)	456.8	673.2	585.5	1,278.9	650.4

Note:
* Estimated by deflating individual expenditure items in current prices by their respective consumer price indexes (rural retail consumer price index and worker cost of living index) as given in *ZGTJNJ* 1991, pp. 235–7, 239–41, 243 and 250.

Sources: *ZGTJNJ* 1991, 298, 280–1; Lin Baipeng, *Zhongguo xiaofei jieguo xue* (Beijing: Economic Science Publishing Co., 1987), pp. 106, 154; *Zhongguo nongcun jingji tongji daquan 1949–1987*, p. 563.

by Deng Xiaoping as early as 1978 and was officially sanctioned by the State Council in 1980. However, the implementation of this policy took place on a narrow experimental basis in selected cities. Due to the low-rent policy and the high price of the average housing unit, individuals had little incentive to purchase their own units. Thus, deregulation made little progress until 1988, when a Housing Reform Working Conference was called by the State Council to formulate an "implementation scheme" for the privatization of urban housing. According to this scheme, housing reform was to be extended to 80 major cities in 1988 and another 150 to 2,000 cities, as well as to 6,000 counties and townships, by 1989; by 1990 it was to be implemented by most cities and towns.[12] With accelerated deregulation of the housing market after

1988 the share of housing expenditure of urban households rose rapidly. In contrast, the share of housing expenditure of rural households rose less dramatically, housing deregulation having started much earlier in the countryside.

It is of interest to examine the consumption composition in *real* terms, since the high rate of inflation in the late 1980s might significantly change the relative prices and so distort real consumption patterns. Table 22.6 shows that consumption patterns in real terms do differ significantly from those in nominal terms. For urban households, it is interesting to note first that while in nominal terms there was an increase in the Engel coefficient between 1985 and 1990, in real terms it had declined. Thus the perverse behaviour of the Engel coefficient observed in nominal terms is apparently due to price distortions. Secondly, while the urban sector's nominal share of non-staple food expenditure increased, the real share actually declined during 1981–90. The decline is apparently due to the derationing of non-staple food, the increased purchase of these goods at higher prices on the free market and the high rate of inflation in the late 1980s. According to the 1988 urban household survey data, urban households purchased 80, 57, 60, 76, 63 and 69 per cent of their fresh vegetables, pork, beef and mutton, chicken, eggs, and fish, respectively, in free markets.[13] Thirdly, while there appears to be a decline in the share of clothing in nominal terms, its share actually increased in real terms. For rural households, the real consumption pattern also differs significantly from the nominal one. The decline of the Engel coefficient and the share of staple food in total household expenditure in real terms is more drastic, compared with nominal measures. But the reverse is true for the share of non-staple food consumption.

To study the change of response of consumer demand to changes in income, income elasticity for two time intervals, 1981–85 and 1985–90, are presented in Table 22.7.[14] As indicated, elasticities of food expenditure were less

Table 22.7 Times series elasticities of expenditures

	Rural		*Urban*	
	1981–85	*1985–90*	*1981–85*	*1985–90*
Food	0.8016	−2.2431	0.2321	0.9497
Staple	0.3038	−14.9579	−0.1077	0.1641
Non-staple	1.2813	5.9684	0.3278	1.1488
Clothing	0.8334	−1.5368	1.5868	0.9365
Housing	1.4803	2.0211	−0.0641	9.6608
Fuel	1.1996	−11.9474	0.8115	0.7090
Daily goods and others	1.5483	6.1158	2.4475	−0.3151
Services	1.3406	43.0105	0.9313	3.8490

Source: Table 22.6.

than unity for both groups of households, while those of staple food were negative and declined steadily for rural households. It is interesting that the elasticities of food of rural households became negative in the period 1985–89. One possible explanation is that Chinese peasants squeezed food consumption in order to make cash available for building new houses, acquiring consumer durables and purchasing services.[15] The elasticity for clothing also declined and remained at a low level between 1985 and 1990. Elasticities for housing and services rose significantly for both groups. For urban households the biggest jump is recorded for housing expenditure, whereas for rural households services displayed the largest increase. While elasticities for daily goods and other consumer durables for rural households increased steadily and remained high, those for urban households declined and became negative during 1985–90, indicating either that consumption of some basic durable goods had reached saturation point, or the diversion of expenditures for private housing construction and ownership.

Despite the shift in the pattern of consumption, the rank order of the major consumption categories in the urban household budget remained fairly stable during 1981–90. Food remained the largest expenditure item, absorbing just under half of the total real expenditure by 1990 (see Table 22.6). The next major category is daily goods and other consumer durables, accounting for about one-quarter. The third is clothing, taking up less than one-sixth, followed by services, housing and fuel. In future, with the abolition of state subsidies on many of these items and the deregulation of the housing market, their shares can be expected to increase substantially.

For rural households there have been more dramatic changes in consumption patterns. Food remained the largest item, accounting for half the family budget in real terms. Clothing, which was ranked second, has dropped to fourth. Second place, as in the urban household budget, has been assumed by daily goods and other consumer durables. Housing rose from fourth to third. Finally, services have come to outrank fuel as the fifth most important item. The rank order of major consumption categories in the rural family budget has thus become closer to that of the urban households.

INTERNATIONAL COMPARISONS

A comparison between the Chinese consumption pattern and that of other comparable Asian-Pacific countries helps, first, to identify whether and to what extent China has succeeded in narrowing its consumption gap with neighbouring countries in recent years, and secondly, to predict the direction of change in China's consumption pattern in the near future. At the same time, any international comparison of consumption patterns is fraught with difficulties. A major problem lies in the choice of an appropriate exchange rate. In order to compare the pattern of Chinese consumption with that of other countries at a similar stage of development it is necessary to measure

China's per capita income in U.S. dollars. But the official exchange rate of the *yuan* is a non-equilibrium rate which undervalues its real value. The use of purchasing power parity (PPP) exchange rate estimated from price comparisons on a product-by-product basis between China and the United States is also problematic, as Chinese prices may not be strictly comparable with American prices.

Another difficulty in placing the Chinese consumption structure in an international perspective is that the budget of urban households is heavily subsidized, particularly with respect to the basic and biggest expenditure items such as food, housing, medicine, fuel and other services.[16] The total value of these subsidies, together with other transfer income, accounted for about 82 per cent of the average wage packet of the urban worker in 1978.[17] The significance of subsidies in urban income and consumption has increased since then as the average subsidies appear to have grown faster than nominal wages.[18] The distortion effect of these subsidies on the urban household consumption pattern is evident from Table 22.8, which presents a modified budget of urban households, in 1981, adjusted for subsidies. Compared with the unadjusted budget, the share of food and housing expenditures is significantly higher, while those of clothing and daily goods and other consumer durables are lower. This indicates that the unadjusted urban family budget data systematically distort the significance of the individual budget items because of the effect of state subsidies.

A third difficulty in comparing China's consumption structure with those of other countries is that Chinese consumer behaviour is distorted by the effects of administered prices and quantity rationing. Chinese consumers may increase their consumption of a good simply because it is impossible to spend money on more desirable goods which are in short supply. Hence, in

Table 22.8 Urban household consumption structure adjusted for subsidies, 1981 (*yuan* per capita)

	Expenditures unadjusted	*Subsidies*	*Expenditures adjusted for subsidies*	*Unadjusted expenditure structure in %*	*Adjusted expenditure structure in %*
Material expenditure	35.56	10.93	46.49	93.40	98.84
Food	21.57	8.82	30.39	56.66	62.00
Clothing	5.63	0.02	5.65	14.79	11.53
Housing	0.59	1.84	2.43	1.55	4.97
Fuel	0.74	0.21	0.95	1.94	1.94
Daily goods and others	7.03	0.06	7.09	18.46	14.46
Service expenditure	2.51	0.02	2.53	6.59	5.16
Total	38.07	10.95	49.02	100.00	100.00

Source: Hu Jian, *Dongdan de xiaofei jieguo (Fluctuating Consumption Structure)* (Beijing: Xueyuan Publishing, Co., 1989), p. 57.

comparison to otherwise similar countries, some goods in China may be relatively over- or underconsumed.[19]

In Table 22.9 the Chinese consumption pattern during 1985-90 is compared with that of Taiwan and Japan at a comparable stage of development (Japan in 1955–60 and Taiwan in the late 1960s), measured in terms of per capita GNP based on official exchange rates. With respect to food consumption Table 22.9 indicates that the Chinese Engel coefficient during 1985–90

Table 22.9 International comparison of consumption levels: China, Taiwan and Japan

	China 1985–90	*Taiwan* 1969	*Japan* 1955–60
GNP per capita	311[1]	343[2]	349[4]
Engel coefficient	56.0[3]	43.6[2]	50.2[5]
Nutrition (per capita daily intake)			
Calories	2,628[6]	—	2,100[5]
Protein (g)	62.0[6]	—	69.7[5]
Fat and oil (g)	41.4[6]	—	22.5[5]
Meat (kg)	18.1[7]	23.8[8]	—
Fish (kg)	5.7[7]	29.0[8]	—
Housing			
m^2 per capita	14.8[9]	12.1[10]	7.28[11]
% urban home with piped water	77.4[12]	—	81.8[5]
with own toilet	39.0[12]	—	88.4[5]
Clothing[13]	121.7	—	100
Durable and semi-durable consumer goods[13]			
Daily goods	96.8	—	100
Culture and recreation goods	96.3	—	100
Service expenditure[13]	29.9	—	100
Overall total[13]	79.1	—	100

Notes and Sources:

1 *ZGTJNJ* 1991, p. 31, official estimates of GNP and exchange rate in current prices.

2 SSB, *Taiwan, Hong Kong, Singapore, South Korea and Thailand, Economic and Social Statistical Data* (Beijing, 1988), pp. 9, 36.

3 Weighted average of rural and urban household coefficient in current prices.

4 SSB, *Guomin shouru tongji ziliao hubian 1949–1985 (National Income Statistical Data Collection, 1949–1985)* (Beijing: Zhongguo tongji chubanshe, 1987) p. 429.

5 T. Mizoguchi, 'Statistical indicators defining poverty levels, using Japanese examples,' *The Philippine Economic Journal*, No. 44 (1980), pp. 99, 108, 115.

6 1984–86, FAO, *Production Yearbook* (1988), pp. 292–6.

7 *ZGTJNJ* 1991, p. 273.

8 Average for 1965–69; USDA, *Pacific Rim Agriculture and Trade Report* (August 1989), p. 42.

9 Weighted average of urban and rural households in 1990: *ZGTJNJ* 1991, p. 306.

10 1975 figure: T. Mizoguchi, 'Socioeconomic characteristics of poverty: macro and micro aspects,' *Asian Development Review*, No. 1 (1990), p. 29.

11 1958–63 figure: Mizoguchi, 'Statistical indicators defining poverty levels, using Japanese examples,' p. 115.

12 SSB, *1988 nian zhongguo chengzhen jumin jiating shouzhi tiaocha ziliao (1980 China's Urban Household Income Expenditure Survey Data)* (Beijing: Zhongguo tongji chubanshe, 1989), p. 20.

13 T. Mizoguchi *et al.*, 'A comparison of consumption level between Japan and PRC,' *Hitotsubashi Journal of Economics*, No. 30 (1989), pp. 23, 26.

was much higher than that of either Taiwan in 1969 or Japan in 1955–60. According to international standards the consumption level is considered poor when the Engel coefficient is as high as 50–59 per cent and moderately comfortable (*xiaokang*) with a coefficient of 40–50 per cent. The relatively high level of the Chinese Engel coefficient, however, should not be interpreted as an indication of a comparatively poor living standard in China, for it may have been caused by overconsumption of food under disequilibrium conditions in the consumer market.

A comparison of nutritional standards between China and Japan shows that the calorie, fat and oil daily intake was higher in China than in Japan in the late 1950s. However, the protein intake was somewhat lower. Though the level of Chinese food consumption was relatively high in relation to per capita income, the quality of diet still leaves much to be desired as plant sources supply more than half the Chinese calorie, protein and fat intake. In 1983 it was estimated that the percentage intake of these three items from animal sources was 7.8, 7.5 and 47 per cent respectively.[20] This is borne out by the relatively low per capita consumption of meat and fish. Compared with 1965–69 Taiwan, Chinese per capita consumption of meat and fish in 1985–90 was only 76 and 20 per cent respectively.

Housing conditions, on the other hand, have greatly improved in China in recent years, especially with relaxation of restrictions on housing construction in the countryside. Per capita floor space rose sharply during 1978–90 from 8.1 to 17.8 square metres per capita for rural households, and from 3.6 to 6.7 square metres per capita for urban households.[21] By 1990, average floor space for all households had reached 14.8 square metres, which was considerably higher than that of Japan in the late 1950s and even exceeded that of Taiwan in 1974. Thus, it appears that housing is a budget item that has been overconsumed in China in relation to the prevailing level of per capita income, especially in the countryside.

In spite of the increased floor space per head, the quality of housing remains relatively poor, especially in urban China. The 1988 urban household survey reveals that around 20 per cent of the dwellings were privately owned. However, the percentage of urban dwellings which had their own toilets and piped water was lower than that achieved by Japan in the late 1950s. Data on the quality of rural housing in China are not available, but there is no doubt that the percentage of dwellings with such facilities is still considerably lower in the countryside.

Clothing also seems to be considerably overconsumed in urban households in China. Table 22.9 indicates that the real consumption of total clothing in the Chinese urban households in 1985 was 1.2 times that of Japan in 1960. The real consumption of durable and semi-durable consumer goods by urban households in China was comparable to that of Japan in the late 1950s. The real services expenditure of the Chinese urban household in 1985 was much lower than that of their Japanese counterparts in the late 1950s, indicating an underconsumption due to limited supply. It approached only about 30 per cent of the Japanese level.

The overall consumption level of Chinese urban households in 1985 amounted to about 86 per cent of that of Japan in 1960. Since the rural consumption standard was only about half that of urban residents in China, whereas in Japan the consumption standard of rural households was not significantly different from that of urban households, the average consumption level of all Chinese households in 1985 must have been considerably less than 86 per cent of that of 1960 Japan.

DIFFERENTIALS AND POVERTY

Consumption and living standard differentials within a nation are primarily determined by consumption disparities within the urban and rural households, and the urban-rural consumption gap. Consumption disparity within the rural households can be inferred from rural income inequality. The Gini coefficient calculated by the State Statistical Bureau reveals that rural income inequality rose during the first phase of the reform (see Table 22.10). For the second phase, 1985–90, the officially estimated Gini coefficient is not available. No estimate of the Gini coefficient for this period from the incomplete rural income data published has been attempted here, since the calculation would require assumptions about average household size and income for each income group to be made which might significantly bias the result. However,

Table 22.10 Rural and urban income distribution: Gini coefficient

	Rural[1]	*Urban*[2]
1977	—	0.186
1978	0.2124	—
1980	0.2336	—
1981	0.2388	—
1982	0.2318	—
1983	0.2459	—
1984	0.2577	0.168
1985	0.2636	—
1989	—	0.174
1990	—	0.180

Notes and Sources:

[1] SSB, *Zhongguo nongmin shouru yanjiu (Chinese Peasant Income Studies)* (Tiayuan: Renmin chubanshe, 1987), pp. 4–7.

[2] Estimated from urban household income and expenditure survey data. *ZGTJNJ* 1990, p. 298; 1991, p. 278; *2000 nian zhongguo de renmin xiaofei (2000 China's People's Consumption)* (Beijing: Zhongguo shehui kezue chubanshe, 1987). p. 75.

since most of the rural disparity is accounted for by regional differences in the rural income distribution, the trend of rural disparity can be inferred from that of regional disparity.

Table 22.11 shows that there is a significant disparity between the

Table 22.11 Regional disparities in per capita net income of Chinese peasants, 1985 and 1990 (in *yuan*)

Provinces/ municipalities	*Agricultural population (1986)*		*Per capita net income*	
	in million	*as %*	*1985*	*1990*
Nation average	848.2	100.0	398	630
East:				
Beijing	3.9	0.5	775	1261
Tianjin	3.7	0.4	565	1069
Shanghai	4.3	0.5	806	1665
Liaoning	22.2	2.6	468	776
Shandong	68.0	8.0	408	645
Jiangsu	51.2	6.0	493	884
Zhejiang	34.1	4.0	609	1045
Fujian	22.9	2.7	397	764
Guangdong	50.0	5.9	495	952
Hebei	48.4	5.7	385	592
Central:				
Heilongjiang	19.7	2.3	398	671
Jilin	14.6	1.7	414	717
Henan	68.9	8.1	329	482
Shanxi	21.0	2.5	358	560
Anhui	44.6	5.3	397	517
Hubei	39.1	4.6	421	602
Hunan	48.9	5.8	395	546
Jiangxi	28.7	3.4	377	580
Sichuan	88.3	10.4	315	505
Shaanxi	25.0	3.0	295	460
West:				
Guangxi	34.6	4.1	303	500
Ningxia	3.3	0.4	321	534
Xizang	1.8	0.2	353	437
Xinjiang	9.3	1.1	394	623
Neimenggu	14.4	1.7	360	607
Yunnan	30.5	3.6	338	490
Guizhou	26.4	3.1	288	435
Gansu	17.5	2.1	255	399
Qinghai	2.9	0.3	343	514
Coefficient of variation, population weighted:			0.7389	0.7556

Sources: Population: PRC's Ministry of Agriculture's Department, *Zhongguo nongcun jingji tongji daquan 1949–1986 (China's Comprehensive Rural Economics Statistics 1949–86)* (Nongye chubanshe, 1989), pp. 12–13. Per capita net income: *ZGTJNJ* 1991, p. 297.

provinces in rural per capita nominal income.[22] For example, per capita income of Shanghai peasants in 1985 was more than three times that of peasants in the poorest province, Gansu. By 1990 the income gap between the two had risen to a ratio of more than four to one. The rising trend of the inter-provincial rural income inequality is also evident from the estimated population-weighted coefficient of variation which rose from 0.7389 in 1985 to 0.75563 in 1990.

Similarly, the consumption disparity amongst urban households can also be inferred from the urban income distribution. Published data, based on the urban household income and expenditure survey, are more detailed and an estimate of the Gini coefficient is therefore possible without having to rely on too many assumptions. As indicated in Table 22.10, urban income inequality declined between 1977 and 1984, but rose again between 1984 and 1990.

Trends in the rural-urban consumption disparity appear to follow the same path as urban income differentials. As the data in Table 22.12 indicate, the urban-rural real consumption gap narrowed from 2.9 to 1 in 1978 to 2.2 to 1 in 1985. This was mainly caused by the rapid growth of peasant consumption, which rose more than twice as fast as in the urban sector. Since 1985 the growth of rural real consumption has, however, slowed, whereas that of the urban household has accelerated. Thus the urban-rural consumption gap has widened again. However, as Lardy points out, the gap is anyway an underestimation since urban households receive huge subsidies which increased even after 1978.

The overall consumption disparity depends also on the percentage share of

Table 22.12 Urban and rural real personal consumption per capita (*yuan* in 1980 prices)

	Rural (1)	*Urban* (2)	*Ratio* (3) = (2)/(1)
1978	147	419	2.85
1979	158	437	2.77
1980	173	468	2.71
1981	187	508	2.72
1982	200	502	2.51
1983	218	512	2.35
1984	245	545	2.23
1985	280	592	2.11
1986	286	635	2.22
1987	298	694	2.33
1988	316	744	2.35
1989	313	723	2.31
1990	310	750	2.42

Source: *ZGTJNJ* 1991, pp. 270–71. Estimation: see note to Table 1.

the urban population or, more accurately, of the non-agricultural population since with a given urban-rural consumption gap, the shift of population from a relatively low rural consumption standard to a higher urban standard will contribute to the overall increase in consumption disparity until the time that half of the population lives in urban areas.[23] As the data in Table 22.13 show, the share of the "real" urban population, namely the non-agricultural population, did increase, but at a low rate.

Piecing together the evidence of rural and urban income inequality, the urban-rural consumption gap and the share of the real urban population, the overall consumption disparity appears to have remained relatively stable or even declined slightly in the first phase of reform, mainly due to the reduction of the urban-rural consumption gap and urban income inequality. But from 1985, with a widening urban-rural consumption gap, and increasing income inequality within the urban and rural sectors, as well as a rise in the share of the non-agricultural population, the overall consumption disparity has been rising again.

The trend in the incidence of poverty (the percentage share of rural and urban households falling below the poverty line) also follows the same pattern as overall income and consumption inequality. In 1985 the official poverty line was 200 *yuan* for the rural population, and 375 *yuan* for the urban population, regarded as reasonable approximations of the cost of a minimum basket of food and other basic needs sufficient to maintain a subsistence

Table 22.13 Urban and rural population data (%)

	Cities and towns[1]	Villages[1]	*Share of* Agricultural[2]	*Share of* Non-agricultural[2]
1957	15.4	84.6	80.7	19.3
1978	17.9	82.1	82.1	17.9
1979	19.0	81.0	81.8	18.2
1980	19.4	80.6	81.1	18.9
1981	20.2	79.8	81.8	18.2
1982	21.1	78.9	81.4	18.6
1983	21.6	78.4	81.2	18.8
1984	23.0	77.0	80.7	19.3
1985	23.7	76.3	79.5	20.5
1986	24.5	75.5	79.3	20.7
1987	25.3	74.7	79.5	20.5
1988	25.8	74.2	79.3	20.7
1989	26.2	74.0	78.9	21.1
1990	26.4	74.0	78.6	21.4

Notes and Sources:
[1] *ZGTJNJ* 1991, p. 79.
[2] Derived from agricultural and non-agricultural population total and per capita personal consumption data, *ZGTJNJ* 1991, pp. 42, 79 and 270.

existence for an average rural and urban resident. Correcting for inflation, it is possible to estimate the changes in the percentage of rural and urban households falling below the poverty line in recent years. As the data in Table 22.14 indicate, the incidence of rural poverty has been much higher than that of urban areas. During the first phase of the reform (between 1981 and 1985) both the rural and urban incidence of poverty declined. But since 1985, while urban poverty continued to fall, rural poverty rose again.

The rate of poverty can be reduced by either increased average income or reduced income disparity. A study of poverty in Japan during 1963–77 reveals that the elasticities of the poverty rate with respect to the average income and the Gini coefficient were -2.90 and 1.95 respectively.[24] Thus the rapid decline of poverty incidence in the rural sector in China during the first phase of the reform was mainly due to the rapid growth of the rural household income. In the urban sector the reduction of the poverty rate during the first phase of the reform was due to both increased income and decreased income disparity.

A closer look at the profile of the absolute poor in China reveals that most of the rural poor reside in the remote and mountainous terrain of its central and western regions. Table 22.15 shows the regional incidence of poverty measured in terms of percentage share of counties with average per capita rural income below 300 *yuan* in 1989. It indicates that the western and central regions contained the largest percentages of poor counties. The relative incidence of poverty was highest in the western region. Provinces with the highest relative incidence of poverty are Yunnan, Guizhou, Shaanxi, Gansu, Neimenggu and Guangxi. The urban poor, on the other hand, are

Table 22.14 Poverty incidence

	1981[1]	*1985*[1]	*1990*[2]
Rural			
Poverty line (*yuan*)	169	200	338
Households (%)	44.3	12.3	13.1[3]
Urban			
Poverty line (*yuan*)	314	375	572
Households (%)	11.2	9.9	3.4[4]

Notes and Sources:

1 Medium scenario estimates of the World Bank cited in S.J. Burki, 'Development strategies for poverty alleviation,' *Asian Development Review*, No. 1 (1990), p. 16.

2 Poverty line adjusted for inflation by using worker cost of living index for urban households and unweighted average of free market and rural consumer retail price index for rural households.

3 Percentage of households with a per capita annual net income below 300 *yuan* only. See *ZGTJNJ* 1991, p. 294.

4 Percentage of households with a per capita annual disposable income of 632. See *ZGTJNJ* 1991, p. 278.

Table 22.15 Regional rural poverty profile, 1989

	% Distribution of counties (1)	*% Distribution of poor counties (2)*	*Relative incidence of poverty (3) = (2)/(1)*
East:	26.1	8.1	0.31
Beijing	0.6	0	0
Tianjin	0.5	0	0
Shanghai	0.4	0	0
Liaoning	3.0	1.7	0.57
Shandong	5.2	0	0
Jiangsu	3.1	0	0
Zhejiang	3.4	0.8	0.24
Fujian	3.0	0	0
Guangdong	4.5	0	0
Hebei	6.6	5.5	0.83
Central:	42.4	42.1	0.99
Heilongjiang	3.1	1.9	0.61
Jilin	2.2	0	0
Henan	5.6	5.8	1.04
Shanxi	4.4	5.8	1.32
Anhui	3.2	2.2	0.69
Hubei	3.5	3.1	0.89
Hunan	4.3	3.9	0.91
Jiangxi	3.7	0	0
Sichuan	8.2	11.1	1.35
Shaanxi	4.2	8.3	1.98
West:	31.5	49.8	1.58
Guangxi	3.5	5.5	1.57
Ningxia	0.8	1.1	1.38
Xizang	2.9	1.4	0.48
Xinjiang	3.3	0.8	0.24
Neimenggu	3.4	5.5	1.59
Yunnan	5.0	19.1	3.82
Guizhou	3.4	10.0	2.94
Gansu	3.4	5.8	1.71
Qinghai	1.6	0.6	0.38

Source: *ZGNYNJ* 1990, p. 415.

characterized by large families, a low employment rate and a relatively large number of dependents.[25]

OUTLOOK FOR THE 1990s: PER CAPITA CONSUMPTION

Prospects for continuing improvement of living standards in the 1990s depend on an assessment of the likely development of those factors which determine the level of per capita consumption. Since this is defined as consumption fund divided by population, and the level of the consumption fund is the difference between national income and accumulation, growth of per capita consumption depends on the growth of national income, the growth of population and changes in the rate of accumulation.

The "Ten-Year Economic Programme" merely reiterates the goal of quadrupling China's 1980 national income by the year 2000 and achieving a 6 per cent growth rate of GNP in the 1990s and a "relatively comfortable" (*xiaokang*) consumption standard for Chinese consumers by the end of the century. Unfortunately, it provides very few clues on the exact level of Chinese consumption and how its pattern is expected to change as China achieves a per capita income of US$1,000. The following discussion therefore has to rely on projections made under the "2000 China" project made earlier by a group of scholars affiliated to the influential State Council's Economic, Technological and Social Development Research Centre.

According to this projection national income is expected to rise at 6.5 per cent for the 1980s and at about 7 per cent in the 1990s (see Table 22.16). The annual average growth of the population is projected at about 1.2 per cent. NMP per capita is scheduled to reach 1,144 *yuan* or US$763 (1980 prices) by the year 2000. The rate of accumulation is expected to decline from 31.5 per cent in 1980 to 29 per cent in the 1980s and 1990s. Real per capita consumption by the year 2000 is expected to be triple that of 1980. Finally, the urban–rural consumption gap is expected to narrow from 2.71 to 1 in 1980 to 1.86 to 1 in the year 2000. As Table 22.16 indicates, the projected income and consumption targets for 1990 appear to have been too conservative inasmuch as they have already been significantly overfulfilled in 1990. With regard to the projected income and consumption targets for the year 2000, the picture is mixed. The projected income target appears to be conservative, since the rate of growth required to achieve it is fairly modest compared with the actual rate of growth in recent years (1985–90). However, the projected consumption targets for 2000 appear somewhat ambitious as the required rates of growth are significantly higher than those achieved in the last few years. This over-optimistic assessment of the level of Chinese consumption in 2000 is mainly due to underestimates of population growth and the rate of accumulation. As Table 22.16 indicates, recent population growth was higher than the projected 1.2 per cent rate of increase; moreover, the rate of accumulation has not declined (as was projected) but has risen, indicating a declining investment productivity. Thus the growth of Chinese consumption in the 1990s depends critically on the future population growth rate and rate of accumulation. If the rising trend of the latter can be arrested and the income growth of the recent past can be sustained over the next decade, then China should be able to double its living standard between 1990 and 2000. If the population growth rate is brought under control and the rate of accumulation is curbed by increasing investment productivity, China's consumption standard in the year 2000 may well be more than double its 1990 level. However, China is likely to face an uphill task in controlling its population

Table 22.16 Projection of Chinese consumption levels and differential in the 1990s

	"2000 China" projection		*Reported achievement in 1990*	*(3)/(1) in %*	*Required growth rate (1900–2000) in %*	*Actual rate of growth (1985–90) in %*
	1990	*2000*				
	(1)	*(2)*	*(3)*	*(4)*	*(5)*	*(6)*
NMP growth rate (in %)	6.5[1]	7[2]	8.7[2]	134		
NMP[3]	6,923	14,271	8,513	123	5.3	7.5
Population (100 million)	11.19	12.48	11.43	102	0.9	1.5
NMO per capita[4]	619	1,144	745	120	4.4	5.8
Rate of accumulation (in %)	29	29	35	121	−1.8	3.7
Total material consumption[3]	4,915	10,132	5,559	113	6.2	5.7
Personal consumption[3]	4,292	8,714	4,612	108	6.6	5.0
Per capita material consumption[4]	439	812	486	111	5.3	4.1
Per capita personal consumption[4]	384	698	403	105	5.6	3.3
of which:						
agricultural population	315	573	310	98	6.3	2.1
non-agricultural population	684	1,066	750	110	3.6	4.9
Ratio of agricultural to non-agricultural pop.	2.17	1.86	2.42	112	−2.6	2.8

Note:
1 1980–90.
2 1990–2000.
3 100 million 1980 *yuan*.
4 1980 *yuan*.

Source: Columns 1 and 2: Medium scenario, see *2000 China's People's Consumption*, pp. 106–14: column 3: Tables 1, 3 and 12.

and the rate of accumulation growth under the existing population structure and economic system.[26]

The projected decline of the urban-rural consumption gap made by Chinese economists is also too optimistic. To reverse the widening gap of recent years, the growth of urban consumption would have to be brought into line with that of rural consumption, and the enormous subsidies provided to urban consumers would have to be reduced drastically – a move that seems politically unacceptable.

CONSUMPTION PATTERN

Changes in real consumer expenditure in different categories of consumer goods depend both on income growth, and income and price elasticities of demand. The difficulty of predicting change in Chinese consumption pattern is that the Chinese consumer market in the past was in disequilibrium. Thus, any income and price elasticities estimated solely on the basis of the observed disequilibrium prices, quantities consumed and expenditure cannot be regarded even as an approximation of actual Chinese consumer behaviour. Neither can they be used as the basis for future predictions.

Projections of future Chinese consumption patterns are numerous. One was made by the above-mentioned "China 2000" project. Another uses the Extended Linear Expenditure Systems (ELES), as presented by Lluch, Powell and Williams.[27] Both projections obtain their Chinese consumer behaviour parameters from data on the disequilibrium prices, expenditures and quantities observed in the early 1980s. The resulting projections in consequence differ markedly from the levels actually achieved.

A more promising method, suggested by Podkammer, is to resort to an international comparison.[28] The average Chinese consumer's behaviour under equilibrium can be inferred from the consumption of other countries which have enjoyed persistent equilibrium conditions in the consumer's market and which are comparable with China in terms of their level of development, climatic and cultural conditions. In the following discussion we choose Taiwan in the 1975–79 period and Japan in 1967 as our reference base for projecting Chinese consumption patterns in the late 1990s. Both Taiwan and Japan had achieved a per capita income of US$1,000 during the periods used for the comparison. Comparing the current Chinese consumption structure with that of Taiwan and Japan during the reference period, it is possible to identify meat consumption, consumer durables, urban housing and services as potential growth areas and bottlenecks.

As mentioned earlier, the current Chinese diet is still very deficient in animal calories and protein, and its per capita real consumption level is very low compared with Taiwan at the same level of development. The growth of income in the 1990s is likely to increase the demand for meat (international studies indicate that the income elasticity of demand for meat is very high).

Since the grain–meat conversion rate is also high, growth of income in the 1990s is likely to increase substantially the demand for grain. If it is assumed that the Chinese consumption of meat, eggs, fish, milk and direct grain in the year 2000 matches the levels of Taiwan during 1975–79 – namely 34.1, 6.6, 36.1, 20.2 and 153 kilograms per capita respectively – with an average conversion rate of 2.2 to 1,[29] the total requirement of grain, including seed, in the year 2000 would amount to 468 million tons per annum.[30] Grain output is projected to increase from an annual average of 404 million tons during 1985–90 to 500 million tons by the year 2000 implying an annual growth rate of 2 per cent. Allowing for a milling rate of 0.87, the availability of Chinese grain would then reach 435 million tons. Compared with the projected requirement, China would face a deficit of 33 million tons in the year 2000. Thus grain imports would have to be almost two and a half times that of 1990. Such imports would have to be even higher if the targeted rate of 2 per cent annual output growth of grain were not achieved or if the population growth were to exceed the targeted 1.2 per cent growth rate during the 1990s.

Apart from meat, another rapidly-growing category of consumption is likely to be "new" consumer durables such as refrigerators, washing machines, air conditioners, vacuum cleaners and motor cars. In general, growth of demand for these items is inversely related to their current coverage rate. As Table 22.17 indicates, the coverage rate of these items in China in 1989, with the exception of television sets, was significantly lower than that of Japan in 1964. Thus, pending the increased availability of piped water and electricity, the demand for washing machines, refrigerators, vacuum cleaners and even air conditioners is likely to soar. However, to catch up with the coverage rate of 1967 Japan by the year 2000, starting from China's low base level and given its enormous population, would require an enormous expansion in the output of these goods. Such a high rate of output growth is likely to be severely constrained by scarce investment resources and foreign exchange constraints.

Urban housing is another potential area of very fast growth. Though rural housing conditions have improved greatly, urban housing conditions still remain relatively poor and basic. The average living space available per person in the urban areas was only 6.7 square metres in 1990 – well below the minimum housing norm of 8 square metres per person. Moreover, the goal of matching the number of housing units with the number of households so that each household has a dwelling place of it's own has not yet been achieved. Many households still live communally, With the lifting of the rural–urban migration ban and the surge in the number of newly-weds, the number of households looking for self-contained units is likely to soar rapidly. At the same time, as income grows, the demand for more living space will also increase. There is little doubt that the Chinese construction industry is capable of meeting this challenge in the 1990s. But since housing construction is

Table 22.17 Comparison of coverage rate of consumer durables (per 100 households), China and Japan

	China[1]	*Japan*[2]	
	1990	*1964*	*1967*
Television set	74	90.3	96.4
Washing machine	38	61.0	84.8
Refrigerator	12	38.0	77.6
Motor car	negl.	—	13.1
Air conditioner	negl.	—	3.9
Vacuum cleaner	negl.	27.0	53.8

Notes and Sources:
1 *ZGTJNJ* 1991, p. 274.
2 *2000 China's People Consumption*, p. 135.

relatively capital intensive and most housing construction so far has been financed by the state, a major question is whether the government will be prepared to tolerate an increased share of these so-called "non-productive" investments in its annual investment budget. If not, the government's policy response is likely to be either to restrain urban housing demand (through price increases or a slowing down in income growth), or to step up the pace of housing reforms and encourage individuals to invest in co-operative and private housing.

Finally, the service sector is a consumer area likely to experience a major expansion in the 1990s. The point has already been made that services are currently "underconsumed" because of their limited supply, especially in rural areas, and a significant service consumption gap exists between China and Japan at a comparable level of development. The income elasticity of demand for services is very high, especially for transport and communications (which averaged 2.7 to 3.2 and 1.4 to 1.7 for the non-agricultural and agricultural household respectively in Japan during 1960 to 1965).[31] As Japan approached and exceeded the threshold of US$1,000 per capita during the 1965–70 period, the share of service expenditures reached almost one-quarter of the family budget for both non-agricultural and agricultural households. In contrast, services made up less than 10 per cent of the Chinese urban and rural family budget in 1990. Some services, such as retail trade, catering, repairs and personal services, are highly labour intensive, and are therefore unlikely to face severe resource constraints. According to the "Ten-Year Economic Programme" the share of services in China's GNP is planned to increase from the current one-quarter to around one-third by the year 2000. Other services, however, such as transport, health and education are relatively capital-intensive and are likely to face severe resource constraints. To fill the gap between the growing capital demand of the service sector and the meagre supply of state capital, it is again likely that the government will have to increase private activity significantly in these areas.

SUMMARY

Since 1978 real per capita material consumption in China has risen at an average annual rate of 7 per cent and more than doubled the standard of living of the average citizen. Nevertheless, China has made only limited progress in improving the qualitativc aspects of life. While consumer satisfaction has significantly increased, thanks to much greater freedom of consumer choice, as welt as improved distribution and allocation of consumer goods and services, the welfare of the average citizen is still adversely affected by widening income disparity, a rising rate of rural poverty, diminishing economic security, increased environmental degradation and unequal access to education and medical care.

During a decade of reforms and under the impact of the open door strategy, the quality of the structure of Chinese consumption also improved markedly. The shares of most of the basic necessities, such as staple food, clothing and fuel, in total household expenditures were significantly reduced, whereas those of mostly non-basic goods, such as non-staple food, housing, consumer durables and services, rose. Despite these changes, Chinese real consumption level has not yet reached the level of 'moderate comfort" (*xiaokang*) and its gaps with the neighbouring Asian-Pacific countries at comparable stages of development have still not been bridgcd. The Engel coefficient remains relatively high and the percentage share of animal sources in daily Chinese nutrient intake, as well as the per capita consumption of services, are still rather low.

Growth of per capita consumption slowed significantly in the second phase of the reforms (1985–90) and was less than half of that achieved in the first phase. This was due to a slowdown of NMP growth, accompanied by a rising rate of accumulation. Thanks to the high rate of inflation even real per capita disposable income stagnated during these years.

Looking ahead in the 1990s, the prospect of accelerating improvements in Chinese living standards depends on the overall economic growth, the growth of population, the rate of accumulation and the continuation of the market-oriented reforms. If population growth is brought under control and the rate of accumulation is curbed, and barring political instability which might result from the leadership succession crisis and the impact of recent developments in the Soviet Union, China's real consumption standard by the year 2000 may well more than double its 1990 level. However, income disparity is expected to increase as well. Non-staple foods, especially meat, the "new" consumer durables, urban housing and services are likely to face the fastest-growing demand. Growth in this sector, however, is likely to be increasingly limited by investment and foreign exchange constraints. To ease the resource constraint, the Chinese government is likely either to restrain consumer demand by way of price increases or a slowdown of income growth or significantly to enlarge private sector participation in the production of these goods and services.

NOTES

1 See Nicholas R. Lardy, "Consumption and living standards in China, 1978–83," in *The China Quarterly*, No.100 (December 1984), pp. 849–65.

2 *2000 nian Zhongguo de renmin xiaofei* (*2000 China's People Consumption*) (Beijing: Zhongguo shehui kexue chubanshe, 1988), p. 108.

3 Since

$$\frac{C}{P} = \frac{C}{Y} \times \frac{Y}{P}$$

where C stands for consumption, Y, national income, NMP, net material product and P, population, hence

$$\frac{\mathring{C}}{P} = \frac{\mathring{C}}{Y} + \frac{\mathring{Y}}{P}$$

4 F. L. Pryor, *A Guidebook to the Comparative Study of Economic Systems* (London: Prentice Hall, 1985), pp. 56, 58.

5 *ZGTJNJ* 1991, p. 269.

6 United Nations, *Human Development Report* (New York: Oxford University Press, 1990), p. 13. The author is grateful to D. Doessel for drawing his attention to this reference.

7 Deborah Davis, "Chinese social welfare policies: policies and outcomes," *The China Quarterly*, No. 119 (September 1989), pp. 577–97.

8 D. H. Perkins, "Reforming China's economic systems," *Journal of Economic Literature* (June 1988), pp. 624–5.

9 S. J. Burki, "Development strategies for poverty alleviation," *Asian Development Review*, No. 1 (1990), p. 17.

10 Wang Zhongmin, "Wo guo manzu jiben xuqiu de zhidu xuanze" ("The choice of basic needs satisfaction system in our country") *Jingji yanjiu ziliao*, No. 3 (1989), pp. 1–18.

11 C. A. Tisdell, *Economic Development in the Context of China: Policy Issues* (London: Macmillan, forthcoming).

12 "Zhufang zhidu gaige shizai bixing" ("Housing reform is inevitable"), *Jingli yanjiu ziliao*, No. 16 (1988), pp. 7–9.

13 *China's Urban Household Income and Expenditure Survey Data, 1988* (Beijing: Zhongguo tongji chubanshe, 1989), p. 21.

14 Income elasticity estimates are based on Engel function

$$e_i/p_i = A(E/p)^a (P_i/p)^b$$

where e_i and E stands for ith expenditure items and total expenditures per capita respectively, and p_i and P are the corresponding price deflators. Since b is relatively small when e_i is defined as a broad category in Table 22.6, income elasticity between year t and t-1 can be directly estimated as

$$a = \left[\log e_{i(t)} - \log e_{i(t-1)}\right] \Big/ \left[\log E_{(t)} - \log E_{(t-1)}\right].$$

See T. Mizoguchi, "Statistical indicators defining poverty levels using Japanese examples," *The Philippine Economic Journal*, No. 2 (1980), p. 101.

15 Y. Y. Kueh, "Food consumption and peasant incomes in the post-Mao era," *The China Quarterly*, No. 116 (December 1988), pp. 634–70 at p. 652.

16 Lardy, "Consumption and living standards," pp. 853–6.

17 Yang Shengmin, *Zhongguo xiaofei moshi de xuanze* (*Choice of Chinese-style Consumption Model*) (Beijing: Zhongguo shehui kezue chubanshe, 1989), p. 157.

18 Lardy, "Consumption and living standards," pp. 862–3; *ZGTJNJ* 1990, pp. 113 and 815.

19 L. Podkammer, "Estimates of disequilibria in Poland's consumer markets, 1965–1978." *The Review of Economics and Statistics*, 1982, pp. 423–31.

20 Yang Shengmin, *Choice of Chinese-style Consumption Model*, p. 224.

21 *ZGTJNJ* 1990, p. 324.

22 Nominal instead of real per capita income is considered here because of the unavailability of price indexes for most of the poorest provinces (Yunnan, Guizhou, Gansu and Qinghai).

23 Perkins, "Reforming China's economic systems," p. 639.

24 D.K. Nanto, "Poverty incidence in Japan," *The Philippine Economic Journal*, No. 2 (1980), p. 153.

25 *Urban Household Income and Expenditure Survey Data*, p. 23.

26 See the assessment of China's population growth and accumulation rate in the articles by Robert Ash and K. C. Yeh in this issue.

27 See Lin Baipeng *et al., Zhongguo xiaofei jiegouxue* (*Studies of Chinese Consumption Structure*) (Beijing: Jingji kexue chubanshe, 1987), and C. Lluch *et al., Patterns in Household Demand and Saving* (New York: Oxford University Press, 1977).

28 Podkammer, "Estimates of disequilibrium." p. 425.

29 This conversion rate is derived from *2000 China's People's Consumption*, p. 223.

30 The seed rate used to derive the demand for seed is taken from F.W. Crook, "China's grain production to the year 2000," USDA. *China: Agriculture and Trade Report*, June 1988, p. 31.

31 For the prospects of achieving the planned target of food grain production in 2000 see the article by Robert Ash in this issue.

23

SOCIAL SECURITY FOR STATE-SECTOR WORKERS IN THE PEOPLE'S REPUBLIC OF CHINA

The Reform Decade and Beyond

Lillian Liu

I SUMMARY

This paper deals only with social security for workers in the urban sector. Social security for the state work force, primarily income security programs for state enterprises, faces unprecedented challenges caused by a decade of policy changes and experiments in social security and enterprise and labor force reforms. Serious problems in funding and administering these programs have surfaced. Social security expenditures are rising rapidly. There are also signs of widespread mismanagement and discrepancies between enterprise implementation and local and central government guidelines, and between local government guidelines and central government regulations. Recent developments suggest that, while the central government is poised to correct some of these problems, some broad policy issues remain: Can China afford the high price of social security for state-sector workers as its population ages? How will Chinese leaders balance their inclination to placate state-sector workers with social security benefits against the need to control these costs?

II INTRODUCTION

In the 1980s the reformist government in the People's Republic of China (PRC) seems to have pursued a bifurcated social welfare policy for the country's rural and urban populations. Government reforms have apparently taken the social safety net from under the rural population while, at the same time, further enriched statesector workers and retirees in urban areas. By decade's end, critics both in China and in the West have pointed to the gross inequity in social welfare treatment between the rural and urban populations. They

Source: US Congress, Joint Economic Committee, *China's Economic Dilemmas in the 1990s: The Problems of Reforms, Modernization, and Interdependence* (Washington, D.C.: US Government Printing Office, 1991), Vol. 1, pp. 270–89.

have especially noted the large sums provided for the welfare of the comparatively small group of state-sector workers and retirees.[1] The "mini-welfare state" (*xiao shehui*) in state work units (*danwei*) seems to be alive and well; state employees therefore are far from being weaned from the "iron rice bowl" that is considered by many reformers as a systemic drag on economic efficiency.[2]

Of the employee welfare expenditures (that is, nonwage compensation), the government-regulated social security programs averaged 72.5 percent during 1978–88.[3] Moreover, in late 1989 and early 1990, as China's economy suffered from the government's austerity program of tightened credits and investment, social security programs for the urban work force have become stabilizing wands the government can wield amidst widespread discontent. Yet all is not well in the freely spending social security programs in the state sector.

III PRE-1978 SOCIAL SECURITY PROGRAMS

A General description

In 1978, on the eve of the post-Mao reforms, formal income security programs for the urban labor force were limited primarily to those employed in the state sector. The state-sector workers, almost 75 million strong, constituted 78 percent of urban workers, albeit only 19 percent of the country's total civilian labor force. They represented two groups: about 80 percent of them worked in state-owned enterprises, and the remainder served in the civil service system that included government and party organizations (*jiguan*) and cultural, scientific, and educational institutions (*siye*).[4] These two groups were protected by two formal social security systems providing extensive cash and in-kind benefits, as stipulated by two sets of regulations for nationwide application. First, the 1951 Interim Labor Insurance Regulations (as amended in 1953 and 1958, with subsequent instructions for implementation) detailed provisions for those working in state-owned enterprises. Second, a separate set of regulations provided comparable but somewhat more extensive benefits to those employed in the civil service system.[5]

The income security programs for those in state enterprises or civil service included: retirement pay of at least 60 percent of an individual's last month's standard wage, paid sick leave (up to 6 months per year) and maternity leave at 90 to 100 percent of pay after 6 years' service, and free medical care for employees and pensioners (50 percent of the cost for their dependents). In addition, these programs offered benefits and grants for workers and dependents in case of long-term disability (work or nonwork related), and for dependents upon the death of the worker or pensioner.[6] Employees did not contribute to the funding of the program, and their continuing eligibility was contingent on their employment at the work unit, which was guaranteed regardless of performance so long as they adhered to the "correct" political orientation. Finally, benefit payments were guaranteed by the state budget for all state work units. In the case of state enterprises, benefit expenditures were thus ensured, regardless of an enterprise's financial solvency.

B Incompatibility with market-oriented economy

Social security programs thus constituted part of a large overall package of nonwage compensation items that characterized the "iron rice bowl" for state-sector employees, a package that also included low-cost housing and extensive food and nonfood allowances. However, these very benefits that seemed to have worked well under a centrally planned economy designed to reward its workers in the industrial sector and to complement a wage policy of ensuring job security and equal compensation have been deemed by reformers as antithetical to "market-oriented socialism." Such programs, it is argued, have tended to foster workers' dependence on the enterprise and the state for their well-being without demanding responsibility in return.

Under pre-1978 programs, state-sector employees were tied to their respective work units, which administered all aspects of the social security programs, from determination of eligibility to benefit payments.[7] This highly decentralized administration, in the absence of an established mechanism for portability of eligibility and benefits, discouraged labor mobility across enterprises, industries or sectors—a precondition to an open economy. To reformers, pre-1978 social security programs were also seen as inadequate for preparing workers to face the brave new world of a market-oriented economy. There were no formal provisions for adjusting benefit payments to price changes, and no unemployment insurance. The special privilege of benefits awarded to only state employees were regarded as a disincentive for workers to seek employment outside the state sector, thus indirectly hindering the development of collective and private enterprises.[8]

The move toward an open economy would by definition entail a contracting state sector and expanding collective and private sectors. The so-called "big" urban collective enterprises (or *de facto* state enterprises) had adopted provisions equivalent to those for state enterprise workers. In addition, some smaller collectives offered modest retirement plans, their finances permitting. For lack of government backing, collective plans were regarded as unstable sources for income maintenance.[9] There was no income security protection whatsoever for workers in the then negligible private sector.

IV MAJOR SOCIAL SECURITY POLICY INITIATIVES, 1978–1989

Despite the reformers' concerns, the social security programs established in the early 1950s are still operative today. The reformist government has kept most of the program regulations intact, making changes in three respects only. First, it improved many of the retirement benefits, including making ad hoc adjustments to pension benefits to offset price changes. Second, in 1986 it set up a special contract workers' retirement pension system for state employees hired under a newly created labor contract system. Finally, it introduced unemployment insurance for state enterprise workers, also in 1986. All three steps reflected the government's efforts to prepare the state-sector labor force for the transition to a market-oriented economy.

A Improvements to existing social security programs

Most of the improvements to the existing social security programs have related to retirement pensions. They were designed to retire older workers and help make room for unemployed youths. For example, the 1978 amendments to the retirement regulations and subsequent instructions in the early 1980s (1) enforced, for the first time, the statutory mandatory retirement age of 60 for men and 55 for women (age 50 for female blue-collar workers); (2) allowed retirement 10 years sooner if poor health was a factor; (3) relaxed minimum qualifying conditions for retirement (for example, the continuous service requirement was reduced from 20 to 10 years); (4) raised pension benefits; (5) promised the hiring of retired workers' unemployed offspring; and (6) offered, to middle- and upper-ranking Communist party and technical cadres, a special preferred pension benefit (*lixiujin*)—at full rate of pre-retirement pay plus all the perquisites associated with their position. Since 1985 the government has approved payments by enterprises of periodic ad hoc subsidies to retirement pensions to compensate for inflation. Concurrent with wage increases for state-sector employees in late 1989, benefits for retirees and the disabled were adjusted upward as well.[10]

B Social security for contract workers

The State Council's 1986 Interim Regulations for Implementation of the Labor Contract System by State-Owned Enterprises support labor force reform by putting new state-sector employees on fixed-term employment contracts.[11] Workers thus employed would have their contracts renewed if they performed satisfactorily; they do not have the protection of life-long employment as permanent workers do. It is expected that the life-tenure system will, over time, phase out of practice as enterprises will be populated by a growing number of contract workers replacing the aging permanent workers.

The 1986 regulations offer workers employed under the contract system a package of retirement pensions, medical care, and other social security benefits comparable to that for permanent workers. There are two major differences in the types of plans offered, however. First, contract workers must help finance their retirement pensions (at 3 percent of their wages, while the enterprise contributes 15 percent toward the buildup of a special retirement fund). Second, instead of individual enterprises, local govemments—specifically, newly created social insurance agencies (SIAs) under city or county labor bureaus—are charged with the administration and fund management of these programs. Presumably, as workers under labor contract gradually outnumber permanent workers in the state sector, the predominant retirement pension will be one funded with worker-employer contributions together with state subsidies, and will be administered by local governments.

C Unemployment insurance for redundant state enterprise employees

As economic reforms continued in the 1980s, the government anticipated the need to provide income security for redundant state enterprise employees. These include workers whose employment contracts expire, employees in bankrupt or near-bankrupt enterprises, and workers who are laid off from state enterprises. The 1986 Interim Regulations for State-Owned Enterprise Workers' Waiting-for-Employment Insurance provide compensation for temporary unemployment to these individuals. Unemployment benefits include medical care as well as 65–70 percent of workers' basic wage for 12 to 24 months, depending on the length of service before unemployment. These programs are financed by the employer, who contributes 1 percent of the standard wage bill, and by local government subsidies. Employees do not contribute.[12]

Having decided to rely on the pre-reform state institutions and enterprises to carry out modernization initiatives, the reformist government seems intent on protecting the privileges of their employees by keeping the pre-1978 social security programs intact and by improving benefits for retirees and workers. On the one hand, the post-1978 social security provisions have thus further enhanced the image of the state work unit as a "mini-welfare state." On the other hand, they represent the government's attempts to remold social security provisions for transition to a new economic order. Provisions have been made to prepare current state employees for contingencies of reforms such as inflation and unemployment. A retirement program requiring contributions from employees under the contract system has been introduced to gradually phase out the noncontributory program for permanent workers.

V PROGRAM IMPLEMENTATION AT THE LOCAL GOVERNMENT AND ENTERPRISE LEVELS

More important than central government policies to social security developments in the 1980s were the practices of city and county governments and of enterprises where central policies and programs were implemented and "experiments" carried out. The Ministry of Labor, which has the responsibility for policy development and oversight of social security programs, has no local offices to implement or enforce compliance of its regulations by individual enterprises. Labor bureaus at provincial, city, and county levels are subordinate bodies of their respective governments, and only *indirectly* subordinate to the labor ministry in Beijing.

Throughout the 1980s the central government allowed local governments and individual enterprises to conduct "experiments" in social security as they adjusted to changing conditions induced by enterprise and labor force reforms. In effect, social security programs as stipulated by the central government could best be regarded as the established "national norm" from which local authorities can and still do deviate for their own purposes. The Ministry of Labor appeared far more effective in promoting particular "experiments" deemed constructive to social security developments than in terminating practices that are contrary to its policies.

This decentralized approach may have been necessary in the absence of institutional control from the Ministry of Labor over local government and enterprise labor officials. It was also in keeping with the reformist government's overall policy of loosening central controls. By the decade's end, it has become apparent that certain earlier improvisations at the enterprise and local government levels have evolved into agendas with broad regional and even nationwide implications. Many, however, remained local and isolated practices with or without central government blessings.

A Retirement pensions and city/county social insurance agencies (SIAS)

1 *Permanent workers*

A good example of how enterprise and local government experiments evolved out of pressures from labor force and enterprise reforms and became adopted by the central government as its policy agenda is the resource pooling for retirement pensions for state enterprise permanent workers.

(a) Rapid rise in retirees adds to administrative and financial burdens of enterprises

In addition to improvements in retirement benefits introduced by the central government, three developments in the 1980s contributed to mass retirement by permanent workers who were middle-aged and older. First, many provincial, city, and county governments took advantage of loosened central control and further improved benefits for retirees under their respective jurisdictions. According to one analyst, by 1988 retirement benefits for workers with 20 years' service ranged from 80–95 percent of the pre-retirement basic wage rather than the 75 percent stipulated under the 1978 retirement regulations.[13] Second, since 1978, the increased opportunity for pensioners to earn extra income by working in a "second employment" has made the option of early retirement more attractive. Wage-earning pensioners continue to receive full retirement benefits, complete with free medical care.[14] Third, starting in 1986, a central government initiative to "optimize labor organization" (*yiuhua laodong zhuhe*) by urging enterprises to reduce surplus and unproductive workers has also led to early retirement of middle-aged and older workers.

Some enterprises, taking advantage of their prerogative to administer social security programs, have relaxed the "poor health" or "total disability" requirements so that employees may retire 10 years sooner than the statutory retirement age.[15] All told, the number of pensioned retirees from the state sector increased from 2.8 million in 1978 to 15.4 million in 1988. Expenditures for pensioners—including retirement pensions, health care, and various subsidies—rose from 1.63 billion yuan to 25.7 billion yuan in the interim.[16]

The vast number of retirees has placed unprecedented administrative and financial demands on enterprises. In older industries, where the number of retired workers makes up a large proportion of or even outstrips the number of active workers, the administrative burden of processing claims and paying benefits places extra demands on active employees' time and productive energy. Moreover, the large and escalating retirement expenses have precluded any prospect of profits and bonuses—a disincentive for active employees to work hard, therefore contrary to the overall objective of improving worker productivity.[17]

(b) Resource pooling and the role of city/county governments

The intense pressure on enterprises with an inordinately heavy financial burden for retirement pensions has prompted them to propose the pooling of retirement funds. Resource pooling, or unified financing (*tongchou*), began in 1984 as "experiments" in isolated cities and counties when hard-pressed enterprises sought assistance from local labor bureaus to help pay pension benefits to their retirees. By year-end 1988, this practice had expanded to 2,141 cities and counties (out of 2,821, total), and 49 prefectures (out of 334). Local governments have had to overcome the resistance of enterprises with a relatively young work force to take part in the pool, often reimbursing them through tax write-offs. As a result of negotiations involving local labor and finance authorities, and considerable promotion efforts by the Ministry of Labor, these city and county governments have adopted compulsory resource pooling for retirement insurance among enterprises across industry lines.[18]

The local labor bureaus have set up subordinate SIAs (the same agencies administering contract workers' pension programs) to take on all the responsibilities involved in carrying out pension pooling for the retirement program for permanent workers—for example, making certain that enterprises keep accurate accounts of their respective total wage bills (the base for computing enterprise contributions to the pool), lists of retirees, and benefit payments due. These agencies must also verify and transact the amount each enterprise owes to the pooled fund or vice versa.[19]

Having begun as an improvisation to pay benefits for enterprises overburdened with a large number of retirees, pension pooling has led to two potentially significant developments that have gone beyond its original purpose. First, the city and county governments have set uniform contribution rates and benefit levels for all participating enterprises under their respective jurisdictions. Furthermore, for the first time, an enterprise's management of its retirement pension program became subject to local government supervision. One report indicates that the trend is heading toward not only expanding the geographic base of pension pooling, but also transferring a part of retirement program administration to local governments. By the end of 1988 one province (Fujian) had begun region-wide pooling in retirement funds. In addition, SIAs in 235 cities and counties (or 11 percent of those practicing resource pooling) assumed the direct responsibility for paying benefits to pensioners.[20]

Nevertheless, the risk sharing is still limited to individual cities and counties, with the exception of Fujian Province. Cities and counties have made their own arrangements with local enterprises, and they have set their own contribution rates and benefit levels, Also, for most city/county governments the role of SIAs at present is largely limited to monitoring pension pooling; the eventual takeover of the administrative responsibilities involving millions of workers remains in the distant future, With enterprises operating at losses or at reduced capacity, or even lying idle, as a result of the government's austerity program that started in September 1988, these agencies have had difficulty in ensuring that participating enterprises make timely payments to the pool, and that there are adequate funds to pay enterprises which stand to benefit from the pool. Under pay-as-you-go financing, SIAs still have to protect the limited reserves (which amount to only 1.9 months of benefit outgo at year-end 1988, nationwide) from erosion in value and from misappropriation. In cases of shortfalls, city/county governments presumably provide subsidies.[21]

2 *Contract workers*

The SIAs monitoring pension pooling for permanent workers are not only responsible for the fund management but also the administration of retirement pensions for contract workers. Because contract workers are comparatively young (typically under age 35) and are years away from retirement, these agencies' primary task at present is the collection of retirement contributions from enterprises, and the registration of contract workers in the retirement program. They have not yet begun to process claims or distribute benefits. At year-end 1988, workers under labor contract exceeded 10 million; only 6.5 million were registered to contribute to the program a year later, however.[22] Protection of these pension funds from erosion in value and from mismanagement is especially important because they are established as a partially funded program. Contributions collected are deposited in special accounts to pay contract workers for benefits due in the future.

B Unemployment insurance and city/county labor service companies

The implementation of unemployment insurance rests with city/county labor service companies (LSCs). These companies were established by city and county labor bureaus as early as 1979. They began by providing job referrals, conducting occupational training, and creating jobs by investing in and setting up collectives for hiring some of the new entrants (averaging about 4.7 million per year during the 1980s) to the urban labor market as a whole. Their responsibilities have expanded since 1986 to encompass the administration of unemployment insurance for dismissed state enterprise employees, including the collection and management of the unemployment insurance fund and payments to beneficiaries. Benefit levels and implementing procedures are subject to specific provisions determined by provincial, city and county governments based on the national norm stipulated in the 1986 Interim Regulations.[23] In some locales, these companies set up branch and subbranch offices in districts (*qu*) and at the street and resident committee level to help register the unemployed, process claims, and make payments to beneficiaries.

By 1989 there were over 3,000 local government LSCs nation-wide. With the majority of their services centering on job training and placement, information is scarce on how well these LSCs have been administering unemployment insurance benefits. National totals are not readily available for the number of state employees who have become unemployed since the 1986 regulations took effect, for those who have since been registered on unemployment rolls, or for those who actually have been receiving benefits. It is believed that, of the average 2.8 million unemployed in the course of 3 years from 1986 to 1988, former state enterprise employees constituted only a small minority. Generally speaking, many enterprises have been reluctant to lay off workers—partly due to lingering commitment to full employment, partly because of the government's belief that keeping workers tied to enterprises can better ease workers' resentment. In late 1989 and early 1990, when, reportedly more than 6,000 enterprises operated at a loss and two-thirds of urban factories were either closed or operating below capacity, many kept their workers on payroll with reduced wages (by 30 to 40 percent), instead of placing them on unemployment rolls.[24]

There are three sources of funding for LSCs: local government appropriations, income generated from affiliated collective enterprises, and contributions to the unemployment insurance fund from enterprises and local governments. Their diverse activities and their major focus on providing jobs for new entrants to the labor force make it difficult to determine whether LSCs have set aside a certain portion of their income for benefit payments to laid-off state enterprise employees. With the central government's rectification campaign in full swing in late 1989, many LSCs have been criticized for laxity in accounting, for widespread misuse and abuse of funds, and for practices such as placing jobs for those with connections rather than ability. Besides, many LSCs and their affiliated collectives have been established as profit-making enterprises with rather unstable existence.[25]

C Medical care and other social security programs

Besides retirement pensions and unemployment insurance, the central government issued no major policy initiatives in social security throughout the reform decade, except for minor improvements.[26] Whereas retirement pension and unemployment insurance programs have had the benefit of local government agencies (SIAs and LSCs, respectively) in monitoring the funding and, in some cases, in taking over the administration of these programs, this is not the case for remainder of the social security programs—such as medical care, work-injury compensation, and cash benefits for sickness and maternity leave. For enterprises that have adopted the enterprise contract responsibility system and are accountable for their own profits and losses, the funding and administration of these social security programs depends entirely on enterprise management. The status of these programs, therefore, has become far more fluid, or unstable, than retirement and unemployment programs.

Other than retirement pensions, the medical care program (whether or not work-related) has been the most costly and problematic. The total of medical care costs for state-sector employees and retirees has constituted a large, if not always the largest, proportion of social security expenditures overall. Medical care costs rose from 2.73 billion yuan in 1978 to 15.24 billion yuan in 1988, and, respectively, constituted 54.6 percent and 40.0 percent of total social security costs. The 1978 per capita expenditure on medical care for employees and retirees—35.3 yuan, or 66.5 yuan when adjusted to the 1988 price level by the urban consumer price index—almost doubled to 132.3 yuan in 1988.[27]

Attempts to control the rapid increase in health care expenses have met limited success, in part because enterprises have no control over health practitioners and/or hospital administrators who are prone to overcharges, waste and abuses (often in collusion with state employees and retirees requesting free medicines for themselves and their families, for example).[28] Some cost-conscious factory managers have introduced various measures (or "experiments") to control health expenditures. The most common approaches adopted, for example, have been to impose co-payments from beneficiaries, or to pay each employee a pre-determined sum per month for medical expenses regardless of actual costs of medical treatments. This latter policy has become especially popular because of its effectiveness in controlling cost and its simplicity in administration. It nevertheless has created hardship for employees and their family members whose treatment for illnesses far exceeds the alloted sum.[29]

The medical care costs cited above represent only the accountable totals of health-related expenditure in social security; paid wages for sick leave, maternity leave, or absence due to work injuries are computed as part of wage totals and not available for inclusion as social security expenditures. Expenses of this type can be substantial, given reports of the widespread practice among workers, who were generally underemployed, taking extended sick leave (available for 6 months per year at full pay after working in the state sector for 8 years) to engage in private businesses or consultative ventures outside the state sector. In some cases, enterprise management has awarded underemployed workers extended leave for as long as 5 years at full or reduced pay as it attempts to "optimize labor organization" or "eliminate" or "digest" (*xiaohua*) surplus and nonproductive workers.[30]

Another problematic aspect in the largely unsupervised enterprise administration of all social security programs is the arbitrary and erratic approach to processing claims. The determination of eligibility and benefit amounts was not always carried out according to central government regulations or local government guidelines, if any. Sometimes there were no observable standards within the same enterprise. Benefit payments were often dependent on the availability of funds, favoritism, or the aggressiveness of the claimant. Such practices have become so prevalent in the administration of compensation for work injuries, for example, that a recent report concluded that government regulations for this program exist only on paper.[31]

Enterprises' disregard for the proper administration of income security programs became evident by the late 1980s. Reports surfaced that the personnel files—including employee information such as position titles, wage records, and service tenure—upon which enterprise officials determine eligibility and benefit amounts, were in disorder and subject to falsification and unauthorized alterations.[32]

Further confounding the breakdown in the administration of social security is the absence of an established appeals system whereby a disgruntled employee can seek redress. The 1987 Interim Regulations for Settlement of Labor Disputes at State Enterprises do not include disputes regarding social security issues. Written complaints have flooded local and central labor offices, reporting nonpayment of benefits and willful reduction in benefits, for example. Many retirees or their offspring visit these offices themselves hoping to get better results. The final resolution of these problems often requires the personal intervention of a local labor bureau chief and other government officials having direct jurisdiction over the enterprise.[33] Certainly, the arbitration of disputes is more difficult if only because of the pervasive discrepancies between enterprise "experiments" and local government guidelines, and between local government "experiments" and central government regulations.

D Summary comments

In the 1980s, as the central government clung to social security programs established in the early 1950s, social security developments in the reform decade have been driven primarily by local government initiatives and enterprise "experiments." The most significant development has been the evolution of resource pooling of retirement pensions because it has made social security less dependent on individual enterprises for funding and administration. However, this development has not reached other social security programs. Also important but with limited impact were experiments in social security cost cutting (as in medical care) carried out by some local governments.

Two critical problems have surfaced. First, the 1980s witnessed the unprecedented rise in social security costs at the expense of enterprises and, ultimately, of the state tax revenues because social security expenditures are operating costs before tax. Total social security expenditures multiplied from 5 billion yuan in 1978 to 38.18 billion yuan ten years later, or 1.4 percent and 2.7 percent of the gross national product (GNP) for the respective years. Annual social security expenditures per covered employee and retiree rose from 77.4 yuan to 331.4 yuan during the same period. The 1988 figure is more than twice the 1978 amount adjusted for inflation (145.8 yuan).[34]

Second, the arbitrary and capricious practices of enterprises in implementing social security programs have made them a less-than-reliable mechanism for income protection. At a time when these programs could have served as effective tools to mollify worker discontent during the 1989-90 economic downturn, the lack of reliability in social security programs may have in itself become a cause of worker frustration. From the perspective of workers, reform-minded experiments such as cutting benefits and imposing co-payments to medical care were regarded as unwelcome violations of central government regulations by enterprises and/or local governments, and as such, they became causes for appeals.

VI RECENT DEVELOPMENTS AND REMAINING POLICY ISSUES

A Recent developments, 1989–90

Central and local government measures in 1989–90 have focused on shoring up financing and administration, and revisions of central government regulations of social security programs. In financing retirement pensions, some local governments have merged the pension pools for permanent workers and for contract workers, hitherto set up as separate accounts. As a result, shortfalls in pension pools for permanent workers (which are financed on a pay-as-you-go scheme, and are thus vulnerable to enterprise losses and shutdowns) can be made up, albeit temporarily, by the accumulated retirement reserves for contract workers.[35] These city and county governments, therefore, have moved another step toward transforming an enterprise-managed retirement system into a social insurance system by broadening the base of risk sharing.

Proposals for setting up reserve funds through resource pooling to finance medical care programs and workers' compensation (cash benefits for work-related injuries) have emerged as well. Whether this practice, following the development of retirement pension pools, will take hold and give rise to localized standardization in programs and to city/county government supervision and control over the administration of these programs, remains to be seen. Medical care and workers' compensation programs are more difficult to administer than retirement pensions because of the complicating role of health care providers. The lack of established standards for determining the degree of injury and disability as well as the level of reimbursable care and compensation also causes administrative problems.[36]

Local governments and central government agencies have taken steps to improve the administration of SIAs and their linkages with the Ministry of Labor. Some city and county labor bureaus have announced their plans to acquire computer technology to enhance the SIAs' ability to monitor resource pooling for pension programs. Presumably, automation will also facilitate the SIAs' gradual takeover from enterprises of the administration of the retirement pension programs. Similarly, the Ministry of Labor has announced its support for the general application of computer technology to the management of social security, including the development of a networking capability between local SIAs and a newly established information retrieval center at the Ministry in Beijing. Moreover, the State Bureau of Technological Assessment (*Guojia Jishu Jianduju*) has approved the issuance of social security numbers to workers beginning in April 1990, another step toward facilitating administrative control of social security programs.[37] Mindful of the inadequacy in the existing institutional setup for asserting centralized control over social security administration, the Ministry of Labor has proposed the creation of a separate agency under its auspices at the central government level. It is not clear, though, whether this agency will have its own subordinate branches and subbranches throughout the country.[38]

There are even indications that the central government at last is poised to revise the existing regulations for the retirement pension and work-injury programs. Details are not yet available. The government's intention seems to reassure workers that the established benefit levels will at least continue, if not be improved. Permanent workers in state enterprises, however, may be expected to contribute to the funding of the retirement program. This would represent a major breakthrough for making workers responsible for part of the costs. There is no sign of reforming the medical care program or of revising the much-abused practice of paid sick leave for extended periods, however. [39]

All these developments seem to follow the general trend of spreading risk-sharing among enterprises and shifting administration of the retirement programs to local governments, instead of depending on individual enterprises for funding and administration. Significant as these developments are in the long-term evolution of a social security system suited for a market-oriented economy, short-term necessities have led to expedient practices that might blunt, if not subvert, this general trend—in particular, practices that reinforce employee dependency on enterprises for their social and economic well-being, or make government funding readily available for social security payments.

As layoffs in late 1989 created resentment among those who became unemployed, the government decided to retain workers in factories at reduced pay in order to avert social disorder. In a January 1990 speech, Premier Li Peng specifically lauded the enterprise's function as a "mini-welfare state," responding to workers' social and economic needs.[40] Thus, the practice of the enterprise's functioning as a "mini-welfare state" has regained official sanction. Efforts to lessen workers' dependence on enterprises in order to facilitate labor mobility appear to have taken a back seat to concerns over social stability.

When the general economic downturn in late 1989 and early 1990 caused two-thirds of urban factories to shut down or operate at a reduced capacity, it also exposed the weak financial base of resource pooling in the permanent workers' retirement pension programs that are funded on a pay-as-you-go basis. Dipping into the reserve funds for contract workers has helped to alleviate the shortfall somewhat. But these reserve funds can be easily exhausted given the large number of retirees and the relatively small number of contract workers contributing into the funds. Information is not available regarding the extent to which retirees have been paid during this period of economic hardship nationwide. Some local governments have issued directives that retirees be paid in full regardless of financial status of their former employers (that is, regardless of an enterprise's ability to contribute to pension pools). They have also offered government funding to make up for enterprise shortfalls.[41] It is likely that local and possibly central government funds have been tapped as a last resort to pay retirement pensions.

It remains to be seen whether this practice of government subsidies to make up enterprise shortfalls is merely a stopgap measure, or whether it will evolve into a routine procedure as during prereform days. The pooling mechanism evolved in the last decade would then become one of channeling local and central government funding to retirement pension payments (or even to medical care and workers' compensation), rather than bona fide pooling of contributions from enterprises.[42]

Recent central and local government measures and proposals have only addressed issues related to developing resources to fund social security (for example, employee contributions to social security, and resource pooling for medical care and work injury programs). No proposals have been put forward to control rapidly rising expenditures. This approach follows the central government's tendency to raise rather than lower benefit levels as evidenced in the 1980s, and probably is also prompted by the current climate of appeasing workers to maintain social stability.[43]

B Implications for transition to a market-oriented economy

During the 1980s, the central government enhanced the social security programs designed in a bygone era and made them the operative programs of today. Only limited progress has been made to adjust social security to a market economy. Both the newly established contract workers' retirement pension program and unemployment insurance program are yet to withstand the test of time. At present, state-sector permanent workers still do not contribute to the funding of social security programs; and they remain tied to their enterprises for receiving social security benefits. As long as resource pooling (for both permanent and contract workers) is limited to retirement pensions at the city/county level, and as long as city and county SIAs operate primarily as clearinghouses for funding rather than administrators of social security programs, the prospect for labor mobility across enterprises even within the jurisdiction of the same city or county will be remote.[44] More important, the central government has yet to set up any government-regulated income security programs for workers in urban collective and private sectors, even though such programs would make these sectors more attractive to new entrants to the urban labor force so not to overload the state sector.[45]

Meanwhile, the skyrocketing cost of providing social security to state-sector employees—a relatively small group of the country's labor force—and its drain on the financial health of enterprises and of the state, is expected to have an adverse impact on the country's national economy. The cost issue will become especially acute as China's population ages and as some 40 percent of its current urban workers retire within the next 20 years. It is estimated that the ratio of employed urban workers to retirees will worsen from 6.4:1 in 1988 to 4:1 by the year 2000. During the same period China's resources will also be needed for investment in economic development and to meet the vast social and economic demands of the rapidly aging rural population who at present must rely on their own resources or family members for support.[46]

C Remaining policy issues

How the government will resolve this dilemma of allocating China's resources among contending population groups and between social versus economic priorities remains the key social security policy issue. The government might begin with reviewing policy alternatives for state-sector social security programs. A continuation of the current arrangements—that is, reliance on local governments and enterprises to initiate "experiments" conducive to the transition to a market-oriented economy—will probably exacerbate ongoing problems of waste and abuse, and will perpetuate the workers' perception that the social security programs are unreliable.

Should the central government, then, begin to assert leadership in social security policy, as it has begun to recentralize management of state enterprises, prices and investment? If so, it may choose to follow the 1980s policy of adhering to the existing programs, all the while expecting that tightened supervision and control from the center will curb waste and abuse. By taking this approach, the government will be putting an end to a decade of local cost-control "experiments," especially in medical care. Besides, given both the lack of an institutional framework for central supervision and control in social security matters, as well as the limited administrative experience of SIAs and LSCs in cities and counties, the savings that can be achieved through regulating administrative procedures, even with the help of computer technology, may be too little and too late to significantly diminish the heavy financial burden in social security over the next two decades.

As an alternative, will the central government decide to reexamine the existing programs and initiate cost-cutting measures as national policy? Will the government overcome its overriding concern for social stability and roll back privileges that state-sector employees and retirees have grown accustomed to expect, especially just after it raised their wages for the purpose of mollifying discontent? Even if that is the direction it takes, to what extent can the central government expect or enforce compliance from enterprise administration?

In sum, at the onset of 1990s, China's leadership faces two policy alternatives. Neither promises easy answers. First, it may continue to use the existing social security system (destabilized as it is) to placate state-sector workers who are disheartened by recent political and economic policies. This will probably drain the country's resources at the expense of meeting the needs of a vast working population outside the state sector, and of further economic development. The second policy alternative is for the central government to decisively control social security costs by modifying existing program provisions and instilling discipline in administration. Meanwhile, it can hold out the hope that an improved economic outlook as the country deepens its economic reforms will help alleviate restlessness among its workers.

ACKNOWLEDGMENTS

Social Science Research Analyst, Office of International Policy, Social Security Administration (SSA), Department of Health and Human Services. The author is grateful to a number of individuals: Christina Harbaugh of the Office of International Research at the U.S. Census Bureau provided many useful sources; her colleagues at the SSA, Lois Copeland and Leif Haanes-Olsen of the Office of International Policy and John Woods of the Office of Research and Statistics kindly reviewed an earlier draft of the paper; and Teh-wei Hu (University of California at Berkeley), Robert Myers (a consulting actuary), and Anthony Pellechio (World Bank) made helpful comments. Ideas expressed are the author's and not necessarily those of reviewers or of their respective institutions. She is solely responsible for any remaining shortcomings.

NOTES

1 D. Davis, "Chinese Social Welfare: Policies and Outcomes" *China Quarterly* (September 1989): 579–97; W. Han, "Woguo zhigongfuli ji qi dui guomin sherufenpei de yingxiang (Welfare for urban workers and its impact on national income distribution, hereafter cited as 'Sherufenpei')," *Jinji Kexue* (March 1990): 12–9; C. Liu, "Lun zhongguo de eryuan shehui jiegou (On the dualistic structure of the Chinese society)," *Shehui* (August 1989): 20–5; Ibid (September 1989): 22–7; Ibid (October 1989): 13–6; Ibid (November 1989): 4–9. For a contrary view see, M. K. Whyte, "Social Trends in China: The Triumph of Inequality?" in *Modernizing China*, eds. A. Doak Barnett and R. Clough (Westview: Boulder, CO., 1986), 103–23. For impact of reform on rural social welfare programs, see D. Davis, "The Provision of Essential Services in Rural China," in *Rural Public Services: International Comparisons*, ed. R. E. Lonsdale and G. Enyedi (Westview: Boulder, CO., 1984), 205–24.

2 For a brief summary of debates on the culpability of the "iron rice bowl" between reformers and defenders of the system, see G. White, "Labor Contract System," *China Quarterly* (September 1987): 365–89; comments on "mini-welfare state," ibid, 366–7. For more recent criticism of enterprises as "xiao shehui", see Z. Wang, "Xiao shehui (Mini welfare state)," *Shehui* (January 1988); 31–2.

3 Social security for purposes of this paper refers to government-regulated cash and in-kind compensation for lost income and for medical care in old age, sickness, disability (work or non-work related), unemployment, or upon death of the bread winner. This definition is in general agreement with that adopted by the International Labor Organization for comparative studies; it is, however, much broader than the U.S. usage of the term. In the United States, "social security" refers only to cash benefits for old age. survivors and disability.

Social security expenditures in this paper include only old-age and diasbility pensions and subsidies; costs of free medical care to retirees, employees (whether or not work-related) and their dependents; funeral grants to retirees and employees; and emergency relief grants to employees. Although cash benefits for sick leave, maternity leave, and temporary diasbility due to work injury are part of social security programs, they are paid out of enterprise budgets for wages and thus are not available for inclusion in social security expenditure. *Zhongguo Laodong Gongzi Tongji Nianjian, 1989* (Chinese Statistical Yearbook of Labor Wages, hereafter *Laodong Nianjian*) (Beijing, 1990), 872–3.

Besides social security, employee nonwage compenastion items include, among others, allowances for transportation and personal hygiene; expenses for educational, cultural, and athletic events, and for employee welfare facilities such as canteens and nurseries.

4 By 1988, 74 percent of state-sector workers were employed in enterprises, and 26 percent in civil services. See Zhongguo Laodong Gongzi Tongji Ziliao, 1949–1985 (Statistics of labor wages in China, hereafter, *Gongzi Ziliao*, Beijing, 1987), 26–7; and *Zhongguo Tongji Nianjian, 1989* (Chinese statistical yearbook, hereafter, *TJNJ*) (Beijing, 1990), 111. For purposes of this paper, *jiguan* and *siye* are referred to collectively as civil service for lack of a better term. J. P. Burns refers to *jiguan* and *siye* as administrative units and service units, respectively. See his "Chinese Civil Service Reform: The 13th Party Congress Proposals," *China Quarterly* (December 1989): 740

5 For a legislative history of state-sector social security provisions, see K. Wang, et al, *Dangdai Zhongguo de Zhigong Gonzi Fuli he Shehui Baoxian* (*Employee Wages, Welfare Benefits and Social Insurance in Contemporary China*) (Hereafter, *Dangdai*, Beijing, 1987), 302–18; an English summary is in N. Chow's *The Administration and Financing of Social Security in China* (University of Hong Kong: Hong Kong, 1988), 22–7.

6 For texts of 1951 Provisional Labor Insurance Regulations as amended in 1953, and 1958 together with implementing regulations, see *Laodong Gongzi Wenjian Xuanbian* (*Selected documents of labor and wages*) (Fujian 1973), pp. 275–306, 407–18, and 447–9.

7 For a detailed listing of various subsidies and allowances in English, see Chow, *Administration and Financing*, 92–4. A. Walder has discussed extensively the predominant role of enterprises in all aspects of workers' lives; see his *Communist Neo-Traditionalism: Work and Authority in Chinese Industry* (University of California Press: Berkeley, CA., 1986).

8 See, for example, "Article Urges Establishment of Comprehensive Labor Insurance System," *JPRS-CAR 89–089*, 33–4.

9 In 1978, about two-thirds of collective workers were covered by some form of income security programs. See, *Zhongguo Shehui Tongji Ziliao, 1987* (Chinese Social Statistics, hereafter *Shehui ziliao*) (Beijing, 1987), 111–2.

10 For a full discussion on the liberalization of retirement regulations in the state-sector income security programs for both government institutions and enterprise workers, see D. Davis, "Unequal Chances, Unequal Outcomes: Pension Reform and Urban Inequality," *China Quarterly* (June 1988): 230–7. For texts of 1978 retirement regulations and subsequent amendments to retirement and social security programs, see *Shehui Wenjiao Xingzheng Caiwu Zhidu Zhaibian* (*Selections on social, educational, administrative and financial systems*) (Beijing, 1979); Zhonghua Renmin Gongheguo Guowuyuan Gongbao (hereafter, Guowuyuan Gongbao) 27 (1989): 973–82; *Xinbian Laodonngzhengce Wenttijieda* (A new compilation of Q and A to labor policies, hereafter *Xinbian*) (Beijing, 1989), 242–54. Improvements to other programs included extending the paid maternity leave from 56 days to 90 days, for example. Senior professional women may now retire at age 60

rather than age 55. "Nugaozhi tui(li) xiu de singuiding (new regulations regarding the retirement of senior professional women)," *Zhongguo Funu* (September 1990): 39.

11 G. White, "Labor Contract System," 365–89. For text of the Interim Regulations, see *Renmin Ribao*, 10 September 1986, 2.

12 For text of Regulations, see *Renmin Ribao*, 10 September 1986, 2.

13 X. Wei, "Chengshi yanglaojin zhidu gaige chuxin chutan (Preliminary discussions on urban retirement pension system reform)," (unpublished manuscript, Beijing, 1988), 2.

14 Some 3.6 million out of 22 million state-sector pensioners are earning wages through "second employment." "Laodong bowen (Labor news)," *Zhongguo Laodong Kexue* (hereafter as *ZLK*) (April 1990): 10.

15 For examples, see X. Wang, "Henansheng anzhi qiye fuyu renyuan de qingkuang (Making arrangements for surplus workers in Henan province)," *ZLK* (January 1989): 46; "Guanyu funu shixing jieduan jiuye de jizhong yijian (Thoughts on the practise of phased-employment for women)," *ZLK* (January 1989): 38–9; "Gaohao laodong zhidu gaige, tuoshan anzhi fuyu renyuan (Improve labor reform, make proper arrangements for surplus workers)," *ZLK* (December 1988): 33–5.

16 *TJNJ, 1989*, 152. Separate totals for state enterprise and civil service retirees are not readily available. In 1988 the number of pensioned retirees from *all* urban employment, including those from collective enterprises, was 21.2 million, receiving 32.1 billion yuan in benefits. By the end of 1989, the totals were 22 million urban reitrees receiving 37.5 billion yuan in benefits. C Gu, "Insurance to Benefit All Chinese Employees," *China Daily* 10 August 1990, 1.

1 yuan equaled 61.3 U.S. cents at year-end 1978, and equaled 26.9 U.S. cents at year-end 1988.

17 S. Pei, "Guanyu gaige tuixiujin zhidu de sikao (Thoughts on the reform of retirement pension system)," *Jingji yu Guanli Yenjiu* (*Economics and Management Research*) 5 (1986): 36–8; and H. Feng, "Shanghaishi quanmin suoyouzhi qiye shixing tuixiufei tongchoude qingkuang (The implementation of resource pooling in state enterprises in Shanghai municiplaity)," *ZLK* (June 1987): 12–5.

18 *Guoying qiye zhigong tuixiu feiyong shehui tongchou banfa huiji* (Collection of resource pooling arrangements for state enterprise retirement pension funds hereafter *Guoyin*) (Beijing, 1987); G, Zhang, "Guangdong shixian quansheng yi shixian wei danwei tongchou tuixiujijin de Guangdong Province," in *Guangdongsheng shehuilaodong baoxian ziliao xuanbian* (*Selected documents on socialized labor insurance in Guangdong Province*), volume 8 (Guangzhou, 1988), 256–66. "Yijiubabanian quanguo tuixiufeiyun shehui tongchou de jiben qingkuang (Status of resource pooling of retirement expenditures in China in 1988, hereafter, Yijiubabanian tongchou,)" *ZLK* (November 1989): 41; and L. Han, "Nuli tuijin shehui baoxian zhidu gaige (Diligently promote the reform of social insurance system, hereafter 'Nuli')," *ZLK* (May 1990): 10–2. Generally speaking, only state enterprises under the jurisdiction of city and county governments must participate in the pool. Provincial-level or national ministry enterprises (such as railway, post, and telecommunications) are exempt.

19 For desriptions of the duties and responsibilities of these resource pooling agencies, see *Guoying*.

20 For example, see Jimo Conty Labor Bureau, "Women shi ruhe dui lituixiu zhigong shixing yanglao baoxian shehuihua guanli de (How we implemented socialized management of old-age insurance for retired workers)," in Qingdao Municipal Labor Bureau's *Qingdaoshi shehui laodong baoxian zhidu gaige cailiao*

huibian (Collection of documents regarding socialized labor insurance system reform, hereafter, *Qingdao cailiao huibian* (Qingdao, 1988), 103–15; and H. Li, "Women shi jenyang yunhao tongchou jijin de (How we effectively manage the pooled fund)," *Dandong Diaoyen* (September 1988): 13–5. See also, "Yijiubabanian tongchou," *ZLK* (November 1989): 41; and *TJNJ, 1989*, 3.

21 M. Fang, "Weishemo zhigong tuixiu yanglaojin shoujiao nan (Why is it difficult to collect contributions to the retirement pension fund)," *ZLK* (April 1990): 32; and "Laodong bumen huyu wanshan yanglaojin shehui tongchou (The labor administration appeals for perfecting resource pooling of retirement pension)," *Jingji Cankao* (Economic Informantion), 22 June 1990, 1; Z. Shi, "Wei baozheng tingchan qiye lituixiu zhigong shenghuo (To guarantee the livelihood of retired workers of non-operative enterprises)," *ZLK* (April 1990): 47; and unpublished data, Ministry of Labor.

22 C. Song, "Yijiubajiunian shangbannian quanguo laodong gongzi qingkuang ji quannian zhanwang (Nationwide labor wages during the first half of 1989 and prospects for the entire year)," *ZLK* (December 1989): 12; L. Han, "Nuli," 10–11.

23 *TJNJ, 1989*, 123; *Xinbian*, 283–4.

24 Z. Ren, "Guanyu jiejue qiye fuyu renyuan wenti de sikao (Considerations regarding the resolution of enterprise surplus workers)," *ZLK* (November 1988): 21–3; G. Yao and M. Fang, "Qiyejia de kunao (Entrepreneurs' dilemmas)," *Shehui* (May 1989): 28–31; "Li Boyong fubuzhang zhai quangou laodong fuwu gongshe gongzhohueyi ji zhongguo laodong fuwugongshi yenjiuhui lishihuiyi shang de jianghua (Deputy Minister Li Boyong's speech at the conference of work of All-China Labor Service Companies and the board meeting of the Research Committee of China Labor Service Companies, hereafter, Li Boyong)," *ZLK* (April 1989): 3–5; U.S. Central Intelligence Agency, "The Chinese Economy in 1989 and 1990: Trying to Revive Growth While Maintaining Social Stability," report presented to the Subcommittee on Technology and National Security, Joint Economic Committee, 28 June, 1990; *TJNJ, 1989*, 123. In 1989, the unemployed were reported to total 3.78 million; see *Zhongguo Tongji Zhaiyao, 1990* (A Statistical Survey of China, 1990) (Beijing, 1990), 18.

25 *ZLK* (March 1990): 36–7; "Guanyu laodong fuwugongsi fazhan he jianshezhong rogan wentide yijian (Thoughts on issues regarding the development of labor service companies)," *ZLK* (April 1989): 47–8; S. Ni, "Shinian laodong jiuye de huigu yu zhanwang (Review of a decade of labor force employment and its future prospects)," *ZLK* (March 1989); 3–7; "Zhongda tanwuan beichachu (A serious case of embezzlement under investigation)," *Zhongguo Laodong Bao* (hereafter, *ZLB*) 6 December 1989, 1; "Ankang diqu qingli zhengdun laodonfuwu gongsi chengji kexi (Rectification of labor service companies in Ankang perfecture brings good results)," *ZLB* 24 March 1990, 3; and "Jichen laodongfuwu gongsi ganbuzhigong 'bapan' ('Eight wishes' of the low-level employees at labor sevice companies)," *ZLB* 10 January 1990, 3.

It is also difficult to assess the effectiveness of these LSCs because reports about these companies do not distinguish the local government LSCs that have the mandate to administer unemployment insurance from some 50,000 other LSCs created by and affiliated with large state or collective enterprises. Enterprise funded and managed LSCs generally engage in profit-making activities to provide job opportunities for their surplus workers and offspring of enterprise employees. Together, all LSCs have 700,000 employees, more than 4,000 vocational schools, and 230,000 service "points" (*dian*) extending to districts, and street and resident committee levels in cities and towns and even to rural towns.

26 In 1988, the paid maternity leave was extended from 56 days to 90 days, for example. *Xinbian*, 254.

27 Derived from data in *Gongzi ziliao, 1949–1985*, 191; *Shehui ziliao*, 1987, 114; and *TJNJ, 1989*, 101, 151–2, 688. Seperate totals for civil service and enterprises are not available for the years 1978 through 1985.

28 For examples, see Y. Xie, et al, "Guanyu guoyin qiye laobao yiliao zhidu gaige de jige wenti (Problems in reforming the enterprise labor insurance medical care system)," *ZLK* (November 1988): 10–3; "Minister Urges Better Medical Care, Lower Costs," *FBIS-CHI-90–050* 14 March 1990, 27.

29 In one city, some 83 percent of sampled enterprises have taken some cost-cutting measures in medical care expenditures. Xie, et al, 10–1; "Woguo gongfei yiliao he laobao yiliaozhidu de gaige (Reform of civil service medical care and labor insurance medical care systems in China)," in *Gaige he wanshan woguo de shehui baozhang zhidu* (Reform and make perfect China's social security system) (Beijing, 1988), 80–8; S. Gui, "Renko laolinghua yu gaige yiliao shoufei (Population aging and reform of co-payment for medical care)," *Shehui* (April, 1987): 18–20.

30 "Qingdaoshi jiaqiang dui 'changqi binhao' guanli (Qingdao city strengthens its management of 'long-term sick leaves')," *ZLB* 10 January, 1990 1; Xie, et al, 10–3; and "Gaohao," 34. It is estimated that, nationwide, about 15 million urban workers engage in a second employment. See Z. Sun, "Guanyu gongzi shenhua gaige mianlinde wenti he duice (Problems and policies regarding wage reform)," *ZLK* (May 1990): 3–9.

31 "Mudanjiangshi laodongju (Mudanjiang city labor bureau)," *ZLB* 8 November 1989, 2; "Dandongshi jiuzheng jiangdi, quxiao zhigong baoxian fuli daiyu de wenti (Dandong city corrects problems in lowering and elimating workers' welfare insurance benefits)," *ZLB* 8 October 1989, 1; "Chengbao buke diulao ([The adoption of enterprise] contract system should not condone negligence of the aged)," ibid, 2; "Qiye zhigong fuli jijin chaozhi yin yinqi zhongshi (Attention should be paid to shortfalls in enterprise employee welfare funds)," *ZLB* 13 January 1990, 1; "Zhigong siwang sangzangfei chaozhi wenti jidai jiejue (Problems of deficits in death and funeral grants for workers urgently await resolutions)," *ZLB* 22 November 1989, 2; X. Zheng and W. Ju, "Xinde gongshang baoxianfagui ying jingkuai chutai (New regulations on workers' compensation should be issued as soon as possible)," *ZLK* (June 1990): 19–21.

32 H. Cai, "Jiaqiang zhigong dangan guanli, wei gaohuo qiye fuwu (Strengthen the management of employee personnel files, facilitate enterprise services)," *ZLK* (November 1989): 23–4; "Zhigaizhong geren dangan zaojia xianxiang yenzhong (The phenomenon of falsifying individual personnel files in the process of revising position titles is considered serious)," *ZLB* 5 May 1990, 3.

33 "Wanshan wuoguo laodong zhengyi chuli lifa ruogan wenti (Several issues concerning the improvement of legislation for settling labor disputes in our country)" *ZLK* 3 (1990): 20–1; "Anshanshi Laodong Ju (Anshan city labor bureau)", *ZLB*, 8 November 1989, 2. For additional reports of complaints in recent years against arbitrary practices of the Labor Insurance Regulations, see items for Shanghai municipal labor bureau, Hebei provincial labor bureau, Mudanjiang city labor bureau, and Hubei provincial labor bureau, respectively, ibid. Apparently, civil service retirees were also suffering from administrative problems. In one case, it took a retired cadre 10 years (from June 1979 to May 1989) to finally settle his appeal to correct his service tenure from 28 to 31 years. *ZLB*, 6 December 1989, 3.

34 *Gongzi ziliao, 1949–1985*, 191; *Shehui ziliao*, 114; *TJNJ, 1989*, 17, 101, 151–2; 688.

35 For examples, see J. Mao and Y. Zhang, "Tuixiufeiyong shehuitongchou jitifangshi chutan (Preliminary investigations into methods for computing contributions to resource pooling for retirement expenditures)," *ZLB* 20 January 1990, 3; "Yenchengshi shixing tuixiu yanglao baoxian yitihua tongchou (Yencheng city implements unitary resource pooling for retirement pensions)," *ZLB*, 28 April 1990, 1.

36 "Sichuansheng zhigong dabin yiliaofei tongchou shidian shouhuanying (Experiments in resource pooling for catastrophic medical care expenditures in Sichuan Province are well received)," *ZLB* 28 March 1990, 2; "Lituixiu zhigong yilaio feiyong shehuitongchou yibi (A look at resource pooling of medical expenditures for retirees)," *ZLB* 14 October 1989, 4; G. Li and Z. Zhang, "Jianli juyou zhongguo tese de gongshang shehui baoxian zhidu (To establish a social insurance system with Chinese characteristics for workers' compensation)," *ZLK* (June 1990); 17–8; X. Zheng, 19–21.

37 For examples, see "Chengdushi shehuibaoxian jigou shixing jisuanjiwanglou guanli chuju guimo (Chengdu city social insurance agency's implementation of computerized management takes shape)," *ZLK* (June 1990): 47; "Laodongbu jiu jisuanji guanli tuixiu yanglao baoxianjijin tichu juti yaoqiu (Ministry of Labor announces requirements for computerized management of reitrement pension funds),' *ZLB* 7 October 1989, 1; Y. Liao, "Woguo shishi shehui baozhang haoma zhidu (China implements social security enumeration system)," *Liaowang* no. 24 (1990): 19–20. The report does not indicate which agency is assigning these numbers or how the adoption of the social security enumeration system is expected to improve the administration of these programs. The author admits that the effective application of the system depends mostly on the pace of automation. At present, individual enterprises keep their own files on employees and retirees manually, and they do not follow and standard procedures or numbering system.

38 This was proposed by the Director of the Department of Social Insurance and Welfare. See, L. Han, "Nuli," 10–1. In late 1988, a State Taxation Administration was established as an independent agency with direct authority over provincial, municipal and county branches. Former Minister of Labor Luo Gan envisioned the resource pooling of retirement pensions at the national level, with a unified system for budgeting, accounting, and auditing. "Renzhen zhili, zhendun, jiji wentoudi tuijin laodong, gongzi, baoxian zhidu gaige (To seriously manage and rectify reforms in labor, wages and insurance systems and to promote them actively but at a steady pace)," *ZLK* (January 1989): 3–9.

39 J. Zhang, "Dui qiye yanglao baoxian zhidu gaige de rogan sikao (Considerations on reforming the enterprise old-age insurance system)," *Jingji Cankao* 14 August 1990, 4 (Mr. Zhang is the director of the Office of Retirement, Department of Social Insurance and Welfare, Ministry of Labor); C. Gu, "Insurance," 1; C. Gu, "Pension System to Undergo Overhaul," *JPRS-CAR-90–040* 29 May 1990, 56; J. Wen, "Reform of workers's insurance under way," *China Daily* 5 September 1989, 1; G. Li and Z. Zhang, 17–8; X. Zheng, 19–21; and "Zhongguo laodong fazhi jianshe ji qushi (The establishment and trends in labor legislation in China)," *ZLK* (March 1990): 3–5. This last reference specifically mentions retirement pension and workers' compensation as among several pieces of legislative proposals already submitted to the State Council for review; labor insurance regulations that stipulate cash benefits for sickness and maternity and medical care are not included.

40 See P. Li, "Gaige kaifang yao yenzhe jiankangde guidao qianjin (reform and open policy must march along healthful tracks)," *Guowuyuan Gongbao* no. 4 (1990): 99–106. In the same speech, Premier Li Peng also supported a labor insurance system financed by contributions from employees, employers, and the government, see ibid, 105.

41 U.S. Central Intelligence Agency, "The Chinese Economy," In Guangzhou city, for example, the government directive instructed the full payment of retirement pensions to beneficiaries of hardship enterprises, and promised making up for shortfalls. Guangzhoushi shehuibaoxian jigou caiqu liudain yingji chuoshi (Guangzhou city social insurance agency adopts six-point emergency measures)," *ZLK* (April 1990): 47.

42 An alternative route to city and county government funding for enterprise shortfalls and central government subsidies for a specific local pension fund would be expanding the base of pooling to the provincial or even national level. If necessary, the central government would make up the deficit for the national fund, raise contribution rates by enterprises and /or employees, or reduce benefit expenditures. However, it may take years to develop provincial or national pooling, because each city or county has negotiated (with local enterprises) its own standards of enterprise contribution rate, retiree benefit level, and various subsidies included in the pension payment. These differences are not easily harmonized.

43 A related question, given the present economic hardship, is whether the government still considers it appropriate to make workers themselves contribute to social security funding as planned and, if so, whether workers will be compensated with higher wages to cushion the blow.

44 Employees also depend on their enterprises for housing and many cash and in-kind allowances in addition to social security provisions. Of the reported total nonwage compensation items, the non-social security portion has been about 28 percent of the total during years 1978–88; the social security portion, 72 percent. See note 4 above.

45 This is not to overlook that about two-thirds of urban collective workers are reported as having access to some income-security programs which depend mostly on the collective's financial solvency. In addition, the People's Insurance Company of China has begun to offer voluntary retirement plans for collective and private sector employees since mid-1980s. None of these programs can compare with the scope and generosity of the state-sector plans. At year-end 1988, 99.8 million workers were employed in the state sector, 35.3 million in urban collectives, and 6.6 million in the private sector. *TJNJ, 1989*, 101.

46 According to one Chinese analyst, the total cost of the benefit package for state-sector employees and retirees, including the reported total of nonwage compensation items (that is, social security, and cash and in-kind allowances), plus unaccounted subsidies (such as housing, fuel, personal use of government vehicles) amounted to 129.6 billion yuan in 1988, or 9.2 percent of China's gross national product for the same year. W. Han, "Sherufenpei," 14; *TJNJ*, 1989, 17.

S. Zheng and C. Chen, "Zhongguo xianxin shehui baozhang zhidude chulu (A way out for the existing social security system in China)." *Shehui* (February 1990): 6–8; and C. Gu, "Pension System to Undergo Overhaul," *China Daily* 10 August 1990, 1, reprinted in *JPRS-CAR-90–040*, 56. The worker/retiree ratios are based on total urban workers and retirees; the 1988 worker/retiree ratio for the state sector was 6.5:1. *TJNJ, 1989*, 101 and 152.

J. Banister estimates that given the current population policy and restrictions on rural migration to cities, "the proportion of the rural population ages 65 and above would rise from 6 percent in 1990 to 7 percent in the year 2000, 13 percent in 2030, 19 percent in 2040. . . ." In comparison, "the proportion of urban population ages 65 and above would increase from 5 percent in 1990 to 8 percent in the year 2000, 27 percent in 2030, 33 percent in 2040. . . ." See J. Banister, "The Aging of China's Urban and Rural Populations," paper presented at the International Academic Conference on China's Population Aging, Beijing, December 1989, 10–1.

24

CHINA'S ENVIRONMENT

Richard Louis Edmonds, William A. Joseph (Editor)

Although changes in the physical environment are difficult to assess over a short time span, Chinese environmental data suggest that in most areas environmental quality has deteriorated since 1950. Problems of deforestation, desertification, soil erosion, water shortages, and levels of pollution are all far more serious today than they were at the time of the founding of the People's Republic of China (PRC). These problems are partly the result of population growth, which puts an insupportable strain on China's natural resources. Recent analysis conducted under the auspices of the country's State Science and Technology Commission and the State Natural Science Foundation Commission suggests that China's current population of 1.2 billion has already exceeded the number that the country can support at a good standard of living. Predictions are that the population could reach a point above which minimal living standards cannot be sustained (1.5 or 1.6 billion people) as early as the year 2015.[1]

Environmental policy was neglected during the Cultural Revolution years; current efforts to deal with ecological problems began in a modest way around 1972. In that year, the PRC sent a delegation to the First United Nations Conference on the Human Environment. At the conference, many developing countries, including China, tried to argue that environmental damage in the Third World was caused by the industrialized countries. However, the Chinese were well aware that they had suffered considerable environmental damage during a period when they had little contact or trade with the major industrial nations. With the founding of China's National Environmental Protection Agency in 1973, environmental planning was included in the national plan, and China held its First National Conference on Environmental Protection. An assessment of Chinese environmental policy was begun, and many research institutes devoted to environmental studies were established. Some Chinese academics and policymakers began to say that economic development could not go ahead without consideration of its impact upon the environment. However, many people believed that economic development inevitably led to environmental pollution and that economic growth had priority no matter what the environmental costs were. They

Source: China Briefing 1994 (Boulder, Colorado: Westview Press, 1994), pp. 143–70.

argued that the countries of the developed world had all gone through a "pollute first and clean up later" phase and that China must do the same. As a consequence, pollution control did not receive as much central support as was needed. However, in 1979 the Environmental Protection Law of the People's Republic of China was promulgated for trial implementation, and from that time environmental-impact statements began to be written for heavy industry, manufacturing, and infrastructure projects. Such analyses did not necessarily have a bearing on the implementation of projects, though, as the state was generally both the instigator and the assessor of development projects.

From 1982 a development strategy began to be discussed that called for, among other things, low waste-high efficiency planning. The concept of harmonious development (*xietiao fazhan*) was adopted as policy at this time. This commonsense but difficult to define idea, which entails increasing efficiency by the initiation of recycling and pollution-abatement measures, has gained support during the past decade as the pace of environmental degradation in the Chinese countryside has accelerated. However, because thousands of new small private entrepreneurs are seeking personal profit without consideration of the environment, harmonious development has proved difficult to implement.

Poverty and lack of education make it especially challenging for China to overcome its environmental problems. Half of China's counties still lack rural extension services. This, combined with high illiteracy rates, means that it is difficult to disseminate ecologically sound techniques. A formal Environmental Protection Law was finally adopted in 1989, but environmental policy decisions continue to be hampered by attempts on the part of the central government to produce a consensus among various factions.

THE THREE GORGES (SANXIA) DAM

The most environmentally controversial project in China today is the construction of the Three Gorges Dam on the Yangzi River in western Hubei Province. The Three Gorges, or Sanxia, area, which extends for 200 kilometers along the river, is rich in historical sites and evokes many ancient Chinese legends. It is also home to a multitude of plants and animals. The sublime beauty of the Three Gorges and their strategic significance have been celebrated for centuries in the works of China's poets and travelers. Today a boat trip through the gorges still offers one of the most breathtaking journeys in China. To build a dam in such a cultural and natural treasure trove is bound to cause unredeemable damage to the nation's heritage.

The proposal for building a dam in the Three Gorges area dates to the 1920s, and arguments for and against the project have persisted among various ministries and provinces since the 1930s. The climate of repression in the aftermath of the Tiananmen demonstrations in 1989 helped to stifle public opposition to the project. In addition, some of the political dissidents who were killed or jailed were likely to have been opponents of the dam. The 1991 Yangzi and Huai river floods brought the issue to the fore; as a principal objective of the dam was flood control, the stance of proponents was strengthened. The project probably was approved at a meeting held under the auspices of the State Council and attended by policymakers in relevant ministries in late summer 1991. Formal approval came at the National People's Congress in the spring of 1992. Although two-thirds of the congress delegates voted for the project, the record-breaking number of delegates voting against it or abstaining represented far greater opposition than the ratio suggests, considering the congress's habit of unanimously approving all that is put before it. Defiant gestures in the congress over the dam issue included an unprecedented walkout by two delegates.

Argument as to whether the dam should be constructed has concentrated on several key questions: flood control, water supply, navigation, and energy supply. The Three Gorges Dam has found strong support because it is intended to help in flood control and in the transfer of Yangzi River waters to water-deficient North China, improve navigation along the river, and provide hydroelectric energy.

At the time of National People's Congress approval in 1992, flood protection was the official reason for constructing the dam. A dam in the Three Gorges would control about half of the Yangzi River's annual volume of flow. The 12 million people and 533,000 hectares of good fields in the Jianghan Plain just below the dam site would receive the greatest flood protection, although benefits could extend to more than 50 million people. The dam supposedly would give the Jianghan Plain 100-year flood protection, as against the 40-year protection calculated to be the optimum obtainable from further investment in existing dikes.

With construction of the Three Gorges Dam, 10,000 dead-weight-metric-ton (dwt) vessels would be able to get as far as Chongqing for more than half of the year, whereas without the dam, no vessels larger than 2,000 dwt can make the voyage. There would be navigation benefits downstream, as the river would be higher in the dry season. As a result, the Three Gorges Dam would reduce present river freight costs from Wuhan to Chongqing by approximately 36 percent.[2]

The Three Gorges Dam is expected to have an 18,200-megawatt generating capacity, which would make it the world's largest hydroelectric generating plant—well ahead of the Itaipu Dam in Brazil. It is estimated that its 26 turbines would supply an amount equal to one-eighth of the PRC's total 1991 electricity supply. Cost estimates suggest that the electricity generated by the dam would be cheaper than that from coal-fired plants. Proponents stress that China will find it virtually impossible to meet its future energy needs by expanding coal production, nuclear power, and other hydropower-generation projects. They point out that building a large dam in the Three Gorges would be more cost-effective in terms of cost per kilowatt hour of power than building a series of small dams on tributaries upstream.

The cost to construct what would become, at 185 meters high and 1,983 meters wide, the world's largest dam in terms of volume of concrete work has been estimated by proponents to be Rmb 50.09 billion at 1993 prices, although some specialists admit that final costs might be up to 50 percent higher. Once generating electricity, the dam would supposedly pay for itself through fees for its electricity supplemented by revenues generated by the Gezhouba hydropower station 38 kilometers downstream.

Proponents say that the dam would be safe from military attack or natural disasters. Some scientists have stated that even multiple landslides into the reservoir would not damage the dam and deny that the reservoir is in a fault zone. According to proponents, no dam has ever burst because of an earthquake induced by the weight of a reservoir, and only two earthquakes have ever produced cracks in dams. They say new techniques ensure that this sort of problem will not occur at the Three Gorges Dam.

Dam supporters also argue that construction will not involve large-scale human dislocation because the reservoir site is in the deepest gorge along the river. More than half of the people to be relocated live in small towns, which would further reduce resettlement costs. The site is also considered to be the best for distribution of electricity up and down the Yangzi River valley, north to Beijing and south to Guangzhou.

Proponents also feel that ecological damage would be minimal. As only 4 percent of the land to be flooded by the dam consists of plains, the loss of good agricultural land would not be serious. Moreover, paddy land for rice is irrigated during the summer, when nutrient-rich Yangzi River silt loads would be least affected by the impounding of water at the Three Gorges Dam. Air and water pollution that would have been generated by coal-fired power plants would be avoided, and there is little evidence to suggest that the reservoir would create breeding grounds for disease-carrying parasites.

Proponents argue that the new landscape formed by the reservoir would be beautiful, with the added benefit of a larger water surface for the Yangzi sturgeon. The reservoir would have great fish-raising potential and a positive effect on microclimate. Historical artifacts located underneath the new water level could be moved to higher locations.

Opposition to the Three Gorges Dam from within China has persisted, although not much has appeared in the press since 1989. However, overseas opposition has been considerable. Opponents see many drawbacks to the project. They argue that flood control would only be relevant to the area directly below the dam because there are a considerable number of tributaries that enter the Yangzi River in the middle and lower reaches. Major rainstorms upstream could lead to the reservoir's flooding upstream areas, particularly around the city of Chongqing, and clear-water releases from the dam could lead to the undercutting of dikes downstream. It has been suggested that raised dikes on lower portions of the river combined with several dams on tributaries would be a far more effective means of flood control, and dike raising is now reportedly going on. Opponents of the Three Gorges project also point out the mutually exclusive functions of a flood-prevention dam and a power-generating dam: a dam used for hydropower generation should have its reservoir largely full of water, whereas one used mainly for flood control should be kept almost empty.

American experts have suggested that a series of small dams along the Yangzi River would benefit navigation more than one big dam. Others argue that further improvements can be obtained merely by increasing efficiency through the use of more-appropriately sized vessels and extending the hours of navigation by using various aids, such as high-quality light signals to control nighttime shipping. Opponents of the dam also suggest that if the silt loads in the Yangzi River continue to increase, the buildup of silt upstream will lead to increased flooding above the dam, and accumulated silt piles at the base of the dam could cause a burst. The burst of the Gouhou Reservoir dam in Qinghai Province on August 27, 1993, killing more than 242 persons, has buttressed arguments against the Three Gorges Dam.

Opponents maintain that since the electricity would have to be transmitted great distances to reach the east coast, considerable amounts could be lost in transmission, and they question the efficiency of the large generators planned for the dam. If the electricity is to be consumed locally, there ought to be a corresponding level of economic development that does not yet exist. Furthermore, the long lead time of 10 years before power generation means that the dam, which is scheduled for completion in 2009, would not be able to solve China's immediate energy problems.

Opponents also suggest that smaller dams built on tributaries would cost less. The spread-out payments from staggered construction would be easier to absorb, and China would recoup costs more quickly because the construction time for each dam would be much shorter. Although supporters of the Three Gorges project suggest that one large dam will generate electricity more economically, opponents argue that they do so by ignoring the ecological and aesthetic losses that could be avoided by building smaller dams in remoter locations.

Population transfers in connection with dam construction supposedly began during late 1993. Approximately 1.13 million to 1.6 million people will have to be relocated by the year 2009. A total of 140 market towns, 11 county seats, and 2 county-level municipalities would end up under water, and Chongqing would lose some of its area. Close to one-third of the total estimated budget for the project is to be spent on resettlement. However, funds may prove to be far from sufficient, since compensation costs will have to increase as rural incomes and inflation rise.

There will also be social problems. It is not clear whether people living in urban areas but lacking urban residence registration will receive full resettlement treatment. It is said that approximately one-third of the people who have been relocated on account of dam construction in China since 1950 are still extremely poor and short of food, and another one-third are no better off than they were before. Therefore, it comes as no surprise that people in the Three Gorges area have been reluctant to move even during the project's "trial" phase.

Opponents cite past dam-construction experiences, pointing out that they do not inspire confidence. For example, after Gezhouba Dam had been under construction for 2 years, the project was stopped and redesigned. Instead of the planned 5 years, Gezhouba took 18 years to finish at a cost close to four times the original estimate. New technical problems should make the Three Gorges project even more difficult.

If construction of the Three Gorges Dam goes ahead, there will be little funding left to carry out any other water-management projects. Based on different calculations, opponents have suggested total costs for the project ranging from two to ten times the official estimate. It has also been pointed out that the official cost analysis does not include change in the future value of China's currency as well as certain social and environmental costs. Some people also suggest that during the construction period, navigation would be disturbed to such a degree as to make the project unprofitable.

Aside from military attack, safety concerns caused by the dam have centered on the instability of the geological structure of the region. The reservoir area is made up largely of weak shale and soluble limestone. It has been postulated that a rise in the water table caused by the reservoir could trigger landslides. One hydrological study concluded that landslides would be a more serious problem than siltation.[3] Opponents also point out that there are three geological fault belts near the reservoir area. Earthquakes greater than 4.75 on the Richter scale have been recorded, and increased pressure on the bottom of the new reservoir could cause stronger earthquakes in the future.

It is estimated that 23,800 hectares of cropland, more than 4,900 hectares of orange groves, and 7,000 hectares of paddy fields will be submerged if the reservoir is constructed. Losses from the alluvial fields that would be flooded could not easily be compensated for by the less fertile lands proposed for settlement. Peasants would undoubtedly be farming on steeper slopes with more potential for soil erosion. If the water level in the Yangzi River is raised during the winter and spring, soils could become waterlogged.

Up to 800 historical sites will be inundated if and when the new dam is built. Recently a working group was formed under the State Relics Bureau to put together a comprehensive plan for the preservation of objects removed from these sites. There are also worries about the effect of the dam on climate, the creation of disease-fostering habitats, pollution from submerged mines, impacts on downstream ecosystems, and the future of some forms of wildlife. A slowed flow rate would reduce the ability of the river to flush out pollutants. It could also result in land being lost along the coast, as the balance between silt being deposited from the river and wave erosion would be altered.

The political situation in the People's Republic is such that domestic public opinion cannot block a project if the leadership is in favor of it. Although the power of a single leader to force a project through is much weaker in the 1990s than in the 1950s, the Three Gorges Dam has the support of Premier Li Peng and General Secretary Jiang Zemin. However, the Canadian government's decision in April 1992 to stop aid to the Three Gorges project suggests that the Chinese could have trouble getting foreign economic assistance. To relieve capital shortages, Deng Xiaoping has suggested the sale of bonds and stocks to finance the dam. Despite possible political and financial impediments, construction of the Three Gorges Dam is likely to begin in 1995.

The Three Gorges Dam seems to be yet another attempt by China to catch up rapidly with developed nations and to solve problems with grand projects like the Great Leap Forward, which was disastrous in terms of human suffering and ecological damage. Statements by proponents of the dam acknowledging that there are problems with the project do not inspire confidence. Furthermore, within the comprehensive plans for the Three Gorges project, as detailed in a March 1992 report by Vice-Premier Zou Jiahua, there are many subsidiary measures that are actually more suitable for sustainable river management than construction of the dam itself. These less spectacular measures include soil conservation and afforestation, reservoir construction on tributaries, improvement of the central- and lower-course dikes, expansion of floodwater-retention districts, dredging of the river and adjoining lake beds, improvement of flood-warning systems, and education of the local populace. If faithfully carried out, these efforts will go a long way toward improving flood control, rapidly generating hydroelectric power, and facilitating navigation without incurring the ecological, economic, and social costs of a superdam.

RESOURCE DEGRADATION

Although pollution has been ubiquitous in recent years, the most threatening of China's environmental problems is still the degradation of the country's natural resources, in particular its water, vegetation cover, and soils. Already the per capita level of China's natural resources is quite low, with levels of land, forest cover, and water resources only 36 percent, 13 percent, and 25 percent respectively of the estimated world per capita levels.[4] Cropland accounts for only 10 percent of China's total area, and both the per capita level and the total quantity of arable land are decreasing. This degradation is due in part to misguided policies, the most damaging of which was the encouragement of population growth.

Water shortage

China currently supports 22 percent of the world's population with only 8 percent of the world's water. Many rivers, lakes, and reservoirs are shrinking or have dried up during the last quarter century, and China has not expanded its irrigated area since the beginning of the 1980s. The groundwater table in northern China has been dropping at a rate of 50 centimeters per annum since the beginning of the 1990s, and in places it is 70 meters below the levels of the 1950s.[5] In 1992 Kunming and Nanning in southern China registered alarming drops in their water tables. Some eastern and northern cities such as Shanghai and Tianjin face considerable subsidence problems because downward settling of the earth's surface has caused unstable conditions. In southern China, a total of 45 cities are reported to be subsiding.

The water-supply problem is most acute around big cities in northern China, where precipitation levels are lower than in the south. Major efforts to recycle and save water, along with water-diversion projects, really only began in the 1980s. A major interbasin water-transfer plan is now under way to convey water from the south of China to the north via the Grand Canal and from the planned Three Gorges Reservoir via the Danjiangkou Reservoir. There is also a plan to pump water from the Yangzi River to the banks of the Yellow River via the Grand Canal route. The water-shortage problem in northern China, however, is likely to get worse before many of these projects are completed.

No matter what public works the Chinese construct to lessen their water problems, conservation of existing water resources is of primary importance. Inefficiency of water use in agriculture and industry is widespread. Water quotas have already been assigned to industries, resulting in some savings. Increased recycling of wastewater in industry should also help. The Chinese are increasing the charges for irrigation water, and those who refuse to pay will have their water supply suspended. Household water use has so far not been very wasteful. However, as incomes increase and more people move from traditional housing into homes with modern plumbing, water consumption will increase. One effective method to save water would be to meter all water use.

Deforestation

Along with water, another seriously degraded resource is China's vegetation cover, particularly its forests. Official statistics indicate that China has forest cover equal to 13.63 percent of the country's total area, which is far below the world average of 31 percent. Vegetation cover has been decreasing since 1949, with occasional rises noticeable only since the 1980s. Among other undesirable side effects, deforestation has meant that drought and flooding are now annual occurrences in all major river basins, and the average area affected by such disasters in the 1980s increased by two-thirds compared with the 1950s.[6]

A Basic Forest Law was ratified in 1986. However, like other basic laws, this law still reads more like a wish list than like concrete regulations. In recent years, planned cutting levels have been greatly exceeded. In some remote areas, lack of state control rules out enforcement of laws. Illegal logging activities have been widespread, especially as the market economy makes it easy to sell timber. The state wood-supply system has been excessively wasteful because of a lack of realistic pricing mechanisms. However, recent moves toward higher, more appropriate prices for timber, retention of earnings by local timber bureaus, tax exemptions, and encouragement to merge state mills with commercial organizations may eventually discourage such waste. Fire and disease also continue to be serious causes of vegetation reduction.

Afforestation efforts since the 1950s have not been very successful. In primary nonproduction forests, management is only token and the natural forests that remain today have been saved largely by their inaccessibility. A complex forestry responsibility system was established in the early 1980s with individuals or households contracting either for individual activities or for management of a portion of forest. The Chinese have been quick to point out examples in which the system has led to increased incomes, but it is still too early to see what effect contract and semiprivatization policies will have on afforestation.

China is aiming to increase its forested areas by 20 percent by the year 2000. If this goal is achieved, China will be able to supply two-thirds of its own demand for wood.[7] Major afforestation programs now under way include the Obligatory Tree Planting Program, the Great Plains Project, the Greening of the Taihang Mountains Project, and the Three Norths Shelter Project. The 18,000-kilometer-long Coastal Protective Forest Project was begun in 1988, and by the end of 1992 it covered more than 6.7 million hectares in 195 counties and cities. A shelter-belt project of 20 million hectares along the middle and upper reaches of the Yangzi River is now being undertaken in 145 counties but is not due to be completed until the year 2030.[8]

The Obligatory Tree Planting Program, adopted in 1981, requires all Chinese citizens above 11 years of age to plant three to five trees each year or do other relevant afforestation work. Most Chinese cities show the benefits of urban tree-planting programs, many of which are also obligatory. However, the total area of public greenery in Chinese cities continued to decrease in 1992 as building construction received priority.

The Three Norths Shelter project (*sanbei fanghulin*), which began in 1978, is the major afforestation project for northern China. This 200,000-square-kilometer shelter belt is a mammoth undertaking that includes small-tree belts, shrub plantings, grasslands, fuelwood forests, timber forests, and plantations of "economic" trees such as fruit or nut trees. Major goals of phase one of this project have included halting soil erosion in Shaanxi, slowing desertification in eastern Inner Mongolia, and protecting Beijing. Although initial reports of the Three Norths project are optimistic, it will take several decades to judge its success.

Soil degradation

China has one of the most serious soil-erosion problems in the world. Conservative estimates suggest that one-sixth of the nation's arable land is affected. Annual soil losses are estimated at between 5,000 and 10,000 million metric tons, with a loss of fertility equal to about 40 million tons of chemical fertilizers, close to China's annual fertilizer production.[9] Rapid soil erosion has contributed to China's overall environmental degradation in several ways. River beds, lakes, and reservoirs are becoming silted and have had their hydroelectric and flood-control storage capacity reduced. The loss of good quality topsoil has reduced arable land and threatens to cause severe food shortages in the near future.

The most severe erosion occurs in the northern portions of the semiarid Loess Plateau of north-central China. According to some reports, the plateau is losing one centimeter of topsoil per annum. The Yangzi River valley is another badly affected area, and there has been serious soil erosion in recent years in areas of the far south, such as Yunnan, Hainan, and Fujian, where formerly there was little erosion. In the far north there are also problems. The Nonni (Nen) River plain in Heilongjiang and extreme eastern Inner Mongolia has soil-erosion problems on more than half of the cultivated land.

China has made considerable effort to stem the erosion of topsoil. Both mechanical engineering solutions and vegetation solutions have been employed—often together. More than half of the 550,000 square kilometers of eroded land that have been improved since the mid-1950s has been afforested, and almost another one-fifth terraced. In addition, about 30,000 check dams have been built across small gullies to control erosion. In recent years methods of erosion improvement have changed from a plot-by-plot to a more systemic basin-by-basin approach. There has also been a shift from reliance on the central government to local government for erosion-control projects. The problem with soil-erosion control is the massive scale of the effort required; as the problem is being addressed in one area, the pace of erosion is picking up in other places.

Control of soil erosion will require regulations keeping farmers off steep slopes as well as the introduction of new farming conservation techniques. The 1985 State Council document entitled "Ten Policy Points for Progress to Enliven the Agricultural Economy" noted, "Cultivated land in mountainous districts with slopes over 25 degrees will have to be progressively taken out of cultivation and returned to forests or to animal husbandry in order to derive maximum benefit from the land. If this results in a lack of food, the state will sell it or supply it on credit."[10] Policies to reduce farming on slope lands and to replace crops with privately managed forests or herding are based on the production responsibility system, which gives individual households control over the management of forest land. However, the areas in which the policy needs to be carried out are generally poor, peripheral, and difficult for the local government to supply with cheap good grain, so the peasants cannot afford the risks nor tide themselves over during the transition from agriculture to forestry or herding.

The Chinese estimate from aerial photographs that between 1975 and 1986, 2,100 square kilometers of "desertified land" (arid or semiarid land that has been degraded into a desertlike barren landscape) were created each year, which is an increase over the pace of desertification prior to 1975.[11] Approximately 1.7 percent of China's area can be considered human-induced desertified land. An almost continuous belt of degraded land now stretches for 5,500 kilometers from the northwest to the northeast of China. Desertification already affects nearly 55 million people and 10 million hectares of pasturage while threatening 3.9 million hectares of cropland, 4.9 million hectares of rangeland, and 800 kilometers of railway lines along with an even greater length of roads.[12] Sandstorms related to desertification now cause about Rmb 4.5 billion of direct economic loss per annum.[13]

Recent desertification is often degradation of agricultural land in the semiarid and subhumid regions that can be restored. However, the northwest arid region is showing a modest increase of desertification that will be hard to rectify. By 1991 the State Council felt that desertification, particularly in the zone where pastoralism and agriculture meet in northern China, was damaging enough to call for the establishment of a National Sand Control Aid Group. In 1992 the Ministry of Forestry began a National Sand Control Ten-Year Plan.

Even where the soils of China are not yet degraded to the point that agriculture becomes impossible, the soil nutritional base is not strong. For example, the rich yields of southern China have only been obtained through heavy labor inputs and the widespread use of manure and composted matter. The natural organic content of the soil averages less than 1.5 percent. It has been estimated that if China were to add no fertilizer to its soils, nitrogen would be exhausted in 20 to 40 years, phosphorus in 10 to 20 years, and potassium in 80 to 130 years.[14]

The second national soil survey undertaken in the 1980s found that overall soil fertility is dropping. In some cases, the drop in soil fertility has been accompanied by desertification, severe secondary salinization, and waterlogging. In part, the drop in fertility is due to reductions of fallow times as farmers seek to maximize output to increase their incomes in the marketized rural economy. The increase in triple cropping and rice monoculture on paddy soils combined with poor drainage systems has led to gleization, a process whereby iron compounds in the soil are depleted of oxygen under anaerobic conditions, or to the formation of "secondary gleyed" paddy soils, which also lowers the growth potential in the paddy. Approximately one-sixth of China's paddy lands suffer from secondary gleization. In addition, the majority of soils in the populous southeast are acidic, which renders the crops there susceptible to acid pollution, more commonly known as acid rain. This possibility is increased by the large amounts of industrial pollutants in the atmosphere.

Although China has improved an estimated 4 million hectares of salinized-alkalized land since 1949, the problems of salinization and alkalization are getting more serious because of inefficient drainage and excessive irrigation, which have increased the levels of salts in the soil. Various estimates indicate that the amount of salinized cropland throughout China is equal to almost one-fifth of all of China's irrigated cropland. It appears that the total area affected by salinization is continuing to grow. Besides salinization and alkalization of the topsoil, overpumping of groundwater in coastal areas has led to salinization of groundwater.

POLLUTION

Whereas one would expect to find resource degradation problems in an underdeveloped and overpopulated agricultural society such as China's, the rapidly developing industrial sector means that serious pollution is also widespread. Reports on pollution in China reveal a whole spectrum of pollution types: water, soil, toxic and solid waste, air, and noise.

Water pollution

As of 1992, just under half of the total length of China's seven major river systems was categorized in the lowest two grades of water quality.[15] Approximately 25,000 kilometers of rivers fail to meet standards for fishing, and the production of fry for four major fish types in the Yangzi River declined from 20 billion in the 1970s to 1 billion in 1992. Pollution of surface water in the cities was even more serious, with 85.7 percent of river sections running through cities failing to meet Chinese safety standards. Some rivers, such as Shanghai's Huangpu River, are getting warmer from all the wastewater dumped into them.

A survey of 27 major cities in the late 1980s concluded that only 6 of them could provide drinking water that met government standards.[16] Water pollution is more serious in populous eastern China than in the west. In general, only lakes and reservoirs that provide drinking water have been protected, and even some of these, such as Guanting Reservoir near Beijing, have levels of ammonia nitrogen higher than the national standards. About one-quarter of lakes surveyed have been assessed as seriously or moderately polluted, and another one-quarter are considered "lightly polluted."

There have been some alarming cases of pollution of the coastal seas and of some estuaries and bays, such as the Yangzi River estuary and Hangzhou Bay, in recent years. Pollution from organic chemicals and heavy metals also has been found in Bohai Bay and at the mouth of the Zhu (Pearl) River, although the situation in these areas was reportedly stabilizing in 1992. Oil concentrations above fisheries standards have been found in coastal waters, especially in southern areas such as Haikou Bay and Beibu Bay, and are increasing. In order to cope with Shanghai's horrific wastewater problem, the municipal government and the World Bank are funding a giant underground flow pipe in an attempt to flush the sewage out of the city into the East China Sea. While this project may improve water quality in Shanghai, its negative impact on neighboring portions of the East China Sea could be serious. Red tides, which refer to sea water discolored by certain types of marine plankton that feed on pollution and are fatal to many forms of marine life, also have been on the increase along China's coastline; they occurred 12 times in 1989, 34 times in 1990, 38 times in 1991, and 52 times in 1992.

The groundwater around some cities has been found to contain phenols, cyanides, chromium, chlorides, nitrates, and sulfates, and exhibits an increasing degree of hardness. Wells have had to be shut down. The lowered water tables around some coastal cities have led to salinization of groundwater.

The water pollution problem is compounded by the favoritism many industries receive from the government, which allows them to operate inefficient equipment with little or no treatment facilities. China's paper-making industry's average output of wastewater, for example, is six times the international average. Official statistics suggest that some progress was made in the treatment of industrial wastewater during the 1980s and early 1990s; however, official statistics are not likely to include wastewater from rural small-scale industries. Other surveys show that industrial wastewater output is higher in total volume than that indicated by official statistics.

Water pollution problems are by no means confined to urban areas. In suburban areas with relatively high densities of farm animals, an increasing number of nitrates can be detected in the soil and water. Many small rivers have become anoxic—no longer able to sustain aquatic life. In the 1980s, many highly polluting urban industrial processes were farmed out to the rural areas. As enterprises in the densely populated lower Yangzi River valley are often in small towns and villages with rivers and canals connecting them, the water pollution from one town often affects the drinking and irrigation water supplies in nearby villages and the surrounding farmland.

There has been moderate success in the control of water pollution in rural towns in recent years. Many rural areas, particularly along the prosperous east coast, have employed complex and intensive waste-recycling systems to produce high-value products such as silk and freshwater fish. In some cases, water pollution in rural areas has been reduced by consolidating small plants so that their wastewater can be treated and minerals recycled. However, the number of serious cases of untreated rural wastewater being discharged is still growing.

Soil pollution

Although China has undertaken many efforts to improve soils in a wide range of environments, soil pollution has negated much of this initiative. Polluted cropland in China is estimated by the Ministry of Agriculture to be about 10 million hectares, causing grain losses of 12 billion kilograms per annum. Such figures are obviously crude estimates, as there were only 220 municipal-sewage-monitoring stations by the end of 1988, and the local industrial-waste monitoring network was not completed until 1990.[17] However, overall monitoring has been expanding rapidly, with 2,172 monitoring stations established at various levels by 1992.

Increased and improper application of chemical fertilizers coupled with increasing livestock production has also led to degradation of soil quality in rural areas. China's average annual fertilizer usage is estimated to be 208 kilograms per hectare, twice the world average.[18] Much of the pollution problem is actually due to the overapplication of human and animal wastes in areas that also employ large quantities of nitrogenous chemical fertilizers. Experiments done in Guangdong during the 1980s have shown that in most soil types, an increase in potassium and phosphorus fertilizers could actually reduce the need for nitrogen fertilizer as well as produce a more stable yield.[19] In some cases, over-application of chemical fertilizers is known to have resulted in soil caking. As a consequence, farmers have been using larger quantities of organic fertilizer since the mid-1980s.

Beginning in 1979, there was an upsurge in the use of organochlorine pesticides such as benzene hexachloride (BHC) and dichloro-diphenyltrichloroethane (DDT), particularly in cotton-growing areas. The production of organochlorine pesticides was banned by the government in 1983, and the percentage of cereal grains with residues exceeding permissible limits went down by the second half of the 1980s. However, overall pesticide use is still increasing. In recent years, cases of illness and death caused by eating vegetables treated with large doses of the chemical methamidophos have been reported. The extensive use of pesticides in the past also means that pests have developed stronger resistance to chemicals.

One method of controlling the introduction of pesticides into the soil and food chain that the Chinese have used with considerable success has been integrated pest management, which was developed in the early 1970s as an alternative to pesticides. By 1979 the Chinese were using this method over a larger area of territory than any other country in the world. However, with the demise of communes and the return to family farming, individual farmers have reverted to the use of pesticides, as integrated pest management can only be effectively practiced over a wide area. Research into pest control is advanced in China. However, practice in the field lags behind that in the model research stations, for peasants and local bureaucrats must resort to labor-intensive techniques that often are not the most appropriate ones.

Toxic and solid waste

Before 1978 manure and household organic waste did not pose a problem because they were used as fertilizer. With the increased availability of chemical fertilizers since around 1980, "night soil" collection has become a problem. Often no one in the towns was willing to undertake management of human wastes, while the population continued to increase. The use of manure and human wastes as fertilizer has increased again since the mid-1980s, but there are worries that now more industrial wastes from the increasing number of rural enterprises are mixed in. Moreover, the amount of imported and domestic chemical fertilizers used roughly doubled between 1980 and 1990.

A partial solution to both the solid waste and the energy-shortage problems in rural China has been biogas, also known as marsh gas or gobar gas, a methane produced by the decomposition of organic matter. The gas can be generated in reactors into which crop waste, animal and human excrement, and fermenting agent are placed. The residual sludge from this process is organic and makes an excellent fertilizer. The Chinese borrowed biogas technology from the Soviet Union and East Germany, but went on to find techniques that were applicable to Chinese communes, especially those in the warmer areas of the south where the reactors would not require heating.

In 1978 the Chinese said there were 7 million biogas reactors in use. However, estimates suggest that these reactors, while important locally, produced less than 2 percent of China's total energy supply.[20] The transformation to family farming generally has hurt the production of biogas, since the communes provided a better scale of operation for reactors and the labor force needed to clean them. Although biogas has made a small comeback in the early 1990s, in 1992 the number of reactors in use was still below the totals for the late 1970s, and it is not likely ever to play more than a minor role in China's total energy production.

With the economic growth of the 1980s, the amount of household rubbish produced grew rapidly. The levels of heavy metals and other inorganic matter found in the rubbish of Shanghai are approaching the levels in developed countries. Tailings of milled ore residues have been allowed to pile up, especially around mining sites in rural areas, and are creating reservoirs of polluted water.

Official statistics suggest that the industrial solid-waste levels stabilized during the second half of the 1980s, and real progress has been made in controlling industrial solid waste from large and medium-sized urban enterprises. As it appears that rural industrial wastes are not included in these official numbers, and many waste-producing industries have been relocated from the urban areas to the countryside over the past decade, these estimates could be overly optimistic. Of the urban waste released by large industry, approximately one-fifth is dumped directly into rivers and streams.

Urban domestic waste grew at a rapid pace during the 1980s. One prediction is that China's urban rubbish will have annual growth rates of 8 to 10 percent up to the year 2000.[21] Chinese urban refuse contains a large amount of coal ash. A shift away from solid fuels to gas would significantly reduce daily per capita rubbish output. Over half of China's urban population now has access to gas. However, natural gas production is stagnating and the urban utilization rate rose by only 3.9 percent in 1992.

Kitchen wastes make up about 31 percent of China's total urban refuse. This means that urban refuse has a high humidity, which makes it difficult to transport and to incinerate. Most urban refuse is removed to farms or rural dumping sites at an ever-increasing distance from cities by lorry or boat, and very little of it is sorted or treated. China has a serious shortage of incinerators and of systems for lining dump sites to prevent polluted water from the rubbish from seeping into the surrounding groundwater. Research into how to bury rubbish only began in 1986 in Tianjin. Recently China completed its first garbage-treatment plant using fermentation technology to produce energy and reduce the bulk of rubbish.

China only recently began to set up toxic-waste storage sites. In September 1991 the Standing Committee of the Seventh National People's Congress approved a motion to adopt the Basel Convention on the Control of Trans-boundary Movements of Hazardous Wastes and Their Disposal, and in 1992 the State Council promulgated the Environmental Policies on the Disposal of Medium- and Low-Level Radioactive Wastes. However, it could be some time before these measures actually take hold. A recent report suggests that people living within 150 kilometers of a nuclear testing site in Xinjiang are showing symptoms of radiation pollution similar to those found among Japanese near Hiroshima and Nagasaki at the end of World War II.[22] A nuclear power station became operational at Qinshan in Zhejiang Province in December 1991, and a station at Daya Bay in Guangdong, along with several in Liaoning, is scheduled to be completed during the 1990s. The proximity of the Daya Bay plant to Hong Kong has made the station a sensitive issue in the territory as the PRC lacks experience in nuclear power generation and has not had a good safety record in many other industries. Many people in Hong Kong regard the chance of a radiation leak as great.

Air pollution

Air pollution plagues most urban areas, although the types of pollutants and their sources vary from region to region. It is estimated that industry accounts for over 80 percent of China's total waste-gas emissions. In recent years, some state-controlled enterprises have improved their gas cleaning. However, since the state sector is largely stagnant in terms of China's overall economic growth as compared with the rapidly expanding nonstate enterprises, such improvements do not necessarily indicate reductions in air pollution.

Particulate levels in Chinese cities are far worse than in most cities in industrialized countries. The push for industrial development has caused China's coal consumption to rise steadily throughout the 1980s. As of the late 1980s, over 76 percent of China's energy was produced by burning coal. This percentage is not likely to go down much until at least 2025.[23] In addition to the sheer quantity of coal burned, China's severe particulate pollution problem is in part due to the fact that only about 17 percent of the coal undergoes washing to remove particulate impurities and in part because most coal is burned in small to medium-sized furnaces, often with poor efficiency. Progress made in particulate control has been largely offset by increased coal consumption.

The percentage of particulates emitted from household chimneys that is recovered by pollution-control devices is much lower than in industry. Most homes in Chinese cities use coal, and coal combustion is responsible for 69 percent of China's particulate emissions.[24] The low smoke-stacks on household stoves further aggravate the particulate problem, with combustion efficiency in nonindustrial uses running as low as 20 to 30 percent.

Particulate levels are especially high in the cities of the north. In 1992 the average daily particulate levels in northern Chinese cities were 403 micrograms per cubic meter ($\mu g/m^3$), whereas in southern cities the levels were around 243 $\mu g/m^3$. The worst daily average urban particulate level in China during 1992 was 663 $\mu g/m^3$; London normally has 48 $\mu g/m^3$, and the World Health Organization recommends 90 $\mu g/m^3$ as a maximum particulate level for safety. As China continues to industrialize, various elements have been added to the particulate pollution. Dust in urban air has been found to contain benzene soluble matter, lead, zinc, copper, arsenic, manganese, iron, cadmium, and molybdenum.

China is the third-largest emitter of sulfur dioxide (SO_2) in the world, after the former Soviet Union and the United States. Sulfur dioxide, like particulates, is closely connected with coal smoke. Estimates suggest that China's sulfur dioxide emissions doubled between 1975 and 1990. As with particulates, levels of sulfur dioxide are more severe during winter in the northern Chinese cities than in the south. Beijing, Xi'an, and Shenyang are among the world's ten worst cities for sulfur dioxide concentrations. However, in the summer months, certain southern cities such as Chongqing, Guiyang, and Changsha can have higher SO_2 levels than northern cities. Northern China urban SO_2daily average levels were 97 $\mu g/m^3$ and southern China levels 90 $\mu g/m^3$ in 1992, with the highest urban daily average level being 463 $\mu g/m^3$. The World Health Organization's safe level for $SO_2$is 60 $\mu g/m^3$. All Chinese city centers have SO_2emission levels that exceed the Chinese legal limits. There are plans to bring SO_2levels in the worst northern cities to below 130–150 $\mu g/m^3$ by the year 2000.[25] In line with this, fines were initiated for SO_2 emissions on a trial basis in late 1992.

Coal combustion is also responsible for two-thirds of the nitrogen oxides

(NO_x) emitted in China. Nitrogen oxide pollution is not yet serious compared to that from particulates and sulfur dioxide. In 1992 the urban daily average nitrogen oxide level for a sample of northern cities was 56 $\mu g/m^3$, whereas southern cities had 40 $\mu g/m^3$, which represents a slight rise in recent years. However, these statistics are roughly the same as levels in the early 1980s and are close to Chinese safety standards. Research into Lanzhou smog in the early 1980s showed that the density of methyl hydrocarbons in the Xigu Industrial District was 70 times that of nitrogen oxides. The increasing quantity of automobile and industrial gasoline fumes suggests that problems associated with carbon monoxide, hydrocarbons, and nitrogen oxides will grow during the 1990s. Traffic congestion in cities has made for levels of NO_x at intersections that often exceed the level the Chinese have set as the maximum for human health. In preparation for an increasing number of photochemical smog problems and ozone alerts, the PRC's National Environmental Protection Agency and the police put together regulations for managing the supervision of automobile emissions in 1990.

China is one of the few areas in the developing world with a major acid pollution problem. Acid pollution in China is caused largely by high levels of domestic sulfur dioxide emissions as a result of burning coal. The problem is particularly serious in southern China, as the high temperatures in the atmosphere there help sulfur dioxide convert to acid faster than in most northern industrial countries. More than half of the rainfall in southern China is now overly acidic. Chlorine and hydrogen fluoride pollution as well as sulfur dioxide have been found to be seriously affecting vegetation. It has been estimated that in the second half of the 1980s, 2.66 million hectares of crops were annually polluted by sulfur dioxide and 1.33 million hectares were polluted by fluoride.[26] Serious corrosion of metal and damage to concrete are also thought to have been caused by acid pollution. Since 1982, 296 acid-precipitation monitoring stations have been established throughout China, and the Chinese have been trying to combat the impact of air pollution on vegetation. Plant varieties found to be resistant to polluting compounds have been recommended.

Noise pollution

With all the other pollution problems facing China, noise pollution has taken a backseat. Prior to 1975, China produced virtually no noise-testing equipment and had no factories producing noise-control facilities. Prior to 1982, there were no standards set for construction materials. Many buildings were built with steel-reinforced concrete panels that were only three or four centimeters thick. When one walks on the stairs in these buildings, the noise that is produced sounds like the pounding of drums.

In 1979 the Sanitation Ministry and the National Labor Bureau decided on 85 dBA (85 decibels on the A scale) as the workplace standard, with 90 dBA set as the absolute permissible high. At constant exposure, the level considered damaging to the ear is 75 dBA, and serious hearing impairment can occur after eight hours of exposure at 100 dBA.[27] Machine sound levels in Chinese factories have often exceeded 90 dBA.[28] Noise in most Chinese cities exceeds the suggested Chinese standards. The target for the mid-1990s is to get all cities to levels below 73 dBA.

Pollution problems continue to grow in China despite significant efforts in recent years to address them. The costs of pollution have been tremendous in economic terms. The message that pollution control can be profitable as well as healthy came home to the Chinese leadership during the 1980s. The task for the 1990s is to experiment with methods to regulate emissions effectively and to get the government to raise its investment in pollution control to a higher proportion of GDP than in the late 1980s.

NATURE CONSERVATION

China is known as a treasure trove of rare species of wildlife. The first nature reserve and laws dealing directly with nature conservation appeared in 1956. Several more reserves were founded in the years up to 1965, although there were no guiding principles for their establishment or distribution. The height of the Cultural Revolution, from 1966 to 1972, was a period of chaos, and no new conservation policies were formulated.

Around 1975, the State Council issued documents to establish planned nature reserves. However, substantial development of reserves did not begin until after 1979. In the early 1980s, a wildlife-protection bureau and an office to control import and export of endangered species were first set up under the Ministry of Forestry, and the China Wildlife Conservation Association was founded. By 1987 the State Council was alarmed enough about the hunting and smuggling of wildlife to issue a directive to local governments admonishing them to increase their surveillance and punishments. In 1988 the government devised China's first wildlife-protection law, which stipulated details on administration and punishments. In 1992 the State Council promulgated the Regulations on the Protection of Terrestrial Wild Fauna of the People's Republic of China, and the government published the first volume of China's *Redbook on Flora: Rare and Endangered Flora.* Local governments have followed suit with similar laws and regulations, but many species continue to dwindle. As of mid-1993, there were 708 nature reserves in China covering close to 6 percent of China's national territory.

Seventy-seven of mainland China's nature reserves, including five coastal fish-reserve zones, are considered national nature preserves. The administration of nature reserves in China is not uniform, however. Different reserves are often administered by different organizations and at different government levels. On the whole, the forestry bureaus tend to dominate because nature conservation work began in the Ministry of Forestry.

Approximately 379 vertebrate species are protected in the PRC at first-class or second-class levels of protection.[29] China has 389 species of plants protected in three categories. Animals and plants receiving first-class protection are those which are endemic, rare, precious, or threatened. Those accorded second-class protection are species whose numbers are declining or whose geographical distribution is becoming more restricted. The third-class species are plants of economic importance for which harvesting is limited. In general, the method for preserving wildlife has been to establish nature reserves in the areas where they live and breed or to establish artificial breeding centers. Certain endangered species are recovering.

However, some animal populations continue to remain low or to decrease. For example, bird's tend to be scarce in China. Explanations for their disappearance include the destruction of their habitats for agriculture, industry, and housing, government eradication policies for certain species, excessive hunting, and pollution from pesticides and industry. Likewise, increased nutrient loading and industrial pollution in lakes, along with the construction of dams and weirs, have led to reductions in fish and crustacean yields and species. Often, in order to increase food production, crab and carp larvae have been stocked in lakes, leading to a reduction of other indigenous species.

International wildlife organizations have been interested in working with China because of its varied environments as well as their concern that many aspects of nature conservation in China could be better managed. In 1979 China became a member of the UNESCO "Man and the Biosphere Programme," and eight Chinese nature preserves are now part of the Man and the Biosphere Programme Network. In 1981 China signed the Convention on International Trade in Endangered Species of Wild Fauna and Flora. Of the plant and animal species protected under this treaty, more than 640 are found in China. China also has ten sites on the UNESCO World Heritage Commission's list. In 1992 the China Council for International Cooperation on Environment and Development was established. Many of the larger reserves have research organizations attached, some of them with international cooperation.

In 1981 an agreement was signed with the International Wildlife Foundation to protect and study the giant panda, with an initial project completed in 1988.[30] Although archaeological evidence indicates that pandas were once distributed widely over southern China, their range now has shrunk to six small areas in southern Shaanxi and in Sichuan. During 1975 and 1976, 138 giant pandas were found dead along the Sichuan-Gansu border. The cause of their death was the deterioration of the arrow-bamboo and square bamboo groves that provide their food.[31] This panda famine stimulated a series of attempts to preserve the animal's habitat. However, in 1983 about 250,000 hectares of arrow bamboo groves, or 46.8 percent of the total arrow bamboo groves along the same mountainous border, again started to die out, and several dozen pandas died from starvation. The total giant panda population of China is now estimated to be about 1,000

As of 1992 there were 13 nature reserves that protect the giant panda. Of these, the Wolong Nature Reserve is by far the largest, occupying one-third of the total area of the panda reserves and containing perhaps one-seventh of the total number of giant pandas found in China.[32] At Wolong there are two major studies of the giant panda currently being undertaken—one related to their breeding in captivity and the other to their behavior in the wild. To keep track of this solitary animal is a difficult task, even though the panda's food range is limited in the Wolong area. Pandas are difficult to capture, and identification of individual animals is not easy. The work is made more difficult by the 4,000 farmers and lumberjacks who live within the nature reserve. Deliberate harm to the pandas has also been committed. In 1987 two gangs of poachers were caught killing pandas and trying to sell the skins; some of the offenders received life imprisonment. Panda killings are still being reported–the number lost in some districts has exceeded those saved. The range of the animal has continued to decrease, from about 20,000 square kilometers in 1970 to 10,000 square kilometers in 1990. In order to help preserve the panda's habitat, the Chinese government recently announced plans to establish another 14 panda reserves.

International cooperation in the conservation of animals other than the giant panda also increased throughout the 1980s. For example, efforts to protect birds were begun in conjunction with the Japanese in 1983, and construction began on a Sino-Japanese Friendship Center for Environmental Protection in the spring of 1992. There is also talk that China might establish "international parks" with Nepal or Pakistan. However, the desire to bring in tourist revenue could compromise the conservation aspects of such parks.

Most environmentalists would argue that China's efforts at nature conservation are too little, too late. The total area for nature reserves is still not what it should be. Other types of nature reserves besides those already in existence are necessary. Also, the distribution of nature reserves is out of balance. Two areas are critically short of nature reserves: the densely populated eastern portions of the country and the Qinghai-Tibetan Plateau.

The Chinese admit that administration of their nature reserves is uneven, with some being run far more effectively than others. Administrative problems for the nature-reserve system as a whole will continue until there is a single government organization supervising national-level operations. Currently, the various units that administer the nature reserves have a tendency to look for short-term economic advantage or to protect only those aspects of the environment that are beneficial to the bureau's interests. The Wolong Nature Reserve in Sichuan has established its own special district government, and this has proved helpful in facilitating management of the reserve. However, even in a showcase reserve such as Wolong, one author found widespread evidence of illegal tree felling, which raises questions about the management of other reserves.[33]

The scale of some of China's nature reserves is too small to be effective. In many cases, state forests or forestry parks are located next to nature reserves; joint management of these could bring increased conservation benefits. The problem of scale is sometimes compounded by attempts to zone reserves for various uses. Once part of a reserve has been zoned for productive or revenue-generating activities, its original preservation function is compromised.

The lack of laws relating specifically to nature reserves prior to 1988 meant there was much confusion, especially as laws regarding ownership of the means of production, land, and so forth were also in flux. Now that laws standardizing procedures for establishing nature reserves, management procedures, and penalties for violations have appeared, there is a need for clear enforcement of local versions pertinent to specific circumstances. Serious cases of killing and smuggling endangered species still exist. A case in point was the recent discovery in northeastern China of a large shipment of frozen bear paws for export.

For laws and their enforcement to be successful, the nature-reserve managers must consider solving the economic and social problems of the local inhabitants. Attempts have been made in some of the nature reserves to compensate local dwellers. At Wolong, farmers have resisted relocation to nontraditional village housing. The government has been trying to solve employment problems for some local people by training them as forest rangers or nature-reserve staff.

Enforcement problems are compounded by the low level of environmental education among the inhabitants of the areas surrounding the reserves. Low levels of education also make it very difficult to find well-qualified staff to manage the reserves. Under such circumstances, some nature reserves are reserves in name only. In many cases, logging and hunting are still going on in areas where such activities are strictly prohibited by law.

Although nature reserves are now a part of China's national annual plans, their overall finance is not included in the annual national or local budget. Nature-reserve officials are expected to maximize income from the reserve lands while preserving their function and character. However, as very little economic assessment of Chinese nature reserves has been done, activities aimed at exploiting renewable resources within reserves often become excessive. One avenue for reserves to generate revenue is through tourism. However, the effects of tourism on China's nature preservation has rarely been positive, and many areas are becoming endangered. For example, some protected areas were opened to foreign hunters in the mid-1980s for a fee. Even though China is a signatory to the Convention on International Trade in Endangered Species, which gives all wildcat species protected status, quotas of skins are regularly set by the Chinese Ministry of Trade.

Most Chinese environmentalists argue for improved management of nature conservation by pointing out the long-term economic value of such a policy. This is the only viewpoint that will attract the attention of a government intent upon rapid economic development. However, China's policymakers must come to understand that nature conservation is a necessity for the country's long-term survival.

PROSPECTS FOR CHINA'S ENVIRONMENT

The Chinese government's standpoint on international environmental cooperation can be summed up by the Chinese delegate's speeches at the United Nations Conference on Environment and Development held in Rio de Janeiro in June 1992. In this view, poverty is the main cause of environmental degradation in developing countries, and thus it is not reasonable to expect these countries to maintain lower emission levels or install expensive equipment to control emissions on their own. Instead, the developed nations should transfer funds and technology to help poorer countries reduce emission levels. Rather than talk of shared responsibility for global warming, the Chinese government argues that it is up to the developed nations to acknowledge their emission of the vast majority of greenhouse gases. This viewpoint echoes the position China took at the 1991 environmental conference of developing countries hosted in Beijing. It can be seen as part of the Chinese government's attempt to make the environment a foreign policy issue and in the process assume leadership of a developing-country environmental bloc. Whether or not China can convince the developed countries to contribute large amounts of funds and technology, improvement in China's environment will require internal political stability as well as international support; even then, it is unlikely that China will be able to halt its ecological degradation within the next couple of decades.

The most threatening of China's environmental problems is the continuing degradation of resources, particularly in poor western and central areas. The fragile ecosystems of the western and border areas are under great strain. Since the 1950s, considerable numbers of Chinese have been relocated westward in order to develop poor areas and reduce population pressure in the east. The expansion of settled agriculture and industry in traditional herding pastures and oases of the west has led to substantial degradation. These areas must no longer be seen as destinations for surplus population. Instead, population densities in parts of the west must be reduced and emphasis put on animal husbandry and forestry where possible.

While resource degradation is also serious in the east, the immediate problem facing the population there is pollution. As small-scale township and village enterprises rapidly proliferate with virtually no government regulation, pollution is becoming widespread in the rural areas. Most rural enterprises use outdated equipment and cannot afford to spend money on pollution abatement. They are inefficient energy users. In particular, rural industries have caused severe water-quality degradation. The central government can only guess at the seriousness of the total picture. It was not until 1989 that any province had completed a basic survey of the levels of pollution from rural small-scale industries. To deal with the rural-industry pollution problem will require a tremendous investment by the Chinese government as well as strict enforcement of regulations.

In China as a whole, the most that can be hoped for is that the pace of water depletion, deforestation, soil erosion, and desertification will slow down in coming years. If efforts at afforestation and population control during the 1980s and early 1990s prove successful, we can expect to see benefits sometime after 2010.

More efficient management would also help reduce environmental problems. It has been suggested that industrial pollution in China could be reduced by 30 percent simply by improving technology management in enterprises.[34] Pollution-abatement equipment is often not installed properly or regularly maintained, and pollution-related accidents are common, with more than 3,000 serious incidents reported between 1989 and 1992.[35] The Environmental Protection Law stipulates that environmental assessments are to be part of construction projects. However, such assessments are rarely carried out for small-scale projects, and their results are often ignored in the case of large-scale projects. In addition to more funds and personnel, much more openness to assessment information will be necessary.

Many analysts see improved economic efficiency, largely from the implementation of pricing mechanisms, as the ultimate key to improving China's environmental problems.[36] Pricing mechanisms have helped to control some forms of degradation, such as pollution in the state-run industries, and have aided in the promotion of environmentally friendly products. Although an array of price reforms has been introduced during the past decade, pressure from government nonetheless remains the main force regulating investment in environmental control since many inputs, such as water, timber, and coal, are still artificially under-priced.

Ultimately, though, China's environmental problems cannot be solved solely through price reform or regulatory policies. If the country is to provide all its people with a good standard of living in the next century, China needs strict population control, extensive environmental education, increased wealth and infrastructure, political stability, and a more open society where information can be obtained and opinions freely expressed. To what degree these goals are met in the coming decade will have far-reaching implications not only for China's environment but for the whole earth.

NOTES

1 "Shengcun yu fazhan" (Survival and Development) (unofficial report of the Chinese Academy of Sciences, 1989), pp. 9, 17.

2 Wang Zuogao, "Navigation on Yangtze River and the Three Gorges Project" (in English with French résumé), *Bulletin of the Permanent International Association of Navigation Congresses*, Vol. 70 (1990), p. 95.

3 Lin Chengkun, *Chang Jiang Sanxia yu Gezhouba de nisha ji huanjing* (Silt and Environment at the Three Gorges and Gezhouba Dam on the Yangzi River) (Nanjing: Nanjing daxue chubanshe, 1989).

4 Wang Xianpu et al., *Ziran baohuqu de lilun yu shijian* (Theory and Practice of Nature Reserves) (Beijing: Zhongguo huanjing kexue chubanshe, 1989), p. 1.

5 Liu Changming. "Underground Water Table under Heavy Pressure," *China Environment News*, no. 44 (March 1993), p. 6.

6 Han Chunru, "Recent Changes in the Rural Environment in China," *Journal of Applied Ecology*, Vol. 26 (1989), pp. 804–5.

7 Stanley Dennis Richardson, *Forests and Forestry in China: Changing Patterns of Resource Development* (Washington, D.C.: Island Press, 1990), pp. 99, 111.

8 *China Today*, August 1990, p. 5.

9 Wang Xianpu et al., preface to *Theory and Practice of Nature Reserves*, p. ii.

10 *Zhongguo linye nianjian* 1949–1986 (China Forestry Yearbook 1949–1986) (Beijing; Zhongguo linye chubanshe, 1987), p. 123.

11 Zhu Zhenda and Wang Tao, "Cong ruogan dianxing diqu de yanjiu dui jinshinian lai Zhongguo tudi shamohua yanbian qushi de fenxi" (An analysis on the Trend of Land Desertification in Northern China During the Last Decade Based on Examples from Some Typical Areas), *Dili xuebao*, Vol. 45, no. 4 (1990), pp. 431–33.

12 Guo Huancheng, Wu Dengru, and Zhu Hongxing, "Land Restoration in China," *Journal of Applied Ecology*, Vol. 26 (1989), p. 790; Han Chunru, "Recent Changes in the Rural Environment in China," p. 805.

13 "1992 Report on the Environment in China," *China Environment News*, no. 47 (June 1993), p.5.

14 Zhao Qiguo, "Woguo de tudi ziyuan" (Land Resources of China), *Dili xuebao*, Vol. 45, no. 2 (1990), p. 155.

15 "1992 Report on the Environment in China," p. 5.

16 Han Chunru, "Recent Changes in the Rural Environment in China," p. 806.

17 Eduard B. Vermeer, "Management of Environmental Pollution in China: Problems and Abatement Policies," *China Information*, Vol. 5, no. 1 (1990), pp. 40–41.

18 Han Chunru, "Recent Changes in the Rural Environment in China," p. 806.

19 Liang Xiaoyan, "Analysis of the Stability of the NPK Effects on Rice in Guangdong Province," in *Soils and Their Management. A Sino-European Perspective*, ed. E. Maltby and T. Wollersen (London: Elsevier Applied Science, 1989), p. 254.

20 Bernhard Glaeser, "The Environmental Impact of Economic Development: Problems and Policies," in *The Geography of Contemporary China: The Impact of Deng Xiaoping's Decade*, ed. Terry Cannon and Alan Jenkins (London: Routledge, 1990), p. 262.

21 Xu Zhuang, "Woguo chengshi laji xingzhi ji wuran zhuangkuang de zonghe fenxi" (Comprehensive Evaluation of the Characteristics and Contaminated Situation of Municipal Domestic Refuse in China), *Huanjing kexue*, Vol. 8, no. 5 (1987), p. 81.

22 "Hece shichang de xishengpin?" (The Sacrificial Product of the Nuclear Testing Grounds?), *Zhongyang ribao* (international edition), November 6, 1991, p. 4.

23 R. Martin Lees, "China and the World in the Nineties," summary report of the

International Conference on Economic Development and Environment in China, January 25, 1991, p. 13.

24 Cao Hongfa, "Air Pollution and Its Effects on Plants in China," *Journal of Applied Ecology*, Vol. 26 (1989), p. 763.

25 Eduard B. Vermeer, "Management of Environmental Pollution in China," p. 43.

26 Cao Hongfa, "Air Pollution and Its Effects on Plants in China," p. 772.

27 Gareth Jones et al., *Collins Reference Dictionary: Environmental Science* (London: Collins, 1990), pp. 107–8, 300.

28 Fang Danqun, "Woguo zaosheng kongzhi jinzhan" (Noise Pollution Control and Prospects in Our Country), in *Zhongguo huanjing kexue nianjian* (China Environmental Science Yearbook) (Beijing: Zhongguo huanjing kexue chubanshe, 1989), p. 177.

29 Zhu Jing, "Nature Conservation in China," *Journal of Applied Ecology*, Vol. 26 (1989), pp. 829–31.

30 *Zhongguo linye nianjian 1988* (China Forestry Yearbook 1988) (Beijing: Zhongguo linye chubanshe, 1988), p. 82; Liu Jianjun, "Saving Wildlife: A Nation Mobilized," *Beijing Review*, no. 16 (April 22, 1990), p. 22.

31 Catherine Shurr Enderton, "Nature Preserves and Protected Wildlife in the People's Republic of China," *China Geographer*, Vol. 12 (1985), p. 135.

32 António Julio Emerenciano Estácio, "Na Terra do Panda Gigante (2): O Panda em Liberdade" (The Land of the Giant Panda (2): The Panda in Freedom), *Macau*, no. 15 (1989), pp. 56–57.

33 Richardson, *Forests and Forestry in China*, p. 107.

34 Zhao Yinwei and Dong Yawen, "Shilun woguo xiaochengzhen shuiwuran fangzhi yu shengtai huanjing jianshe" (On the Discussion of the Water Pollution Control and Eco-environment Construction in Small-Sized Cities and Towns of China) (1990), p. 35.

35 *China Environment News*, June 15, 1993, p. 5.

36 For example, Lester Ross, *Environmental Policy in China* (Bloomington: Indiana University Press, 1988), p. 132; and Liu Tianqi, "Zhongguo huanjing guanli de fazhan licheng" (A History of the Development of Environmental Management in China), in *China Environmental Science Yearbook*, p. 354.